SKIP HEITZIG

THE BIBLE FROM 30,000 FEET™

HARVEST HOUSE PUBLISHERS
EUGENE, OREGON

Cover by Darren Welch Design, Mount Juliet, TN

Interior design by Janelle Coury

Editing by Steve Miller

Published in association with William K. Jensen Literary Agency, 119 Bampton Court, Eugene, Oregon 97404.

The Bible from 30,000 Feet is a trademark of The Hawkins Children's LLC. Harvest House Publishers, Inc., is the exclusive licensee of the trademark THE BIBLE FROM 30,000 FEET.

THE BIBLE FROM 30,000 FEET™

Copyright © 2017 Skip Heitzig
Published by Harvest House Publishers
Eugene, Oregon 97408
www.harvesthousepublishers.com

ISBN 978-0-7369-7029-7 (hardcover)
ISBN 978-0-7369-7030-3 (eBook)

Library of Congress Cataloging-in-Publication Data
Names: Heitzig, Skip, author.
Title: The Bible from 30,000 feet / Skip Heitzig.
Other titles: Bible from thirty thousand feet
Description: Eugene, Oregon : Harvest House Publishers, 2017. | Description
    based on print version record and CIP data provided by publisher; resource
    not viewed.
Identifiers: LCCN 2017003963 (print) | LCCN 2017015669 (ebook) | ISBN
    9780736970303 (ebook) | ISBN 9780736970297 (hardcover)
Subjects: LCSH: Bible—Introductions.
Classification: LCC BS475.3 (ebook) | LCC BS475.3 .H45 2017 (print) | DDC
    220.6/1—dc23
LC record available at https://lccn.loc.gov/2017003963

Printed in the United States of America

17 18 19 20 21 22 23 24 25 / ML-JC / 10 9 8 7 6 5 4 3

This book is dedicated to all of God's people
who believe the Bible is important enough
to read,
to learn,
to know,
to apply,
and to obey.

"Your words were found, and I ate them,
and Your word was to me the joy and rejoicing of my heart"
(Jeremiah 15:16).

Acknowledgments

A depth of gratitude is due to the late Dr. George Campbell Morgan, who pastored Westminster Chapel in London during the early 1900s. He was always a man of one book. He knew the Bible and was committed to teaching the books of the Bible to his Friday night Bible class, which thousands attended weekly. His famous bird's-eye view outlines of books of the Bible gave me the initial inspiration for this work.

Dr. J. Vernon McGee also must be mentioned since his daily radio broadcast, *Thru the Bible,* was my daily bread for years in the early part of my Christian walk. His practical, rubber-meets-the-road approach gave me great encouragement.

Pastor Chuck Smith was my pastor for many years, as well as a friend and mentor. Inspired by both aforementioned men, Chuck took his congregation through every book of the Bible, giving me both a satisfied heart and a hunger for more. All three of these great expositors have passed from the earthly scene, but their influence lingers on in my life. All three, as the writer of Hebrews declares, "being dead yet speaketh" (Hebrews 4:11 KJV).

My heart is full of gratitude for my wife, Lenya. She kept insisting that this book be written to equip people with the principles of Scripture. She has faithfully been by my side for decades and has poured more encouragement into me than any other single human being.

Quentin Guy has helped out immensely by taking my rudimentary notes on each book of the Bible and working closely with me to craft a literary expression. Because of him, this book is readable! Thanks, Quent.

Thanks to Brian Nixon and Lorin Bentley for their labor of love in providing both helpful advice and actual content.

Thanks to my faithful assistant, Laney St. Martin, who made sure that my writing schedule was kept sacred so I could finish the manuscript.

A humble shout-out to the flock of Calvary Albuquerque! I love their love for Bible teaching. Every time I wonder, *Aren't they sick of me yet?,* I look out to see them coming back for more.

Special thanks to Bob Hawkins and the fine folks at Harvest House Publishers for believing in this *cruising altitude* approach to Scripture and for their insights, edits, and support.

CONTENTS

Old Testament

New Testament

GIVE ME A YEAR, AND I'LL GIVE YOU THE BIBLE

It takes just under seventy hours to read the Bible straight through at a moderate rate. But most people would never approach it nonstop like that. To do so would be tedious. However, if that reading time were spread out over the course of an entire year, it would average out to about an hour and twenty minutes per week.

This weekly approach breaks down the Bible into more bite-sized chunks, allowing you to set aside time for meditating upon and applying the Bible's meaningful truths. In your hand is a tool that will help you to do exactly that. In fact, I want to make a deal with you: Give me a year—fifty-two weeks—and I'll give you a working understanding of the message of the Bible. I will help you to see it as a whole, understand and apply the main principles of all sixty-six books, and show you how it all fits together, revealing a panorama of God's mind and plan as revealed in Scripture.

When you fly at 30,000 feet (the relative cruising altitude for most commercial aircraft), a glance out the window reveals a broad, curved horizon and the shifting blur of the ground below. You have a sense of the massiveness of heaven and earth, but not the details of everyday life—no buildings or cars or people, and certainly none of the triumphs or struggles of human hearts as they engage with one another at ground level. So when you consider the title of this book, *The Bible from 30,000 Feet,* you might wonder how you could get anything meaningful from looking at the Bible from such a great height. *Just think of all the things you'd miss,* you might say. And while that would be a struggle with any other book you might read, the Bible is different.

The Bible is unlike any other book you will ever read, unlike any book that has ever been written. It's both personal—a love letter from God to us—and historical—an account of God's interactions with His people over thousands of years. It

gives us the big picture—God creating the world and everything in it, the forming of nations, God's plan of redemptive history—and the intimate details—Jesus pouring His heart out to His Father in Gethsemane, David describing his brokenness after his affair with Bathsheba, Hannah praising God for her miracle child Samuel. It is certainly worth the effort to consider every single paragraph and verse, and the nuance of every word. But there is also value in stepping back from the details and considering the larger scope. We can sometimes "miss the forest for the trees" and lose our bearings of the larger story amid the numerous details. Therefore both approaches are needed—up close and farther away.

Reading the Bible ought to be a lifetime commitment. God is deeply concerned with the ins and outs of your life, and nothing does His work in your heart like His Word. But I am concerned, even alarmed, because the tendency in our age is to drift away from listening to God's voice in His Word. The biblical understanding of past generations has become the biblical illiteracy of modern ones. Researchers tell us that only 19 percent of churchgoers read their Bibles daily.* I've written this book in part to counter that trend. God's Word is a living thing—and it can do His work in your life, even from 30,000 feet. "His powerful Word is sharp as a surgeon's scalpel, cutting through everything, whether doubt or defense, laying us open to listen and obey. Nothing and no one is impervious to God's Word. We can't get away from it—no matter what" (Hebrews 4:13 MSG). No matter who or where you are, the Bible can still speak to you and show you vital truths about God—His love for you, and His plans for your life.

I want to give you a taste of God's Word, a movable feast you can eat over a year's time, in chapter-sized portions. In *The Bible from 30,000 Feet* I've covered the whole Bible in fifty-two chapters. So if you'll give me a year, I'll give you the Bible. Stick with this plan for the next fifty-two weeks, and I promise you that you won't regret it; in fact, your appetite for the Scriptures will increase. You'll gain a clearer sense of the big picture, the grand plan of God for the world…and for *you*.

In order to give you an overview of each book, I've provided a flight plan at the beginning of each chapter, using FLIGHT as an acronym:

Facts: The basics about who wrote the book and when it was written

Landmarks: A brief overview of the major themes of each Bible book

Itinerary: The key points—the distinguishing topics and memorable moments in each book

* Rankin, Russ. "Study: Bible Engagement in Churchgoers' Hearts, Not Always Practiced," LifeWay Research, accessed March 15, 2017, http://www.lifeway.com/Article/research-survey-bible-engagement-churchgoers.

Gospel: Jesus is in every book of the Bible, and this tells where to find Him

History: A bit of context to set the scene for each book

Travel Tips: Points of application to keep in mind as you travel through the Bible

The **In Flight** portion of each chapter is a compact version of my teaching on each of the Bible's books. You'll find that, even from this surveyor's perspective, the Bible is full of amazing people, stories, and events—and most of all, an amazing God. My hope and prayer is that your appetite will be whetted—that after reading this book, you'll go back to *the* Book and dig in, hungry for more. An airplane can take you on incredible adventures, whether for work or play, but the Bible can change your life—even from 30,000 feet.

Finally, one of the advantages of our flyover vantage point is the ability it gives us to see what has been called the Bible's *scarlet thread of redemption*—God's redemptive plan through the ages. From the very beginning God planned to redeem mankind from sin and restore us to intimate relationship with Himself. At this altitude, we see clearly that the Bible is really all about one person, Jesus Christ. The Old Testament points toward Him through prophecy and types, and the New Testament describes the immediate and ultimate effects of His first and second comings.

So as we prepare to take this yearlong flight together, make sure you buckle your seatbelt, place your heart in an upright position, and don't hesitate to ask your flight attendant, the Holy Spirit, for any assistance you'll need along the way.

Skip Heitzig

OLD TESTAMENT

GENESIS
FLIGHT PLAN

Facts

Author

Moses authored Genesis, the first of the five opening books of the Bible, which Jesus called the "Law of Moses" (Luke 24:44). Moses lived 120 years (Deuteronomy 34:7). His life can be split into three parts: his life in Egypt (around 1500 BC), in Midian (the mid-1400s BC), and in the wilderness (the early 1400s BC).

Date Written

We don't know where or when Moses wrote Genesis, but he could have started to collect the facts about God and His people after he was taken into Pharaoh's house. He probably finished writing the book sometime prior to his exile in the wilderness of Midian.

Landmarks

Genesis is the foundation of God's work as Creator and Redeemer of His creation. It all begins here—creation, sin, God's remedy for sin, family, government, and the origins of the nation of Israel. To get a grip on all these beginnings, we'll follow a set of landmarks: four great events—the formation, the fall, the flood, the fallout from man's rebellion—and a foursome of great men.

Itinerary

- Four Great Events (Genesis 1–11)
  - The Formation (Genesis 1–2)
  - The Fall of Man (Genesis 3–5)
  - The Flood (Genesis 6–9)
  - The Fallout from Rebellion (Genesis 10–11)

- Four Great Men (Genesis 12–50)
    - Abraham (Genesis 12–25)
    - Isaac (Genesis 21–28, 35)
    - Jacob (Genesis 25–37, 42–43, 45–49)
    - Joseph (Genesis 37–50)

Gospel

The Old Testament predicts the coming of a *Superman,* One who will repair the damage caused by Eden's evil interloper, a dark prince who spoiled God's creation. Numerous prophecies, predictions, and allusions point to both the first and second coming of the Messiah, Jesus Christ. These form the trail mapping God's plan to save mankind—a scarlet thread of redemption woven throughout the Scriptures.

The first thread was woven after the fall, when Jesus was introduced as the Seed of the woman who will overcome Satan (Genesis 3:15). We also see a symbol of salvation in Noah's ark (like Jesus, the sole means of salvation), Jacob's ladder (presaging Jesus as the only connection we have to God in heaven), and in the parallels between Joseph and Jesus: both were betrayed by loved ones and sold, and both played mediators between life and death. God's redemptive plan goes back to the beginning of time.

History

The story of Genesis unfolds in the Fertile Crescent of the Middle East, starting with Mesopotamia (modern Iraq). Some controversy exists as to how long ago "the beginning" was, but simple math indicates that Genesis covers at least 2500 years of human history, focusing on the emergence of the Hebrew people. Noted biblical archaeologist Dr. Steven Collins places the human record of Genesis between 3300 BC (the Stone Age) and 1800 BC (the Middle Bronze Age).

Travel Tips

The challenge of Genesis is to personalize these well-known stories, understand that they are real accounts of real events and real people, and learn practical lessons from them. That begins with three points of recognition:

- Recognize God is the Creator (Genesis 1). God created all things for a purpose. As the Bible unfolds, this purpose is ultimately found in

Jesus Christ. First, all people must recognize their need for a relationship with their Creator through Christ. How do we do that? Read on.

- Recognize you are a sinner (Genesis 2). Humans are fallen beings in need of redemption. One of the key moments in Genesis is when God established a relationship with Abraham through his seed—down the line, that was Christ. Ultimately, Christ will crush the serpent (Satan). Part of this "crushing" of sin in the world is to make new creations of people who turn from their sin and to Jesus Christ.

- Recognize that God has a purpose for you (Genesis 12–37). As you read Genesis, you'll find all types of characters and narratives. All of them come into contact—for better or worse—with God. God is the great conductor, leading the symphony of life according to His purposes. When you turn to God, know that He has a plan for your life: "to be conformed to the image of His Son" (Romans 8:29). As a Christian, your purpose is to grow more Christlike day by day until Christ either comes for His church or calls you home. Your growth starts here in Genesis.

In Flight

The Formation (Genesis 1–2)

The record of the formation of the universe is simple, straightforward, and unambiguous: God created it all (Genesis 1:1-5). That's it. If you can accept that first verse of the Bible, you should have no problem believing the rest of it.

> If you can accept that first verse of the Bible, you should have no problem believing the rest of it.

Here's a rundown of Earth's first week:

- Day one: God turned on the light, dividing day from night.
- Day two: God set up the hydrological cycle, separating the water in the sky from the water covering the earth. This "firmament" was different from the sky we have now; it has been described as a "vapor canopy" that surrounded the earth and lasted until the flood.

- Day three: God pooled the waters into oceans (possibly even a single ocean), creating land masses (possibly even a single continent). Then, because it now had a place to grow, God produced plant life, vegetation of all sorts, each with its own ability to reproduce itself through seeds.

- Day four: God installed some celestial bodies—the sun, moon, and stars—and instituted days, seasons, and years.

- Day five: God put birds into play, along with sea life—both examples of amazing diversity and complexity.

- Day six: God generated the animal kingdom in all of its remarkable variety and then topped off His creation with its pinnacle: human beings, created in His own image (Genesis 1:27). He arranged food for everyone, set Adam and Eve in charge of taking care of His creation, and called it all "good" (Genesis 1:31).

- Day seven: His work completed, God rested (Genesis 2:1-2).

Creation itself is amazing—a perfect balance of conditions that make life on earth possible—but even more powerful is the thought that God cares so much about the people who live in it. Right away, God gave Adam an equal counterpart and helper, Eve (Genesis 2:18-25), and made them caretakers of His creation.

The Fall (Genesis 3–5)

Up to this point, God had given mankind only one negative command: not to eat from a particular tree in the garden, the "tree of the knowledge of good and evil" (Genesis 2:17). Everything else—all the good things in Eden—was theirs to do with as they pleased. However, God also gave us free will. From the start, we had the ability to choose our actions.

Prohibition becomes an invitation, and Satan knew it. He questioned God, God's Word, and God's motives (Genesis 3:1-7). Eve's first mistake was engagement with this clever, single-minded entity. Adam's mistake was just standing there while she did it.

That day marked the beginning of what the Bible calls *the world*—a term used especially in the New Testament to describe the system of thinking and behaving that opposes God (1 John 2:16; 5:19). God established His creation, the physical world, and called it good, and now Satan intruded with his *modus operandi,* the spiritual world of deception and destruction. Satan came to commandeer God's world, and Adam handed him the title deed.

> ### This is the darkest day in the history of the human race, where all our problems began.

This is the darkest day in the history of the human race, where all our problems began (Romans 5:12). Death spread and reigned from Adam to Moses. When Adam took that fruit and sinned against God, he acted as the representative of every human being ever—so that the effects of what he did spread to everyone throughout all history. Every human being to be born would now have a sin-imbued nature.

It was a game-changer for Satan too. When God laid out the consequences for Adam and Eve's disobedience—bearing children in pain and working the ground to feed their family, among other things—He nailed down Satan's future as well: At some point in the future, God would provide a way to defeat him (Genesis 3:15). This marked the beginning of God's long-term plan of redemption. Eventually, a descendant of Eve—specifically, a woman from God's chosen people Israel—would give birth to the Savior, a Son who would undo everything Satan accomplished in Eden and crush him in the process. It set Satan on a narrower path, one intended not just to bring down mankind but to end the godly line through whom this Messiah would come. God's rescue operation for the world was now set in motion.

Satan set about polluting everything God had made, looking to destroy the human race and end the threat to his power on earth. The end result was a human race so twisted and wicked that God decided to reboot life on a global scale (Genesis 6:17).

The Flood (Genesis 6–9)

When God decided to wipe mankind off the face of the earth, He chose a single individual to live so that the human race could begin again. Noah alone was considered righteous by God (Genesis 6:5-8), so God made him the instrument of mankind's physical salvation.

If you look back to Satan's desire to disrupt God's ultimate plan to save mankind and crush him, he and his minions probably responded with a resounding cheer to God's decision to send a flood: *Yes! He's going to wipe all of them out. Game over.* But, as usual, the enemy of our souls underestimated the Lord of the universe. God established His covenant with Noah (Genesis 6:18), and told him to build a boat. "Here are the specs," He told Noah (Genesis 6:14-16), and Noah obeyed. No doubt, Noah took a lot of grief from his neighbors as he faithfully built this enormous vessel. His very work on it was a witness to the unbelieving world (Hebrews 11:7). And then it started to rain.

And boy, did it rain (Genesis 7:11)! The foundations of the earth broke up, releasing gushing torrents that had been stored in subterranean cavities. The vapor canopy dissolved, pouring down water from the heavens. More water than most had ever even imagined was suddenly released—for forty straight days. Hills were covered, then mountains, and if you weren't on the boat, you died, wiped away like grime off a windshield (Genesis 7:17-24). Meanwhile, God kept life and hope alive on one boat.

God's Word tells us He unleashed a worldwide flood but preserved life and kept His promise to maintain the eventual line of the Savior through Noah and his family. Even in judgment, then and now, God is just and merciful. The shame of it is what mankind did with its second chance.

> ## Even in judgment, then and now, God is just and merciful.

The Fallout (Genesis 9–11)

After the flood, people and animals followed God's command to "be fruitful and multiply" (Genesis 8:17; 9:1). Mankind established a new social order, ordaining human government with the authority to exercise capital punishment as a just response to murder (Genesis 9:5-6). There was also a new physical order. The protective vapor canopy, a sort of thermal blanket that had surrounded earth since its creation, had been destroyed as a result of the floodwaters bursting forth, resulting in a more dangerous environment (storms, earthquakes, hurricanes, tornadoes, and drought, plus higher exposure to solar radiation) that contributed to a general shortening of human lifespans.

That didn't stop people from multiplying. Genesis 10 is called the Table of Nations because it records how Noah's sons, Shem, Ham, and Japheth, had their own children, who eventually became various people groups and nations around the world. However, the second half of God's command was to "fill the earth"—*to spread out*, in other words. Instead, they did the opposite, coming together to build a superstate that stood in rebellion against God (Genesis 11:1-4).

God, of course, saw what they were doing, but more than that, He saw why. The people were united in opposition to God's direct instruction, so He decided to head them off at the pass, confusing their language and forcing them to abandon the tower at Babel (Genesis 11:5-9).

God's response to man's rebellion was the beginning not just of historical Babylon but spiritual Babylon. Everything that Satan did and does to disrupt God's plan to bring salvation through His people, the Jews, and to deceive and destroy mankind in general can be categorized as spiritual Babylon. It's what we mean when we speak of *the world* or *the world system*, in contrast with God's kingdom and kingdom values. The choice between the two shapes each of our lives, as it did the next phase of God's plan for mankind, led by four great men.

The Foursome (Genesis 12–50)

As is so often the case throughout history, God uses people to accomplish His purposes. The rest of Genesis is the account of four such people—four great men whom we call the patriarchs: Abraham, Isaac, Jacob, and Joseph.

Abraham

The first time they met, God told Abram, "I want you to leave everything you're familiar with; get out of your comfort zone. Though it's going to be hard to leave all of that behind, what I'm going to replace that with—how I'm going to bless you—is incalculable, mind-blowing. So leave everything that has shaped your life up till now, make a clean break, and come follow Me." And in a remarkable show of faith, Abram obeyed (Genesis 12:1-4).

One of the key events in the Bible is the covenant God made with Abram (Genesis 15). It was a one-sided promise, whereby God would do all that was necessary to fulfill the conditions. Abram's part was to trust God—to remain patient, hopeful, and full of belief. Abram had concerns and he shared them, but God didn't get mad at Abram. Instead, He took him for a walk and repeated His promises (Genesis 15:5). It was a comforting, reassuring moment—and a reminder of two important things: God can handle your hard questions, and He always keeps His promises.

Abram responded with faith (Genesis 15:6), and from that moment on, God said, "You're righteous. I'm taking your faith and crediting it to you, calling you righteous because of your faith." It was a pivotal moment, establishing a precedent for how God arranges everything so that unrighteous people can be made righteous in His sight.

In the meantime, however, Abram's wife, Sarai, was getting impatient. She thought, as so many of us do when we're tired of waiting on God's promises, *I'm going to help God out. After all, God helps those who help themselves.* Not only is that idea nowhere to be found in the Bible (Benjamin Franklin popularized this ancient sentiment in his *Poor Richard's Almanack*), the main thrust of Scripture is the exact opposite—that God helps the helpless.

That's exactly what God did here. He cleaned up the mess Sarai caused when she gave her servant Hagar to sleep with Abram in order to produce a child (Genesis 16). God would bless Ishmael, the son Hagar had with Abram, but He would keep His promise and give Abram and Sarai a son, Isaac, through whom He would keep the line of Jesus going. As a symbol of His faithfulness, God also changed their names to Abraham and Sarah.

On His way to destroy the wicked cities of Sodom and Gomorrah with a pair of angels, God dropped in on Abraham to let him know that his son would be born within a year (Genesis 17:15-21). Sodom and Gomorrah were doomed (Genesis 19:13), but God is always looking to save any who want to be saved. For Abraham's sake, He saved Abraham's wayward nephew Lot from the destruction (Genesis 19:29).

A bit later, God gave Abraham the hardest test ever, telling him to offer his precious son Isaac as a sacrifice (Genesis 22:1-2). Whatever thoughts Abraham may have had about why, his only response was obedience. Another remarkable point is that God felt it necessary to identify Isaac as the son "whom you love" (Genesis 22:2). This is the first use of the word *love* in the Bible, and it was written about a father loving his "only son" and preparing to offer him in sacrifice. It clearly foreshadows God's own plans for His only Son, who would be sacrificed on the same mount years later.

Abraham embraced God's will through a process. He obeyed God's command, but he also thought about what he knew of God's nature and character, and that gave him confidence that God would work everything out for the best. His faith was tested severely and he passed God's test, leaving a legacy of godliness for Isaac.

Isaac

As Abraham's life drew to a close, he sent a servant out on a final mission—to find a wife for Isaac. His own wife Sarah had recently died (Genesis 23:2), and he was discharging at long last a common duty, ensuring his son's happiness and the continuation of his line. God orchestrated the match, bringing Abraham's servant Eliezer to Rebekah, confirming the match, and then blessing his journey home with the young bride-to-be (Genesis 24:12-63).

It's a beautiful love story, and Isaac's part in it is touching. While Eliezer was away he waited patiently and sought God, trusting his father's judgment to make a match. It was a beautiful beginning for the relationship. I wish I could tell you that they all lived happily ever after, but they didn't.

Here's a quick flyover: Rebekah was infertile, like her mother-in-law Sarah had been, so Isaac prayed for her and she became pregnant. However, it was a difficult pregnancy, and she asked God why. The Lord replied, "Two nations are in your womb" (Genesis 25:23). Rebekah's twins would indeed become fathers of nations: Esau was born first, red-haired and hairy, and then came Jacob, grabbing at his brother's heel to pull him back inside the womb.

Their names fit—Hairy and Heel-catcher—and their personalities made their differences even clearer. Isaac encouraged Esau's sportiness and Rebekah doted on Jacob's indoor acumen (Genesis 25:28). Of course, as whenever parents pick favorites, it went poorly.

Jacob

God had predicted that Rebekah's secondborn would rule over her firstborn (Genesis 25:23), but it seemed highly unlikely that Jacob would take Esau's position and inheritance. Esau was their father's favorite, strong and outgoing, an obvious provider. However, he was also ruled by his urges. Jacob made up for his lack of outdoor skills by being clever and even conniving. He bided his time, waiting to make a play for his brother's birthright—the inheritance and property rights of the firstborn—based on Esau's weakness.

Jacob's cunning swindled Esau twice. The first time, he got his brother to abandon his birthright for a bowl of stew (Genesis 25:29-34). The second time, with his mom's help, Jacob dressed up like Esau in pelts, sprayed on some *eau d'Outdoorsman*, and tricked his dad into giving him his brother's blessing while Esau was out hunting at their father's request. Isaac was blind in his old age, and Jacob got away with this. But Jacob had to flee when Esau became enraged over his brother's deception and wanted to kill him (Genesis 27:41-45).

Despite all the massive family dysfunction going on, God was sovereign. He let Jacob know He was with him, giving him a dream of a stairway full of angels connecting heaven and earth, and repeating the promise He had made to Jacob's ancestors (Genesis 28:13-15). It was the first of two key moments in Jacob's faith. God's timing was perfect, because Jacob was in for a rough season with his uncle Laban, a man as tricky and self-serving as he himself had been.

Jacob fell hard for Laban's younger daughter, Rachel, and Laban agreed to their marriage in return for Jacob's service to him (Genesis 29:9-20). Jacob jumped at the chance to earn his bride's hand and said, "I'll serve you seven years if I can marry Rachel." Laban agreed and played it cool, but he also played Jacob for a lovesick fool.

Sure enough, after Jacob met the terms of their deal, Laban switched daughters on the wedding night. Ironically, he pulled a reverse-Jacob, switching his firstborn daughter Leah for his secondborn, Rachel, Jacob's intended (Genesis 29:18-25). Payback! Jacob went to Laban and said, "You tricked me!" But Laban slickly siphoned another seven years off of him, and Jacob ended up working fourteen years for two wives.

That kind of family drama was a constant companion. Rachel and Leah ended up competing to see who could bear Jacob the most sons, even bringing in their handmaidens, Hagar-style, to up their totals. Leah won the babython, eight sons to four, and with a total of twelve sons, Jacob was *really* blessed.

Eventually, Jacob left Laban and headed home to Canaan. He got word that Esau was coming to meet him. That led to Jacob's second pivotal moment of faith. He sent his family on ahead and hung back to wait for Esau, thinking there was a decent chance his brother would kill him. That night, the incredible happened: Jacob wrestled "a Man" who turned out to be God—and whom Jacob did not let go of until he received God's blessing (Genesis 32:24-26). It was at that point that God changed Jacob's name, calling him Israel in honor of his struggle (Genesis 32:28). God also blessed Jacob's meeting with Esau, which went without incident.

Jacob learned the hard way that it's more important to ask "Am I on God's side?" rather than the more typical question, "Is God on my side?" It was a question one of his sons also learned to ask as he went through various trials on the way to the triumphs God had in store for him.

Joseph

The story of Jacob's second-to-last son is one of the most epic in the entire Bible. Though I'll just hit the highlights, his impressive biography and incredible personal journey unfolds for us in Genesis 37–50.

Joseph was a dreamer shaped by the school of hard knocks, a believer molded in a crucible of pride, betrayal, and a series of sudden rises and falls into a model of perseverance and faith. Most people are familiar with the Sunday-morning highlight reel of Joseph's life: Drama was a fact of life for Jacob's eleventh son (and Rachel's first). He was Daddy's favorite (another family theme), was given a fancy technicolor coat that pretty much screamed "Hate me!," shared some dreams that depicted him lording it over all his jealous brothers—and his parents, got thrown into a hole by his fed-up brothers, and was sold into slavery in Egypt. That's just Act I.

In Act II, Joseph caught the eye of his owner, Potiphar (an official in Pharaoh's court), moved upstairs to run the household, and got hit on by the first desperate housewife, Mrs. Potiphar. When he refused her advances on ethical grounds, she ratted him out and got him thrown in jail, where, even though he interpreted some dreams for some of Pharaoh's key guys, he languished, forgotten by everyone except God.

In the final act, Joseph was recalled from prison to interpret some troubling dreams for Pharaoh himself. God gave him the meanings of the dreams and eventual favor with Pharaoh, who put him in charge of plans to prepare Egypt to survive the famine the dreams foretold. Everyone in Egypt got fed, and people came from all over the region to buy food, including Joseph's brothers from Canaan.

When Joseph revealed himself to his brothers, they thought they were dead men, fearing their younger brother's revenge. But Joseph summed up the whole affair by crediting God for turning their evil into a blessing for many, including them (Genesis 50:20)! Pharaoh insisted that Joseph bring his whole family down to a temporary land of plenty in Goshen, father and son were lovingly reunited, and the family was reconciled.

Enjoy this moment, because when we pick up the story in the book of Exodus, things will have changed. The children of Israel will have multiplied greatly, in keeping with God's promise to Abraham, Isaac, and Jacob. But they will have fallen out of favor with Egypt's rulers and been made slaves. In Egypt, they were allowed to grow and become a great nation. They thrived and God blessed them, but Egypt was never meant to be their home. God had promised His people the land to which He had called Abraham, and He would rescue them from Egypt, calling them to go home.

EXODUS
FLIGHT PLAN

Facts

Author

Jesus stated that Exodus was written by Moses (Mark 12:26), and the earliest Jewish scribes agreed. It is the second book of the Torah, known as the five books of Moses or "the Law of Moses" (Luke 24:44).

Date Written

Exodus was probably written shortly after the book of Genesis, possibly between 1445 and 1405 BC. Exodus covers the period of time during which God freed the Hebrew people from servitude in Egypt and they wandered for forty years in the wilderness.

Landmarks

The two major themes of Exodus are redemption and identification. God delivered His people *from* slavery, and then He decreed *to* His people how to live free. That one-two punch at the heart of Exodus reflects the Christian life: Once Jesus redeems you from your sin, you start reading your Bible and going to church as a way to identify yourself with Him. Israel's great deliverance can be seen in four phases: domination, liberation, revelation, and identification.

Itinerary

- Domination: The Bondage of Egypt (Exodus 1–12)
  - A Misplaced Recollection
  - A Misguided Emancipator
  - A Transformative Manifestation
  - A Mousy Messenger
  - A Monumental Encounter

- Liberation: The Barrenness of the Wilderness (Exodus 13–18)
  - Miraculous Reminders
- Revelation: The Bringing of the Law (Exodus 18–31)
  - A Must-Read: God's Top Ten List
  - Major Consequences and Merciful Maximums
- Identification: The Birth Pains of the Nation (Exodus 32–40)
  - The *Uh-oh* Moment
  - A Holy Meeting Place

Gospel

When God gave Moses the law to guide the Israelites' lives and worship of Him, He was also pointing to the eternal covenant that came in Christ. Under the covenant of the Law, Moses mediated between God and His people, but under the covenant of grace, the perfect Mediator came in the person of Jesus Christ—fully God and fully man.

The Passover—including the death of Egypt's firstborn, the shedding of a lamb's blood, and the departure from bondage—is one of the clearest and most dramatic pictures of salvation in Christ in the entire Bible. New Testament authors point this out frequently (John 1:29, 36; 19:14; Acts 8:32-35; 1 Corinthians 5:7; 15:3-4; 1 Peter 1:19-20; Revelation 5:6-9).

The details of the tabernacle, recorded in Exodus 26–27 and 30, foreshadow heaven and Christ Himself. Jesus, the Great High Priest, made it possible to have fellowship with the Father. The tabernacle eventually became the temple, and Jesus eventually became the ultimate fulfillment of the temple as "the Word became flesh and dwelt among us" (John 1:14).

History

The book of Exodus covers about a forty-year period, beginning 350 years after Joseph's death. The historical time frame of the Exodus wanderings is controversial; people have differing opinions about the exact dates and locations of the events. Most agree Exodus is set in the Bronze Age, but scholars debate whether it occurred earlier (1400s BC) or later (1200s BC) in that era. The identity of the pharaoh described in Exodus is also debated, depending on an early view (Thutmose III or Thutmose IV), or a late one (Rameses II).

Travel Tips

We've all had a Genesis—a beginning—but not everyone has had an Exodus—a deliverance from bondage. Much more than history, the Bible is *His* story—God's story of the redemption of His creation. How does Exodus relate to you today?

- Recognize your need for deliverance. At some point in your life, you will have to come to terms with your need for redemption. Part of observing the Passover includes retelling the Israelites' redemption story so that God and His deliverance won't be forgotten. Your redemption story—how you came to know Jesus—should be part of your testimony too.

- Recognize that Jesus is the deliverer. Moses said, "The LORD your God will raise up for you a Prophet like me from your midst. Him you shall hear" (Deuteronomy 18:15). God gave His people a new life when He liberated them from Egypt, but, mighty as it was, that deliverance only pointed to a greater liberation by the One who delivered the whole world from sin's grip: Jesus Christ.

- Resolve to spend more time with the God who loves you and saved you. God established the law and the tabernacle to teach His people how to worship Him properly. However, He was also making it clear that He wanted to spend time with them, in their presence, enjoying and blessing them.

> **Resolve to spend more time with the God who loves you and saved you.**

In Flight

As we fly over the book of Exodus, we're going to witness the birth of a nation. Births are exciting, but also painful; ask any mother. *Exodus* means "going out." Abraham's descendants through his grandson Jacob came into Egypt as a family of seventy people. They would leave after 400 years as a nation of around two million (Genesis 15:13). God had bigger plans in mind for His people, but they came with a challenge.

Domination: The Bondage of Egypt (Exodus 1–13)

A Misplaced Recollection

Between the end of Genesis and the beginning of Exodus, 350 years had passed, long enough for any nation to forget its roots, its history. All that Joseph had done to save Egypt from famine had been forgotten, along with respect for God and favor for Israel. God blessed the people of Israel anyway, and their numbers increased dramatically. In order to curb the growth of this exploding minority, Pharaoh issued a terrible order to the Hebrew midwives: kill the firstborn sons (Exodus 1:15-16). Because they feared God, they found a way around the order; God blessed them for their civil disobedience and multiplied His people even more (vv. 17-21).

It was under this heavy oppression that God produced His deliverer: Moses, one of the most amazing men in the Bible—in his character, in what he withstood, in his closeness to God. He became Pharaoh's adopted grandson and was raised with all the wealth and privilege of an Egyptian prince. Egypt was the mightiest kingdom in the known world at the time, a progressive culture of science, mathematics, academia, architecture, and engineering. According to the Roman-Jewish historian Josephus, Moses was next in line to be Pharaoh.[1]

A Misguided Emancipator

Apparently, though, Moses was aware of his Jewish roots, and he felt some kind of empathy for the Israelites' troubles. Admittedly, he expressed it in a rather misguided way, killing an Egyptian taskmaster who was beating one of his fellow Hebrews. Moses "looked this way and that way"—but, unfortunately, not up—"and when he saw no one, he killed the Egyptian and hid him in the sand" (Exodus 2:12).

Seems to me that, because sand blows away so easily, that it's not the best material to use for burying a corpse. Moses's dirty deed and sandy cover-up made for a rocky landing. The good news is that Moses was not an accomplished murderer; the bad news, for him, was that he was found out pretty quickly and forced to flee. He ended up all the way across the Arabian Peninsula in Midian.

It's been well said that Moses spent forty years of his life as a prince, trying to be something, the next forty as a shepherd, discovering he was really nothing, and the final forty as Israel's leader, proof that God can take nothing and make something out of it.

A Transformative Manifestation

God made contact with Moses in an unusual way, fitting the path of Moses's life: a burning bush. When a flaming shrub calls your name, you stop and look. When that flaming shrub tells you you're standing on holy ground, you take off your sandals as instructed. When the flaming shrub identifies itself as the God of your ancestors, you hit the ground face-first (Exodus 3:1-6). God was bringing Moses into the loop of the covenant He made with Abraham and reiterated to Isaac and Jacob—and Moses was going to be His guy to get His people back on track to the land He had promised to the patriarchs.

Also, whereas God introduced Himself to Abraham by telling him to leave home, He identified Himself to Moses by His name: "I AM WHO I AM" (Exodus 3:14). He had not done so with any of the patriarchs (Exodus 6:2-3), but here God said, "Thus you shall say to the children of Israel, 'I AM has sent me to you'" (Exodus 3:14).

A Mousy Messenger

While Moses was clearly impressed with God, he just as clearly felt unequal to the task. God responded to his excuses, one by one: Moses said, "What if they don't believe me?" and God upgraded Moses's shepherd's staff to a snake-stick. Throw it down and it becomes a snake; grab it by the tail and it's a staff again (Exodus 4:1-5). Then God had him put his hand in his coat, turned it white with leprosy, and then healed it when Moses stuck his hand back in his coat. Then God told him, "If those two tricks don't get their attention, just pour some river water on dry land; it'll turn to blood."

Moses should have exclaimed, "Wow! Cool! I've never seen anything like that. They'll be blown away." Instead, he came up with another excuse: "I never took speech in high school; public speaking gives me butterflies." God was ready for that one too (Exodus 4:11-12): "Look, Moses. I made your mouth, right? Trust Me, and I'll give you the words to put in it."

Any inability you have can be overshadowed by the ability God has.

Any inability you have can be overshadowed by the ability God has. This should've been enough for Moses, but it wasn't. Moses's final protest was less of an excuse than the heart of his other excuses: "Send somebody else—anyone, Lord!" That's when God got a little upset (vv. 14-17): "You have a brother, Aaron, right? Take him with you. I'll tell you what to say, you tell him, and he'll say it. So, take your stick, do your signs, and don't let a flaming branch smack you on the way out!"

A Monumental Encounter

God's chosen leader Moses, with Aaron as spokesperson, opposed the king of Egypt himself, *mano a mano*, in an epic showdown. God warned Moses in advance that He would harden Pharaoh's heart (Exodus 4:21-23). God had revealed Himself to Moses; now He would reveal Himself to Pharaoh and the entire nation of Egypt, through a series of plagues—each one a tailor-made judgment designed to attack different aspects of their false belief system.

The Egyptians worshipped a whole host of gods and goddesses. God told Moses, "Against all the gods of Egypt I will execute judgment: I am the LORD" (Exodus 12:12). Moses was just the messenger; the real showdown was between Pharaoh, leader of an economically advanced and militarily powerful dynasty who was hiding behind his deceitful deities, and almighty God, the Great I AM. We know it was no contest, but Pharaoh had yet to learn that. God used plagues to teach him:

Plague one: The water of the Nile River turned to blood (Exodus 7). False god attacked: Osiris, the river god. The Nile was the principal resource of all Egypt, considered the source of all life. This was an attack against a key part of both their worship and ecological systems.

Plague two: Frogs covered the land (Exodus 8:1-14). False god attacked: Heket, the patroness of childbirth and creation. It was a major offense to kill a frog in Egypt, so when the plague put frogs in every nook and cranny, the Egyptians couldn't do anything because it was illegal to kill them!

Plague three: The dust became lice (Exodus 8:16-19). False god attacked: Geb, god of the earth. The word translated "lice" could also mean "sand flies"—nasty little biting bloodsuckers.

Plague four: Flies swarmed across the land (Exodus 8:20-32). False belief attacked: These flies may have been scarab beetles, an Egyptian symbol of eternal life worshipped and placed in sarcophagi, either physically or symbolically, to symbolize their version of the afterlife. As God made clear here, their plan had some serious bugs in it.

Plague five: The livestock were afflicted with pestilence (Exodus 9:1-6). False god attacked: Mnevis, Hathor, or Apis, all livestock-related fertility deities. As was often the pattern with these plagues, only the Egyptian people and their property suffered. In all of these first five plagues, we read that "the heart of Pharaoh became hard" (v. 7).

Plague six: Boils broke out on people and animals (Exodus 9:8-12). False belief attacked: Egyptian priests would throw a handful of ashes into the air and speak a blessing to the people. Moses initiated this one by scattering a handful of soot in front of Pharaoh. When it settled, boils broke out. Also, for the first time, we see that it was "the LORD [who] hardened the heart of Pharaoh" (v. 12).

Plague seven: A mixture of hail and fire obliterated people, livestock, and crops (Exodus 9:13-35). False god attacked: Nut, the Egyptian sky goddess. Further, the devastation of the early crops (flax and barley) showed up Seth, the god of wind and storms, and Isis, the goddess of life, who was often depicted working with flax.

Plague eight: Locusts destroyed the rest of the crops (Exodus 10:1-20). False god attacked: Min, whose annual start-of-harvest festival was ruined by the swarms. It's a safe bet that these locusts were what scientists know today as the short-horned grasshopper, a quick-breeding, fast-moving, voracious group of crop-eaters that still plague the region to this day.[2]

Plague nine: Darkness covered the land (Exodus 10:21-29). False god attacked: Ra, the sun god. This "darkness which may even be felt" (v. 21) sounds pretty creepy. It's possible it was a physical manifestation of the spiritual oppression of Egypt's false worship system.

After the first five plagues, Pharaoh hardened his own heart. It's not until the sixth plague that we see the Lord hardening his heart. It's as if God was saying, "Over and over, you've chosen to go against Me. Now, I'm going to solidify your choice in your heart." If Pharaoh had any perspective at all, he would have been terrified. His stubbornness set the stage for the final and most terrible plague.

Plague ten: The death of the firstborn (Exodus 11:1-10; 12:29-30). God's final, crushing blow did two things: it delivered His people from Egypt, loaded down with Egyptian riches that became theirs for the asking (Exodus 11:2), and it established the Passover as one of the most important, widely observed Jewish festivals— and a foreshadowing of the redemption Christ would purchase on the cross for all mankind. Through Moses, God instructed each Hebrew family to sacrifice a lamb, smear its blood on the lintel and doorposts of their homes, and prepare a special meal commemorating the historical night about to happen (Exodus 12:1-11).

God moved through Egypt that night, striking down every firstborn, whether human or animal—unless the doorframe was smeared with blood. Those houses He would pass over, sparing the inhabitants (Exodus 12:12-13). God did not save people because they were Jewish; He did not condemn people because they were Egyptian. Anyone who was inside a house marked with lamb's blood would be spared. Any firstborn who was outside or in an unmarked house that night would die.

The Passover was all about the blood—the sacrifice—that provided a substitute for the life required by the plague of death. In effect, the blood of a lamb set the slaves free. And it still does. John the Baptist would say of Jesus, "Behold! The

Lamb of God who takes away the sin of the world!" (John 1:29). No wonder God told them, "You shall observe this thing as an ordinance for you and your sons forever" (Exodus 12:24).

Liberation: The Barrenness of the Wilderness (Exodus 13–18)

Miraculous Reminders

After that dreadful night of widespread death, Pharaoh basically kicked Israel out of Egypt, for the Egyptian population was now terrified. Now they were free! As God had predicted, the Egyptians sent the Hebrews out with gold, silver, clothing, and livestock: "Thus they plundered the Egyptians" (Exodus 12:36). It all sounds good—and it was for Israel—but Pharaoh was still a wild card. God hardened His enemy's heart again, knowing he would give chase.

As the Hebrews left Egypt, God initiated a signature mark of His presence: He led them during the day by a pillar of cloud and by night with a pillar of fire, neither of which left the people at any point (Exodus 13:21-22). Later Jewish writings called these signs the *Shekinah*—the "resting place"—that described God's presence in the tabernacle and temple. They were in a barren wasteland but with a divine GPS! God's glory was their rear guard, so that as Pharaoh chased them to the edge of the Red Sea, he couldn't close the gap.

By God's power, Moses split the waters of the Red Sea and the people passed through on dry ground (Exodus 14:22). Pharaoh sent his army right in after them, but God messed with their chariots and made it clear that they were fighting a losing battle because He was with Israel (vv. 23-25). He told Moses to stretch out his hand, and the waters rushed back in, completely wiping out the mightiest army on earth and winning the respect and belief of Israel (vv. 26-31).

However, despite God's continuing presence and provision, Israel had an ongoing trust issue as they traveled; the recurrent theme in the next several chapters is their grumbling and complaining. It was like the worst family vacation ever, with the people trapped in the family station wagon with no air conditioning and no satisfying answer to the question, "Are we there yet?"

Journeying across the Sinai Peninsula—picture serious desert here—they ran out of provisions. They weren't shy about letting Moses know—"at least we had food in Egypt"—but God was ready for them. He brought them quails that night (Exodus 16:12-13), drew water from a rock (Exodus 17:5-6), and dropped bread from heaven for them each morning (Exodus 17:4, 14-15). When they first saw the bread, the people asked, "What is it?"—which in ancient Egyptian was *mon* (translated into English, *manna*). The name stuck, and so did the menu for the next forty years.

Revelation: The Bringing of the Law (Exodus 19–31)

In Exodus 19, the emphasis shifts from liberation to legislation—the laws that God gave Israel to tell the people how to live with Him and each other. He wanted them to be constantly aware of His holiness and their need for grace. In giving Israel His Law, God was anchoring them to their history with Him and giving them their identity as His chosen people, so they would know who they were, where they had come from, and where they were going.

Three months after leaving Egypt, Israel set up camp in the wilderness at the base of Mount Sinai (Exodus 19:2). God called Moses up the mountain and laid out the bottom line: "Remember where you were, what I've done, and how I've cared for you. If you will obey Me, I'll bless you beyond belief." God brought the people out of Egypt, where they had at one time known regular meals, taken them way out in the middle of nowhere, where there was no natural protection or provision, and provided miraculously for them in the wilderness.

> **The purpose of the Law was to make it clear that we couldn't match God's standard of holiness.**

When Moses reported God's message to the people, they got on board (Exodus 19:8): "God has a law? Bring it on; we'll do it." They sounded sincere, but the fatal flaw of the law was the weakness of the human heart to keep it (Deuteronomy 5:29). This didn't become fully clear until Christ came. The purpose of the Law was to make it clear that we couldn't match God's standard of holiness (Romans 3:19). The apostle Paul said, "The law was our tutor to bring us to Christ, that we might be justified by faith" (Galatians 3:24). That's what the new covenant of grace in Christ is all about, but the law came first.

A Must-Read: God's Top Ten List

The law made it clear that God expects two things from His people: supreme devotion to Him and sincere affection for others. He began with His Top Ten, the Ten Commandments, but that was just the beginning. There were many more laws in the chapters to come, but the Ten Commandments work as a summary (Exodus

20:3-17). The first four are about supreme devotion to God, and the last six focus on sincere affection for others:

1. No other gods before God (v. 3)
2. No carved images of any created thing (vv. 4-6)
3. No taking God's name in vain (v. 7)
4. Keep the Sabbath (vv. 8-11)
5. Honor your parents (v. 12)
6. No murder (v. 13)
7. No adultery (v. 14)
8. No stealing (v. 15)
9. No bearing false witness (v. 16)
10. No coveting (v. 17)

These laws look simple, but how many have *you* broken—either inwardly by your desires, or actually? This list reveals God's holiness. He is fundamentally different than we are, set apart by the perfection of His nature and qualities. That came across loud and clear: The people told Moses, "You speak with us, and we will hear; but let not God speak with us, lest we die" (Exodus 20:19). Moses responded, "Do not fear; for God has come to test you, and that His fear may be before you, so that you may not sin" (v. 20). He drew the direct connection between recognizing God's holiness, respecting it, and not sinning.

Major Consequences and Merciful Maximums

God was serious about consequences for breaking His laws. For example, there's a whole host of regulations about capital punishment, beginning with "He who strikes a man so that he dies shall surely be put to death" (Exodus 21:12). Capital punishment predated Moses, going all the way back to Noah's time (Genesis 9:6). While taking any life is definitely not something to be taken lightly, the Law of Moses viewed capital punishment as righteously administered judicial execution.

There were stipulations for people who harmed someone but their victim recovered sufficiently. However, if anyone harmed someone in a lasting way, then the *lex talionis*—the law of exact retribution—came into play (Exodus 21:23-27). The idea was that the punishment must fit the crime. Versions of it appear in the earliest written laws—the code of Hammurabi, for example—and in each of those instances, it was a legal guarantee of payback.

But God included it for a different reason: He wanted to limit vengeance. God understood that human nature isn't satisfied with exact retribution. Our nature is to say, "You poked out one of my eyes? *Thou shalt be blind in both of thine!* You knocked out one of my teeth? *Thou shalt wear dentures forevermore hence!*" We want to keep going until it feels right, not realizing that, at a certain point, we've made it worse than the original crime.

God also ordained laws to regulate three feasts that the Jews were to observe each year (Exodus 23:14): Passover (also called the Feast of Unleavened Bread, celebrating their redemption), Pentecost (also known as the Feast of Harvest, celebrating God's provision), and Tabernacles (also called the Feast of Ingathering and Sukkot, the Feast of Booths, celebrating God's protection in the wilderness). God has always been big into fellowship. People would gather from all over Israel, flooding to Jerusalem at these three times each year, spiritually and socially uniting in worship and celebration.

Identification: The Birth Pains of the Nation (Exodus 32–40)

This is where most people slow down as they read through the Bible. This section is the graveyard of many Christians' New Year's resolutions. All the great stories of beginnings in Genesis draw them in, and the deliverance of Israel in Exodus is thrilling stuff, but then come the details—social laws, moral laws, spiritual laws, property rights, governance—and the enthusiasm dries up. I'm not going to say it's as fast-paced and emotionally stirring as what came before it, but everything here—and in Leviticus, Numbers, and Deuteronomy—is here for a reason. God cares about the details of everyday life. But, since we're cruising at 30,000 feet, I'll just hit a few highlights.

The *Uh-oh* Moment

Everything seemed to be cruising along at this point, but while Moses was up on the mountain receiving all of this instruction from the Lord, the people had a major *uh-oh* moment: the golden calf. Moses was up on the mountain, receiving the law and instructions for the tabernacle from God Himself. In the midst of this powerful revelation, the people down below turned in a snap to idolatry, worshipping an idol they forged from melted-down jewelry. *Anyone seen Moses lately? No? All right, then—it's pagan party time!* Uh-oh.

God told Moses to hightail it back to camp, where his "anger became hot" (Exodus 32:19) and he chucked the stone tablets—freshly hewn and engraved by God's own finger!—down, broke them, mixed up the dust with water, and made everyone chug it (v. 20). *You want to party? Have some wrath-flavored punch.* Moses, incredulous, asked Aaron how it happened. Aaron's response is Classic Buck-Passing 101: "So they gave [their gold] to me, and I cast it into the fire, and this calf came out" (v. 24). *It was amazing, bro—I chucked all this gold in the fire and poof! Instant calf.* More like intentional sin.

Moses made the people choose sides: "Whoever is on the LORD's side—come to me!" (Exodus 32:26). The sons of Levi joined him, but it's not clear if anyone else did. He commanded them to "let every man kill his brother, every man his companion, and every man his neighbor" (v. 27). Three thousand men were killed that day, which sounds harsh, but think of it this way: If they would dare to sin so soon after God's deliverance, right beneath the mountain where God was talking with Moses, there was a serious problem in the camp. Moses cut it out like surgeon removing a tumor.

A Holy Meeting Place

Chastened by the whole episode with the calf, Israel responded with humility and obedience. The people built the tabernacle, resting on each seventh day and following God's specifications (Exodus 40:17-19). This was almost a full year after they had left Egypt. Moses put the replacement set of tablets God had given him, a pot of manna, and Aaron's rod (collectively called "the Testimony") in the ark, inserted the poles through the rings to lift the ark, and set the mercy seat on top.

Once the ark was in the Holy of Holies and everything had been set up properly, God's glory settled over and throughout the tabernacle (Exodus 40:34-35). From that point on, the Hebrews waited on God. When the cloud lifted up from the tabernacle, they packed up and moved on; when it settled, they stopped and set up camp. At that moment, though, the nation rested at the foot of Mount Sinai.

> **God wants to deliver you from the slavery caused by your sin, and take His rightful place at the very center of your life.**

The tabernacle was at the very heart, both geographically and spiritually, of the encampment of Israel. It's a great way to end the book: God's presence dwelling among His people. The grumbling and groaning weren't over yet—far from it!—but the story of Exodus ends in a good place. God delivered His people from the furnace of Egypt into the fiery wilderness, where He provided for, preserved, and protected them. The message of Exodus is this: God wants to deliver you from the slavery caused by your sin, and take His rightful place at the very center of your life.

LEVITICUS
FLIGHT PLAN

Facts

Author

Both internal evidence (more than thirty times we read that "the LORD spoke to Moses") and external evidence (early Jewish testimony) point to Moses's authorship of Leviticus, the third book of the Torah.

Date Written

Leviticus was written sometime in the fifteenth century BC, probably after the completion of the tabernacle. The initial revelation of the law was given to Moses at Mount Sinai (Leviticus 25:1) and during the wilderness wandering.

Landmarks

Leviticus divides into two sections. The first focuses on establishing the law and the way to God through sacrifice. God clarified how people were designed to live and how they could atone for their sins. The second section emphasizes walking with God through sanctification—the process by which we become holy, or set apart, for God's purposes. In a word, we should be *different*.

Itinerary

- The Way to God Through Sacrifice (Leviticus 1–17)
  - Laws of Personal Proximity
  - Laws of Professional Activity
  - Laws of Ritual Purity
  - Laws of National Sanctity
- A Walk with God Through Sanctification (Leviticus 18–27)
  - The Difference of Holiness
  - The Moral Difference

- The Organizational Difference
- The Devotional Difference
- The Community Difference
- The Voluntary Difference

Gospel

The scarlet thread of redemption is clearly woven into the nature and practice of the law and the tabernacle sacrifices. Beyond the veil separating the Holy of Holies in the tabernacle lay the mercy seat, the golden lid of the Ark of the Covenant, upon which the blood of atonement was poured. Jesus became our mercy seat, transforming a place of judgment into a place of mercy.

There are also clear parallels between the sacrifice and scapegoat on the Day of Atonement and Jesus's sacrifice and atonement on the cross. The law made clear God's holiness, and Jesus met its requirements so that anyone can draw close to holy God through Him.

History

Historically, Leviticus is set right after the events of Exodus. Egypt was the reigning regional power and had been for more than 1500 years. It was in the midst of polytheism, building projects, and Pharaoh worship that God, through Moses, not only delivered the Hebrews from slavery but also established the codes of worship for Israel.

Travel Tips

Leviticus has a sort of planned obsolescence; it wasn't made to last. The principles of sacrifice, sanctification, and holiness still hold power for us, but because of the blood of Jesus, we no longer have to make regular, ritualistic sacrifices.

- True sacrifice is voluntary, not forced. Though the Law of Moses contained a lot of mandatory sacrifices, people could offer many sacrifices out of their own free will (Leviticus 27)—a grateful, heartfelt response to what God had done for them.

- Take time to celebrate what God has done for you. The national days of feasting and sacrifice prescribed in Leviticus reminded the Jews of God's deliverance from Egypt and provision in the wilderness.

Celebrate the moments in your life during which God has shown Himself strong on your behalf.

- Be thankful that God is concerned with every detail of your life. Much of the law deals with the human body—dietary restrictions, how to treat illnesses, and how to avoid contamination. God wants you to take care of your body as well as your soul.

Be thankful that God is concerned with every detail of your life.

In Flight

In Genesis, we saw the condemnation for sin. Then we came to Exodus and saw God's redemption for sin as He delivered Israel from bondage. Now, in Leviticus, God showed the people how to have separation from their sin: blood. It's mentioned eighty times and makes one thing abundantly clear: Sin has an awful cost—the lifeblood of an innocent animal must be shed to pay for human sin. That blood *atoned* for sin—that is, *paid its price*—thus purchasing peace with God.

The Way to God Through Sacrifice (Leviticus 1–17)
Laws of Personal Proximity

The first seven chapters of Leviticus answer the question, "How can I approach God?" Israel's first encounter with God in Exodus filled them with dread and holy awe (Exodus 19:16), but God had clearly expressed an interest in having a relationship with the people. But how could they draw near their Creator—physically, emotionally, spiritually—in His terrifying holiness? God's answer to Israel was to approach Him through the blood of animal sacrifice. That animal would take the place of the person offering it. Today, God is looking not for animal sacrifices but the heart that worships Him "in spirit and truth" (John 4:23). We don't need the blood of animals because of Jesus: His blood covers all our sins.

Leviticus begins with descriptions of five offerings God prescribed. The first three were mostly optional "sweet aroma" offerings—the idea being that, when you brought them, they made a pleasing scent to the Lord. They were about surrender and thanksgiving—the Old Testament equivalent of presenting an offering as your "reasonable service" (Romans 12:1). The second two were obligatory—you had to bring them because sin requires payment, in blood, because everyone sins (Romans 3:9-12). Here are the different ways people could draw closer to God:

The burnt offering (Leviticus 1): Sometimes burnt offerings were voluntary, and other times, required (v. 3). People brought livestock—bulls, rams, goats, lambs, and even birds—to be burned on the altar. God's was a very visual worship system. That is, people didn't just hear about the consequences of sin; they saw it every time the priest slashed an animal's throat and let the blood run into the basin.

The grain offering (Leviticus 2): For the times when someone just wanted to thank God for who He is or all He had done, the law included grain offerings. This was the only nonbloody offering. Cakes made of fine flour, sometimes unleavened, would be "anointed with oil" (v. 4) and burned on the altar. A portion of it was given to the priests to be their bread at home, part of God's provision for them since they didn't work in the fields or at a trade.

The peace offering (Leviticus 3): The peace offering was similar to the burnt offering: You brought your animal, it was killed at the door of the tabernacle, and the blood was poured at the base of the altar. It was different, however, in that part was given to the priest, again for their meal at home, and then the one who brought the animal enjoyed the rest with family—sort of like a holy barbeque. The peace offering was an invitation to intimate fellowship with God.

The sin offering (Leviticus 4): Sin isn't just a deliberate infraction. It can also be an accidental failure, which God took into account with the sin offering, where a bull was offered for an unintentional offense (v. 2). Even if it was an accident, sin is still sin—that is, falling short of God's standard.

The trespass offering (Leviticus 5): The Bible makes a distinction between a sin and a trespass. One is intentional, and the other is unintentional. We are sinners by nature *and* by choice. If you didn't realize you had broken God's law, you made the trespass offering. It involved a public confession and a public demonstration (vv. 5-6). God was giving you the freedom to say, "Yes, I blew it, but I'm going to be forgiven of it, and avoid it from now on."

Laws of Professional Activity

The people needed sacrifices, but also a sacrifice-*er*—a priest. They couldn't approach God with their offerings on their own. God gave that role to the tribe of Levi, establishing a high priest and priests serving under him. However, even the Old Testament priests couldn't just rush into the Holy of Holies and say, "I'm cool with God. After all, I'm a professional." To approach God, they had to offer a sacrifice like everyone else, for the same reason: Blood had to be shed for their sins.

The priests' ordination service was unusual, to say the least (Leviticus 8:22). Moses sacrificed a ram, then put some of its blood on Aaron's right ear, right thumb, and right big toe, and did the same with Aaron's sons. The blood and its placement signified the role of the priest: The blood on the right ear meant he was called to hear God's voice. The blood on his right thumb meant he was called to do His will, and the blood on his right big toe meant he was called to walk in His ways.

After a series of sacrifices and offerings, Moses and Aaron went into the tabernacle, came out and blessed the people, and then God's glory appeared and fire from heaven consumed the burnt offering. However, despite a successful start, things went south quickly—in the very next chapter, actually. It's hard to imagine, but on the very first official run-through, Aaron's sons Nadab and Abihu "offered profane fire before the LORD" (Leviticus 10:1). God didn't like it, and He killed them. This was the showdown at the Not-OK Corral!

No one honestly knows what this "profane fire" actually was. It could have been fire from the outer courtyard instead of the prescribed fire from the altar. Some scholars think Aaron's sons might have been drunk, offering a sacrifice while ritually unclean, or with impure hearts, disrespecting God before the people. Whatever the case, one thing became clear: The worship God accepts is the worship God prescribes.

The worship God accepts is the worship God prescribes.

The Bible never flatters its heroes. Even in this important moment, we get the full truth. Aaron must have been shell-shocked to see this case of divine justice, but Moses laid it out for him: "This is what the LORD spoke, saying: 'By those who come near Me I must be regarded as holy; and before all the people I must be glorified.' So Aaron held his peace" (v. 3). The priests had a serious job with serious expectations.

Laws of Ritual Purity

The next group of laws answered the question, "How can I stay clean before the Lord?" It's the beginning of the concept of sanctification, the journey of walking in a holy way with a holy God. There were a variety of laws about how to be ritually cleansed from defilement, which is the idea of being made dirty, sometimes physically, but in a way that also creates spiritual separation. These were issues of diet, hygiene, disease (particularly leprosy), and bodily discharges—it's all in there! God wanted His people to walk with Him in every phase of their lives.

God began by laying out which types of animals were all right to eat. These dietary restrictions were given for two basic reasons. First, following them would show that Israel was different from the surrounding peoples, which is the idea behind being holy. Holiness means separate from the masses, unlike the status quo. God told His people to be holy because He is holy (Leviticus 11:45).

The second reason was for sanitary purposes. Three thousand years ago, there wasn't an FDA. God knew which animals were healthy and which were unhygienic, were poisonous or ate unclean things, or were more likely to carry diseases. So in order to protect His people from diseases, He gave laws (vv. 46-47).

There were also laws regarding childbirth. As soon as a baby was born, a mom had to wait for a period of ritual cleansing (Leviticus 12:2-5). Directly afterward, she had to bring a burnt offering and a sin offering. It's telling that cleansing was needed so soon in a child's life. That's the nature of sin, and it's the nature we are born with. Even those little bundles of joy carry the imprint of sin—and if you don't believe it, just wait a few years!

Disease is one of the key consequences—and proofs—that creation has been altered by sin. In that ancient world of premedical care, God gave specific instructions in Leviticus 13–15 on dealing with leprosy and running sores. The term translated "leprosy" was kind of a catchall descriptor for a number of skin diseases, all of which were highly contagious. For the good of the sick person and the whole community, he or she was to be brought into isolation and inspected.

Part of the priest's function, then, was acting like a doctor—isolating people, quarantining them if necessary, and then over time examining a sore or a scab to see how it would progress. He would pronounce the patient unclean or cleansed based on that progress. So whether it was food placed in the body, a baby produced by the body, or a disease positioned on the body, God laid out clear expectations for how to deal with it. God cares about your soul *and* your soma.

Laws of National Sanctity

The final section of laws directed how Israel as a nation should obey God. They really were to become *one nation under God*. Israel's highest and holiest day was Yom Kipper, the Day of Atonement (Leviticus 16). It was a special day in the Hebrew calendar, in many ways the center and culmination of all of their festivals. However, it was different—it wasn't a joyous celebration, but rather a time of serious contemplation. God wanted it set aside as a time of personal reflection and confession of sins.

On that special day, the high priest would bathe himself, get dressed in his distinctive garments, and take a bull and two goats to the tabernacle. Aaron cast two lots, one for God and one for what God called the scapegoat. The goat that God's lot fell on became a sin offering for Aaron, purifying him so that he could offer the other goat for all of Israel's sin. The other goat was presented to the Lord as payment for the sin of the whole nation, after which it was released into the wilderness (Leviticus 16:8-21).

Once the scapegoat was out of sight, there would be a celebration; the only joy that day was that their sin, which caused the death of one goat and the exile of another, was taken away. It was an annual observance, passed down through every generation, that began with solemnity and ended with festivity.

Leviticus 17 is a hinge between the first part of the book and the second. God established laws for various offerings and the rules governing the priesthood in the first part. In the second, He would give more laws for Israel, but in between are the key verses to the whole book:

> I will set My face against that person who eats blood, and will cut him off from among his people. For the life of the flesh is in the blood, and I have given it to you upon the altar to make atonement for your souls; for it is the blood that makes atonement for the soul (Leviticus 17:10-11).

You might think, *No worries! I will have no problem keeping this commandment!* But back then, the people in some of the pagan countries actually did eat blood. They thought that if they drank an animal's blood, they would take on its characteristics—becoming strong as an ox, ferocious as a lion, or swift as a gazelle. Here, God forbade the Israelites to act like those around them. Once again, blood—in this case, a forbidden use of it—was the basis of their relationship with God. Blood was to be used exclusively in worship to portray and enable atonement. It made holiness possible.

A Walk with God Through Sanctification (Leviticus 18–27)
The Difference of Holiness

From a fallen human perspective, God's holiness is probably His least attractive attribute, generally speaking. Most people would choose some other aspect to advertise God with—His love, His mercy, His creative nature, or maybe His sovereign control, power, or even infinite knowledge. Here's where the Bible surprises us, talking more about God's holiness than any other attribute or facet of His nature. What's more, there is a correlation between who God is and who God wants His people to be: "Be holy, for I am holy" (Leviticus 11:45). We can't pick and choose which attributes of God we like and toss the rest. We take the whole package as God reveals Himself to us.

The first step in holiness is repentance.

The first step in holiness is repentance. When a person turns *from* sin and *to* God, the separated life begins. It's a package deal, and what results from doing both is holiness. God reminded Israel of the authority behind this message: "I am the LORD your God" (Leviticus 18:2). It's a phrase that recurs forty-two times in Leviticus. We ask, "Why should I do this?" and God responds, "Because I am the LORD your God." Our perception of reality matters less than God's declaration of His sovereignty. His holiness is the difference.

The Moral Difference

The difference was to be seen in Israel's moral conduct. By applying the Ten Commandments to various issues, the law brought the nitty-gritty of holiness into everyday life. Morally speaking, Leviticus 18–20 contains a list of pretty ugly sins revolving around the misuse of sex: incest, homosexuality, and bestiality—all of which were practiced by various Egyptians and Canaanites. People say the sexual revolution started in the 1960s, but all of the stuff that kicked in then and is going on today is as old as the hills and twice as dusty. Christians are to be different in all areas of their lives, and certainly in the moral areas. If the Holy Spirit is living in you, you are going to become holier and holier—more and more different from the culture around you—and it's going to turn up in every area of your life, from the dining room to the boardroom to the bedroom.

History has shown us over and over that, where the family crumbles, the nation will follow.

One of the things God did with this list is put a protective hedge around the family. Otherwise, in the face of adultery and incest and homosexuality, the family can disintegrate—and along with it, the foundational core of society. History has shown us over and over that, where the family crumbles, the nation will follow. And all of society's euphemistic terms for these sins—taming adultery by labeling it *an affair*, co-opting words like *gay* and *diversity* to describe homosexuality and transgenderism—can't hide the truth about their effects.

The truth about the Hollywood version of sex is that what's fashionable is actually destructive and even fatal. An unbiblical approach to sex can hurt you physically, emotionally, and spiritually. It will also hurt your family, breaking trust and unity, and others outside your family—from relatives, friends, co-workers, and fellow Christians to your hindered witness to unbelievers. Most of all, your sexual sin hurts God's heart.

That's not something to be taken lightly. While Christians need to maintain a respectful and winsome attitude, showing authentic care for those who disagree and practice replacement lifestyles, we should never forsake what God has said is true. No good can come of it. So when we read that God said, "You shall not lie with a male as with a woman. It is an abomination" (Leviticus 18:22), notice that it does not say homosexuality is an alternative lifestyle condoned by God. It doesn't say it's normal since God *made* them that way, or that because it's been around so long that it's about time we all lightened up and just let people love who they want to love. God calls these things sin, and they're not God's highest or best for anyone.

God's Word conveys restrictions but it also tells us over and over that He loves us—He knows what makes life work best. He designed us to get the most out of sex in a marriage between one man and one woman who are committed to each other as long as they live. Obeying God in all of these ways would result in a moral difference in Israel, distinguishing her people from those of the surrounding nations.

The Organizational Difference

The ministry standards for the priesthood were pretty high, both for the ordinary priests and for the high priest. As you look through the law, you'll see the word *defile* a lot, as the priests had to be very careful not to make themselves unclean in any way—ceremonially, sexually, or morally. That included regulations about touching dead people, going unshaven, who they could marry, and which Levites could make offerings.

There were also instructions for how priests were to be ceremonially cleansed if they became defiled. The reason behind all of these priestly requirements and restrictions is, once again, holiness (Leviticus 21:6). The whole community of Israel was to be holy, and within the community, the priests were also to be set apart from the ordinary man or woman. Why? Because the priests were the link between God and men. They stood in a unique place and played a unique role. Therefore, God said, "You're all to be holy, but I'm holding you priests to an especially strict standard."

God's expectation is the same for those in ministry today: The higher your position organizationally, the higher your responsibility. The expectations Paul gave Timothy for those in leadership (1 Timothy 3) are similar to the priestly standards in the Old Testament. The priests had to separate themselves from the community and were not allowed to touch certain things or go with certain groups. There was a high degree of separation and loneliness. So approach any ministry with prayer and careful forethought. You may be called, but be ready to count the cost so you can be prepared for the challenges you will face and those your family will face.

The Devotional Difference

Israel was to have a unique devotional life. The priests and people were to be fully committed as they engaged in all the offerings and rituals. With the exception of the Day of Atonement, all the festivals and observances shared one common factor: joy. Three times a year, all the males within the proximity of Jerusalem were to gather at the temple to celebrate Passover, Pentecost, and Tabernacles. If you lived elsewhere, it was always your life's dream to come to Jerusalem for those three feasts.

In fact, God *commanded* His people to rejoice (Leviticus 23:40). Why would He have to do that? Haven't you noticed our tendency to dwell on the wrong things and walk around grumpy and depressed half the time? God understood that life is hard, so He wanted the people to come to His feasts and have some sanctified fun.

The way some church folks act, you wouldn't know that this command is in the Bible. I grew up in a church where we called weekly attendance our "Sunday obligation." There was no joyful, voluntary exuberance or excitement. It was nothing we looked forward to; it was something we had to do. Yet eighteen times in the book of Psalms we read, "Make a joyful shout to the LORD" or "Make a joyful noise to the LORD."

Sometimes you won't feel the joy. Sometimes you just have to obey the command, and trust that the joy and emotion will follow. Rejoicing when you don't feel like it isn't hypocrisy; it's obedience. Emotion is sometimes like the caboose on the train—it follows the engine of decision. You decide to show the right behavior and then, as you walk in obedience, the emotion comes along as a consequence of being obedient. The hour or so of worship at church ought to be *happy hour*, the happiest people on earth at the happiest place on earth, celebrating the God who gives us joy.

Rejoicing when you don't feel like it isn't hypocrisy; it's obedience.

The Community Difference

God's holiness was to define the entire life of Israel's community—a considerate family caring for one another and sharing the same territory. Leviticus 25–26 lays out how the people were to treat workers, relieve debt, and give farmed land a chance to recover—pretty practical stuff. The Sabbath year was the method God prescribed. You would work for six years, and the seventh year you would let the land lie fallow; you wouldn't work the land, trusting that whatever grew on its own would be sufficient (Leviticus 25:1-7). God promised blessings for their obedience in this.

In making clear the importance of keeping His commands, God made a conditional promise based on obedience: *If* you do this, *then* I will do this. He began by saying, "If you walk in My statutes and keep My commandments, and perform them, then I will..." and He went on to elaborate all the ways He would bless them (Leviticus 26:3-13): rain in season, harvests with produce that lasted from reaping till the next sowing, full bellies, peace in the land, and victory over their enemies.

Obedience is the ground of blessing in the Old Testament. This is one of the differences between the Old and New Testaments. If you're a Christian and you fail to do all that God wants you to do (and we all do), God made a covenant with you through Christ that is unconditional. It is not based on your ability to perform it, but upon Jesus Christ, who fulfilled it. I'm not saying to go ahead and live any way you want to and disobey God because you'll be blessed anyway. You do that, and you'll live a miserable life. Holiness still matters—to you as an individual, to the church, and to the community in which you live.

> **The heart of true worship is voluntary rather than compulsory.**

The Voluntary Difference

Israel was to choose each day to be like God in holiness. Leviticus concludes with God speaking about voluntary vows, as opposed to obligatory worship. They weren't required, as were the festivals or the trespass or sin offerings. Rather, they were vows that you made to God because you felt like it—you just wanted to. The heart of true worship is voluntary rather than compulsory. It doesn't have to be coerced. It doesn't result from getting a group all pumped up like at a pep rally. If it's not in your heart, you can't manufacture it. It starts with presenting yourself to God each day as a living sacrifice (Romans 12:1), and saying, "God, here I am, body, mind, and soul. What do You have for me today? Show me what You want me to do. I'm all Yours."

God's instructions to Moses indicated as much: "Every devoted offering is most holy to the LORD" (Leviticus 27:28). If you give it, give from your heart, knowing that God can tell the difference between a voluntary offering and one given out of obligation or coercion. We want to be grateful and happy to devote our tithes and offerings to God and His work. Joyful giving recognizes that God owns everything, not just your tithe, and you get to participate in what He is doing. That voluntary, heartfelt attitude is a mark of holiness, and it was part of God's commandments for His people.

Joyful giving recognizes that God owns everything.

NUMBERS
FLIGHT PLAN

Facts

Author

The authorship of the book of Numbers is attributed to Moses (see Numbers 1:1; 33:2). It is the fourth book in the Torah, or Pentateuch (meaning "five scrolls," or the five books of the Law).

Date written

Like the first three books by Moses, Numbers was written sometime during the fifteenth century BC. The book of Numbers details a thirty-eight-year period between the exodus and the end of the Israelites' wanderings.

Landmarks

The book of Numbers isn't about mathematics, but a pair of censuses. It describes two generations of Israelites: the first generation that left Egypt, and then the one that actually made it into the Promised Land. It's an eleven-day journey from Mount Sinai to the entrance of the Promised Land at Kadesh Barnea (Deuteronomy 1:2), but it took Israel almost forty years to make it. Their story here is "How to Turn a Two-Week Trip into a Forty-Year Trial." How's that for numbers?

Itinerary

Three words capture the whole flow of Numbers: *organization, disorganization,* and *reorganization*:

- Organization (Numbers 1–4)
    - Counted Because They Counted
    - Coordinating the Camp
    - Classifying the Clergy
    - Consecrating the Community

- Checking for Continuation
- Disorganization (Numbers 5–25)
  - The Contagion of Complaint
  - A Contrast with Cowardice
  - A Coalition of Criticism
  - A Costly Crackdown
  - A Copy of the Cross
  - A Con Artist of Consequence
- Reorganization (Numbers 26–36)
  - Confirming the Committed

Gospel

In the book of Numbers, God established cities of refuge, where murderers could seek asylum. They could safely stay in one of these sanctuary cities until the death of the high priest, after which they could return home. It's a striking concept: While the high priest was alive, you were safe, but when he died, you were set free. It's a beautiful picture of our Great High Priest, Jesus Christ, who gave His life to set us free and save us from the sting of eternal death.

History

The book of Numbers covers the nearly forty years that Israel spent wandering in the desert. Some historians place that period between 1445 and 1405 BC.

Travel Tips

Numbers is full of lessons about the importance of our attitude toward God. Based on God's promises to be with you and care for you, are you still willing to follow Him, even when you don't know where He is leading you?

- Both faith and unbelief are contagious. To be around someone with strong faith is inspiring. In Numbers, however, unbelief spread like wildfire among the people of Israel. Be careful how you transmit your faith, especially to the next generation.

- Accountability is important to God. Rather than participate in our culture's pervasive attitude that always looks to lay blame somewhere else, accept responsibility for your choices. Remember, your sense of identity and worth is found in Jesus Christ.

Your sense of identity and worth is found in Jesus Christ.

- God didn't give the tribe of Levi their own place in the camp of Israel because their place was with Him, serving Him as a set-apart priesthood. Similarly to the Levites, we as believers are a royal priesthood (1 Peter 2:9), chosen by God for His service.

In Flight

In Numbers, the children of Israel organized themselves, took a census, and began to march through the wilderness in an orderly fashion. They then became disorganized because of unbelief, eventuating in a reorganization of their priorities.

Organization (Numbers 1–4)

Counted Because They Counted

Two years after God brought Israel out of Egypt, He instructed Moses to number the people. Moses organized a census of all the adult men in order to create a draft for military service (Numbers 1:2-3). The list of names and numbers taken for the draft isn't exactly scintillating reading, but for Israel, all those numbers and names were a beautiful gesture of God's love to a beleaguered nation—as if He was saying as He counted, "I love you and you and you…"

Whenever God counts people, it's because people count to God.

In Egypt, the Jews were an innumerable hoard of nameless slaves; the individual was expendable. Here, under God's care, names of tribes, families, and individuals were recorded. Whenever God counts people, it's because people count to

God. Nobody gets lost in God's crowd; you're much more than a number to Him. The Bible indicates that God knows every name, every hair of our heads, and values each of us (Luke 12:7).

Coordinating the Camp

The twelve tribes of Israel were then divided up into four camps—three tribes on each side of the tabernacle (Numbers 2). Each camp had a standard—a banner featuring the tribe's emblem. Each group of three tribes had a lead tribe: to the east of the tabernacle, Judah's flag featured a lion. Ephraim camped to the west and flew a banner featuring an ox. On the south side, Reuben's symbol was a man, and to the north, Dan's was an eagle. The Levites were in the center of the entire encampment, surrounded by the other camps.

Later, the prophet Ezekiel saw in a vision four living creatures—each with the face of a man, a lion, an ox, and an eagle (Ezekiel 1:5-10). Later still, the apostle John described his vision of the throne of God in heaven, noticing four living creatures surrounding it, with parallel descriptions: "the first...was like a lion, the second...like a calf, the third...had a face like a man, and the fourth...was like a flying eagle" (Revelation 4:7).

Each of the four Gospels has a similar focus: Matthew showed Jesus fulfilling Hebrew prophecy—the Lion of the tribe of Judah (Genesis 49:9-10)—the ideal Jewish Messiah. Mark depicted Jesus's servitude as He set about doing His Father's will and work, just as an ox, the ancient beast of service, would set to work plowing a field. Luke, the physician, highlighted Jesus as the Son of Man, focusing more on Jesus's humanity than the other Gospel writers. And John portrayed Jesus as deity, the Creator and sustainer of everything, a symbol of the ascending flight and power of the eagle. All of these fourfold representations began with the placement of the camps of Israel.

And just to top it off, if we were to assume a bird's-eye view of the layout of the camp of Israel, we would see an arrangement in the shape of a cross, with the lower branch of the cross being a bit longer due to the population of those tribes. I picture the Holy Spirit smiling as everyone got situated, knowing how predictive it all was in the Father's mind of all these things' fulfillment in Christ.

Classifying the Clergy

The tribe of Levi, led by Aaron, was not counted in the first census. They had their own numbering, a tally of the priests of Israel. God assigned the entire tribe of Levi to this work (Numbers 3:7-9). There was too much work in the tabernacle for any one man or small group to perform, so the load was spread out across many shoulders.

The Levites were organized by families: Gershon, Kohath, and Merari. The Gershonites camped on the west side of the tabernacle (Numbers 3:23) and maintained everything to do with the tent coverings (vv. 25-26). The Kohathites camped to the south and tended to the articles of furniture, the Ark of the Covenant, the altar of incense, the golden lampstand, the table of showbread, and all the holy implements used in service in the tabernacle (v. 31). The sons of Merari camped to the north and looked after the tabernacle's infrastructure: the poles, bases, and stands that held the curtains around that courtyard (vv. 36-37). Moses and Aaron and his sons camped on the east side of the tabernacle as overseeing caretakers (v. 38).

Consecrating the Community

As part of the organization of the people, God also arranged for their consecration—the rules of holy cleanliness. It seems a bit harsh—people got put out of the camp for having various diseases or touching a corpse (Numbers 5:2). But if it seems that God was being too hard on those poor people, who couldn't help it if they caught leprosy or if someone keeled over dead next to them and defiled them, think of it as an act of love. God was quarantining those that might have certain diseases so that those maladies didn't spread to the rest of the camp. Though God's love is personal, it is also practical.

Checking for Continuation

Having set up the camp and instructed the people how to keep it holy, God then told them how to move. They weren't in the Promised Land yet, so Israel was living a nomadic lifestyle, waiting on God's leading. They moved when God moved them, following the peculiar guidance system of the pillar of cloud by day and fire by night. When the cloud of His presence in the tabernacle moved, they would pack up and follow—whether it had been a couple of days, a few months, or a year (Number 9:22). God provided this unique navigational system throughout their years in the desert, and they got off to a good start.

This portion of Israel's journey paints a picture of obedience and faithful following. Their mistake came when the people started relying on their own wisdom, trusting in the numbers of the army rather than in the God of their army. A wise mentor once told me, "If you defend yourself, God will let you." So often when something challenging happens, we want to jump in and start defending ourselves, instead of letting the Lord be our defense—our shelter and shield—and letting

Him carry us through the trial. This tendency disrupted the Israelites' organized start and drove them way off God's path.

Disorganization (Numbers 5–25)
The Contagion of Complaint

Despite a good beginning, the people soon began to grumble and complain. What changed? Just think of all they had seen: God opened up the Red Sea and destroyed the Egyptians. Manna appeared daily on the ground and water gushed from a rock. Their faith should have been rock solid. But here's the thing: They got used to it. God's wonders became old hat to them. That's when the whining started.

> ## When the seed of discontent is planted, a crop of disgruntlement grows.

Complaining can be contagious, and among large groups, it can create chaos. There were a lot of people—probably more than three million—out in the desert. God's blessing of growth, taken for granted, became a perceived lack of concern—the idea that the bigger they got, the less personal attention they got. People started putting themselves above the good of the whole, complaining that God wasn't caring for them now that they were out of Egypt. And when the seed of discontent is planted, a crop of disgruntlement grows.

God's response was instantaneous—fire fell from heaven—a clear indication of His attitude toward grumbling and complaining among His people, whether it's just one person, a few, or many doing the infecting. He hates it. It's a strong word, but one used in other places to describe how opposed God is to something (Proverbs 6:16-19). And the saddest part? Despite God's immediate judgment of the people's faithless complaining, many responded with further unbelief and ingratitude.

The children of Israel suffered from selective memory disorder. They forgot that they had been redeemed not from freedom but slavery. They reacted as if Egypt had been a paradise, conveniently forgetting that they weren't sweating in the brickyards anymore, suffering under the cruel whips of their taskmasters. Granted, they were in the middle of the Sinai desert, but God was taking care of them with water, food, clothing, and shelter. Yet none of it was good enough.

A Contrast with Cowardice

The malfunction was community-wide. Take, for example, the time God had Moses send spies into Canaan to check out the land He intended to give to the people (Numbers 13:1-2). Their mission was to spy out the land, check out the terrain, and inspect the inhabitants for numbers, strengths, and weaknesses.

The spies returned after forty days with a mixed report: "The land where you sent us...truly flows with milk and honey, and this is its fruit" (Numbers 13:27)—a huge cluster of grapes that took two men to carry, straddling it between them. But, they said, "the people who dwell in the land are strong; the cities are fortified and very large; moreover we saw the descendants of Anak [a race of gigantic warriors] there" (v. 28). They were holding the proof of God's blessing, but harboring the panic of fearful children.

One of those scouts, Caleb, a tenacious man of faith and courage, stood up and said, "God is with us. Let's go for it!" Caleb knew God would give them the victory He had promised, but the other spies (except Joshua) said, "Are you kidding? Did you see the size of those giant dudes? We can't beat them!" That unfavorable report freaked everyone out, and they all started to complain to Moses and Aaron—"If only we had died in the land of Egypt! Or if only we had died in this wilderness!" (Numbers 14:2). Their complaints continued: "Why has the LORD brought us to this land to fall by the sword, that our wives and children should become victims?" (v. 3). They used their kids as an excuse for their faithlessness.

The people even threatened to replace Moses and go back to Egypt. At that point, Caleb stood up with Joshua, who eventually became the leader of Israel, and pleaded with the people to trust God rather than, in their fear, rebel against Him (Numbers 14:9-10). However, their courageous faith fell on hard hearts: "All the congregation said to stone them with stones" (v. 10).

That's when God stepped in, ready to wipe out the lot of them. He would have been just in His judgment, but Moses interceded and begged God for mercy. God spared the people, but would not allow them to enter the land: "Your little ones, whom you said would be victims, I will bring in...But as for you, your carcasses shall fall in this wilderness" (vv. 31-32). Ouch! Except for Caleb and Joshua, that whole generation would die in the wilderness, and their children would inherit the Promised Land.

A Coalition of Criticism

God rebooted Israel by addressing the core problem: sin. He told Moses to instruct the people once again about various offerings to pay for their sins (Numbers

15:1-31). Sin wasn't any more popular a topic then as it is now, largely because people are guilt-averse. Israel's lack of ownership of their unbelief led to harsh but just results. God was reminding them of His provision for making it right.

Unfortunately, the whine had become Israel's national anthem at this point. A prominent Levite, Korah, led a coalition of 250 other leaders in rebellion against Moses's leadership and authority (Numbers 16:1-3). Their basic complaint? "Moses, you have way too much power for one guy." What did Moses do? He said, "We're going to have a showdown and let God decide who is holy."

Moses laid out the terms of the contest (Numbers 16:28-30): "If Korah and all these other 250 guys die of natural causes—if they just grow old and die—then the Lord isn't speaking through me. But if the earth opens up and swallows them alive, then I'm the guy God sent." How's that for a spiritual challenge? God didn't waste any time with His reply: Once Moses stopped speaking, the ground cracked open and devoured the entire contingent of complainers. The earth closed up and *bam!* No more rebellion.

After dealing with Korah and company, God confirmed the priesthood through Aaron and his sons. He caused Aaron's staff to germinate overnight, His choice among staffs from all the tribal leaders (Numbers 17:2-8). This foreshadowing of a resurrection—something dead coming to life at God's touch—served as validation of the priesthood of Aaron and his line. Such miracles of life conquering death reached full fruition in the ministry of Jesus Christ.

A Costly Crackdown

The people of Israel broke down in the wilderness because they failed to walk with God. They took Him for granted, treated His commandments as optional, and trusted their emotions instead of His promises. The result was death. Stuck circling the wilderness of Zin since the first census, the older generation began to pass away. Numbers 20 begins with death—Moses's sister Miriam's—and ends with death—Aaron's.

When they arrived again at Kadesh, where they had entered the wilderness all those years ago, Moses must have had a case of déjà vu. Thirty-seven years earlier he had sent out the twelve spies from Kadesh, and here they were again, with little more than faithless wandering in between.

Naturally, the people were complaining again—this time, about a lack of water. They weren't going to enter the Promised Land, but they still expected God to provide its blessings at their beck and call. God told Moses to take his staff, speak to a rock in front of the whole group, and He would make water come out of it. Moses and Aaron gathered everyone together, but rather than speak to the rock as God had instructed, Moses gave the people an earful: "'Hear now, you rebels! Must we bring water for you out of this rock?' Then Moses lifted his hand and struck the rock twice with his rod; and water came out abundantly, and the congregation and their animals drank" (Numbers 20:10-11).

It was a great miracle, and God provided for His people yet again. However, there was a problem. Moses didn't obey God's instructions. Back in Exodus 17, when they were all camped at Rephidim, God had told Moses to strike a rock to provide water for the people, and Moses did it. He had even named the place Massah and Meribah—*tempted* and *contention*—because the people had questioned God's presence and provision there (Exodus 17:1-7). But that time, he didn't lose his cool and yell at everyone. But because he did so here at Kadesh, there would be a consequence: God would not allow Moses and Aaron to enter the Promised Land (Numbers 20:12).

Harsh and unfair? Seems that way at first glance. After all, God had invested a lot of time in developing Moses as a leader—forty years' preparation in Egypt, forty in Midian, and forty leading Israel. And poor Moses! He'd put up with the constant whining and rebellion for decades. But he failed God in three ways here:

- Disobedience: Plain and simple, Moses disobeyed God. Any time you let emotion control you, you run that risk.

- Distortion: Moses didn't represent God correctly. In this instance, Moses's anger distorted God's attitude, presenting it as angry, and God wasn't angry at this point.

- Dominance: In self-exalting pride, Moses said, "Must we bring water for you out of this rock?" *We?* Who is *we*? Moses had no power to bring water from a stone; only God had such power. But Moses, whether he meant to or not, took credit for God's miracle.

Moses had served well in so many ways, but he didn't this time, and lest we forget, sin has a cost—even for a mighty servant of God like Moses.

A Copy of the Cross

Israel sang their national whine one last time in Numbers. Disobedience forced the people to avoid going through Edom (the Edomites had previously denied them passage through their lands), and they were discouraged. Naturally, they complained. "No water and no food but this lousy manna? Egypt was way better!" By this time, God was done with their whining. He sent a bunch of venomous snakes into the camp to bite and kill. This got their attention, and Israel got spiritual on the double-quick; they came to Moses, pleading with him to plead with God on their behalf.

When Moses prayed for the people, God gave an interesting response. He had Moses make a metal snake and fasten it on top of a pole, and whoever looked at it would survive (Numbers 21:8-9). Some must have thought, *This is stupid. I'm dying here, and I'm supposed to look at a snake on a stick?* After all, there is nothing about a bronze snake on a pole that could possibly heal anyone—*logically*. And that's exactly the point: the theological isn't always logical.

Furthermore, it worked. Why? Because, in order to be healed, a person had to take a step of faith. Moses probably attached the bronze serpent to one of the banner poles the tribes of Israel flew to represent their camps. The framework of those poles included a horizontal crossbar up top, to which the flag would be attached— it was built like a cross. So to have a bronze serpent on a cross-like pole was indicative of what would happen when Jesus Christ came. In fact, Jesus used this very incident to refer to His crucifixion (John 3:14). Putting a metal snake on a stick may seem silly, but the cure was real and simple: All the Israelites had to do was look at it. But even doing that required two things: an admission of guilt and a statement of faith—the same things required for coming to Christ.

A Con Artist of Consequence

The picture of the cross is followed by the puzzle of Balaam in Numbers 22–25. Balaam is an enigma, a paradox. Here's a diviner, someone on speaking terms with God, hired by an enemy of Israel to curse them. As Israel traveled through the wilderness, they were getting something of a reputation—or, rather, God was. God had given Israel military victories over the Canaanites (Numbers 21:1-3), the Amorites (Numbers 21:21-32), and Og, king of Bashan (Numbers 21:33-35). Those nations had been far stronger and better established, but, of course, they were no match for God. Moab was next in Israel's path, and their king, Balak the son of Zippor, was frustrated and fearful (Numbers 22:2-3).

Balak's response was to hire Balaam, a Mesopotamian *baru*—a type of priest who used astrology and divination to create oracles and signs, often by reading animal entrails, oil drops, or tea leaves. Balak requested that Balaam come and place a curse on Israel, trusting in Balaam's supposed ability to bless or curse. Even though Balaam was a pagan, God spoke to him audibly, telling him not to go to Balak or bother cursing Israel (Numbers 22:9-13).

Balaam obeyed God, but Balak sent back an entourage to convince him to change his mind. Balaam said all of Balak's gold and silver wouldn't be enough to convince him to go against God. God then sent Balaam on a mission, instructing him to go to Balak but to say "only the word which I speak to you" (Numbers 22:20).

Balaam saddled up his donkey and headed out, but apparently he went with the wrong attitude or motive, because along the way, God got mad at him and sent an angel to block his path. The donkey, seeing "the Angel of the LORD" in the path three different times, stopped. Balaam hit the donkey each time she stopped because he didn't see the angel. The donkey was more spiritually perceptive than this so-called prophet!

God gave the donkey the ability to speak so she could express her displeasure (Numbers 22:28-29). She asked, "Why are you hitting me?" And Balaam replied, "Because you keep putting on the brakes! I'm so mad I could kill you!" What's great here is that not only did the donkey speak, but Balaam answered her right away, as if he were used to carrying on a conversation with her. They go back and forth for a minute until, finally, God opened Balaam's eyes. When he saw the angel, he dropped to the ground and bowed down.

God permitted Balaam to continue. Balak took Balaam to three different high places so he could pronounce a curse on Israel, and each time, Balaam spoke God's message instead, offering a prophecy in praise of God and His blessings on Israel (Numbers 23:7-11, 18-24, and 24:3-9). Even though Balaam couldn't curse a people God hadn't cursed (Numbers 23:8), the people of Israel brought trouble on themselves again at a place called Peor. They joined the local tribe, the Moabites, in their religious rituals, which involved having sex as part of their Baal worship. It isn't shocking that God wasn't thrilled (Numbers 25:1-3).

Israel's abrupt idolatry was unexpected, and it remained unexplained until several chapters later, when Moses filled in the rest of the story. After God had given Israel a victory over the Midianites, the army brought captive women and children back to Moses instead of killing them. Moses wasn't pleased, and here's why: "Look, these women caused the children of Israel, through the counsel of Balaam, to trespass against the LORD in the incident of Peor" (Numbers 31:16).

So even though it looked like Balaam had been moved by God to pronounce blessings (or at least prevented from uttering a curse), secretly, he must have taken Balak aside and said, "Look, I can't curse whom God has blessed, but guess what? We don't have to curse them. All you have to do is send your women into their camp to seduce their men with their worship rituals. Israel's jealous God will curse them for their idolatry." So although Balaam had a supernatural encounter with God, his heart was unchanged. The result of his deception was destruction for all those "who were joined to Baal of Peor" (Numbers 25:5), a spiritual housecleaning in the form of a plague God sent that resulted in 24,000 deaths (v. 9).

Reorganization (Numbers 26–36)

Confirming the Committed

It was time to reset the counter. The older generation's failure had brought death; now, this next generation would bring life. God told Moses and Eleazar, Aaron's son and the new high priest, to take a new census (Numbers 26:2). There had been essentially a zero-population increase over those thirty-seven years, a fitting testimony to Israel's struggles to grow spiritually.

The new generation needed a primer on the kinds of offerings and sacrifices that God had ordained earlier (Numbers 28–30). The older generation, distracted by their griping and idolatry, had not adequately passed on God's requirements to their progeny. But while the people were changing, God hadn't. Moses taught the new generation the Law, and then the people moved on for the first time in almost four decades. God helped them defeat the Midianites and cross the Jordan River, and they finally arrived in the Promised Land.

Not everyone crossed the Jordan, though. The tribes of Reuben and Gad and the half-tribe of Manasseh asked to stay on the east side of the river and take their inherited land there. It's certainly a beautiful area, grassy and well-watered by rain, with lots of oaks and pistachio trees. Moses was concerned that their staying behind would discourage the rest of the people as they prepared to go fight for the land God promised them, but eventually they struck a deal. The two-and-a-half tribes agreed to stand with the rest of Israel, going back to their new homeland only when the rest of the tribes had secured theirs (Numbers 32:18-19).

Finally, God gave them the boundaries of the land, south, west, north, and east (Numbers 34:1-12). The land was distributed to the remaining tribes, along with the locations of cities for the Levites (Numbers 35:1-8) and cities of refuge (Numbers 35:9-15). Everything seemed like it was back on track, but here's the tragedy: If you tally up the land within the boundaries God gave Israel, it comes to about 300,000 square miles of land. However, at the peak of their history, Israel occupied only 30,000 square miles of land. They only laid claim to one-tenth of what God had promised them. Because Israel shortchanged itself in the wilderness and afterward, the numbers just never added up.

DEUTERONOMY
FLIGHT PLAN

Facts

Author

Deuteronomy is the fifth book in the Torah, the five books of Moses. All but the last chapter of the book are attributed to Moses. Joshua, Moses's successor, may have written the last chapter after Moses's death.

Date Written

Moses wrote the book after he gave the three messages in the book and sometime before his death in 1406 or 1405 BC.

Landmarks

After the forty years of wandering described in the book of Numbers, the Israelites were finally ready to enter the Promised Land. Because Moses was speaking to a new generation about God's work and ways, he wanted to make sure to cover several vital elements. The key word here is *covenant*, speaking of the special relationship that God established with His people. The book of Deuteronomy can be organized around the three farewell messages Moses gave while the Israelites camped on the plains east of the Jordan River before crossing it.

Itinerary

- First Sermon: Review of the Past (Deuteronomy 1–3)
- Second Sermon: Regulations for the Present (Deuteronomy 4–26)
- Third Sermon: Readiness for the Future (Deuteronomy 27–30)
- Rest at the End of an Era (Deuteronomy 31–34)

Gospel

Deuteronomy is the book that Jesus Christ quoted most often while on earth. The scarlet thread of redemption is most obvious in a prediction Moses made: "The LORD your God will raise up for you a Prophet like me from your midst, from your brethren. Him you shall hear" (Deuteronomy 18:15). "Prophet" is capitalized because translators believe it refers to the Messiah, Jesus Christ. The Lord said, "I will raise up for them a Prophet like you from among their brethren, and will put My words in His mouth, and He shall speak to them all that I command Him" (v. 18). In that sense, Moses was a type of Christ, and Christ fulfilled the Mosaic ideal (John 1:21).

History

Moses's retelling of the vital features of the law took place on the plains of Moab, east of the Jordan River. The Hebrews had traveled from Kadesh, past the Dead Sea, and were about to enter the Promised Land. The book of Deuteronomy says that Moses died at Moab. He was 120 years old and died around 1406–1405 BC.

Travel Tips

More than a review session, Deuteronomy was a reinforcement of the value God places on relationship with Him. Under the old covenant, relationship came through the keeping of the law; under the new covenant, it comes only through the blood of Christ. Under both covenants, God not only made it clear what His people must do to draw close to Him, He also showed that He wanted us to.

- The law is like a mirror, reflecting the truth about our sinful condition. A mirror may reveal the dirt but is powerless to wash it away. What the law ultimately does is point you to Christ, the only one who can make you presentable before God.

What the law ultimately does is point you to Christ, the only one who can make you presentable before God.

- Perspective is everything. God moved Israel from Egypt to the Promised Land in order to help the people to grow. We prefer the mountaintops to the valleys, but God is with us in both places. And while growth often happens in the valleys, you probably won't find much spiritual depth on the mountaintops.

- Faith means acting on God's commands. Moses summarized the importance and power of this when he said, "Choose life, that both you and your descendants may live...[and] love the LORD your God, that you may obey His voice, and that you may cling to Him, for He is your life" (Deuteronomy 30:19-20a). Moses's command wasn't just for the current generation of Israelites but also for the next one.

In Flight

Review of the Past (Deuteronomy 1–3)

Deuteronomy begins with a reminder that Israel managed through persistent disobedience and rebellion to turn an eleven-day march into a forty-year meander (Deuteronomy 1–3). They went from walking to wandering, from ambling to rambling. Moses informed them that God had finally given them their marching orders: "You have dwelt long enough at this mountain. Turn and take your journey" (Deuteronomy 1:6-7). Don't you love that? God said, "You've been here long enough—go, already." God gave the people specific directions, reminding them of the boundaries of the land He had promised their ancestors Abraham, Isaac, and Jacob (vv. 7-8).

Moses then recapped and highlighted laws, lessons, and events, adding his own thoughts, perhaps offering the people a different perspective from their leader than they had heard before. For example, he said, "I spoke to you at that time, saying: 'I alone am not able to bear you'" (Deuteronomy 1:9). He told of the plan to set capable men over them to help him govern, and "you answered me and said, 'The thing which you have told us to do is good'" (v. 14). In recounting the plan to send spies ahead into the land to scout it out, Moses told them, "The plan pleased me well; so I took twelve of your men, one man from each tribe. And they departed...and spied it out" (vv. 23-24).

As he described the failures that followed, Moses was honest and forthcoming about his own flops as well, saying, "The LORD was also angry with me for your sakes, saying, 'Even you shall not go in there'" (v. 37). For this new, younger generation preparing to enter the land of promise, it probably made this legendary figure more human, even as they were reminded of their obligation to stay true to God.

Because of their outstanding commitment and obedience, only Joshua and Caleb would enter the Promised Land (vv. 36-38). A conservative estimate of the number of people who had died in the wilderness is 1,200,000 over a period of thirty-seven-and-a-half years. That's an average of eighty-five funerals per day, or seven people kicking the bucket every waking hour. Death became a way of life. How dramatic an illustration was that for the children of Israel? Every day, for more than three-and-a-half decades, people all around them were dying, being buried, being left behind. It was a sober reminder to the people that the wages of sin is death. A whole generation died in the desert.

Regulations for the Present (Deuteronomy 4–26)

Moses's second farewell speech offered regulations for the present—principles to govern their life in the new land they would soon occupy (Deuteronomy 4–26). He shifted from the historical to the legal, and from what God had done to what He was doing at that point, including what He required for right living. Moses went back over all of those laws and requirements from Exodus, Leviticus, and Numbers. New generations need old truth. Truth doesn't change; some principles—especially biblical ones—are eternal and overarching.

The first thing Moses told Israel makes it clear that God doesn't want anyone messing with His Word. "You shall not add to the word which I command you, nor take from it, that you may keep the commandments of the LORD your God which I command you" (Deuteronomy 4:2). We mustn't add or subtract from the Bible according to what we prefer—"Well, I like this portion of the Bible but not that one. I like most of the red words—Jesus said some nice things—but I don't need all the ones in black." It's not only an error-prone approach to Scripture, it's warned against in Scripture itself.

Moses focused the children of Israel on passing the baton of Scripture to each successive generation—teaching God's Word to their children and grandchildren, ensuring directly that God's truth gets passed down. To that end, he recapped the law and its application: the Ten Commandments (Deuteronomy 5–11), ceremonial laws (Deuteronomy 12–16), civil laws (Deuteronomy 16–20), and social laws (Deuteronomy 21–26). Let's do a flyover of some of the highlights:

The Sh'ma Yisrael: Moses presented the "Sh'ma Yisrael"—the Jewish confession of faith—which begins, "Hear, O Israel: The LORD our God, the LORD is one!" (Deuteronomy 6:4). The Hebrew word translated "one" here is *echad*, which doesn't mean an absolute singularity (as in one and one only), but a compound unity. It's the same word used in Genesis 2:24 to describe a husband and wife becoming *one* flesh. It also allows for the validity of the doctrine of the Trinity—one God in three Persons: Father, Son, and Holy Spirit are unified as God. Though the Jews would not have thought of it that way, the meaning of the word *one* points to that truth of tri-unity.

The First and Greatest Commandment: "You shall love the LORD your God with all your heart, with all your soul, and with all your strength" (Deuteronomy 6:5). Jesus referred to this as "the first and great commandment" (Matthew 22:38). Moses emphasized the importance of being deliberate about it, teaching children God's Word, modeling it in behavior and words on a consistent, daily basis (Deuteronomy 6:6-7). Repetition ingrains the information and forms the habit. But it had to be real, or their kids (and everyone else) would see right through their religious veneer. It wasn't about being perfect, but about providing a steady example that would stimulate their children to follow God.

Beware, Lest You Forget: God wanted His people to remember the blessings that living by His commands carried, even if it meant looking back to the wilderness, the time when God "led [them] all the way these forty years in the wilderness, to humble [them] and test [them], to know what was in [their] heart, whether [they] would keep His commandments or not" (Deuteronomy 8:2). It's an ongoing theme in Deuteronomy: "Beware, lest you forget." Slow down from time to time, deliberately reminding yourself what God has done in the past and applying it in the present.

Fear of the Lord: God made His expectations clear—to fear Him, walk with Him, love Him, serve Him wholeheartedly, and keep His commandments (Deuteronomy 10:12-13). Don't think of fear as cringing in dread of God. God isn't frowning from heaven, just waiting to swat you for every little infraction. *Fear of the Lord* is reverential awe that produces a humble submission to a loving God. If there is any fright involved, it's that we're afraid that we would do something that wouldn't please the Lord. Moses made sure that the people of Israel understood that their desire to please God would result in His blessings.

> *Fear of the Lord* is reverential awe that produces a humble submission to a loving God.

Readiness for the Future (Deuteronomy 27–30)

In his third and final farewell address, Moses addressed what God was going to do next (Deuteronomy 27–34). He prophesied Israel's future, near and far—what would happen soon and what would happen to them ultimately. It's a fascinating section, particularly chapter 27. Moses gave instructions that "on the day when you cross over the Jordan to the land which the LORD your God is giving you" (v. 2), the people were to set up great stones, whitewash them, and write the law on them (vv. 2-8). These were to be rock-solid reminders of their spiritual underpinnings.

Then the people were to move to the central ridge in the land of Canaan, eventually known as Samaria, and divide into two groups. Half of the tribes would stand on Mount Gerizim, and the other half would stand across from them on Mount Ebal, with the Levites standing in the valley between the two groups. The first group would call out blessings on Israel, and the other would call out curses. The Levites also called out curses, to which the people responded with a resounding "Amen!" The word of God echoed across the valley, from mountaintop to mountaintop, recognizing and solidifying Israel's status as God's special, chosen people (Deuteronomy 27:11-26).

Next, Moses recounted the benefits of obedience: "If you diligently obey the voice of the LORD your God...that the LORD your God will set you high above all nations of the earth. And all these blessings shall come upon you and overtake you" (Deuteronomy 28:1-2). Notice the word *if* near the beginning—a tiny word with gigantic impact. That *if* shows us that what's going to happen to them in the future is conditional upon what they do. The blessings were dependent on their obedience.

Then Moses flipped the coin to reveal the consequences of disobeying: "*If* you do not obey the voice of the LORD your God, to observe carefully all His commandments and His statutes which I command you today, that all these curses will come upon you and overtake you" (v. 15, emphasis added). The curses were specific and widespread: "Cursing, confusion, and rebuke in all that you set your hand to do, until you are destroyed and until you perish quickly, because of the wickedness of your doings in which you have forsaken Me" (v. 20).

God basically made two different kinds of covenants: conditional and unconditional. A conditional covenant is bilateral (two-sided)—both parties do something. An unconditional covenant is unilateral (one-sided)—God makes a declaration, and it doesn't matter what you do or don't do; He's going to keep His promise. Significant biblical covenants include:

- ***The Edenic covenant:*** God made a *conditional* covenant with Adam and Eve in the Garden of Eden, where He would bless them if they obeyed Him, took care of the garden, multiplied, and did not eat from the Tree of the Knowledge of Good and Evil. Adam and Eve blew it and were kicked out of Eden.

- ***The Abrahamic covenant:*** God *unconditionally* promised land to Abraham and his descendants throughout all generations.

- ***The Mosaic covenant:*** This *conditional* covenant is what we have been looking at, God's *if-then* promises to bless Israel for obedience and curse them for disobedience.

- ***The Palestinian covenant:*** Theologians use this term to describe the promise laid out in Deuteronomy 29–30. It had both components, conditional and unconditional. God's promise of the land to Abraham, Isaac, and Jacob is an *unconditional* covenant. In the end, their descendants will have the land because God will make it happen—but not completely until the millennial reign of Christ. However, their occupation of the land is *conditional*; it works generation by generation, based on whether or not they kept the Mosaic covenant. God knew they would disobey, but He also knew He would bring them back.

Moses wrapped up this final address by summarizing all he had said (Deuteronomy 30:19-20), underscoring God's heart for His people—any regulations He gives, any rules, mandates, commandments, or obligatory statements He prescribes are so that you might have life, and have it more abundantly (John 10:10).

Rest at the End of an Era (Deuteronomy 31–34)

Moses had written the entire Bible up to this point, and now his time had come (Deuteronomy 31–34). God took him up to Mount Nebo, a beautiful vantage point in modern-day Jordan, 2680 feet above sea level, just east of the Dead Sea (Deuteronomy 34:1-4). Moses gave his farewell address (Deuteronomy 31:1-2), reminding Israel that God had told him he wouldn't be crossing over the Jordan into the Promised Land with them, but that the "LORD your God Himself crosses over before you; He will destroy these nations from before you, and you shall dispossess them. Joshua himself crosses over before you, just as the LORD has said" (v. 3). In other words, they were in good hands. God was still God and would go with them as He had promised.

Furthermore, God had provided a new leader, Joshua, who had been faithful to God and Israel for a long time. Joshua hadn't complained or tried to promote himself under Moses's leadership; along with Caleb, he had advocated taking the land under God's promises and protection (Numbers 14:6-9), and now God raised him up to lead the nation. Moses encouraged Joshua, telling him, "Be strong and of good courage, for you must go with this people to the land which the LORD has sworn to their fathers to give them, and you shall cause them to inherit it. And the LORD, He is the One who goes before you. He will be with you, He will not leave you nor forsake you; do not fear nor be dismayed" (Deuteronomy 31:7-8). Moses didn't begrudge Joshua his new role, but blessed him with words that had probably lifted his own spirits over the years.

Deuteronomy 32 is a long song Moses composed and presented to the gathered people. In some ways, it's the country music song of the Old Testament, covering Israel's failures, foibles, fiascoes, and flops. I don't know how the tune went, but it would be interesting to hear a 120-year-old dude sing it (I hear it as a twelve-bar blues). Moses was finally given the stage to vent some of his frustrations over Israel's persistent rebellion and disobedience: "Of the Rock who begat you, you are unmindful, and have forgotten the God who fathered you" (v. 18).

With that out of the way, Moses's final recorded words to Israel were gracious and full of blessing. Deuteronomy 33 is a happy chapter. Moses blessed all the tribes of Israel, his last recorded words full of grace, blessing, and praise for each tribe, predicting days of strength and victory for each of them. "Happy are you, O Israel! Who is like you, a people saved by the LORD, the shield of your help and the sword of your majesty!" (v. 29). Make sure your last words are gracious words—that's how you'll be remembered.

Make sure your last words are gracious words—that's how you'll be remembered.

Moses then went up to Mount Nebo, where God showed him a spectacular view of the Promised Land. I believe it was a winter day, because that's the clearest time to see the entire land, especially after a rainfall: no wind, no dust, with pleasant, crisp temperatures. God showed him the Promised Land and said, "'I have caused you to see it with your eyes, but you shall not cross over there.' So Moses the servant of the LORD died there in the land of Moab, according to the word of the LORD" (Deuteronomy 34:4-5).

Flavius Josephus, a Jewish-Roman historian, wrote an account of Moses's death, likely based on an oral tradition passed down through the generations:

> Amidst the tears of the people, the women beating their breasts, the children giving way to uncontrolled wailing, Moses withdrew. At a certain point in the ascent he made a sign to the weeping multitude to advance no further, taking with him only the elders, the high priest Eleazar, and the general Joshua. At the top of the mountain, he dismissed the elders, and then, as he was embracing Eleazar and

> Joshua, and still speaking to them, a cloud suddenly stood over him, and he vanished in a deep valley. [3]

Coupled with the account in Deuteronomy, it's a sad note to end on, but not a final note. During the transfiguration of Jesus, Moses appeared with Him and Elijah on the mountain within the boundaries of the Promised Land of Israel (Luke 9:28-36), so he did get to enter the land after all. The law couldn't get him in, but the grace of Jesus Christ did. Furthermore, many believe that, during the future seven-year Tribulation period coming on the earth, Moses will be one of the two witnesses who appear and testify to the gospel (see Revelation 11).

Among the Jews, Moses's reputation and legacy were secured: "Since then there has not arisen in Israel a prophet like Moses, whom the LORD knew face to face, in all the signs and wonders which the LORD sent him to do in the land of Egypt, before Pharaoh, before all his servants, and in all his land, and by all that mighty power and all the great terror which Moses performed in the sight of all Israel" (Deuteronomy 34:10-12). His testimony is still an encouragement for those who want a closer walk with God.

JOSHUA
FLIGHT PLAN

Facts

Author

After the death of Israel's leader and lawgiver, Moses, God chose Joshua as the new leader. Joshua also become Israel's general, leading the new nation of tribes as they conquered the land and parceled it out. Joshua, an eyewitness, wrote the first twenty-three chapters. The priest Eleazar or his son Phinehas (Joshua 24:33) may have written chapter 24, which records Joshua's final speech and death.

Date Written

The first twenty-three chapters were probably written shortly after their events occurred, sometime around 1405–1398 BC. The last chapter was most likely recorded around 1380 BC, after Joshua's death.

Landmarks

Think of all the miracles Joshua had seen: the plagues of Egypt, the parting of the Red Sea, daily manna and water from a rock, clothes and shoes that didn't wear out for forty years, and the fall of Jericho's walls. God used Joshua in an uncommon way to oversee an uncommon work in bringing Israel into the land. The book of Joshua can be divided into three slices of this key time in Israel's history: entering the land, conquering the land, and distributing the land.

Itinerary

- Entering the Land (Joshua 1–5)
  - A Smooth Handoff
  - A Pair of Spies and an Unlikely Savior
  - A Spiritual Priority

- Conquering the Land (Joshua 6–12)
  - A Sudden Epiphany
  - A Startling Strategy
  - A Selfish Blunder
  - A Supernatural Adventure
- Distributing the Land (Joshua 13–24)
  - The Strength of Seasoned Warriors
  - An Unsettling Situation
  - A Series of Careful Strategies
  - The Slippery Slope of Assumption
  - A Strong Finish

Gospel

One of the most obvious gospel connections in the book of Joshua is the name *Joshua*, which is our pronunciation of the Hebrew name *Yeshua*, the Greek translation of which is *Jesus*. But the parallels go deeper than that. Under the leadership of Moses, great and godly though he was, Israel did not inherit the land because they repeatedly disbelieved and disobeyed God. They never qualified to receive it under the Law. But, here in Joshua, God said, "I'm giving you this land" (see Joshua 1:3). What they couldn't qualify for under the Law of Moses, God gave them as a free gift. It would be a process to claim it, but it was theirs. If that sounds familiar, it is—it's grace. As the apostle John said, "The law was given through Moses, but grace and truth came through Jesus Christ" (John 1:17).

History

Joshua is the first book of the Bible that specifically highlights the history of the Hebrew nation in their own land, long anticipated by their forefathers. It marks the transition from the books of the law to the books of history. At this point, the threats of Egypt, Babylon, and other empires were not a concern to Joshua and the Jews. Various Canaanite tribes were the dominant force at this time in history, known as the Late Bronze Age, with the Hittite people of Asia Minor rising in power and influence.

Travel Tips

Joshua read all of the Law of Moses to the people (see Joshua 8:34-35), and took a stand before the community to show that he would obey all he had read (see Joshua 24:15). No matter what he was doing, Joshua remained faithful, because he knew that God was faithful.

- Whatever God starts, He finishes. He is the author and finisher of your faith (Hebrews 12:2), and the book of Joshua is a great example of God keeping His promise to Abraham, Isaac, and Jacob—a promise of which you, as a believer, are a recipient.

- Conviction requires a response. Rahab and her family seem to have been the only ones in all of Jericho who actually moved from their fear of the Lord to some kind of faith in God (Joshua 2:8-13). It's one thing to know you need to get right with God, and another to act on it.

- God's promises include blessings not just for the next life, but this one too. While we have seasons of battle in this life—hardship and trials—God also gives us times of rest and recovery.

- Learn to trust God on a day-by-day basis. God didn't just want Israel to conquer, He wanted them to trust Him as they did so, step by step, day by day.

Whatever God starts, He finishes.

In Flight

Entering the Land (Joshua 1–5)

A Smooth Handoff

Joshua begins where Deuteronomy left off, with Moses's death and God promoting Joshua: "Now therefore, arise, go over this Jordan, you and all this people, to the land which I am giving to them—the children of Israel" (Joshua 1:2). We don't have a lot of details about Joshua's early life, although it makes sense that he would have been born a slave in Egypt. According to the historian Josephus, Joshua was eighty-five years old when he replaced Moses,[4] and he had previously served as Moses's assistant and Israel's first military commander (Exodus 17:8-16). Along with Caleb, he was one of twelve spies sent to check out Canaan, and with Caleb, the only ones to offer a positive report on what they found there (Numbers 13:16-30; 14:6-9).

God first laid out the boundaries of the land in Genesis 15, but now He told Joshua, "Every place that the sole of your foot will tread upon I have given you, as I said to Moses" (Joshua 1:3). The land was a gift Israel didn't earn or deserve, but God promised it to Abraham, well before Joshua's generation was even around. Like any gift, however, they had to receive it. The implication of God's statement was that He wanted to give them all of the Promised Land, but they would have to claim it step by step.

If it had been up to Joshua alone, all of the land would likely have been claimed. God promised to be with him, encouraging and supporting his efforts: "Be strong and of good courage" (Joshua 1:6). And Joshua understood the basis for his courage and success: meditating on and obeying God's laws. He took God at His word, but, just as Moses had to deal with stubborn and unbelieving people, so did Joshua. Conquest and occupation were theirs, *if* they obeyed God.

A Pair of Spies and an Unlikely Savior

Joshua sent out a pair of spies to check out the terrain, particularly the high walls of Jericho, the first major city in their path. The spies ended up at the home of a local prostitute, Rahab, who protected them by hiding them from the city authorities (Joshua 2:1-7). Rahab's actions were an act of faith, a response to the stories that she had heard about what God had done on Israel's journey through the wilderness. She stated her belief in God and said that nothing would stand in God's way. Then she asked for protection for herself and her family when Israel invaded, which the spies granted.

Rahab didn't just fade from view afterward, either; she is mentioned both in the book of Hebrews' hall of faith (Hebrews 11:31) and in the genealogy of Jesus Christ (Matthew 1:5). Her unlikely faith stood out not only among her own people, but among God's people too. Amazing, isn't it, that the first convert in Canaan was a call girl? The call girl became a *called* girl!

Joshua's spies escaped and returned with a good report: "Truly the LORD has delivered all the land into our hands, for indeed all the inhabitants of the country are fainthearted because of us" (Joshua 2:24). Joshua must have been thinking, *I knew it! That's what I said forty years ago! Those other ten yo-yos were saying, "We're like grasshoppers compared to them," but now God has put fear in their hearts.* The time had come to step out in faith.

A Spiritual Priority

The crossing of the Jordan River is a beautiful story of unity and faith. Joshua organized the people for their march: the priests were to go first—not the army or the generals—carrying the Ark of the Covenant, a symbol that God would go before them and open up the way. Indeed He did, splitting the waters of the Jordan so that Israel could pass through on dry land (Joshua 3:12-13). God gave this new generation a miracle of their own—and it wouldn't be the last.

Israel set up base camp in Gilgal (Joshua 4:19). Once word got around how they had miraculously crossed the Jordan, the locals lost heart. It was an ideal time to attack from a human standpoint, but not from a spiritual perspective. First, the children of Israel had to take care of some unfinished business with God. This new generation of males hadn't been circumcised, which was part of the covenant of the land. Also, they hadn't kept the Passover for a long time. They needed to establish their spiritual priorities before they did anything else. Consecration must precede conquest.

Joshua wasted no time obeying God. He made knives of flint and carried out the ritual of circumcision (Joshua 5:2-8). They had to stop and wait to recover, trusting that their obedience to God's command would keep their window of opportunity open. Circumcision is clearly a physical procedure, but it's symbolic of a spiritual operation: God wanted them to cut out of their lives anything carnal so that they could focus on the spiritual.

After the men had healed, everyone observed the Passover. For forty years, they had lived by sight: They saw a fiery pillar every night, and followed a pillar of cloud by day. They had manna every day. As soon as they entered the land and renewed the covenant, these visible tokens of God's presence ceased. But it wasn't a sad moment; it meant they were growing up spiritually. To wake up with no visible sign of God's presence and say, "I believe by faith that God is with me" is a sign of spiritual maturity. For the moment, at least, the children of Israel were ready to enter the land. It was time to "walk by faith, not by sight" (2 Corinthians 5:7).

Conquering the Land (Joshua 6–12)

A Sudden Epiphany

Joshua was about to lead Israel to one of the most remarkable victories in the Bible at Jericho, but the most important part of that battle came before the people drew near those famous walls. As he scouted the territory, Joshua came face to face with the commander of God's armies, "a Man" who stood with sword drawn. Joshua asked him, "Are you a friend or a foe?" The answer is interesting: "No, but as Commander of the army of the LORD, I have now come" (Joshua 5:14).

Joshua was Israel's leader, its general, handpicked by God and commissioned by Moses, but he clearly recognized that he was talking to his commanding officer. He dropped to his knees and worshipped, asking for guidance. The commander told Joshua to take off his sandals, "for the place where you stand is holy" (Joshua 5:15). Joshua was ready to fight, but was told first to worship. This is a lot like Moses's commission at the burning bush—an encounter with God that made the ground he was on holy because of the unique encounter with God at that place.

This preamble to Jericho reminds us that public victories are a result of private visits with the Lord. It's not by might, it's not by power, it's not by Joshua's ingenuity, but by the Spirit of God (Zechariah 4:6). Spiritually speaking, if we forget that God is in charge and just go rushing out, we're going to be defeated.

> **Public victories are a result of private visits with the Lord.**

A Startling Strategy

Joshua's worship paid dividends beyond Israel's military capabilities. God gave him the strategy to take the city, but it was a peculiar and very nonmilitary approach. Laying siege to a walled city was a lengthy, painstaking process. Ramparts had to be built under fire from enemy archers manning the walls, which in Jericho's case were forty-five feet tall. The city had to be surrounded and its supply routes cut off.

But God didn't need a massive army, marching in lockstep formation and brandishing gleaming weapons—a bunch of dudes in robes blowing horns will do nicely, thanks. Oh, and on the seventh day, when the priests blow their trumpets, have everyone give a big shout and "then the wall of the city will fall down flat" (Joshua 6:5). Then you can just go on in and take the city—no problem.

As strange as their strategy was to them, imagine watching it play out as a citizen of Jericho. The stories of Israel's crushing military victories have your mind racing. Then you see them on the horizon, and your heart clenches up. As they surround your city, your stomach ties itself in knots. But then, they wait. And you wait, anticipating the worst. Tension thickens the air. Then, finally, Israel marches—not toward your walls, but around them. They complete a circuit and go home. Part of you is relieved, while another part wonders what they could possibly be doing.

The next day, you join your neighbors on the walls and watch Israel march around Jericho again. *What's with the guys leading the way, blowing rams' horns? Are those priests? That hardly seems military.* And then they go back to their camp again. Fear still hovers in the air, but not quite as strongly. As Israel marches around the city over the next four days, the dread dissipates, to the point where you're even mocking them. This is no mighty, all-conquering army. To think you had reason to be afraid, behind these mighty walls! Tomorrow, though, you'll sing a different tune.

On the seventh day, Israel marched, the trumpets blared, and Joshua gave the command to shout. The fighting men of Israel hadn't done anything but march in a loop for six days, walking and going home, so all of that pent-up emotion and energy came out in their victory shout. Fear roared back into Jericho's citizens, and as their mighty walls began to wobble, teeter, and then crumble, they realized that everything they had heard was true: God marched with Israel.

A Selfish Blunder

Joshua warned the people before they entered Jericho to take only the gold and silver for God's treasury, but to leave behind the "accursed things" (Joshua 6:18)—items used in idol worship. They kept their promise to spare Rahab and her family, but failed to obey Joshua's warning about the cursed things, something they didn't discover until their second battle, when they were routed by the men of Ai (Joshua 7:1-5). God was suddenly not with them—but why? It turned out to be one guy, Achan the son of Carmi, who had sinned, but God had let the consequences of that sin spread to the whole army.

Ai was nothing compared to Jericho, but Israel lost three dozen men in that battle because of Achan's disobedience. Here's the deal. God said, "When you go into the land, in the very first city, Jericho, you can't take all of the spoils of war. You have to devote them all to the Lord for His work and His purpose, but you can't touch them for yourself." But Achan, whose name literally means "trouble," brought trouble on the whole group. He took and hid a Babylonian garment and some money, and it ended up costing him his life (Joshua 7:21-25).

Once Achan had been dealt with, God gave the city of Ai to Israel (Joshua 8:1-30). God often used foreign nations and armies to punish His people, but He never let them get away with bragging about or taking credit for their victories themselves. After Ai's defeat, Joshua did what Moses had commanded back in Deuteronomy 27: He divided the people in half, sent one group to Mount Gerizim to shout blessings, and the other to holler curses from Mount Ebal. Joshua also read the Scriptures to all the people, making sure that the Word of God was central in their community. You might say that Israel became a *textual community*—a group whose fellowship was based on the text of Scripture.

A Supernatural Adventure

God continued to give Israel victory, including the taking of Jerusalem from the pagan Jebusites, often using miraculous methods—selective, smart-bomb-style hailstones destroyed most of the Amorites at Gibeon (Joshua 10:8-11), and Joshua was allowed to command the sun to stand still in the sky while Israel mopped up the rest (vv. 12-14). This may be the most perplexing miracle in the whole Bible, but the point is, do you believe God could do this? How big is your view of His power? Because if God can't do this miracle, He can't do any of them. If God can't account for whatever physical effects might result from stopping the sun in the sky for a day—as staggering a thought as that is for us—then He is confined to the very creation He made, and He isn't really in control at all.

The Promised Land was not an easy place to take. God didn't bring the Israelites to the French Riviera just to hang out, soak in the rays, and enjoy the good life. Rather, the people fought for seven years to conquer the land, and it took another eighteen to settle and distribute it. The Christian life is very much like settling the land of Canaan. When you become a believer you come to rest in Christ, yes, but as soon as you pray that prayer, it's almost as if you can smell the smoke of the battlefield. Jesus never promised us a vacation. If you play the spiritual pacifist, saying you don't believe in fighting, the devil will beat you up.

The good news is that you're on the right side. As the apostle John said of Jesus, "He who is in you is greater than he who is in the world" (1 John 4:4). Even if the ultimate victory is a ways off, God will give you smaller victories each day you walk with Him. God would say to you, "I've given you the land; now walk through it, get your feet wet if need be, and take all that I've given you." Joshua embraced that call and led Israel to conquer the land.

> **Even if the ultimate victory is a ways off, God will give you smaller victories each day you walk with Him.**

Distributing the Land (Joshua 12–24)

The Strength of Seasoned Warriors

Now that Israel had arrived, it was time to distribute the land. The rest of the book reads sort of like a real estate contract, with lots of details about the boundaries of each tribe's portion. Joshua shifted into a more mundane—but no less important—job. He would survey the land and dole out the real estate to each tribe. Even so, he and Caleb, both now in their eighties, were still going strong, still leading Israel in word and deed.

As far as serving God is concerned, getting old is no reason to slow down. He told Joshua, "You are old, advanced in years, and there remains very much land yet to be possessed" (Joshua 13:1). No one likes to be reminded of their age, and getting older scares most people. It's typically where the biggest trials of life fall. Joshua, however, seemed to be just getting started in his usefulness to God. It's easy to read God's observation as blunt, but God knew Joshua's enthusiasm. He was just telling him, "Big job ahead—show 'em age is just a number."

Caleb was the same way. Together, his and Joshua's strength and service were definitely needed, because there was still a lot of land to take. Israel's initial conflicts with the Philistines began here (v. 2), but the game plan stayed the same: God named all the inhabitants of the land, then said, "I'll take care of your enemies; you use lots to distribute the land."

God cleared the way, and when distribution day came (Joshua 14), the method used to figure out who was going to live where doesn't sound very spiritual: casting lots. No one knows exactly what they did or how it worked. The closest equivalent is to flipping a coin, perhaps with sticks or stones, with God superintending the result—the idea being, "The lot is cast in the lap, but its every decision is from the LORD" (Proverbs 16:33).

Afterward, Caleb came to see Joshua at Gilgal, claiming the land God had promised him (Joshua 14:7-8). Both had served together valiantly forty years earlier. Caleb was still going strong at age eighty-five and had no plans to stop being of use if God would use him—"Give me the land God promised me and then turn me loose on the enemy; if God is with me, I'll drive them out!" As great as the stories are of people God has delivered from drug addiction or while in prison, the greatest testimony is that of the person who has walked faithfully with God throughout his or her entire life. That was Caleb.

An Unsettling Situation

As the allotment of the land continued, an unfortunate pattern developed. Instead of driving out the Canaanites, the tribes of Israel let them stay, where they would disrupt, distract, and destroy Israel's relationship with God through their pagan religious practices. Why? Motivated by materialism, the tribes thought, *Hey, why should we kick these guys out? We can use them for cheap labor.* That was a big mistake because, as we'll discover in the book of Judges, those very same people, the

Canaanite slave laborers, would form a coalition with the Philistines and other enemies of Israel and defeat them, turning the Jews into forced laborers.

Even a little bit of evil or compromise in your life will eventually bite you. You
know where you're most vulnerable to sin, and if there's a pet sin you don't deal
with immediately, harshly, and radically, it will grow. Sin is not something we can
control, especially as it grows. It is a virus that will ultimately control and destroy
us if we neglect to get rid of it.

> ## Even a little bit of evil or compromise in your life will eventually bite you.

A Series of Careful Strategies

Next, in a move that would affect Israel for hundreds of years, Joshua moved
headquarters from Gilgal to Shiloh, a more geographically central location. It
would be the new center of worship for the next 369 years. Strategically, Shiloh
was valuable high ground from which Israel's leaders could survey all the surrounding valleys, a great military and defensive advantage.

Seven tribes had yet to receive their land, but Joshua expected them to take
some initiative (Joshua 18:2). God had promised, twice, that everywhere they put
their feet would be theirs—but they still had to go get it. Groups representing each
tribe went out to survey the land; they brought back their findings, and Joshua cast
lots for them at Shiloh (v. 10).

Next, God had Joshua establish special cities called cities of refuge. If a person committed involuntary manslaughter—they unintentionally killed someone—
they could flee to one of these cities of refuge and wait for a fair trial by the judges
at the gate. They could bring their family and live without fear of reprisal, until
either their case was judged or the high priest died. If it was the latter, they could
then return safely home (Joshua 20:1-6).

Another group of cities was designated for the tribe of Levi (Joshua 21). Because
the Lord was their inheritance and they would live off donations from the rest of
the tribes, they received forty-eight cities scattered throughout the land. The cities were placed in such a way that anyone in Israel was never more than ten miles
from a Levitical city. There was always a priest or priests nearby if you had questions about the law or Scripture or their applications.

The Levites fulfilled ceremonial and priestly duties critical to God's worship, but they were also to follow Moses's instruction to "teach Jacob Your judgments, and Israel Your law" (Deuteronomy 33:10). God's heart in all generations, then and now, is that the Lord's people learn His Word. He wants us to be taught, to be spiritually fed by consistent exposure to biblical truth.

The Slippery Slope of Assumption

Joshua 22 brings us to a sad episode, an example of the lowest form of communication: assumption. This almost divided the nation of Israel, setting it on a course toward civil war. The two-and-a-half tribes who had settled east of the Jordan had fulfilled their duty and returned home. The fighting men of Reuben, Gad, and Manasseh had endured a long separation from their families while helping the other tribes conquer the land.

On their way home, though, they built a big altar on the Jordan River's west bank (v. 10). When the other tribes heard about it, "the whole congregation of the children of Israel gathered together at Shiloh to go to war against them" (v. 12). They were clearly upset about it, but enough to go to war with their fellow Israelites? Questions were definitely in order.

The obvious question was, "Why did you build this altar?" The only true altar of sacrifice had been built for the tabernacle at Shiloh. Why build another, especially since the old generation had built a false altar at Peor, which resulted in God sending a plague that killed 24,000 (Numbers 25:1-11). It was a stinging memory that led Phineas (the son of Eleazar the high priest) and a delegation of ten leaders, one from each tribe west of the Jordan, to react harshly. Fearing heresy, they reacted to hearsay, prepared for war, and only then asked questions.

What they found out when they confronted their brothers was not apostasy, but a show of unity. It turned out that Reuben, Gad, and Manasseh feared being cut off from the rest of Israel. With the natural border of the Jordan between them, they were afraid that the descendants of those west of the Jordan would say to their descendants, "What have you to do with the Lord God of Israel?" (Joshua 22:24). They explained that their altar was meant to be a replica, not an alternate—the last thing they wanted was to rebel against God (vv. 28-29).

The delegation from the ten tribes was satisfied with their response and everyone parted in peace, but it was a close call. The danger was that Israel assumed rebellion when the cause was fear of isolation. It's a lesson we would do well to remember, both individually and as the body of Christ.

A Strong Finish

The crisis at the Jordan was averted, and years of peace followed. The time came for Joshua's farewell speech. He pointed the people back to their true champion, the One who defeated their enemies and gave them a homeland: "The Lord your God is He who has fought for you" (Joshua 23:3). Joshua's testimony was simple but profound: If you do your part in these ways, God will do His.

Everything God had promised to do for Israel, He had done—providing land Israel didn't work for, houses they didn't build, and gardens they didn't plant. The commitment Joshua demanded—"Serve the Lord!" (Joshua 24:14)—was a logical response to God's provision—but it required an intentional decision and an absolute promise: "And if it seems evil to you to serve the Lord, choose for yourselves this day whom you will serve...But as for me and my house, we will serve the Lord" (v. 15). The people responded with a commitment to serving God, and Joshua recorded their covenant.

Commitment to following the Lord begins at home.

Commitment to following the Lord begins at home. Joshua knew a nation is only as strong as the families that comprise it, beginning with the designated spiritual leader, the man. He and Caleb were ready to fight, and to hold others accountable. His powerful pledge set a strong standard for the young nation.

JUDGES
FLIGHT PLAN

Facts

Author

The writer of the book of Judges is unknown. Some scholars believe the prophet Samuel wrote parts of it. However, some of the events described in Judges occurred after Samuel's death, so another author would have had to complete the writing.

Date Written

Like the author, the date the book was written is unknown. Proposed dates range from 1005 to 1000 BC, prior to David's reign. The events described took place between 1380 and 1000 BC.

Landmarks

The book of Judges is not about courtroom proceedings or judicial practices, but a detailed history of the 350 years after the death of Joshua. The judges were stopgap leaders, some military, some only regional, but none with the spiritual authority of Moses or Joshua. There were thirteen judges—twelve men and one woman—who provided leadership and deliverance during a chaotic period characterized by a cycle of sin.

There were four phases to this sin cycle—rebellion against God, retribution by God, repentance toward God, and restoration from God—but Israel repeated the pattern over and over again. As a result, they went from conquest to compromise to chaos.

Itinerary

- Conquest (Judges 1–2:9)
- Compromise (Judges 2:10–16)
- Chaos (Judges 17–21)

Gospel

The book of Judges is a series of case studies on mankind's inability to break the cycle of sin. Although Jesus Christ's sacrificial work on the cross paid the price for sin once and for all, people continue to turn from God's grace. This pattern existed before Jesus's time and will continue till the end of the age. There is no direct mention of the coming Messiah in Judges, but we see mankind's great need for Him.

Judges highlights the cosmic conflict and kingdom warfare that began in Genesis when the battle lines were drawn between the "Seed of the woman" and the "serpent" (see Genesis 3:15). The imperfect deliverers in the book of Judges anticipate and give contrast to the eventual Deliverer who offered Himself for this nation.

Even after seven cycles of rebellion, retribution, repentance, and restoration, the Israelites continued to forsake God and follow idols. Jesus broke the cycle of sin and death on the cross, but Judges makes it clear that, even in the current age of grace, God will judge unrepentant sinners. Furthermore, God gave the people of Israel judges to guide and deliver them during that ugly season. But when Jesus returns, He will be the ultimate Judge of both the living and the dead of all nations and peoples.

History

The book of Judges covers between 300 and 400 years of history, roughly the years from Joshua's death in 1380 BC to when Saul was appointed king in 1050 BC. Judges covers seven historical cycles of apostasy (turning away from God), slavery (conquered and in servitude to another people), and deliverance (God rescuing His people, only to have them turn away again). Many regional peoples oppressed the Israelites during this time—the Midianites, Ammonites, and Philistines in particular.

Travel Tips

By the time you finish the book of Judges, even flying over it from 30,000 feet, you'll be sick of Israel's relentless cycle of sin, repentance, deliverance, and sin again. God was certainly sick of it too, but He never gave up on the Hebrew people—or on humanity—which He showed when He broke the cycle of sin once and for all at the cross. Be encouraged by the knowledge that even when we're at our darkest, God's light can still shine on us and guide us home.

- God often uses the least likely people to accomplish His work. Judges is full of unlikely characters and heroes, each a forerunner of Paul's description of God's methods: "God has chosen the foolish things of the world to put to shame the wise...[and] the weak things of the world to put to shame the things which are mighty" (1 Corinthians 1:27).

- God is holy. He cannot abide the presence of sin. Judges makes it clear again and again that sin has consequences. Yes, we live in the age of God's grace, but as Paul said, "Shall we continue in sin that grace may abound? Certainly not!" (Romans 6:1-2).

> **God often uses the least likely people to accomplish His work.**

In Flight

Conquest (Judges 1–2:9)

Judges begins with success for Israel. The people were fired up, and God gave them victory over the Canaanite tribes. At first, they asked God's counsel and obeyed His instructions, with good results—defeating the tyrant Adoni-Bezek and 10,000 of his men (Judges 1:1-7). Unfortunately, their good start did not lead to a strong finish. Over the next several battles, Israel made less and less progress, winning only partial or temporary victories because they didn't completely follow God's command to drive out the inhabitants of the land.

Unable to conquer and settle the land, eventually the people fell to a point where the inhabitants turned around and drove them out (Judges 2:10-15). Israel needed God's spiritual support, of course, but they also needed His help in a military sense. Compared to the Canaanites, Israel was constantly outnumbered and outgunned. The enemy's iron chariots proved more formidable than the Israelites' primitive weaponry. But that was the whole point. God wanted to give them victory not *because of*, but rather *in spite of* the military disparity—as He would do later through the leadership of Deborah and Gideon. Their victories came through God's might, not theirs.

The main problem, though, wasn't that Israel didn't have the right artillery or vehicles, but that they left the shelter and strength of God's promise to give them the land. God's promise was the portal to God's power. Conversely, diminished power is the result of diminished faith. The root of the problem was that the people didn't fully believe—as shown by a willingness to obey God and root out all of the previous inhabitants and their pagan practices. Some enemies don't go away easily. Some enemies, in fact, aren't even people but are habits and ways of thinking that are sowed over a long period of time. The people had fallen too easily into relying on their own strength instead of God's promises.

Compromise (Judges 2:10-16)

The children of Israel had experienced a time of blessing and prosperity. After 400 years of slavery in Egypt and forty years of wandering through the wilderness, they had come to the Promised Land, conquered their foes, and distributed the land. Things were good for a while, but it didn't take long for prosperity to become complacency, which then turned to compromise. With each successive generation, they forgot more and more of what God had done, taking His blessing for granted. Times of prosperity are more dangerous than times of adversity.

You could call it *next-generation syndrome*; they got bored with the older generation's stories of what God had done in their time, but didn't seek their own experience with God. Until a new generation experiences God for themselves, they are prone to a downward progression of philosophy and behavior—the sin cycle. So it was with Israel. They ditched God and took up with the local idols, Baal and the Ashtoreths, engaging in the sex-based worship of those Canaanite fertility gods.

This was the first stage of the sin cycle: *rebellion*—questioning the validity of the true God because of the sensual enticements offered by the Canaanite religions. Like metal to a magnet, young Israelites gravitated away from God and toward Baal and Astarte. Rebellion led to *retribution*. Infuriated by Israel's infidelity, God stopped protecting Israel and strengthened their enemies. They then fell into the hands of their enemies. The retribution led to *repentance*. Eventually, Israel's oppression brought a level of displeasure that only increased as they realized that they couldn't defeat anyone without God on their side. They cried out to Him for help, which led to *restoration*. God delivered them, sending Israel a hero to overthrow their enemies and restore their freedom.

It would have been drastic enough if this whole sequence described one particular episode in Israel's history, but it became the pattern for the next 350 years: rebellion, retribution, repentance, and restoration—over and over and over again, sinning and suffering, then sighing and saving.

That's a staggering, depressing thought—unless you factor in one key element: God's pursuing, vigilant, incessant love. Israel blew it, they cried out, God saved them. They blew it again, cried out again, and God saved them again—over and over. Anyone who says that the Old Testament is all about God's wrath and the

New all about His love should think again. God pursued Israel repeatedly, like a husband who just wouldn't give up on an unfaithful wife. The bulk of Judges covers seven cycles of deliverance: seven times they fell away, seven times other nations enslaved them, and seven times the Lord delivered them.

In raising up judges, God often followed His typical protocol of selecting the least likely candidates. This is one of the few delightful aspects of the book. Ehud, for example, was left-handed, a rare attribute that afforded him the necessary stealth to sneak in and assassinate the Moabite king who was oppressing Israel (Judges 3:15-30). Shamgar killed 600 Philistines with an ox goad—not your typical weapon, but very effective with God guiding his hands (Judges 3:31). The only woman judge, Deborah, was also a prophetess—and tough as nails to boot! She even wrote a victory song to commemorate God's defeat of their foes (Judges 4–5).

Gideon might have been the least likely judge God picked (Judges 6–8). The Midianites were the oppressors *du jour*, and they would come in and take whatever crops the Israelites had grown. So Gideon, by his own admission the weakest in his family, which was the weakest in their tribe, was hiding out down at the bottom of a hill, threshing his wheat in a winepress. The Angel of the Lord appeared to him and said, "The LORD is with you, you mighty man of valor!" (Judges 6:12). I can see Gideon looking over his shoulder, wondering who the angel was talking to. But the angel wasn't being sarcastic—God was sending a message designed to strengthen Gideon's faith: "You can do what I'm about to ask you to, Gideon, because I am with you." Gideon needed a little convincing, but ultimately, God gave him victory over the Midianites—with an army whittled down from 32,000 men to 300!

Availability ranks higher on God's list of qualifications than ability.

God would rather use a few whose hearts are all-in than an army of halfhearted hangers-on. You don't need tons of people; you just need the right people—people of faith—ready to risk it all because they expect great things from a great God. The great missionary Hudson Taylor was once asked why God chose him for such a lofty task. He replied, "Because I was weak enough!" It seems that *availability* ranks higher on God's list of qualifications than *ability*.

Jephthah was another unlikely leader, the son of a prostitute who was denied his inheritance by his stepbrothers (Judges 11). He found another band of brothers, though, a gang of ne'er-do-wells who ran around the countryside raiding others—until Israel was oppressed again and called on Jephthah to lead their armies against their current enemy, the Ammonites. For all of his own crazy behavior, Jephthah sought God's blessing before he went into battle, a wise but all-too-rare move in Israel in those days. God gave him victory, but Jephthah had previously made a foolish vow that ended up costing him his youngest daughter, who likely stayed a virgin her whole life and never had children to carry on the family name.

The most famous judge was Samson (Judges 13–16). Imagine Superman's strength, driven by Hugh Hefner's morality. This *Terminator* of the Old Testament has a sad story. God used Samson to defeat Israel's enemies repeatedly, but he could have been so much more. His mother had been previously barren, but the Angel of the Lord told her that not only would she bear a son, but he would also deliver his people from their enemies. God required that Samson take the vow of a Nazirite, setting himself apart for God's service. He set the table for this judge to be a man of God, but Samson turned out to be a man of the flesh. Having both natural advantages and supernatural privileges, Samson would've been a great big brother, but he turned out to be a not-so-great son.

Samson was driven by impulse—lust and rage and ego. He wanted what he wanted when he wanted it, and expected others to provide it for him, including his parents, from whom he demanded compliance. When he didn't get his way, bad things happened. He married a Philistine girl for her looks, but ended up killing most of the Philistine groomsmen in their wedding party over some clothing. The Philistines responded by marrying her off to the best man—such loyalty!—and Samson retaliated by tying the tails of a bunch of foxes together, placing torches between their tails, lighting the torches, and sending the blazing foxes through the Philistines' crops. They couldn't get back at him, so they burned his wife and father-in-law in their house. Samson responded to that by slaughtering a thousand of them with a donkey's jawbone. He had the physical strength of a superhero, but the spiritual character of a wimp.

In all his ways, Samson more closely resembled an enemy of God than a man of God. He was selfish, vengeful, and violent—and yet God still used him to accomplish His purpose, which was punishing the Philistines for their wrongful treatment of Israel. Samson didn't turn his temptations over to God or trust God to be his strength. He thought he was entirely self-sufficient, needing no accountability, and finally, it caught up with him. He fell hard for a Philistine woman, Delilah, who nagged him into giving away the secrets of his Nazirite vow, particularly the cutting of his hair. Now, just to be clear, the hair wasn't magic. Rather, finally, all of Samson's foolishness finally caught up with him, like a rechargeable battery that hasn't been plugged in for far too long.

Samson never acknowledged God until he was shaved, blinded, beaten, and chained to a pair of pillars as an object of scorn in a Philistine temple. His sin had finally enslaved him. It was only then that Samson found it within himself to ask God for help. God responded and gave him the strength to collapse the pillars with his bare hands, crushing himself along with his enemies. Samson was a brute force, but he could've been a better force—channeled by God and used for many more years to deliver and strengthen God's people.

Chaos (Judges 17–21)

The rest of Judges is just a sad descent into chaos, featuring cross-sections of life that show God's people given over to depraved behavior—idol worship, gang rape, a horrific murder, and the threat of civil war being the lowlights. There were alarming consequences without God's righteous governance. "In those days there was no king in Israel; everyone did what was right in his own eyes" (Judges 21:25), and so Judges actually ends in a worse place than it began. Israel's downward spiral reveals a principle: With the absence of authority comes the presence of anarchy.

RUTH
FLIGHT PLAN

Facts

Author

The author of the book of Ruth is unknown. Timewise, some scholars link Ruth with the book of Judges, pointing to the prophet Samuel as the author of both books. Also, since Ruth contains elements of prophecy—correct predictions about the line of David through Boaz, for example—Samuel seems to be the best candidate.

Date Written

Because of the references to David, his throne, and his genealogy, Ruth was probably written around 1010–970 BC. However, the exact date is unknown.

Landmarks

In this quick flight over the book of Ruth, we see a story of romantic grace unfold before us. Ruth was a foreigner among the Israelites, a Moabite woman whose husband had died. She and her mother-in-law, Naomi, moved to Bethlehem at the beginning of barley harvest, where she met Boaz. Boaz eventually married her and became her kinsman-redeemer, a type of Christ.

Ruth is the only book in the Old Testament named after an ancestor of Jesus Christ, the only one named after a non-Jew, and one of only two in the entire Bible named after a woman. Ruth's name means "friendship," and she really showed her quality in that area. Hers is a story of God's providence and redemption overlaying the main story line of human love and relational interaction. Love is at the center of each of Ruth's four chapters.

Itinerary

- Love's Resolve (Ruth 1)
- Love's Response (Ruth 2)

- Love's Request (Ruth 3)
- Love's Reward (Ruth 4)

Gospel

In the book of Ruth, hints of the coming Messiah can be seen in the character of Boaz, who is presented as a kinsman-redeemer (see Leviticus 25:25). Like Jesus, he was both qualified and willing to redeem his people. Just as Boaz eventually did for Ruth, Jesus became our redeemer who paid all our debts, our avenger who defends us against our adversaries, and our mediator, accomplishing our reconciliation with God the Father. And just as Boaz ended up marrying Ruth, so Jesus is the Bridegroom of His church. Like Christ, Boaz was an affectionate bridegroom who bought a field to get a bride—a Gentile bride, like the church (see Matthew 13:44).

History

Ruth was most likely written around the reign of David, but the story takes place during the time of the book of Judges. Therefore, Ruth should be understood, historically speaking, within Judges' timeframe. Judges covers 300–400 years of history, from roughly 1380 BC, when Joshua died, to 1050 BC. For the Hebrew people, this period of history was one of unrest and faithlessness toward God. Yet the book of Ruth paints for us a picture of the enduring faithfulness of a few, as well as the deep love they had for one another and God.

Travel Tips

Ruth and Naomi's story not only shows us the value of relationships, but also the power of faith. Neither woman took for granted what she had in the other—trust, loyalty, sincerity, and love. And God honored Ruth's faith and obedience by grafting her onto the same family tree from which Jesus would come.

- The worst God has for you is better than the best the devil has for you. When Naomi lost her husband and sons, her mind turned to the Lord (Ruth 1:6-9). It's easy to excuse unbiblical behavior during times of stress and trial—to think that your way will work better than God's way given the circumstances. But the repercussions of going your own way will affect you and those you love.

> ## The worst God has for you is better than the best the devil has for you.

- God keeps His commitments and expects us to keep ours. Ruth's commitment to Naomi played a key part in establishing the genealogy of the Messiah. You never know how being a person of your word can change your world—but it will.

- Kindness is the key to successful relationships. What attracts people to Christ is not your outward appearance but your inward character. There is nothing wrong with looking good, but when you regularly show kindness, respect, and gratitude, God will shine through you.

In Flight

Love's Resolve (Ruth 1)

The story of Ruth happened during the time of the judges—a period of widespread apostasy and ungodly fervor in Israel. In terms of the sin cycle that Judges details—Israel's rebellion, God's retribution, Israel's repentance, and God's restoration—it was a time of retribution, specifically a famine that brought food shortages to an all-time low. The Law of Moses established God's intent that the productivity of the land—rain and fruitful harvests—would come in direct proportion to the obedience of the people. Famine indicated that the people were out of order.

Sin affects everyone and everything, on both global and personal levels. So even though there weren't too many righteous people in Israel in those days, those who stayed true to God still had to trust Him through the hard times. That's how it was for Naomi and her daughter-in-law, Ruth. Naomi had lost her husband and sons, so under the laws of the land, she also stood to lose her inheritance. She was inches from being out on the street.

Ruth, for her part, was from Moab, a beautiful spot in the highlands east of the Dead Sea. The problem was that the Moabites were historical enemies of Israel, worshippers of Chemosh, a fierce god who demanded child sacrifice. However, during the famine, Naomi had heard that God had provided bread for His people in Moab. Suffering had made her God-conscious in the way that it often does, and so she told her widowed daughters-in-law to head home to Moab. One of them went, but Ruth committed to staying with Naomi. And so the two women set out and traveled to Bethlehem.

It was a small beginning with monumental historical impact. Here's why: Jesus Christ was born in Bethlehem, the city of David, according to prophecy. Bethlehem was called the city of David because David was born there, the youngest of the sons of Jesse, the son of Obed. The father and mother of Obed were Boaz and Ruth. If Ruth hadn't chosen to stick with Naomi no matter what, none of those dominoes would have been set to tumble the way they did. This is a striking example of God's providence—working supernaturally through natural means to achieve a purpose. God worked through a loyal, loving, and noble decision made by a humble woman who wasn't even of the house of Israel.

Ruth's resolve shows the difference between involvement and commitment. She wasn't just along for the ride; she intended to stay by Naomi's side and to worship Naomi's God. Ruth was all-in.

Love's Response (Ruth 2)

Naomi was once a part of an aristocratic family that owned a lot of land around Bethlehem. One of the heads of this family, Boaz, came out to his fields to greet his workers and saw Ruth gathering grain. This was called gleaning, which according to Mosaic law allowed poor folks to come gather what was left over after the initial harvest. Boaz demonstrated that he was a godly boss, greeting his crew with a blessing and receiving one in return (unlike most of the work crew/boss interactions I've been around), and then turning his attention to Ruth. She hadn't caught his eye as a mere matter of physical attraction, either; he had heard her story and was determined to help her.

Ruth was blown away to find such favor. She had no expectations that she would get the benefit of the doubt from anyone—not as a woman or a Moabitess. At the same time, her trials hadn't crushed her spirits. Even though she had suffered immensely and lost considerably, she still showed grace. She just wanted to be allowed to work in Boaz's fields so she could provide for Naomi. Boaz, though, had far more generosity in mind. He praised her for her loyalty and commitment, and told his workers to let her glean from the best parts of the fields. Their relationship, though in its nascent stages, was off to a great start, building on kindness, respect, and sensitivity.

God takes ordinary events in life and arranges them for an extraordinary result.

Naomi was thrilled with Ruth's report that evening. She was as committed to Ruth's welfare as Ruth was to hers. Their mutual care and commitment point to the central undercurrent of the book: the providence of God. God takes ordinary events in life and arranges them for an extraordinary result. For example, Naomi and Ruth showed up in Bethlehem at a very particular time, the harvest. Ruth would be able to get work. Also, Bethlehem was a very particular place, the breadbasket of ancient Israel, and there she would meet Boaz in the fields. God was behind the scenes, weaving natural elements together to produce a supernatural outcome.

Love's Request (Ruth 3)

Naomi slipped into matchmaker mode, thinking, *This is really good. You want to know this guy; this could be from the Lord.* She gave Ruth practical advice, telling her to put her best foot forward: "Sweetheart, wash and perfume yourself; put on your best dress. Make yourself appealing, and then go in and pop the question to him; don't let this guy get away."

Ruth followed Naomi's advice, doing the Sadie Hawkins thing according to the laws regarding her situation in Deuteronomy 25—written centuries earlier as if God anticipated this very moment! The idea was that if a husband died and the wife was left childless, she would go to his brother or near relative for him to "raise up a seed"—that is, have a kid—so that the husband's family wouldn't disappear in Israel. Boaz knew all of this and was impressed that Ruth followed Israel's laws. He agreed to her request, but they had to wait because there was another relative who had the right of first refusal.

Boaz praised Ruth for her virtue and made the symbolic gesture of inviting her to "lay at his feet until morning" (Ruth 3:14). There was nothing immoral or impure about this; it was a common custom in the Middle East representing his intent to protect her and marry her if it all worked out. And the next morning, he sent her home to Naomi with a lot of extra food to show his honorable intentions.

Love's Reward (Ruth 4)

Boaz had to conclude the matter legally before honoring his intent to marry Ruth and secure her family's property and financial future. In ancient times, if a Jewish family lost their property, they could buy it back at the appropriate time. Title deeds always held this redemption clause. In order for it be activated, the person—known as the kinsman-redeemer—had to meet certain qualifications: he had to be a relative, he had to be able to pay whatever price was stipulated, and he had to be willing. Boaz met all three.

Boaz followed the law to a T, sealing his purchase of the land in front of witnesses, and by law arranging to do something that was otherwise strongly frowned upon—marrying a converted Gentile. So Boaz took Ruth, and she became his wife. Their first child, Obed, was David's grandfather, a key point the book makes at its conclusion by including a brief genealogy of David's line. As for Ruth, it was like the women told Naomi: "Your daughter-in-law, who loves you…is better to you than seven sons" (Ruth 4:15). Ruth had committed to follow her mother-in-law Naomi and adopt the country, culture, and God of the children of Israel. Love's reward was a happy ending for this couple and for Naomi, and a happy continuation of the messianic line of David leading to Jesus Christ.

1 SAMUEL
FLIGHT PLAN

Facts

Author

The author of 1 Samuel is not known for certain. Many scholars believe that the prophet Samuel compiled the information in the book and communicated it to the prophets Nathan and Gad, who then wrote it down. What we do know is that 1 and 2 Samuel were originally one book.

Date Written

If Samuel, Nathan, and Gad wrote the book of 1 Samuel, it was likely written sometime during the eleventh century BC. Samuel was born around 1105 BC, and David was born close to 1040 BC. Since the book covers their history, it's likely to have been written during or shortly after the events occurred.

Landmarks

After the time of the judges, Israel was on a collision course with chaos and captivity. True leadership was sadly lacking, primarily because the people had strayed from God. The book of 1 Samuel covers a period of about ninety-four years, from the birth of Samuel to the death of Saul. It tells stories of men and women who, in their distress, called on the Lord. As a result, God gave them one of the most wonderful gifts anyone could receive—the gift of influence. Among them were three major figures, leaders for a nation in desperate need of direction: a prophet, a politician, and a poet. All three men had flaws, but all of them influenced Israel, playing their roles in briefly uniting the kingdom.

Itinerary

- The Role of a Prophet (1 Samuel 1–8)
  - A Righteous Request
  - A Ready Heart

- A Regretful Removal
- A Rash Recourse
- The Rule of a Politician (1 Samuel 9–15)
  - Repeated Foolishness
  - A Royal Regret
- The Rise of a Poet (1 Samuel 16–31)
  - A Refreshing Replacement
  - A Well-Placed Rock
  - A Ruler's Wrath
  - A Respectful Runaway
  - A Reasonable Intervention
  - A Prudent Return
  - A Remorseful Ruination

Gospel

Many wonder if Israel asking for a king was God's will. A prophecy in Genesis reveals that it had always been God's plan that someday, He would reign through a king: "The scepter shall not depart from Judah, nor a lawgiver from between his feet, until Shiloh comes" (Genesis 49:10).

However, the Israelites pushed the issue and didn't wait on God's timing; that's why they ended up with Saul (who was from the wrong tribe, Benjamin) as their first king rather than David, the man after God's own heart. David, of course, was also of the tribe of Judah, an ancestor of Jesus, the King of kings, the prophesied Son of David. And Jesus, like His forefather King David, was from Bethlehem. The preacher Phillips Brooks would one day pen this thought in what became a famous Christmas song:

> Yet in thy dark streets shineth
> The everlasting Light;
> The hopes and fears of all the years
> Are met in thee tonight.

History

First Samuel begins with the birth of Samuel, follows the transformation of Israel from tribal alliances to a united monarchy, and concludes with the death of Saul, events that occurred roughly from 1105 BC to 1000 BC. One of Israel's greatest threats during this time was the Philistines, who lived in coastal areas along the Mediterranean Sea.

Travel Tips

First Samuel shows the importance of letting God have the greatest influence in your life. We all have to make a choice in that sense: to go either the way of Saul's self-service, or the way of David's God-service.

- Saul could have done things differently. He could have taken his sin seriously, for one, and placed character over reputation—as God does. Saul didn't take advantage of strategic friendships with godly men like Samuel, Jonathan, and David. Isolation is dangerous; God made us for fellowship.

- To the extent that you are influenced by God, you will influence others for His glory. Who has had the biggest positive impact on your life? Now, look at your own footprints. Who are you influencing—family, neighbors, fellow Christians, co-workers?

- God looks at a person's heart; we so often look at their appearance. He regularly chooses to use unlikely people, and He does it to remind us that He is in charge. How would your life—and the lives of others—change if you looked for the best in others?

To the extent that you are influenced by God, you will influence others for His glory.

In Flight

The Role of a Prophet (1 Samuel 1–8)

A Righteous Request

This account of influence in Israel began with a woman. Hannah, like a number of other godly, effective women in Scripture, was barren. She prayed, pouring her pain out before God, promising Him that if He gave her a son, she would dedicate the child to Him. Her desire was not to have a son who would be the richest or smartest or best-looking, but one who would serve God with total dedication.

Perhaps God was waiting for just such a prayer, because He gave Hannah a baby boy, whom she named Samuel. When he was a bit older—maybe around twelve—she brought him to the house of the Lord in Shiloh and left him in the care of the priest Eli to train the boy in ministry. Samuel's dedication to God stood in contrast with the corruption of Eli's sons, who worked as priests but served themselves first instead of God. During the time of the judges, God rarely spoke to His people, probably because they weren't listening. But in Samuel, He found open ears and a willing heart.

A Ready Heart

God introduced Himself to Samuel one night, calling out his name. Once Samuel figured out it wasn't his mentor Eli summoning him, he waited for God's call to come again. When it did, Samuel responded right away, "Speak, for Your servant hears" (1 Samuel 3:10). He didn't hedge his bets by waiting to see what it was that God wanted him to do; he was committed to serve from the moment God called on him.

God then revealed the unfortunate truth about Eli's sons—that they were immoral and corrupt and the Lord was going to put an end to their lives and influence. God told Samuel that Eli's failure was in never correcting or restraining them. Samuel didn't want to tell Eli the bad news, but he obeyed his calling, and Eli accepted God's message. Word got around that God had a new prophet in Shiloh.

A Regretful Removal

God carried out His word through Israel's enemies, the Philistines. Following a sound defeat, Israel's leaders called for the Ark of the Covenant—the sacred box that symbolized the presence of God among His people—to be brought from Shiloh, thinking it would lead them to victory over the Philistines. Because they trusted in their talisman more than the God it represented, Israel was slaughtered in battle, losing 30,000 men, including Eli's sons, Hophni and Phinehas. The Philistines also captured the ark. When old Eli got the news, he keeled over, broke his neck, and died, which brought an end to his forty years of service as a judge.

This horrible moment was captured best in the name of Phinehas's newborn son, who was born during the battle. When Phinehas's wife heard what had happened, she named the child *Ichabod*, which means "no glory." "The glory," she said, "has departed from Israel, for the ark of God has been captured" (1 Samuel 4:22). She understood that, more than a token of God's blessing, the ark was the physical symbol of God's presence, glory, forgiveness, and mercy. Once a year, the high priest sprinkled a lamb's blood on the mercy seat on the top of the ark—atoning for the sins of the nation. How would Israel now approach God for forgiveness? After so many years of idolatry, immorality, and self-serving behavior, God had given Israel what she kept asking for: for Him to leave her alone. His glory had departed.

But God wasn't about to let the Philistines determine when and where His glory would come and go. After they put the ark before a statue of their god Dagon, they returned the next morning to find the statue had fallen forward, as if in worship of the God of the ark. It seems that God was exhibiting His sense of humor, demonstrating the helplessness of this false god in His presence. God then blistered the Philistine capital of Ashdod with destruction and its citizens with tumors, so that they ended up returning the ark. The ark stayed in seclusion for the next twenty years in the town of Kirjath Jearim.

A Rash Recourse

Samuel remained a faithful judge in Israel his entire life, but his sons did not follow in his moral footsteps. The people saw another situation coming similar to the days of Eli's sons and told Samuel they wanted a king. Samuel was bummed, but God told him, "It's not you they've rejected; it's Me. Give them what they want."

The Lord then told Samuel to inform Israel about what it would mean to have a king—military conscription of sons for the army and royal conscription of daughters for duties in the palace, taxes on everything from produce to livestock, and servitude to a mere man rather than the God who had liberated them and provided for them all these generations. The people didn't care: "We want a king like everyone else has." They got a king all right, but otherwise, it was all wrong: the wrong timing, the wrong tribe (Saul was from Benjamin, not Judah), and the wrong temperament.

The Rule of a Politician (1 Samuel 9–15)

Repeated Foolishness

Saul certainly looked the part of a king. He was tall and handsome, and he was from a good family—a winner in every obvious way. What wasn't obvious was Saul's prideful and political heart, which cast a shadow over his reign. He was a smooth-talking poser, the Old Testament equivalent of a carnal Christian—on a spiritual roller coaster his whole life, with the promise of his early walk with God canceled out by poor choices as he aged. As God would later describe it, "I gave you a king in My anger, and took him away in My wrath" (Hosea 13:11).

Years later, Saul himself would inadvertently provide his own nine-word biography: "Indeed I have played the fool and erred exceedingly" (1 Samuel 26:21). This tragic admission could have been the banner over his life. He started out humbly, expressing disbelief that Samuel would anoint him of all people. But eventually he came to believe his own press: "Wow, man, you're so tall and good-looking, and from such a good family—you should be king!" Such pride and arrogance will drive any life into a wall of destruction, and Saul was a case study.

A fool habitually turns from wisdom, repeating mistakes till his life implodes. Saul played the fool in a few different ways:

Arrogance: Saul took credit for other people's victories—even those of his own son Jonathan—promoting himself over the nation he served (1 Samuel 13:1-4). He compounded his error by carrying out a burnt offering on his own, instead of waiting for Samuel to fulfill his God-given role as priest. This snubbing-of-the-nose to God was noticed by Samuel, who told Saul that his days as king were now numbered, because "the LORD has sought for Himself a man after His own heart" (1 Samuel 13:14)—"and Saul, it ain't you!" Pride always breaks what God builds.

Pride always breaks what God builds.

Indifference: Saul cared more about his reputation than the people under his care. At one point, Israel's army had been reduced to only 600 men. Saul was sitting under a tree, waiting for something to happen. His son Jonathan was not a sitter but a fighter, so he got up, took his armor bearer, and went on a two-man sortie into Philistine territory, saying, "The Lord can win with a lot of us or a few." Sure enough, God gave the two men victory (1 Samuel 14:6-14). The dynamic duo set an example, inspiring the rest of the army to follow them into battle.

Saul, in the meantime, had issued a senseless order, forbidding any of the men to eat until all the enemies were defeated, under penalty of death. The men had been forced to battle all day without eating, so everyone was beyond exhausted. Jonathan, out on his raid, hadn't heard the king's order, and stopped at one point to refresh himself with some wild honey.

When Saul found out what Jonathan had done, he told him, "You're a dead man." Jonathan responded with the obvious—that Saul's ridiculous demand had left all his men so weak from hunger that the army had been prevented from winning an even greater victory (1 Samuel 14:29-30). The people stood up for Jonathan, recognizing that his leadership had won the day, but Saul's jealousy and tactical ineptitude betrayed a stunning indifference toward anyone's welfare but his own.

Disobedience: Samuel told Saul that when he went to battle against the Amalekites, Saul was to "utterly destroy all that they have, and do not spare them" (1 Samuel 15:3). No exceptions. God intended to use Israel to punish the Amalekites for an old injustice, an ambush in Moses's day that led to the slaughter of women, children, and the elderly (Deuteronomy 25:17-19). They were a cancer in the Promised Land, and God had promised to cut them out completely.

Saint Augustine's "just war" theory was based upon this understanding—that warfare is sometimes necessary to restrain the rise of evil. But Saul thought he knew better than God. Israel was victorious, but Saul spared not only the best of the livestock but Agag, the Amalekite king. As a result, the Amalekites would continue to plague Israel for years to come.

A Royal Regret

God told Samuel, "I greatly regret that I have set up Saul as king" (1 Samuel 15:11). Samuel was grieved for Israel and cried out all night in prayer, but when he went to see Saul the next morning, Saul had the nerve to tell him that he had obeyed God's commandment. Samuel said, "Then what's all this animal noise I hear, sheep bleating and oxen moaning?" Saul shrugged it off, saying, "Oh, that? Those are for a sacrifice to God—but hey, we killed the rest!"

Saul sounded very pious and spiritual, but Samuel knew better—that defying God is not piety but rebellion. He told Saul to zip it—that God delighted more in obedience than in burnt offerings. It was a matter of the heart, and Saul had none. God was fed up with Saul, and Samuel proclaimed His rejection. Saul would keep his crown for the time being, but God would not be with him, and God's replacement was waiting in the wings.

Samuel had nothing more to do with Saul, and he mourned for him the rest of his life (1 Samuel 15:35). Saul's life and reign could have ended happily, but his disobedience destroyed Israel's stability. As F.B. Meyer wrote, "This is the bitterest of all—to know that suffering need not have been; that it has resulted from indiscretion and inconsistency; that it is the harvest of one's own sowing; that the vulture which feeds on the vitals is a nestling of one's own rearing. Ah me! this is pain."[5]

The Rise of a Poet (1 Samuel 16–31)

A Refreshing Replacement

Israel's first two kings provided a direct contrast in what matters to God. Saul had a rock star mentality; he wanted people to think that he was impressive and he wanted to be served. David, his replacement, had the mindset of a shepherd—a man after God's own heart. God told Samuel to anoint a king among the sons of Jesse of Bethlehem. This time, though, God avoided the big, handsome guy and went with the least likely selection. Jesse's youngest son, David, wasn't even among his brothers when Samuel arrived. He was out tending sheep in the fields. When they brought him to Samuel, God said, "That's the guy." Everyone was stunned, but God clarified the principle behind His choice: "Man looks at the outward appearance, but I look at the heart" (1 Samuel 16:7).

Samuel anointed David as the next king, and as God's Spirit came upon him, it also left Saul, replaced by "a distressing spirit from the LORD" (v. 14). David soon came to Saul's attention as a capable warrior and musician, and Saul brought the young man in to play for him and soothe his troubled spirit. David was Saul's personal iPod. What's more, Saul loved the guy—at least at first. He couldn't help sensing God's hand on David.

So David came to Saul's court and played his harp whenever Saul was under duress, refreshing Saul and driving away the evil spirit that plagued him. It would return, though, and over time, David would lose favor with Saul, even though he never once mentioned that he had been tapped by God as the future king. David saw himself as no one special—just a shepherd kid with a harp who had been blessed by God and suddenly brought to the king's courts, which is part of what God loved about him. David honored Saul because he wanted to honor God; whatever Saul's faults, God had chosen him as Israel's first king, and David respected God in all His ways. It was that trait that led to the young shepherd-poet's most famous moment—the defeat of the Philistine giant, Goliath.

A Well-Placed Rock

For the first twenty-three years that Saul was king, Israel was at war with Philistia. At one point their armies met between two hills in the valley of Elah, and the Philistines sent out their big gun for a one-on-one, winner-take-all fight. Goliath was so huge that his name has become a synonym for gigantic things. Standing almost nine feet tall, Goliath's body armor weighed over 150 pounds and his spear was about 26 feet long—with a 17-pound head![6]

Israel's army looked at him and collectively said, "We want no part of that." David looked at him and said, "So what? He's defying God. He's a dead man walking." David understood that to mess with God's people is to mess with God Himself—and that God takes it personally when you hassle His people.

Saul tried to equip David with his own armor, but it didn't fit. David just took the weapons of his trade as a shepherd—a sling, some rocks, and his bare hands—and went forward in God's name. Goliath saw David and was insulted, saying, "Am I a dog, that you come to me with sticks?" (1 Samuel 17:43). He didn't know it at the time, but he was outmanned and outgunned. When David struck this giant down with a well-placed shot from his sling, he wasn't chucking a rock—he was unleashing a Spirit-guided smart bomb, and it was lights out for Goliath. The secret to killing giants is to have a greater respect for a giant God.

The secret to killing giants is to have a greater respect for a giant God.

A Ruler's Wrath

The rest of 1 Samuel describes the change in the relationship between King Saul and young David. Saul's attitude toward David went from respect to resentment. His jealous hatred of David, manifested in his ongoing attempts on David's life, is the unfolding tale in the rest of this book. There's a contrast between how Saul related to people—insecure in his self-reliance—and how David did—secure in God's strength and provision.

As a result of the presence of the Spirit of the Lord in David's life—and the lack in Saul's—David behaved wisely and Saul irrationally, till the end of his life. Saul sent David out on dangerous missions, trying to get him killed, but David succeeded because God was with him. That's why Saul invented a new twist on a classic childhood party game called Pin the Spear in the Worship Leader. He tried to kill David twice that way, but his son Jonathan, who had become fast friends with David, helped him escape.

A Respectful Runaway

Through it all, David did not once retaliate, though he could have on a few occasions, including once when he came upon Saul as Saul relieved himself in the cave where David and his men were hiding (1 Samuel 24). It's not that David couldn't have harmed Saul—after all, there was a reason the women sang that Saul had killed his thousands but David his ten thousands. But David honored God's anointing on Saul as king. Instead of fighting back, he ducked, dodged, and darted, avoiding Saul and staying on task with what God had called him to do.

Even though David became a fugitive, he didn't allow Saul to steal his joy in the Lord. In fact, while he was on the run, David penned some powerful poetry describing his dependence on God's help and venting his frustration with his enemies. A number of the psalms have their background in this period of his life.[7] Some of the best songs in history were written during the worst periods of pain in people's lives. As C.H. Spurgeon said, "The music of the sanctuary is in no small degree indebted to the trials of the saints. Affliction is the tuner of the harps of sanctified songsters."[8]

David survived by leaning hard on God, but also by using the tools God had given him, including cunning and guile with his enemies and righteousness with his allies. At one point, he pretended to be insane, drooling and scratching at the city gates, in order to hide out among the Philistines—while all the while secretly striking at them under God's supervision (1 Samuel 21). Another time, he promised protection to the priest Abiathar, whose father Ahimelech had been executed, along with other priests, by Saul for harboring David, whom they didn't know was at odds with the king (1 Samuel 22). David's generosity and righteousness won him a loyal following among seasoned soldiers and regular citizens.

A Reasonable Intervention

After Samuel's death, David went out into the desert, the Wilderness of Paran (1 Samuel 25), where a story unfolded of beauty and the beast—the beauty being Abigail, who was married to a foolish lout of a man called Nabal (whose name means "fool"). Abigail also tamed the beast in David, saving her husband's life after he disrespected David's efforts to protect his shepherds and livestock from roving bandits. When David asked Nabal for some food for his men for their services, Nabal went against every social convention of the time and refused. When David heard about it, he didn't just get mad, he went nuclear, threatening to kill every man that worked for Nabal.

When Abigail heard about the situation going to DEFCON 1, she stepped in, humbly going to David with food and gifts and dissuading him from taking vengeance into his own hands. David thanked her for her intervention, and, after God struck Nabal dead a week and a half later, David proposed to this wise and gracious young woman. The hardhead met the hothead, but the cool head prevailed. Interesting dating technique!

There was no time for a honeymoon, though, because Saul continued his pursuit. Once again, however, David had the advantage but didn't take it, sneaking into Saul's own tent in his camp and taking the spear and water jug lying right next to Saul's sleeping head (1 Samuel 26). David retreated, completely undetected, to a nearby hill and called out to Saul's commander, Abner, "How come you're not protecting your king?" Saul recognized David's voice, and David told Saul, "Why are you chasing me, a flea, all over Israel? I've got your spear, but I spared your life because you are the Lord's anointed." Saul started weeping like a baby—"David, I love you; you're so good to me. I messed up"—but it was just an emotional show. He would turn again, and soon, his seemingly honest and meaningful confession dissolved in a heart hardened toward God.

A Prudent Return

On the run again, David returned to Philistia, this time not as a drooling whackhammer but a welcome guest (1 Samuel 27). The Philistines were preparing a major offensive into Israel, but David again played his cards wisely, laying low among God's enemies, pretending to attack the Israelites while really raiding their enemies, while he waited to see what God would do with Saul.

A Remorseful Ruination

As the armies of the Philistines gathered to attack Israel, David got his answer: Saul finally went off the deep end of stupid, consulting a clairvoyant to summon Samuel's spirit from beyond the grave (1 Samuel 28). Saul wasn't just disobeying the law of Moses by dealing with a medium (Deuteronomy 18), but also going against his own edict, for he had banned them from Israel.

Why did Saul do this? God had been giving Saul the silent treatment. He wasn't speaking to him through any of the normal means of prophets and priests, and even though it was his own fault, Saul grew desperate and searched out a medium.

The séance didn't go well. Once the woman conjured up Samuel's spirit, the dead prophet said, "Why did you disturb me? Can't you see I'm a dead guy? But for the record, tomorrow there is going to be a battle. Israel will lose, you and your sons will die, and you will be where I am." This was too much for Saul to handle and he collapsed, depleted of physical energy and bankrupt of spiritual vitality.

Meanwhile, the Philistine king, Achish, sent David back to Ziklag (the town he had gifted to him a few chapters back) after some of his nobles gave him grief for having a noted Philistine-killer with him, even though David had completely fooled Achish into thinking he was an ally (1 Samuel 29). David returned and dealt with an Amalekite raid in which Ziklag was set aflame and the townspeople, including his family, captured. He won them back, but it meant he wasn't present at Saul's final showdown at Mount Gilboa, when Samuel's terrible prophecy of Saul's doom came to pass: "Saul, his three sons, his armorbearer, and all his men died together that same day" (1 Samuel 31:6).

Saul's demise reflected the despair that had taken hold of his life. Severely wounded, he ordered his armorbearer to finish him off before the Philistines closed in on them, but the man refused out of fear. Saul then fell on his sword, taking his own life. It's one of the seven instances in the Bible of suicide. The Philistines cut his head off and hung his corpse in plain sight on the wall of their city Beth Shean. Men from Jabesh Gilead, right across from the Jordan, came across, took Saul's body, and gave him a decent burial. Saul played the fool to the end, but it didn't have to be that way. Had he truly repented, God would have forgiven him. Instead, his is a sad conclusion to a life of unrealized opportunity.

2 SAMUEL
FLIGHT PLAN

Facts

Author

First and 2 Samuel were originally compiled as one book, but were divided into two separate books sometime during the early first century BC. As with 1 Samuel, the author is unknown, though some have suggested Samuel, Nathan, and Gad probably wrote the book.

Date Written

Like 1 Samuel, 2 Samuel was written after the reign of David, possibly during the reign of David's son Solomon, around 925 BC.

Landmarks

Second Samuel tells the story of how David went from shepherding livestock to serving as God's sovereign king in Israel. Following the latest Philistine invasion, Saul was killed, along with his sons. This opened the door for David, whom the prophet Samuel had anointed some twenty years before, to rise to the throne. The book of 2 Samuel falls into three sections showcasing David's rise and fall.

Itinerary

- David's Triumphs (2 Samuel 1–10)
    - Crying Over the King
    - Coronation as the King
    - Confirmation as King
    - Compromise of the King
    - The Covenant with the King's King
- David's Transgressions (2 Samuel 11–12)
    - A Costly Decision

- A King's Confession
  - David's Troubles (2 Samuel 13–24)
    - The Consequences of a King's Sin
    - A King's Careless Indecision
    - A Crushing Resolution
    - A Costly Counting and a Precious Purchase

Gospel

The scarlet thread of redemption winds unmistakably through the life of David. God promised He was going to build David a house—a lineage or a dynasty (2 Samuel 7)—which would be established forever. In addition to this Davidic covenant (mentioned later this chapter), David himself prefigured the greater Son of David, Jesus Christ. When Jesus came to Jerusalem, the city that would reject Him and eventually kill Him, He didn't get angry. Rather than fume and say, "Oh, you'll get what's coming to you, Jerusalem," He wept (Luke 19:41-44). His heart broke knowing the suffering that would come to the people at foreign hands because they had rejected God. Similarly, David wept over King Saul and God's rejection of Saul as king. Saul had driven David from his home, out into the wilds, into cold nights and dark caves. And yet David refused to scorn him, honoring God by respecting God's chosen king—even after Saul's fall from grace.

History

During this period in Israel's history (1010–970 BC), David conquered many of Israel's enemies in the land of Canaan, ultimately making Jerusalem his royal city and Zion the religious center of the nation (see 2 Samuel 5:7).

Since its foundation, Jerusalem has been demolished twice, sieged twenty-three times, attacked fifty-two times, and captured and recaptured forty-four times. Many archaeologists believe that the oldest remaining part of the city was settled in the early Bronze Age, during the fourth century BC.

Travel Tips

The book of 2 Samuel shows us how even the best people can fall into sin, and how God is still willing to forgive and help deal with the consequences:

- Augustine defined the progression of sin as a thought first, then a form, a fascination, and a fall. David's sin with Bathsheba began as an idle thought in an idle moment. When it took form, it became adultery covered up by deceit and murder. There will always be consequences for sin; still, it's far better to confess your sin and know you are forgiven as you deal with it.

One of our greatest needs—if not the greatest—is to be forgiven.

- Forgive because God forgave you. One of our greatest needs—if not the greatest—is to be forgiven. Make forgiveness—both offering it and receiving it—a priority in your life.

In Flight

David's Triumphs (2 Samuel 1–10)

Crying Over the King

When David first heard about the deaths of his king, Saul, and his dear friend, Jonathan, he wrote a lament—a song of mourning commemorating their exploits and bravery (2 Samuel 1). David's response is remarkable in light of all that Saul had done to David—chasing him all over Israel, trying to kill him. David didn't dance and sing, "Ding-dong! The witch is dead!" He had always respected Saul's anointing and authority as king; never once had he retaliated against Saul, and now he mourned him publicly.

In eulogizing Jonathan, David wrote, "How the mighty have fallen in the midst of the battle!" (2 Samuel 1:25). There was no doubt that David and Jonathan had a special relationship. After David had slain Goliath and come to serve in Saul's court, "the soul of Jonathan was knit to the soul of David, and Jonathan loved him as his own soul" (1 Samuel 18:1). We see that bond in David's lament for his fallen friend: "I am distressed for you, my brother Jonathan; you have been very pleasant to me; your love to me was wonderful, surpassing the love of women" (2 Samuel 1:26).

Some have forced from those words a homosexual relationship between David and Jonathan. But that stretches credibility and ruins a beautiful, heartfelt tribute. Yes, David didn't have the best marriage to Jonathan's sister Michel—or a good track record with marriage in general, despite his fruitful career. Despite that, there is no evidence to suggest that David went against God's law and participated in homosexuality. The rigors of battle and admiration for a godly heart drew David and Jonathan together, and David honored his friend in death.

Coronation as the King

God sent David to Hebron in Judah, where he received his first public anointing as king (2 Samuel 2:4). Samuel had anointed him privately when David was just a boy at his dad's house, but now the men of Judah proclaimed him as their king. The kingdom wasn't united yet; Judah represented only the southern portion of Israel, so David still had work to do to unite all twelve tribes. That work started with Saul's surviving son, Ishbosheth. Saul's former commander, Abner, set Ishbosheth over all of the tribes except Judah, setting the stage for a civil war between Saul's appointed heir and God's anointed king.

In the war that followed, "David grew stronger and stronger, and the house of Saul grew weaker and weaker" (2 Samuel 3:1). Abner saw the writing on the wall and, at one point, met with David. He told him, "Look, David, the cards are on the table. You're the next king, so let's negotiate a handover. I know that God has selected you, and I'm willing to turn my master and all of his house and holdings over to your hands." And so he did, negotiating the treaty that would unite the kingdom (even if it was just to ensure his own survival).

Confirmation as King

David was king over Judah and the south for seven years before he was made king over all of Israel. Having consolidated his rule, David was anointed a third and final time at Hebron—this time by representatives of all the tribes as king over all of Israel (2 Samuel 5:3). The tragedy of civil war had ended as all of Israel gathered and told their God-appointed king, "Indeed we are your bone and your flesh" (v. 1). Among other things, they recognized that fighting their fellow Jews was out of line with God's desire for His people.

Next, David took Jerusalem. Originally settled by the Jebusites, a Canaanite tribe, Jerusalem was strategically located, built on the natural fortification of a hilltop, and fed by the natural spring of Gihon. The original inhabitants of the city were arrogant, thinking David could never take away the high ground from them. They even told him, "The blind and the lame will repel you" (v. 6). That made David angry—he showed a pattern of being temper-prone, especially when he perceived that God's good name had been slighted—and he took the city in the full confidence that he was God's anointed, and that God was establishing a kingdom through him. He conquered the city, then built it up and expanded his family, taking wives and concubines from Jerusalem who bore him sons and daughters. Jerusalem became and remains the geographical heartbeat of the Jewish people.

Compromise of the King

The next episode we see shows us the danger of doing the right thing the wrong way—making compromises in the name of being practical and pragmatic. David set about with a righteous purpose: bringing the Ark of the Covenant up from the countryside house where it had been stored for the past forty years (1 Samuel 7). The ark's proper place was in the central room of the tabernacle, the Holy of Holies. Once each year, the high priest sprinkled blood over its lid, known as the mercy seat, as atonement for Israel's sins. So for decades, Israel had gone without the main rite that represented God's salvation, His mercy and forgiveness in the chief place of His presence and worship. Having been God's instrument to unify the kingdom, David wanted to remedy that.

David gathered Israel's best men, 30,000 strong, and set out in a great procession, accompanied by musicians, to bring the ark to Jerusalem. They recalled how the Philistines returned the ark all those years ago, bringing it back on a cart, and thought, *Hey, we'll build a new cart and do this the right way.* However, while they were doing the right thing, they were doing it the wrong way. The Law of Moses prescribed a specific protocol for moving the ark anywhere (Numbers 4). Only one tribe could carry it, the tribe of Levi. Only one family in Levi could carry it, the family of Kohath. And the Kohathites had to carry it in a very special way: the ark had a little ring on each of its four corners, and two poles were slid through those rings so that the ark could be lifted up using the poles, which were hoisted upon their shoulders.

But David was thinking, *Times have changed, and this is a modern era. Let's speed it up a little bit. After all, it's a nine-mile jaunt uphill, so why have the priests carry the ark on their shoulders when we can put it on a nice cart?* However, when God prescribes a specific way of doing things, it's best to do them His way. So when the cart hit a bump and a guy named Uzzah reached out to steady the ark with his hand, God got angry and struck him dead (2 Samuel 6:6-8). David wasn't happy, but he recognized where he had gone wrong—that the ends don't always justify the means.

Three months later, when David tried again, he went above and beyond to honor God, sacrificing oxen and sheep every six paces, dancing, playing music, and rejoicing the entire nine miles until the ark was safely brought back to Jerusalem.

The Covenant with the King's King

Second Samuel 7 is one of the most important chapters in the entire Bible. The rest of the Bible's message rests upon this chapter and the promise God made to David in it. It all started when David looked around, saw that God had given him victory over his enemies, and that the land was at peace. He looked at the house he had built for himself, and then looked at God's ark, sequestered in tent curtains, and said, "That's not right." He wanted to build God a proper temple, to honor his King. God responded through His prophet, Nathan, "Actually, I don't really care about a big monument or a big building; I've been happy in the tent."

"In fact," God said, "You want to build Me a temple, but I'm going to build *you* a house"—a lineage—"and establish your throne forever" (see 2 Samuel 7:13). It was an unconditional covenant; that is, God would do all the work. He would raise up a son of David—Solomon—to build the temple, and He would also eventually raise up a Son of David—Jesus Christ—to rule from David's throne in Jerusalem forever.

Like many Old Testament covenants, there were two fulfillments: one that happened close to the time it was made, and one that was (or will be) fulfilled later on. In this case, David's dynasty would last until the Babylonian captivity, which began in 586 BC. His descendant, Jeconiah, was such a wicked king that God cut off the line of his offspring. God, however, would keep the line of the future Messiah going through another son of David, Nathan, an ancestor of Jesus's mother, Mary (see the explanation in "Matthew, Mark, Luke").

David didn't know all these messianic implications, but even so, he was overwhelmed by God's greatness and his smallness. God had promised him that not only would his son sit upon the throne, but there would also be an everlasting lineage and an everlasting kingdom, and he was humbly grateful.

David's Transgressions (2 Samuel 11–12)

A Costly Decision

David was a passionate man full of deep feelings and driving principles. Sometimes, though, passion can build a prison. In David's case, all the power and authority that served him as he worked to unify the kingdom became a problem in peacetime. With the kingdom settled, he took liberties and it cost him, setting him on a troubled path for the rest of his days.

David had geared up and gone out to battle in springtime for years and years, but this time, he stayed home (2 Samuel 11). He sent his commander Joab and his troops out to fight the Ammonites, but he stayed in Jerusalem. Maybe he thought, *War is a young man's game. I've earned the right to stay home this time.* Whatever David was thinking, he made a mistake. He had often been compassionate with his mortal enemies, but perhaps in his middle age he had grown complacent about his true enemy, the devil—and the devil nailed him.

When David first saw Bathsheba bathing on a rooftop, he couldn't have imagined all the trouble his eyes were going to cause. His first glance turned into a lingering gaze, which turned into lust, then fascination, and then intention. Finally, he acted upon his fascination, met with her, slept with her, and so he fell.

David probably thought he'd get away with it—*I'm the king, after all, and it's just one night*—but then Bathsheba got pregnant, and he went into cover-up mode, sending for her husband Uriah to come home and have a little R-and-R with the wife. When Uriah refused to take a luxury his fellow soldiers couldn't enjoy with their wives, David then sent him to the front lines, where he would be a likely target for the enemy. Sure enough, Uriah was killed, and after Bathsheba's period of mourning, David took her as his wife.

Sin always comes out into the light, revealed for the twisted and ugly creature it is.

A King's Confession

David compounded his sin by trying to hide it, but sin always comes out into the light, revealed for the twisted and ugly creature it is. The Bible does not cover up sin, even with such a man as David: "the thing that David had done displeased the LORD" (2 Samuel 11:27). Sin is expensive because it offends a holy God. After all, God, by His holiness, defines what sin is. There were other ramifications, of course, but David's sin struck God's heart first. David realized that singular fact and immortalized it in song: "Against You, You only, have I sinned, and done this evil in Your sight" (Psalm 51:4).

David went almost a year without that confession, though. He carried on outwardly as if nothing had happened. Internally, however, the hollowness of his isolation gnawed at him, and his conscience ate at his peace of mind, worsened by his lack of confession. He ignored the warning light on his dashboard, so to speak, and the malfunction got worse (see Psalm 32).

God, however, wasn't content to leave David in the pain of his isolation, so He sent him Nathan, a prophet who carried God's word to the king (2 Samuel 12). Nathan approached David's issue through a parable, telling him the story of two men, one rich and one poor. The rich guy had plenty of livestock, but he took the poor man's only beloved lamb to feed a guest.

When David heard the story, he was furious. "Who is this guy? He deserves to die, after he pays the poor guy back four times over!" Nathan responded, "*You* are the guy!" He held up a verbal mirror, reminding David of all that God had given him throughout his life, and all that God would have given him if he only asked. Instead, David took another man's only lamb (Bathsheba) to consume her by his own lust. And because he sinned in secret, his punishment would be public: God would allow notorious grief and hardship in David's own home.

David's Troubles (2 Samuel 13–24)
The Consequences of a King's Sin

The consequences of David's sin begin to reverberate throughout his family, imprisoning all of them in a web of deceit, betrayal, and death. David had six wives, a bunch of concubines, and a pack of kids, and if you think that sounds like potential for a lot of conflict, you're right. David's household was a convoluted mess, and one disturbing example of this came when his daughter Tamar was raped (2 Samuel 13). Now, this was tragic in and of itself, but another factor made it even worse: her own half-brother Amnon committed the crime.

Amnon was sick with lust for Tamar. The Bible says he loved her, but it was just a case of hormonal overdrive. He conspired to have his way with her, pretending to be ill and asking David himself to send Tamar to him with some snacks to nurse him back to health. David sent Tamar to Amnon, who then forced himself on her and raped her. The so-called love he felt was immediately replaced by disdain, and he kicked her out.

Tamar tore her robe and smeared ashes on her head—both signs of serious grief. Her full-blood brother, Absalom, found her and figured out what had happened. When David found out, he was furious, but he did nothing. He probably thought, *I lost the moral high ground, the right to discipline my son in an area of sexual promiscuity, because I failed in this area.* But his failure actually made him the ideal person to speak to his son—someone who knew firsthand the perils of allowing lust to take root. Unfortunately, his fear of being perceived as a hypocrite only made the injustice worse.

Absalom, for his part, bided his time, waiting a full two years before taking matters into his own hands, killing Amnon during a family get-together that David didn't attend. Once the deed was done, Absalom fled to Geshur, where he stayed for three long years. Back home, David mourned his sons—first, the death of his firstborn Amnon, and then, as the years healed that pain, the self-banishment of Absalom. Though he later pardoned Absalom and let him return to his home, David's relationship with his son was broken.

A King's Careless Indecision

David seemed to have forgiven Absalom, but hadn't forgotten the incident. Instead of an embrace or talking it through and resolving it, David offered only silence, content that he had been merciful about his son's transgression. However, David being dead right wasn't worth a dead relationship. Eventually, bitterness over the lack of communication took hold of Absalom's heart, indifference settled in, and he openly rebelled against his father.

God had promised David that an adversary would rise up in his own house, and it turned out to be Absalom, whose good looks camouflaged a bad heart. David's sin-chickens were coming home to roost. Absalom began to publicly campaign against his father, hearing people's complaints and cases as they entered Jerusalem and then lamenting that he was not a judge who could take care of the matter for them (2 Samuel 15:2-6). He played to the people, hearing them, hugging them, and stealing their hearts. David came off as a distant, unconcerned ruler compared to Absalom's political glad-handing, and the embittered young man gained a large following. Eventually he made his move, staging a coup in Hebron (2 Samuel 15:10).

When David got word of Absalom's treachery, he fled Jerusalem. It shocked the people, but he did it because he loved the city and didn't want to see it become the center of bloodshed, with innocent citizens caught in the crossfire between him and his wayward son. Also, David knew how to handle himself out in the sticks after his fugitive days spent running from Saul. After he left, Absalom moved into the palace in Jerusalem and, in fulfillment of God's prediction after David's sin with Bathsheba, slept with several of David's concubines, who had been left behind to take care of the palace (2 Samuel 16).

Despite the coup, God was at work. Absalom employed a couple of royal counselors, one of whom was a brilliant strategist named Ahithophel. When Absalom asked him what he should do next, Ahithophel said, "I know exactly what you ought to do. Send an army out after David right now, take him by surprise, and preemptively kill him." Absalom thought that sounded good, but then he asked the other counselor, Hushai, what he thought, and Hushai told him, "Get organized first. David is an experienced warrior and if you go after him now, you'll be dead meat."

Now, Hushai was doing this on purpose because he was loyal to David. Everyone agreed that his plan was better than Ahithophel's, and so Absalom waited. Ultimately, though, it was all part of God's plan: "For the LORD had purposed to defeat the good advice of Ahithophel, to the intent that the LORD might bring disaster on Absalom" (2 Samuel 17:14). The overarching lesson is that God is sovereign, even in times of betrayal, political upheaval, and war. It can be tough to swallow, but it's true.

> **God is sovereign, even in times of betrayal, political upheaval, and war.**

A Crushing Resolution

When the battle between father and son finally came, David's practical experience trumped Absalom's political momentum. David used a classic tactic, dividing his troops into three different brigades, each with the specific order to capture Absalom alive. The king's troops routed Absalom's Israelites, and Absalom fled. As he rode away on his mule (fast mules in those days), his famously long hair got caught in the branches of a terebinth tree.

There he was, dangling by his locks, when a soldier spotted him. He reported to Joab, who chastised him for not striking Absalom dead. The man told him, "You couldn't pay me enough to kill the king's son against his wishes." Joab, however, as was his tendency, did what he wanted and thrust three spears through the helpless Absalom.

David was devastated by the news. His haunting lament stands out, even today: He wept, and "as he went, he said thus: 'O my son Absalom—my son, my son Absalom—if only I had died in your place! O Absalom my son, my son!'" (2 Samuel 18:33). How tragic that this father and son never reconciled. Over the years, I've seen this particular regret played out over and over—in hospital rooms, at deathbeds, after funerals—faces dropping and lives shattering with the gaping emptiness left by the unrepaired relationship, the unavoidable truth that whatever had divided the deceased and the one left behind was nothing compared to the chasm of death that now stretched between them.

What seemed a victory for David and the kingdom turned to mourning with the king's broken heart. The weakening of relationships between the northern part of Israel and the south started here. Following David's departure and Absalom's rebellion, the tribes argued over the perceived vacuum in leadership, which led to a split among Israel's tribes. Led by a rebel named Sheba, ironically a Benjamite like Saul, every tribe but Judah abandoned David (2 Samuel 20:2).

A Costly Counting and a Precious Purchase

Second Samuel ends with an account of David's mess and God's mercy. We read that God was angry with Israel (no specific reason is given), and "He moved David against them to say, 'Go, number Israel and Judah'" (2 Samuel 24:1). However, over in 1 Chronicles, the account of the same event tells us, "Satan stood up against Israel, and moved David to number Israel" (1 Chronicles 21:1). The reports seem conflicted—who moved David to take a census, God or Satan? To get the complete picture, you have to do a little detective work. The accounts dovetail nicely, so it's worth the effort to put it together.

To start with, kings numbered people regularly. They would take a census to find out how many people there were in order to tax them and see how many soldiers they had. Here's where it got sticky for David: He took the census for prideful reasons. His motivation to do it, which Satan incited and God allowed, was to find out how strong his army and treasury were.

Instead of trusting the Lord for both resources, David wanted to satisfy his ego, to see just how great a king he was. After he had done the census, though, he knew he had messed up. He didn't need a prophet to bust him this time; his own "heart condemned him after he numbered the people" (2 Samuel 24:10). He confessed his sin to God, and God sent him a prophet to confirm his error and give him three choices: seven years of famine, three months of running from enemies, or three days of plague.

David chose door number three, trusting in God's mercy during a plague. "From Dan to Beersheba seventy thousand men of the people died" (2 Samuel 24:15). When the angel came to drop the hammer on Jerusalem, God stopped him at "the threshing floor of Araunah the Jebusite" (v. 16). The prophet Gad then told David to build an altar to the Lord there. David went to Araunah, who wanted to give him the place for free, but David told him, "Thanks, but I won't make offerings to God with something that costs me nothing." David purchased the floor, built an altar, and offered sacrifices to God, who then withdrew the plague.

Now, it seems that everything worked out—David learned his lesson, and God showed mercy. But there's more: The threshing floor of Araunah wasn't just a random spot where the angel happened to be standing when God stopped him. It was located at the top of Mount Moriah, where Abraham had offered Isaac. It would also be the site of Solomon's temple. Most importantly, the mountainous ridge ascends outside the city walls to what was then the future location of the crucifixion of Jesus. Today, it's called the Temple Mount—the most contested piece of real estate on the planet. David, as he did in so many other ways, kept the ball rolling toward the pivotal moment in history: the coming of the Messiah, Jesus Christ.

1 KINGS
FLIGHT PLAN

Facts

Author

This book, though it has long been in the Hebrew canon, is of uncertain origin. The author is unknown. Tradition suggests the prophet Jeremiah, but this can't be proven.

Date Written

Because 1 Kings does not mention Israel's return from Babylon in 536 BC, many scholars believe it was written between 562 and 536 BC.

Landmarks

Like 1 and 2 Samuel, 1 Kings is a story of Israel's leadership, the reigns of its kings. And like several other historical books of the Bible, it shows the failure of the nation's leadership to obey God. An increase of national prosperity was undermined by a decrease in national spirituality. While Israel grew physically and militarily, they grew weak spiritually through idolatry and rebellion against God. The book's organization reflects that contrast: the first part covers a united kingdom, and the second, a divided one.

Itinerary

- The United Kingdom (1 Kings 1–11)
    - An Exacting End
    - An Enlightened Decision
    - Some Excellent Achievements
    - An Early Warning
- The Divided Kingdom (1 Kings 12–22)
    - Moral Failures

- Massive Division
- A Monstrous Monarch vs. a Man of God

Gospel

Solomon's greatest achievement, the temple, was a visible, tangible place in the center of the nation where God's people could visit and know that He was present with them. But this was just a foreshadowing of a much greater temple to come: the body of the believer. God's presence took on a new form in the incarnation of Christ; Jesus was God become flesh. And after His resurrection and ascension, God's presence changed again. The apostle Paul, preaching among the temples of the Areopagus in Athens, alluded to this truth when he said, "The Most High does not dwell in temples made with hands" (Acts 7:48). If you are a believer, God dwells within you (see 1 Corinthians 3:16)—not in manmade temples, but in the people who have received Jesus Christ as their Lord and Savior.

A more important illustration of redemption is this: Solomon was a son of David, who brought a level of glory previously unknown to the nation of Israel. However, Jesus, the greater Son of David, would far outshine Solomon in both wisdom and glory. He came as one "greater than Solomon" (Matthew 12:42). That greatness would be demonstrated by His sacrificial atonement on the cross, and will be demonstrated to the world in His earthly, millennial reign.

History

The dates of 1 Kings range from the death of David in 970 BC to the reign of Ahaziah of Judah (841 BC). The book chronicles a history of amazing heights of wealth and prestige under Solomon and the weakness, poor leadership, and division that followed his reign.

Solomon was the mastermind behind the construction of the temple, which was dedicated to the Lord (Yahweh) and housed the Ark of the Covenant. Early rabbinical references state that the temple lasted for 410 years. The first-century historian Josephus wrote that "the temple was burnt four hundred and seventy years, six months, and ten days, after it was built."[9]

Anytime human wisdom tries to replace God's sovereign wisdom, there will be trouble.

Travel Tips

The book of 1 Kings further establishes what we already know: that we live in a chaotic world. Anytime human wisdom tries to replace God's sovereign wisdom, there will be trouble.

- Solomon had a "largeness of heart" (1 Kings 4:29) to go with his famous wisdom—a great combination for any leader. You can have all the smarts you need, but the Bible says that knowledge puffs up, while love builds up.

- Wisdom lasts only as long as you keep it in front of you. Despite his wisdom and generosity, Solomon broke almost all of God's commands for kings laid out in Deuteronomy—from limitations on horses and women (he had more than 700 wives) to his own palace. He over-taxed his people and spent the funds lavishly and primarily on himself. What got lost in all of those projects and weddings was his time spent in God's Word.

- Even great men and women of God hit low points in life. Elijah should have enjoyed the victory God gave him over the prophets of Baal; instead, he became discouraged. God is there when you can't see beyond your pain or circumstances—and especially when you are in your darkest hour.

> **God is there when you can't see beyond your pain or circumstances—and especially when you are in your darkest hour.**

In Flight

The United Kingdom (1 Kings 1–11)

An Exacting End

The end of David's life was not tranquil or peaceful. He seems to have had all sorts of problems growing older, from needing nursing care to experiencing a touch of senility—forgetting his promises and some of his contracts—and managing a rebellion in his own household. He was about seventy years old at this point

(2 Samuel 5:4), but they were a hard-lived seventy years. David was burned out. Everything he had faced and done—from shepherding to living on the run to soldiering—had taken its toll.

To top it off, he also had to deal with his fourth son, Adonijah, who took advantage of his father's infirmity to declare himself the new king. Adonijah was Absalom's brother, also good-looking and also, apparently, embittered by his dad's failure to confront or discipline his children—an approach that had resulted in the deaths of two sons, Amnon and Absalom. If Solomon hadn't been merciful, this bitterness would have contributed to Adonijah's demise (although Adonijah crossed Solomon later and paid for it with his life). David commanded a nation, but couldn't control his own kids.

Adonijah's failed coup forced David to repeat his promise that Solomon would inherit the throne. His wife Bathsheba and the prophet Nathan seemed to have to remind him, but once they did, David not only confirmed his promise but moved to expedite it (1 Kings 1:24-35). Before David died, he took Solomon aside and gave him some practical instructions regarding some necessary political housecleaning. David's cabinet of leaders served him and Israel well, by and large, but could have posed potential problems for the young, inexperienced Solomon. David knew how to handle loose cannons like Joab, his military commander, but it was payback time for Shimei, a relative of Saul's who had cursed David during Absalom's revolt. David did all he could to smooth his son's path to the crown.

Solomon ascended to the throne without further controversy, and David died shortly afterward. His obituary was short and sweet: "So David rested with his fathers, and was buried in the City of David. The period that David reigned over Israel was forty years; seven years he reigned in Hebron, and in Jerusalem he reigned thirty-three years" (1 Kings 2:10-11). David's life was over, but his legacy was just beginning. God had future plans for the throne of King David, including the end-times reign of his distant relative, Israel's future Messiah, Jesus Christ.

An Enlightened Decision

God firmly established Solomon's reign, not least because "Solomon loved the LORD, walking in the statutes of his father David" (1 Kings 3:3). One evening at a local worship center called Gibeon, Solomon sacrificed a thousand burnt offerings to the Lord. That night, God came to him in a dream and basically gave him a blank check: "Ask! What shall I give you?" (1 Kings 3:5). It was like the ultimate winning lottery ticket—but not without pressure. After all, Solomon could ask for anything, but this was *God* making the offer. Solomon needed to give a good answer.

Solomon was excited to be king, but the weight of having responsibility over his dad's kingdom was sinking in at this point. He knew he needed to handle people, make decisions, expand the kingdom, and build the temple that David had planned—in short, he needed God's wisdom. Solomon prayed hard and he prayed well: "Give to Your servant an understanding heart"—literally, a *hearing* heart— "to judge Your people, that I may discern between good and evil. For who is able to judge this great people of Yours?" (1 Kings 3:9).

Solomon wanted to hear God's voice advising him on how to rule, to make decisions that reflected what God was saying about them as His people. God gave Solomon's request a divine thumbs-up, commending him for not asking for a long life or wealth or the heads of his enemies on a stick. He gave him not only great wisdom but wealth, honor, respect, "and largeness of heart like the sand on the seashore" (1 Kings 4:29). In other words, he had the best possible combo a leader could ask for, the perfect balance—a brainy mind and a big heart.

Some Excellent Achievements

Solomon's gifts were put to good use. He built a temple for God, created infrastructure in Jerusalem—new streets and public buildings—expanded Israel's borders, and presided over a court that attracted curious kings and queens from all over the world. He composed 1005 songs and wrote 3000 proverbs, along with three books of the Bible (Proverbs, Ecclesiastes, and the Song of Songs). His reputation was unimpeachable among both scholars and rulers.

One of Solomon's greatest achievements was building Jerusalem's first temple for the worship of the true God. According to a parallel account in 1 Chronicles 28, David had already drawn up some of the plans for the structure, but God didn't allow him to build it, so he passed his blueprints on to his son. Solomon took to the task with gusto. First, he formed a partnership with a family friend, Hiram, king of Tyre, up in Lebanon on the Mediterranean coast. Lebanon was famous for its abundance of cedars, and Solomon and Hiram agreed on an exchange of Israel's wheat and olive oil for Lebanese lumber and experienced woodworkers. Tens of thousands of people worked on the project, going to and from Lebanon, carrying supplies, quarrying stone in the mountains, and supervising the work itself—183,000 personnel in total!

The temple of Solomon represents the very pinnacle of his glory. It became the heart of Judaism and Jewish social life. Their scholars commented that the temple was the epicenter of God's plan and program on earth.[10] Solomon's temple was twice the dimensions of the tabernacle (see Exodus 26). It was roughly 2700 square feet, relatively small compared to other buildings of similar renown, but it was astonishing—made with the finest cedar and cypress, limestone, and overlaid with gold (1 Kings 6). All the stone was cut at the quarry, so that no hammers were heard on-site during construction, and the stones were fitted together with such precision that not even a knife blade could be slid between the stones. The temple took seven years to construct, and the value of materials and labor—including stonework, woodwork, gold, silver, brass, embroidery, implements, and musical instruments—would today doubtless add up to billions of dollars!

When the work was finished, the dedication began. Solomon filled the treasury with silver and gold that David had dedicated for that purpose, brought temple furnishings and implements into the courtyard and inner rooms, and had the priests carry the Ark of the Covenant into the Holy of Holies, accompanied by massive numbers of animal sacrifices. Once it was all done, God showed up: a cloud—the Shekinah glory—filled the temple so that the priests couldn't see and had to vacate the premises (1 Kings 8:10-11).

An Early Warning

Solomon demonstrated wisdom with people and with God, but no one is perfect; one of Solomon's far-reaching problems was money management. He was a tax-and-spend king. He overtaxed and overburdened the people, a key factor in the kingdom's eventual split. His palace took twice as long to build as God's temple and was far larger. He himself lived in glory and splendor on a yearly wage of twenty-five tons of gold—described as "six hundred and sixty-six talents of gold" in 1 Kings 10:14. It's a fascinating number, seen only one other time in the Bible—in Revelation 13:18, where we read of another overbearing ruler in Jerusalem associated with the number 666. It is as if Solomon's father David became a type of Christ, while Solomon himself became a type of the Antichrist.

I wonder how well Solomon knew the book of Deuteronomy. It required that every king of Israel write his own copy of the Law of Moses—an attempt to guarantee his familiarity with God's statutes. Given Solomon's repute as a wise man, it seems he would have been familiar with such stipulations as "[the king] shall not multiply horses for himself" (Deuteronomy 17:16)—but Solomon had famous stables all over Israel—40,000 of them, in fact (1 Kings 4:26). The law also said that the king shouldn't "multiply wives for himself, lest his heart turn away" (Deuteronomy 17:17), a commandment that was no doubt debated among his 700 wives and 300 concubines (1 Kings 11:3)—as "his wives turned away his heart" (v. 3). The law continued, "Nor shall he greatly multiply silver and gold for himself" (Deuteronomy 17:17), but his 666 gold-talents-a-year salary broke that commandment too. Solomon's shortcomings set the stage for a disastrous result.

The Divided Kingdom (1 Kings 12–22)

Moral Failures

In 1 Kings 5–10, we read about all the great and marvelous things that Solomon did and said. However, when we get to chapter 11, we read, "*But* King Solomon..." (v. 1), which is never a sign of good things to come. It sets up the contrast of a series of pending failures. Case Study A: "But King Solomon loved many foreign women, as well as the daughter of Pharaoh: women of the Moabites, Ammonites, Edomites, Sidonians, and Hittites" (v. 1). Beyond the obvious issue of the challenges of being married to more than one woman, period, God had long commanded the children of Israel not to intermarry with foreign tribes because "they will turn away your hearts after their gods" (v. 2). And so they did with Solomon, dividing his heart, which then divided the nation. That was his legacy. He wrote the book of Proverbs, but he should have read and followed his own advice!

> ## All the wisdom in the world means nothing without a godly moral compass.

All the wisdom in the world means nothing without a godly moral compass. Solomon fell, offering sacrifices and building altars to false gods—even though God had personally appeared to him twice!—and so God punished him for his offense. God told Solomon—not through a prophet, but by direct revelation—"I will surely tear the kingdom away from you and give it to your servant" (1 Kings 11:11). The Lord honored his covenant with David, telling Solomon that He would give one tribe to Solomon's son, for David's and Jerusalem's sakes. Solomon spent the rest of his reign fighting foreign foes and resisting local rebellions. When he died, his throne went to his son Rehoboam, but the rest was lost to political rivals.

Massive Division

After Solomon, the kingdom was divided between two men, each of whom would form a lineage of kings: Jeroboam, the son of Nebat, from up north, ruled the ten northern tribes of Israel, and Rehoboam, the son of Solomon, ruled in Judah. And Rehoboam didn't even start out right, as his father had. Solomon at least began with a prayer meeting, seeking God for wisdom; Rehoboam ignored everyone but his boyhood pals, who were neither wise nor levelheaded.

Before the nation split, Jeroboam came to Rehoboam and asked him to lower the taxes, which had been heavy under Solomon. The inexperienced Rehoboam told him to come back in three days so he could think about it. When he consulted his older advisors, they told him to ease up on the taxes. Rehoboam's rat pack, however, told him to ratchet them up to even higher levels than they had been under Solomon (1 Kings 12:6-11). He followed their lead, thinking he would control the nation by force.

Jeroboam returned, heard about Rehoboam's new plan, and said, "Forget you." He won the allegiance of every tribe but Judah, and set himself up as king in the north. From here on out, there were two countries and two kingdoms—ten tribes in the north calling themselves Israel, and two in the south, known as Judah.

Rehoboam was smart enough to stay in Jerusalem because he knew the emotional heart of Israel was still the temple. People would still feel pulled to return to the temple to worship God. Jeroboam realized the same thing and devised an obvious but misguided solution. He said, "I'll put up two new sites of worship in the north: one at Bethel, in the center of the country, and one at Dan, in the north. We'll have a priesthood and a temple and false gods and goddesses and a whole idolatry system and everything!" Everything but the one true God, that is.

The rest of the book is a pathetic running parallel account of these two kingdoms and their respective kings—eight kings in the north and four in the south—all of whom are also mentioned again in the books of 1 and 2 Chronicles. The rest of 1 Kings gets pretty confusing, with the narrative bouncing back and forth between these split kingdoms. The two consistencies are that the two sides fought each other regularly, and that all of Israel's kings were horrible—rotten leaders and spiritual apostates. The eight kings of Israel in the north were Jeroboam, Nadab, Baasha, Elah, Zimri, Omri, Ahab, and Ahaziah. All of them were idolaters and pagan worshippers. In the southern kingdom of Judah, the kings were Rehoboam, Abijam, Asa, and Jehoshaphat. Only the last two did right in God's eyes.

A Monstrous Monarch vs. a Man of God

One northern king in particular stood out as the worst of the worst: Ahab (1 Kings 16:30-33). He married a witchy woman named Jezebel, whose name has become synonymous with evil. Jezebel was a princess from Sidonia who brought Baal worship into the highest level of Israel's government. It got really bad, which is usually when God enacts a really good plan. He sent in a prophet named Elijah, who was articulate, fiery, and uncompromising.

First Kings 17–22 records the conflict between the man of God, Elijah, and the man of the world, King Ahab. Elijah was a miracle worker; eight miracles are mentioned in this book. When we first meet him, he suspended the rains for three-and-a-half years as a message from God that Israel was off track (1 Kings 17:1). He also built his résumé as a man of God by making a poor widow's oil and flour last during that whole drought. He even brought the same woman's son back to life. Not a bad start!

God then sent Elijah to visit Ahab, who was already upset with Elijah for stopping the rains. Suspending the rain was humiliating to Baal worshippers because they believed that seasonal rains were a sign of Baal's favor. So, when it didn't rain for more than three years—despite their prayers to Baal—they were awfully embarrassed. That was a good thing because it brought about a confrontation. Ahab's greeting suggests such a conflict was already brewing: "Is that you, O troubler of Israel?" (1 Kings 18:17). Elijah's response clarified things for him: "I have not troubled Israel, but you and your father's house have" (v. 18). He didn't mess around with pleasantries, but proposed a showdown at Mount Carmel: all of Baal and Asherah's prophets (850 in total) against God's one prophet, him.

Elijah set up the stakes: if God wins, follow Him; if Baal wins, follow him. He then laid out the rules: one bull each, cut up and placed on wood, no fire. "Then you guys bring all of your prayers and crazy incantations and call down fire from Baal to consume it." Baal's prophets called on him all morning, with a growing sense of frenzy as time passed by, eventually hopping and leaping all around the altar—but to no avail. Around noon, Elijah started giving them a hard time: "Maybe he can't hear you? Could he be busy—you know, relieving himself? He might even be sleeping. Maybe he needs you to make a louder alarm clock!"

Baal's boys cried out in rage, then began to cut themselves, a customary practice apparently designed to get a false god out of the outhouse and back on the playing field. No answer. By evening, they had exhausted themselves, no doubt collapsing in a bloody heap near their altar. At that point, the supposed showdown became a one-way throwdown. Elijah stepped up, built an altar of twelve stones, and dug a trench around it. He piled up his wood, killed and cut up his bull, placed the pieces, and then told the attendants to pour four pots of water on the whole thing. "And then do it again...okay, one more time...all right, once more." The altar was soaked and the trench filled.

Elijah then offered a simple, short prayer, which ended, "O Lord, hear me, that this people may know that You are the Lord God, and that You have turned their hearts back to You again" (1 Kings 18:37). *Foosh!* Fire fell from heaven and completely burned every cut of beef and each drop of water. The people completely panicked, running like rats from a sinking ship and shouting in terror, "The Lord, He is God! The Lord, He is God!" (v. 39). Elijah had all of the prophets of Baal rounded up and executed. He then turned to Ahab and said, "Go have a party. You got your rain back." Moments later, a huge black cloud rolled up and drenched the thirsty earth.

Ahab was so upset he went and told his evil wife on Elijah. Jezebel threatened to kill Elijah, who fled to the wilderness (1 Kings 19). Whatever momentum Elijah thought had been gained at Mount Carmel—headlines reading "Baal worship crushed! Israel returned to God!"—quickly evaporated and he became depressed, perhaps out of sheer exhaustion. Cowering at Mount Sinai, this great prophet was feeling so low that he actually wanted to die. He cried out, "God! Take my life!" Instead, God sent him an angel, who baked him a cake.

We tend to become self-centered when we suffer, and with Elijah, God started with a gentle reminder that the solution wasn't physical death, but in dying to self. Once God took care of Elijah's need to be nurtured and heard, He got Elijah's attention with a reminder: "I have reserved seven thousand in Israel, all whose knees have not bowed to Baal" (1 Kings 19:18). He sent His wounded prophet to find them and continue in the work that He had for him. Elijah returned to the battle, standing up for God against Ahab and others, a necessary force for good in a nation whose God-inspired light was dimming from the top down.

2 KINGS
FLIGHT PLAN

Facts

Author

Originally, 1 and 2 Kings were one book. It wasn't until the first century BC that the books were divided. Traditionally, the prophet Jeremiah—who was alive to see the siege and fall of Jerusalem—is said to have written Kings, but the text itself does not tell us who the author was, leaving the matter a mystery.

Date Written

The book of 2 Kings may have been written sometime between 562 and 536 BC.

Landmarks

The book of 2 Kings covers a period of Israel's history that looks a lot like a reality TV singing competition—you've got a few strong contestants, but most are really, really bad. Instead of singers, though, we have sovereigns—kings whose lives and policies were at the center of these best and worst of times. When we left Israel in 1 Kings, it had gone from a united kingdom to a divided one, split into the northern kingdom of Israel and the southern kingdom of Judah—made up of ten tribes and two, respectively.

The division detailed in 1 Kings bottoms out here in 2 Kings with the collapse of the two struggling kingdoms: Israel, failed by godless leadership, was conquered by enemies and brought into captivity. And the surviving kingdom, Judah, lasted another 132 years before falling to Babylon.

Itinerary

- The Struggling Kingdoms (2 Kings 1–17)
    - A Memorable Exit
    - A Marvelous Successor
    - A Mortified Dignitary

- A Malevolent Endeavor
- A Missing Mentor
- A Meritorious Moniker
- A Mandatory Undertaking
- A Menacing Development
- The Surviving Kingdom (2 Kings 18–25)
  - A Mighty Force
  - Malignant Monarchs

Gospel

In 2 Kings, we see how Satan worked hard to destroy God's chosen people in a political and spiritual battle of leadership. Satan's goal was to terminate the messianic line—something he had been trying to do since God predicted that the offspring of the woman Eve would crush his power (see Genesis 3:15).

His nefarious plan wove in and out of Israel's history as part of the wickedness that led to Cain killing Abel, the judgment of the flood, Esau's hatred of Jacob, Pharaoh's order to kill the firstborn sons of Israel in Moses's time, Saul's hunting of David, Haman's attempted genocide in the book of Esther, and here in the books of 1 and 2 Kings, it led to the idolatry and havoc caused by various kings of Israel and Judah, particularly when Athaliah ordered the slaughter of the royal household of Judah and only baby Joash was rescued (see 2 Kings 11).

Satan's subterfuge hinged on the premise that God's promise of redemption required the existence of a nation and the continuance of that nation. Thus, if Satan could destroy that nation, he could thwart God's plan. He failed here in 2 Kings, just as he did on every other occasion; and God was determined to weave His redemptive thread even throughout Israel's darkest times.

When you read of the many bad rulers and few good ones in 2 Kings, keep in mind that more was going on than just issues of politics and leadership. The heart of God's people, and His longstanding plan to buy them back from sin's grip, were at stake in the midst of questionable reigns and the decline of the nation.

History

Second Kings tells the history of the divided kingdoms, Judah in the south and Israel in the north. It begins with the reign of Ahaziah (841 BC) and concludes with Jehoiachin being released from prison (598 BC). During this period of time, more than two dozen kings ruled Judah and Israel, culminating with the fall of the northern kingdom in the siege of Israel (722 BC) and the fall of the southern kingdom and Judah's captivity in Babylon beginning in 586 BC.

Travel Tips

The book of 2 Kings shows what happens when individuals and nations depend on their own sense of what's right and wrong instead of God's. It's hard not to take matters into our own hands when God doesn't let us in on what He is doing. But Israel and Judah's struggles should encourage us to draw closer to God; they show that He is there through good times and bad, even as we fight through trials and deal with the consequences of our mistakes.

- A godly mentor can help guide you toward God in evil times, but you still have to develop your own relationship with God. One of the few godly kings during this time was Jehoash, who "did what was right in the sight of the LORD all the days in which Jehoiada the priest instructed him" (2 Kings 12:2). After Jehoiada died, Jehoash began to listen to and lean on other leaders, who led him into idolatry.

- A kingdom is only as strong as its king. Israel and Judah's good kings only seemed like halfhearted, stopgap measures between the bad ones, and the people eventually fell into captivity because their rulers led them away from the Lord. Still, 2 Kings shows that God is always with you, especially when you need to get back on track with Him.

God is always with you, especially when you need to get back on track with Him.

In Flight

The Struggling Kingdoms (2 Kings 1–17)

After the division of the kingdom, Israel and Judah suffered from degenerative spiritual heart disease. Despite God's continually outstretched, pursuing hand of mercy and forgiveness, the vast majority of kings in both kingdoms hardened their hearts, choosing idolatry and wickedness. That's God's pattern throughout the

Bible—and, I believe, throughout history—to warn people and offer a heart transplant before bringing judgment. In both 1 and 2 Kings, God sent a pair of prophets to try and defibrillate His people: Elijah, and his successor Elisha.

A Memorable Exit

Second Kings opens with Ahaziah, king of the north, getting injured in a fall. He sent people to consult the false god Baal-Zebub (literally, "lord of the flies") and see whether he would live or die (2 Kings 1). God sent Elijah to intercept them and ask, "What? Is there no God in Israel that you've got to go ask Fly Lord?" Elijah told them, "Go tell your boy this: He's finished." When they reported back to Ahaziah, he asked them what the guy who sent the message looked like. They said, "A hairy man wearing a leather belt" (v. 8). "Ah," he said, "that would be Elijah."

When Ahaziah sent a captain along with a company of fifty soldiers to confront Elijah, the prophet called fire down from heaven and torched them. The same thing happened with the second captain and company of fifty. Finally, the third guy approached Elijah on his knees, pleading, "Please, I'm just the messenger! The king wants to see you." Elijah went and repeated his original message to Ahaziah, who died of his injuries.

Elijah had an exit scene worthy of his stature: God sent a fiery chariot and a whirlwind to take him directly to heaven (2 Kings 2:1-11). Before he went, Elijah passed his prophetic mantle—which was both a cloak and a prophet's symbolic glory—to his apprentice, Elisha, who asked for a "double portion of [Elijah's] spirit" (v. 9). A "double portion" simply meant that Elisha wanted to be Elijah's successor, with the same powerful working of God's Spirit in his life. In the law, a firstborn son was entitled to receive twice the inheritance of a father's other sons and was also entitled to the right of succession (Deuteronomy 21:17). Elijah told him, "You have asked a hard thing" (2 Kings 2:10)—he knew how difficult it was to be a prophet, to speak God's truth into whatever situation He called him, facing personal dangers, discomfort, and even spiritual depression.

As the two prophets were walking along chatting, a fiery chariot pulled by fiery horses pulled up between them. Elijah said, "That's my ride," and off he went in a whirlwind, an exception to the rule, "It is appointed for men to die once, but after this the judgment" (Hebrews 9:27). Now, I believe that ultimately, he will die. The prophet Malachi said that God would send Elijah in the last days as one of the signs of His coming final judgment of earth (Malachi 4:5-6). Jesus also affirmed that Elijah would come in the future (Matthew 17:11, Mark 9:12). It's entirely possible that we see Elijah mentioned in the book of Revelation, one of two unnamed witnesses sent from heaven (the other likely being Moses) to work wonders and testify in Jerusalem of God's judgment (Revelation 11:3-12).

A Marvelous Successor

Elisha did indeed pick up where Elijah left off, boldly speaking God's truth to the kings of Israel and Judah. When, in a rare display of camaraderie, Jehoram, king of Israel, allied with Jehoshaphat, king of Judah, against their common enemy, Moab, Jehoshaphat (one of the even rarer good kings in those days) called for a prophet so they could seek God's will for their campaign. Elisha showed up and said to Jehoram, "Go talk to your mama's prophets. If it wasn't for Jehoshaphat here, I'd have nothing to do with you" (see 2 Kings 3:10-14).

Like his predecessor, Elisha went around performing miracles. He helped a destitute widow pay off her creditors by enabling her single jar of olive oil to fill a bunch of borrowed jars so that she could sell the oil, pay off her debts, and live on the rest (2 Kings 4:1-7). Elisha also prophesied a child for a barren couple who had prepared him a room to stay in whenever he traveled through their village, Shunem, in Galilee. The woman had a son, and a few years later, the little boy suffered some kind of head trauma and died. The woman went out looking for Elisha and found him near Mount Carmel.

In her grief, she fell at Elisha's feet, but his servant Gehazi tried to push her away. Elisha told him, "Let her alone; for her soul is in deep distress, and the LORD has hidden it from me, and has not told me" (2 Kings 4:27). That God hadn't revealed the woman's plight to him was shocking to Elisha. Can you imagine being so in tune with God that you are surprised when He doesn't reveal something to you? It wasn't a matter of ego or presumption, though, because Elisha truly cared for the woman and her family. He went to her house, prayed, stretched himself over the child, and revived the boy.

A Mortified Dignitary

Elisha's reputation carried into neighboring Syria, where the king's military commander, an honored soldier named Naaman, suffered from leprosy (2 Kings 5). One of his household servants was an Israeli girl who had heard of Elisha and recommended that Naaman seek out the prophet to see if he could be healed. Leprosy was a catchall term for a number of dreaded skin diseases, and the Syrian king wanted to see his right-hand man cured, so he sent Naaman to Jehoram, the king of Israel.

Naaman and his entourage showed up at Elisha's house in full military regalia, chariots, horses, and all. Normally when a dignitary honored your home with his presence, you'd go greet him, saying, "We're so honored to have you, etc." Well, Elisha sent only a messenger to tell Naaman to go wash in the Jordan River seven times and he'd be healed. For all its impressive reputation, the Jordan wasn't much to look at, with its narrow banks and shallow, mud-browned waters. Elisha, as a servant of God, didn't play favorites or pander to this big shot, but just told him to go dunk himself in a muddy trickle of a river and he'd be fine.

Naaman had expected some big, religious show—or at least a customary greeting. Elisha didn't meet his expectations, and Naaman was furious, saying, "We've got better rivers back in Syria, if that's all it takes!" He stormed off, which demonstrates a typical reaction when God or God's people do things differently than expected. Some people don't want an answer from God or His Word as much as to be coddled or indulged. Naaman's servants seemed to recognize the difference and appealed to him to give Elisha's remedy a shot. Reluctantly, he agreed.

Seven times Naaman dipped himself in the muddy puddle of the Jordan, no doubt mortified that a man of his stature should be reduced to such desperate measures. But guess what? It worked. He came out of the river healed, his skin as clean and fresh as a child's. Sheepishly, he went back to Elisha and pledged his loyalty to the one true God (2 Kings 5:15-19). Maybe he didn't receive Elisha's personal attention, but his cure was clearly more than enough for him to give honor where honor was due.

God provided a witness to both Israel and Judah through the various miracles Elisha performed—making an ax head float, revealing clandestine enemy tactics, and predicting market values and future heads of state (2 Kings 6–8). And boy, did Israel and Judah need that witness! Ahab and Jezebel's son Joram was now ruling in Israel and following in his parents' ways—though not nearly at their level of wickedness—and Jehoram, son of the good king Jehoshaphat, had become first co-regent with his father, and now, his father's replacement on the throne of Judah. But marrying the wrong person can destroy it all! Jehoram married Ahab's daughter, who turned him from his own father's worship of God to follow Baal.

Those idolatrous, pagan practices now spread from the north to the south, infecting everyone with its disease. However, God was merciful to Jehoram, "for the sake of His servant David" (2 Kings 8:19), because of His promise that the tribe of Judah would be protected because it held the line of the Messiah (Genesis 49). If you go back to Genesis 3:15, you'll recall that the promise of the Messiah was also a promise to eventually end Satan's reign. And so, throughout Israel's history, the devil has tried to disrupt and destroy the nation. So all the intrigues, division, warfare, and idolatry were part of the war being waged behind the scenes in the spiritual realm and showing up from time to time in the physical world.

A Malevolent Endeavor

This included a particularly close call in the history of salvation. Jehoram's son Ahaziah had become king of Judah, and he continued in his father's Baal worship. God raised up Jehu to rule in Israel, and used him to destroy Baal worship throughout the land. Jehu became a rod of God's punishment, killing Joram and his mother Jezebel in the north and Ahaziah in the south, and tearing down Baal's worship centers (2 Kings 9–10). When Ahaziah's mother, Athaliah, heard her son was dead, "she arose and destroyed all the royal heirs" (2 Kings 11:1). In other words, she had everyone killed from the house of David in the tribe of Judah who could succeed to the throne—all except one. Ahaziah's sister Jehosheba rescued her brother's son, Joash, from the queen's regicide and managed to hide him for six years. Eventually, Joash would become king of Judah.

All this intrigue reveals an intense spiritual battle taking place. On the human level, the lineage of King David was almost wiped out. If Athaliah had completely succeeded, that would have prevented the Messiah's coming. No royal seed from David's house would mean God's promises would be thwarted. Because that just doesn't happen, the tiny but resilient scarlet thread of redemption was preserved through a boy named Joash. Athaliah's rampage was among Satan's failed attempts at the time to end the messianic line, one of a series of deceptions and murders going back to the Garden of Eden.

And Joash, when he ascended the throne at the venerable age of seven, became that rarest of things: a king who "did what was right in the sight of the LORD" (2 Kings 12:2). There was a qualification, though: Joash (also called Jehoash) did what was right "all the days in which Jehoiada the priest instructed him" (v. 2). Because of Jehoiada's mentoring and influence, Judah had a godly king, one of the few who lived by the book and according to the Spirit of God. One problem remained, however. King Jehoash did not get rid of the "high places"—the locations where Baal and other false gods were worshipped—and he allowed people to continue to give offerings in those places. That's the kind of compromise that has brought down many good people—letting a known evil flourish so as not to cause trouble or give offense. When God is offended by something, we should be too.

When God is offended by something, we should be too.

A Missing Mentor

As long as Jehoiada the priest was alive, King Jehoash did okay, especially in the maintenance and upkeep of the temple (2 Kings 12:4-16). But as soon as the king's spiritual mentor died, his spiritual life fell apart. He caved in to the political pressure to worship idols. God sent prophets to snap Judah out of it, but the people wouldn't listen. Jehoash even ended up killing Jehoiada's son, a prophet named Zechariah, who spoke against what Judah's leaders were doing. Jehoash didn't have his own relationship with God, so he was easily swayed away from the good he had done under Jehoiada's influence. The lesson is sobering: If your faith can only be propped up by other people, you'll stumble when the props are taken away.

A Meritorious Moniker

Another name worth mentioning is that of King Azariah, often better known by his other name, Uzziah (2 Kings 15). He was sixteen years old when he became king (2 Chronicles 26:1), which seems awfully young. But not only did Uzziah reign for fifty-two years, he ended up being one of Judah's finest kings. He brought spiritual reform and expanded Judah's borders. The secret to his success was simple but profound: "He did what was right in the sight of the Lord, according to all that his father Amaziah had done" (2 Kings 15:3). He had a good example and followed it, and continued to honor God in many ways even after his father died.

Uzziah is probably best known as the king mentioned in the prophet Isaiah's vision of heaven: "In the year that King Uzziah died, I saw the Lord sitting on a throne, high and lifted up, and the train of His robe filled the temple" (Isaiah 6:1). After Uzziah's half-a-century reign ended with his death, the people were shaken and wondered, "What are we going to do? We had a great leader, and now he's gone." Through Isaiah, God reminded them, "Even though your earthly king has left you, I, the heavenly King, have not. I am still sitting on the throne; I haven't vacated it and I'm fully in charge."

As good a king as Uzziah was, he still had his shortcomings and failures, including the ever-persistent *letting-the-high-places-stand* issue. As he got older, he thought he was high enough on God's list to justify dressing up as a priest and offering incense. He even got uppity when the true priests—the Levites—called him on it. Now, God has never held back from making it clear when even His favorite leaders sin, and Uzziah was no exception: God struck him with leprosy for the rest of his life, and he had to dwell apart from everyone else. It seems like the hardest thing to do in life is to finish well. Without God's grace, how could it even be possible?

A Mandatory Undertaking

After another couple of bad kings, there was an especially good one, Hezekiah, who "did what was right in the sight of the LORD, according to all that his father David had done" (2 Kings 18:3), *including* the ever-elusive removal of the high places. Bravo! He also destroyed the bronze serpent that Moses had made at God's instruction way back in Numbers 21 as a cure for a plague the people had brought down on their own heads. Evidently this bronze serpent had been kept and preserved down through the centuries, despite having no healing properties in and of itself. Instead, it had become an idol.

The danger of relics is that what begins as a reminder of God's faithfulness often ends up becoming an object of faith. Hezekiah, however, grouped the bronze serpent with the poles and pillars used to worship Baal and Asherah and tore it down, reminding them that it was just a piece of brass. The great rarity of leaders like Hezekiah, who sought God and had a zero-tolerance policy toward idolatry, was the key reason behind the fall of both kingdoms.

A Menacing Development

The northern kingdom was first to collapse. Like their forefathers in the wilderness under Moses, they were a stiff-necked, unfaithful people, persisting in their idolatry and rejecting God repeatedly until, finally, God rejected them, delivering them into their enemies' hands. In 722 BC, Assyria conquered Israel and hauled most of the people away, replacing them with other conquered people from Babylon and other pagan nations—which led to intermarriage and intermixed religion. All the pollution that Israel had flaunted during its rebellious days now continued during its status as a slave state to Assyria. Part of this northern kingdom became known as Samaria, which eventually hosted an unofficial, rival temple claiming to be as legitimate as the one in Jerusalem, thus widening the rift with the south even more.

The Surviving Kingdom (2 Kings 18–25)

A Mighty Force

The surviving kingdom, Judah, lasted another 150 years. Assyria, conqueror of the northern kingdom, approached Jerusalem twice. In 713 BC, the Assyrian king, Sargon II, threatened Jerusalem but was paid off with a tribute. The second time, in 701 BC, Sargon's successor Sennacherib, fresh off his conquest of the rest of Judah, sent his chief of staff to the gates of Jerusalem with an intimidating letter promising destruction. Assyrian troops, at the time the mightiest army in the world, surrounded the city, preparing to lay siege. King Hezekiah spread out the letter before the Lord (2 Kings 19:14), praying for God to intervene and save his people. Isaiah the prophet came in and encouraged the king, telling him, "Don't sweat it; God is much bigger than Assyria."

Because Hezekiah, who had been chastised by God for issues of pride, humbled himself before God, God took care of Assyria and became the strong deliverer for Israel, sending a single angel to wipe out 185,000 Assyrian troops (2 Kings 19:35). Assyria's army was destroyed, which left it open to being conquered by a new world power, Babylon. A century and a half passed after God spared Judah in Hezekiah's time, with various successor kings taking Judah's throne. But only one of them, Josiah (Hezekiah's great-grandson), did right by God.

Beginning in 604 BC, Babylon, led by Nebuchadnezzar, made the first of three successive attacks against Jerusalem. In the first attack, he took captive a bunch of choice young men, including Daniel, who would go on to become God's man in Babylon. Eventually, during the third attack in 586 BC, Judah fell to the Babylonians.

Malignant Monarchs

After Josiah, the last good king, died, his son Jehoahaz sat on the throne. He was there for only three months before he was deposed by the Egyptians, who put his brother Eliakim on the throne and changed his name to Jehoiakim (2 Kings 23:26–24:6). The prophet Jeremiah warned him (Jeremiah 38:2), basically telling him, "God's hand is moving through the Babylonians, so do whatever Nebuchadnezzar says." But Jehoiakim rebelled against Nebuchadnezzar and was ousted by the Babylonians, who replaced him with a guy named Jehoiachin (the names are just close enough to be confusing).

Jehoiachin lasted about three months before he was deposed and taken captive to Babylon. His replacement, Zedekiah, staged a coup, which the Babylonians dealt with by killing his sons in front of him and then putting his eyes out before taking him in chains to Babylon (2 Kings 25:7). The Babylonians plundered the temple and burned the palace and all the houses of the rich. "For because of the anger of the LORD this happened in Jerusalem and Judah, that He finally cast them out from His presence" (2 Kings 24:20). Despite the clear hand of God's judgment upon them, none of the kings after Josiah turned back to God.

> We have to choose the realm we will
> serve: the kingdom of our selfish cause,
> or that of the sovereign Christ.

In the end, the national leaders determined Judah's national legacy. The kings who ruled made the difference in each kingdom's fate. The fact that Judah had a handful of kings who honored God helped them maintain their freedom as a nation longer than their northern counterpart—but eventually, their lack of dependence on God ended with their captivity too. The difference, then, between a good king and a bad one was that the good kings honored God, which brought God's blessings on their people. The question that each king answered with his choices is one all of us must ask at some point: Who is in charge of my life? We all live in the kingdom of the physical world, but spiritually, we have to choose the realm we will serve: the kingdom of our selfish cause, or that of the sovereign Christ.

1 CHRONICLES
FLIGHT PLAN

Facts

Author

Jewish tradition states that Ezra (or possibly Nehemiah) was the author of the books of 1 and 2 Chronicles. The author likely compiled various writings and documents that existed in his day. Since Chronicles has a priestly focus and perspective—such as its unique knowledge of the temple—the priestly scribe Ezra may be the best candidate for authorship.

Date Written

Scholars suggest many dates for the writing of 1 Chronicles, ranging from 460–430 BC. The book was written after the Babylonian exile. However, the lack of Hellenistic descriptions in 1 and 2 Chronicles indicates that the books were compiled and composed before Alexander the Great swept across and conquered the known world (ca. 331 BC). This gives a more focused time frame in which the book could have been written.

Landmarks

When we hear the word *chronicle*, we typically think of a newspaper—a reporter's journal of the events in a community. That's not far from what we are going to see in the books of 1 and 2 Chronicles: a vantage point of the history of the nation, especially the southern kingdom of Judah, the city of Jerusalem, and the reign of David. It's a chronology with a spiritual perspective, though, a divine editorial on the state of the nation.

First Chronicles covers much of the same ground as 2 Samuel and 1 and 2 Kings, recorded by Ezra, a priest who came back from the Babylonian captivity to encourage the people of Israel to rebuild their nation. The book divides neatly into two slices, both related to David, Israel's second king: The first part speaks of David's rightful ancestry—essentially a list of names and genealogical tables covering the 3000 years from Adam to David—and the second part documents David's royal activity, focusing on the forty years of his reign.

Itinerary

- David's Rightful Ancestry (1 Chronicles 1–9)
  - After God's Ordained Captivity
- David's Royal Activity (1 Chronicles 10–29)
  - After God's Own Heart
  - After God's Royal Covenant
  - After David's Preparations
  - After a Thousand Years

Gospel

The references to the throne of David and the Son of David in 1 Chronicles 17 point ahead to the coming of Christ and to His eventual reign on earth in the end times, revealing the massive scope of God's redemptive plan. Here, God promised that David would have a lineage that will last forever and ever. Part of the covenant God made was fulfilled in David's son Solomon, who reigned from the throne of Israel. But a large portion of the covenant is still waiting to be fulfilled in Jesus Christ and His second coming.

Until you get a grasp on 1 Chronicles 17, it will be hard to understand the ministry of Jesus Christ and eschatology in general (the study of the last days). The New Testament itself begins with the words, "The book of the genealogy of Jesus Christ, the Son of David" (Matthew 1:1). Right off the bat, Matthew wanted to make it clear that Jesus fulfilled the promise God made to King David back in 1 Chronicles 17. When the angel Gabriel appeared to Mary, he said, "Behold, you will conceive in your womb and bring forth a Son, and shall call His name Jesus. He will be great, and will be called the Son of the Highest; and the Lord God will give Him the throne of His father David" (Luke 1:31-32).

After Jesus's death and resurrection, on the day of Pentecost, Peter began his sermon by saying, "Men and brethren, let me speak freely to you of the patriarch David, that he is both dead and buried, and his tomb is with us to this day. Therefore, being a prophet, and knowing that God had sworn with an oath to him that of the fruit of his body, according to the flesh, He would raise up the Christ to sit on his throne" (Acts 2:29-30).

History

The historical period 1 Chronicles covers is the same as that of 1 and 2 Samuel. However, differently from the books of Samuel, the genealogy of 1 Chronicles begins with Adam and continues through David and Solomon, thus covering the period from creation to about 970 BC. The difference in perspective between the two histories is important to note: 1 and 2 Samuel concentrate on the political life of Israel, while 1 and 2 Chronicles focus on the religious and spiritual life of Israel, founded in the genealogy that would eventually bring the Messiah.

The frequent use of and reference to numerical and chronological documents in both 1 and 2 Chronicles, mixed with detailed history, shows that the author had historical reasons for writing the books. The author wanted to ensure the Hebrew people had access to the information in these historical documents so they could have a record of their past.

> **Compared to God's eternal plans and promises, our self-made plans are, at best, well-intentioned but off target.**

Travel Tips

The book of 1 Chronicles reminds us that though the nature of this world is fleeting, God sees us as people of long-term potential. Compared to God's eternal plans and promises, our self-made plans are, at best, well-intentioned but off target, and at worst, shortsighted and dangerous. Studying David's glory days should encourage us to keep our eyes on our heavenly Father, who has great plans and important roles for each of us to play.

- In the center of a cathedral archway in Milan, Italy, is this inscription: "Nothing is important except that which is eternal." Both pleasant and troublesome things will happen to you, but that's all momentary compared to the eternal. When you navigate your life focused on God and His ways, then you'll truly grow to be a man or a woman after His own heart.

- You can never outgive God. The Lord's generous heart shone through in His covenant with David. Anytime there is a desire in your heart to serve the Lord in some capacity—"God put it on my heart to get involved over there; I'm going to do something for God"—know that God sees and loves your heart, and He will bless you and do great things in and through you.

- Rejoice that God is faithful to finish the works that you start but might not see completed in your lifetime. When God told David that he would not be the one to build the temple, David didn't sulk or complain. He rejoiced in God's promise that his son would be a "man of rest" (1 Chronicles 22:9). He was content to add his own simple brushstrokes to God's bigger painting.

In Flight

David's Rightful Ancestry (1 Chronicles 1–9)

The first nine chapters make up the most extensive chronological list of genealogies in the Bible. The first three establish a line going from Adam to David. After the list of Jacob's sons—the founders of the twelve tribes of Israel—the line goes nine generations from Judah to Jesse, David's father (1 Chronicles 2:1-12). There is also a list of David's brothers, in case you were wondering who didn't get chosen to be king of Israel (vv. 13-15), as well as of his official nonconcubine sons and their various mothers (1 Chronicles 3:1-9).

Why all the hullabaloo about names and genealogies? Simply stated, God has been at work from the beginning of human history to develop and preserve a people who would become the national receptacle for the Savior of the world. As has often been stated, history is *His* story!

After God's Ordained Captivity

The selective nature of the list draws attention to the direct connection between Adam and David. Because David is the end point, those closest to him are included. Along with the history of the tribe of Judah, Saul's lineage through the tribe of Benjamin is in there, along with David's descendants from Solomon to Jeconiah, the king whom God cursed because of his wicked ways (Jeremiah 22:24-30).

Keep in mind who wrote the book: Ezra was trying to encourage the postcaptivity Jews as they rebuilt their homeland and temple. After seventy years in Babylon, he wanted them to see that God had a plan extending all the way back in human history to Adam and continuing through King David and now to them.

Genealogical records aren't really attention grabbers, but they are every bit the

Word of God that John 3:16 is. They may not seem relevant now, but without them, we wouldn't have a historical verification of the lineage of the Messiah. Tracing David's ancestry ties him to Adam, and when we get to Matthew and Luke in the New Testament, they tie David to Jesus.

The Jews kept these records for three reasons: First, as proof of tribal heritage for the purpose of land transactions, so the buyer and seller knew the land was staying within the twelve tribes of Israel. Second, when people came back to Israel from Babylon, a lot of them didn't know which tribe they came from. Only Levites were allowed to serve as priests, so genealogies cleared up who could serve in the temple. Third, it helped verify the identity of the Messiah. If someone claimed to be the Messiah, the records of the tribe of Judah could be searched to see if his lineage could be traced back to David.

David's Royal Activity (1 Chronicles 10–29)

Having established a thorough record of who was whom, Ezra spent the rest of the book on David's forty-year reign over the kingdom of Israel. He began with the account of Saul's death and David's royal ascension. More than that, he offered a divine editorial on the historical facts of Saul's reign and death: "So Saul died for his unfaithfulness which he had committed against the Lord, because he did not keep the word of the Lord, and also because he consulted a medium for guidance. But he did not inquire of the Lord; therefore He killed him, and turned the kingdom over to David the son of Jesse" (1 Chronicles 10:13-14).

After God's Own Heart

Think back to when God dispatched the prophet Samuel to Bethlehem to anoint Israel's second king in the house of Jesse. Saul was still alive and kicking, but God was fed up with his arrogant disobedience. God told Saul through Samuel, "You're finished. You've disobeyed Me habitually, and I want a man after My own heart." David is the only person in Scripture described as "a man after [God's] own heart" (1 Samuel 13:14). Looking at David's life, his flaws, and his failures, some say, "How can the guy who did those things be a man after God's own heart?"

And I get it—David wasn't perfect. But God Himself said it, and the phrase can be translated a few different ways from the original Hebrew that help shed some light. "After [God's] own heart" can also mean after God's own *mind*—that is, thinking His thoughts, or a man with the *will* to fulfill God's intentions. David, in other words, was constantly asking, "What is God's heart in this? What is He saying? How can I fit into what He is doing?" David, though noticeably flawed, set spiritual priorities on a consistent, habitual basis so that even when he sinned, he knew where to turn to find his center again.

That spiritual perspective distinguishes 1 Chronicles from the other accounts of David's life in 2 Samuel and 1 and 2 Kings. Some of the same events are included—for example, both 1 Chronicles 13 and 2 Samuel 6 have the story of how David tried to rush in bringing the ark back to Jerusalem and God struck Uzzah for putting out his hand to steady it. Others are omitted here in 1 Chronicles, like David's struggles with Saul, his affair with Bathsheba, and the tragic betrayal of his son Absalom. Ezra kept his focus on the positive—not because anyone denied David's sins and shortcomings, but because the postcaptivity audience needed to be encouraged for their future by all the good that happened when David stayed focused on God.

First Chronicles captured the idea that God chose David because of what He could see in his heart (1 Samuel 16:7). God saw David, warts and all, very differently than we see David. David committed adultery and arranged a murder to cover it up; by human calculation, that cancels out the good he did. But while God didn't hide those facts—they're right there in the Bible, after all—the point of view in 1 Chronicles isn't revisionism, it's revelation: God saw David as more than his sins, not as a failure but as the king of Israel who would bring forth the Messiah through his genealogy.

Good men were drawn to David while he was still on the run from Saul, likely sensing God's anointing, and there is a list of these "mighty men of valor" (1 Chronicles 12:8) and their feats. Military officers and skilled warriors joined him by the thousands, soldiers from each tribe who defected from Saul's army came and pledged loyalty to David. They supported him as he ascended to the throne and joined him in his ongoing campaign against Israel's longtime foe, the Philistines. David's victory over their champion Goliath had set the Philistines back for a while, but they heard he had become king and decided to seek revenge.

God gave David victory...because prayer was key to his military policy.

Ezra gave insight into this great warrior's prayer life. When David heard the Philistines were on the move, he asked God, "Shall I go up against the Philistines? Will You deliver them into my hand?" (1 Chronicles 14:10). God told him to go for it. Then, the next time David inquired, God told him to hold back and take a different approach (vv. 13-16). God gave David victory both times because prayer was key to his military policy.

After God's Royal Covenant

Having set the king He wanted on the throne, God changed the game completely. After God established his reign, David took a moment to reflect on his life (1 Chronicles 17). He realized that while he was living in a palace, God was living in a tent. He determined to build God a proper house—a temple. But God told him, "I never asked you for a house." Through the prophet Nathan, God reminded David that He had been with him through thick and thin and brought him from the sheepfold to the palace (v. 8). But God loved the heart David displayed in desiring to build something special for Him, so He said, "Hey David, I'm going to build something for *you*, your son, and My people—a royal dynasty" (see 1 Chronicles 17:9-10).

David had been thinking of building God a literal house of worship, but instead, God promised David a dynastic house. What a legacy! "When your days are fulfilled...I will set up your seed after you, who will be of your sons; and I will establish his kingdom. He shall build Me a house, and I will establish his throne forever" (1 Chronicles 17:11-12).

As for the temple, David made the plans and came up with the financing, but his son Solomon built it. The eternal establishment of the throne, however, wasn't through Solomon—he died, after all. But God promised that the throne of David would reign forever through the Son of David, Jesus Christ.

God's covenant with David had two parts. In the first, God said, "David, you're going to have a son, and he is going to build a temple." This referred to Solomon. The second part was that the throne of David would be established forever—and that would come through the greater Son of David whom Solomon foreshadowed: Jesus Christ.

After David's Preparations

Much of the rest of 1 Chronicles explains the construction and worship protocols for the temple. In essence, David gathered and prepared materials for it, and Solomon ended up overseeing its actual construction. David explained to his son that because of his history as a soldier, he would only help with the preparations, and that his son, a man of peace, would do the building (1 Chronicles 22:7-8). As a man of blood, the conquering unifier of Israel, David could not be involved in the construction of something as holy as a building that would be inhabited by God's very presence.

Solomon benefitted from his father's sacrifice, though. David had not only organized the materials for the temple, he had also gathered all those who would serve in it—priests, officers, judges, gatekeepers, singers, and musicians—all of whom would play their part in the worship of the Lord (1 Chronicles 23–27). He then called a public leadership meeting to announce God's design for the temple and everything in it, explain God's plan for Solomon, and exhort all of the people to step into the task wholeheartedly (1 Chronicles 28).

> ## When it comes to God's work, it's amazing God allows us the privilege to be involved.

Next, David took an offering (1 Chronicles 29). The building program ahead of them would cost a lot of money, and he gave the people a chance to get involved in this great work honoring God. That's always the reason for an offering—allowing human participation in a divine operation. When it comes to God's work, it's amazing God allows us the privilege to be involved. David set the tone for giving himself, describing his own heartfelt offering of a massive amount of gold and silver. The people's response was overwhelming, equal in generosity and sincerity to David's (1 Chronicles 29:9). He would not build the temple himself, but he saw that his preparations would not be in vain; he could die a happy man, knowing that temple would be built.

David led the people in a blessing, and they all bowed down and worshipped God. Thousands of animals were sacrificed, leading to a huge celebration, eating and drinking and anointing Solomon as their new king. The final verses summarize David's reign: He ruled for forty years and "died in a good old age, full of days and riches and honor; and Solomon reigned in his place" (v. 28). For those moments, things were good—really good—a precursor of the happy ending all God's people can look forward to when Jesus returns to reign on the earth.

After a Thousand Years

As a closing point, let's look far down the road—to when Christ will rule this earth from Jerusalem for a thousand-year period we call the millennium. The purpose of the millennium is twofold. First, the earth will need about ten centuries to recover from the devastation that will occur during the Tribulation, the period of God's judgment directly preceding it. We should preserve the earth as best we can—it's a matter of stewardship—but with all due respect to the environmentalists, if you think the earth is messed up now, you ain't seen nothing yet! The millennium will be needed to redeem creation from the curse of the fall (see Genesis 3) and from God's judgments during the Tribulation.

Second, the millennium will be needed for God to fulfill the rest of the promises He made to His people in the past, especially David. His covenant with David promised David a kingdom in his day and a greater one to come. God's prophets predicted a coming kingdom in two phases, one earthly and the other heavenly. The first installment of that promise is the millennium, an earthly kingdom in which Christ will literally rule from the city of Jerusalem over a renewed and restored earth. The second phase of that kingdom is what we call the eternal state. Jesus will close accounts on this world, destroy the present earth altogether, and create the new heaven and earth, establishing the New Jerusalem as its capital city, which will hover above the new earth like a gleaming satellite metropolis (Revelation 21–22).

That kingdom theme provides bookends to 1 Chronicles. From the beginning of mankind, starting with Adam, God has preserved a people and a lineage that has led to King David. Then He promised David a kingdom that includes his own offspring. If God can preserve this line from eternity past all the way through to David and his reign, then take heart; build the temple and build the city.

First Chronicles is a record of a key time in salvation history: God establishing through David's line His promise of the Messiah and His eventual earthly reign. By the time that promise is completely fulfilled, God will have answered the prayers of the saints for the last 2000 years: "Thy kingdom come, Thy will be done in earth, as it is in heaven" (Matthew 6:10 KJV). Make sure that when that ultimate chronicle is completed, your name is written in the genealogy of God's family through Jesus Christ.

2 CHRONICLES

FLIGHT PLAN

Facts

Author

As with 1 Chronicles, the author of 2 Chronicles is unknown. Tradition links the postcaptivity priest and prophet Ezra—or even Nehemiah—to the text. While not a verification of authorship, the writer of 2 Chronicles refers to himself as the "Chronicler."

Date Written

Second Chronicles was written shortly after 1 Chronicles, possibly sometime between 450 and 425 BC.

Landmarks

In our journey through the book of 2 Chronicles, we'll fly over King Solomon's reign, catching the spiritual roller coaster that began at his death and then picked up speed as Israel splits into two kingdoms. The book of 2 Chronicles can be divided into three sections: the distinctive glories of Solomon's rule, the division of the kingdom after his death, and the eventual decline of the southern kingdom, Judah.

Itinerary

- The Distinction of Solomon's Kingship (2 Chronicles 1–9)
- The Division of the Singular Kingdom (2 Chronicles 10–12)
- The Decline of the Southern Kingdom (2 Chronicles 13–36)
  - Good Fruit with a Few Bruises
  - A Few Good Apples in a Bad Bunch
  - Rotten Fruit in a Burning Barrel

Gospel

Second Chronicles relates how Solomon built God's temple on Mount Moriah. Moriah was a historically significant place for the Jewish people because it was where Abraham almost offered his precious son Isaac as a sacrifice to the Lord. The temple, of course, later became the central location for offering sacrifices to the Lord. This pointed to and foreshadowed a future event that happened on the same craggy ridge of Moriah, just slightly north, at Golgotha: God the Father offered His only Son, Jesus Christ, as a sacrifice for all of mankind.

The temple itself prefigured Christ. As Jesus said, referring to Himself, "Yet I say to you that in this place there is One greater than the temple" (Matthew 12:6). Speaking of His own body, He also said, "Destroy this temple, and in three days I will raise it up" (John 2:19). Toward the very end of the Bible, the apostle John witnessed the New Jerusalem coming out of heaven, but "saw no temple in it, for the Lord God Almighty and the Lamb are its temple" (Revelation 21:22). In Solomon's time, God lived among His people by way of the temple, and after the captivity in Babylon, a second temple was built, but both were just foreshadowing what Christ came to do: fulfill the sacrificial purpose of the temple at the cross and one day come to dwell with His people in a new and eternal city.

History

The history of 2 Chronicles picks up where 1 Chronicles left off—with the rule of Solomon (971–931 BC)—and ends with the Jewish exile and captivity in 586 BC. Some interesting events that happened during this time include the prophet Isaiah's ministry, which began in 755 BC, and the discovery of the book of the Law of Moses—the first five books of the Bible—in 624 BC.

Travel Tips

Second Chronicles captures the glory of the temple in all its meaning and magnificence, including the ways in which it pointed to Christ. Second Chronicles also relates the history of how God's people lost sight of His vision for them and the relationship He desired with them, and how they subsequently divided and were conquered.

- Have you lost sight of your eternal home? Jesus said, "Let not your heart be troubled; you believe in God, believe also in Me. In My Father's house are many mansions; if it were not so, I would have told you. I go to prepare a place for you" (John 14:1-2). Jesus created the world in six days; imagine what He has done in the 2000-plus years since He ascended! Heaven is going to be marvelous.

- God loves humility. Humility is a combination of two things: an honest self-appraisal and a good God-appraisal. When you look at yourself in the light of who God is, you become what Jesus described in the Sermon on the Mount as "poor in spirit" (Matthew 5:3). Being poor in spirit leads to mourning, and mourning leads to meekness, which leads to a hunger and thirst for righteousness.

> **Humility is a combination of two things: an honest self-appraisal and a good God-appraisal.**

In Flight

The Distinction of Solomon's Kingship (2 Chronicles 1–9)

Solomon ruled Israel for forty years. His was the golden age of Israel, sort of like post-World War II America—an age of progress, prosperity, and peace. The reason? "The LORD his God was with him and exalted him exceedingly" (2 Chronicles 1:1). Solomon started out strongly, leading the people in worship at the tabernacle in Gibeon and sacrificing a thousand burnt offerings. That led to God rolling out the red carpet and asking Solomon what gift He could give him. Solomon responded, "I will need wisdom to govern this great people of Yours." Because of Solomon's heart, God blessed him with more wisdom than any other king had ever possessed or ever would. He also promised Solomon tremendous wealth and honor, so that "the king made silver and gold as common in Jerusalem as stones, and he made cedars as abundant as the sycamores" (2 Chronicles 1:15).

Solomon then began two major building projects—a temple for God, and a royal house for himself. The temple provides another framework for the entire book: The first nine chapters detail how God blessed Solomon as he built it, and the rest of the book focuses on the kings of Judah who maintained it. Of all the kings of Judah after Solomon, most did evil in God's sight. But in 2 Chronicles, Ezra focused primarily on the highlights of the good kings, who brought reform, reinstituted the Passover, and repaired the temple. The book opens with the temple being built by Solomon and closes with the first temple being destroyed and an encouragement to build the second temple.

Solomon laid a foundation for the house of the Lord on Mount Moriah, at the site David had purchased from Araunah years before, which was the place where Abraham had almost offered Isaac as a sacrifice. Solomon was looking to do everything bigger and better than it had been in the tabernacle, and the temple's dimensions doubled those of the tabernacle: ninety feet deep, thirty feet wide, and forty-five feet tall. Every detail testified to God's holiness, power, grace, and beauty. The temple took Solomon seven-and-a-half years to finish, and he timed its dedication to fall during the seventh month during the Feast of Tabernacles—when the children of Israel were celebrating God's provision in the wilderness.

It was quite a shindig—priests sacrificing sheep and oxen in droves, the Ark of the Covenant being carefully transported into the Holy of Holies, and a festival of worship music, singers, and musicians praising God (2 Chronicles 5:13). At the peak of all the activity, a cloud descended and "the glory of the LORD filled the house of God" (v. 14). This is a tangible sign of God showing up in the Old Testament, a sign of His presence among His people, and they responded with worship. It was so wonderful and powerful that the priests had to stop what they were doing, no doubt joining the rest of the congregation in worship.

For Ezra's audience, many years later struggling to rebuild their decimated hometown and temple, it was encouraging to be reminded of Solomon's glory days—his visit from the queen of Sheba, the splendor of his court, his gold-overlaid ivory throne, his hundreds of shields of hammered gold and twelve lion statues on the steps ascending to his throne, and the constant retinue of musicians, merchants, and rulers from around the world, as well as his annual salary of 666 talents of gold.

The Division of the Singular Kingdom (2 Chronicles 10–12)

Unfortunately, the glory days of Israel lasted only as long as Solomon's life. As soon as he died, it all went to pot. His son Rehoboam took over, a weak leader whom stronger, more opportunistic men leveraged for control and, ultimately, the division of the kingdom. The next generation would pay the hefty price tag of that disobedience.

An old political enemy of Solomon's, Jeroboam son of Nebat, returned from self-imposed exile in Egypt and approached Rehoboam (2 Chronicles 10). He told the new king, "Do us all a favor: Now that your dad is dead, consider easing his tax burden. He was crushing us, and I know this palace really looks great, but now's your chance to earn some love from your people." After getting advice from two groups—wise, older men who told him to heed Jeroboam's request and show the people some love, and a bunch of young bucks Rehoboam had grown up with— the king settled on the counsel of the latter group and told Jeroboam, "You think Dad was bad? I'm going to make his taxes look like toll fees."

Jeroboam was prepared for such an answer. During Solomon's reign, a prophet named Ahijah had given him a message, saying that God was going to take Solomon's kingdom away because of his idolatry and give Jeroboam ten of the tribes to rule (1 Kings 11:31-38). So his response to Rehoboam—"Fine, then; I'm out of here and I'm taking ten tribes with me"—came as a result of God's judgment on Solomon's sin. However, despite God's promise to bless him if he stayed true, Jeroboam instituted idol worship, abandoning the God who had put him on his throne. From that point on, the kingdom was divided, with Israel in the north and Judah in the south.

Despite the division, the next three years were years of blessing because Rehoboam was honoring God and following in David and Solomon's footsteps. In the fourth year, though, Rehoboam abandoned the source of his blessings. He took credit for all the infrastructure and military might he had built and went his way instead of continuing in God's, taking the nation down with him (2 Chronicles 12:1). In his fifth year, God sent regional superpower Egypt to attack Jerusalem as a judgment against Rehoboam. The prophet Shemaiah came to Rehoboam and said, "You blew it; you should have listened to God." The king was convicted and repented, and God spared him and Judah from Egypt's attack.

Rehoboam's reign is summed up in a single verse: "He did evil, because he did not prepare his heart to seek the LORD" (2 Chronicles 12:14). That moment of humility and repentance was just that—a moment. And his lack of consistent obedience to God only created more division—between most of Judah's kings and God, and between the kings of Judah and Israel.

The Decline of the Southern Kingdom (2 Chronicles 13–36)

The rest of the book focuses on the southern kings of Judah and largely omits, with a few exceptions, the northern kings of Israel. Nineteen more kings are mentioned, from Abijah to Zedekiah, and most of them were poor leaders, disobedient to God, engaged in idol worship that lowered the spiritual standards of the entire nation. The few good kings stood out like very few stars against a very black night, and even the good they did wasn't enough to prevent Judah from plunging into judgment and captivity. We'll give them the 30,000-foot flyover treatment, comparing them thematically with a barrel of apples.

Good Fruit with a Few Bruises

Abijah

Rehoboam's son Abijah replaced him as king of Judah, and he actually took a stand for God against his father's old enemy Jeroboam (2 Chronicles 13). Standing on a mountain between his army of 400,000 and Jeroboam's army of 800,000, Abijah said, "Do you really think you can stand against God and His priests and His army with your golden calves and false priests?" While he was talking, though, Jeroboam sent an ambush to attack from the rear. When Abijah realized he had been surrounded, he cried out to God. The priests blew their trumpets, Judah's army shouted, and "God struck Jeroboam and all Israel before Abijah and Judah" (v. 15). Abijah's troops killed 500,000 Israelite soldiers that day, and Jeroboam never recovered, dying shortly afterward. God showed favor to Abijah and Judah "because they had relied on the Lord God of their fathers" (v. 18).

Asa

After Abijah died, his son Asa replaced him and did a lot of good, bringing religious reform, rebuilding some of the regional temples that had fallen into disrepair, and destroying the pagan altars. But as good as he was, he had some hang-ups. He allied Judah with a long-time adversary, Syria, against Israel, when God wanted him to go against Syria so that He could give Asa a decisive victory against a foe that would come back to bite them (2 Chronicles 16:7-9).

Jehoshaphat

Asa's son Jehoshaphat succeeded him, a great king who sought God and "walked in the former ways of his father David" (2 Chronicles 17:3). He continued the reforms and revival Asa had begun, specifically by involving the priests in the work. He sent them to the towns around Judah to hold Bible studies and teach people the Scriptures, the Law of Moses, and the words of the prophets so they would know what God was doing among them. Like David, Jehoshaphat was fiercely monotheistic, tolerating no rivals to God, ridding the land of false worship. "His heart took delight in the ways of the Lord" (v. 6).

While Jehoshaphat had a godly heart, it seems he wasn't the brightest bulb in the box. He allied himself with Ahab, the truly wicked king of Israel, marrying one of Ahab's daughters and getting caught up in Ahab's wars (2 Chronicles 18). Fortunately, God had Jehoshaphat's back. After a prophet had told Ahab that God planned for him to die in a coming battle, Ahab came up with his own plan. He told Jehoshaphat, "Tell you what, son-in-law: Why don't you wear your royal robes into this battle with Syria, and I will go in disguise?" And Jehoshaphat said, "Sure thing, Ahab!" During the battle, the Syrians' plan was to target only the king of Israel. They didn't know what Ahab looked like, so they just went after the guy in robes. Jehoshaphat cried out to God, who saved him from his own foolishness, but Ahab got taken out by a random arrow and died that evening.

Both warriors and worshippers were crucial to Jehoshaphat's next battle against Ammon and Moab. When word came that the enemy was on the way, Jehoshaphat set a good tone, bowing to and praising God. The people joined him in worship, led by the Kohathites and the Korahites—Judah's worship teams—who went out ahead of the army, singing and praising God. Picture it: the singers, not the soldiers, led the way into battle. They had it all right: the perspective, the patience, and the position, marching forward with praise on their lips: "Praise the LORD, for His mercy endures forever" (2 Chronicles 20:21). Ammon and Moab fell, turning against each other, so that Judah didn't even have to fight. All that was left to them was to collect the spoils of their dead enemies.

A Few Good Apples in a Bad Bunch

Jehoram, Ahaziah, and Athaliah

After Jehoshaphat's death, things got ugly for a while with a run of bad kings (2 Chronicles 21–25): Jehoram ruled for eight years, and his first official act was to kill all his brothers and eliminate his competition for the throne. Ahaziah came next, an idolater who died of battle wounds after a year on the throne. There was a brief power vacuum at the top, which Ahaziah's mother, a nasty piece of work named Athaliah, filled. She killed all the possible royal heirs, but her grandson Joash escaped, hidden away from her for the six years she was in charge. Joash reemerged at the ripe old age of seven to be proclaimed king; his reappearance led to Athaliah's death under the charge of treason. Everyone threw a party, which shows how popular she was.

Joash

Joash did a good job, at least while he was under the counsel of Jehoiada the priest. He took up a collection from among the people to rebuild and restore the temple and its treasury. After Jehoiada died, though, Joash started listening to the wrong advisors, who turned his heart from God toward idol worship. He even ended up killing Jehoiada's son for prophesying against his wicked turn, a move that eventually led to his own assassination at a servant's hands. Not a good end for Joash.

Amaziah

Amaziah, Joash's son, then reigned for twenty-nine years. I wish I could say he did an amazing job, and he did put on a good show at first, "doing what was right in the sight of the LORD, but not with a loyal heart" (2 Chronicles 25:2). But his first move was to execute the people who had killed his dad. He then turned from God completely and engaged in idolatry. That led to another lowlight of his reign—his capture in a battle against Israel, which ironically was led by a king with the same name as his father, Joash, leaving the temple to be plundered. Booooo!

Uzziah

God gave Judah a break with their next king, Amaziah's son Uzziah, who took the throne at sixteen. Age isn't always a good gauge of spiritual ability or commitment, and Uzziah turned out to be one of Judah's best kings. He ruled for the lengthy sum of fifty-two years, loving the Lord, doing what was right in God's eyes, fortifying Jerusalem's walls and building up infrastructure, "and as long as he sought the LORD, God made him prosper" (2 Chronicles 26:5). "As long as" implies that he didn't always seek God, and sure enough, once God had blessed Uzziah, strengthening and enriching him, Uzziah got a big head, took all the credit for his success, and had to be taken down a few pegs. He ended up a leper, which underscores the importance of sticking with God all the way through life.

Hezekiah

A few kings later, a breath of fresh air took the throne. Hezekiah re-opened the temple, brought the priests back to Jerusalem, and cleansed and sanctified it for use (2 Chronicles 29). He broke down the altars and idols throughout the area and encouraged the people to return to God, who gave them "singleness of heart to obey the command of the king" (2 Chronicles 30:12). Hezekiah also reinstituted the Passover, long neglected and forgotten during all the years of the bad kings.

This change of heart and renewal of faith came at just the right time, because soon afterward, Assyria invaded Judah. Having conquered the northern kingdom of Israel some years earlier, Assyria, led by King Sennacherib, prepared to lay siege to Jerusalem. Hezekiah prepared to resist, building up the city walls and watchtowers and forging weapons and shields. He encouraged the people not to fear Assyria, saying, "With him is an arm of flesh; but with us is the LORD our God, to help us and to fight our battles" (2 Chronicles 32:8).

Sennacherib, however, was a master of psychological warfare. He sent messengers and letters to discourage everyone in Jerusalem. "Don't think your God can save you," they said. "Every other nation we've conquered built up their defenses and trusted their gods—and it did them no good. It won't help you, either. Save yourself the trouble and surrender now." They hollered these messages in Hebrew to further discourage the people. Given Assyria's track record, their threats had weight and credibility—but they did not have the God that Hezekiah served. Their arm of flesh was no match for God's arm of unrestricted power!

Hezekiah and the prophet Isaiah led the people in crying out to God to deliver them, and God came through big time: "The LORD sent an angel who cut down every mighty man of valor, leader, and captain in the camp of the king of Assyria" (v. 21). Assyria had an army of 185,000, but Judah had a majority of One. Assyria talked smack and God smacked them down because His people trusted Him in their hour of need.

Hezekiah didn't end particularly well; he got cocky after God won his battles and blessed him with wealth and power, and God had to straighten him out, humbling him with a major illness. Also, when Babylonian ambassadors came to check out all of Hezekiah's wealth and splendor, "God withdrew from him, in order to test him, that He might know all that was in his heart" (v. 31). Hezekiah flunked, showing the Babylonians all the wealth in the treasury, which enticed his visitors to put Jerusalem on their list of Places We Must Invade and Conquer Someday, which happened about thirty years after he died.

Manasseh

Manasseh, Hezekiah's successor, started out as the worst king ever, Ahab times two. He repaired all the altars Hezekiah had torn down, burned his own children in pagan sacrifice, and even put an idol in the temple. But God still tried to get through to him and the people. When they didn't listen, the Lord moved to more extreme measures to get the king's attention: the Assyrians captured Manasseh and took him in chains to Babylon.

There, he sort of woke up and realized he had sinned against God. Manasseh repented, humbling himself and asking God to forgive him. And God did, restoring the throne and the kingdom to Manasseh, who responded by cleansing the temple of the idols he had installed there, and casting the other altars and shrines to false gods out of the city. He repaired God's altar and offered peace and thank offerings on it, "and commanded Judah to serve the LORD God of Israel" (2 Chronicles 33:16). His is truly one of the most fascinating and dramatic conversion stories in the Bible.

Josiah

If the first part of Manasseh's reign put him among the worst rulers of Judah, his successor Josiah was among the best. Josiah was another early starter, becoming king at age eight. During his thirty-one year reign, he became—and remained—Judah's godliest monarch. While he was still young, he began to seek God for himself, and God used him to spark a dramatic revival in Judah.

Josiah purged the city and land of idols, pounding them to dust and chopping down the high places of false worship. Then, at age twenty-six, he decided to repair the temple. As his workers were taking the trash out, removing the rubble, restoring the stones, and refurbishing the floors, one of the priests found a copy of the Law—the first five books of Moses. You would expect to find a Bible in the temple, but apparently it had been neglected during all of the bad times, maybe hidden away by a faithful priest to protect it from an evil king. It was like a fresh revelation to Josiah—and a convicting one, at that. "When the king heard the words of the Law...he tore his clothes" (2 Chronicles 34:19)—a cultural sign of grief and mourning.

Josiah was heartbroken and afraid. However, a prophetess told him, "God saw your tender heart, your humility, your brokenness, and He has promised to spare you the consequences that He will bring on this place." Josiah gathered all the people of Judah at the temple and read them the Law. He then pledged to follow God's commandments, and demanded a promise from everyone present to do the same. He held the greatest Passover feast since Samuel's day. And, later, when Egypt attacked Judah, Josiah couldn't let Jerusalem go undefended so he went out to fight, sustaining an injury that eventually killed him. Everyone—priest, prophets, and people—mourned him. A good start *and* a good finish—A+ for Josiah.

Rotten Fruit in a Burning Barrel

After Josiah, it was all downhill into captivity. Josiah's son Jehoahaz barely got the throne warm when he was deposed by the Egyptians after three months as king. Egypt was contesting control of the Middle East with Assyria and Babylon; all of them caused trouble for God's people. Assyria had conquered Israel almost 150 years earlier, and now Egypt was threatening from the south and Babylon from the north and east.

The Egyptians carted Jehoahaz off to Egypt and put his brother Eliakim in charge in his place, and changed his name from Eliakim to Jehoiakim. No one knows why, but it might have been a power move to show they were now in control of Judah. Jehoiakim kept the throne for eleven years. The prophet Jeremiah warned him not to resist the king of Babylon, but Jehoiakim—who was yet another bad king in God's eyes—ignored the prophet's warning and got himself carried off to Babylon in chains. The Babylonians then thought, *Let's make this name thing really confusing*, and put Jehoiakim's son Jehoiachin in his place as king.

Jehoiachin, who was only eight, got three months and ten days—during which time the naughty boy managed to do evil in God's sight. Babylon continued to administer God's spankings and he was deposed and taken to Babylon. His uncle, Zedekiah (who also did evil), then became the final king of the house of David before the captivity. He ignored the warnings God sent by the prophet Jeremiah and decided he could take a stand against Nebuchadnezzar of Babylon, which, as you can imagine, did not go well.

After two previous assaults from Babylon in 605 BC and 597 BC, the final year of destruction was 586 BC. God had continued to send prophets and warnings, giving His people every chance to get it together and turn around back to Him, but they just weren't having it (2 Chronicles 36:15-16). Finally, it was too late. God's judgment came in the form of the merciless king of Babylon, who broke down Jerusalem's walls, killed Judah's young men, plundered the treasuries of the king and the temple, and then burned the temple, the palace, and the houses of the rich.

God forced the people to honor His commandment to give the land a rest, and so they did, for seventy years, while they were enslaved in Babylon. Eventually the kingdom of Persia overthrew Babylon, and God moved Persia to let His people return to their land. Ezra the priest was among those who returned, and he ended the book on a hopeful note, telling how Cyrus, king of Persia, was commanded by God "to build Him a house at Jerusalem...Who is among you of all His people? May the LORD his God be with him, and let him go up!" (v. 23).

EZRA
FLIGHT PLAN

Facts

Author

Jewish tradition states that Ezra himself wrote the book of Ezra, though the book does not name its author. In early Hebrew versions of the Scriptures, Ezra and Nehemiah were included as one book. Ezra is written in first person and uses elements of Nehemiah's firsthand accounts, lending credence to the priestly scribe Ezra being the best candidate for authorship.

Date Written

If Ezra wrote the book of Ezra, he probably did so shortly after he arrived in Jerusalem in 458 BC. The book is postexilic—that is, it was written after the Jews had been exiled in Babylon under the reigns of Artaxerxes I and Darius II.

Landmarks

The book of Ezra is called the Second Exodus. Roughly a thousand years after the first exodus of Israel from Egypt—after the eras of judges and kings, a unified kingdom and a divided one, and seventy years' captivity in Babylon—the Jews returned to the Promised Land. There had been three exiles—three different occasions when the Babylonians captured Jews and took them to Babylon, in 605, 597, and 586 BC. And there would be three returns, under Zerubbabel, Ezra, and Nehemiah. Ezra covered the first two in his book, which provides a natural outline: Zerubbabel's return, a national restoration, and Ezra's return, Israel's spiritual reformation.

Itinerary

- National Restoration (Ezra 1–6)
  - The Return

- The Rebuilding
- The Resistance
- Spiritual Reformation (Ezra 7–10)

Gospel

Where do we see Jesus in the book of Ezra? Ezra isn't quoted in the New Testament, though its companion book Nehemiah is (John 6:31). Nevertheless, the book is a history book, recording not only the dealings of the Jewish nation and the temple, but the continuing line of David as well. Zerubbabel, empowered by God to be the chief builder of the temple (see Ezra 3:2), was a descendant of the royal line of the house of David and an ancestor of Jesus Christ. The destruction of the scarlet thread of redemption was narrowly averted when Ezra responded to the mixed-faith marriages of the Jewish leaders in Jerusalem by speaking out against them—and when the leaders, in turn, responded by repenting and divorcing their non-Jewish wives. It was a radical move that essentially preserved the purity of the lineage of Israel. In particular, it preserved the line of the tribe of Judah, from whom it was prophesied the Messiah would come (see Genesis 49:10).

The name of the high priest is worth noting. *Jeshua* means in Hebrew and Aramaic "God is Salvation." *Jeshua* (pronounced Yeshua) is translated in the New Testament as the name Jesus. It's fascinating that the high priest in charge of the reconstruction of the temple was a man named Jesus. The New Testament refers to Jesus as our great High Priest (Hebrews 4:14), and He will be the center of focus in the temple that will be built in Jerusalem in the millennial kingdom.

History

The book of Ezra begins with Cyrus's decree in 538 BC that the Jews could return to Jerusalem. About two years later, in 536 BC, thousands of Jews flooded into Jerusalem and began the temple project. However, economic and political problems caused delays with the project between 535 and 520 BC. The temple was finally finished around 515 BC, and Ezra arrived in Jerusalem to teach the law of God to the people in 458 BC. In that fifty-eight-year gap between the temple's completion and Ezra's arrival, the events of the book of Esther were taking place in Persia (modern-day Iran). At the same time as Ezra, God also raised up two other prophets, who in turn have their own books in the Bible, Haggai and Zechariah.

Travel Tips

Ezra was overwhelmed by God's faithfulness, especially when contrasted with the unfaithfulness of the Jewish people. Ezra understood that we don't always respond to God the way we ought to, but that God is willing to respond to our sincere desire to change and follow Him.

- Ezra's prayer (Ezra 9) revealed a lot about his heart toward God and his attitude as a leader. Confronted with Israel's sin, he prayed, first and foremost. He also identified with the sins of the people, including himself as he asked God for mercy. Finally, he resigned himself to the will of God and trusted in God's mercy and love. No wonder the people responded!

The Word of God does the work of God in the lives of the people of God.

- The Word of God does the work of God in the lives of the people of God. As they rebuilt the temple, the people became discouraged and stopped building. But two prophets—Haggai and Zechariah—came and encouraged them "in the name of the God of Israel, who was over them" (Ezra 5:1) to continue the work. When they ran into opposition from the Persian government, they stuck to God's commandment to rebuild, trusting that He would see them through the trials. What enemy can stand against the power of God's Word?

- Whatever God has put on your heart to do for building up His house and His kingdom, do it. If it's risky, good—God will show Himself able and strong. Do what He has called you to do.

In Flight

National Restoration (Ezra 1–6)

Three words sum up Ezra 1–6: *return*, *rebuilding*, and *resistance*. Under the leadership of Zerubbabel, a group of Jews returned from captivity to Israel, began to rebuild the temple, and resisted a group of enemies who were standing against their work.

The Return

The Jews' return to Jerusalem began with Cyrus, the king of the Medo-Persian Empire, who ruled the known world at that time. He had united the Medes and the Persians, who had overthrown the Babylonians, who had in turn overthrown Assyria as the dominant power in the Middle East, Europe, northern Africa, and western Asia. Cyrus had a repatriation policy, meaning that when he conquered a kingdom, rather than keep the people as slaves in Persia, he sent them home to govern their land under his ultimate authority. In 539 BC, he gave that command to people from Israel and Judah.

Ezra put a spiritual perspective on this development: By God's leading and in fulfillment of a prophecy by Jeremiah, Cyrus, the ruler of the world, said that God had commanded him to send the Jewish people back to Jerusalem to build a new temple (Ezra 1:1). He not only invited the Jews to return to their homeland, he encouraged their neighbors to support their efforts with silver and gold and livestock, plus offerings for the temple when it was rebuilt. He also returned the temple furniture and worship articles, which Nebuchadnezzar of Babylon had removed when he attacked Jerusalem before the captivity.

Ezra tallied up a total of 49,897 people who returned with Zerubbabel (Ezra 2:64-65). Many more stayed behind, comfortable with their situation in Babylon. Before the captivity, God had told the children of Israel to settle in and make the best of their captivity (Jeremiah 29:5-7). They settled down, all right, but most of them became a little too settled. Fifty thousand returned to Jerusalem, but a million stayed behind.[11] Fast-forward to Jesus's time, when five million Jews still lived outside of Israel,[12] and it becomes clear that, going back to Ezra's day, only a small percentage felt led to return.

Of those who returned, a good ten percent were from the tribe of Levi—the priests and those dedicated to God's work in the temple—along with non-Jewish people who served in nonpriestly roles in the temple. Because of the diaspora—the dispersal of Jews—that began with Assyria and the ten northern tribes of Israel and continued with Babylon's conquest of the remaining two tribes in Judah, it was sometimes hard to verify who was from which tribe. This was particularly important when it came to the Levites, who were the only ones God allowed to serve as priests. That was one of the reasons Ezra made a list—so he could tell who was a Levite and fit to serve as a priest.

The Rebuilding

Even before the foundation of the temple was laid, Zerubbabel and the priest Jeshua built the altar and were keeping the prescribed feasts and making daily burnt offerings (Ezra 3). The first thing on their agenda was to get a center of worship up and running, and the center of their worship was sacrifice. Why? Because the law said, "The life of the flesh is in the blood, and I have given it to you upon the altar to make atonement for your souls; for it is the blood that makes atonement for the soul" (Leviticus 17:11). For New Testament believers, the law was fulfilled in the sacrifice of Christ on the cross.

The Old Testament system of sacrifices anticipated Christ. The center of Christian worship is the blood of Jesus, a point Paul made when he wrote, "I determined not to know anything among you except Jesus Christ and Him crucified" (1 Corinthians 2:2). Christians commemorate the sacrifice Jesus made by celebrating communion; the Jews celebrated what God had done for them by keeping the feasts and offering regular sacrifices. What made it even better when Zerubbabel and company held their spiritual party after their return was the fact that Cyrus and the Medo-Persian government had footed the bill for the whole thing.

The party continued at the laying of the foundation. Most people were shouting God's praises and signing responsively—one group singing "For He is good" and another responding "For His mercy endures forever toward Israel" (Ezra 3:11)—but some of the older priests and tribal heads wept loudly, perhaps still living in the past. The Babylonian Talmud (Jewish commentaries on the Bible) said that Zerubbabel's temple was missing five things that Solomon's temple had: the Ark of the Covenant, the holy fire that lit the altar, the Shekinah glory of God, the Spirit of prophecy, and the Urim and Thummim (the two stones used to discern the will of God).[13] So, even with Cyrus's support, the second temple was not nearly as large or grand as Solomon's; maybe these older folks felt something had been lost that would never be regained. It's hard to move forward when you're always looking backward. In fact, that's a pretty good recipe for a miserable life.

God's glory and work aren't diminished by anything people do. Some forget Him, others lose sight of His mission, but the size of a temple or an offering are nothing compared to a heart dedicated to God's worship and service. And most of the returnees rejoiced with full hearts. God had promised that this day would come—that after seventy years' captivity, Babylon would fall (Jeremiah 25:11-12) and Israel would return (Jeremiah 29:10). There was cause for celebration, not least because they were moving forward. God's work in their lives wasn't finished—and that's what is so wonderful about God: He has done great things, but He is also doing great things now, and He will do great things in the future too.

God's glory and work aren't diminished by anything people do.

The Resistance

The rebuilt temple brought the light of God's blessing back to Jerusalem. Any light also attracts bugs, and that was the case here: the enemy came, subtle and political. Isaac Newton's third law—that, for every action, there is an equal and opposite reaction—is a spiritual law too: When God acts, the devil reacts.

By the spring of 535 BC, the temple foundation was laid. A group, alternately called "the adversaries of Judah and Benjamin" (Ezra 4:1) and "the people of the land" (v. 4), lobbied to stop the work on the temple. They had come to Zerubbabel and Jeshua and asked to help build the temple, but had been turned away. They claimed they had worshipped God since the days of Assyria—the empire that had conquered and dispersed the ten northern tribes of Israel. Red flag! Assyria's policy had been to send in foreign people to marry the remaining Jews, muddying their religion with pagan practices. By Jesus's day, this mixed group would be known as the Samaritans; they had their own system of worship and their own temple, where they worshipped their own version of the one true God.

After suffering years of captivity in a foreign land for their nation's disobedience of God, Zerubbabel and his leaders wouldn't have anything to do with such a misguided mélange, and these adversaries took it personally: They "tried to discourage the people of Judah. They troubled them in building" (v. 4), bribing officials to slow the work down and writing letters to the Persian king in protest. Cyrus, who had let the Jews return to Israel, was now dead, and the favor God had given the Jews with him was also gone.

Persia's current leader was Artaxerxes, and the detractors in Jerusalem wrote to him, telling him that the Jews had a history of rebelling against any foreign power occupying their land. They painted themselves as good citizens of the Persian Empire, unwilling to see Artaxerxes's honor besmirched by these rebellious Jews—even though they had been willing to help build the temple. Word came from Persia to stop the project, under penalty of military action, and work on the temple stopped until the next guy, Darius, was in charge in Persia (vv. 18-24).

For sixteen years, the work stopped. No one lifted a tool or moved a stone on the temple site. People didn't want to risk Persia's wrath; they lost momentum and grew discouraged with the rubble from the captivity laying in heaps all around them. So God sent two prophets to snap them back to attention and get them back to building—Haggai and Zechariah, both of whom have books in the Bible. Haggai preached four sermons to Zerubbabel and Jeshua, and Zechariah rebuked the people for building up their own homes and leaving the house of God in ruins. The two leaders responded to the prophets' urging, and got back to work on the temple (Ezra 5:2).

The preaching of God's Word inspired the people to go through with the work. Full trust in God to keep His promises, to be faithful to His character, means knowing that He will always do the right thing even when you don't know what the path ahead looks like. Haggai and Zechariah reminded the people of that, and they were then able to face their foes with their confidence fully placed in God.

The locals who had been giving them a hard time came and grumbled again, threatening to appeal to the king. Zerubbabel and Jeshua told them, "Write to Darius if you must, but we are God's servants and we are going to finish the mission that King Cyrus sent us to complete. Check your records and see." Sure enough, when Darius went back to the scrolls, he found the decree of Cyrus, which included mention of his financial support for the whole undertaking (Ezra 6:1-5).

Darius wrote to the troublemakers, telling them, "Back off and let the Jews work. Furthermore, use the taxes from your lands to fund their work, giving them whatever they need to make sacrifices to God." What's so satisfying about the tables being turned on these snitches is that Zerubbabel and Jeshua didn't defend themselves—they left it to God to uphold their cause, and He came through big time! They finished the temple a few years later and dedicated it with a big celebration.

Spiritual Reformation (Ezra 7–10)

Between chapters 6 and 7 is a fifty-eight-year gap. Zerubbabel, Jeshua, and company completed the temple, and then, almost six decades later, Ezra the priest arrived with another group of Jews returning from Babylon. Incidentally, during that in-between period, the whole book of Esther took place in Persia, another picture of life for the Jews during these challenging years. We'll get to Esther's story in a few chapters.

Ezra introduced himself through a genealogy that established his Levite lineage going all the way back to Aaron, Moses's brother (Ezra 7:1-5). He provided his credentials as a priest because a lot of people returning to the land claimed to be related to Aaron but couldn't prove it and weren't allowed to serve in the temple. Ezra was. He was also a scribe, trained in reading, interpreting, translating, and copying Scripture.

There was a science and a methodology to writing down the Word of God, counting the columns vertically and horizontally, and if everything didn't match precisely at the end of a page, the scribe would rip it up and start all over again. Their craft is one of the reasons the Scriptures have been passed down so exactly and faithfully through the ages. Jewish tradition says that Ezra also founded the Great Synagogue, a group of scholars who met and decided which books would form the canon of Old Testament Scripture.

Along the way, Ezra set up camp at Ahava, where he led his group in fasting and prayer for three days, asking for God's protection on their journey. Other Levites and priests joined them there, and Ezra divvied up the money Artaxerxes had given him among twelve of the priests, telling them, "You are holy to God, and so is this offering; when you get to Jerusalem, put it in the temple treasury." This seed money was an act of faith and hope in the efforts all of them would make once they arrived.

And they got there just in time. Once the group arrived and settled in a bit, the leaders of the Jews already in Jerusalem came to Ezra and told him that most of the Jews had married pagan husbands and wives—including the priests and Levites already there. And their kids were marrying the locals too. Ezra came unglued in a priestly sort of way, tearing his clothes and ripping out some of his hair and beard as signs of grief and mourning (Ezra 9:1-3). *Ouch!* He couldn't believe the people had already fallen back into the same sins that had gotten them sent into captivity in the first place. "Then everyone who trembled at the words of the God of Israel assembled to [him]" (v. 4), and they spent the rest of the day fasting and praying, no doubt feeling desperate and helpless.

Ezra turned to God, confessing the people's sins, weeping and bowing down. A large group of men, women, and children joined him, moved by his example. They were starting to feel the weight of their sin, and some came to him and confessed, asking for him to lead them in trying to put things right. In the chill and heavy rain of a Jerusalem December, Ezra challenged those who had married pagans to separate from them in order to get in line with God's commandments (Ezra 10:10-12). Now, this isn't a scriptural precedent for getting a divorce because you think your spouse isn't holy enough; it was a specific solution at a specific, fragile time in Israel's history. It took a few months to get everything sorted out, but Ezra was God's instrument to help get the nation back on track.

A final thought: If the idea of a regathered Israel seems ancient and irrelevant, consider the prophecy of a second regathering, which was proclaimed by Isaiah: "It shall come to pass in that day that the Lord shall set His hand again the second time to recover the remnant of His people who are left" (Isaiah 11:11). That happened in

1948, when Israel reformed as a nation for the first time since the Roman diaspora in AD 70. All the conflicts that these books of history in the Bible describe—Israel's struggles to occupy the Promised Land, the ongoing conflicts with the tribes and nations surrounding them—are still happening now. God has been and is working all things together for all mankind, including His special possession Israel. Everything that is past and present is prelude to what will happen in the end times, and Israel will remain the epicenter of history, now and into eternity.

NEHEMIAH
FLIGHT PLAN

Facts

Author

Because Nehemiah is associated with the book of Ezra (they were originally one book in the Hebrew Scriptures), many scholars believe that Ezra wrote the book of Nehemiah. However, others believe Nehemiah himself wrote the book. Another possibility is that Ezra used the memoirs of Nehemiah and his own skills as a scribe to create what we now know as the book of Nehemiah.

Date Written

If Ezra wrote the book of Nehemiah, he probably wrote it around the year 400 BC. If Nehemiah wrote it, an earlier date is more probable, possibly around 425 BC. Either way, the book was penned sometime between 425 and 400 BC.

Landmarks

Nehemiah went from being a cupbearer in Persia to a construction-builder in Jerusalem. He was a contemporary of Ezra, the priest who led the second group of Jews back from captivity in Babylon to a new start in Israel. About fourteen years after Ezra left, Nehemiah led the third and final group back to Jerusalem to rebuild the city.

Rebuilding is often a more daunting task than building from scratch. It requires digging through debris and rummaging through rubble, torn between memories of what had been and fears that things will never be the same again. Nehemiah returned to a broken-down Jerusalem, a city experiencing a whole gamut of emotions and trying to find hope in God. The book breaks down into three sections, each centered on Jerusalem: rebuilding its protection, reviving its passion, and resettling its population.

Itinerary

- Rebuilding a City's Protection (Nehemiah 1–7)
- Reviving a City's Passion (Nehemiah 8–10)
- Resettling a City's Population (Nehemiah 11–13)

Gospel

In the book of Nehemiah, the scarlet thread of redemption is woven into the walls of Jerusalem itself. To borrow from Jesus, the very "stones...cry out" His praises (Luke 19:40). From the beginning, God set Jerusalem apart from every other city on earth. Earthly conflicts continued to scar it—for instance, in AD 70, the Romans destroyed what Nehemiah had rebuilt, just as Jesus had predicted—but a glorious future awaits it. God said, "In Jerusalem I will put My name" (2 Kings 21:4), and Psalm 87:2 says, "The Lord loves the gates of Zion more than all the dwellings of Jacob." God has a special interest in this city, this epicenter of biblical activity.

Jerusalem is the *geographic center of the earth biblically* (Ezekiel 5:5). Whenever the Bible mentions cardinal directions—north, south, east, and west—they are all presented relative to one city—Jerusalem. It is also the *salvation center of the earth spiritually*. The only place where the salvation of all mankind was purchased is just outside the city walls at Mount Calvary. And Jerusalem is also the *storm center of the earth prophetically*. Every world leader knows that events that happen in a single neighborhood in Israel have more international consequence than just about anywhere else in the world. Furthermore, the Bible predicts the nations of the world will gather against Israel in the latter days. Finally, Jerusalem is the *glory center of the earth ultimately*! The very place that Nehemiah and others were building up would one day be established by God as His kingdom headquarters (Isaiah 2:2-3).

History

The events described in the book of Nehemiah took place between 458 and 420 BC. King Artaxerxes I of Persia, the world's dominant power of the time, allowed the Jews to return to Jerusalem and rebuild its walls. Nehemiah, a cupbearer in the king's court, stayed twelve years in Jerusalem until the project was finished. Shortly after construction was complete, Nehemiah returned to serve Artaxerxes I in Persia. He returned again to Jerusalem for the last time around 425 BC.

Travel Tips

The book of Nehemiah is, of course, about building up the walls around God's chosen city. It's also about a man who was in the right place at the right time with the right mindset.

- Each member of the body of Christ has their part to do in building up God's kingdom. The book of Nehemiah serves as a great reminder that church isn't a spectator sport, but a filling station—you don't just watch; you gas up, get involved, and go out!

- Large doors swing on small hinges. In his position as the king's cupbearer, Nehemiah took advantage of the requirements of his position to hear news of what was going on in Jerusalem and then to get involved for God's glory.

- Many Christians feel ashamed to just sit down and think. "Let's get going!" is the favorite call to arms for gospel workers, but thinking and planning are needed when undertaking a task for the kingdom. Stop, sit down, think it through, and pray it through. Get a God-given plan, *then* go for it.

> **Each member of the body of Christ has their part to do in building up God's kingdom.**

In Flight

Rebuilding a City's Protection (Nehemiah 1–7)

Nehemiah was serving as a cupbearer to King Artaxerxes of Persia when his brother, Hanani, visited him from Judah and gave him an account of the goings-on among the Jews who had returned from captivity in Babylon. It wasn't a good report: "The survivors who are left...in the province are there in great distress and reproach. The wall of Jerusalem is also broken down, and its gates are burned" (Nehemiah 1:3). Nehemiah's response was emotional, profound, and immediate: He broke down, weeping, fasting, and praying for days, confessing Israel's sins and crying out for God's mercy. Nehemiah also asked God for a favorable response from his boss, the king, for the request he was about to bring to him.

A cupbearer sounds like a guy who brings the king his royal lemonade, but he was actually an important officer in the king's court. He served as the king's personal assistant; he had to be cultured, conversant in legal and political matters, a trustworthy gatekeeper for the king's many appointments and appearances. Because of his access to the king and the inner workings of the court, Nehemiah heard this report about Jerusalem and was in a position to seek the king's help. First, though, he sought God's help.

Part of the cupbearer's job was to be happy in the king's presence. No one wants to work with a Debbie Downer, but in the Persian court, it could be fatal. Bumming the king out could mean your head! So when Nehemiah carried his heartbreak over the state of Israel into the workplace, it didn't matter that he "had never been sad in his presence before" (Nehemiah 2:1). When the king asked him, "What's with the sad face?" it wasn't a question of "Oh, isn't this a nice king?" but "Is my boss going to kill me?" Nehemiah was risking not just his job, but his life. No wonder he was "dreadfully afraid" (v. 2)! Still, he summoned the courage to speak the truth—carefully, and with great respect: "May the king live forever! Why should my face not be sad, when the city, the place of my fathers' tombs, lies waste, and its gates are burned with fire?" (v. 3).

Solomon wrote, "The king's heart is in the hand of the LORD, like the rivers of water; He turns it wherever He wishes" (Proverbs 21:1). So when King Artaxerxes asked Nehemiah what he requested, Nehemiah recognized God's hand at work and shot up a quick prayer—something like "Help me, God, give me Your grace"—and then asked to be sent to rebuild Jerusalem. He approached the king respectfully and submissively; he didn't say, "Listen, King, I'm heading to Jerusalem, whether you like it or not." Likewise, Christians should show the utmost respect for earthly authorities—speaking courteously, paying taxes, honoring employers and law officers—because God has put them in those positions of authority (Romans 13:1-7). It worked for Nehemiah; Artaxerxes sent him with his blessing, letters of safe conduct, and financial support. Talk about having a confirmation from God!

When Nehemiah arrived in Jerusalem, a couple of local officials, Sanballat and Tobiah, were waiting for him. They were bugged that anyone would come seeking to help the Jews. Nehemiah played his cards close to the chest and told no one, not even the Jews, of his reason for visiting. For a few days, he just checked things out, wanting to see what he was up against. Finally, having gotten the lay of the land, he shared the plan God had laid on his heart, and the Jews were receptive. When "they set their hands to this good work" (Nehemiah 2:18), though, that just got their enemies riled up.

> ### When God does a work, Satan reacts to that work by trying to mess it up any way he can.

Sanballat, Tobiah, and Geshem the Arab got wind of Nehemiah's plan and confronted him, mocking, "What? Are you going up against the king?" Nehemiah gave them a firm, direct answer: "The God of heaven Himself will prosper us; therefore we His servants will arise and build, but you have no heritage or right or memorial in Jerusalem" (Nehemiah 2:20). He was ready to answer them because he understood that, when God does a work, Satan reacts to that work by trying to mess it up any way he can. That's just the devil's MO. Remember, since his expulsion from Eden, he has been doing his best to disrupt God's plan of salvation; he certainly didn't want God's people to return to Jerusalem and rebuild anything.

Despite the opposition, Nehemiah and company got busy. The high priest, Eliashib, and his fellow priests began Jerusalem's extreme makeover by rebuilding the Sheep Gate, which was the door in the walls through which the sacrificial animals were led. Various groups also jumped in and repaired other gates, towers, and the wall between each, and made great progress. In chapter 3, the phrase "next to" is used sixteen times—this group building *next to* this group, this guy doing repairs *next to* that guy—thirty-eight individuals and forty-two groups mentioned by name as contributors. It's a great image of how God's people, particularly the body of Christ, are to get along and each do our part. No single person, regardless of talent or skill, can do the job alone, partly because of the massive, global scope of the work but mainly because God wants us to work together, cooperating and supporting the overall mission of building His kingdom.

Their corporate enthusiasm was met with continual opposition. When Sanballat wasn't publicly mocking and accusing the Jews, he was privately meeting with the local army, making plans to attack them. "He spoke before his brethren and the army of Samaria, and said, 'What are these feeble Jews doing? Will they fortify themselves? Will they offer sacrifices? Will they complete it in a day? Will they revive the stones from the heaps of rubbish—stones that are burned?'" (Nehemiah 4:2). The short answer is yes, they will. When the wall was built to half its full height, Sanballat conspired to attack the workers, but Nehemiah was praying the entire time, keeping his hands to the work and keeping an eye on his enemies.

The Jews were beginning to get discouraged by the difficult labor and the plots of their adversaries, which became evident in their speech: "There is so much rubbish that we are not able to build the wall" (Nehemiah 4:10). When did the stones used to build Jerusalem's walls become "rubbish"? Building God's city became an impossible task when the Jews took on the language used by their enemies.

But Nehemiah responded, once again with prayer, and then with a plan. He positioned armed men near the walls and encouraged them to not be afraid: "Remember the Lord, great and awesome, and fight for your brethren, your sons, your daughters, your wives, and your houses" (v. 14). When their enemies found that they had lost the element of surprise, they held off, and everyone got back to work on the wall—watchfully, with tools in one hand and a weapon in the other.

Now aware of their anti-Semitic enemies, Nehemiah and the Jews then faced another kind of opposition, this time from within—greed. The local government had raised taxes—probably in response to Persia giving their tax income to help the Jews—so people were out of money and there was famine in the land. Loan officers in Jerusalem were charging exorbitant interest rates, even Jews charging other Jews. Nehemiah found out, scolded them, and set up stringent accountability measures for the economic woes (Nehemiah 5:6-13). Persia made Nehemiah Judah's governor at that point and he set a godly standard for the job, refusing the food and luxuries that came with the job and keeping his workers and servants from doing so in order to keep the burden off the people.

Sanballat kept after Nehemiah, trying to get him alone to hurt him, accusing him of having royal ambitions, and employing Jewish informers to try and ruin his reputation. But Nehemiah stayed true to God and to his task—trusting that God would avenge him against his foes—and the wall was finished in record time: fifty-two days (Nehemiah 6:15). "When all our enemies heard of it, and all the nations around us saw these things...they were very disheartened in their own eyes; for they perceived that this work was done by our God" (v. 16).

Reviving a City's Passion (Nehemiah 8–10)

Ezra 8–10 in a nutshell is the people, the Bible, and a water gate revival. With the wall's construction completed, it was time for the people's consecration. Nehemiah recorded that Ezra the priest gathered everyone at the gate near the city water supply and read the Bible to them. Ezra had already been in Jerusalem for more than a dozen years, serving as Israel's spiritual leader. Here, he led everyone in an epic Bible study, from morning till midday, with the other priests serving to lead worship and explain the law (Nehemiah 8:1-8).

It was the first day of the seventh month, the Jewish New Year, known as Rosh Hashanah—a time of celebration and rejoicing in God's blessings. But we read that Nehemiah joined Ezra and told everyone, "'This day is holy to the LORD your God;

do not mourn nor weep.' For all the people wept, when they heard the words of the Law" (Nehemiah 8:9). Why the tears? Because, as Ezra read the Law—the first five books of the Bible—he came to Deuteronomy, right around chapter 28. That's where Moses had recorded not just the blessings for obeying God's commandments but the curses for disobedience.

You can always tell the depth of a well by how much rope has to be lowered; the law showed the people how far they had fallen when God rescued them from their deserved captivity. The Bible convicted them, and they grieved for their sin and its effects. Nehemiah, however, reminded them that this was a day for celebration: "Do not sorrow, for the joy of the LORD is your strength" (Nehemiah 8:10). They "went their way to eat and drink, to send portions and rejoice greatly, because they understood the words that were declared to them" (v. 12).

This is a great example of the effect that the simple teaching of the Word of God can have on people. There has never been a true revival apart from it. Before the captivity, God's Word revived Judah under Josiah, and it revived the people here during the time of Ezra and Nehemiah. They kept the Feast of Tabernacles for the first time since Joshua's day (v. 17), building booths and living in them to commemorate how God sheltered their ancestors in the wilderness with Moses. The Word of God is what does the work of God in the lives of the people of God.

The time to grieve their sin came a few weeks later, and the "children of Israel were assembled with fasting, in sackcloth, and with dust on their heads" (Nehemiah 9:1), all signs of mourning and distress. They spent the next three hours reading the Scriptures, confessing their sins, and worshipping. They were declaring their dependence on God. Nehemiah 9:6-38 is the longest prayer recorded in Scripture (thirty-four lengthy verses). Ezra drew on his knowledge of the Bible, pulling history and teaching from all of it, Genesis through Chronicles. His appetite for God's Word fed Israel, providing an example for us too—to be reading Scripture every day, learning about God and preparing for whatever any given day might bring.

Ezra's prayer ended with a promise to make and seal a covenant to follow God's Law, and we're given a list of eighty-four men who signed it (Nehemiah 10:1-27). Beginning with Nehemiah and the priests, Levites, and leaders, they committed to following God, joined by everyone who could understand what was being required—wives, sons, daughters—and "entered into a curse and an oath to walk in God's Law, which was given by Moses the servant of God, and to observe and to do all the commandments of the LORD our Lord, and His ordinances and His statutes" (v. 29). Their hearts had been moved to be holy—set apart as God's people—and their promise became their practice as they established a tax to support the work and upkeep of the temple and a tithe of their very best to honor God. Israel turned back to God, and He resuscitated the people's hearts.

Resettling a City's Population (Nehemiah 11–13)

Despite having rebuilt walls and a strong revival, Jerusalem had a problem: It was basically a ghost town. Only 50,000 or so had returned over the three different journeys from Babylon, and more of them lived outside of the city walls, in little towns and villages around Judah, than inside. Nehemiah faced the question, What do you do when you rebuild an amazing city and no one moves in? His solution was unusual but effective: a tithe of the people. One out of every ten people was called to live in Jerusalem (Nehemiah 11:1). The leaders already resided there, but everyone else cast lots to see who would relocate to the city.

The next couple of chapters list those families, inside Jerusalem and outside, and the priests and Levites who returned. Finally, the culmination of all their work, the service dedicating Jerusalem's walls, took place, with a strong emphasis on joyful praise. These returned and revived Jews were at a great point in their relationship with God, and they were unashamed to praise Him (Nehemiah 12:27). In this passage, singing is mentioned eight times, thanksgiving six times, rejoicing seven times, and musical instruments three times. There were choirs on the walls, musicians at the gates, and singers at the temple, "so that the joy of Jerusalem was heard afar off" (v. 43). It was party time in the holy city!

The last thing Nehemiah addressed in the book is a trio of problems (Nehemiah 13). First, the Levites had not been adequately supported by the people, as the Bible required. Second, people were breaking the Sabbath, working and selling stuff when they were supposed to be resting. Third, Jews were still marrying foreigners in the land, to the extent that half their kids couldn't even speak Hebrew. Each one of these issues had presented a huge problem for Israel in the past; each was a key factor leading to the captivity from which they had just returned. Nehemiah took each problem head on, and as he did, he prayed the same prayer: "Remember me, O my God" (vv. 14, 22, 31). He wanted God to keep in mind the good he had done in reestablishing the defenses, devotion, and denizens of Jerusalem, God's special city.

ESTHER
FLIGHT PLAN

Facts

Author

This book is named after its chief character, not its unknown author. Some speculate that Ezra or Nehemiah wrote it, due to its close association with those books. However, Esther's point of view is clearly that of a Persian Jew, as we see in the detailed knowledge of life in the Persian royal court and the pro-Jewish attitude throughout the story, leading many to ascribe authorship to Mordecai, a relative of Esther.

Date Written

The book of Esther took place after the Jewish exiles returned to Jerusalem, covering roughly a ten-year period that some scholars pin between 483 and 473 BC. If these dates are correct, then the book was likely written shortly after its events occurred, possibly around 460 BC. From the standpoint of biblical chronology, Esther may have been composed between Ezra chapters 6 and 7.

Landmarks

This flight in the book of Esther takes us eastward over the ancient Persian Empire. The purpose of this book was to record the institution of the Feast of Purim and the people's obligation to its perpetual observation. Throughout the history of the Jews to this day, Esther has been read at Purim to commemorate the great deliverance of the Jewish nation brought about by God through Esther.

The book of Esther reads like a cross between a fairy tale and mystery story. Brave and beautiful Esther is the fair maiden, so to speak, who becomes the queen of the kingdom of Persia. The villain Haman launches his attack to destroy her people, the Jews, but she—along with her kin, the hero Mordecai—thwarts his plot and risks her life to save her people. Esther's story begins with supernatural providence, sets up a satanic plot, and ends with God's sovereign protection.

Itinerary

- Supernatural Providence (Esther 1–2)
  - Wining and Dining
  - Whining and Denying
  - Winning and Designing
- Satanic Plotting (Esther 3–5)
  - Wrangling and Devising
  - Waiting and Daring
- Sovereign Protection (Esther 6–10)
  - Worsening and Divulging
  - Writing and Delivering

Gospel

Even in a book where God goes unmentioned, we can still see the strands of the scarlet thread of redemption. When God moves in human history, most of the time He moves through ordinary events, stringing them together in such a way that His will is ultimately done. He moves in many different ways through these everyday events, including *appearance* (creation of the universe and intermittent appearances through a theophany), *maintenance* (He keeps the universe running), *interference* (miracles that supersede natural law), and *providence* (His most common method of superintendence, weaving everyday events into the fabric of His perfect will).

John Nelson Darby put it this way: "God's ways are behind the scenes; but He moves all the scenes which He is behind."[14] God's work isn't always obvious, visible, or audible. Like Jesus said, the kingdom of God does not come through outward observation (Luke 17:20). So, though unmentioned, God's providential presence is all over the book of Esther, particularly in preserving His people and, through them, the line of the Messiah.

History

If the traditional time period attributed to the book of Esther is correct, then the events therein took place when Ahasuerus (better known by his Greek name, Xerxes), son of Darius I and father of Artaxerxes (the king who sent Nehemiah back to Jerusalem), was king of Persia (486–465 BC). At the opening of the book of Esther, Ahasuerus had recently lost a key naval battle to the Greeks at Salamis, followed by a defeat by combined Greek forces at Plataea, and had regrouped by settling in at his capital city, Shushan (also known as Susa). Shushan is where the majority of the events in Esther took place (Esther 1:2).

God never wastes a life dedicated to Him.

Travel Tips

The book of Esther shows the importance of developing the kind of character that God honors. Even when it may seem like God isn't watching, we should live in a way that shows the integrity of a heart seeking to honor Him, because what we say and do truly matters to Him. It may not be obvious how God is working in a given situation, but He is indeed at work.

- Esther caught the king's eye with her physical beauty, but she won his heart with her character. The character and integrity God will develop in us from the time we spend with Him will far outlast any physical beauty.

- As you work for God, seek His approval, not men's accolades. Mordecai helped thwart a plot to kill the king, but neither sought nor received recognition for a long time.

- God never wastes a life dedicated to Him. When you give your life to the Lord, He takes you at your word. He is faithful to mold and shape you, both in your heart and through the circumstances in which you find yourself.

In Flight

Supernatural Providence (Esther 1–2)

Israel had forgotten about God during the time of their exile and the events of the books of Ezra and Nehemiah, but God had not forgotten about them. The book of Esther shows His ongoing providence under the least likely circumstances and in a culture unsympathetic to Jewish interests.

Wining and Dining

Esther's story starts during Israel's exile in captivity. The Babylonians had conquered Judah, but had in turn been conquered by Persia (modern-day Iran). In the third year of his reign, King Ahasuerus threw a huge party, inviting all the upper crust of Persian society—nobles, princes, officials—and showing off his kingdom for half a year. He ruled 127 provinces and showed representatives from each of them a great time. In displaying his wealth and costly possessions, the king was trying to sell these guys on a war plan. The wining and dining was necessary because a new threat to the kingdom was rising in the west, under Philip II of Macedon.

Philip had united the regional warlords of Macedonia and Greece, building a strong military coalition that could threaten Persia's supremacy in the area. Philip's son, Alexander, would do just that, conquering Persia on his way to ruling the known world. Alexander would make Greek language and culture common throughout his empire, and build roads that the Romans would expand after him, setting the scene for the coming of God's Messiah and the expedient spread of the gospel. So while Ahasuerus was concerned about a burgeoning power to the west, God had a much bigger picture in mind.

After the six-month party ended, Ahasuerus threw party number two—a seven-day feast thanking all his palace officials for their help with the first party. His wife, Queen Vashti, threw her own party for the women in the palace—standard protocol in that culture. On the last day of his party, "when the heart of the king was merry with wine" (Esther 1:10), Ahasuerus sent for Vashti. In his inebriated condition, he wanted to parade his trophy wife around and show off her renowned beauty.

Vashti, however, wasn't having any of it. She refused to come, refused to obey the command of the guy who was so confident in his rule that he had just spent the last half-year partying. It's not clear exactly why she refused. Maybe she didn't want to cat-walk before her drunk husband and his cronies, or perhaps she was pregnant with little Artaxerxes and worn out from all the recent festivities. Whatever it was, she was willing to risk the king's wrath—and this was a guy with a reputation for getting hot under the collar. According to the historian Herodotus, Xerxes once had the Hellespont—a body of water in north Turkey separating Europe and Asia—whipped when a storm destroyed a bridge he'd built over it.[15] That's right—he exercised his royal prerogative to get mad at a strait. So Vashti had to have known she was taking her chances.

For his part, Ahasuerus got mad, but he was also confused about what to do. He had never faced feminism before, never had anyone say *no* to him. So he consulted a few of his princes, who gave him the following sage advice: "If the king's wife is doing that, women all over the empire will be disobeying and disrespecting their husbands. If you think Philip is trouble, just try a nation full of angry women. Take her crown, put her under house arrest, and send out an edict telling wives to do what their husbands tell them." The king and princes all liked the sound of that, so Ahasuerus sent out an edict and squashed the first women's liberation movement in the Persian Empire. Then something unexpected happened for the Persian king.

Whining and Denying

There is a gap between chapters 1 and 2, during which Ahasuerus, also called Xerxes, went out and fought a famous battle against the Greeks at Thermopylae. Even though Persia's troops eventually overwhelmed a much smaller Greek force, victory came at a high cost—20,000 of Persia's finest killed while the Spartan-led Greeks suffered the loss of 1000 soldiers. It was as humiliating as a victory could be, and it slowed Persia's mighty army down long enough for the Greeks to muster enough resistance to defeat Persia a few years later at Plataea. In between that expensive victory and the decisive defeat, Ahasuerus returned home to lick his wounds.[16]

"After these things, when the wrath of King Ahasuerus subsided, he remembered Vashti, what she had done, and what had been decreed against her" (Esther 2:1). He got lonely and needed a hug after losing to the Greeks. But he couldn't go back on his royal decree—it was against the law in Persia for a king to reverse his own edict. His valet came up with an idea: "Let's find you a new queen, your majesty. What you need is a virgin search—we'll round 'em up, clean 'em up, and you decide which one to give a thumb's up." And so Ahasuerus hosted the first recorded beauty contest.

Winning and Designing

It didn't take the king long to choose a winner. It was a dream opportunity for a lot of families and a huge crowd of young women gathered at the royal palace at Shushan. Mordecai, a Jew whose ancestors had been captured by the Babylonians when Jerusalem fell, brought his niece, whom he had raised after her parents' death, a young woman named Esther. Her Hebrew name was Hadassah (Esther 2:7), which means "myrtle." But she was known, and still is, by her Persian name, Esther, which means "star." And that she was—not just because of her beauty but also her character: "The king loved Esther more than all the other women, and she obtained grace and favor in his sight" (v. 17). So this new Hebrew star walked onto the Persian stage.

Esther was crowned as the new queen, and it's not a surprise that Ahasuerus threw a party and proclaimed a holiday. However, there were a couple of issues.

First, Mordecai had entered Esther into the contest, likely unaware that the Law of Moses forbade intermarriage with a pagan, even if said pagan was ruler of the known world. Remember, there's no mention of God in this book, no mention of prayer; pragmatism ruled the day.

The other issue was that no one in the palace knew Esther was a Jew. Before she entered the palace, Mordecai had told her to keep her heritage a secret. But, again, God was behind the scenes, designing His plan to protect His people. When the big reveal came, it was at a very providential time. And before then, God strategically positioned Mordecai to be of service to Esther's new husband.

Esther must have used her influence to get her uncle an official position at the palace, because we read that "Mordecai sat within the king's gate" (Esther 2:21)—an indication of his position of authority and clout. It was there that he overheard a plot against the king's life. He told Esther, who told Ahasuerus, who had an inquiry made, leading to the two conspirators' arrest and execution (vv. 21-23). Mordecai didn't get credit, at least not publicly, for his critical role in foiling the plot. But apparently he wasn't seeking it either, because no mention is made of him complaining. His concern as the king's servant was the king's safety, and he carried out his duty honorably.

Satanic Plotting (Esther 3–5)

We've met the good guys; now it's time to meet the villain of the story. "After these things King Ahasuerus promoted Haman"—insert ominous bad-guy theme—"the son of Hammedatha the Agagite, and advanced him and set his seat above all the princes who were with him" (Esther 3:1). The king told everyone to bow down before this guy Haman and praise him, but Mordecai wouldn't do either.

Wrangling and Devising

Haman hated Mordecai for not kissing up to him. But he didn't want just to get rid of Mordecai, whom he had found out was a Jew; he went ballistic and "sought to destroy all the Jews who were throughout the whole kingdom of Ahasuerus—the people of Mordecai" (Esther 3:6). If you thought Ahasuerus overreacted by getting rid of Vashti for not coming to his party, that was nothing. Haman went to the king and got him to write one of his famous edicts—this one condemning a group of people in the kingdom whom Haman didn't name but accused of having different laws and disobeying the king's laws. Haman even offered to pay a boatload of money to have them all killed. Ahasuerus not only agreed, he gave Haman his signet ring—his royal stamp of approval—to carry out the plan.

If that sounds fishy, remember that Ahasuerus was not at his best after his military struggles at Thermopylae. He was down and trying to figure out how to preserve his kingdom. That doesn't make him right, but it's not the craziest decision the guy ever made (whipping the Hellespont, anyone?). He had official letters sent out across all 127 of his provinces, instructing his governors to destroy every single Jew—man, woman, and child—on the same day. "Oh, and steal all their stuff too," he added (Esther 3:8-14).

This was nothing less than legalized anti-Semitism. And it's easy to see Satan's hand in this plot too. If Haman were to be successful, it would change the course of redemptive history. If God's plan of salvation depended on the existence of a people group—through the Jew would come the Bible and the Messiah—then to eliminate that group would thwart God's plan. I will say, though, that's a big *if*. God isn't easily thwarted.

Waiting and Daring

Mordecai heard the news and viscerally reacted, tearing his clothes, putting on sackcloth in mourning, and crying out. He stopped coming to the palace, and Esther had to send a servant to find him and see what the deal was. When it turned out to be a very big deal, she expressed her reticence to barge into the king's presence to protest his decision because it could cost her her life. Mordecai reminded Esther of her own roots, saying that her being queen wouldn't save her from sharing the fate of the rest of the Jews. He hinted at God's providence: "If you remain completely silent at this time, relief and deliverance will arise for the Jews from another place, but you and your father's house will perish" (Esther 4:14).

Then, however, Mordecai offered a note of encouragement: "Yet who knows whether you have come to the kingdom for such a time as this?" (v. 14). In other words, maybe God made her queen so she could be in a position to save her people—and thwart Haman's evil scheme. Esther appears to have taken that idea to heart, because she responded to her uncle with strong conviction. She told Mordecai to get all the Jews together and fast and pray for her. "And so," Esther said, "I will go to the king, which is against the law; and if I perish, I perish!" (v. 16). It was Persian law that one didn't just go visit the king on a whim. If you showed up uninvited, you were at the mercy of the king's golden scepter. If he held it up, you could approach him; if he didn't, you were just taken out and beheaded. Esther hadn't gone to see the king in a month, but too much was at stake. If she said nothing and was discovered to be a Jew, she'd be killed on the specified day, but if she didn't see the scepter, she'd be executed immediately. The way Esther saw it, she was dead either way, so she went for broke. And once again, God was moving the players on His chessboard into position.

Esther went to the king and "found favor in his sight" (Esther 5:2). He held up the scepter and asked her, "Tell me what you want, Queen Esther—name it and it's yours. Half the kingdom? No problem!" Instead, Esther asked for a dinner party— just him, her, and Haman. She found Ahasuerus's sweet spot—a good time. He sent a servant to go grab Haman, and they went to Esther's banquet. That night, the king offered her up to half the kingdom again, but Esther just asked for his and Haman's attendance at another dinner the next night.

The next day, Haman was walking around town, feeling pretty special—until he saw Mordecai. *I hate that guy*, he thought, and it ruined his whole afternoon. He went home and bragged to his wife about being the only one beside the king invited to Esther's party, and then complained about Mordecai. His wife gave him some really warped Agagite advice: "Honey, why don't you build a seventy-five-foot tall gallows and ask the king to hang Mordecai on it—then go and have a nice time at your dinner!" The points she got for being a supportive wife were canceled out by her suggestion of a public execution for someone her husband didn't like.

Haman had the gallows made, probably on a public building or city wall to get the desired height. Also interesting is that the Hebrew word translated "gallows" can be translated as "a stake," which implies the impaling of the victim—a form of crucifixion, in other words. It could be that Haman planned to impale or crucify Mordecai. Though the Romans would later perfect crucifixion as a method of execution, the Persians invented it.

Sovereign Protection (Esther 6–10)

Even though the satanic plot was in place, God was still orchestrating matters providentially. The night of Esther's first banquet, the king had insomnia. He had some kingdom records brought to him—legal briefs, court records, board minutes—the perfect remedy for sleeplessness. As the servants read, they came to the account of how Mordecai had saved the king's life awhile back. Ahasuerus asked, "What honor or dignity has been bestowed on Mordecai for this?" (Esther 6:3). When they told him that nothing had been done, he called for whatever officer was available in the court. Haman just happened to be there, on his way to ask the king to execute Mordecai. Ahasuerus summoned him and asked him what he thought the king should do to honor someone—not Mordecai specifically, but just a theoretical person whom the king wanted to recognize.

Haman, of course, thought the king was talking about him, so he came up with a big public parade, dressing the honoree up in a royal robe the king had worn, on a horse the king had ridden, led around the city square by one of the princes, giving him a big shout-out as he went. "Great idea!" said Ahasuerus. "See that all of that gets done for Mordecai the Jew!" At that moment, Haman probably would have tipped over in the slightest breeze. The blood drained from his face, and he slunk home until dinnertime.

Worsening and Divulging

Haman's day took a fatal turn at dinner. He and King Ahasuerus showed up for Esther's second banquet, and over wine, the king asked his wife to tell him her petition. "Anything you want, up to half the kingdom!" Picture the scene: The king didn't know Esther was Jewish, and neither did Haman. She was about to drop the bomb. Esther asked for her life and the life of her people. "For we have been sold, my people and I, to be destroyed, to be killed, and to be annihilated" (Esther 7:4).

The king immediately asked who the scoundrel behind this was, and Esther answered, "The advisory and enemy is this wicked Haman!" (Esther 7:6). Haman had planned and schemed genocide over a bruised ego, but after all of his moves were made, God moved His queen into place on the board and said, "Checkmate." Haman was left begging Esther for his life while the king stormed out into the garden to process what he'd just heard.

It only got worse when Ahasuerus returned, because he found Haman sprawled across the couch where Esther was sitting, pleading for mercy. The king said, "Is this guy also trying to make a pass at my wife, the queen?" He had Haman arrested on the spot, and while he was trying to figure out what do with him, one of his servants helpfully said, "Hey, there's the gallows Haman made for Mordecai!" They hanged Haman—or impaled him; either way, it wasn't pretty. And then "the king's wrath subsided" (v. 10). Maybe not as satisfying as flogging the ocean, but definitely more significant in avoiding genocide.

Writing and Delivering

The satanic plotter was dead, but there was still a problem: The king's irreversible edict had gone out to all 127 of his provinces. Everyone was under orders to kill any Jews they found on that certain day, perhaps still expecting to get paid for it. Esther, realizing this, went to Ahasuerus and begged him, weeping, to undo the evil Haman had caused (Esther 8:3). The king showed her the golden scepter again—which also indicates that she spoke to him again at great risk to herself, at least legally—and he gave his signet ring to Mordecai. He told him, "Write your own decree to save your people and seal it with my ring." In other words, "You write the order, and I'll sign it!"

Mordecai dictated a letter to the royal scribes, who then carried it across the empire on the king's fastest horses, getting the message out and averting a holocaust. Jews everywhere threw a huge feast, and a lot of people even converted to Judaism "because fear of the Jews fell upon them" (Esther 8:17). Think about that: This was Persia—modern-day Iran—and a whole bunch of natives became Jews. That's monumental all by itself, but it turned out that it also saved them, because on the big day when the Jews had originally been scheduled for extermination, the tables were turned and the Jews "overpowered those who hated them" (Esther 9:1).

Mordecai was placed into Haman's post, wielding a level of power and authority second only to the king (Esther 10:3), and all the officials, fearing him, turned on the Jews' enemies, killing 500 men in the capital at Shushan, including the ten sons of Haman. It got pretty intense, and the Jews were given permission across the empire to defend themselves against those who would have killed them; they killed 75,000 enemies (Esther 9:16). With Esther's royal approval, Mordecai made it an official holiday for the Jews, the feast of Purim, which they were to observe at that time each year "as the days on which the Jews had rest from their enemies, as the month which was turned from sorrow to joy for them, and from mourning to a holiday" (v. 22).

No matter how Satan arranges his plan and pieces, the board will always ultimately belong to God.

Even at a point in their history when God had exiled the Jews to a foreign land and they weren't seeking Him or calling on Him by name, He still sovereignly protected them and delivered them from their enemies. God was keeping His promise to extend the life of the nation through which the Messiah would come, and no matter how Satan arranges his plan and pieces, the board will always ultimately belong to God.

JOB

Facts

Author

Though the author (or compiler) of the book of Job is unidentified, most scholars think that it was a Jew who was familiar with Job's story and the circumstances that befell him and his family, possibly Solomon or Ezra. If it was written early in the history of the Jews, Moses or even Job himself are good candidates for authorship. If Moses was the author, it's possible he wrote the book after first hearing an oral account of Job from his father-in-law, Jethro, during his time in Midian.

Date Written

Like the author of Job, the date of the book's composition is unknown. Some of the words and terms used in the book lead some scholars to believe it was written in the Iron Age, sometime after 1200 BC and around the time of Solomon's reign. However, other terms used in the book point to an earlier date. Though the exact date of its writing may never be known, many scholars believe Job is the oldest book in the Bible.

Landmarks

Even from 30,000 feet, the book of Job is still bumpy terrain, with pivotal peaks of trust in between death-shrouded valleys of doubt. Job's is a story of suffering that asks two of the hardest questions in the world: First, why do good people suffer? God called Job "a blameless and upright man, one who fears God and shuns evil" (Job 1:8)—but God allowed some horrible things to happen to this godly man.

That fact leads into the second question: How can a good and loving God allow such horrible suffering in the world? It's an age-old issue, and a whole topic of discussion that philosophers and theologians call *theodicy*. We all ask at some point how to reconcile a loving God and a suffering world—because you don't have to go to seminary to know what it is to suffer. We can all identify with Job on some level. From our broad angle, we're looking at the spiritual division of

Job's story: his physical malady, the spiritual reality, his mental agony, and the ultimate victory.

Itinerary

- Physical Malady (Job 1–2)
- Spiritual Reality (Job 1–2)
- Mental Agony (Job 3–37)
- Ultimate Victory (Job 38–42)

Gospel

Job preached the first Easter message thousands of years before it happened (Job 19:25-27). Essentially he said, "Even though I know that I'm going to die—and it's pretty evident that soon I will die—I also know that I'm going to live." But how can you live if you die? The answer is resurrection. When Job said, "I know that my Redeemer lives" (v. 25), he was anticipating God's Messiah. With those prophetic words, Job pierced through the seemingly impenetrable veil of death and saw a future full of the promise of immortality—of everlasting life. He believed he was going to die, yet he knew he was going to live. If you're looking for Jesus Christ in the book of Job, there He is—a suffering man who was able to look ahead to a living Redeemer who would suffer to guarantee Job's own resurrection. How's that for redemption's scarlet thread?

History

Because the time period in which Job took place is unclear, we don't have a thorough understanding of what was going on in the larger world at the time. We know that Job lived in the land of Uz, which was located somewhere in northern Arabia, possibly near the Euphrates River by the city of Damascus (the Dead Sea Scrolls—one of the oldest biblical documents—refer to Uz being "beyond the Euphrates"). Genesis 10:23 states that a man named Uz was the son of Aram, a grandson of Shem, Noah's son. We also know that Job was a wealthy and respected leader in his community, and that he lived to a ripe old age. He most likely orally communicated his story to the next generation, who eventually passed that story down to Moses and others.

Travel Tips

This book takes us through the whirlwind of Job's troubles: his physical malady, the spiritual reality behind his suffering, his mental agony from wrestling with the why of suffering, and his eventual victory as he discovered that God uses suffering for purposes he could never understand but could still accept by faith.

- Suffering sometimes makes us feel like divine playthings, and it can be unnerving. On earth, we often feel like we're center stage, but on heaven's greater stage, we're not. That doesn't mean God doesn't care about you; it just means He is keeping a bigger picture in mind as He allows certain things to happen in your life.

- It's one thing to say that God gives and takes away, but can you also say, as Job did, "Blessed be the name of the Lord" (Job 1:21)? Faith is not primarily about certainty, but trust.

Faith is not primarily about certainty, but trust.

- Walk softly around a broken heart. When someone has experienced a loss or is going through a trial, be tender and careful. It's a valuable ministry just to sit and commiserate with a wounded soul.

- Suffering is real and should be grieved and attended to. However, not everything that hurts is bad. Think of Jesus being beaten and crucified to pay the price for your sins. Rather than getting stuck on what you don't understand about God, camp out on what you know to be true about your good, loving, gracious, all-knowing, all-powerful, always-present Father in heaven.

In Flight

Physical Malady (Job 1–2)

Faith is never tested more than when suffering interrupts a life that's going well. God had blessed Job with seven sons and three daughters; thousands of sheep, oxen, camels, and donkeys; and a household full of servants. He honored God, sacrificing to Him both for sins he knew of and ones he didn't, taking no chances that his children's sins would go unatoned. Job was honored and admired throughout the region—and most importantly, by God Himself. That alone made him a target for God's enemy. Unbeknownst to Job, God gave Satan permission to ruin his life. God didn't ask Job if it was okay to do so, didn't give him a heads up. Suddenly, Job's life was in tatters, and while we know that the devil did it, Job didn't.

Once unleashed, Satan didn't waste any time. While we don't see Satan striking Job directly, he orchestrated four rapid-fire disasters to fall on Job and his family: raiders stole his oxen and donkeys and killed his servants, lightning struck his sheep and shepherds, Babylonians stole his camels and slaughtered the drivers, and a tornado flattened the house where all of his children had gathered for a party. Only four servants were left, one to report each of the catastrophes.

What was Job's response after all this? Remarkably, "he fell to the ground and worshiped" (Job 1:20). We are told that "in all this Job did not sin or charge God with wrong" (v. 22).

When Satan came before God to give his next report, God asked him, "How do you like my friend Job now?" Satan said, "He hasn't cursed you because you haven't let me touch him physically." God gave Satan another crack at breaking Job, and Satan afflicted him with a physical malady.

Pulling together a few verses creates a composite of Job's condition. First, he had inflamed lesions that caused intense itching, which he scratched with a piece of broken pottery (Job 2:8). Second, those lacerations in his skin must have attracted maggots: "My flesh is caked with worms and dust, my skin is cracked and breaks out afresh" (Job 7:5). Third, Job developed some sort of osteopathy: "My bones are pierced in me at night, and my gnawing pains take no rest" (Job 30:17). Fourth, his skin blackened and fell off in patches (Job 30:30). Finally, add on top of all that night terrors—horrific dreams and visions driven by the maddening physical pain (Job 7:14-15). The entire picture is of a man afflicted by the unleashed powers of hell. It would have been like enduring a personal version of the Great Tribulation. And just as in that coming conflict, there was more going on than met the eye.

Spiritual Reality (Job 1–2)

On the flip side of physical reality is the spiritual realm. This unseen reality is every bit as active and important as the world we can see. It's crucial to realize that when troubles arise. Sometimes God calms the storm for us, and we love it when He does. Other times, though, God calms us in the storm, as He did here with Job, anchoring him so that Job was able to wholeheartedly bless God's name in spite of his pain and turmoil.

How you feel about God in your darkest hour of suffering is how you really feel about God. Job knew what happened, but not why. He knew nothing of God's interactions with Satan in heaven; he didn't know how highly God thought of him—that God held him up as an example of integrity matched in the Bible only by Noah and Daniel (Ezekiel 14:14; James 5:11).

How you feel about God in your darkest hour of suffering is how you really feel about God.

Here's why Job's story is so unsettling: One minute, he was safe, comfortable, blessed with family, trusting God, blameless, upright. The next moment, he lost it all. The sudden shock of his suffering is unnerving because his story could be ours. Suffering among God's people is a common enough theme in the Bible, but there's no escaping its impact when you read Job. There's no avoiding the fact that trusting in Jesus Christ does not exempt you from suffering. But there's that unseen spiritual reality behind the suffering.

The opening of the book of Job goes behind the scenes, behind the curtain of what we can physically perceive, to the spiritual reality of heaven. There, in God's throne room, the *ben Elohim*—the sons of God, the angels—gave an account of themselves to God (Job 1:6-7). Satan was among them, unexpectedly to us perhaps, but not to God, and God asked him, "Where have you been lately?" Satan knew there was no point in lying to God, so he replied, "Hanging out on earth, going all over the place." This brief interaction offers two important facts about the devil: one, he is accountable to God; and two, he is not omnipresent—he can't be everywhere at once.

God then asked Satan if, during his roaming, he had seen Job, a God-fearing man of integrity—"There's no one like him on earth," God said. Satan, true to form, rebutted God, saying, "Sure, You've given him everything anyone could want—a full household, career success, and material wealth. Take it all away and see if he still honors You." God then gave Satan permission to destroy all He had given Job, but not to touch Job himself. Right away, we have information and a perspective that Job does not. We're privy to these scenes, but Job was just living his life, trying to honor God and do right by his family and employees.

Satan's accusation was that Job was a mercenary—that he honored God only because God had blessed him. Strip that away, Satan said, and the guy will curse You to Your face. God, however, seemed confident in Job's faithfulness, because He gave Satan leeway to strike Job. That's a third thing about Satan: He can only attack God's people with God's permission. Job was at the center of a celestial controversy over his faith.

Satan is an expert people-watcher. He and his minions study us, pulling out the same bag of tricks every time because they're so effective in every generation. Note that God asked Satan, "Have you considered My servant Job?" (Job 1:8). "Considered" means "to study," like a military general would study how best to attack an opponent. And it's better translated not as a question but a statement: "You have been studying My servant Job." God knew that Satan had been scrutinizing Job, had seen this righteous man and targeted him. It's similar to when Jesus told Peter that Satan had asked to sift him like wheat—to see what he was really made of (Luke 22:31).

It's a pretty frightening thought, isn't it, that the devil has studied you? Jesus told Peter, "I have prayed for you, that your faith should not fail; and when you have returned to Me, strengthen your brethren" (v. 32). That's spiritual warfare, though: Satan sees us representing God well and wants to destroy us, but we have Jesus praying for us, speaking directly into God's ear from His seat at the Father's right hand (Romans 8:34).

But while the devil is powerful, with an insidious and enormous intellect driving his wicked agenda, he is on a leash. When he came before God and asked to harm Job, God said, "Yes, but only to this extent." And when Satan returned to ask again, God limited him again. And while he has been against you your whole life, any suffering God allows him to inflict won't last forever. God always keeps His eye on you, especially in hard times. He doesn't let Satan stick you in the oven, and then go on vacation and leave you baking.

And whatever circumstances Satan is using to bake you, they are common to all of us. At some point, we all face disease, decay, and death. We all struggle with various temptations to sin. But God is still in control. As Paul wrote, "God is faithful, who will not allow you to be tempted beyond what you are able, but with the temptation will also make the way of escape, that you may be able to bear it" (1 Corinthians 10:13). Now, that doesn't mean that God will bring a loved one back to life or heal you from every disease. He will, however, strengthen you when you turn to Him. He will mature your faith, and help you shine in the darkness of your suffering as a witness to His eternal grace. That seems like small potatoes at times, but the pain of this life is temporary compared to the eternal stakes.

It's human nature to focus on what's directly in front of us and miss the bigger picture, which for the believer should always include the spiritual realm. Job's wife, for example, couldn't look past her grief, so when she saw her husband scraping his boils in the ash heap, she got angry and said, "Do you still hold fast to your integrity? Curse God and die!" (Job 2:9). It's easy to say, "Wow, thanks for the great, godly counsel, Mrs. Job," but notice Job's response: "'You speak as one of the foolish women speaks. Shall we indeed accept good from God, and shall we not accept adversity?' In all this, Job did not sin with his lips" (v. 10). He kept God's will and purposes in mind, even if he didn't understand the way they were playing out.

Job loved God more than all that God had given him. That doesn't mean Job didn't have some questions, that he didn't get frustrated, that he wasn't deeply hurt and grieved by all he'd lost. "Job arose, tore his robe, and shaved his head; and he fell to the ground and worshiped" (v. 20). The first part of that was expected—cultural signs of deep grief and lamentation. He hated what he was experiencing. But the second part is remarkable: Job worshipped. "Naked I came from my mother's womb, and naked I shall return there. The LORD gave, and the LORD has taken away; blessed be the name of the LORD. In all this Job did not sin nor charge God with wrong" (vv. 21-22).

Job's spiritual perspective is a good reminder when we look at the world around us and wonder what's going on. *Why can't Israel and Palestine sort out their mess? Why can't we have political candidates who espouse godly values? Why is my boss such a terrible person?* Remember, there is always something going on behind the curtain, beyond what we can see, and it's spiritual in nature. Recognizing that there is a spiritual reality is just the beginning, though. Seeking God is critical, but it only helps us frame the battle from a biblical point of view. We still have to keep on trusting Him as we go through the hardship, and even with His peace guarding us, it's not easy.

Mental Agony (Job 3–37)

When you're suffering in an obvious and visible way, as Job was, people will wonder what's going on. Some of them might even wonder if God is judging you for something. So on top of whatever you're going through, you might have others Monday-morning-quarterbacking why you're going through it. That's what happened to Job when his so-called friends showed up, supposedly to comfort him. It ended up as mental agony for Job.

Job's three friends—Eliphaz the Temanite, Bildad the Shuhite, and Zophar the Naamathite—heard about his hardship and "came to mourn with him, and to comfort him" (Job 2:11). I quoted that last part because I want you to see that they got off to a good start. They came and wept and did the whole robe-tearing and ash-sprinkling-on-the-head thing to show their sympathy, and they just hung out with him for a week, saying nothing, "for they saw that his grief was very great"

(v. 13). Actually, all of that is beautiful; they practiced the silent ministry of presence—just being there and grieving quietly with their friend. They should've quit while they were ahead!

Initially, Job's friends understood that someone who is suffering doesn't need a sermon on theodicy, or a pep talk about heaven. They just hung out and mourned with him. And when Job finally spoke up and vented some of his grief, expressing his sorrow and the full realization of his worst fears (Job 3), they should have kept quiet. The problem started when they broke the silence and went into speech mode.

Eliphaz got the ball rolling for what turned into a two-dozen-chapter-long discourse, each of the visitors giving his take on Job's agony, and Job rebutting it. Eliphaz was a Temanite, a people known for their wisdom. He was probably the eldest of the three, and his commentary is a bit more tempered and balanced than his friends' speeches (Job 4–14)—but just a bit. Basically, he said, "Job, you have sinned somewhere along the line and God is punishing you." And that's the softest approach of the three.

When Eliphaz asked, "Who ever perished being innocent? Or where were the upright ever cut off?" (Job 4:7), he was touching on the false notion that if you are truly godly and faithful, you'll never suffer. He went on for two chapters about how Job's affliction could only have resulted from his own sins. Finally, Job responded, saying in part, "Even if I had sinned, brother, shouldn't you be comforting me instead of accusing me of something you're not even sure is true?" (Job 6:14).

Then Bildad weighed in, offering a gentle critique in which he called Job a blowhard and said the reason his kids had died is because they sinned (Job 8:1-4). Job's retort asked God to reveal His reasons: "Does it seem good to You that You should oppress, that You should despise the work of Your hands, and smile on the counsel of the wicked?" (Job 10:2-3). He got a little feisty with God—not uncommon for someone in his situation. Job was addressing God but telling Bildad, "You don't know what I'm feeling, but you're judging me and my family anyway."

Friend number three, Zophar, then did what many knowledgeable Christians would be tempted to do but shouldn't under the circumstances—correct Job's theology (Job 11:14-15). The gist of his take was, "Repent, Job; change your thinking and your ways and you'll have nothing to fear from God." He wasn't wrong theologically, but he made things even worse for his friend. Job already had the devil after him, trying to break him; he didn't need his friends piling on too.

Job reached a breaking point and let his visitors have it: "You are all worthless physicians...Your platitudes are proverbs of ashes, your defenses are defenses of clay. Hold your peace with me, and let me speak, then let come on me what may!"

(Job 13:4, 12-13). God had already allowed so much to happen, and even though Job wasn't going to question God, he wasn't going to put up with his friends' accusations, either. After all, what did he have to lose?

His next statement is one of the highlights of the book: "Though He slay me, yet will I trust Him. Even so, I will defend my ways before Him. He also shall be my salvation, for a hypocrite could not come before Him" (vv. 15-16). What a great stance to take: "If I lose it all but I have God, that's all I need. He can do what He wants with me, even if I'm innocent—which, by the way, guys, I am."

What a transforming thought! Job understood that what was hidden from his eyes was not hidden from God's; furthermore, He knows everything and He is in control. "I cannot perceive Him...I cannot behold Him...But He knows the way that I take; when He has tested me, I shall come forth as gold" (Job 23:8-10). To get your heart around that is to revolutionize your times of pain and darkness. You won't understand all that God is doing, but you know He has His eye on you, and that somewhere in all of it are His purposes, driven by His will and goodness and righteousness.

Job's response to the accusing, worldly voices of his friends left Satan with nothing to say on his next visit to heaven. God won the wager, as Job proved that God can be worshipped apart from His gifts. Job was left with nothing but God, yet he continued to follow and trust God. Whether God blessed him or buffeted him didn't matter, because he knew that one day he would die and stand before his God, resurrected (Job 19:25). Finally, everyone exhausted their supply of hot air, and that's when God stepped in.

Ultimate Victory (Job 38–42)

God must have been waiting backstage for the right time to step in and straighten these guys out. When He did, though, He didn't just part the invisible veil and appear; He spoke from the middle of a huge storm (Job 38:1-3), an awesome display of power. He addressed Job directly, ended the debate, and in the end, restored Job.

Job had been seeking an audience with God, and he got one. However, his claim that he would lay his questions and arguments before God never materialized. God made it clear from the outset that Job (and certainly the others, as well) were "darkening counsel" with all their foolish words (Job 38:2). The absurdity of the creature criticizing the Creator was quickly impressed on all of them— both the vain fist-shaking and the holier-than-thou defense of God's righteousness. As the ultimate stage manager, God told Job, "You see the play, but you have no clue what's going on backstage."

A simple science quiz served to make God's point, two chapters of simple questions about the natural world—biology and physics and astronomy—questions that scientists have mostly answered by now, but here's the point: God set all of that in motion. Birds and light and wind—they all came from the mind of God. Developing an understanding of how they work means very little when you consider their origins and design. God made everything and maintains it; He reserves the right to remind us when necessary.

> **God made everything and maintains it; He reserves the right to remind us when necessary.**

Imagine a bear caught in a trap. Its captor, a research scientist, intends to free the bear once he culls the information he wants. But the bear doesn't know that's what the scientist is thinking. The bear becomes frantic and fearful, supposing this stranger is a harmful aggressor. The scientist must tranquilize the beast to calm him enough to release him. The tranquilizing dart serves only to further agitate the bear, which uses every bit of strength to counteract the scientist's will. Smokey isn't thinking, *What a good and helpful man this is*, but *He's trying to kill me!* The bear can't grasp the man's compassion, kindness, and care any more than we can understand God's.[17]

Job got the point. The thrust of God's argument was, "Job, if you can't understand the way of things in the physical world, how can you understand the spiritual realm, which you can't even see?" Job humbled himself, recognizing his place before his Creator: "I know that You can do everything, and that no purpose of Yours can be withheld from You...I have uttered what I did not understand, things too wonderful for me, which I did not know" (Job 42:2-3).

God then had a few choice words for Job's friends. He sent them to go make burnt offerings, "and My servant Job shall pray for you. For I will accept him, lest I deal with you according to your folly" (Job 42:8). They hustled off to take care of their business, and "the LORD restored Job's losses when he prayed for his friends. Indeed the LORD gave Job twice as much as he had before" (v. 10). God gave Job the chance to forgive his friends, and then his family came and comforted him. Eventually, he had ten more kids and twice as much livestock as he'd owned previously. Job lived another 140 years, saw four generations of grandchildren, and "died, old and full of days" (v. 17).

> **Suffering in the hands of an all-powerful and absolutely loving God can be a wonderful tool for us, giving perspective to our grief and hard times.**

It was a good way to go, blessed in his old age, but Job died with the scars of that difficult time in his life. The notion that suffering in the hands of an all-powerful and absolutely loving God can be a wonderful tool for us, giving perspective to our grief and hard times. In fact, God consistently makes something good come out of really bad things. And the times we don't see the good, we can still trust that God is still at work. That's faith.

PSALMS
FLIGHT PLAN

Author

The book of Psalms is a collection of songs, prayers, and poetry written by many authors. Of the 150 psalms, seventy-three are attributed to the poet and musician King David. Other psalms were written by Asaph (twelve), the Korahites (twelve), King Solomon (two), Moses (one), Heman (one), Hezekiah (one), and Ethan (one). The remaining psalms are anonymous.

Date Written

The Psalms were written and compiled over a 1000-year period, beginning with Moses (around 1450 BC) and ending with the Jewish captivity in Babylon (around 585 BC). The Psalms were most likely collected during the time of Ezra.

L**andmarks**

In this flight, we cruise over the book of Psalms, a collection of songs, prayers, and poetry expressing the deepest human emotions. It is an intersection where two dimensions transect: the horizontal (earthly experience) and vertical (heavenly expectation). It is a record of the prayers, praises, and protests of God's people. Not only do the Psalms contain more chapters than any other book in the Bible, but these chapters are among the best-known and best-loved in the Old Testament. During the kingdom period, which began with the reign of King David, the Psalms were used as the temple hymnbook. They can be classified into ten different types, including messianic, historical, and hallelujah psalms.

The Psalms are filled with lyrics that reflect almost every human experience and emotion on the spectrum. From the greatest sorrow and depression to the most thrilling expressions of joy and gladness, one theme in the book is constant: a complete dependence on the love and power of God. The Psalms are divided into five sections, which reflect the themes of the first five books of the Bible: relationship with God (Genesis), God's deliverance (Exodus), the sanctuary of God (Leviticus), the steep price of rebelling against God (Numbers), and the renewal of spirit God's Word brings (Deuteronomy).

Itinerary

- Songs of Relationship (Psalms 1–41)
- Songs of Redemption (Psalms 42–72)
- Songs of Refuge (Psalms 73–89)
- Songs of Rebellion's Cost (Psalms 90–106)
- Songs of Revival (Psalms 107–150)

Gospel

The book of Psalms plays an integral role in the grand unfolding of the gospel story. Jesus quoted the Psalms eleven times—more than any other book of the Bible. Furthermore, there are seventeen messianic psalms that predicted the Messiah's birth, life, death, burial, resurrection, second coming, universal reign, and glories of His kingdom, among other things.

How incredible that Jesus Christ was foretold, described, and honored in the book that Israel used for worship in the temple—a collection of songs from very different authors who expressed a myriad of emotions over a long period of time. For reference, the following psalms are considered messianic: 2, 8, 16, 22, 23, 24, 40, 41, 45, 68, 69, 72, 89, 102, 110, 116, and 118.

History

Though the book of Psalms was written over a period of about 1000 years, the individual songs refer to time periods that range from creation to consummation—from the beginning of time to the end. The authors of the psalms praised God for His creative acts, recalled the history of His people Israel, cried out for help and deliverance from their present enemies, and foretold the coming Messiah and the end of the age. The book of Psalms is truly universal in scope.

The Psalms give us a model for honest interaction with God.

Travel Tips

The book of Psalms speaks honestly about humanity's struggles with faith, doubt, God's presence in hard times, and physical and emotional suffering. That's why it's been such a comfort to God's people for thousands of years. Furthermore, the Psalms give us a model for honest interaction with God.

- When you talk to God, you can—and should—be honest. This is because, first of all, you can't fool Him. But second, He can handle it. He knows your heart and what you're going through, so tell Him the things you can't tell anyone else.

- Anchor yourself to God through His Word. Psalms 1 and 119 emphasize over and over the value and importance of knowing God's character and ways through Scripture—like a daily meal you can't afford to skip.

- Read through the Psalms and you'll discover consistency. God was brought into every area of life, everything a person goes through, and somehow it was all related to the praise and worship of God. The psalmists did not relegate their worship of God—their honoring of His value and holiness—to a once-a-week experience. They didn't separate their church life from their social life or their work life. For them, all of life was beautifully integrated and brought under submission to God.

- You can pour anything on your heart into the ears of God. Think of Psalm 59. Transparency before God is all part of viewing the ups and downs of human existence through the lens of faith.

- The Psalms are realistic. Just because you are a believer doesn't mean you are not going to go through very dark valleys of the shadow of death, deep times of depression or hardship. To read many of the psalms is to watch the psalmist say in various ways at various times, "I want to crawl under a rock right now, but God is still in control and I will praise Him." We should always come back to God's greatness and faithfulness, depending on Him in all circumstances.

You can pour anything on your heart into the ears of God.

In Flight

Songs of Relationship (Psalms 1–41)

Psalm 1: Rooted in God

Psalm 1 taps a rich vein of theology that runs throughout the book—in this case, the doctrine of God's blessings on His obedient children. For the person who takes pleasure in reading and thinking about God's law, there is the promise that they "shall be like a tree planted by the rivers of water, that brings forth its fruit in its season, whose leaf also shall not wither; and whatever [they do] shall prosper" (Psalm 1:3). By contrast, those who do not follow God have a bad life with a bad ending—and God knows the difference between who follows Him sincerely and who doesn't (v. 6). It sets the tone for the whole collection.

Psalm 2: A Foolish Rebellion

If Psalm 1 is anthropocentric—centered on man's response to God—then Psalm 2 is theocentric, focusing on God's response to mankind's rebellious ways, which is to provide a means of reconciliation—the Messiah, Jesus Christ. Psalm 2 is the first of a large group that we call messianic psalms. God has had His plan of redemption in play since before the world began, so it shouldn't be surprising that so much of the Old Testament reflects the coming and future reign of the Messiah.

It reflects not mankind's general state of rebellion against God but a specific rebellion. "Why do the nations rage, and the people plot a vain thing? The kings of the earth set themselves, and the rulers take counsel together, against the Lord and His Anointed" (Psalm 2:1-2). "Anointed," in the original Hebrew text, is *mashiach*—the root of our word *Messiah*. In Greek, the word is translated *Christos*. So when the nations huddle up and plot to stand against God, they specifically rebel against Jesus Christ. It's not hard to imagine such a scenario today, where most people seem to be open to any kind of spirituality as long as it's not a serious interpretation of Christianity.

What is God's response? Well, He isn't hiding from this coalition of humanity's leaders, cringing in the corner, wondering, *Whatever will I do?* No, God laughs, scorning the foolishness of their plans, because ultimately, nothing can stand against His plan to redeem mankind (Psalm 2:4-5). The unknown psalmist referred to Christ's first coming—"Yet I have set My King on My holy hill of Zion…You are My Son, today I have begotten You" (vv. 6-7)—and His second coming—"I will give You the nations for Your inheritance, and the ends of the earth for Your possession. You shall break them with a rod of iron; you shall dash them to pieces like a potter's vessel" (vv. 8-9).

In light of those realities, the world's leaders are advised to "serve the LORD with fear, and rejoice with trembling. Kiss the Son, lest He be angry, and you perish in the way, when His wrath is kindled but a little. Blessed are all those who put their trust in Him" (vv. 11-12). This unnamed narrator was describing the work of the Holy Spirit—gently, patiently, and firmly pointing the way to peace with God through Jesus Christ.

Psalm 19: A Remarkable Work

One of David's best-known psalms, Psalm 19, is a great example of how God speaks through His general revelation—His creation. "The heavens declare the glory of God; and the firmament shows His handiwork. Day unto day utters speech, and night unto night reveals knowledge" (vv. 1-2). People often wonder these days why God is silent, but the things He made speak to all of us. These natural wonders tell us about power, beauty, balance, timing, consistence, and variety. If the art hanging in the skies can take our breath away, how much more remarkable is the Artist Himself!

> **People often wonder these days why God is silent, but the things He made speak to all of us.**

While the natural world points generally to God's glory, He is also revealed through His special revelation—His Word. David shifted from the wonders of the stars and sun to the majesty of God's Word: "The law of the LORD is perfect, converting the soul; the testimony of the LORD is sure, making wise the simple" (v. 7). He then went on to cover the amazing power of Scripture to transform our lives.

Here is the flow of the psalm: You are outside, checking out nature, and all of it reveals something about God, but it doesn't reveal enough. The heavens tell you about God's power and glory, but not His love. Constellations and comets are magnificent, but even more astonishing is the Creator's humility and sacrifice in sending His Son to pay for our sin—the thing that separates us from Him. To get that part of the story, you have to go to God's special revelation, the Bible, the words He inspired and spoke through men over a period of thousands of years.

Psalm 22: A Righteous Prophecy

Another of David's psalms was messianic, opening with a line familiar from New Testament accounts of Jesus's crucifixion. In the fourth of Jesus's seven famous sayings from the cross, He quoted Psalm 22:1: "My God, My God, why have You forsaken Me?" (Matthew 27:46; Mark 15:34). That's just the beginning of a remarkable prophetic declaration of the Messiah's suffering. Reading David's words, the scene at Golgotha comes clearly into view, Jesus's physical suffering and mental anguish over His separation from His Father:

> Why are You so far from helping Me, and from the words of My groaning?...All those who see Me ridicule Me; they shoot out the lip, they shake the head, saying, "He trusted in the LORD, let Him rescue Him; let Him deliver Him, since He delights in Him!"...I am poured out like water, and all My bones are out of joint...They pierced My hands and My feet; I can count all My bones...They divide My garments among them, and for My clothing they cast lots (Psalm 22:1, 7-8, 14, 16-18).

There's no episode in David's life that fits these agonized cries, no piece of Jewish history that parallels these particular struggles. In fact, it's a clearer description of Jesus's crucifixion than anything we find in the New Testament. It fits perfectly: Jesus's distress over being separated from the Father as He felt the separation caused by our sin laid on Him; the mocking He endured, the beatings and lashings administered—which lacerated His flesh but broke not a single bone; the piercing of the nails that fastened Him to the wooden pole and beam; the Roman soldiers throwing dice to see who would get His cloak. When David wrote this, crucifixion hadn't yet been invented, making the detailed description even more astonishing in its prophetic power.

Psalm 23: A Shepherd's Rod

The most famous psalm is also possibly the most misunderstood. Typically when you think of Psalm 23, it's being read at a funeral or when people are on the verge of death—because of the phrase "Yea, though I walk through the valley of the shadow of death" (v. 4). But it's actually a psalm about life, not death. After all, the psalmist is *walking* through the valley, not being carried by pallbearers. It's a description of living life in God's care, having a relationship in this life with the Great Shepherd.

The figure of speech, the picture of a shepherd caring for his flock, is one of the most beloved and biblical of all illustrations of how God's people relate to Him. Jesus employed the image to describe that relationship: "I am the good shepherd. The good shepherd gives His life for the sheep...I know My sheep, and am known by My own" (John 10:11, 14). Being an actual shepherd, David would have naturally loved this analogy. Because he had kept and protected sheep, David grasped the principle behind "The Lord is my shepherd" (Psalm 23:1), which is this: The quality of a sheep's life is directly proportional to the quality of the shepherd's care. A sheep with a lazy, careless shepherd is going to have a short, unhappy life. Sheep just aren't good at making it on their own. But a cautious, vigilant, loving shepherd is going to provide a sheep with a happy, well-fed, secure existence.

When David wrote that God was his shepherd, he was bragging, telling the other sheep, "Hey! Look how awesome my Shepherd is!" God leads His sheep to good grazing places, gives them times of refreshment near "still waters," guides them through danger and the tendency to wander, comforting them and providing for them, even amongst enemies and hard times. Best of all, in the end, He leads His sheep home, where we "will dwell in the house of the Lord forever" (v. 6).

Songs of Redemption (Psalms 42–72)
Psalms 32 and 51: The Relief of Confession

We see in the Psalms many of the ways that David was a man after God's own heart. That includes David's response to his own sins, in particular his adultery with Bathsheba and arrangement of her husband Uriah's murder (2 Samuel 11–12). He went a year without confessing these sins, until Nathan the prophet busted him. After that he wrote a pair of psalms about the matter, reflecting on the power of God's redemption.

Psalm 32 begins, "Blessed is he whose transgression is forgiven, whose sin is covered. Blessed is the man to whom the Lord does not impute iniquity, and in whose spirit there is no deceit" (vv. 1-2). After a year of keeping under wraps the terrible things he had done, David was so relieved to have them out in the open, to confess his sins and have God forgive him. "When I kept silent, my bones grew old through my groaning all the day long. For day and night Your hand was heavy upon me; my vitality was turned into the drought of summer" (vv. 3-4).

David hadn't gone around during that year of silence feeling like he'd gotten away with what he had done. He was distraught, sleepless, every waking moment colored with the knowledge that God knew what he had done and that there would be a reckoning. Now, sin is bad because it breaks your relationship with God, but one of the side effects of that is that all the worry, fear, and stress are bad for your mental and physical health too. Finally, David reached the breaking point: "I said, 'I will confess my transgressions to the Lord,' and You forgave the iniquity of my sin" (Psalm 32:5).

David understood that though others had suffered because of what he had done, he had sinned first and foremost against God: "Against You, You only, have I sinned, and done this evil in your sight" (Psalm 51:4). As painful as it was to confess the sin, David experienced relief—not from the consequences of his actions as they played out in the world, but in knowing God forgave him and still loved him. "You are my hiding place; you shall preserve me from trouble; you shall surround me with songs of deliverance" (Psalm 32:7).

Psalm 59: A Reliable Judge

Psalm 59 is an example of what is called an imprecatory psalm. To *imprecate* means to call God's judgment down on someone, to curse them. The first verse tells us that David wrote this when Saul was hunting for him, looking to kill him, and he was on the run, a fugitive from his own father-in-law for a decade. Just to remind you, David had done nothing to deserve such treatment. He stood up for God against the Philistines, killed Goliath, and became Saul's house musician. But Saul had heard the songs others were singing—*Saul has slain his thousands, David, his ten thousands*—and became jealous. God's Spirit abandoned him for his own disobedience, replaced by an evil spirit that compelled him to try to kill David.

David's prayer here was specific: "Deliver me from my enemies, O my God; defend me from those who rise up against me. Deliver me from the workers of iniquity, and save me from bloodthirsty men" (Psalm 59:1-2)—Saul and his men, in other words. David's prayer also appraised the situation as he wrote, considering what was happening and what he wanted God to do: "They run and prepare themselves through no fault of mine. Awake to help me, and behold!" (v. 4). He recognized that these guys hated him even though he hadn't done anything to them. That they weren't acting in a godly way gave him the confidence to approach God boldly with his request, even as he was careful to do so in a godly way himself: "I will wait for You, O You his Strength, for God is my defense...Do not slay them, lest my people forget; scatter them by Your power, and bring them down, O Lord our shield" (vv. 9, 11).

David figured that Saul's own sin would undo him, but even so, he didn't hold back from being deeply honest before God. In *The Message*, Eugene Peterson translated David's request this way: "Don't make quick work of them, GOD, lest my people forget. Bring them down in slow motion, take them apart piece by piece...Finish them off in fine style! Finish them off for good!" (vv. 11, 13). Sounds like a mafia prayer, doesn't it? But it was a worship song; David included the musical style and notation. Worship includes this kind of total honesty. God can handle it.

> Worship includes total honesty. God can handle it.

Songs of Refuge (Psalms 73–89)

Psalm 73: A Realistic Struggle

Asaph, one of David's choir directors, is listed as the author of Psalms 73–83, which had a common theme of an honest approach to life and worship. Psalm 73 in particular deals with a challenging, ongoing issue for believers—the problem of evil. Asaph began with an affirmation of his faith: "Truly God is good to Israel, to such as are pure in heart" (Psalm 73:1). It's an important declaration, because most of the rest of the psalm describes experiences that shook that faith, challenging Asaph's beliefs. He ended by confirming his faith once again, proving that God is our refuge in life's storms, but in between is a story of hard times and doubts about God.

One of Asaph's big questions focuses on how God can allow the wicked to get away with so much, even to prosper. Asaph looked at bad people who seemed to be doing well, who didn't anguish over doing the right thing, didn't suffer for their selfishness and poor treatment of others. Looking at what they seemed to be getting away with, he wrote, "My feet had almost stumbled" (v. 2). But as Asaph worked through his feelings, he uncovered the root of his frustration: his own envy of their perceived lack of problems. It was a classic case of being green with envy and ripe for trouble.

Envy took Asaph's eyes off God and set them on the problems he saw. To his credit, he wrote honestly and frankly about struggling through the issue, and eventually returned to a spiritual perspective: "When I thought how to understand this, it was too painful for me—until I went into the sanctuary of God; then I understood their end. Surely You set them in slippery places; You cast them down to destruction" (vv. 16-18). Being among God's people in His holy place evoked eternal thoughts about the nature of sin, the price of rejecting God, and God's faithfulness to His children. Instead of looking at God through the lens of suffering, he looked at suffering through the lens of God.

Looking at the horizontal through the lens of the vertical set Asaph's heart on a different track. He realized that whatever disappointment he might have felt toward God should have driven him to seek Him more, not less—to go to church more, not less, to devote more time and thought to God instead of giving in to the human tendency to pull back and self-isolate. Singing songs of praise among God's people and hearing His Word taught put pain in its proper place, back under God's sovereign hand. P.T. Forsyth, a Scottish theologian, once said, "It is a greater thing to pray for pain's conversion than for its removal."[18]

Psalm 84: A Restful Shelter

The sons of Korah were one of the families (along with the sons of Asaph) who led worship in the temple (they had no relation to the rebel Korah back in Moses's day). They were not only worship leaders, but they also had a specific job to do in the tabernacle and temple: They served as gatekeepers (1 Chronicles 9:19), like security guards for the building and its treasury. For them, the temple was a true place of encounter with the living God—something we see in this psalm.

"How lovely is Your tabernacle, O LORD of hosts! My soul longs, yes, even faints for the courts of the LORD; my heart and my flesh cry out for the living God" (vv. 1-2). They loved the temple, not just for its value to the community but because it was where they encountered God personally. The idea of gathering with God's people to worship Him is exciting because there was blessing in it: "Blessed is the man whose strength is in You, whose heart is set on pilgrimage" (v. 5). For all those who lived outside of Jerusalem, the desire to travel there on feast days and worship in the temple was profound.

All who came in a true spirit of worship were welcome. "Even the sparrow has found a home, and the swallow a nest for herself, where she may lay her young—even Your altars, O LORD of hosts, my King and my God. Blessed are those who dwell in Your house; they will still be praising You" (vv. 3-4). Sparrows and swallows were common birds, the first considered worthless (Matthew 10:29) and the second, restless and wandering until they find a home—at which point, they sing. Both found one among God's people and in His presence. What is worthless to people, the psalmist would say, can be valuable to God. God makes room in His house even for the sparrow, and gives the swallow rest and reason to sing its song. As Augustine said, "Our heart is restless until it finds its rest in Thee."

This led the sons of Korah to write, "For a day in Your courts is better than a thousand. I would rather be a doorkeeper in the house of my God than dwell in the tents of wickedness" (v. 10). It wasn't glamorous to be a gatekeeper—a doorkeeper—but doing it for God made all the difference. Why? Because there was a relationship supporting the work. The desire to serve God lifted the task above the ordinary, and a menial task done for the Lord's house beat lounging around in a wicked person's penthouse.

Songs of Rebellion's Cost (Psalms 90–106)

Psalm 90: A Responsive Reflection

This is the only psalm ascribed to Moses, which makes it the oldest in the entire book. The background is Numbers 20, in which three major events happened to Moses: His sister Miriam died, he struck the rock twice (disobeying God and resulting in being forbidden to enter the Promised Land), and then his brother Aaron died. The entire nation mourned those losses, and Moses lamented his own disappointment. Israel's persistent rebellion had cost them all, but Moses pursued his normal practice and turned to God.

Moses began by drawing on a family-centered image: "Lord, You have been our dwelling place in all generations" (v. 1). "Dwelling place" can be translated as "refuge" or even "den"—the idea being that God had been a constant, comforting presence all those long years in the wilderness. Despite his disappointment about the Promised Land, Moses knew his intimacy with God wasn't over, that their relationship would continue into eternity.

Still, it was hard not to reflect on life's brevity: "A thousand years in Your sight are like yesterday when it is past, and like a watch in the night. You carry them away like a flood; they are like a sleep" (vv. 4-5). We all reach a tipping point in life where time seems to speed up, the years fly by, and suddenly we're dealing with getting older. Looking back at the years of watching a whole generation die off, Moses observed, "We have been consumed by Your anger...You have set our iniquities before You, our secret sins in the light of Your countenance. For all our days have passed away in Your wrath; we finish our years like a sigh" (vv. 7-9). The reality of sin's cost—death—was hitting close to home for this great man of God.

Ask God to help you make each day count for something of eternal value.

Sin leads to death, always—the death of relationships, one's health, and ultimately to the second death if it goes unrepented of, unchecked, unforgiven. The priority, then, is in Moses's prayer: "So teach us to number our days, that we may gain a heart of wisdom" (v. 12). Because time flies, it's up to you to be the navigator. Decide wisely where you will spend your moments, your leisure, your work. Ask God to help you make each day count for something of eternal value.

Songs of Revival (Psalms 107–150)

Psalm 119: The Revitalizing Word

This is the longest chapter in the whole Bible at 176 verses. And its theme *is* the Bible—God's Word. It's as if the Holy Spirit, through the psalmist, is reminding us of the most important expression of God that we have, outside of Jesus Himself. Over and over again in these verses, we see the author's love of the Word of God in the very language. Several words, each a euphemism for God's Word, are mentioned a couple dozen times each: "law" (25), "testimony" (22), "precepts" (21), "statutes" (21), "the way" (11), "commandments" (22), "judgments" (23), and "the word" (39). God's Word revitalizes us, refreshing and renewing our weary spirits.

Another remarkable aspect of Psalm 119 is that it's set up as an alphabetical acrostic. That is, it has twenty-two sections, each subtitled after one of the letters of the Hebrew alphabet, *alef* to *tav*. Each section has eight verses, but more than just poetic pedantry, it's the psalmist's way of showing that the word of God covers the A-to-Z of our lives. It's helpful every day in facing each day's challenges. A sampling of its verses shows the daily value of God's Word:

> How can a young man cleanse his way? By taking heed according to Your word (v. 9).

> Open my eyes, that I may see wondrous things from Your law (v. 18).

> Before I was afflicted I went astray, but now I keep Your word (v. 67).

> It is good for me that I have been afflicted, that I may learn Your statutes (v. 71).

> Your word is a lamp to my feet and a light to my path (v. 105).

Think this guy loves the Bible? That's what it's all about. I know we're fluttering over this field of flowers like a butterfly, but my hope and prayer is that our view from 30,000 feet will inspire you to go back and drink more deeply from each blossom, like a bee extracting every ounce of nectar. While one verse is enough to change your life, you never know on any given day which verse it might be, unless you familiarize yourself with all of them.

Psalm 139: Our Rare and Wonderful Father

David wrote God's personal profile in this psalm. It's a great dose of doctrine—which, by the way, shouldn't be a scary word, or a diminished one: *Doctrine* just means "teaching." You can't be fully into Jesus without being fully aware of all the

Bible says about Him. All the things the Bible teaches about God—His ways, character, laws, and so on—gives us a moral and spiritual compass for navigating life. If we are off in our thinking about God, we will be off in our thinking about everything else—morality, human nature, sin, death, love—you name it. All the sincerity in the world can't compensate for a Godless approach to life. David laid out the basics of knowing God:

> ## If we are off in our thinking about God, we will be off in our thinking about everything else.

God is omniscient: He knows everything. "O Lord, You have searched me and known me. You know my sitting down and my rising up; You understand my thought afar off. You comprehend my path and my lying down, and are acquainted with all my ways. For there is not a word on my tongue, but behold, O Lord, You know it altogether" (vv. 1-4). He knows you inside and out, better than you know yourself—not to mention His knowledge of His creation, which would dwarf the collected works of all the libraries, think tanks, and research labs in the world. God's knowledge is innate, intuitive. He knows all things before man can even think the thought. "Such knowledge is too wonderful for me; it is high, I cannot attain it" (v. 6)

God is omnipresent: He is everywhere. "Where can I go from Your Spirit? Or where can I flee from Your presence? If I ascend into heaven, You are there; if I make my bed in hell, behold, You are there" (vv. 7-8). God is always everywhere present in the totality of His person, in the totality of His being. Simply put, that means you can run, but you can't hide. Not in broad daylight, not in the shadows, not even in death—and certainly not anywhere on earth.

God is omnipotent: He is almighty. "For You formed my inward parts; You covered me in my mother's womb. I will praise You, for I am fearfully and wonderfully made; marvelous are Your works, and that my soul knows very well. My frame was not hidden from You, when I was made in secret, and skillfully wrought in the lowest parts of the earth. Your eyes saw my substance, being yet unformed. And in Your book they all were written, the days fashioned for me, when as yet there were none of them" (vv. 13-16).

God can do anything, and as a proving point, David referred to human pregnancy as the quintessential example of God's skill and power. He also recognized the wonders of the heavens (Psalms 8, 19), but the point here is clear: the Bible acknowledges personhood from the moment of conception. From zygote to old age, we are *imago dei*—made in God's image.

God is obeisant*:* He lowers Himself to consider and care for us. "How precious also are Your thoughts to me, O God! How great is the sum of them! If I should count them, they would be more in number than the sand; when I awake, I am still with You" (vv. 17-18). Try counting the number of grains in a handful of sand just to get some perspective on that. This is the most staggering truth of all.

How astounding is it that omnipresent, omniscient, omnipotent God is mindful of you? He didn't just make you and set you spinning off into the universe; He humbles Himself to take as much interest in your life and thoughts as He does angels and planets and galaxies—more even.

> ## How astounding is it that omnipresent, omniscient, omnipotent God is mindful of you?

You might say that before God formed the universe, He had you in mind. He was thinking about you. If you've ever had someone walk up to you and tell you that you've been on their mind and in their prayers, you know how good it feels to hear that. Picture God saying, "I think about you all the time, more than there are grains of sand."

Psalm 150: Our Worthy Recognition

After such a wonderful series of thoughts about God, it's clear how deserving of praise He is. The final psalm focuses on praise—a word used thirteen times in just six verses. The Hebrew phrase "Praise the LORD" is *Hallelujah*! You can go to any country and say "Hallelujah" and someone will know what that means. "Praise God in His sanctuary; praise Him in His mighty firmament! Praise Him for His mighty acts; praise Him according to His excellent greatness!" (vv. 1-2).

We are to praise God for all those things, and to praise Him with music—a joyous, loud celebration of who He is. Even if you can't play an instrument or sing, you're still included: "Let everything that has breath praise the LORD" (v. 6)—and then the psalm closes with another "Hallelujah!" If you remember nothing else, remember that Psalms opens with encouragement to anchor yourself to God and ends with praise to Him. He is both the reason and the purpose for which you exist.

PROVERBS
FLIGHT PLAN

Facts

Author

The book of Proverbs is attributed to three main authors: Solomon, Agur, and Lemuel. Little is known of Agur and Lemuel, but some think Solomon either knew them personally or had access to their writings. Some even believe these were aliases for Solomon. Some proverbs are anonymous, going by the title "Sayings of the Wise."

Date Written

Solomon wrote his proverbs between 970 and 930 BC. Because we do not know about Agur and Lemuel, specific dates for their compositions can't be determined. King Hezekiah compiled all the proverbs, sometime between 729 and 686 BC.

Landmarks

The book of Proverbs is part of the Bible's wisdom literature, along with the books of Job and Ecclesiastes. It is one of the most read books in the Bible, and one of the most practical. Proverbs is the greatest how-to book ever written, and those who have the good sense to take its lessons to heart will quickly discover godliness, prosperity, and contentment are theirs for the asking.

As we fly over Proverbs from 30,000 feet, four mountain peaks come into view, each one drawing a theme from various verses scattered throughout the book.

Itinerary

- Peak 1: The Fear of the Lord vs. the Fear of Man
- Peak 2: The Diligent Person vs. the Lazy Person
- Peak 3: The Wholesome Mouth vs. the Polluted Mouth
- Peak 4: Friendship/Fellowship vs. Isolation

Gospel

In Proverbs 8, wisdom is personified and seen in its perfection. It is divine, the source of biological and spiritual life; it is righteous and moral and available to all who receive it. Paul referred to Jesus as "the wisdom of God" (1 Corinthians 1:24). He also described Christ as the One "in whom are hidden all the treasures of wisdom and knowledge" (Colossians 2:3). Proverbs 11:4 also makes the bold declaration that "righteousness delivers from death," a truth that is fully expanded on in the New Testament as Christ's righteousness on the cross.

In Proverbs 30:4, Agur wrote a clear reference to the sovereignty of God and His Son—another example of Christ as wisdom personified:

> Who has ascended into heaven, or descended?
> Who has gathered the wind in His fists?
> Who has bound the waters in a garment?
> Who has established all the ends of the earth?
> What is His name, and what is His Son's name,
> If you know?

Part of the life of Christ in the believer is the wisdom He gives us through the Holy Spirit and the Word to live righteously.

History

Much of the history surrounding the book of Proverbs revolves around Solomon. The Bible says that Solomon was the wisest man who ever lived, and that he spoke 3000 proverbs (1 Kings 4:29-32). His reign was the time in Israel's history when prosperity and intellectual sophistication were at their height (970–931 BC).

Travel Tips

The book of Proverbs is divided into thirty-one chapters, which makes it great to read for daily devotions over the course of a month. The more you read the proverbs, the more likely they are to resonate in your mind, and so in your behavior.

* A wise man or woman is always learning. They don't say, "Don't tell me; I already know these things." They are always open to increasing their knowledge, not content to stop learning. The Talmud said, "He who adds not to his learning only diminishes it," a thought reflected throughout Proverbs.

- Solomon's life is a cautionary tale: Practice what you preach. Even though the Bible called him the wisest man who ever lived, he died a fool. He built God's temple but turned toward idolatry because he married 700 women and had another 300 concubines who turned his heart from God. No wonder the Bible says, "Be doers of the word, and not hearers only, deceiving yourselves" (James 1:22).

In Flight

We live in an age of overwhelming knowledge. With high-end computers in our pockets and a social media presence that glorifies uninformed opinions, it's hard to know which end is up most of the time. As one pastor noted, "We have largely traded wisdom for information, depth for breadth. We want to microwave maturity."[19] Something in us resists this trend, though—something that craves deeper understanding and practical advice that has endured through the ages. That's why the book of Proverbs is one of the most frequently read and referenced books in the Bible.

King Solomon asked God for wisdom, and God didn't hold back in supplying it, moving Solomon to write 3000 proverbs—wise sayings—some 500 of which made their way into this book. The Spanish novelist Miguel de Cervantes is credited with saying, "A proverb is a short sentence based on long experience." Every culture has proverbs, ours included: *Nothing ventured, nothing gained. Look before you leap. Don't throw the baby out with the bathwater.* And so on. The difference here is that these proverbs were inspired by God—more than just good advice, they are God's advice.

Dividing the book is difficult because it covers a variety of topics without a common thread linking them as you read. That's why, for our purposes, I'm going to focus on four big mountaintop themes, drawing from different verses throughout Proverbs. The unifying focus is laid out in the first verse, Solomon's mission statement: "To know wisdom and instruction, to perceive the words of understanding, to receive instruction of wisdom, justice, judgment, and equity; to give prudence to the simple, to the young man knowledge and discretion—a wise man will hear and increase learning, and a man of understanding will attain wise counsel" (Proverbs 1:2-5). Knowledge requires wisdom, and here is where you can find it. When you take God out of the mix, you lose the foundation of wisdom, so let's fly over His mountaintops and seek it.

Peak 1: The Fear of the Lord vs. the Fear of Man

Without proper filters, we have no hope of figuring out what true wisdom is or how to apply it. Right off the bat, though, Solomon told us, "The fear of the Lord is the beginning of knowledge, but fools despise wisdom and instruction" (Proverbs 1:7). "Beginning" can also be translated as the "chief part," the "first and best." So "the fear of the Lord" is the best and most important component of what you learn in life.

> ## Without proper filters, we have no hope of figuring out what true wisdom is or how to apply it.

What does "the fear of the Lord" mean? Let me start by saying what it's not: It's not a superstitious dread of God, as if God is sitting up in heaven frowning down on you and waiting for you to mess up so He can strike you down. The idea of "fear" in the Hebrew text is *reverence*, something like how you might be afraid of disappointing your parents. "The fear of the Lord," then, is a reverential awe that produces humble submission to your loving Father in heaven. The only dread is that you would displease God. It's built on relationship, not rules. Because you love Him, because He has adopted you as His child, redeeming you from sin's curse, you respond to His commandments in love.

There are benefits for that reverent fear too: First, it keeps you from evil. "By the fear of the Lord one departs from evil" (Proverbs 16:6). Fear of displeasing God keeps you away from things you shouldn't be involved in. How do you break a bad habit? Develop a fear of the Lord. In Proverbs, wisdom often takes on a narrative voice, becoming a character representing this aspect of God. "I, wisdom, dwell with prudence, and find out knowledge and discretion. The fear of the Lord is to hate evil; pride and arrogance and the evil way" (Proverbs 8:12-13). I think of Joseph, sold into slavery in Potiphar's house. When Mrs. Potiphar came on to him—hormones raging, no one around—Joseph knew God was watching. He rejected her advances, saying, "How then can I do this great wickedness, and sin against God?" (Genesis 39:9).

Fear of the Lord will also increase your quality of life. "In the fear of the Lord there is strong confidence, and His children will have a place of refuge. The fear of the Lord is a fountain of life, to turn one away from the snares of death" (Proverbs 14:26-27). This is what Jesus called an abundant life: "I have come that they may have life, and that may have it more abundantly" (John 10:10). We all want quality of life. You can live life turned up to ten through the fear of the Lord. This contrasts directly with the fear of man, which is living in constant anxiety over what people will think, especially if they find out you're a Christian. Solomon summed up the order of priority nicely: "The fear of man brings snare, but whoever trusts in the LORD shall be safe" (Proverbs 29:25).

Fear of the Lord will increase your quality of life.

Peak 2: The Diligent Person vs. the Lazy Person

A second major theme of Proverbs is that, as redeemed followers of Christ, we should be concerned about the quality of our work. Work isn't part of the curse of the fall; one of the first things God did in the Garden of Eden was give Adam a job. The curse is that we do it by the sweat of our brow. Knowing that work done well is going to be difficult, we can, generally speaking, go one of two ways. We can follow the idea of the author who wrote, "I like work; it fascinates me. I can sit and look at it for hours."[20] Or we can look to the example of Teddy Roosevelt, who said, "Whenever you are asked to do a job, tell 'em, 'Certainly I can!' Then get busy and figure out how to do it."[21]

Biblically speaking, Solomon pointed us toward an example from nature: "Go to the ant, you sluggard!"—that is, you slothful person, you hater of work. "Consider her ways and be wise, which, having no captain, overseer or ruler, provides her supplies in the summer, and gathers her food in the harvest" (Proverbs 6:6-8). We should be able to tell our employer or would-be employer, "You hire me, and I will be the best worker you've got." There's pressure in keeping a promise like that, but that's where you draw on your fear of the Lord, putting the fear of man aside and trusting God to help you.

Part of representing God well means finishing what you start.

Part of representing God well means finishing what you start. "The lazy man does not roast what he took in hunting" (Proverbs 12:27). Picture a guy who rolls out of bed, goes out and bags dinner, but then gets home and doesn't bother to cook it. This is the type of person who struggles with his Rice Krispies in the morning: "A lazy man buries his hand in the bowl, and will not so much as bring it to his mouth again" (Proverbs 19:24). God always finishes what He begins, from the work of creation to the work of sanctification that is ongoing in the believer's life (Philippians 1:6). He expects us to strive toward the same goal—without excuses.

Lazy people rationalize their ways: "The lazy man says, 'There is a lion outside! I shall be slain in the streets!'" (Proverbs 22:13), and "will not plow because of winter; he will beg during harvest and have nothing" (Proverbs 20:4). His idea of work is to imitate a door: "As a door turns in its hinges, so does the lazy man on his bed" (Proverbs 26:14)—swinging back and forth, stuck in the same place. That rolling over from hot side to cool is tough—especially if you just flipped your pillow half an hour ago! The images would be hilarious if they weren't so pathetic.

Wisdom has little patience for lazy people: "How long will you slumber, O sluggard? When will you rise from your sleep? A little sleep, a little slumber, a little folding of the hands to sleep—and so shall your poverty come on you like a prowler, and your need like an armed man" (Proverbs 6:9-11). You may have heard the saying, "An excuse is the skin of a reason stuffed with a lie." There is no excuse, biblically speaking, for a Christian to be a lazy worker, either at home or on the job. Certainly, in these busy days, we have to prioritize our activities, often choosing between good, better, and best. But when we pick the best, we should do it to the best of our ability.

Peak 3: The Wholesome Mouth vs. the Polluted Mouth

If the thought of filtering, guarding, and controlling what you say makes you squirm, join the club. This is an issue for every one of us. As James said, "No man can tame the tongue. It is an unruly evil, full of deadly poison" (James 3:8). But it can be given over to the Lord; in fact, evidence of a Spirit-controlled life will be a tongue that is wholesome. And God feels pretty strongly about that: "These six things the LORD hates, yes, seven are an abomination to Him" (Proverbs 6:16). That's a huge statement right there, because as children of God who walk in the fear of the Lord, we want to love what God loves, and hate what God hates. When we are given a list of what God hates, we should take it to heart. And what's the second thing on this list? "A lying tongue" (v. 17). The last two things also have to do with our speech: "A false witness who speaks lies, and one who sows discord among brethren" (v. 19).

The solution to avoiding the things God hates is to do what He loves. Instead of a lying tongue, have an honest tongue; instead of bearing false witness, speak the truth; instead of sowing discord, bring people together, and so on. We all say things we wish we could take back, but listen to what it means to make wholesome speech your goal: "A word fitly spoken is like apples of gold in settings of silver" (Proverbs 25:11). When we choose our words carefully, they're beautiful—but, as Mark Twain once said, "The difference between the right word and the almost right word is the difference between lightning and the lightning bug."

> ## The solution to avoiding the things God hates is to do what He loves.

Words have power to build us up or tear us down emotionally. Indeed, "death and life are in the power of the tongue" (Proverbs 18:21). That's not so much about a command a king might give to live or die, but the scope of the feelings words affect. "There is one who speaks like the piercings of a sword, but the tongue of the wise promotes health" (Proverbs 12:18). We've all met verbal terminators, those who can slice and dice with a few well-chosen words; in fact, some of us may be one of them. But to speak in this way is to live on the flip side of being verbal healers whose words can encourage, build up, and bring peace and joy. "Anxiety in the heart of a man causes depression; but a good word makes it glad" (Proverbs 12:25).

Words impact relationships. For those who aren't natural communicators, think of words as a useful tool to cultivate healthier relationships. "Pleasant words are like a honeycomb, sweetness to the soul and health to the bones" (Proverbs 16:24). The next time a conversation gets heated, remember that "a soft answer turns away wrath" (Proverbs 15:1). There are also all kinds of warnings against gossip. "A perverse man sows strife, and a whisper separates the best of friends" (Proverbs 16:28). You can usually tell when someone has been whispering about you when you get the cold shoulder from someone who has previously been warm and receptive. Even if they know better, the words they heard, true or not, have given them pause for thought about you. That's why Solomon warned, "A talebearer reveals secrets, but he who is of a faithful spirit conceals a matter" (Proverbs 11:13). There is great wisdom in guarding your tongue.

Peak 4: Friendship/Fellowship vs. Isolation

One of the greatest titles you could ever give another person is *friend*. You can have a few really good ones in your life, and what an honor it is to be one. But while the term is not to be used lightly, having friends is necessary. "A man who isolates himself seeks his own desire; he rages against all wise judgment"

(Proverbs 18:1). When people have been burnt by relationships, hurt because of what others have done, and they get to a point in life where they become calloused, it's dangerous. Their attitude is, "Why bother? Why should I even do this again? It's better if I just withdraw and go it alone." I understand the inclination, but to do so is against God's order. Basic relationships 101: "It is not good that man should be alone" (Genesis 2:18). Our Creator recognized we need each other, even though we sometimes *needle* each other. Those sharp edges of our personalities can hurt, but they can also be softened as we rub up against each other in fellowship. It's all part of God's design.

Unless you form meaningful relationships with people where there is openness, frankness, honesty, and accountability, you become more isolated. You don't grow emotionally or spiritually. It seems like you are a wonderful person when you are alone with yourself. You are never sweeter, never godlier, never more fun to be with. But where life really tests you is when your personality rubs up against somebody else's personality. The phrase *mutual incompatibility* is often used to describe any relationship that's lasted longer than two weeks. Our flaws create friction, and God's wisdom is the best way to survive the heat.

> ## Our flaws create friction, and God's wisdom is the best way to survive the heat.

Ask God to bring the right people into your life—not perfect people who agree with all your brilliant ideas and habits, but people who love and support you even after they find out what a mess you are. When you find those people, it's a true gift: "A friend loves at all times, and a brother is born for adversity" (Proverbs 17:17). A true friend inspires you to be your best self: "As iron sharpens iron, so a man sharpens the countenance of his friend" (Proverbs 27:17). For your part, bear in mind that a "man who has friends must himself be friendly"—a general reminder to be kind and respectful to everyone you encounter—"but there is a friend who sticks closer than a brother" (Proverbs 18:24). When you find that friend, treasure the relationship.

When you see a potential friend, take the initiative. Ruth reached out to Naomi, saying, "Wherever you go, I will go" (Ruth 1:16), and Jonathan reached out to David and "made a covenant, because he loved him as his own soul" (1 Samuel 18:3). Let there be no stewing in your own juices and saying, "Nobody really cares about me; nobody is interested in me." *But you don't understand, I'm shy.* Listen, you are not alone. So many people you meet are also shy. Someone has to take the initiative, and you will find that, when you are friendly, it will draw out friendliness; when you love and reach out, it will draw out love and outreach.

> ## When you love and reach out, it will draw out love and outreach.

One of the greatest examples of this give and take, this mutual blessing, is in a godly marriage. That thought underscores the topic of Proverbs 31, credited to King Lemuel, whom some think may have been a pseudonym for Solomon. Either way, it details a wonderful relationship between a husband and wife, particularly in the husband's extolling of his wife's virtues: "Who can find a virtuous wife? For her worth is far above rubies. The heart of her husband safely trusts her; so he will have no lack of gain. She does him good and not evil all the days of her life...Her children rise up and call her blessed; her husband also, and he praises her: 'Many daughters have done well, but you excel them all'" (Proverbs 31:10-12, 28-29).

Remember the power of words to build up. This guy was basically saying, "There are a lot of women out there, honey, but there is only one for me, and that's you. You surpass everyone I have ever met." Telling your wife that at the altar is great, but she won't mind hearing it each day, either. And if she hasn't heard you say it in a while, there's no better time for those fitly spoken words than now.

Consider this appeal from Wisdom, personified as if she were standing on the streets of the city, calling out to passersby (Proverbs 8:1-3):

> Now therefore, listen to me, my children, for blessed are those who keep my ways. Hear instruction and be wise, and do not disdain it. Blessed is the man who listens to me, watching daily at my gates, waiting at the posts of my doors. For whoever finds me finds life, and obtains favor from the LORD; but he who sins against me wrongs his own soul; all those who hate me love death (Proverbs 8:32-36).

Pick one of these little truth bombs today, meditate on it, memorize it, apply it as you go about your business, and do the same tomorrow and the day after, until wisdom is a habit that marks your walk with God.

ECCLESIASTES
FLIGHT PLAN

Facts

Author

Ecclesiastes 1:1 attributes the book to "the son of David, king in Jerusalem." The best candidate for this description is David's son, Solomon. Though some contest Solomon's authorship, thinking Ecclesiastes was written during the postexilic period after Solomon's time, the internal evidence in the book points to him. The book also corresponds to his life as king and role as a writer. Because of the fragments of Ecclesiastes found among the Dead Sea Scrolls, most scholars now place the book during the reign of Solomon.

Date Written

The book of Ecclesiastes was most likely written toward the end of Solomon's reign, around 940 BC, as he looked back to reflect on the meaning of life and warn readers about wrong choices.

Landmarks

One of the big questions of life—if not the biggest—is "Why am I here?" Solomon, in all his wisdom, asked that as well. He wrote the book of Ecclesiastes as a journal of his search for life's meaning and purpose. Here you'll find his reflections on experience, honest and open about both the ups and downs. While his thoughts meander at times, there are themes that form an outline: Solomon's search, his sayings, and his solution.

Itinerary

- Solomon's Search (Ecclesiastes 1–4)
- Solomon's Sayings (Ecclesiastes 5–10)
- Solomon's Solution (Ecclesiastes 11–12)

Gospel

Even though you won't see specific references to the Messiah in Ecclesiastes, you'll see redemption's necessity in bold relief. Solomon was weary with the pursuit of meaning. He spoke of the fatiguing vanity of life "under the sun" (a phrase that recurs 29 times in this book). Life under the sun, according to Solomon, was toilsome, difficult, predictable, and meaningless. That's the natural result of focusing on the horizontal (the world around you with all of its challenges, mysteries, and philosophies) and not on the vertical—that is, God and His Word and ways.

But that's the dark before the dawn, and it provides the needed contrast to "life under the Son"! We need to bring God into the equation to have the right perspective of Jesus Christ. Without Him, life is vanity—empty and futile. With Him, life is full of purpose. Jesus said, "I have come that they may have life, and that they may have it more abundantly" (John 10:10). As Solomon discovered, all the riches and power in the world can't bring true satisfaction. Medical science can add years to your life, but only Jesus can add life to your years.

History

The book of Ecclesiastes is an illuminating commentary on the life of King Solomon. Solomon started off as a mighty king (ca. 970 BC), bringing the nation of Israel to its wealthiest and strongest point. However, made content and complacent by his fame and fortune, Solomon began to disobey God by pursuing the empty things described in Ecclesiastes. It was probably toward the end of his life that he realized that he had chased after the wrong things, that he should have spent his time getting to know God more, growing in God's wisdom even into his latter years.

Travel Tips

Ecclesiastes reveals the thoughts of a man who lived life to the maximum—the good and the bad, the secular and the godly. Solomon noted, "There is nothing new under the sun" (Ecclesiastes 1:9). While those words are true, it's also true that there is new life under the Son, Jesus Christ. When you have God at the center of your outlook on life, things become a lot less confusing and a lot more purposeful. Here are three takeaway points:

- Fear God. Like in the book of Proverbs, fear refers to reverential awe that produces loving and humble submission to holy God. Because He is your loving Father, you won't want to disappoint Him.

- Obey God. Obedience follows fear. Enthusiasm is a lot easier than obedience. You might get worked up in a worship experience about Jesus, but unless you keep His commandments, you're missing the point. Obedience doesn't show weakness, but the will to submit to God's higher authority for your own good.

- Prepare to give an account. One day, you will stand before God and give an account for your life. Life is a God-given opportunity, life without God is empty, and death without God is a calamity.

> **Life is a God-given opportunity, life without God is empty, and death without God is a calamity.**

In Flight

Solomon's Search (Ecclesiastes 1–4)

As Solomon conducted his grand search for life's purpose, he collected and compiled various philosophies based on his own experience, interviews, and observations. The Hebrew name for this book, *Qoheleth*, means "one who assembles or teaches the public"—a name reflected in Solomon's choice to refer to himself in its pages as "the Preacher" (Ecclesiastes 1:1). The Greek name *Ecclesiastes* means roughly the same thing, although you could say Solomon was more of a searcher than a preacher here.

Solomon immediately introduced his key word, a summation of his searching: "'Vanity of vanities,' says the Preacher; 'Vanity of vanities, all is vanity'" (Ecclesiastes 1:2). In Hebrew, "vanity" means "breath," a "vapor"—something that quickly comes and goes. The implication is that everything in this life is fleeting and ultimately empty, mysterious and even meaningless. Everything is soap bubbles, said Solomon—floating and iridescent, capturing our attention for a moment, then *pop!* gone in the next, never to be recovered.

At that point in his life, most likely toward the end, Solomon found himself dissatisfied with all life had to offer. He had tasted it all—wealth and power, wine, women, and song—and it all came to nothing for him. He was mired in pessimism—like two men who meet for dinner and, instead of shaking hands, just shake their heads. But even in that dark place, Solomon struck a chord of truth: "What profit has a man from all his labor in which he toils under the sun?" (Ecclesiastes 1:3).

On the horizontal plane of existence—the experiences and events confined to this earthly realm—ultimately, nothing satisfies beyond the moment. Once you've sucked the marrow out of life, you'll still be hungry for something more, something lasting. If there was ever an Old Testament book that anticipated the new covenant under Jesus Christ, Ecclesiastes is it. Without a meaningful relationship on the vertical plane—with God—it's all soap bubbles. "All things are full of labor; man cannot express it. The eye is not satisfied with seeing, nor the ear filled with hearing. That which has been is what will be, that which is done is what will be done, and there is nothing new under the sun" (Ecclesiastes 1:8-9).

Solomon's description of life's day-in, day-out grind suggests that you can't appreciate a happy, hopeful life without understanding what an unhappy, cynical one looks like first. He began with the tedium of life, the predictability of life and death, sunrise and sunset, rivers that run constantly but never fill the sea. "Is there anything of which it may be said, 'See, this is new'? It has already been in ancient times before us. There is no remembrance of former things, nor will there be any remembrance of things that are to come by those who will come after" (Ecclesiastes 1:10-11). In other words, "What's the point?" This is not the Solomon who wisely tested a mother's love back in the day (1 Kings 3:16-28); here, he would've said, "Do what you want. That baby is going to have a miserable life anyway." Yikes!

Now, I don't want to completely contradict the man that the Bible called the wisest ever to live (2 Chronicles 1:12). But, while Solomon was correct in his observations, his conclusions were missing something. If life proves unsatisfying, it's because you weren't made to be satisfied with the things of this world—not in any permanent way.

If life proves unsatisfying, it's because you weren't made to be satisfied with the things of this world.

Paul later wrote, "For the creation was subjected to futility"—emptiness—"not willingly, but because of Him who subjected it in hope" (Romans 8:20). "Basically," Paul was saying, "God put a hole in your soul that only eternal things can fill." Solomon sensed this, saying, "Also He has put eternity in their hearts, except that no one can find out the work that God does from beginning to end" (Ecclesiastes 3:11). That hope came in the form of Jesus Christ, but Solomon wasn't in the right frame of mind to consider the prophecies of God's Messiah.

While Solomon realized that God made mankind for more than just this life, he couldn't grasp God's full purpose in doing so, and it frustrated him. For a guy that knew as much as he did, it was even worse: "In much wisdom is much grief, and he who increases knowledge increases sorrow" (Ecclesiastes 1:18). But here was the problem: He was only looking inward, not upward: "I communed with my heart...And I set my heart to know wisdom and to know madness and folly" (vv. 16-17). The human heart is a tricky thing, and to leave its thoughts unfiltered by God's Spirit and Word is a surefire recipe for depression.

Clearly, intelligence was not the issue, and neither were education or lack of life experience. Solomon tried all sorts of things to fill the gap—pleasure, drinking, sex, possessions, projects, money, human greatness—and even with his great wisdom as a filter, it all came up vanity. All that information is nothing without a spiritual revelation, which Solomon had only in part. He was limited to his own perspective on life, and it made him miserable. "Therefore I hated life because the work that was done under the sun was distressing to me, for all is vanity and grasping for the wind" (Ecclesiastes 2:17). His horizontal searching only made the hole in his heart bigger, and wine and women only dulled the pain temporarily.

Even in his spiritually downtrodden state, Solomon expressed his search simply and eloquently: "To everything there is a season, a time for every purpose under heaven" (Ecclesiastes 3:1). The familiar verses that follow convey a sense of boredom, anxiety, and fatalism in all of the various activities of life—a time for every old thing under the sun. Finally, though, he began to bring God back into the picture: "I know that whatever God does, it shall be forever. Nothing can be added to it, and nothing taken from it. God does it, that men should fear before Him...God requires an account of what is past" (vv. 14-15) There was just a little glimmer of light as this horizontal thinker looked at life under the sun, then added God to the equation.

Looking up began changing Solomon's outlook. "I said in my heart, 'God shall judge the righteous and the wicked, for there is a time there for every purpose and for every work'" (Ecclesiastes 3:17). Bringing God into the equation moved him from bewilderment and pessimism to beauty and purpose. Though he didn't understand all of life, even at the end of this journey, things started to make more sense. The confusion began to dissipate. Enough of the dots began to connect for him to understand that life has purpose, even in the seemingly mundane events. The key is in relationships—with God and others.

By God's design, you need other people, and they need you.

Even though Solomon's ode to vanity continued—oppression is vanity, working and making money is vanity, and so are political power and competition for success—he stuck an almost-hidden gem in the midst: "Two are better than one, because they have a good reward for their labor" (Ecclesiastes 4:9). He connected with a basic biblical principle—that it's not good for man to be alone (Genesis 2:18). By God's design, you need other people, and they need you. He built people to be interdependent in relationship, as sticky and hard as that is. "For if they fall, one will lift up his companion. But woe to him who is alone when he falls" (Ecclesiastes 4:10). That "falling" is physical, emotional, and spiritual—part of the principle that "a threefold cord is not quickly broken" (v. 12). And any relationship or network where God is the third cord will be stronger than any without Him.

Solomon's Sayings (Ecclesiastes 5–10)

Solomon shifted from the philosophical to the proverbial over the next handful of chapters, covering similar thematic territory but in sayings that distill the matter to its essence. Vanity is still the big idea—found here in legalistic religion, wealth, and earthly justice (Ecclesiastes 5–10). Let's look at a few highlights.

Loving money is vanity: "He who loves silver will not be satisfied with silver; nor he who loves abundance, with increase. This is also vanity" (Ecclesiastes 5:10). Now, wealth itself is not soap bubbles, but the love of it is. Abraham was wealthy, as were Job and Joseph. They were godly men who blessed others with what they had. However, hoarding it, being dominated by it, or prioritizing it is idolatry. Money for many unbelievers is exactly like Jesus is for believers: They trust in it, looking to it to secure and save them.

Solomon knew from experience the folly of this: "The abundance of the rich will not permit him to sleep. There is a severe evil which I have seen under the sun: riches kept for their owner to his hurt. But those riches perish through misfortune; when he begets a son, there is nothing in his hand" (Ecclesiastes 5:12-14). The more money you have, the more worries that come with it. You work hard, and with the right perspective, that's good. But if money is your driving inspiration and objective, at some point you will feel the weight of its ultimate emptiness; you can't take it with you, and it can be lost in a heartbeat.

Solomon then moved from the practical to the spiritual, bringing the soul into the equation. "All the labor of man is for his mouth, and yet the soul is not satisfied" (Ecclesiastes 6:7). The material world satisfies your flesh, but not your soul—the inner, eternal part of you. Just like your body, your soul needs nourishment too, and just like your body, it matters what you feed it. That kind of soul food includes studying the Word of God, worship, prayer, discipleship, fellowship, witnessing, and obedience to the commands of Scripture. All of those exercise and strengthen your soul so that your soul can dominate your flesh, rather than the other way around (which is the default setting).

That spiritual fitness includes a reality check, which Solomon put this way: "Better to go to the house of mourning than to go to the house of feasting, for that is the end of all men; and the living will take it to heart" (Ecclesiastes 7:2). It sounds strange, but if you have a choice between attending a wedding or a funeral, go to the funeral. It's a reminder that you too will die one day, and that it's good to be sad if it helps you make your days count.

American and Western culture will do just about anything to eradicate suffering, pain, or anything else that makes us uncomfortable. But only a fool denies that those things are part of life; if God permits them, then there must be purpose in them—a depth of understanding and empathy that only they can bring. "Sorrow is better than laughter, for by a sad countenance the heart is made better. The heart of the wise is in the house of mourning, but the heart of fools is in the house of mirth" (Ecclesiastes 7:3-4). There is something healthy in grieving and moving on, as opposed to just ignoring it or failing to prepare for it. As Robert Browning said:

> I walked a mile with Pleasure;
> She chattered all the way;
> But left me none the wiser,
> For all she had to say.
> I walked a mile with Sorrow,
> And ne'er a word said she;
> But, oh! The things I learned from her,
> When Sorrow walked with me.

Trials and tribulations are so hard, but in God's hands, they can sow unique growth. It's better to ask *what* you can get out of them, rather than *how* you can get out. Otherwise, you end up stuck in such observations as, "There are wicked men to whom it happens according to the work of the righteous" (Ecclesiastes 8:14). When good things happen to bad people, and vice versa, it's easy to say it's all soap bubbles—and Solomon did: "The race is not to the swift, nor the battle to the strong, nor bread to the wise, nor riches to the man of understanding, nor favor to men of skill; but time and chance happen to them all" (Ecclesiastes 9:11). While it seems that he slipped back into a horizontal view, once again, he wasn't wrong: Life is unfair. But there are greater purposes than fairness in life's struggles.

> **Trials and tribulations are so hard, but in God's hands, they can sow unique growth.**

Rain and sunshine fall on the godly and ungodly alike. That injustice, though, is tempered by acknowledging that mankind's innate sin is the culprit: "Wisdom is better than weapons of war; but one sinner destroys much good" (v. 18). Solomon echoed that thought, particularly in chapter 10, extolling the virtues of wisdom and the downfall of fools in a style similar to his work in the book of Proverbs: "Folly is set in great dignity, while the rich sit in a lowly place" (Ecclesiastes 10:6). People of proven worth end up replaced by the foolish, which is both unfair and unwise. Life's enigmas were wearing on Solomon at this point, and you can hear the *whatever* tone in his words. Life had lost its spark, its zest, and he had gotten to a point where his attitude was just "Whatever."

Solomon's Solution (Ecclesiastes 11–12)

Up to this point in his search and his sayings, Solomon had used only observable data. His conclusions were based on what he could see and touch and hear and feel in the material world around him. Here's what that tells you: The finite can never grasp the infinite. Something infinite—without boundaries or borders—can never be fully grasped by a finite mind. You can't put the ocean in a teacup. To try, and to think that all of life is bounded by that teacup, can only lead to cynicism, pessimism, and despair. Fortunately, Solomon tempered some of that, factoring in the unfathomable, considering God as he sought a solution to the situation.

Solomon looked at life's full scope, from birth to youth to old age and death. From that experienced perspective, he advised those younger than himself. "As you do not know what is the way of the wind, or how the bones grow in the womb of her who is with child, so you do not know the works of God who makes everything" (Ecclesiastes 11:5). It's not possible for a person to fully grasp all of God's plans or methods. By admitting that God is able to hold all of life's different situations and emotions and keep them in check, Solomon expanded past vanity into infinity. God doesn't struggle with uncertainty or the search for meaning the way people do; He knows everything and has a plan that encompasses both the universe and each individual life.

God is not against having fun, especially when it's wholesome and interactive and blesses you and others.

That was a reason to celebrate: "Rejoice, O young man, in your youth, and let your heart cheer you in the days of your youth; walk in the ways of your heart, and in the sight of your eyes" (v. 9). In other words, there's something to be said for having fun while you can—enjoying the energy and curiosity of being young. God is not against having fun, especially when it's wholesome and interactive and blesses you and others.

There is still a balance, though: "But know that for all these God will bring you into judgment" (v. 9). That's not meant to be a comedown but an encouragement: You can avoid the vanity of life by doing all that you do in alignment with the joy and peace of belonging to God, balanced with that healthy, reverent fear of displeasing Him. "Remember now your Creator in the days of your youth, before the difficult days come, and the years draw near when you say, 'I have no pleasure in them'" (Ecclesiastes 12:1). It takes you a lifetime to prepare for old age, and if God isn't part of your life from an early stage, those challenges will be even greater. It will be less of a habit to consider Him, to put Him back into the equation.

Solomon's poetic description of the rigors of old age is picturesque and poignant. His vivid explanation of one's mental lucidity before intellectual powers began to fade is evocative: "While the sun and the light, the moon and the stars, are not darkened, and the clouds do not return after the rain" (v. 2). Metaphorically, the body follows, as limbs weaken ("the keepers of the house tremble and the strong men bow down" in v. 3), teeth are lost and worn down ("the grinders cease because they are few" in v. 3), and sight worsens ("those that look through the window grow dim" in v. 3).

As the modern saying goes, "Old age ain't for sissies!" In contrast, the modern habit is never to think about it while we're young. And Solomon would agree to a certain extent, telling you to enjoy your youth while it lasts, even as you keep the thought of your march toward eternity in mind. I think he would also agree that it arrives much faster than you ever could have imagined. Making the most of the moments God has given you, regardless of your age, is a good way to avoid vanity. Rather than just counting time, make time count!

Rather than just counting time, make time count!

The searcher wrapped up his ruminations a few verses later: "Let us hear the conclusion of the whole matter: Fear God and keep His commandments, for this is man's all. For God will bring every work into judgment, including every secret thing, whether good or evil" (vv. 13-14). Solomon lived life fully, in all its ups and downs, and though he was weary of it as he neared his death, He still gave God His due respect. Sadly, though, the vanity of a mostly horizontal view robbed him of his joy in God's peace and salvation. It's a sobering reminder that life under the sun alone is empty, but life under the Son of God is an opportunity, an adventure, and a blessing.

SONG OF SOLOMON
FLIGHT PLAN

Facts

Author

The first verse of Song of Solomon identifies King Solomon as the book's author. We know from 1 Kings 4:32 that Solomon wrote more than 1000 songs. This was most likely one of the best "love songs" he composed, singled out as a separate work and canonized in Scripture.

Date Written

Most scholars believe that Solomon wrote the Song of Solomon when he was a young man, possibly around 950 BC.

Landmarks

While Solomon's other books, Proverbs and Ecclesiastes, focus on the intellectual and philosophical issues of life, the Song of Solomon centers on emotion. It's a poem that depicts the wooing and wedding of a country girl to King Solomon and the deep passions that ensue in their married lives. Solomon wrote more than 1000 songs, but this is his greatest hit, his "song of songs" (v. 1). It reflects on a two-year period in their relationship, providing an outline for the book: the engagement, the wedding, and the marriage.

Itinerary

- The Engagement (Song of Solomon 1:1–3:5)
- The Wedding (Song of Solomon 3:6–5:1)
- The Marriage (Song of Solomon 5:2–8:14)

Gospel

Although Song of Solomon tells a true love story between a husband and wife, it also points to the kind of love God has for His people. Without straining the meaning or consigning it to allegory, the Song of Solomon effortlessly hints at a truth unpacked in the New Testament. A number of passages, mostly written by Paul, draw a connection between human marriage and God's love for Israel and the church (2 Corinthians 11:2; Romans 7:4; and Ephesians 5:25-27).

Marriage between a man and a woman is a microcosm of divine love, a picture of the great love Jesus Christ has for the church. This idea is especially reflected in one of the best-known verses in the book: "He brought me to the banqueting house, and his banner over me was love" (Song 2:4). A banner's purpose was to clearly identify the people who gathered beneath it, whether they were soldiers or members of a tribe. In the context of the verse, Solomon's bride was enjoying an unmistakable public display of her husband's love for her.

> **If you ever doubt God's love for you, all you have to do is look at the cross.**

Similarly, God's banner of love over the Christian is the cross. If you ever doubt God's love for you, all you have to do is look at the cross, the visible sign of His sacrificial, eternal, perpetual love. It's humbling to think of what Jesus suffered to show God's banner over us. In going to the cross, Jesus not only showed us His passion to fulfill the will of the Father, but He also showed us the commitment and sacrificial love that a successful, godly marriage requires.

History

The Song of Solomon is believed to be the first of Solomon's three works in the Bible, likely written in the early years of his reign. Along with Proverbs and Ecclesiastes, it chronicles Solomon's thoughts and ideas during his rise to power, his wise ruling during Israel's golden age of unification, and ultimately his falling away from God, painting a revealing picture of his reign (ca. 970–931 BC).

Travel Tips

Solomon's song reminds us of the power and passion of God's love. While the book's focus is a passionate and committed marriage between Solomon and his very first wife (the first of hundreds, unfortunately), it's also a reminder that God is not a stuffy prude. When God instituted marriage between Adam and Eve, "they were both naked, the man and his wife, and were not ashamed" (Genesis 2:25). Even so, it takes time, trust, transparency, and tenacity to make a marriage work.

- Put character first. Solomon's bride was first and foremost attracted to his character—his good name (Song 1:3)—more than anything else.

- Sex is for marriage. If you're dating, courting, or in a relationship that's headed for marriage, beware not to go too far physically. God designed sex to be an expression of intimate love within the boundaries of marriage. Since sexual impulse is God's invention, it must be God-guided and God-governed. Your patience will be rewarded in marriage.

- A godly marriage takes hard work, humility, forgiveness, respect, and kindness. The key to having a successful marriage is the same in your walk with Christ: deny yourself.

In Flight

The Engagement (Song of Solomon 1:1–3:5)

The Song of Solomon is the story of a young man named Solomon, who just happened to be the king of Israel, and a young woman, called the Shulamite, who came from a little village called Shulem in the Jezreel Valley, Israel's breadbasket up in the north. Scholars think that she worked on a farm owned by Solomon, alongside her family, tending a vineyard. Somehow the two met, took a liking to each other, a beautiful relationship unfolded, and then an engagement.

The Song is primarily a dialogue, with Solomon (also called the Beloved) and the Shulamite exchanging words like characters in a play. Every now and then, a few other groups join in. The Daughters of Jerusalem were young women who likely served in the king's court and attended the Shulamite as the relationship blossomed. The Shulamite's brothers and relatives also weigh in later on. I like their contributions simply because they show the importance of not pursuing a relationship in isolation. It's good to have people who care about you sharing their encouragement and concerns and giving godly advice as you go through the ups and downs of a relationship.

At this point, during the engagement, it was all ups. Some commentators think that this was Solomon's first marriage (he ended up with 700 wives and

300 concubines), and the song transmits that kind of passion. As it begins, this country bride daydreamed of her betrothed: "Let him kiss me with the kisses of his mouth—for your love is better than wine. Because of the fragrance of your good ointments, your name is ointment poured forth; therefore the virgins love you" (Song 1:2-3). The virgins were the young women working in the palace who shared the Shulamite's good opinion of her beloved's character—his good name—and rejoiced in her good fortune (v. 4). I love that: Even though she loves his kisses, she is first attracted to his character. That's paramount in any healthy relationship, especially one intended to end in marriage, because beauty will fade, but you'll be stuck with that character for the long haul.

The Shulamite, like almost all other young people, was concerned about her appearance. "I am dark, but lovely, O daughters of Jerusalem, like the tents of Kedar"—the black wool tents used in the desert by the Bedouins—"like the curtains of Solomon. Do not look upon me, because I am dark, because the sun has tanned me" (vv. 5-6). In those days, pale skin was considered the standard of beauty, the sign of a woman of means and comfort. Tanned skin indicated that you were a manual worker, stuck outside, grinding out your daily bread. Clearly, Solomon didn't care, but the thought that he might crossed her mind.

It's typical for people to spend more time in front of the mirror during the engagement than afterward. It's human nature—and it's fine to care about your looks as long as it doesn't become an obsession. Studies show that the more you're exposed to cultural standards of beauty (these days, mainly through the media), the less satisfied you tend to be with your own image. Fortunately, despite her concerns about whether she was attractive to Solomon, the Shulamite had her dignity and valued her own purity: "Tell me," she asked him, "O you whom I love, where you feed your flock, where you make it rest at noon. For why should I be as one who veils herself by the flocks of your companions?" (v. 7). Prostitutes wore veils then, so she was saying, "I want to spend time with you, but I won't chase after you like a hooker."

She wanted this relationship, but she wasn't going to force it. One of the mistakes that people make, whether it's young couples getting married for the first time or people in a rebound relationship, is wanting to move too quickly. They are determined that *this is it*, this is the one; no one can dissuade them, and Christians can get even weirder about it—saying things like, "God spoke to me and said you were the one." In which case you could respond, "Fine, but you'd better be saying that in five years—and ten and twenty—because you are bringing God into something that should last." That's called accountability. It's pretty rare when a couple has known each other for a month or two, and are suddenly engaged. More often than not, that's a red flag that they're rushing things. Of course, on the flip side, you can be engaged for too long, which might indicate a lack of ability to fully commit. But either way, it's better to make sure you know a person's character before getting married.

The engagement period was the time in Solomon's day that couples used to get to know each other better. They were committed to getting married, but after the engagement, it was appropriate to spend time together. Clearly, the young king and his bride-to-be were liking what they got to know. Solomon said, "O fairest among women...I have compared you, my love, to my filly among Pharaoh's chariots" (vv. 8-9). Keep in mind that Solomon loved horses. He had thousands, knew all about them, so to call his girl his filly was a high compliment to her statuesque beauty. I've heard it said that if a man has enough horse sense to treat his woman like a thoroughbred, she'll never turn into an old nag.

As the betrothal progressed, their intimacy grew. Solomon praised her, gushing, "Behold, you are fair, my love! Behold, you are fair! You have dove's eyes" (v. 15). Before you wonder why telling her she has bird eyes is romantic, let me explain. Doves can focus on only one thing at a time, so Solomon was saying that she had eyes only for him. Better, right? For her part, the Shulamite told him how handsome he was (v. 16) and described the scenery—"the beams of our houses are cedar, and our rafters of fir" (v. 17)—indicating that they were on an outing and that being with him in nature made her feel as if she were in a palace. Ah, the power of love goggles!

The relationship progressed quickly, the scene shifting from an outdoor picnic to an official banquet. "He brought me to the banqueting house, and his banner over me was love" (Song 2:4). Now, instead of just being alone with her somewhere, she was invited into his public life. He was not ashamed to be seen with her. She sensed his growing affection, along with the dangers of increased intimacy. As she told her companions, "I charge you, O daughters of Jerusalem...do not stir up nor awaken love until it pleases" (v. 7). In other words, don't stimulate love prematurely; don't make the relationship go too fast.

It's a theme repeated throughout the book. More than simply advising her friends, she was looking for accountability from them. She understood that her passion could get the better of her, and she wanted to make sure she waited for the relationship to unfold at the right pace so that she and Solomon could marry and enjoy sexual love in a beautiful, intimate, God-ordained way.

This interaction should help dismiss the idea that God is some old-fashioned prude, down on sex, approving it only for procreation. I invite you to read the whole book—but only if you are not in a position where its frank language might compromise your purity. God invented sex, but because He did, it must be God-guided and God-governed. Sexual love has its safe place. Soil is good in a garden, but not in the living room. Fire is good in a fireplace, but not on the carpet. In the wrong place, outside of marriage, sex grows out of control and destroys relationships.

Solomon also understood that marriage is God's only intended environment for sexual love: "Drink water from your own cistern, and running water from your own well. Should your fountains be dispersed abroad, streams of water in the streets? Let them be only your own, and not for strangers with you. Let your fountain be blessed, and rejoice with the wife of your youth" (Proverbs 5:15-18). Within marriage, sex can refresh and delight you; outside of marriage, it's like drinking from a gutter.

Solomon prepared for that level of commitment by getting to know his fiancée as well as possible. "O my dove, in the clefts of the rock, in the secret places of the cliff, let me see your face, let me hear your voice; for your voice is sweet, and your face is lovely" (Song 2:14). He pursued her, telling her, "I want to know everything there is to know about you," and that's a good thing to have in a courtship, that pursuit of understanding the complete person. Better to be honest during the engagement than to cover up things that can't possibly stay hidden once you're married.

Through this process of discovery, others held the couple accountable. The Shulamite's brothers advised them, "Catch us the foxes, the little foxes that spoil the vines, for our vines have tender grapes" (v. 15). At first glance, it seems like they're telling her to get back to work in the vineyard, but I believe this is a metaphor: The vineyard is the couple's relationship, and the foxes are all those pesky habits and potential conflicts that too often take root and destroy marriages. The brothers' advice is to take care of those things before they said, "I do."

Marriages don't disintegrate overnight. A breakup in a relationship is a slow leak, never a blowout. Infidelity and divorce are most often products of longstanding issues, dozens of smaller, unresolved conflicts and issues that, like the little foxes, nibble at the vines until the vineyard is ruined. The engagement should be a time of getting to know each other as well as possible to see if you are both in a position to make as serious a commitment as marriage.

The Wedding (Song of Solomon 3:6–5:1)

In those days, the wedding began with a procession. If you were a bride, you would get ready in your parents' house—the house in which you grew up. The bridegroom wouldn't tell you when he was coming; he would just show up with the wedding party, and you had to be ready to go. The procession would move from your parents' house to his own house—in the case of Solomon and the Shulamite, the palace in Jerusalem.

The bride described her view of the procession: "Who was this coming out of the wilderness like pillars of smoke, perfumed with myrrh and frankincense, with all the merchant's fragrant powders?" (Song 3:6). Imagine what it would have been like for this young bride, madly in love with the king, to look outside and see the procession coming: Solomon in his royal palanquin—a portable throne surrounded by silver pillars on a gold base—incense billowing up and mingling with the dust of horses, surrounded by dozens of attending soldiers, swords gleaming, the crowd trailing behind for hundreds of yards.

She would have felt thrilled and safe, protected by her groom and his men. She would also have felt apprehensive, knowing that she was marrying royalty, bringing new responsibilities and pressure (v. 11). She knew what she was getting into. Marrying the king meant that much of his time would be occupied by affairs of state and royal decision-making—that she would have to share him with the nation. Still, she surrendered herself willingly and with joy.

After the wedding ceremony came the consummation of their relationship. Solomon's song goes into detail about her looks as he compliments her appearance. The images require similar explanation to the dove's eyes—"hair like a flock of goats" and "teeth like a flock of shorn sheep" (Song 4:1-2), meaning black, lustrous locks, and beautiful straight, pearly whites—but trust me when I say that he praised her. Solomon was good with words, a real sweet talker, and he used them here to make his new bride feel more at ease as the evening went on. "Until the day breaks and the shadows flee away, I will go my way to the mountain of myrrh and to the hill of frankincense. You are all fair, my love, and there is no spot in you" (vv. 6-7).

How gentle Solomon's words were for his beloved. He put no pressure on her, or himself, to live up to any outside expectations, desiring that they should simply enjoy each other's company and warm to the moment in due time. He even expressed appreciation for the gift of her purity that night: "A garden enclosed is my sister, my spouse, a spring shut up, a fountain sealed" (v. 12). Simply put, here is a girl who saved herself for marriage. She stayed pure all of her life, kept herself closed and guarded until she could give herself away—and that's God's will: abstinence until marriage, fidelity in marriage, and enjoyment of marriage. Solomon and the Shulamite were, in the best Garden of Eden sense, naked and unashamed.

Following God's path to the marriage bed brought His approval: "Eat, O friends! Drink, yes, drink deeply, O beloved ones!" (Song 5:1). Many scholars believe that this is God's blessing on the couple—an exhortation to enjoy each other. "You're doing this the right way, and I am blessing this relationship; it's holy to Me."

The Marriage (Song of Solomon 5:2–8:14)

In the last few chapters of the book, the marriage matures. The honeymoon is clearly over at this point. Something seems to have divided Solomon and his bride, some argument or spat that put them at odds. Interestingly, it starts right after God's blessing: "I sleep, but my heart is awake; it is the voice of my beloved! He knocks, saying, 'Open for me, my sister, my love'" (Song 5:2). So he is not in their bedroom; he might even be locked out. She is awake but pretending to be asleep, thinking, "I have taken off my robe; how can I put it on again? I have washed my feet; how can I defile them?" (v. 3). Having gotten ready for bed, she doesn't want to get up and open the door for him. What happened to the sweet talk, the breathless excitement?

> **Some of the best advice I've heard is to keep your eyes wide open before marriage and half shut afterward!**

She wants to open the door for him but hesitates, and when she finally decides to, he's gone (vv. 4-6). She goes out looking for him, but he's nowhere to be found: "I charge you, O daughters of Jerusalem, if you find my beloved, that you tell him I am lovesick!" (v. 8). Something has happened with our love-struck newlyweds, but what has sparked such drama? Let me just say it's nothing out of the ordinary. They've had a conflict and they need to resolve it. That happens even in the best of marriages. Some of the best advice I've heard is to keep your eyes wide open before marriage and half shut afterward!

It's not because they are incompatible—*everyone* is incompatible with everyone else, if they know each other for more than a week or two. The key is to have a good fight (yes, there is such a thing, when it's full of honesty and grace), to be able to resolve the issue so the outcome is achieved in a way pleasing to God, allowing the couple to move forward together in unity. Anything less lets the little foxes run free in the vineyard, destroying what's been grown and eroding the soil of the relationship—the foundation of trust.

The Shulamite and her royal husband do eventually resolve the conflict. The details of how they do so aren't in the song, but the results are: "Before I was even aware, my soul had made me as the chariots of my noble people" (Song 6:12). Yeah, I know: *What?* It's pretty obscure, but the idea is that Solomon set her in his royal chariot in front of all the people, an indication that they were reconciled.

Once you make a habit of resolving conflict, your marriage will mature. That's how it was for our couple here. They are romantic once again, but it's a mature romance based on commitment, not hormones. At least one year after their marriage and honeymoon, they're keeping the romantic fires burning between them. Once again, Solomon extolled his bride's beauty, and in return, she declared the power of their commitment to one another:

> Set me as a seal upon your heart, as a seal upon your arm; for love is as strong as death, jealousy as cruel as the grave; its flames are flames of fire, a most vehement flame. Many waters cannot quench love, nor can the floods drown it. If a man would give for love all the wealth of his house, it would be utterly despised (Song 8:6-7).

She understood that she was treasured, the first and most important of all his human relationships, and she reserved her best affections only for him. "My own vineyard is before me. You, O Solomon, may have a thousand" (v. 12). In other words, Solomon was wealthy; he could buy anything he wanted or have any woman he wanted. All she had to give him was her heart, but she gave it freely and completely. Based on his words in this song, it was a gift he received gladly and with honor.

Some years back, I read a good reminder: "Getting married is easy. Staying married is more difficult. Staying happily married for a lifetime should rank among the fine arts."[22] How do you do that? With effort. Work toward consistency in giving yourself, humbling yourself, and putting your spouse first. If you both do that, you will love each other well, even to the point of modeling how God loves His people. This beautiful, tender love story in the Song of Solomon—a young couple's love sprouting, blossoming, being pruned, but then blossoming even more abundantly a year later after the conflict was resolved—points us toward the reconciliation and love we find in Christ—and how we as His bride long for our Bridegroom to return.

ISAIAH
FLIGHT PLAN

Facts

Author

The first verse of Isaiah tells us that the book was written by the prophet Isaiah, the well-to-do son of Amoz, a claim reinforced throughout the book. His poetic and eloquent writing style reveals that he was well educated; most biblical scholars think he was well acquainted with the royal court of Judah.

Date Written

Isaiah wrote his book between 739 and 700 BC, during the reigns of four kings of Judah: Uzziah (d. 740 BC), Jotham (750–732 BC), Ahaz (735–715 BC), and Hezekiah (715–686 BC).

Landmarks

This flight in *The Bible from 30,000 Feet* requires us to gain quite a bit of altitude in order to take in the entire book of Isaiah, the Shakespeare of prophets. His ministry to Israel and Judah lasted about fifty years, and the New Testament quotes him more than any other prophet.

The book of Isaiah offers both some of the clearest prophecies about the Messiah and a fascinating and uncanny parallel with the narrative of the whole Bible. Just as the Bible has sixty-six books, there are sixty-six chapters in Isaiah. The Bible is split into two testaments: the Old Testament contains thirty-nine books, and the New Testament twenty-seven. Isaiah contains a similar natural thematic division: its first thirty-nine chapters focus on God's condemnation, and the last twenty-seven emphasize God's consolation.

Itinerary

- Prophecies of Condemnation (Isaiah 1–39)
    - Act I: Denunciation of Judah (Isaiah 1–12)
    - Act II: Vengeance on Enemies (Isaiah 13–23)

- Intermission: Isaiah's Apocalypse (Isaiah 24–27)
- Act III: Warnings for Judah and Israel (Isaiah 28–35)
- Act IV: Assault on Assyria (Isaiah 36–39)
- Prophecies of Consolation (Isaiah 40–66)
  - Act V: Israel's Salvation (Isaiah 40–48)
  - Act VI: Israel's Savior (Isaiah 49–57)
  - Act VII: Israel's Splendor (Isaiah 58–66)

Gospel

The New Testament quotes Isaiah twenty-one different times, making him its most quoted prophet. Jesus began His own ministry in Nazareth by reading a passage from Isaiah: "The Spirit of the Lord is upon Me, because He has anointed Me to preach the gospel to the poor" (Luke 4:18, quoting Isaiah 61:1).

Isaiah is called the messianic prophet because of his emphasis on God's Anointed One: He spoke of the virgin birth of the Messiah in Isaiah 7:14 (the Immanuel prophecy), prophesied both Christ's birth and His coming kingdom in Isaiah 9:6-7, and alluded to His atoning work on the cross in Isaiah 53. Salvation, mentioned thirty-one times in the book, is a major theme. Even Isaiah's name (*Yeshayahu* in Hebrew) means "God is salvation."

One of the main places we see the scarlet thread of redemption in Isaiah is in the oft-repeated word *servant*. While it sometimes refers to David (Isaiah 37) or the nation of Israel (Isaiah 41), most often it describes the Messiah. In four passages known as "the Servant Songs" (Isaiah 42:1-4; 49:1-6; 50:4-9; 52:14–53:12), we see the work and calling of God's ultimate servant, Jesus Christ.

The messianic focus of so much of Isaiah's prophecies shows us that it was always God's plan to make the most precious and powerful of sacrifices to bring His people—both Jews and Gentiles—back into relationship with Him.

History

Isaiah served as God's prophet from around 740 to 690 BC. His ministry hit its stride when the northern and southern kingdoms came under threat during the Assyrian crises (735–701 BC). When Hezekiah became king, Isaiah served as a powerful positive influence on his leadership, along with two other prophets of the time, Micah and Hosea.

Four kings reigned in Judah during Isaiah's life: Uzziah (d. 740 BC), Jotham

(750–732 BC), Ahaz (735–715 BC), and Hezekiah (715–686 BC). You can read more about this period of Israel's history in 2 Chronicles 26–32.

Travel Tips

Isaiah pointed out the people's need for God and called them on going through the motions with their worship. Over and over, he pointed to the Messiah, who would come to redeem mankind from sin, and would one day return to reign. Isaiah dispensed plenty of good advice for how to live until then:

- Call sin what it is. Sin shouldn't be dismissed or diminished as a mistake or a product of one's environment; it shouldn't be winked at or shrugged off. God hates sin—though He loves sinners.
- Remember that God is on the throne, no matter who is the president or leader of a country, and no matter how broken a system of politics appears to be. While Christians should be involved in politics, we should never forget in whom we place our ultimate trust.
- God often disciplines His people before He comforts them. The difference between the two sections of Isaiah reflects this pattern. He brings judgment and institutes consequences for sin so that He can then rescue and restore.
- God's Word speaks to the condition of your heart in all seasons of life, sometimes challenging you, sometimes comforting you. God knows when you need conviction and when you need consolation, and His Word provides both.

God knows when you need conviction and when you need consolation, and His Word provides both.

In Flight

Prophecies of Condemnation (Isaiah 1–39)

Act I: Denunciation of Judah (Isaiah 1–12)

Beyond his powerful prophecies, Isaiah was also a social reformer. He foretold the future, but he also criticized God's people on their failure to trust the Lord, and cautioned them on the alliances they were making with foreign powers. The ten tribes of the northern kingdom of Israel had been trying to hold off Assyria for 150 years before Isaiah was born. Their bribes and alliances had failed, and by the time Isaiah became a prophet, Assyria had conquered Israel in 722 BC and was marching through Judah toward Jerusalem.

Under the circumstances, Isaiah pulled no punches. He made it clear why God had permitted their enemies to draw so near: "The LORD has spoken: 'I have nourished and brought up children, and they have rebelled against Me...They have forsaken the LORD, they have provoked to anger the Holy One of Israel, they have turned away backward'" (Isaiah 1:2, 4). Isaiah was brave enough to call it like it was—Israel's problem was not a mistake, not a product of their environment, but *sin*.

Despite His disgust with their behavior, God was not content to leave the people floundering in their sin—He never is. Even as judgment approached, He appealed to them to return: "'Come now, and let us reason together,' says the LORD, 'Though your sins are scarlet, they shall be white as snow; though they are red like crimson, they shall be as wool'" (v. 18). While God was calling His people to return to heartfelt worship and obedience to the law, He was also using images that pointed to the cross of Christ and the ultimate sacrifice that He would offer to cleanse the hearts of any who would receive Him.

Isaiah used a poetic style in the opening twelve chapters of his book, alternating with historical prose as he told the story between the prophecies. The poetry works well to underscore the emotion of God's appeal to Israel's hearts. Referring to spiritual neglect despite the beautiful, fertile home God had provided in Jerusalem, Isaiah wrote, "What more could have been done to My vineyard that I have not done in it? Why then, when I expected it to bring forth good grapes, did it bring forth wild grapes?" (Isaiah 5:4). He went on to describe those wild grapes—a multitude of sins, including empty worship, drunkenness, oppression, materialism, injustice, and pride—condemning "those who call evil good, and good evil" (v. 20).

Isaiah painted a bleak picture, but not a hopeless one. God was faithful to raise up prophets to let His people know He was still there, still in control, still worthy of trust. As an example, Isaiah described his own calling: "In the year that King Uzziah died, I saw the Lord sitting on a throne, high and lifted up, and the train of his robe filled the temple" (Isaiah 6:1). Winged seraphim hovered in His presence, shaking the pillars with their praise: "Holy, holy, holy is the LORD of hosts; the whole earth is full of His glory!" (v. 3).

It was loud and smoky, with terrifying six-winged angels shouting and a palpable sense of God's holiness. Isaiah responded in the only reasonable way: abject fear. "Woe is me, for I am undone! Because I am a man of unclean lips, and I dwell in the midst of a people of unclean lips: for my eyes have seen the King, the LORD of hosts" (v. 5). One of the seraphim then touched his lips with a burning coal from the altar, cleansing his mouth, the vessel of the overflow of his heart: "Your iniquity is taken away, and your sin purged" (v. 7). A special cleansing was needed before a special calling. God asked, "'Whom shall I send, and who will go for Us?' Then I said, 'Here I am! Send me'" (v. 8). In the midst of pending doom in a leaderless kingdom, God made it clear: He is on the throne, and those who seek Him will be transformed. And so He sent Isaiah.

From early on in Isaiah's ministry, his messages contained powerful and elegant prophecies of the Messiah—particularly His birth and reign—couched in predictions of fast-approaching events. As Judah came under attack from Assyria (allied with Israel, no less), King Ahaz panicked, but Isaiah spoke to him, telling him not to fear "these two stubs of smoking firebrands...It shall not stand, nor shall it come to pass" (Isaiah 7:4, 7). He encouraged Ahaz to ask God for a sign, but Ahaz, trying to sound pious, refused to "test" the Lord.

Isaiah, wearied by his king's small faith, told him, "The Lord Himself will give you a sign: Behold, the virgin shall conceive and bear a Son, and shall call His name Immanuel" (v. 14). It's a familiar prophecy, but notice the context. God would deliver Judah from Assyria, but in the long run, He was also preparing to deliver the entire world from its biggest enemy, sin, through His Son, Jesus Christ. In many ways, that's Isaiah in a nutshell: storm and gloom one moment, glory and hope in the next.

In the midst of promised judgment against Judah came a promised hope: "There shall come forth a Rod from the stem of Jesse, and a Branch shall grow out of his roots" (Isaiah 11:1). What an image—the tree of David almost totally chopped off, the kings of Judah brought to an end in captivity—but just when it looks like that tree will never spring back, a little bud will sprout in the chopped-off stump, and it will be none other than the Messiah, Christ Himself. "The Spirit of the LORD shall rest upon Him, the Spirit of wisdom and understanding, the Spirit of counsel and might, the Spirit of knowledge and the fear of the LORD" (v. 2). The severity of Judah's condemnation was tempered by their eventual restoration.

Act II: Vengeance on Enemies (Isaiah 13–23)

Having established both Judah's coming punishment and her eventual restoration, Isaiah turned his attention to the nations that God had used and would use to bring about His judgment. All nine of the nations he mentioned were connected with Israel in some way. Typically they were condemned because of how they treated Israel, in keeping with the scriptural principle established in Genesis 12:3: Bless Israel and be blessed; treat Israel poorly and be cursed.

Judah's future captor got first mention: "The burden against Babylon which Isaiah the son of Amoz saw" (Isaiah 13:1). Next to Jerusalem, Babylon is mentioned more in the Bible than any other city. The capital of a magnificent, advanced historical empire also became a spiritual symbol of godlessness—the epitome of man's vanity and pride, fueled by spiritual evil. "And Babylon, the glory of kingdoms, the beauty of the Chaldeans' pride, will be as when God overthrew Sodom and Gomorrah" (v. 19). It would fall at the hands of the Medes (v. 17). The amazing thing is that Isaiah predicted Babylon's downfall before it (or the Medes) had even risen to power.

Babylon is long gone, but a list of the other condemned nations reveals some familiar names, modern nations still in conflict with Israel: Assyria and Philistia (Syria and Gaza) in chapter 14, Damascus in chapter 17 (Syria again), Egypt in chapter 19, and Tyre in chapter 23 (Lebanon). Babylon gets another warning in chapter 21, along with Edom, whom some scholars identify with modern-day Palestinians.

A highlight of (or perhaps a blotch on) this section is the fall of Lucifer, the great liar and originator of the world's problems and patron saint of Babylon (likely unbeknownst to the Babylonians themselves). In describing the eventual demise of the earthly "king of Babylon" (Isaiah 14:4), God also detailed the expulsion from heaven of Babylon's spiritual forefather: "How you are fallen from heaven, O Lucifer, son of the morning! How you are cut down to the ground, you who weakened the nations! For you have said in your heart, 'I will ascend into heaven, I will exalt my throne above the stars of God...I will be like the Most High'" (vv. 12-14). It's fitting that the one responsible for the creation of what we call the world system and its anti-God agenda should be included in this portion about the punishment of Israel's enemies.

Intermission: Isaiah's Apocalypse (Isaiah 24–27)

In the middle of these prophecies of condemnation is a brief parenthetical intermission featuring a rather vague series of future judgments and divine glory. It's often called "Isaiah's little apocalypse." It highlights one of the most important features of prophecy: In looking to the future through the vision God gave them, prophets often had what we might call spiritual bifocals. That is, there was an immediate fulfillment and a long-term one, both in the same prophecy. They saw a template that foretold what would happen in the near future, yet also modeled a greater-scale version of a related event in the distant future.

Previously, Isaiah had prophesied about local events, then broadened the scale as far as Israel's regional neighbors. In this section, however, his vision expanded to a global scale—a distant time of worldwide destruction and judgment that would end in the kingdom age. It's consistent with Revelation 6–20, which describes the Tribulation period, the day of the Lord and His great global judgment, and the millennial kingdom of Christ that follows.

To begin with, the earth will suffer God's wrath: "Behold, the LORD makes the earth empty and makes it waste, distorts its surface and scatters abroad its inhabitants...The earth mourns and fades away, the world languishes and fades away; the haughty people of the earth languish" (Isaiah 24:1, 4). With regard to the God-given role mankind has as stewards of God's creation, we have come up short.

However, many have taken up the fight for the environment as a battle honoring "Mother Earth," removing God the Creator from the picture, leaving a lot of people who care about nature caught in an unwholesome blend of environmental atheism and naturalistic animism (where created things have spirits attributed to them—trees and rivers and even the earth itself). Their hope will be destroyed when God judges the earth and finishes the decimation humanity has begun. He'll do it in order to judge human evil and wipe the slate clean for a new beginning, but it's going to get ugly first.

For their blasphemy, God will mete out Levitical punishment: stoning (Leviticus 24:10-16). According to Revelation 16:21, hundred-pound hailstones will rain down across the globe, resulting in the devastation that Isaiah described: "The earth is violently broken, the earth is split open, the earth is shaken exceedingly. The earth shall reel to and fro like a drunkard, and shall totter like a hut; its transgression shall be heavy upon it, and it will fall, and not rise again" (Isaiah 24:19). The level of ruination is difficult to imagine, but God's judgment will be just on a world of hardened, idolatrous hearts.

Even in the midst of global judgment, however, God will protect those whom He has adopted by the blood of Christ, giving them shelter: "Come, my people, enter your chambers, and shut your doors behind you; hide yourself, as it were, for a little moment, until the indignation is past. For behold, the LORD comes out of His place to punish the inhabitants of the earth for their iniquity; the earth will also disclose her blood, and will no more cover her slain" (Isaiah 26:20-21).

Even in the midst of global judgment, God will protect those whom He has adopted by the blood of Christ.

And in the kingdom to come, the 1000-year reign of Christ on the earth, Israel will become not only the center of government but of outflowing blessing to the world—blessings both physical and spiritual: "Those who come He shall cause to take root in Jacob; Israel shall blossom and bud, and fill the face of the world with fruit" (Isaiah 27:6). This promise of ultimate blessing for God's people is as sure as His promise of judgment for the world.

Act III: Warnings for Judah and Israel (Isaiah 28–35)

Isaiah then turned his attention back home, giving six specific warnings to Israel and Judah. Each begins with the word *woe*—and really, even though it's a different word than the command used to stop a horse, it works the same way here. He was trying to keep Israel and Judah from continuing down certain destructive paths. If they didn't listen to His command to "Whoa—slow down and consider"—there would indeed be woe.

Isaiah's first warning was for the ten northern tribes of Israel, here called by the eponym *Ephraim*: "Woe to the crown of pride, to the drunkards of Ephraim, whose glorious beauty is a fading flower which is at the head of the verdant valleys, to those who are overcome with wine!" (Isaiah 28:1). Isaiah warned Judah and Israel not to partner with Egypt. Judah listened, but Israel, frightened by the threat of Assyria, didn't—which meant more woe. "'Woe to the rebellious children,' says the LORD, 'who take counsel, but not of Me, and who devise plans, but not of My Spirit, that they may add sin to sin'" (Isaiah 30:1). Israel's alliance with Egypt failed, and Assyria conquered them and sent their citizens into captivity in 722 BC. Judah held out a while longer, until Babylon, who conquered the Assyrians, took them captive in 586 BC.

Israel chose to trust Egypt's military strength rather than God—and the result was another woe: "Woe to those who go down to Egypt for help...but who do not look to the Holy One of Israel, nor seek the LORD!" (Isaiah 31:1). That was bad enough, but it also established a pattern for the future. Their rejection of God resulted in their captivity back then, but later, their rejection of God's Son would leave them in captivity to sin—and in the end times, susceptible to the charms of a powerful world leader whom Paul called "the man of sin" (2 Thessalonians 2:3)—the Antichrist. Jesus predicted this, telling the Jewish leaders of His day, "I have come in My Father's name, and you do not receive Me; if another comes in his own name, him you will receive" (John 5:43).

In the midst of this warning came wonder. Isaiah also looked beyond the days of Israel's self-deception to the kingdom age, a time when Christ will make things right on earth for a season, reigning from Jerusalem itself. "The wilderness and the wasteland shall be glad for them, and the desert shall rejoice and blossom as the rose...They shall see the glory of the LORD, the excellency of our God" (Isaiah 35:1-2). Parts of the Middle East are so desolate that they make the moon look lush, but during the millennial reign of Christ, the whole region will be verdant and fertile, full of life. It will be a glorious time for people too: "Then the eyes of the blind shall be opened, and the ears of the deaf shall be unstopped. Then the lame shall leap like a deer, and the tongue of the dumb sing. For water shall burst forth in the wilderness, and streams in the desert" (vv. 5-6). These verses suggest a dramatic change in earth's hydrological cycle, brought about by Christ's repairs.

God wanted to reason with His people, to draw them back to Him, but even when they refused, He remained faithful to His promises to Abraham and David, and this future era will be a key part of that. There will be no broken homes, no broken hearts, no diseases, no hospitals, no wheelchairs, no funerals, no sadness. They will all be eradicated in the kingdom age.

Act IV: Assault on Assyria (Isaiah 36–39)

Isaiah then turned his attention back to Judah's enemies—specifically, Sennacherib, king of Assyria. He also shifted from his poetic style to a straightforward, prose style in these four chapters, recording the history as it played out (Isaiah 36:1). Sennacherib was looking to finish the job that his predecessor had begun by conquering Israel a few decades earlier.

Assyria's king deployed his right-hand man, the field general known as the Rabshakeh, to Jerusalem's walls with an army and a letter to Judah's king Hezekiah, which basically said, "Your God won't save you. All these other forty-six cities we have conquered trusted their gods. We wiped them out. Don't think your Yahweh is going to help you at all. Give up." The letter had the intended effect. When Hezekiah heard its words, he did the equivalent of getting ready for a funeral, tearing his clothes and putting on sackcloth. But he also went to the temple to seek God (Isaiah 37). He knew he had no strength to stand up to Assyria's might, but he believed God could do something about it, if He would.

Hezekiah sent for the prophet Isaiah himself, who replied with an encouraging message: "Thus says the LORD, 'Do not be afraid of the words which you have heard, with which the servants of the king of Assyria have blasphemed Me. Surely I will send a spirit upon him, and he shall hear a rumor and return to his own land; and I will cause him to fall by the sword in his own land'" (Isaiah 37:6-7). Sennacherib, distracted by a battle with another foe, sent the Rabshakeh with another letter, repeating his threats.

Hezekiah took the letter and laid it out in the temple before the Lord. He prayed for deliverance, and God gave Isaiah another message: Sennacherib wouldn't so much as fire an arrow over the walls, "for I will defend this city, to save it for My own sake and for My servant David's sake" (v. 35). Then God sent an angel into the Assyrian camp, where he killed 185,000 soldiers (v. 36). Overnight, the battle was won, and the initial prophecy would be fulfilled almost instantly with a disgraced Sennacherib hearing of a plot and returning home, where he was killed in a coup (vv. 37-38).

While Hezekiah didn't finish on the best of notes (Isaiah 38–39; 2 Kings 20), Isaiah remained a steady voice on God's behalf to the end of the king's days. Unfortunately, the end of Hezekiah's reign marked not a turning point toward God but another step toward the condemnation Isaiah foretold.

Prophecies of Consolation (Isaiah 40–66)

Act V: Israel's Salvation (Isaiah 40–48)

Isaiah 40 begins with welcome words after thirty-nine chapters of convicting predictions of doom: "'Comfort, yes, comfort My people!' says your God. 'Speak comfort to Jerusalem, and cry out to her, that her warfare is ended, that her iniquity is pardoned; for she has received from the LORD's hand double for all her sins'" (vv. 1-2). "Comfort" replaces "woe" as the key word. This change is not dissimilar from an effective parenting technique: discipline first, then comfort. God knows how to find that balance so beautifully.

Isaiah's shift in emphasis parallels the change between the Old and New Testaments. The first thirty-nine chapters deal with the law, Israel's failure to keep it, and the judgment that resulted. The last twenty-seven focus on God's love and grace, and the first chapter in this section connects directly to the beginning of the New Testament, with John the Baptist quoting Isaiah 40:3: "The voice of one crying in the wilderness: 'Prepare the way of the LORD; make His paths straight'" (Matthew 3:3). What's more, the last two chapters in Isaiah speak of the new heaven and earth (Isaiah 66:22), centuries before John also foretold them at the end of the New Testament in Revelation 21. So, as you read, keep both lenses handy—the near and the far.

All four Gospels record John the Baptist quoting Isaiah 40, which predicted him as the forerunner of the Messiah, Jesus Christ. More immediately, though, Isaiah was foretelling the return of Israel from captivity in Babylon—again, approximately a century before Babylon even rose to power. But after the condemnation that would come Israel's way, God would eventually comfort them by clearing a straight path to bring them back home.

As the people considered Isaiah's prophecy about Babylon, its fulfillment must have seemed far off, in that way where anything that isn't happening in the next few weeks does. But Isaiah offered a different perspective: "All flesh is grass...The grass withers, the flower fades, but the word of our God stands forever" (Isaiah 40:6, 8). The first part is common physics, known as the second law of thermodynamics: the essence of entropy is that everything is winding down, decaying over time. Creation will eventually lose its battle to regenerate itself, and great rulers come and go. Mighty civilizations rise in a cosmic blink only to blow away with time's breeze.

Fortunately, God gave us His Word as an anchor, to keep us from being overwhelmed by the grand scope of prophecy while we're stuck in time, feeling only its slow, inexorable march toward death and eternity. The Word of God is the only thing that "stands forever." So when your world is crumbling, immerse yourself in God's Word, His promises and mercies, His wisdom and grace. It will produce stability and generate joy.

> When your world is crumbling,
> immerse yourself in God's Word.
> It will produce stability and generate joy.

David wrote, "Turn my eyes from worthless things, and give me life through your word" (Psalm 119:37 NLT)—a prayer that Israel and Judah had apparently failed to lift up in Isaiah's day, evidenced in his question, "Why do you say, O Jacob, and speak, O Israel, 'My way is hidden from the LORD, and my just claim is passed over by my God'?" (Isaiah 40:27). They had untethered themselves from God's Word and were drifting in life, away from Him and closer to the catastrophe of captivity.

Isaiah called them back: "The everlasting God, the LORD, the Creator of the ends of the earth, neither faints nor is weary. His understanding is unsearchable. He gives power to the weak, and to those who have no might He increases strength" (vv. 28-29). To wait on God is to be lifted up on eagles' wings, strengthened supernaturally for the challenges ahead. Israel would be refreshed at that future date as they returned across the desert from captivity—but God's rejuvenating words are also for you right now. They are the personal message you've been waiting for, so plug into His Word now and be revitalized, have your purpose renewed, and rest in the peace only He can give.

> **To wait on God is to be lifted up on eagles' wings, strengthened supernaturally for the challenges ahead.**

Act VI: Israel's Savior (Isaiah 49–57)

At the heart of God's purpose for you is servanthood. It's a concept that comes up in different ways in Isaiah, with different servants. For example, God was vested in Israel because they were a special people—"My servant, Jacob whom I have chosen, the descendants of Abraham My friend" (Isaiah 41:8). Isaiah's common theme of *God's servant* applies to Israel, but also to David (Isaiah 37), King Cyrus of Persia (Isaiah 44), and Jesus Christ. In each case, Israel's savior served God's purposes.

There are four sections in Isaiah called Servant Songs (Isaiah 42, 49, 50, and 52–53). They focus on God's Messiah, His ultimate Servant, Jesus Christ: "Behold! My Servant whom I uphold, My Elect One in whom My soul delights! I have put My Spirit upon Him; He will bring forth justice to the Gentiles" (Isaiah 42:1). During Jesus's first mission, He fulfilled the qualities ascribed to Him here: "He will not cry out, nor raise His voice, nor cause His voice to be heard in the street. A bruised reed He will not break, and smoking flax He will not quench; He will bring forth justice for truth. He will not fail nor be discouraged, till He has established justice in the earth; and the coastlands shall wait for His law" (vv. 2-4). Jesus came to show God's heart, treating people with gentleness, compassion, and encouragement.

While Jesus came first as mankind's Savior, He will return as our sovereign King. Isaiah foretold it all, issuing God's challenge to the nations of the world to match His prophetic track record:

> Who among them can declare this, and show us former things? Let them bring out their witnesses, that they may be justified; or let them hear and say, 'It is truth.'...I, even I, am the LORD, and besides Me there is no savior. I have declared and saved, I have proclaimed (Isaiah 43:9, 11-12).

Prophecy is one of God's unique calling cards. It's the distinguishing characteristic among all the so-called holy scriptures of the world. God alone has a perfect record, 100 percent spiritually and historically accurate in His predictions, and there is no reason to think that will change. Isaiah's prediction of Babylon's rise to power is just one example of hundreds, as is his foretelling of Israel's return from captivity and the future reign of the Messiah.

The mention of King Cyrus and the Jerusalem temple is noteworthy (Isaiah 44:28). At the time of Isaiah's writing, the temple was standing in Jerusalem, yet the verse said that a foundation would be laid, which implies that the current temple would have to be destroyed. That happened 140 years later, in 586 BC. Cyrus wasn't even alive at the time this prophecy was given! According to the Jewish-Roman historian Josephus, Cyrus read Isaiah's prophecy and was divinely inspired to send the Jews back to rebuild Jerusalem[23]—making him a savior to Israel as a servant of God's purposes.

This predictive power permeates the Servant Songs. The second foretold Jesus's birth: "Listen, O coastlands, to Me, and take heed, you peoples from afar! The LORD has called Me from the womb; from the matrix of My mother He has made mention of My name" (Isaiah 49:1). You know the story—how the angels spoke to Mary, then to Joseph, and then to the shepherds, that Jesus was born in Bethlehem, just as Isaiah already explained in chapters 7 (the Immanuel prophecy) and 9—"Unto us a Child is born, unto us a Son is given" (Isaiah 9:6). These three prophecies go hand in hand.

The third song depicts Christ as the submissive servant, particularly as it relates to His commitment to the mission God the Father gave Him: "I gave My back to those who struck Me, and My cheeks to those who plucked out the beard; I did not hide My face from shame and spitting" (Isaiah 50:6). Jesus allowed cruel men to shame and beat Him in order to accomplish God's will.

The final Servant Song is the Mount Everest of messianic prophecy. Beginning in Isaiah 51:12, the Messiah's sovereignty is described, the divine might that the whole world will see one day. However, starting in Isaiah 52:13, He becomes the suffering servant, pouring Himself out in substitutionary death. There are more details in Isaiah 53 about Christ's suffering and crucifixion than in any of the four Gospels. Crucifixion hadn't been invented yet, which makes this prophecy all the more remarkable.

First came the beating Jesus sustained during His trial before Pilate—and His ultimate purpose in permitting it: "His visage was marred more than any man, and His form more than the sons of men; so shall He sprinkle many nations" (vv. 14-15). He would grow up "as a root out of dry ground" (Isaiah 53:2)—blooming in that parched, hardened earth of Israel's stony hearts. Remember Isaiah 5, when God lamented that such wild fruit had grown from the good soil He had given Israel? That was the environment in which Jesus ministered, and so was "despised and rejected by men" (v. 3).

Theologians call what Jesus did on the cross a "vicarious atonement." He took our place, paid our price as the recipient of God's judgment against sin. As our substitute, "He was wounded for our transgressions, He was bruised for our iniquities; the chastisement for our peace was upon Him, and by His stripes we are healed. All we like sheep have gone astray; we have turned, every one, to his own way; and the Lᴏʀᴅ has laid on Him the iniquity of us all" (vv. 5-6). These are familiar verses, but let them sink in: God treated His Son as if Jesus committed every single sin ever perpetrated by everyone. He let Him be crushed, pierced, separated, and humiliated instead of us. God treated Jesus like you and I deserve to be treated so that He could treat you and me like Jesus deserves to be treated!

> **God treated Jesus like you and I deserve to be treated so that He could treat you and me like Jesus deserves to be treated!**

Act VII: Israel's Splendor (Isaiah 58–66)

Though Israel had blown it—both in the sin that would lead to captivity in Babylon, and later in failing to receive their Messiah when Jesus came—God wasn't through with them yet. He still isn't. In fact, Israel will be center stage in the end times, and Jerusalem will be Christ's capital in the millennium. Apart from their internal issues with God, Israel has been a specific target for Satan down through the ages, subject to the fury of the Roman Empire, the Spanish Inquisition, and Nazi Germany, to name a few better-known attempts to wipe out the Jewish people.

However, Isaiah affirmed God's ongoing protection and preservation of His people: "When the enemy comes in like a flood, the Spirit of the Lᴏʀᴅ will raise up a standard against him. 'The Redeemer will come to Zion, and to those who turn away from transgression in Jacob'" (Isaiah 59:19-20). On the day of the Lord, God will "recover the remnant of His people who are left" (Isaiah 11:11) and establish them as "The Holy People, the Redeemed of the Lᴏʀᴅ; and you shall be called Sought Out, A City Not Forsaken" (Isaiah 62:12).

Despite God's promises of ultimate splendor for Israel, Jesus lamented her hardheartedness as He entered Jerusalem the week before His crucifixion: "If you had known, even you, especially in this your day, the things that make for your peace! But now they are hidden from your eyes" (Luke 19:42)—a fulfillment of the prediction in Isaiah's commission as a prophet: "Make the heart of this people dull, and their ears heavy, and shut their eyes; lest they see with their eyes, and hear with their ears, and understand with their heart, and return and be healed'" (Isaiah 6:10).

It wasn't that God didn't want them to return to Him. Rather, He knew they wouldn't—not fully, and not until the kingdom age, as Isaiah predicted: "For behold, the darkness shall cover the earth, and deep darkness the people; but the LORD will arise over you, and His glory will be seen upon you. The Gentiles shall come to your light, and kings to the brightness of your rising" (Isaiah 60:2-3). This messianic age is just as sure to happen in God's eyes as the rise of Babylon and Israel's eventual captivity and release.

Israel's future splendor was built on the healing work of the Messiah. Isaiah encapsulated Jesus's ministry so powerfully and succinctly that Jesus quoted it in His first public sermon, claiming that He had fulfilled it that day (Luke 4:21):

> The Spirit of the Lord GOD is upon Me, because the LORD has anointed Me to preach good tidings to the poor; He has sent Me to heal the brokenhearted, to proclaim liberty to the captives, and the opening of the prison to those who are bound; to proclaim the acceptable year of the LORD, and the day of vengeance of our God; to comfort all who mourn (Isaiah 61:1-2).

Dr. Harry Ironside preached on the comma that followed the phrase "acceptable year of the LORD," saying that the pause between it and the day of God's vengeance has lasted 2000 years.[24] We are living in the time between Jesus's first coming and His second, between His past work as the Lamb of God, shedding His blood to cover our sin, and His future work as the Lion of Judah, executing God's righteous wrath and judgment. The first time He came, wicked men judged Him; the second, He will judge them (Isaiah 63:3-4).

The day of God's vengeance is highlighted by the so-called Battle of Armageddon, a one-sided affair in which Jesus will easily destroy all the nations of the world aligned against Him, His robe dipped in the blood of His enemies (Revelation 19:13-21). His victory accomplished, the peace of Christ will reign on earth. "'The wolf and the lamb shall feed together, the lion shall eat straw like the ox, and dust shall be the serpent's food. They shall not hurt nor destroy in all My holy mountain [that is, Jerusalem],' says the LORD" (Isaiah 65:25). This incredible, unprecedented peace will last for 1000 years (Revelation 20:1-3).

The millennium will accomplish two purposes: first, to redeem creation from the curse of the fall and the judgment of God during the Tribulation. Earth will be a wreck, and Jesus will heal it during this time, answering the prayer, "Your kingdom come. Your will be done on earth as it is in heaven" (Matthew 6:10).

The second reason is to fulfill God's promises to Israel—specifically, His pledge to David that he would have a spiritual and material kingdom, a throne on Mount Zion from which his descendant the Messiah would rule (2 Samuel 7:16). Afterward, Jesus will defeat Satan for good, and usher in a new heaven and earth: "'For as the new heavens and the new earth which I will make shall remain before Me,' says the Lord, 'so shall your descendants and your name remain'" (Isaiah 66:22). Israel's best days—and yours as a believer in Christ—are yet to come.

JEREMIAH
FLIGHT PLAN

Facts

Author

The prophet Jeremiah, son of the priest Hilkiah, wrote the book of Jeremiah. He was raised in a small town outside Jerusalem called Anathoth and composed most of his book with the help of his secretary, Baruch. Baruch likely assembled his notes into a book at some point after the Jews' final exile into Babylon.

Date Written

Jeremiah wrote his book between 625 and 580 BC. This era in Israel's history, which spanned the reigns of Josiah to Zedekiah, is covered in 2 Kings 22–25. Jeremiah continued to prophesy after the destruction of Jerusalem and subsequent Babylonian captivity in 586 BC.

Landmarks

Flying over the book of Jeremiah takes us from the heights of God's divine perspective on His people and their enemies to the figurative—and literal—bottom of a well. Jeremiah comprises a series of oracles—prophetic writings—transcribed over a period of more than forty years during the reigns of several kings in the southern kingdom of Judah.

Jeremiah had the unsavory assignment of declaring to the nation of Judah that the sky was falling. Judgment was coming, but just like Chicken Little, he got little to no response. The Babylonians were coming, but Jeremiah was up against a group of false prophets who were saying everything was just fine, that there was nothing to worry about.

We can divide Jeremiah into three sections, bookended on one end by the story of the prophet's calling and on the other by an appendix reviewing the history of Jerusalem's fall and exile. In between are various proclamations, both of God's impending judgment and of His promises of restoration and renewal.

Itinerary

- Preparation of Jeremiah Formulated (Jeremiah 1)
- Proclamations of Jeremiah Foretold (Jeremiah 2–51)
  - Concerned Criticism (Jeremiah 2–4)
  - Counterfeit Counsel (Jeremiah 5–6)
  - Consternation with the Congregation (Jeremiah 7–10)
  - Colorful Case Studies (Jeremiah 11–20)
  - Certainty of Conquest (Jeremiah 21–29)
  - Change of Covenant (Jeremiah 30–33)
  - Cost of Consistency (Jeremiah 34–38)
  - Care after the Captivity (Jeremiah 39–51)
- Predictions of Jeremiah Fulfilled (Jeremiah 52)

Gospel

Jesus and Jeremiah shared a lot of character traits. When Jesus asked His disciples who people were saying He was, they mentioned Jeremiah as a possibility (Matthew 16:14). Like Jeremiah, Jesus could be tough; both confronted their enemies over and over again for their hypocrisy. On the other hand, both were tenderhearted and deeply loved Israel, weeping over her sin.

Jeremiah is called the weeping prophet because of his sorrow and frustration over the conduct and eventual fate of God's people. He didn't just prophesy judgment on them; he felt every high and low with them. He didn't relay God's judgment and then add his own "That's what you get. I'm out of here"; he wept over their sin and its consequences. But he also never failed to see the light at the end of the tunnel. Despite rightly predicting the captivity and desolation of his people, Jeremiah also predicted that they would be gathered to the land again seventy years later and in the final messianic age of this world.

Jesus was similarly brokenhearted over sin. He didn't come solely to declare God's judgment and the repentance of sins; He came as a man, experiencing everything we do and then willingly giving His life to pay the penalty for our sin. He wept over Jerusalem with compassion when He saw it for the last time before His crucifixion (Matthew 23:37: Luke 19:41-44). Both hearts broke for sin's cost, but

Jeremiah pointed to a day when God would restore Israel's homeland and renew her heart during Christ's reign on earth.

History

Jeremiah's ministry lasted through the reigns of Josiah (640–609 BC), Jehoahaz (609 BC), Jehoiakim (609–598 BC), Jehoiachin (598–597 BC), and Zedekiah (597–586 BC). His call to ministry came in approximately 627 BC, the thirteenth year of Josiah's reign. That same year, Assyria's last great king, Ashurbanipal, died, leading to the establishment of an independent Babylonian state. It was during Jehoiachin's reign that the king of this state, Nebuchadnezzar, rose to power and attacked Jerusalem, sending Jehoiachin captive to Babylon. Nebuchadnezzar set up Zedekiah as a figurehead over Judah and eventually laid siege to and destroyed Jerusalem and the temple in 586 BC.

Travel Tips

Jeremiah's example is a reminder to stick to the ministry God has called you to no matter the challenges and hardships. Resistance from others shouldn't surprise you—in fact, you should expect it. As the cultural climate grows increasingly hostile to God's truth and the gospel, you need to rely on God more than ever, seeking the right balance of love and truth the world needs to hear.

- God views life as sacred. He told Jeremiah His plans for him began before he was even born (Jeremiah 1:5). God knows each of us from the moment of conception and has a meaningful plan for our lives (Jeremiah 29:11).

- Even though God must judge your sin, He longs for true intimacy with you. One of the first things God told Jeremiah to tell the Jewish people was that He remembered how well they had started out after the exodus in showing kindness and love (Jeremiah 2:2).

> **Even though God must judge your sin, He longs for true intimacy with you.**

- Only the living water Jesus offers can quench your spiritual thirst. Through Jeremiah, God mentioned two evils His people had committed: leaving Him, and trying to dig their own broken cisterns, or wells (Jeremiah 2:13)—a metaphor for trying to find satisfaction in something other than God. But only the Lord, the "fountain of living waters" (Jeremiah 2:13), can truly satisfy.

- Let God's Word sink into your heart. If you've been going to church for a while or if you've read the entire Bible, you might think you've heard it all. But God's Word is a living thing that you can apply to your life in ways you could never imagine (Hebrews 4:12)—if you remain open to it.

In Flight

Preparation of Jeremiah Formulated (Jeremiah 1)

Jeremiah's forty-year preaching ministry spanned the reign of five different kings—the last five kings of Judah, in fact, before Babylon conquered it. God called Jeremiah when he was a young man, making it clear that His plans preceded Jeremiah's birth: "Before I formed you in the womb I knew you; before you were born I sanctified you; I ordained you a prophet to the nations" (Jeremiah 1:5). Given that Jeremiah would later encourage God's people with God's promise of good thoughts and plans for them (Jeremiah 29:11), it's fitting that God began by encouraging this young prophet in all the work He had set aside for him.

What's also clear is that Jeremiah was overwhelmed by the task: "Ah, Lord God! Behold, I cannot speak, for I am a youth" (Jeremiah 1:6). Jeremiah's response earned him membership in a large group of people used mightily by God who didn't think they could handle the job—Moses, Gideon, Isaiah, and Paul among them. Of course, the truth is that, without God, they couldn't have done anything they ended up doing. But with God they did astonishing things. And so God encouraged Jeremiah: "Do not say, 'I am a youth,' for you shall go to all to whom I send you, and whatever I command you, you shall speak. Do not be afraid of their faces, for I am with you to deliver you" (vv. 7-8).

The value of God's presence can't be overstated. Without Him, nothing gets done; with Him, there is nothing that can't be done. That must have been a welcome thought for Jeremiah, because God didn't hold back in telling him how hard it was going to be. Jeremiah would speak truth to power—kings, princes, and priests of Judah—and the common people too, but they wouldn't thank him for it: "'They will fight against you, but they shall not prevail against you. For I am with you,' says the Lord, 'to deliver you'" (v. 19). As God touched Jeremiah's mouth, imprinting His message on the young prophet's lips (as He had also done with Isaiah), Jeremiah had every reason to get excited. But it didn't quite work out as he might have hoped.

Without God, nothing gets done; with Him, there is nothing that can't be done.

In four decades of preaching, Jeremiah didn't see a single conversion. He wasn't celebrated but persecuted. On the surface, that might have seemed like a failure—as if he was, in fact, too young and inexperienced. But God knew what He was doing; He always does. No one took Jeremiah's words to heart—at least not until the captivity, when his words comforted God's conquered people, as they would for generations to come. By then, Jeremiah's words were a life preserver to a nation drowning in despair.

Proclamations of Jeremiah Foretold (Jeremiah 2–51)
Concerned Criticism (Jeremiah 2–4)

Jeremiah's words to Jerusalem, though denunciatory of her sins, are striking because of their tenderness and pathos and their colorful use of metaphor. God's broken heart broke Jeremiah's heart, and that often comes through in his message: "Thus says the LORD: 'I remember you, the kindness of your youth, the love of your betrothal, when you went after Me in the wilderness'" (Jeremiah 2:2). Though the exodus from Egypt was centuries prior, for God it was like looking back on the early days of a beautiful new relationship. God brought His people out of slavery and into the desert, and they had only Him to trust in.

God provided all they needed—bread from heaven and water from rocks. They followed Him, walking under His protection and trusting Him daily. He was telling them, "I miss that. I loved it when it was just you and Me, and there wasn't all of the fancy organizational rigmarole that you have placed between us." It was more than nostalgia, though; Israel had fallen into the mess that would lead them into captivity because they had complicated their relationship with God, doing what they felt was right rather than obeying Him. Like the church in Ephesus, whom Jesus accused of having left their "first love" (Revelation 2:4), Israel left the simplicity of walking with God. Whether it's with God or in a marriage or a friendship, a relationship doesn't break down overnight. It's a slow erosion made up of dozens of decisions, most of them small, that gradually smothers the flame.

Israel had quenched her love for God through "two evils: They have forsaken Me, the fountain of living waters, and hewn themselves cisterns—broken cisterns that can hold no water" (Jeremiah 2:13). There were two ways of getting water back then. One was through rivers or streams, and the other was collecting rainfall in cisterns. The Jews called the former "living water" because its constant movement kept it from stagnating. The latter came primarily through the annual winter rainfall, and was carefully collected in large, hewn-out pools called cisterns to stave off the dry months. The problem was that, without great care in their construction and maintenance, cisterns developed fissures—cracks in the rock that were covered by plaster but slowly leaked, draining the supply.

God's point was that Israel and Judah had left His living water—His constant, reliable source of refreshment and rest—and replaced it with broken manmade cisterns—their alliances with other nations like Egypt and Syria. As Jesus told the Samaritan woman at the well, "Whoever drinks of this water will thirst again" (John 4:13). As a result of refusing true refreshment, Israel's strength drained away. Short of drawing close to God, whatever you seek happiness in—human relationships, work, wealth, popularity—will leave you dried out at some point, wanting something more that you can't find anywhere else but in God.

Jeremiah described Judah's wayward behavior using a term with which we're familiar in the church today: "backsliding"—mentioned seven times in Jeremiah 3 alone. In the church today, this refers to someone who has known and even walked in God's truth but has recently returned to their old, presalvation ways. In ancient Judah, it meant the people had committed idolatry. Despite the infidelity it indicates, God's message is the same today as it was then: "Return, you backsliding children, and I will heal your backslidings" (Jeremiah 3:22).

Jeremiah described Judah and Israel's faithlessness in many ways—a broken cistern, an unfaithful wife, and a backsliding child. These figurative images distinguish his prophecies. For example, instead of just telling people to return to following God's ways, he said, "Break up your fallow ground, and do not sow among thorns" (Jeremiah 4:3)—or as another translation puts it, "Plow up the hard ground of your hearts! Do not waste your good seed among thorns" (v. 3 NLT).

Counterfeit Counsel (Jeremiah 5–6)

One of the big problems God had with both Judah and Israel during this time was the preaching of false prophets: "They have lied about the LORD, and said, 'It is not He. Neither will evil come upon us, nor shall we see sword or famine. And the prophets become wind, for the word is not in them...Because you speak this word, behold, I will make My words in your mouth fire, and this people wood, and it shall devour them'" (Jeremiah 5:12-14). Politicians made alliances with other nations instead of trusting God to defend them against the coming threat. Prophets preached feel-good messages, tickling people's ears and not offering any challenge to return to their first love. They preached peace when there was none (Jeremiah 6:14), offering a Band-Aid for an arterial bleed.

But they weren't fooling God. "Because from the least of them even to the greatest of them, everyone is given to covetousness; and from the prophet even to the priest, everyone deals falsely" (v. 13). In the hustle and bustle of life, they chose expedience, and once they committed to doing things their way instead of God's, no one could sway them otherwise. God told them to "ask for the old paths, where the good way is, and walk in it" (v. 16); He sent them "watchmen" (v. 17) to sound warnings, but they wouldn't listen. As the nation's captains, they told their passengers to eat, drink, and be merry, oblivious to the fact that the ship was headed for disaster. They were off-course, and the warnings coming in from God's radio were being ignored. They were setting themselves up for a Titanic-like catastrophe.

Consternation with the Congregation (Jeremiah 7–10)

That didn't stop God from sending those warnings through His true prophets, however. He sent Jeremiah to the temple gates with a tough message: Even if you're in the temple, attending the three great feasts (Passover, Pentecost, and Tabernacles) every year, being there won't save you if you worship falsely and live selfishly. "Behold, you trust in lying words that cannot profit" (Jeremiah 7:8)—and as a result, they oppressed the poor, stole, murdered, swore falsely, burned incense to idols, and then came to the temple and said, "We are delivered to do all these abominations" (v. 10). The temple had become the "den of thieves" (v. 11) that Jesus later criticized (Matthew 21:13; Mark 11:17; Luke 19:46).

Once again, these temple discourses weren't just targeting the people but their politicians and priests—the leaders who were steering them off course. It had gotten so bad that God told Jeremiah not to bother praying for them anymore—"nor lift up a cry...for them, nor make intercession to Me; for I will not hear you" (Jeremiah 7:16). They had chosen to devote themselves to worshipping a ritual and so worsened their relationship with the only One worthy of worship—and God was fed up with it. This is the only time in the Bible you'll find God telling one of His servants, "Don't pray, because I won't even listen."

Jeremiah responded with tears—both for the doom coming on his people and the pain of knowing how badly they had messed up. "Oh, that my head were waters, and my eyes a fountain of tears, that I might weep day and night for the slain of the daughter of my people!" (Jeremiah 9:1). Again, God pointed the way back: "Let not the wise man glory in his wisdom, let not the mighty man glory in his might, nor let the rich man glory in his riches; but let him who glories glory in this, that he understands and knows Me" (vv. 23-24). Israel and Judah had gotten fat and sassy doing just the opposite; in their God-given prosperity, they forgot their divine provider—a sure indicator of a nation in decline. Jeremiah had been the warning prophet; now he became the weeping prophet, lamenting both the condition of and the consequences for his people.

Colorful Case Studies (Jeremiah 11–20)

Over the next several chapters, God instructed Jeremiah to do some performance prophecy—unusual visual aids that probably made him look crazy to the hardened hearts around him. For the first one, God became Jeremiah's fashion consultant. He had the prophet wear a beautiful linen sash, similar to what a priest might wear, as a symbol of Judah's pride. Jeremiah then buried the sash near a river, dug it up several days later, and brought it out, muddy and ruined, to let the people know where their pride was leading them (Jeremiah 13:1-11).

Another time, God forbade Jeremiah to go to funerals or places of feasting as a demonstration that there was no point in mourning Judah and nothing to celebrate either. To that end, He told Jeremiah not to get married and have kids, because they would "die gruesome deaths; they shall not be lamented nor shall they be buried, but they shall be like refuse on the face of the earth" (Jeremiah 16:4) when the Babylonians came. Good incentive to stay single!

God also had Jeremiah visit a potter, where the prophet watched a flawed pot be reshaped into a useful one. God made it clear that He could shape Judah similarly, doing whatever He pleased with them (Jeremiah 18:4-11). When Jeremiah shared that particular lesson, the citizens of Jerusalem scoffed, saying, "That is hopeless! So we will walk according to our own plans" (v. 12). In other words, "You bum us out, dude! We're just going to keep doing what we're doing, Debbie Downer." More than that, though, they began to plan retaliation: "Let us devise plans against Jeremiah; for the law shall not perish from the priest, nor counsel from the wise, nor the word from the prophet. Come and let us attack him with the tongue, and let us not give heed to any of his words" (v. 18).

God's response was to send Jeremiah after a dried pot, which he then shattered in front of the priests and leaders outside the Potsherd Gate, which led to the Valley of Hinnom, often used as the city dump (Jeremiah 19). Just in case the visual was lost on them, Jeremiah proclaimed God's promise: "Behold, I will bring such a catastrophe on this place, that whoever hears of it, his ears will tingle...Even so I will break this people and this city" (vv. 3, 11).

Apparently the ears of the priest in charge of the temple, Pashhur, tingled at Jeremiah's prediction. He had Jeremiah beaten and thrown in stocks near one of the temple gates. Mocked and discouraged, Jeremiah decided to quit the ministry, saying of God, "I will not make mention of Him, nor speak anymore in His name" (Jeremiah 20:9). He was ready to hand in his official prophet card—and given the treatment he had endured, it's easy to see why he felt that way.

Jeremiah wanted to quit, but he couldn't: "His word was in my heart like a burning fire shut up in my bones; I was weary of holding it back, and I could not" (v. 9). At the point of personal burnout, God's Word fueled him on. Even as he struggled to continue, he knew God was with him and would deliver him from his prosecutors. Therapy can help you through a hard time and vacations are nice, but immersing yourself in God's Word uniquely revives and restores your spirit. God had upped the ante with Jeremiah's extravagant, peculiar presentations of His truth, but He covered His prophet with that same truth, assuring him of His presence in the midst of persecution.

Certainty of Conquest (Jeremiah 21–29)

Reinvigorated by God's promises, Jeremiah got back to work. In the next several chapters, he illustrated the certainty of Judah's captivity. Babylon would come against Judah three different times over a period of about twenty years, wearing the people down physically and depleting them socially. In 605 BC, Babylon took a number of young people captive as a tribute paid by Judah to avoid being overthrown—among them a young man of great promise named Daniel. The second time, in 597 BC, thousands more were exiled, including a large number of political, social, and religious leaders. Finally, in 586 BC, a full siege resulted in the breaching of the walls, the leveling of the temple, the burning of the city, and the deportation of most of Jerusalem's remaining citizens.

These desperately sad messages from Jeremiah included foretelling the breaking of David's royal line with Jeconiah (also called Coniah) and Jehoiachin (Jeremiah 22:28-30). God would find another way to keep His promise that David would have a descendant on Israel's throne. God's plans for His people included an end-times return to the land, where the Messiah—"a Branch of righteousness" from the house of David (Jeremiah 23:5)—would rule the world.

In another colorful metaphor, God compared His people to two baskets of figs—one good and one spoiled (Jeremiah 24). They were all going to be taken captive, but the "good figs" would be preserved in Babylon, because God would watch over them, prosper them, and bring them back. The "bad figs" were false prophets and leaders, specifically King Zedekiah and his princes, and they would die in captivity. Sharing that forecast got Jeremiah some death threats, but he had rooted himself in God's promise: "Know for certain that if you put me to death, you will surely bring innocent blood on yourselves, on this city, and on its inhabitants; for truly the LORD has sent me to you" (Jeremiah 26:15). The threat was real: Another prophet had been killed by the king for prophesying the same message, but God protected Jeremiah (vv. 20-24).

God even had Jeremiah put an animal's yoke around his neck to demonstrate His power to harness the kings of the earth to His will (Jeremiah 27:2). God would use Babylon to accomplish His purposes, and He called anyone who was saying anything else a liar (vv. 7-10). However, He also made it clear that He would eventually break Babylon's oppressive yoke and bring the captives home (Jeremiah 28:2-6).

Later, Jeremiah captured the essence of God's promises in a letter that he sent to the captives in Babylon. All of Jeremiah's prophecies had come true, revealing him as God's true prophet, and no doubt that doubled the people's regrets. Not only were they conquered captives in a strange land, the prophet they had persecuted turned out to be right all along. But neither God nor Jeremiah wanted to rub it in their faces; the letter was meant to encourage, restore hope, and remind them of God's good promises. It accomplished all of that and more:

> After seventy years are completed at Babylon, I will visit you and perform My good word toward you, and cause you to return to this place. For I know the thoughts that I think toward you, says the LORD, thoughts of peace and not of evil, to give you a future and a hope. Then you will call upon Me and go and pray to Me, and I will listen to you. And you will seek Me and find Me, when you search for Me with all your heart (Jeremiah 29:10-13).

The captivity was not the end of Israel and Judah's relationship with God, but a spanking administered by a loving parent looking to break through the hard hearts of His children. God used Babylon to break Judah's will, but He preserved their spirits with His promises. Even in their current state, the people took comfort in the idea that God's promises of their captivity had come true, so surely His pledge to restore them would too.

Change of Covenant (Jeremiah 30–33)

Beyond the promise of a return from captivity was God's ultimate plan to unite and restore His people, a new covenant that would be instituted by His Messiah. The old covenant of the Law, broken again and again by a faithless Israel, would be replaced by a new, deeply personal bond for each and all of them: "I will put My law in their minds, and write it on their hearts; I will be their God, and they shall be My people" (Jeremiah 31:33). The old covenant of the Law had a shelf life. There was coming a day when God would no longer relate to people based on their broken promises to keep His laws. Eventually He would send Jesus, whose perfect life and sacrificial death would provide the basis for a new relationship.

What a difference between the law and grace! Whereas the old covenant tried to control your conduct, the new covenant promises to change your character. Going beyond the sheet music of the law, which confined you to the notes on the page, the new song would be intuitive, played by ear, deep in the fiber of your being.

Jeremiah trusted God's promise enough to invest in it. Even though he was imprisoned for preaching the truth of Babylon's coming, he arranged to buy the title for a parcel of family land because God had promised that "houses and fields and vineyards shall be possessed again in this land" (Jeremiah 32:15). It was an act of faith, not just in Judah's return in seventy years, but in the everlasting kingdom God had promised through His Messiah, Jesus Christ (Jeremiah 33:14-18). Jeremiah had taken God up on His promise—"Call to Me, and I will answer you, and show you great and mighty things, which you do not know" (v. 3)—and it comforted him while he suffered for God's truth.

Cost of Consistency (Jeremiah 34–38)

Jeremiah recounted more of his ups and downs than any of the other prophets in the Bible—not just the message God gave him but his own thoughts about them, plus the details surrounding how, when, and where he delivered it and the subsequent reactions (which often ended with him being beaten or jailed). The upshot of it all is a personal perspective in the middle of a tumultuous time, a reminder that the scope of God's plans involves both nations and individuals.

Jeremiah learned the cost of a consistent stand for the truth. With God's words burning in his heart, he stayed on point with the message God gave him—and boy, did those stubborn people get sick of him. Judah's leaders didn't care that he took to heart the doom he was prophesying, that he wept over Judah's troubles and interceded for the people until God told him to stop. They just wanted him to shut up—even permanently, in some cases: "The princes said to the king: 'Please, let this man be put to death...For [he] does not seek the welfare of this people, but their harm'" (Jeremiah 38:4). King Zedekiah, who had been the subject of many of Jeremiah's unfavorable prophecies, told them, "Hey, do what you got to do." So they arrested Jeremiah and lowered him into a dungeon—basically, a deep pit with a muddy bottom.

It was literally the lowest point in Jeremiah's entire life, but even then, God didn't forget him. One of the king's eunuchs, Ebed-Melech, advocated for the prophet's release on the grounds that he would starve in the dungeon because the city's bread supplies had run out—as a result of Babylon's siege. Ironically, the proof that Jeremiah had been right the whole time seemed good enough reason for the king to permit his removal from the pit. In fact, Zedekiah may even have been curious to see what else Jeremiah was right about, because he had a frank discussion with the prophet about his own future as king.

Jeremiah promised to shoot straight with the king if he promised not to put him back in the hole, and the king agreed. But there was no secret to what Jeremiah told Zedekiah; it was a reiteration of what he had been saying over and over (vv. 15-23): "If you surrender to Babylon, you and your family will live and the city will not be burned; if you resist, the opposite will happen." God's judgment was a done deal; the best Judah could hope for was to trust Him while in exile. Zedekiah was grateful for the message and honored his promise, but the best he could do under the circumstances was to arrange for Jeremiah to be kept under house arrest in the royal courtyard. That's where Jeremiah was when Babylonian forces breached Jerusalem's walls and captured the city.

Care after the Captivity (Jeremiah 39–51)

Jeremiah recorded his eyewitness account of the fall of Jerusalem (more of that in the next chapter, Lamentations). Underlying all the horrific details is a foundational principle: You can't compromise with God. Try to have it both His way and yours, and you'll end up having neither. God will stay true to His essential character—holiness, love, and grace—just as the world will still stay true to its basic nature—self-service and survival at any cost. Their opposing objectives are why you can't serve two masters.

> You can't compromise with God. Try to have it both His way and yours, and you'll end up having neither.

The Babylonians allowed Jeremiah to stay in Judah, where he continued to receive messages from God and minister. Babylon's captain of the guard, Nebuzaradan, told Jeremiah he was free to decide where he wanted to go—either to stay or to go to Babylon. Jeremiah chose to stay as part of a small remnant of Jews (Jeremiah 40:1-12). Before Nebuzaradan left, though, he himself preached a condemning word against the Jews: "The LORD your God has pronounced doom on this place. Now the Lord has brought it, and has done just as He said. Because you people have sinned against the Lord, and not obeyed His voice, therefore this thing has come upon you" (vv. 2-3). It's one thing to have God's prophet telling you you've messed up; it's another entirely to have a pagan be the bearer of God's truth.

Jeremiah worked with a governor appointed by Babylon, Gedaliah, who echoed an earlier prophecy of Jeremiah's in telling the people how to treat their captors (Jeremiah 29:4-7): "Do not be afraid to serve the Chaldeans. Dwell in the land and serve the king of Babylon, and it shall be well with you" (Jeremiah 40:9). Despite the assurance of God's protection, various political factions conspired against Gedaliah, killing him and a number of Babylonian officials.

Caught between staying in Judah, where Babylon would surely send troops to retaliate, and fleeing to Egypt, where God had warned them not to go, the people asked Jeremiah to seek God for them. The message he brought was unmistakable: They were to rely on God's promise not to fear Babylon and not to travel to Egypt, where, despite the seeming promise of peace and safety, God's fury would be poured out on them for their disobedience (Jeremiah 42:17-18).

Jeremiah anticipated that the people would ignore God's word: "For you were hypocrites in your hearts when you sent me to the Lord your God, saying, 'Pray for us to the Lord our God, and according to all that the Lord your God says, so declare to us and we will do it'" (Jeremiah 42:20). Sure enough, the leaders didn't want to seek God to see what His plans were; they wanted Him to approve of theirs. They accused Jeremiah of lying about having received such a warning from God, gathered everyone up, and headed south to Egypt (Jeremiah 43:1-7).

Despite Judah's deliberate rebellion, God continued to send His word to the people through Jeremiah in Egypt, warning them that to stay there was to court disaster. They responded like spoiled children (Jeremiah 44:15-19), saying, "You say God has told us not to worship like everyone else does down here? Well, guess what, you foolish prophet—we're going to do it even more!"

Jeremiah responded by predicting that God would give Egypt to Babylon—punishing their host for harboring a disobedient people (vv. 29-30). The remnant of renegade Jews would also die in Egypt; "none shall return except for those who escape" (v. 14). Because of their obedience, God promised Jeremiah and his assistant Baruch that He would preserve their lives "as a prize in all places" (Jeremiah 45:5). Given Jeremiah's broken heart for his people, however, this was probably a small comfort.

Life would come at a premium for many of the surrounding nations, as Jeremiah prophesied doom on Egypt, Philistia, Moab, Ammon, Damascus, and various others, including Babylon. God was fed up with His people, but the nation that

He used to chasten her would not go unpunished for the arrogance they demonstrated and the pleasure they took in Judah's destruction. Written at a point when it looked like Babylon would reign forever and Judah would fade from history, Jeremiah's prophecy didn't hold back:

> "Let the violence done to me and my flesh be upon Babylon," the inhabitant of Zion will say...Therefore thus says the Lord: "Behold, I will plead your case and take vengeance for you. I will dry up her seas and make her springs dry. Babylon shall become a heap, a dwelling place for jackals, an astonishment and a hissing, without an inhabitant" (Jeremiah 51:35-37).

Woven throughout these promises of devastation for Judah's enemies were pledges of God's protection for His people—prophecies that foretold how He would preserve a remnant of His people and eventually bring them back to their homeland relatively soon, in seventy years' time, and in the distant future, during the millennial kingdom of Christ.

Predictions of Jeremiah Fulfilled (Jeremiah 52)

When Baruch penned the final chapter of Jeremiah, twenty-five years had passed since the previous predictions were made. It's a historical supplement that shows prophetic fulfillment. Regarding Babylon's rise and conquest of Judah, everything that Jeremiah had predicted—and Isaiah, centuries before—had come to pass.

Following a two-and-a-half-year siege at Jerusalem, Babylon's forces broke through the walls on July 18, 586 BC,[25] capturing King Zedekiah and Judah's princes. The princes were put to death at Nebuchadnezzar's command shortly afterward, while the king was blinded and taken in chains to Babylon (Jeremiah 52:6-11). General Nebuzaradan burned the temple and the houses of the wealthy and razed the walls. He took everything of earthly value from the temple and sent it, along with a group of captives, back to Babylon. You can still see the soot marks on the ruins of the Old City in the Kidron Valley.

Jerusalem's fall came to pass as predicted, but her restoration would come seventy years later, as promised. Three different groups of Jews would be sent back by the kings of Medo-Persia, the empire that fulfilled Jeremiah's prophecy and conquered Babylon. And in the future, just as Israel will receive her God-given place at the center of Christ's millennial kingdom, so Babylon—risen in the last days as the spiritual antithesis of everything to do with God—will ultimately fall, her place as the wicked representative of godless values erased from history forever: "Babylon the great is fallen, is fallen, and has become a dwelling place of demons, a prison for every foul spirit, and a cage for every unclean and hated bird!" (Revelation 18:2).

As a final thought, consider the importance of communication—a message not just sent but received. Almost everyone has a cell phone these days, making them available constantly. At the same time, they are able to vet their calls and decide whose they will answer. Cell phones are a great invention, but like any piece of technology, they come with their share of frustrations. Finland hosts an annual mobile phone-throwing championship—an opportunity for people to break the hold of high-tech gadgets by chucking phones as far as they can. Sounds like fun, but it points me back to the original purpose of a phone: two-way communication.

> **God placed a call to each of us when He sent His Son Jesus to save us from sin.**

God placed a call to each of us when He sent His Son Jesus to save us from sin. And it was necessary primarily because mankind has been historically poor about calling on God. "Call to Me, and I will answer you, and show you great and mighty things, which you do not know" (Jeremiah 33:3). Jeremiah called Judah for forty years, and not one soul responded. But he remained faithful to stay on the line, both with God and on God's behalf. When God gives you a call, knocking on the door of your heart, answer Him; you'll be amazed at all He has to show you.

LAMENTATIONS
FLIGHT PLAN

Facts

Author

Jewish tradition attributes authorship of the book of Lamentations to the prophet Jeremiah, though he goes unnamed in the book. Extrabiblical sources (that is, sources outside the Bible), such as the Greek Septuagint and Jewish Targum, point to Jeremiah as the author. Style and content similarities between Jeremiah and Lamentations also point to Jeremiah as the best candidate.

Date Written

Babylon sacked Jerusalem and the southern kingdom, Judah, in 586 BC; the book of Lamentations was written shortly thereafter.

Landmarks

This melancholy flight passes over the book of Lamentations. We will see why, as he grieved the destruction of Jerusalem, Jeremiah is referred to as the weeping prophet. This poetic book reveals a man distressed for a nation under the consequences of its own sin and ends with a prayer for restoration of the nation from captivity. The book of Lamentations is made up of five acrostic poems (poems beginning with a certain letter of the Hebrew alphabet), each a eulogy to the kingdom of Judah.

Itinerary

- Jerusalem Personified (Lamentations 1)
- Judgment Pronounced (Lamentations 2)
- Jeremiah's Proclamation (Lamentations 3)
- Justice Publicized (Lamentations 4)
- The Jews' Petition (Lamentations 5)

Gospel

Jesus is plainly evident in the tears of the weeping prophet in Lamentations. Looking out over Jerusalem's devastation, Jeremiah wrote, "For these things I weep; my eye, my eye overflows with water; because the comforter, who should restore my life, is far from me. My children are desolate because the enemy prevailed" (Lamentations 1:16). The sorrow sin causes overwhelmed the prophet's heart, just as it later did the Messiah's, when Jesus wept over Jerusalem's failure to recognize her Redeemer the week before she crucified Him (Luke 19:41-44).

The ultimate hope of Christ that provides the one bright spot in Lamentations—the single break in the clouds among five funeral dirges—came when Jeremiah recognized God's compassion in the midst of his sorrow: "Through the LORD's mercies we are not consumed, because His compassions fail not. They are new every morning; great is Your faithfulness" (Lamentations 3:22-23). The Hebrew word for "mercies" is *chesed*, which can also be translated as "lovingkindness," or "covenant love."

It's the kind of love that comes as a by-product of God's covenant with His people. Seventy years after their exile to Babylon, God brought the Jews back to the land because, in His mercy and lovingkindness, He said He would. When God makes a covenant, He keeps it. Even in the worst of times, Jeremiah understood this essential quality of God and praised Him for it.

But as wonderful as that covenant was for the Jews, God's new covenant through Jesus Christ's sacrifice on the cross is much better: If you have accepted Jesus as your Lord and Savior, then God is your Father and you are His child—no matter who you are. Your past, present, and future sins are all forgiven, and you have constant access to God's great mercy and unfailing faithfulness through the blood of Jesus. Though there are still consequences for sin, that sin has no control over the child of God. Plus, we have the assurance of heaven to look forward to: No matter what we go through in this life, we'll arrive safely home with Jesus one day.

> No matter what we go through in this life, we'll arrive safely home with Jesus one day.

History

The events described in the book of Lamentations took place when the Babylonians, led by King Nebuchadnezzar, destroyed Jerusalem in 586 BC. Jerusalem's walls were taken first, and then the temple, palaces, and other buildings followed. More than 4500 Jewish men (and probably 10,000 to 13,000 women and children, who were not included in the biblical account according to the numbering tradition of the day) were taken as prisoners and sent to Babylon.

The siege of Jerusalem began on July 10, 586 BC. The Jewish historian Josephus, writing much later in the first century AD, gave a record of the event, echoing 2 Kings 25:1-21, 2 Chronicles 36:15-21, and Jeremiah 52:4-30.[26] Jeremiah had previously predicted all of it, and because of his relentless commitment to proclaiming God's message, he had been thrown in prison by Zedekiah and his officials. Ironically, Jeremiah was released from prison by Nebuchadnezzar and set free (Jeremiah 39:11–40:1), while Zedekiah and his cronies went into captivity.

Travel Tips

Lamentations is a stirring reminder of two realities: God's judgment *and* His grace, love, and mercy. The judgment side of things gets more exposition here because of its immediate nature—the Jews were still grieving their losses at this moment in history, after all. But, as Jeremiah attested, God's steadfast faithfulness and mercy are what give us hope when hardship threatens to overwhelm us.

- God wants you to turn to Him in hard times. Jerusalem's downfall resulted from God's people persistently turning to other sources— nations and idols—for help and protection, instead of trusting God to protect and sustain them.

- Relationship beats religion and rituals any day. As Jeremiah lamented over how the presence of Judah's enemies defiled the temple, he noted how the Jews had misplaced their trust by putting it in a building rather than in the God for whom that building was created (Lamentations 1:10). Our spiritual lives should not be about a place, but a Person. The temples we create in our lives—work, activities, and even ministry—are empty and vulnerable to destruction.

- Sin is best confessed to God and turned from—ruthlessly. It's not easy, but it beats all the other ways you could deal with your sin—denial, dismissal, and drawing on your wisdom instead of God's are all popular on the broad path of destruction.

> ## Our spiritual lives should not be about a place, but a Person.

In Flight

Jerusalem Personified (Lamentations 1)

A lamentation is an expression of grief, typically a song or a poem mourning loss or destitution or pain. Regarding grief, Solomon observed, "Better to go to the house of mourning than to go to the house of feasting, for that is the end of all men; and the living will take it to heart" (Ecclesiastes 7:2). Take what to heart? That you will be there someday, sooner than you think. Read with a proper perspective, Lamentations isn't so much a book about death and destruction as much as it is about life and restoration and the God who makes it possible to bring the latter out of the former. Darkness reminds us how much we need light. As Jesus said, "Blessed are those who mourn, for they shall be comforted" (Matthew 5:4).

Jeremiah had good reason to mourn. Jerusalem—the city that he loved, the city of God's name and God's promise—had been conquered and burned by the Babylonians. He knew judgment was coming and had been the instrument of God to warn, repeatedly and without effect, the people of Judah. So the outcome wasn't a shock to him intellectually. Emotionally and spiritually, though, it was devastating, and Jeremiah wrote of Jerusalem, personifying the city as an afflicted woman whose sins had come home to roost.

Imagine a camera panning across Jerusalem, taking in the destruction from the outside looking in: "How lonely sits the city that was full of people! How like a widow is she, who was great among the nations! The princess among the provinces has become a slave!" (Lamentations 1:1). For most of her history, Jerusalem has been a crowded place, especially during the major religious feasts. David observed how "all the tribes of Israel—the LORD's people—make their pilgrimage here" (Psalm 122:4 NLT), and modern Jerusalem is still wall to wall with people today. I've seen it, though, during a partial evacuation, when word of a possible attack led to officials cordoning off the Old City near the Damascus Gate, and the emptiness of the streets was eerie.

Jeremiah expressed that haunting feeling of desolation as an enslaved princess fallen from royal suites to the gutter, betrayed by the false friendships she had once cultivated: "She weeps bitterly in the night, her tears are on her cheeks; among all her lovers she has none to comfort her" (Lamentations 1:2). Aside from the physical bleakness of the burned city, this is a picture of feeling alone in a crowd, that emotional and spiritual loneliness darker than midnight. In Jerusalem's case, she was surrounded by nations with whom she had built alliances, only to have them fail her in her hour of need.

God had warned Judah's leaders over and over again not to ally themselves with Egypt and Edom and Tyre—not to trust the strength of any army to protect them against Babylon—because it wasn't a matter of military might but God's just punishment for Judah's sin that had doomed her. As various kings and priests had looked out over the crowded streets, filled with pilgrims and vendors and families, somehow they concluded that striking alliances with pagan governments was a better option than drawing close to the God who had founded and established them. Turning from God to man's help was her downfall.

No doubt that was part of the anguish that wracked the tiny remnant left behind, as "all her friends have dealt treacherously with her; they have become her enemies" (Lamentations 1:2). The drifting away from God took place over the years as the people put their faith in the temple itself, rather than the God who was supposed to be worshipped within its walls and courts. They thought that the presence of the building itself, and the rituals they carried out within, guaranteed good standing with God.

But Judah's worship didn't come from her heart, so it didn't translate into everyday life, didn't result in wisdom or peace or righteousness. And now, looking at the scorched ruins of the temple, Jeremiah saw the unimaginable had happened: "The adversary has spread his hand over all her pleasant things; for she has seen the nations enter her sanctuary, those whom You commanded not to enter Your assembly" (v. 10). When Babylon sacked the temple, it was an outward manifestation of Judah's inward deterioration.

Jeremiah then shifted his point of view, taking on the voice of the broken city, confessing her sin: "The LORD is righteous, for I rebelled against His commandment. Hear now, all peoples, and behold my sorrow; my virgins and my young men have gone into captivity" (v. 18). When it comes to sin, there are a few typical ways people respond. The first is straight denial; either sin doesn't actually exist, or it's relative, or what they've done just isn't sin. Another way is to compare themselves to someone else, saying, "It's not like I'm a serial killer or a terrorist." Still others actually admit they've sinned, but they try to take care of it themselves, reading self-help books or going to therapy—both of which can help, but only to certain extent, and not in any way that deals with the ultimate issue: We've all sinned and fallen short of God's glory (Romans 3:23).

The best way to deal with sin is the biblical way—to agree with God that sin is sin, to admit that you've sinned, to ask God to forgive you for your sin, and then to turn away from it for good. Let God clean you up internally, and then you can partner with Him to move away from any external situations. Anything less and your sin will linger, rooted deep in your heart and mindset, and it will grow again—as Jerusalem discovered to her dismay.

Judgment Pronounced (Lamentations 2)

The second dirge pictures God as the one dismantling Jerusalem—a one-man wrecking crew acting on the admonition later recorded in the New Testament: "It is a fearful thing to fall into the hands of the living God" (Hebrews 10:31). Persistent sin and failure to confess and repent meant God's best option was to get His people's attention through drastic means. "How the Lord has covered the daughter of Zion with a cloud in His anger! He cast down from heaven to the earth the beauty of Israel, and did not remember His footstool"—the temple—"in the day of His anger" (Lamentations 2:1).

Babylon was God's agent, but God orchestrated Judah's downfall. "The Lord was like an enemy. He has swallowed up Israel, He has swallowed up all her palaces; He has destroyed her strongholds, and has increased mourning and lamentation in the daughter of Judah" (v. 5). This is the hard truth: Jeremiah mentioned Babylon some 160 times in the book of Jeremiah as the nation that would besiege, pillage, and destroy the city, but here, talking about the same events, he portrayed God as the agent. God worked sovereignly behind the scenes, directing events and people so that Nebuchadnezzar would rise to power and come against Jerusalem, and God allowed him to topple its walls.

Now, this wasn't God orchestrating His people's suffering because He was in a bad mood or has a hateful personality. This was a divine spanking, a concept any parent can understand, and one used to describe God's discipline throughout the Bible. Solomon said, "My son, do not despise the chastening of the LORD, nor detest His correction; for whom the LORD loves He corrects, just as a father the son in whom he delights" (Proverbs 3:11-12). Sometimes, a child is on a bad path, bent by the will and pride of human nature, and the only way to get him off that path and back on God's path is a painful act of discipline—which is actually an act of love. The writer of Hebrews quoted Proverbs 3 on the same subject and added that "no chastening seems to be joyful for the present, but painful; nevertheless, afterward it yields the peaceable fruit of righteousness to those who have been trained by it" (Hebrews 12:11).

Part of the pain of that discipline, though, was God abandoning the temple. "The Lord has spurned His altar, He has abandoned His sanctuary; He has given up the walls of her palaces into the hand of the enemy. They have made a noise in the house of the LORD, as on the day of a set feast" (Lamentations 2:7). The Babylonians came and partied in God's house because God let them. He let them do so because, by their legalism and idolatry, it was what the Jews had been asking for, even if indirectly, for centuries. They needed to get back to the intent of the law, a heart committed to pleasing God.

Jeremiah was a powerful example of what it meant to connect with God's heart. He gave voice to his personal response to all the heartache he saw: "My eyes fail with tears, my heart is troubled; my bile is poured on the ground because of the destruction of the daughter of my people, because the children and infants faint in the streets of the city" (v. 11). After all he had seen and been through—the wickedness and false teaching of Judah's leaders, and the persecution he had endured at their hands—he could easily have become desensitized, hardened to the heartbreaking effects of sin. But he didn't; he stayed connected to God, and knew that even in His anger, God's heart was always to reconcile with His wayward children. In order to accomplish that, however, He had to act as a chastening parent, an agent of discipline to awaken them to their need for Him.

Jeremiah's Proclamation (Lamentations 3)

Jeremiah was God's eyewitness in this difficult season. "I am the man who has seen affliction by the rod of His wrath" (Lamentations 3:1). In other words, "I, Jeremiah, watched God spank this nation." On the surface, it is one of the least enviable ministries ever recorded—no conversions during his lifetime, witness to Jerusalem's destruction and Judah's exile, mocked and beaten and imprisoned—and yet he didn't give in to despair or bitterness, didn't jump on a judgment bandwagon and crow over Judah's just desserts.

So when you read Jeremiah's account of his reaction to the suffering he saw, you're not looking at the words of a whiner. You're seeing the pain of sin's cost, its fatal wages, as it wore down a good man. And even in his anguish, Jeremiah kept his eyes on God and accepted the hardship that God had allowed. For starters, it gave him a healthy outlet for his pain: "He has led me and made me walk in darkness and not in light. Surely He has turned His hand against me time and time again throughout the day...I have become the ridicule of all my people—their taunting song all the day" (Lamentations 3:2-3, 14). Watching Jerusalem burn and his people go into exile, Jeremiah's agony tore at his heart and turned his stomach, the deep fear that came as he realized that God, in working out His purposes, had indeed abandoned His people to their own devices.

Even though Jeremiah had obeyed God and faithfully carried out his job as prophet, he felt Judah's isolation, the sense of separation from God: "Even when I cry and I shout, He shuts out my prayer. He has blocked my ways with hewn stone; He has made my paths crooked" (vv. 8-9). God had warned him not to pray any longer for Judah's deliverance (Jeremiah 7:16; 14:11), but to see that He really wasn't listening any longer was crushing. God's invitation to call on Him and be shown wonderful, unknown things (Jeremiah 33:3) had been revoked.

Jeremiah was left with a choice: to despair and give up, or to go back to what God had already promised. He reviewed what he knew about God's character and anchored himself to that truth. It produced the most hopeful moment in the book: "This I recall to my mind, therefore I have hope. Through the LORD's mercies we are not consumed, because His compassions fail not. They are new every morning; great is Your faithfulness" (Lamentations 3:21-23). This is the single sunbeam breaking through the gray, the diamond in the coal mine, and it's a beauty.

God's promise to bring His people back home after a season in captivity fueled Jeremiah's hope. "'The LORD is my portion,' says my soul, 'Therefore I hope in Him!' The LORD is good to those who wait for Him, to the soul who seeks Him. It is good that one should hope and wait quietly for the salvation of the LORD" (vv. 24-26). This remarkable resolve didn't come because things were going well for Jeremiah, or because he had never suffered. His eyes still stinging with an overflow of tears, Jeremiah turned to the one true thing in his life: his God.

Grieving over his people's slaughter and frustrated over the lack of justice for all the times he had been humiliated and punished, Jeremiah left vengeance in God's hands and trusted that God would make it all right: "You drew near on the day I called on You, and said, 'Do not fear!' O Lord, you have pleaded the case for my soul; You have redeemed my life" (vv. 57-58). He knew God was sovereign and loving: "For the Lord will not cast off forever. Though He causes grief, yet He will show compassion according to the multitude of His mercies" (vv. 31-32). Jeremiah looked beyond his circumstances and saw his Savior.

Justice Publicized (Lamentations 4)

The fact that Jeremiah had re-anchored his hope in God didn't mean that his current situation wasn't still a huge mess. The fourth funeral dirge laments the carnage throughout the once-glorious city of Jerusalem. "How is the gold become dim! How changed the fine gold! The stones of the sanctuary are scattered at the head of every street" (Lamentations 4:1). Perhaps he referred to the few remains of the temple treasury or even one of the gemstones dislodged from the high priest's bejeweled breastplate, scattered in the streets like so much garbage.

The horror of the damage was inescapable—spirits broken, starving children, wealth discarded, the slain better off than the living. And yet God's justice was being realized. "The LORD has fulfilled His fury, He has poured out His fierce anger. He kindled a fire in Zion, and it has devoured its foundations" (v. 11). Even worse was the knowledge that all the surrounding nations understood that Judah's shame had come as a result of her own disobedience. "The kings of the earth, and all inhabitants of the world, would not have believed that the adversary and the enemy could enter the gates of Jerusalem" (v. 12).

It was as if all the surrounding pagan nations knew that Judah had a special deal with God. They could see that He blessed the Jews, their land and leaders, protecting them in battle and prospering them through the reigns of men like David and Solomon. Maybe the reason for Judah's fall, then, was as clear to them as it was to Jeremiah: "Because of the sins of her prophets and the iniquities of her priests, who shed in her midst the blood of the just" (v. 13). The leadership was corrupt. "They wandered blind in the streets; they have defiled themselves with blood, so that no one would touch their garments" (v. 14).

The very individuals who were to represent God to the people, and represent the people before God, had lost their fear of the Lord—their reverent, humble awe of the God they served. They got caught up in status, power, and wealth, turning their attention to seeking and maintaining those things rather than the work God had given them. And in their positions as leaders, they provided that example to the people, turning their hearts from God and setting the nation on a disastrous path.

The Jews' Petition (Lamentations 5)

Jeremiah's final lament was a prayer, pleading with God to keep His promises, not to forget the people in their darkest hour. "Remember, O LORD, what has come upon us; look, and behold our reproach! Our inheritance has been turned over to aliens, and our houses to foreigners...Our fathers sinned and are no more, but we bear their iniquities" (Lamentations 5:1-2, 7). And oh! What a list of consequences it was: famine and fever, rape and oppression, hard labor and fear of gathering publicly. "The joy of our heart has ceased; our dance has turned into mourning. The crown has fallen from our head. Woe to us, for we have sinned!" (vv. 15-16).

Jeremiah asked an honest question—one that, if we are equally candid, we would admit we have also put to God at some point: "You, O LORD, remain forever;

Your throne from generation to generation. Why do you forget us forever, and forsake us for so long a time?" (vv. 19-20). Yes, Judah had messed up—her leaders, her prophets, her people by and large chose their own way over God's and drove God to these desperate measures to snap them out of their sin. But for how long, O Lord? How long?

And even so, there were holy people among them, Jeremiah and others, who stayed faithful and got grouped in with the masses of selfish sinners. It's not unreasonable for them to ask God, "Are You still up there? Do You still care?" That hope and fear mingled in Jeremiah's final statement, a prayer the book leaves unanswered. "Turn us back to You, O Lord, and we will be restored; renew our days as of old, unless You have utterly rejected us, and are very angry with us!" (vv. 21-22).

I can only hope that Jeremiah turned to the law, to the passage where Moses foretold everything that had just happened. Back when Moses was indoctrinating a new generation, the one that would actually enter the Promised Land after the previous generation had blown it and died off in the desert, he made a fateful prediction:

> I call heaven and earth to witness against you this day, that you will soon utterly perish from the land which you cross over the Jordan to possess; you will not prolong your days in it, but will be utterly destroyed. And the Lord will scatter you among the peoples, and you will be left few in number among the nations where the Lord will drive you. And there you will serve gods, the work of men's hands, wood and stone, which neither see nor hear nor eat nor smell. But from there you will seek the Lord your God, and you will find Him if you seek Him with all your heart and with all your soul. When you are in distress, and all these things come upon you in the latter days, when you turn to the Lord your God and obey His voice (for the Lord your God is a merciful God), He will not forsake you nor destroy you, nor forget the covenant of your fathers which He swore to them (Deuteronomy 4:26-31).

Let that sink in. Even at a moment of renewal, God told His people that they would blow it and that He would punish them for it. But He also told them that, in His mercy, He would listen when they cried out to Him from their captivity, and He would bring them back into the land He had promised their ancestors. So in that sense, Lamentations ends with hope, in spite of suffering, in spite of Judah's sin. Even through the tears, Jeremiah knew that God's mercy and faithfulness was new every morning. It only looked like they had used them all up, but God would bring them through the consequences of their sin to a new day, and He would guard them even in the midst of those consequences, looking to draw their hearts back to Him. Great is God's faithfulness!

Great is God's faithfulness!

EZEKIEL
FLIGHT PLAN

Facts

Author

According to Ezekiel 1:1, Ezekiel the priest authored the book that bears his name. Ezekiel was the son of Buzi and came from a priestly family. His wife—"the desire of [his] eyes" (Ezekiel 24:16)—was taken from him suddenly while in exile in Babylon; we don't know if they had any children.

Date Written

Ezekiel began his ministry in the fifth year of King Jehoiachin's reign, 593 BC, which was when he began to write his book. He then probably finished sometime in 571 BC.

Landmarks

Ezekiel's prophetic ministry began with a dramatic vision near the Chebar River near Babylon. His spectacular and strange visions of God's glory were further enhanced by his bizarre performances that accompanied them—on different occasions, at God's behest he shaved his head and beard, played army, and lay on one side in public for months. These things were done to help his audience understand the concepts he was trying to convey. The message of his book can be summarized in four words: commission, correction, castigation, and conciliation.

Itinerary

- Commission of the Prophet (Ezekiel 1–3)
- Correction of the Problem (Ezekiel 4–24)
- Castigation of the Peoples (Ezekiel 25–32)
- Conciliation of God's Purpose (Ezekiel 33–48)

Gospel

The bright scarlet thread of redemption is found in Ezekiel 36, where God made a three-tiered promise to Israel that they would be regathered to their land, that their hearts would be regenerated spiritually, and that His kingdom would be reestablished among them. The first part of that promise was fulfilled when Israel became a nation in 1948, and the third part will be fulfilled at Jesus's second coming when He establishes His kingdom on earth (Ezekiel 40–48). The second part—the promise of regeneration—points to the work Jesus did on the cross.

Jesus is our "great High Priest" (Hebrews 4:14), who gave Himself as the ultimate sacrifice for sin. Under this new covenant, His blood regenerates us spiritually, cleansing us of sin and making us new creations. This covenant is foreshadowed in Ezekiel 36: "Then I will sprinkle clean water on you, and you shall be clean; I will cleanse you from all your filthiness and from all your idols" (v. 25).

In the Jewish rights of purification, the priest would sprinkle lamb's blood on the "dwelling places," the vessels used for worship, and on the people themselves in order to cleanse them. Ezekiel's use of "sprinkle" predicted the priestly work the Messiah would do in cleansing the nation of Israel through His own suffering on the cross.

Israel lost its temple—its means to atone for sin—not long after Jesus walked the earth. But here in Ezekiel, God promised to provide atonement for them. Isaiah used similar language when he prophesied that God's Servant (Jesus) would "sprinkle many nations" (Isaiah 52:15). This foretold the great truth that salvation isn't just for the Jews, but for the whole world.

History

Ezekiel was taken to Babylon by Nebuchadnezzar with the second wave of Jewish captives in 597 BC, so his writing followed closely after Daniel's—who was taken with the first wave of captives in 605 BC and just prior to Jerusalem's fall in 586 BC.

Jeremiah, who had been prophesying for more than thirty years by the time Ezekiel began his ministry, was left in Jerusalem at that time. All three prophets foretold the impending doom of Judah, the need for the Jews to return to God, and God's plans to make that possible.

Travel Tips

Ezekiel's main message is that no matter what God's people are facing—a hostile culture, the loss of jobs and homes, widespread fear and depression—they can trust God's promises to restore that which is lost. While you may struggle to understand what God is doing when you face challenging and dark days, you can also rest in the knowledge that He gives you His Spirit to empower and sustain you.

- God equips those whom He calls. Ezekiel had a tough message to deliver and a lot of physical challenges that went with it. The only explanation for how Ezekiel was able to persevere throughout his ministry is that God's Spirit empowered him (Ezekiel 2:2; 3:24).

God equips those whom He calls.

- God is holy. The Jewish temple played a crucial part in Ezekiel's prophecies, adding to the sorrow of the people's exile and the joy of their return, since the temple provided their only access to God. For New Testament believers, the temple is a reminder of who God is and all that He has done and will do for His people. God is still perfectly holy, but we no longer have to go through a complicated series of rituals and sacrifices to get to Him. The blood of Jesus Christ saves us and gives us access to His presence, and we are now God's temple on earth (1 Corinthians 6:19-20).
- Jesus calls all believers to be watchmen: "Watch therefore, for you do not know what hour your Lord is coming" (Matthew 24:42). Not only should you be aware of the events in the world that Jesus said would be precursors of the end times, you should also be about His business in the meantime, whatever that may look like in your daily life.

In Flight

Commission of the Prophet (Ezekiel 1–3)

Ezekiel was a contemporary of both Jeremiah and Daniel—two other prophets who received spectacular visions. There are no indications that they knew each other, but each had his unique and powerful ministry—Jeremiah to God's people in Judah, Daniel to the royal courts of their captors, and Ezekiel to God's people in Babylon. While Jeremiah did some pretty unusual things to get God's message across, Ezekiel took it to another level. He lived out the message even more radically, at various points shaving his head and beard, building a military diorama, laying on his side for more than a year, and baking bread using cow dung as fuel. Acting out God's message drove it home on a deeper level—though the words were pretty intense too!

Ezekiel committed himself fully to a ministry that he didn't set out to do, but that God called him to. Picture having a goal or a plan that requires you to work and study and train for years—such as starting your own business or becoming a doctor. But then, at the moment all your diligence is supposed to come to fruition, something happens to prevent it—a loss or injury so unexpected that you have no idea what to do next. If you can imagine the confusion and devastation you would feel, you would know what it would have been like to walk a mile in Ezekiel's sandals.

Ezekiel had trained his whole adult life to become a priest of God in the temple in Jerusalem. That all fell apart in 597 BC, when he was deported in the second phase of the Babylonian conquest of Judah. We find him in Babylon as the book begins: "It came to pass in the thirtieth year, in the fourth month, on the fifth day of the month, as I was among the captives by the River Chebar, that the heavens were opened, and I saw visions of God" (Ezekiel 1:1). One of Ezekiel's trademarks is his precise dating, and here he gives us the month and day and his age, thirty—which was the age at which priests could begin serving the Lord in the temple.

On one hand, Ezekiel was spared the doom of Jerusalem's fall and the destruction of the temple; on the other, he was likely disappointed he never got to serve as a priest. Maybe he was even wondering what he was supposed to do with his life—and then God called him to serve from captivity. It was a remarkable introduction, a spectacular, strange vision of God in His glory: a fiery whirlwind containing "four living creatures" (Ezekiel 1:5) and God seated above them on a sapphire throne, a figure of fire and rainbow light.

The creatures looked like men, and each had four faces and four wings and flashed around like lightning, but always moving straight ahead, wherever the spirit led them. Rather than the result of a late-night pepperoni pizza, these were a special class of angelic being called *cherubim* (Ezekiel 10:15) who escort God's presence and glory and stand sentinel over man's access to Him. Cherubim had prevented Adam and Eve from re-entering Eden after the fall, and a pair of carved cherubim sat atop the mercy seat on the Ark of the Covenant.

In Ezekiel's vision, each cherubim had four faces: those of a man, a lion, an ox, and an eagle. Many theologians see possible patterns there of a model of God's throne in heaven. Back in the wilderness, when the children of Israel camped out for forty years, they always set up their encampment in the same arrangement. The tabernacle was at the center, with a group of three tribes on each of the four sides. Each group had a lead tribe that flew a banner: Judah's emblem was a lion, Ephraim's was the ox, Reuben's was a man, and Dan's was an eagle. God wanted to camp out with His people, and the setup was a precursor of His promise to set His throne among them as their Messiah.

That leads us to the New Testament, where we find the story of God's Messiah in not one but four Gospels. Each has a different focus on Jesus: Matthew spoke of Him as the Lion of the tribe of Judah, the promised King. Mark presented a compact, immediate picture of Jesus as God's humble, diligent servant—an ox set to the task of salvation. Luke revealed Jesus's role as the Son of Man, come to identify with us, to heal and save. Finally, John portrayed Christ as the Son of God, symbolized as a soaring eagle. These different facets of Jesus's ministry and character also come to the fore at the end of the Bible, where John saw four living beings, with similar characteristics to the ones in Ezekiel, around God's throne in heaven (Revelation 4:6-8).

Even wilder is the method of transportation accompanying these cherubim. Beside each of them was an amber-colored gyroscopic wheel-within-a-wheel that moved where and when they did (Ezekiel 1:15-20). The rims of each wheel were also tricked out with eyes, giving an overall impression so unworldly as to invite attention from a whole host of fanciful speculators, who have called the wheels everything from UFOs to a Talmudic secret to a source of Kabbalah (a form of Jewish mysticism). The correct answer is "none of the above": Rather, this is a tricked-out, angel-powered vehicle moving God's presence wherever He wants it to go—and possibly, given that eyes often depict omniscience in Scripture, everywhere there *is* to go.

Up to this point, Ezekiel had just been looking under the hood, checking out the chassis and the body of this divine vehicle—but then he heard a voice, saw a human-like figure seated on a throne above the cherubim, and it clicked: "This was the appearance of the likeness of the glory of the LORD" (Ezekiel 1:28). That's when he hit the deck, getting face-down in the dirt before God. The Lord told him to get up, the Holy Spirit set him on his feet, and God spoke to him, calling him "son of man" (Ezekiel 2:1, 3, 6-8). That phrase is one of the hallmarks of Ezekiel's writing, used 100 times over the course of the book. It emphasizes man's mortality—as if God wanted to make something crystal clear: "Hey, Israel and Judah: I am God and you are not." No matter how much stature a man has intellectually, physically, or spiritually, he is still flesh, still prone to sin, still limited in ways that God is not nor ever will be. Amidst all the hardship of his ministry—the physical toll, the social rejection—Ezekiel survived because the Holy Spirit indwelled and infused him with supernatural power and knowledge. Because of the Spirit's presence, Ezekiel was able to take in the message God had for him—"lamentations and mourning and woe...[which] was in my mouth like honey in sweetness" (Ezekiel 2:10; 3:3)—and deliver it to the hardhearted people of Israel, whom God said would not listen to him because they wouldn't listen to their God (Ezekiel 3:7). Nevertheless, God sent Ezekiel, because a son of man with the Spirit of God in him, who internalizes and applies God's Word, will become a powerful tool.

Specifically, God told Ezekiel, "I have made you a watchman for the house of Israel; therefore hear a word from My mouth, and give them warning from Me" (Ezekiel 3:17). A watchman was an essential role in those days. He stood watch from towers atop a city's walls, looking for any signs of trouble—an approaching enemy, an impending storm, or a fire in the city. *Watchman* is a fitting job description in the sense that prophets were originally called *seers*, those who received visions from God. Ezekiel would see things from God's perspective and declare it with power to the masses.

Correction of the Problem (Ezekiel 4–24)

The first demonstration of God's word to the captives in Babylon depicted the siege of Jerusalem (Ezekiel 4–24). Since Ezekiel had been deported in the second group of captives, news of what was happening back home would have caught most Jewish ears. The news wasn't good, though. God told His prophet to draw a picture of Jerusalem on a clay tablet, but then to build up clay siege mounds around it and set model camps and battering rams around the walls (Ezekiel 4:1-3). Trouble was coming to Jerusalem.

I don't know if boys played with toy army men back then, but Ezekiel got to—and for an extended period too because God also wanted him to metaphorically bear Israel and Judah's sin. He was to lay on his side each day—one day for each year of Israel's sin (390 days) and then switch to the other side and bear Judah's sin too (another forty days). That was a tougher job than it might sound like at first, even if he only had to do it during daylight hours or some other period of time each day.

If nap time seemed rough, snack time was worse. God wanted Ezekiel to eat bread each day "and bake it using fuel of human waste in their sight" (Ezekiel 4:12)—as a symbol of the unkosher food the Jews would be eating in exile. As someone who had stayed kosher his whole life, a priest, Ezekiel protested the baking fuel. God let him off the hook and let him use cow dung instead. Only comparatively would that seem like a relief, but it must have been because Ezekiel didn't complain again. Beyond the symbolism of Israel's sin, the idea was that under siege, there would be no wood to cook fires, so dried-out manure would have to be used. The image of Jerusalem's future desperation was taking shape—and it was going to be an eyesore.

God was telling His people the details in advance not because they could do anything about it—they were already captive in Babylon, it was too late for them to help Jerusalem. Rather, He told them so that, as it all unfolded, they would understand one thing: God was saying, "Know that I am the Lord" (Ezekiel 6:7). That phrase is used sixty times throughout the book for that very reason: God is unique, holy, and different than His creation. He can control it, make demands on it, and work out its details to achieve a certain objective.

That's a concept that should have been familiar to Israel and Judah because it was true of their temple: On the one hand, the temple that meant God could be approached and that He wanted relationship; on the other hand, He had to be approached carefully, through offerings and sacrifice, and not everyone could do it. There were separate courts for Gentiles, women, men, and priests. All of that spoke to His holiness, but Israel and Judah had forgotten, and there would be a reckoning.

Jeremiah and Isaiah covered a lot of the same material—the inevitability of judgment, the false hopes raised by the leaders, the horror of life under siege, the wrath of God through the hand of Nebuchadnezzar. Ezekiel emphasized God's promises to bring the people back and restore them, but focused primarily and graphically on the harsh nature of the punishment to come. The spanking worked; the captivity did its job of correcting Israel's behavior. When the people returned home after seventy years in Babylon, they never again fell into the kind of blanket idolatry they engaged in before the captivity.

Castigation of the Peoples (Ezekiel 25–32)

God here began to shift his focus to the punishment He would visit on the nations who had enjoyed and celebrated His discipline of Israel and Judah. Again, it's similar material to what was covered by Jeremiah and Isaiah—doom on the Ammonites, Moabites, Philistines, Egyptians, and so on—with Ezekiel making his familiar distinction that the reason these hardships would befall them was so that they would know that God is the Lord (Ezekiel 25:7).

Ezekiel talked about one particular city more than any other prophet, forecasting the fall of Tyre. A major port city located within heavy walls on a rocky island off the eastern Mediterranean coast north of Israel, Tyre was a prized target for Nebuchadnezzar and other conquerors after him. After Ezekiel denounced various other rulers, he spoke of the ruler of Tyre in unusual terms—seemingly on one level as a human ruler and on another as a demonic one, possibly even Satan himself. God told Ezekiel to address the pride of "the prince of Tyre" (Ezekiel 28:2).

The Hebrew word for "prince" is *nagid*, indicating an earthly ruler, the man at the top. At this time Tyre had a prince named Ethbaal,[27] who ruled from 590–572 BC. He took an inordinate amount of pride in his city's wealth and defensive capabilities, something Ezekiel touched on: "Thus says the Lord GOD: 'Because your heart is lifted up, and you say, "I am a god, I sit in the seat of gods, in the midst of the seas," yet you are a man, and not a god...Behold, therefore, I will bring strangers against you'" (Ezekiel 28:2, 7). God emphasized Ethbaal's mortality and pride in detailing his coming downfall, but then something peculiar happened.

God told Ezekiel to send a lamentation to the "king of Tyre" (Ezekiel 28:12). Ezekiel employed the Hebrew word *melek* ("king"), which he rarely used, and only once in conjunction with the kings of Judah (for Jehoiachin in Ezekiel 1:2). Tyre had a prince, not a king, at this time. Was Ezekiel just looking for a different word for *leader*? You might think so, at least until he described this king of Tyre, using details that could fit no earthly ruler: "You were in Eden, the garden of God; every precious stone was your covering" (Ezekiel 28:13). Even if this was royal hyperbole used to make Ethbaal seem like a legendary monarch, the description of those covering stones—nine of the twelve listed were also found on the breastplate of a priest—stands out as distinctive.

The next detail—"The workmanship of your timbrels and pipes was prepared for you on the day you were created" (v. 13)—suggests a musician, not a ruler. The mention of the day of this king's "creation" suggests not a typical birth but a special act of formation. "You were the anointed cherub who covers; I established you; you were on the holy mountain of God; you walked back and forth in the midst of fiery stones" (v. 14). Now, Ethbaal probably lived large, but this isn't a description of earthly wealth or position or origin.

We saw cherubim back in chapter 1 in Ezekiel's vision at the river; there is no way Ethbaal looked anything like one of them, or had their role as angelic guardian of God's presence. There is a connection, though. Remember, Ethbaal was being called out for his vanity, which ties him to the fall of the angelic being—a former worship leader in heaven—who was denounced and banished for his excessive, blasphemous pride. "How you are fallen from heaven, O Lucifer, son of the morning! How you are cut down to the ground, you who weakened the nations! For you have said in your heart: 'I will ascend into heaven, I will exalt my throne above the stars of God'" (Isaiah 14:12-13).

In declaring Ethbaal's doom as ruler of Tyre, Ezekiel drew a parallel with Satan's fall, giving us a glimpse into the spiritual power behind the kingdoms that set their hearts against God and His people. For the role they played and the awful pride they took in it, even as agents under the control of God's sovereign hand, the punishment of these nations was just.

Conciliation of God's Purpose (Ezekiel 33–48)

God turned Ezekiel's attention back to Israel for the remainder of the book, describing His plan to restore them after their captivity. The ultimate conciliation, though, is still to come, when Israel becomes the center of Christ's millennial kingdom reign—and Ezekiel pointed to this too.

God began this section by reminding Ezekiel of the importance of his role as a watchman (Ezekiel 33:1-7). Not only was the prophet to stay true to God's calling—speaking the truth God gave him whether the people responded or not—but he could do so knowing that God would vindicate his ministry, that when all the predicted doom and destruction came, then "they will know that a prophet has been among them" (v. 33). Part of that message included speaking to the false prophets and shepherds of Israel, who had taken advantage of their authority and fleeced the people under their care.

Ezekiel made it clear that God would not let them get away with their abusive ways, and that His long-term plan was to provide Israel with a true Shepherd, Christ (Ezekiel 34:22-31). God made a three-part promise to Israel, which included being regathered to their land physically (Ezekiel 36:23), having their hearts regenerated spiritually (vv. 25-27), and then re-establishing His kingdom on earth eventually (Ezekiel 40–48).

The fulfillment of all these promises seemed unlikely at the time Ezekiel predicted them, and yet Israel did indeed return to their land after seventy years in Babylon, and centuries later, after a massive dispersal during Roman times in the first century, the state of Israel was reformed in 1948. That fulfilled God's promise: "I will take you from among the nations, gather you out of all countries, and bring you into your own land" (Ezekiel 36:24). To visit Israel today is to experience fulfilled prophecy as the Jews there speak their historic Hebrew language in their ancient homeland.

The regathering served as a precursor to a future reawakening: God will revive Israel spiritually during the end times, in the kingdom age, something Ezekiel predicted: "I will give you a new heart and put a new spirit within you; I will take the heart of stone out of your flesh and give you a heart of flesh. I will put My Spirit within you and cause you to walk in My statutes, and you will keep My judgments and do them" (Ezekiel 36:26-27). That promise encompasses both Israel and the rest of the world as part of the new covenant forged by Jesus Christ on the cross and fulfilled ultimately in the millennium (see **Gospel** on page 282).

Ezekiel's prediction of that atonement is memorably illustrated in a vision of a valley filled with dry bones (Ezekiel 37). God showed Ezekiel this image as a representation of Israel's spiritual state—their capital, temple, and hearts dead and dried out in a valley of despair and dispersal. He asked, "Son of man, can these bones live?" (v. 3). Ezekiel replied that God alone could know such a thing, and God responded, "Prophesy to these bones, and say to them, 'O dry bones, hear the word of the Lord!'" (v. 4). This was a vivid picture of Ezekiel's ministry—that the people had not responded to his warnings any more than a pile of bones would.

Yet God had regeneration and revival in mind despite how futile it seemed. God said to the bones, "Surely I will cause breath to enter into you, and you shall live" (v. 5). The Hebrew word for "breath" here is *ruwach*, which means "spirit." God would cause His Spirit to enter these dead people and resurrect them, a powerful visualization of what Christ accomplished on the cross. Further, God promised to be with Israel afterward, a scenario that is key to the end times: "I will set My sanctuary in their midst forevermore" (Ezekiel 37:26).

> God would cause His Spirit to enter these dead people and resurrect them, a powerful visualization of what Christ accomplished on the cross.

Israel's revival precedes the next events Ezekiel described, his famous vision of the war against God and Magog (Ezekiel 38–39). There's more to unravel here than our high-altitude vantage point permits, so I'll just lay out a few basic details. God told Ezekiel, "Son of man, set your face against Gog, of the land of Magog, the prince of Rosh, Meshech, and Tubal, and prophesy against him" (Ezekiel 38:2). All the strange names refer to a group of nations that will attack the regathered Israel in the end times. *Gog* means "leader," but the rest are old names for peoples from the table of nations in Genesis 10.

With the help of ancient historians like Herodotus[28] and Josephus,[29] we can piece together a broad idea of what Ezekiel prophesied. Magog appears to be composed of parts of modern Russia and its allies, including Iran (ancient Persia, which also included parts of Iraq), Ethiopia, and Libya (Ezekiel 38:5). Gomer and Togarmah (v. 6) are believed to be part of Turkey. Even though in Ezekiel's day there were no connections or ties among any of these nations, they all have one thing in common: at some point or other, they have all expressed and acted on hatred of Israel and the Jewish people.

Today, many of those nations, spearheaded by Russia, have formed alliances that point to a fulfillment of these prophecies. It's something that's bound to happen at some point, and it's good to stay tuned in and watchful. But the bottom line is this: Whoever these nations are and whenever they decide to join up and attack, God will defeat them. "You shall fall upon the mountains of Israel, you and all your troops and the peoples who are with you; I will give you to birds of prey of every sort and to the beasts of the field to be devoured" (Ezekiel 39:4). This battle with Gog and Magog will likely be the catalyst that turns Israel's hearts back to God, opening them up to receive Jesus as their Messiah and Savior.

The last nine chapters of the book describe a vision of a rebuilt temple. When Ezekiel foretold this, the first temple was still several years away from being destroyed by the Babylonians, and hundreds of years from being rebuilt and destroyed again by the Romans. There is no temple in Jerusalem now, but during the millennium, it will be rebuilt again, and Israel's national life will be restructured around the presence of Christ in it. A purifying river will flow from the temple down to the sea as God heals the land (Ezekiel 47:1-10), and each of the twelve tribes will receive an allotment of land (Ezekiel 48) and "the name of the city from that day shall be: The Lord Is There" (v. 35).

The purification of the earth and Israel's place in the center of the millennial kingdom will set the stage for history's final act. After the 1000 years end, God will get rid of the old heaven and earth and replace them with a new, eternal heaven and earth, the capital of which will be New Jerusalem, "coming down out of heaven from God, prepared as a bride adorned for her husband" (Revelation 21:2). There won't be a temple in the eternal state, "for the Lord God Almighty and the Lamb are its temple" (v. 22). Despite the hardship that Ezekiel described and foretold, his message looked beyond Israel's idolatry and captivity to the time when God would draw His people close and stay in their presence forever.

DANIEL
FLIGHT PLAN

Facts

Author

The prophet Daniel, whose name means "God is my judge," is the author of the book of Daniel. Not only did Daniel claim authorship (Daniel 12:4), but Jesus also stated that Daniel wrote the book (Matthew 24:15).

Date Written

Daniel wrote his book in Babylon, probably sometime after 536 BC, the date of the last recorded event in the text. Some scholars suggest the year 530 BC.

Landmarks

The book of Daniel offers some of the most astonishing and astounding views of the prophetic past and future in the Bible. Daniel fits in both the prophetic and historic sections of Scripture, chronologically linking the time between the reigns of the kings in 2 Chronicles and the restoration of Jerusalem in Ezra. The book of Daniel begins by describing the Jewish deportation to Babylon and ends with Daniel's vision of the seventy weeks. It can be divided into two major sections: the historic (seven different historical narratives that deal with prophetic history) and the prophetic (four prophetic visions interpreted by the angel of the Lord).

Itinerary

- Historic Providence (Daniel 1–6)
  - Divine Plan (Daniel 1:2)
  - Daniel's Purpose (Daniel 1)
  - Daunting Premonition (Daniel 2)
  - Dazzling Pride (Daniel 3)
  - Divine Punishment (Daniel 4)

- Damning Postcard (Daniel 5)
  - Defiant Prayer (Daniel 6)
- Prophetic Preview (Daniel 7–12)
  - A Royal Horde (Daniel 7)
  - Reckoning Horns (Daniel 8)
  - Revelation's Hinge (Daniel 9)
  - A Righteous Hope (Daniel 10–12)

Gospel

Jesus Himself verified the prophetic accuracy of the book of Daniel when He called Daniel a prophet (Matthew 24:15). Many of the prophecies in this book have indeed proven to be remarkably accurate, predicting both the first and second coming of the Messiah. As a Jew, Daniel knew that Israel lived in expectation and anticipation of a coming kingdom ruled by their Messiah. No doubt he was troubled when he had his vision of Gentile nation after Gentile nation ruling the world, wondering when that Messiah would come. But then the messianic prophecies started pouring in, leaving us with some of the most profound and accurate predictions about the Messiah in all of the Bible.

In Daniel 2, we see the Son of Man, the Messiah, as a smiting stone that comes out of heaven. In his vision of the dominant kingdoms of the earth, Daniel described how "a stone was cut out without hands...And the stone...became a great mountain and filled the whole earth" (Daniel 2:34-35). Jesus is that Rock, and He will set up a kingdom that will never be destroyed (Revelation 11:15-19).

Daniel prophesied about this kingdom in the same chapter, saying that "the God of heaven will set up a kingdom which shall never be destroyed" (Daniel 2:44). This prophecy is echoed throughout the rest of the book, including Daniel's prediction that the Messiah would return to earth in glory to rule: "His dominion is an everlasting dominion, which shall not pass away, and His kingdom the one which shall not be destroyed" (Daniel 7:14).

Daniel 9 is considered the very backbone of biblical prophecy. It lays out a specific timetable of events having to do with Jesus's first and second comings. Jesus once again validated this timetable and the prophecies of Daniel when He wept over Jerusalem and said, "If you had known, even you, especially in *this your day*, the things that make for your peace! But now they are hidden from your eyes" (Luke 19:42, emphasis added). Jesus was referring to the day Daniel had prophesied, the sixty-ninth week, when the Messiah would enter Jerusalem to accomplish God's greatest rescue mission (Daniel 9:25-26).

The final week referred to in the text (Daniel 9:27), often called "Daniel's seventieth week," is the seven years of the tribulation, the events that will precede Jesus's second coming. The book of Daniel provides us with some of the most specific information about the Messiah, continuing to weave that scarlet thread of redemption throughout the intricate tapestry of God's story.

History

Daniel was born in Judah under the reign of King Josiah (around 621 BC). He was taken into captivity by Babylon during the first Jewish deportation, sometime around 606–605 BC, and put under the service of King Nebuchadnezzar, eventually taking a key administrative role.

The historical events in the book of Daniel are the same events that took place during the lives of the prophets Ezekiel and Jeremiah. Daniel was a captive in Babylon, along with thousands of other Jews. He lived and ministered in Babylon for close to seventy years, probably from about 605 to 536 BC. During his captivity, Babylon passed through the hands of at least four major rulers: Nebuchadnezzar, Belshazzar, the Median king Darius, and the Persian ruler Cyrus.

Travel Tips

Men and women of character will rise to meet a challenge. Daniel stood out above those around him, honored God, and influenced his world. The challenge his story and prophetic visions offer us is to rise up, be counted, be different, and above all, be pleasing to God.

- Human-based governments don't last. Daniel's visions make it clear that mankind cannot successfully govern itself in a lasting way, either nationally or individually. He saw mighty kingdom after mighty kingdom fall. Only God can give your life true meaning, value, and purpose, so let Him govern it. After all, only His kingdom will be left standing in the end.

- Suffering often makes us question God. So often we think that hardship is for other people—even other believers—but not us. *I know He allows others to suffer, but me? No way.* But if God is truly sovereign and loving, then that means He's in charge of your bad times too.

- All of history centers on Christ's atoning work on the cross. The pivotal moment in all creation was when God sent His Son to die for the sins of mankind. The "seventy weeks" prophecy of Daniel 9 shows God's plan for this moment in history, revealing the tremendous love He has not only for His people, Israel, but also for all of mankind. The accuracy of Daniel's prophecies serves as a great reminder to take refuge in God's promises in uncertain times—Daniel did so, and we should too.

> **Rise up, be counted, be different, and above all, be pleasing to God.**

In Flight

Historic Providence (Daniel 1–6)

Divine Plan (Daniel 1:2)

God controls both history as well as prophecy. He governs all things past, present, and future. In 605 BC, under the leadership of Nebuchadnezzar, Babylon swept down into Israel from Carchemish in northern Syria, fresh off a power-shifting victory over Egypt. Its target? Jerusalem. In the first of three waves of attack, siege, and capture, Babylonian forces deported a group of Jerusalem's finest young people, including a teenager named Daniel.

Daniel spent the rest of his life in Babylon, becoming a prophet of God and an advisor to a handful of different kings. The first half of his book tells his story, infusing remarkable events with interpretations of vivid dreams and visions. The second half records a series of prophetic visions Daniel received, acting as an appendix of sorts to the first section.

The blend of history and prophecy is so incredibly detailed that skeptics have said that the book couldn't have been recorded in Daniel's day, claiming there is no way he could have predicted so many events with such accuracy. But if that were so, Daniel would have been no prophet, and his book would have been a forgery. But Jesus Himself called Daniel a prophet (Matthew 24:15), verifying Daniel's authorship and prophecies. Rather than a forgery, then, Daniel is a monument of prophetic literature.

Daniel opens by setting the historical context: the siege, destruction, and pillaging of Jerusalem. Nebuchadnezzar is named as the agent of the city's downfall, but God was the architect: "*The Lord gave* Jehoiakim king of Judah into [Nebuchadnezzar's] hand" (Daniel 1:2, emphasis added). So even though Nebuchadnezzar, a mighty king riding high off his victory over the region's reigning power, carried off treasure and captives to Babylon, he was only a pawn on God's chessboard.

The predictions made by Isaiah, Jeremiah, Ezekiel, and others had come to pass. God handed His people over to their enemies as punishment for their persistent idolatry and hardheartedness toward Him. Beyond that, however, God also had plans for this young man Daniel, who would be a vibrant contrasting light to all the pagan worshippers of that land, glorifying God as He gave Daniel the backbone of all prophetic Scripture—and the spine to follow Him in a strange land.

Daniel's Purpose (Daniel 1)

Nebuchadnezzar's program included selecting the cream of Judah's crop, its finest youth from its best families, and indoctrinating them in Babylonian language and culture (Daniel 1:3-5). Daniel and three of his friends—Hananiah, Mishael, and Azariah—were among the chosen. They were immediately given Babylonian names to rob them of their Jewish identity and conform them to the king's standards. Daniel was called Belteshazzar and his friends were renamed Shadrach, Meshach, and Abed-Nego. But God had a purpose for Daniel's heartache, and Daniel found purpose in his own heart.

Daniel led his friends in deliberately resisting this Babylonian brainwashing: "Daniel purposed in his heart that he would not defile himself with the portion of the king's delicacies, nor with the wine which he drank; therefore he requested of the chief of the eunuchs that he might not defile himself" (v. 8). Part of this pagan programming involved bringing in the finest chefs in the royal court to cater sumptuous meals so that these young men would see how good things could be in Babylon. Where it appeared that their God had abandoned them, Nebuchadnezzar would step in and show them how good it was to serve him and his gods. Daniel wasn't buying it.

It would've been the easiest thing in the world for Daniel to cave in and enjoy his new status as one of the king's chosen few. Instead, he anchored himself firmly to God. We see Daniel's resistance evident in the phrase "purposed in his heart." Daniel was focused on God, and he decided that he would follow Him in Babylon just as he had back home. He stayed true to God and resisted temptation, and God gave him favor with the people in charge, enabling him to show his intelligence and skill while living on a humble, kosher diet. His star began to rise.

Daunting Premonition (Daniel 2)

After some time passed, God gave Daniel an opportunity to get into Nebuchadnezzar's personal good graces. The king was feeling the pressure of the power he had accumulated, and he "had dreams; and his spirit was so troubled that his sleep left him" (Daniel 2:1). Problems by day became fears by night, and he called on the guys he employed to sort out that type of issue—his magicians, astrologers, and sorcerers. They played it safe, asking him to provide the details, which they would interpret. Nebuchadnezzar was smarter than that, though; he told them that if they were worth their salt, they'd give him both the details and the meaning—upon pain of dismemberment.

These wise guys tried to buy time but that only angered the king, so he sent out an order to have all the wise men of Babylon killed. Daniel and his friends were considered part of that larger group, so they were rounded up. Daniel asked the king for time, and he gave it. The young man intended to seek God and asked his friends to join him in prayer. Not all dreams are messages from God, but these were, and only a servant of God would be able to interpret them. Daniel made that clear when Nebuchadnezzar asked for the dream's interpretation, saying, "There is a God in heaven who reveals secrets, and He has made known to King Nebuchadnezzar what will be in the latter days" (v. 28).

Daniel went on to tell the king about the image in his dream, the magnificent statue with a gold head, silver chest and arms, bronze belly and thighs, iron legs, and iron and clay feet—all of which was, in the end, shattered by an enormous boulder (Daniel 2:31-35). Nebuchadnezzar's astonishment must have grown with every passing detail—and even more so when Daniel laid out the dream's meaning (vv. 36-45).

In essence, Daniel told the king, "You are sleepless, worried about your future, wondering how long you're going to be top dog, and what will come after you. God is giving you a glimpse of the kingdoms that will follow." The sweep of future history encompassed in the dream covered the major empires of the world up to the establishing of Christ's kingdom at His second coming—represented by the great stone "cut out of the mountain without hands" (v. 45)—God's "kingdom which shall never be destroyed" (v. 44).

Later, Daniel would have his own nighttime vision that corroborated Nebuchadnezzar's dream (Daniel 7), but at this point, the king was blown away. God had used an image that he as a pagan monarch would grasp—an idol—to make His point. Nebuchadnezzar praised God and made Daniel a provincial governor and overseer of the wise men. Daniel stayed loyal to his friends, petitioning the king to give them positions of responsibility, which he did; by God's grace, provision, and plan, these four young men were doing well in a hostile environment. Just how hostile, they would find out eventually.

Dazzling Pride (Daniel 3)

By the beginning of Daniel 3, sixteen years had passed. Nebuchadnezzar had grown in power and pride, and made a gigantic statue, probably of himself, out of gold and demanded that everyone worship it. He hadn't forgotten that he was only the head on the statue he had dreamed of all those years before; in fact, he probably took it as inspiration—"Forget the silver and bronze parts to come! I'm still the top guy, it's still my golden age, and I'm going all out to hang onto my spot." This thing was ninety feet tall; he had it set up on the plain of Dura and commanded everyone that, once they heard the Chaldean Philharmonic Orchestra kick in, it was either bow or burn.

Maybe Nebuchadnezzar thought his Jewish advisors wouldn't think it was a big deal to give Big Nebbie some love; perhaps he presumed that, by this time, they had surely forgotten their God and His laws. But they hadn't. Commandments one and two were still at the forefront of their minds and actions: no other gods and no making or worshipping manmade images. Hananiah, Mishael, and Azariah just weren't going to go along with bowing down before a giant statue of the boss.

Sticking up for God all these years had made these guys some bitter enemies in the royal court, and some Babylonian muckety-mucks ratted them out to the king, who first threw a fit and then threw Shadrach, Meshech, and Abed-Nego into a huge, superheated furnace—so hot that it killed the men who threw them in. Nebuchadnezzar then spotted a fourth man with them in the flames (Daniel 3:25). Some scholars think this was a Christophany—a pre-incarnate appearance of Jesus. But one thing is certain: God was faithful to them in their trial, honoring their faithfulness to Him. For his part, Nebuchadnezzar not only praised God for delivering the men, he made it illegal to speak out against the God of Daniel (vv. 28-29).

Divine Punishment (Daniel 4)

Nebuchadnezzar should have opened the first waffle shop because he went back and forth so much—"I'm top dog! No, God is! Worship the giant, golden me, everyone, or die! No, God is awesome and no one can say otherwise!" It all suggests a recognition of God's majesty without a personal acknowledgement of His sovereignty, and it all caught up with Babylon's monarch. His up-and-down journey continued with a narrative unique in all of Scripture—a pagan, Gentile king penning part of a chapter.

Nebuchadnezzar gave a first-person account of a lesson God taught him (Daniel 4). As happened the first time God made Himself known to the king, a dream was involved. And like the first time, all of his New Age quacks couldn't figure it out, but God gave Daniel the meaning. The dream, however, was different. In it, the king saw a tree so tall it could be seen from one end of the earth to the other. It was beautiful to behold; full of fruit; a shelter for animals, birds, and people. The tree was Babylon, but there was an even higher authority, represented by "a watcher, a holy one" (v. 13), who shouted down from heaven to cut the tree down to its stump.

Furthermore the watcher—an angelic being of some sort—proclaimed that the one the tree represented would "graze with the beasts on the grass of the earth. Let his heart be changed from that of a man, let him be given the heart of a beast, and let seven times pass over him" (vv. 15-16). No one could figure out the meaning of the dream until Daniel arrived. He told the king, "I wish this wasn't you, O king, but it is. You're going to be driven out into the fields like an animal until you understand that 'the Most High rules in the kingdom of men, and gives it to whomever He chooses'" (v. 25). Daniel encouraged him to repent in the hope that God might lengthen the time before it happened.

True to form, though, Nebuchadnezzar soon went back to his egotistical ways. The story's point of view had shifted back to Daniel as he interpreted the dream, and next we're told how it came to pass. A year later, Nebuchadnezzar was walking the palace grounds, admiring all the splendor. He said, "Is this not great Babylon, that I have built for a royal dwelling by my mighty power and for the honor of my majesty?" (v. 30). You're probably thinking, *He's asking for it!*—and you'd be right. The answer to Nebuchadnezzar's question came instantly—a voice from heaven that sentenced him to insanity and declared he would eat grass in the field like an ox for seven years. "His body was wet with the dew of heaven till his hair had grown like eagle's feathers and his nails like birds' claws" (v. 33)—until he recognized God's sovereignty.

God gives earthly kingdoms to whomever He chooses. The narrative now back in the first person, Nebuchadnezzar wrote of his deliverance from the pasture and the recovery of his reign. "My understanding returned to me; and I blessed the Most High and praised and honored Him who lives forever" (v. 34). The lesson was not lost on Nebuchadnezzar, and it shouldn't be lost on us: We can vote and pray for elected officials (and we should), but God chooses who is in charge. That means He permits leaders both good and bad to rule, and through all of it, He is in complete control.

> God permits leaders both good and bad to rule,
> and through all of it, He is in complete control.

Damning Postcard (Daniel 5)

Nebuchadnezzar's grandson, Belshazzar, followed in his father's footsteps—both as king and in his pride. Just as his grandfather had built a huge monument to his own ego, Belshazzar threw Babylon's final party, hosting all the nobles and using golden chalices ransacked from the temple in Jerusalem to toast their little gods of metal, wood, and stone. At that point, having denigrated Almighty God to a defeated deity, God pulled the plug—not just on the festivities, but on Babylon as an empire.

A hand appeared and wrote a message on a wall, which, once again, only Daniel could interpret (Daniel 5). Once he was sure he wasn't having a drunken hallucination, the king sent for his grandfather's right-hand man, who was about eighty years old at this point. Just as he had with Nebuchadnezzar, Daniel gave Belshazzar, whose knees were literally knocking in fear, the straight scoop. The king offered him a top-three position ruling the kingdom, but Daniel said, "Keep your gifts. You've forgotten how God blessed your grandfather and how He humbled him for failing to acknowledge His ultimate power. You knew all that but still thought it was a good idea to toast idols using goblets meant to honor God." Daniel then gestured toward the postcard on the wall. "Here is what He has to say about that."

It wasn't pretty. The writing on the wall (and yes, this is the origin of that phrase) was comprised of four words: MENE, MENE, TEKEL, UPHARSIN (Daniel 5:25-28). Those mysterious words boiled down to a stunning message: "God has numbered the days of your kingdom, and they are finished. You personally have been found wanting, and your kingdom will be given to the Medes and Persians." The end wasn't a matter of years or even days away, but hours. That night in 539 BC, Belshazzar was killed and the kingdom passed to Darius the Mede. Bye-bye, Babylon.

Defiant Prayer (Daniel 6)

Babylon was now under new management, the Medo-Persian Empire. Cyrus ruled the whole thing and Darius served as his viceroy—kind of a co-ruler specifically over Babylon. Even though Daniel was eighty-seven at this point, Darius made him one of three governors overseeing the 120 satraps (sort of like county managers) who helped run the kingdom. You'd think a guy pushing ninety might just ask for a nice chalet down near the Euphrates, but Daniel stepped right in and "distinguished himself above the governors and satraps, because an excellent spirit was in him" (Daniel 6:3). Darius even considered setting him over the whole region.

Daniel's excellence in all he did earned him the jealousy of the men under his charge. They conspired to bring him down, but there were no skeletons in his closet, and they realized that the only way they could possibly bring him down was to try and use his relationship with God against him. The satraps and other governors went to the king and persuaded him to pass a law saying that "whoever petitions any god or man for thirty days, except you, O king, shall be cast into the den of lions" (v. 7). I guess furnaces were now out of fashion. They knew the law of the land was that once the king signed a decree, there was no taking it back—and they also knew that Daniel would never obey such a decree.

And they were right. Daniel knew about the petition but went about his usual business, praying three times a day, clearly visible through the window he opened toward Jerusalem. His detractors caught him in the act and reported him to Darius. When the king found out who his new law had just busted, he was seriously bummed out because he admired Daniel, and so he worked all day to figure out a loophole. When those sneaky rat-traps—or satraps, rather—reminded him that his decree was permanent, Darius consented to let them throw Daniel in the lions' den. But he didn't like it. He told Daniel, "Your God, whom you serve continually, He will deliver you" (v. 16).

After a sleepless night, Darius rushed to the den, which had been sealed with a stone marked by the king's own signet ring (his official stamp of approval). He called out to see if God had delivered Daniel, who called back, "Piece of cake!" Actually, Daniel was courteous, showing Darius respect as he proclaimed his God's power and his own innocence: "O king, live forever! My God sent His angel and shut the lions' mouths, so that they have not hurt me, because I was found innocent before Him; and also, O king, I have done no wrong before you" (vv. 21-22). *Oh, and don't wake the lions; they're sleeping.* But they were definitely awake when Darius threw all the conspirators and their families in with them. The lions tore them to pieces before they even hit the ground. Darius, just as Nebuchadnezzar had before him, wrote an official decree praising God for His power and faithfulness to His servant Daniel (vv. 25-28).

Daniel was comfortable with leaving his life completely in God's hands—if the lions had attacked him, he probably would have thought, *Guess I wasn't innocent before my Lord*. He didn't fear what men thought of him or might do to him more than he feared displeasing God. He kept his eyes on God through thick and thin, turning the eyes of the least likely—great kings and rulers of his day—toward heaven to offer God His just praise. What a picture: a king with insomnia on his royal bed and a prophet snoozing in a lion's den because he knew that his God was in charge of the fieriest, fiercest trials.

Prophetic Preview (Daniel 7–12)

A Royal Horde (Daniel 7)

Prophecies, visions, and revelations marked Daniel's career. The book shifts at this halfway point to an appendix of sorts, recording visions in the order Daniel received them, each one a cornerstone of God's prophetic record. History vindicates the accuracy of Bible prophecy. When events unfold as predicted, you've got an accurate prophet; that was Daniel. There are few more stunning examples of this than his vision of the four beasts (Daniel 7). It mirrors the dream he interpreted for Nebuchadnezzar back in chapter 2, but it came to him years later, during Belshazzar's reign.

Daniel saw not four types of metal on a statue but four beasts that arose from the sea—itself a symbol of the mass of humanity across the world—each of which served as an avatar of an empire. A lion with eagle's wings represented the golden head of Babylon, followed by a bear symbolizing Medo-Persia's silver chest and arms, then a winged leopard that stood for Greece's bronze torso and thighs, and finally, a metallic beast that trampled the earth, the iron legs of Rome.

The contrast between Daniel and Nebuchadnezzar's visions illustrates two different perspectives of the same events: Babylon's king saw the secular perspective, the building of humanity from feet of clay to a head of gold, the constant improvement of mankind as time passes—without realizing that, from God's top-down perspective, the metals decrease in value from gold down to miry iron. By contrast, in Daniel's vision, God drew out His view of mankind's alleged progress by picturing these kingdoms as beasts, each more threatening and frightening than the previous.

Even in a brief summary, the match of prophetic and historical details is astonishing. Archaeological digs have revealed statues of winged lions guarding the palace gates in the ruins of Babylon, symbols of its glory and power. The Medo-Persian bear, raised up on one side, signified the greater power that Persia wielded in that alliance, and its mouth full of three ribs indicated nations that it had conquered to rise to power (thought by many to be Babylon, Assyria, and Egypt). The leopard of Greece predicted Alexander the Great's speedy ascent and conquest of southern Europe, northern Africa, the Middle East, and central Asia, and its four wings stood for the four generals who split his kingdom after his equally quick demise.

The beast of Rome conquered with its mighty military and strict rule of law—the iron teeth and bronze claws of Daniel's vision.

After this fearsome fourth beast came a single horn—a prophetic symbol of power—that made war against God's people until He came and stopped it. This was a picture of Christ defeating the Antichrist in the last days and setting up God's kingdom on earth. Whereas people tend to see things as getting better and better, God sees them as getting worse and worse, and one day, He will intervene to set things right.

We look at this vision and think, "Cool! What an amazing view of history past and history to come"—and it is—but Daniel didn't enjoy it as much. Even though the vision ended with the establishment of the millennial kingdom (Daniel 7:24-27), Daniel said, "My thoughts greatly troubled me, and my countenance changed; but I kept the matter in my heart" (v. 28). In other words, he was in shock.

For Daniel, remember, the vision came at a time of uncertainty. Israel was still captive in Babylon, still waiting for God's anger to cool, still hoping for the time when He would return them to their homeland. But here, God gave him a vision of four powerful, terrifying empires, two of which he had seen close up and personal, and there was no indication of where God's people fit into this except as objects of persecution. Even with the promise of eventual restoration and God's kingdom on earth, who knew when that would be? Knowing that God will ultimately be victorious is comforting, but in the midst of tribulation, that victory can't come soon enough.

Reckoning Horns (Daniel 8)

Another vision Daniel received during Belshazzar's time helps to narrow down the timeframe of the previous scenario. In this vision, Daniel saw the transfer of power from Medo-Persia to Greece (previously seen as the bear and the leopard). Daniel saw a two-horned ram battling a single-horned goat, with the ram pushing its way in almost every direction and taking over before the goat charged in from the west without touching the earth—turbo goat!—and clobbered him (Daniel 8:1-8).

While history revealed the identity of most of the beasts in the first vision, the angel Gabriel left no doubt as to who the ram and goat were: two-horned Medo-Persia and the uni-goat of Alexander's Greece (vv. 20-21)—including the fact that four smaller horns (kingdoms) would rise out of Alexander's busted horn (v. 22). After Alexander's death, his empire was divided among four of his generals—Cassander, Lysimachus, Seleucus, and Ptolemy.

At this point, Israel came back into view, under attack from one of the four regions—"a little horn which grew exceedingly great toward the south, toward the east, and toward the Glorious Land" (Daniel 8:9), which can only be Israel. This horn "even exalted himself as high as the Prince of the host; and by him the daily sacrifices were taken away, and the place of His sanctuary was cast down" (v. 11). The identity of this powerful, blaspheming ruler wasn't given by the angel, but history made it clear: this was Antiochus IV, the eighth ruler of the Seleucid Empire, who named himself Antiochus Epiphanes, "God made manifest." Not too egotistical, right?

Actually, more than just a mere egotist, this guy was a precursor of the Antichrist himself, a king "having fierce features, who understands sinister schemes. His power shall be mighty, but not by his own power...He shall even rise against the Prince of princes; but he shall be broken without human means" (vv. 23-25). The thought of his coming made Daniel sick (v. 27). In 168 BC, Antiochus IV ransacked Jerusalem, destroyed part of the second temple (which hadn't even been built yet in Daniel's time), put up a statue of Zeus in another part, and outlawed the practice of Judaism, sacrificing a pig on the altar of sacrifice in the main courtyard.[30]

This act became known as the "abomination of desolation" (Daniel 11:31; 12:11, see also 9:27), something Jesus referred to when He later described the similar actions of the Antichrist in the end times (Matthew 24:15). All the horns of human kingdoms—powers ancient, present, and future—can ultimately do very little in the face of the one true power in the universe—the God who set them in place, predicted their demise, and calls them to a reckoning.

Revelation's Hinge (Daniel 9)

Daniel 9 is the Mount Rushmore of prophecy, instantly recognizable and lasting in impact. During the first year of the reign of Darius, God gave Daniel incredible insight regarding the prophecies of Jeremiah and the seventy-year period of Jerusalem's captivity. Daniel was praying, praising God for His faithfulness and confessing the sins of Israel. He hadn't committed any of those sins himself, but he counted himself among those who had, making prayers of intercession because "all Israel has transgressed Your law, and has departed so as not to obey Your voice" (v. 11).

As Daniel prayed, the angel Gabriel arrived—how cool is that!—to give him God's message in person: "O Daniel, I have now come forth to give you skill to understand...for you are greatly beloved" (vv. 22-23). Just as God had protected Jeremiah when Babylon sacked Jerusalem, preserving his freedom in return for his faithfulness over the years, so God sent one of His top angelic generals to let Daniel in on His ultimate plans for Israel: the seventy-weeks prophecy:

> Seventy weeks are determined for your people and for your holy city,
> to finish the transgression, to make an end of sins, to make reconcil-
> iation for iniquity, to bring in everlasting righteousness, to seal up
> vision and prophecy, and to anoint the Most Holy (v. 24).

"Determined," in Hebrew, indicates setting something aside for a purpose. God has set aside a period of time, here called "seventy weeks," on the divine timetable. Literally, seventy weeks is seventy *sevens*—seventy sets of seven something—it could be days, weeks, or years. "Weeks" comes from the consensus of most Christian and Jewish scholars that these are periods of seven years; seventy sevens, then, would be 490 years.

Here's how it plays out: Gabriel told Daniel, "Know therefore and understand, that from the going forth of the command to restore and build Jerusalem until Messiah the Prince, there shall be seven weeks and sixty-two weeks; the street shall be built again, and the wall, even in troublesome times" (v. 25). Seven "weeks" of years would be forty-nine years, and sixty-two "weeks" would be 434 more years, for a total of 483 years.

The exact time of the Messiah's arrival in Jerusalem was predicted: "After the sixty-two weeks Messiah shall be cut off, but not for Himself; and the people of the prince who is to come shall destroy the city and the sanctuary. The end of it shall be with a flood, and till the end of the war desolations are determined" (Daniel 9:26). After the end of these sixty-nine weeks (these 483 years) the Messiah would come to the city and be killed—"cut off"—not for Himself, but for His people.

This information begs the question, When did the countdown begin on those 483 years? That date is in the prophecy: "From the going forth of the command to restore and build Jerusalem" (v. 25). Our historical vantage gives us that specific date: When God prompted the Persian kings to start sending the Jews back to Jerusalem, King Artaxerxes told Nehemiah to return to Jerusalem on March 14, 445 BC. It was the fourth decree that Persian kings had issued to the Jews, but the first to instruct them to rebuild its streets and walls. Counting 483 years—173,880 days—from March 14, 445 BC, we land on April 6, AD 32—the day Jesus entered Jerusalem on the back of a donkey's colt, fulfilling the prophecy of Zechariah 9:9 and beginning the week that ended with His crucifixion and resurrection. God's wristwatch is impeccably precise!

God's wristwatch is impeccably precise!

The wonder of this prophecy is that it demonstrates an important truth: All of history surrounds the atoning work of Jesus Christ on the cross. That sixty-ninth week is the fulcrum of history, dividing time into a before-and-after based on God's plan of salvation. The seventieth week has yet to occur; it is the seven-year period known as the tribulation, when "the prince who is to come"—the Antichrist—"shall confirm a covenant with many for one week; but in the middle of the week"—that is, three-and-a-half years into the tribulation—"he shall bring an end to sacrifice and offering. And on the wing of abominations shall be one who makes desolate, even until the consummation, which is determined, is poured out on the desolate" (Daniel 9:27).

Of course, there's much more to be said about those end-times scenarios, and we will view various aspects of them as we continue our journey, especially in the book of Revelation. The seventy-weeks prophecy offers crucial information about the timeframe of God's plan of atonement in Christ and Christ's return to reign at the end of the world's darkest hour—a time that will make the captivity in Babylon and the desecrations of Antiochus IV look like a beach party. Fortunately, God has designs to save both those in the world and His specific people, offering forgiveness to anyone who would receive it, Gentile or Jew.

A Righteous Hope (Daniel 10–12)

The last three chapters of the book form the account of a final vision Daniel received. It covered a lot of the same territory as his other visions, but in greater detail. Once again, it was no comfort to him to see all the difficulty and devastation to come, and he mourned and didn't eat or bathe much for three weeks. It also didn't help that the messenger was terrifying: an angel in a gold belt whose body glistened like a gem, with flaming eyes, a face that flashed like lightning, and a voice like an enormous chorus. The guys who were with Daniel couldn't see anything but ran away in fear, and Daniel fainted (Daniel 10:4-10). This is why angels have to say, "Don't be afraid," which this one did.

This angel also called Daniel a "man greatly beloved" (v. 11), an encouraging echo of Gabriel's words back in chapter 7. We get some brief insight into the nature of spiritual warfare, too, as the angel explained how it had taken him three weeks to arrive in answer to Daniel's prayers because "the prince of the kingdom of Persia withstood me" (v. 13) and the archangel Michael had to come assist him. This wasn't a human prince but a demonic being put in charge of Persia—perhaps assigned by Satan to influence the human kings of Persia.

The message the angel delivered is astonishing but far too detailed to get into from our vantage point. The first thirty-five verses of Daniel 11 provide 135 prophecies, all of which were fulfilled before Christ's first coming. They start in familiar territory, with Persia growing in power with each passing king until it attacks Greece, which will eventually defeat it under Alexander. There were no rams or goats here, just nations with human kings desiring power and fighting to gain it.

After Alexander's death and the quartering of his empire, one of those four kings would grow strong—"the king of the south," as the angel called him—and be in continual conflict with a guy called "the king of the north." As is true throughout the Bible, north and south are relative to Israel, the most important nation to God. So, north of Israel was the Seleucid Empire, and south was the Ptolemaic Empire. History is full of conflicts between the two, and many of their key battles are predicted in this chapter.

For our purposes, Daniel 11:1-35 deals with battles that take place during Daniel's sixty-nine weeks—the 483 years leading up to Christ's death and resurrection—and verses 36-45 focus on Daniel's seventieth week, the tribulation. They still feature kings of south and north, but these will be future nations and rulers, one of whom will be the Antichrist. He will invade Israel, rolling over its defenses, before he meets his end. "At that time Michael shall stand up, the great prince who stands watch over the sons of your people; and there shall be a time of trouble, such as never was since there was a nation, even to that time. And at that time your people shall be delivered, every one who is found written in the book" (Daniel 12:1).

In the angel's description of the Day of Judgment, we see the first mention in the Bible of the phrase *everlasting life*: "And many of those who sleep in the dust of the earth shall awake, some to everlasting life, some to shame and everlasting contempt" (v. 2). There's also an implied instruction to share the gospel—the one thing that can open the door to life and close the door on death: "Those who are wise shall shine like the brightness of the firmament, and those who turn many to righteousness like the stars forever and ever" (v. 3).

> The smartest thing you can do in light of prophecy is make sure you are in the hands of the One who guarantees it.

And with that, the angel told Daniel to "shut up the words, and seal the book until the time of the end" (v. 4). There have been and will continue to be a lot of people running around in the meantime, freaking out, trying to figure out the future and their place in it. The insight in Daniel's prophecies gives us reason to rest in God's promises—to follow the advice the angel gave Daniel as they parted: "You, go your way till the end; for you shall rest, and will arise to your inheritance at the end of the days" (v. 13). The smartest thing you can do in light of prophecy is make sure you are in the hands of the One who guarantees it. God promises hope to those who dare to trust Him, honor Him, and fight for Him as dark future days unfold as He foretold.

HOSEA
FLIGHT PLAN

Facts

Author

Hosea the prophet, the son of Beeri, wrote the book named after him (Hosea 1:1). At God's instruction, Hosea married a harlot named Gomer. Their marriage later came to symbolize God's relationship with Israel, as Hosea was troubled by her constant infidelity. The book of Hosea is the first of the Minor Prophets, a title that simply refers to the length of the books, not their significance.

Date Written

Hosea wrote this book during the reigns of several kings of Israel and Judah, covering the years 755 to 715 BC. He died in 713 BC.

Landmarks

The book of Hosea is a bittersweet journey through the nature of human infidelity. Hosea was called to prophesy to the northern kingdom of Israel during the reign of King Jeroboam II (and during the reigns of Uzziah, Jotham, Ahaz, and Hezekiah in Judah). His message was clear: God's people had rejected Him, so they would be sent into exile and become wanderers in other nations. We'll divide the book of Hosea into three sections that show the power of faith in both the private and public spheres of life.

Itinerary

- A Faithless Wife (Hosea 1–2)
- A Future Restoration (Hosea 3)
- A Fickle Nation (Hosea 4–10)
- A Faithful God (Hosea 11–14)

Gospel

The message of Hosea is the message of the gospel: God has gone to the utmost lengths to offer us life in exchange for pain, suffering, and death. Just as Hosea was to be forgiving and willing to receive his adulterous and wandering wife, God will forgive and restore those who have drifted from Him. So many people think God wants to take the joy out of life, what with all of His commandments and thou-shalt-nots. *Who wants to follow God,* they think, *when all He does is focus on the negative?* But people who think that way have it backward: Sin is the root cause of the suffering in the world, not God's rules. Jesus came so that, in His own words, we "may have life, and that [we] may have it more abundantly" (John 10:10). Jesus died so that He could give us something we could never attain on our own: eternal life—life to the full!

> **God has gone to the utmost lengths to offer us life in exchange for pain, suffering, and death.**

And that's the offer of the gospel: an overflowing life of love and grace here on earth, and eternal life with God in heaven. The book of Hosea shows all the ugliness of a people abandoned to the consequences of their selfish desires, but their situation was only temporary. Yes, God promised that He would "punish [Israel] for the days of the Baals" (Hosea 2:13), but in the very next verses He promised He would "allure her...and speak comfort to her...I will betroth you to Me forever" (vv. 14, 19). Hosea's marriage was a model of redemption, revealing God's justice and kindness, His holiness, faithfulness, and deep, abiding love.

History

Hosea was born in the northern kingdom of Israel toward the end of the reign of King Jeroboam II (793–753 BC). He grew up and ministered under the rule of several other kings of Israel (Zechariah, Shallum, Menahem, Pekah, Pekahiah, and Hoshea). Jeroboam II's rule was one of political and economic prosperity, but the underlying spiritual decay in the nation eventually became manifested during the reigns of his successors. These kings brought with them political unrest and spiritual chaos, culminating in the Assyrian captivity of Israel in 722 BC. Many Jews turned to the idolatry and other practices of the Assyrian religion, further rebelling against the Lord.

Hosea ministered and prophesied to the people around the same time as the prophets Amos and Jonah. This was some 250 years after the time of David and Solomon and about 650 years after the twelve tribes of Israel first entered the Promised Land. At this point in its history, civil war had divided God's covenant people into two nations: the ten northern tribes made up the kingdom of Israel, and the other two tribes, Judah and Simeon, became the southern kingdom of Judah.

Travel Tips

The book of Hosea is the story of a heartfelt message from a heartsick prophet about a heartbroken God. Hosea's life bore the scars of a torn and tattered marriage, but he continued to speak on behalf of the Lord, telling the people of Israel about God's plan to win them back.

- Your relationship with God centers on His faithfulness, not yours. He guides and disciplines you as a father does a child, but He loves you sacrificially the way a husband should his wife. The only appropriate response to such a loving and caring God is to fear Him—having a healthy respect and awe for Him—and to love Him by doing what He says (John 14:15).

- Sin is sin is sin. Hosea didn't hesitate to call sin what it was, calling out Israel for its disobedience and rebellion. Because he first proclaimed this hard truth, his words of encouragement resonated even more later on—after all, truth begets truth. "I will heal their backsliding," God said of the people of Israel, "I will love them freely" (Hosea 14:4). When we confess and repent of our sins, turning our hearts back to God, then He can begin to heal and bless us.

Your relationship with God centers on His faithfulness, not yours.

In Flight

A Faithless Wife (Hosea 1–2)

In the time of the divided kingdoms of Israel and Judah, God called Hosea to prophesy, specifically in the form of taking a wife who would be unfaithful to him, just as God's chosen people had been unfaithful to Him. "The LORD said to Hosea: 'Go, take yourself a wife of harlotry and children of harlotry, for the land has committed great harlotry by departing from the LORD'" (Hosea 1:2). So Hosea the prophet married Gomer the go-go girl.

There's been a lot of debate over whether Hosea knew in advance that his wife, Gomer, was a prostitute, or if she proved unfaithful after they were married. Rather than get caught in the particulars of that matter, the overarching idea is that their relationship provided a tangible illustration of how God loves people. His love is not a cheap thing, even if people treat it like that, so when He instructed Hosea to make his marriage an example of the pain of infidelity, it's not like He was saying, "Hosea, just treat it like a play—you're just acting." Instead, God invited Hosea to share in His pain, to partake of the suffering caused by a cheating spouse.

When Gomer turned her back on her marriage and slept with other men, Hosea experienced what God felt every time Israel turned their back on Him to worship other gods. Beyond the typical prophetic messages of denunciation or conciliation, Hosea felt what God feels, much like what Paul called "the fellowship of His sufferings" (Philippians 3:10). And how he must have suffered! He married Gomer and they had kids, each named at God's instruction as a symbol of what God would do to Israel (Hosea 1:3-11): Jezreel ("God Will Sow," an indication of the wrath to come), Lo-Ruhamah ("No Mercy"), and Lo-Ammi ("Not My People").

Hosea foretold Assyria's conquest of the northern kingdom, saying that God would "bring an end to the kingdom of the house of Israel" (v. 3), showing no mercy and rejecting His people, but that He would, for the time being, preserve the southern kingdom: "Yet I will have mercy on the house of Judah, will save them by the LORD their God, and will not save them by bow, nor by sword or battle, by horses or horsemen" (v. 7). And that's just what he did, delivering Judah and Jerusalem from Assyria's onslaught during King Hezekiah's time, answering the king's prayer and sending an angel to wipe out 185,000 enemy troops (Isaiah 37). Israel would fall in 722 BC, but Judah would stand until God allowed Babylon to breach its walls in 586 BC.

In His holiness, God must judge sin, but in His love, He promises mercy and restoration. That's why we have Him saying, on one hand, "You are not My people, and I will not be your God" (v. 9), but then promising that "the number of the children of Israel shall be as the sand of the sea...And it shall come to pass in the place where it was said to them, 'You are not My people,' there it shall be said to them, 'You are sons of the living God'" (v. 10). God made covenants with the Jews, promising to turn their pain into a "door of hope" (Hosea 2:15), a door that will always swing on the hinges of those promises. That's at the heart of every believer's testimony—that God rode in and saved the day when things looked bleakest, when hope seemed most distant, when sin and cynicism seemed strongest.

> **God is often greatly misunderstood: He doesn't take the fun out of life; He puts fullness into it.**

God is often greatly misunderstood: He doesn't take the fun out of life; He puts fullness into it. To those who trust in Him, He withholds deserved punishment (that's His mercy) and then gives undeserved blessings (that's His grace) That's why He told Hosea, "In that day you will call your brothers Ammi—'My people.' And you will call your sisters Ruhamah—'The ones I love'" (Hosea 2:1 NLT). For Israel's infidelity, God said, "I will punish her" (v. 13), but in His mercy, He said, "I will allure her...and speak comfort to her" (v. 14). The abandonment would be temporary; the restoration will be eternal.

The overarching theme of Hosea is redemption, couched in terms of relationship. God is all about having a relationship with you—as a father and a child, guiding and nurturing, as a husband to a wife, steeped in committed intimacy and faithfulness, and as a master and servant, His challenge and support enabled by your obedience. Hosea demonstrated all of these with his own life and marriage, powerfully summarized in one brief chapter.

A Future Restoration (Hosea 3)

Hosea 3 is only five verses long, but it portrays the essence of redemption. God stepped out of heaven into humanity in order to buy us back from sin's clutches. That's what the Hebrew and Greek words translated *redeem* mean—for the original owner to ransom, to buy back from the marketplace. Like Hosea's wife Gomer, we have sold ourselves to the world, to its desires and priorities, and God through Jesus Christ bought us back for Himself. Hosea's marriage reflected the stages of mankind's relationship with God: engagement, marriage, adultery, estrangement, and restoration.

"The LORD said to me, 'Go again, love a woman who is loved by a lover and is committing adultery, just like the love of the LORD for the children of Israel, who look to other gods and love the raisin cakes of the pagans.' So I bought her for myself for fifteen shekels of silver, and one and one-half homers of barley" (vv. 1-2). Apparently Gomer was a slave, and Hosea purchased her to marry her and give her a better life. Her sense of gratitude was a lot like the Hebrews' when God brought them out of slavery in Egypt—she almost immediately went after other lovers, even though she and Hosea had children and a life together. Hosea's heart, like God's, was broken.

But God told Hosea to take her back, to forgive and love her. Hosea told her to stay true, and that he would do the same: "You shall stay with me many days; you shall not play the harlot, nor shall you have a man—so, too, will I be toward you" (v. 3). God's commitment to Israel was the same—including the consequences for their failure to stay faithful to Him and His promise to be there when they returned to Him: "For the children of Israel shall abide many days without king or prince, without sacrifice or sacred pillar, without ephod or teraphim" (v. 4)—no godly priests or false household gods.

God was saying to Israel, "I am going to grant you no access to spiritual support, either true or false." He was going to give the people time to think it over, to see what life was like when that part of them was cut off. "Afterward the children of Israel shall return and seek the LORD their God and David their king. They shall fear the LORD and His goodness in the latter days" (v. 5). This is one of the most remarkable prophetic statements in all of Scripture.

Here's why: The phrase "many days" (v. 4) is ambiguous; it could mean any number of days—twenty days or a hundred years. That's peculiar because God is typically exact. For example, He told Jeremiah that He would restore Judah from captivity after seventy years, and Abraham that his descendants would live in a foreign land for 430 years. But here, through Hosea, God said Israel would be "many days" without a king. Remarkably, since the last king of Judah, Zedekiah, it has been almost 2500 years! That nation rejected the King whom God sent when Jesus came the first time, and the current state of Israel has no monarch. What has God been doing those "many days"?

He has been calling out another people to Himself, the Gentiles. For those of us who are not Jews, God has a special plan as well. As the apostle Paul wrote, "Blindness in part has happened to Israel until the fullness of the Gentiles has come in" (Romans 11:25). God extended the promise of relationship to the world through Jesus Christ, a time we are still living in, and when He decides that time is up, God will turn back to the Jews, and "so all Israel will be saved" (v. 26). Those are the "latter days" Hosea mentioned (3:5), the kingdom age, when the kingless throne of Israel will be filled by the throneless King of heaven.

A Fickle Nation (Hosea 4–10)

In the next few chapters Hosea played the role of God's prosecuting attorney, leveling charge after charge against Israel: spiritual apathy and atrophy, uncertainty, and idolatry. Their fickleness toward God would cost them, and Hosea wanted to add his voice to those of the many prophets God had sent to warn His people of their sins and the coming reckoning.

The first charge, spiritual apathy, came because Israel stopped hungering after God, and so they stopped growing spiritually. Hosea said, "There is no truth or mercy or knowledge of God in the land" (Hosea 4:1), with the result being "My people are destroyed for lack of knowledge" (v. 6). When they rejected God's law and knowing Him through His Word, the people of Israel destabilized themselves as a nation. It affected them individually, but also collectively, something God made clear: "Because you have rejected knowledge, I will also reject you from being priest for Me; because you have forgotten the law of your God, I also will forget your children" (v. 6).

It's unwise to pursue knowledge for its own sake, but you don't want to reject it out of hand, either. You need a balance, knowing what God has to say but then living by it; you can't do the latter without knowing the former. To reject, ignore, or reinterpret God's truth to fit the times is courting disaster, and so Hosea warned Israel of the cost of their apathy toward God.

> **To reject, ignore, or reinterpret God's truth to fit the times is courting disaster.**

The second charge against the nation was uncertainty. The people deliberately chose not to trust God; instead, they formed political alliances with pagan nations, thinking that military might would make them stronger than staying under God's good right hand. This error in judgment was a natural consequence of turning from God's Word: "Ephraim [another name for Israel] is oppressed and broken in judgment, because he willingly walked by human precept" (Hosea 5:11). Human wisdom left them hollow, but they tried to compensate without seeking God, making even more mistakes. "When Ephraim saw his sickness and Judah saw his wound, then Ephraim went to Assyria and sent to King Jareb; yet he cannot cure you, nor heal you of your wound" (v. 13).

The result of this wishy-washy attitude and behavior was that Israel could only come up with half-baked schemes. As Hosea pointed out, "Ephraim has mixed himself among the peoples; Ephraim is a cake unturned" (Hosea 7:8). Imagine trying to eat a pancake that was cooked on only one side. That's what Israel was doing when they allied themselves with Assyria, the enemy who would eventually overthrow them. Trying to do life with only a halfhearted view of God was their undoing. His holiness demanded their total commitment, and His love guaranteed their protection. But because they didn't have the first, He took away the second.

The third charge was idolatry. Like a holy prosecutor, Hosea warned, "Ephraim is joined to idols, let him alone" (Hosea 4:17). Israel's priests had failed in their duty to connect the people with their God; instead, they had blended false gods into their worship, abusing their authority as leaders—and God told them He would hold them accountable: "Hear this, O priests! Take heed, O house of Israel! Give ear, O house of the king! For yours is the judgment" (Hosea 5:1). God would let them have what they wanted—worshipping idols—but in a land where there was no other way to worship, where any attempt to worship the one true God would not be tolerated. Hosea described the futility of this approach: "They sow the wind, and reap the whirlwind" (Hosea 8:7).

The law of the harvest typically revolves around the idea that, by sowing a handful of seed, you can reap acres of produce. That's a good thing if you are sowing godly seeds of righteousness and producing a harvest of blessing. But if you sow a few seeds of apathy, water them with uncertainty, and fertilize them with idolatry, then you'll reap more corruption and wickedness than you ever thought possible. Ask Israel. "Ephraim is stricken, their root is dried up; they shall bear no fruit. Yes, were they to bear children, I would kill the darlings of their womb" (Hosea 9:17).

A Faithful God (Hosea 11–14)

Fortunately, the last few chapters of Hosea showcase God's faithfulness to His people as the metaphor shifts from husband and wife to father and child. Hosea made it clear that Israel had sinned, but that God's heart was to forgive and restore them. In the end, his message wasn't about finger-pointing but about God's desire to show His people how far from Him they had moved, and then welcome them back to His open arms.

Hosea first depicted Israel as a runaway child: "When Israel was a child, I loved him, and out of Egypt I called my son. But the more they were called, the more they went away from me" (Hosea 11:1-2 NIV). In other words, Israel ran from God despite His gentle, fatherly care for them. "It was I who taught Ephraim to walk, taking them by the arms; but they did not realize it was I who healed them. I led them with cords of human kindness, with ties of love. To them I was like one who lifts a little child to the cheek, and I bent down to feed them" (vv. 3-4 NIV). The more God lovingly pursued His children, the more they ran in the opposite direction. "My people are bent on backsliding from Me. Though they call to the Most High, none at all exalt Him" (v. 7). It doesn't make sense, but it does reflect human nature to run from a caregiver at the point of accountability.

By chapter 12, the beloved child had grown into a rebellious teenager. "Ephraim feeds on the wind, and pursues the east wind; he daily increases lies and desolation" (v. 1). Specifically, the alliances with foreign powers are mentioned, but it's the attitude behind those partnerships that is most concerning. God likened Israel to their historical namesake, Jacob, who tricked his brother and father into getting what he wanted, and had to flee Esau's wrath (way back in Genesis 27). God said Israel was acting like Jacob, taking matters into their own hands instead of trusting Him, and for that, God said He would "punish Jacob according to his ways; according to his deeds He will recompense him. He took his brother by the heel in the womb, and in his strength he struggled against God" (Hosea 12:2-3).

There was a historical precedent for Israel's rebellion in one of its national ancestors. Like Jacob, Israel would be driven into the strange land and find itself at the mercy of strangers. But, like Jacob, the nation would not be alone. On the run in the wilderness, Jacob "struggled with the Angel and prevailed; he wept, and sought favor from Him. He found Him in Bethel, and there He spoke to us—that is, the LORD God of hosts" (vv. 4-5). Though God's people would find themselves with rocks for pillows, struggling with men and God in Assyria, God would not completely abandon them. Israel's foolish rebellion would lead to great pain, but God would eventually restore them.

That's the image Hosea closed with, a restored adult. "O Israel, return to the LORD your God, for you have stumbled because of your iniquity" (Hosea 14:1). Hosea didn't hesitate to call sin what it was, to tell Israel how they had fallen. He didn't enjoy doing it, but by not shying away from the harsh reality of sin, he drew an effective contrast with God's offer of forgiveness and restoration.

The first step toward doing that is to admit that the sin exists. A doctor can tell you you're sick, but unless you admit the disease exists and agree with the prescribed course of treatment, nothing will change. The disease will run its course, wreaking havoc on your body and mind and possibly ending in death. The only difference between disease and sin is that sin is guaranteed to end in death and separation from God beyond death.

Hosea advocated confession. "Take words with you, and return to the LORD. Say to Him, 'Take away all iniquity; receive us graciously, for we will offer the sacrifices of our lips. Assyria shall not save us, we will not ride on horses, nor will we say anymore to the work of our hands, "You are our gods." For in You the fatherless finds mercy'" (vv. 2-3).

The Prussian king Frederick the Great was said to have toured a prison in Berlin, where he encountered prisoner after prisoner protesting his innocence and asking to be let out. Finally, he came to a prisoner who said nothing at all. Frederick said, "I suppose you are going to tell me you are innocent too." The man's words surprised him: "Your Majesty, I am not innocent. I robbed a bank and I deserve the punishment that has been leveled against me." Frederick called the guard over and said, "Release this rascal before he corrupts all of these fine, innocent men." God, too, is all about releasing people from deserved punishment—offering grace when we admit our guilt.

Solomon noted that "he who covers his sins will not prosper, but whoever confesses and forsakes them will have mercy" (Proverbs 28:13). Hosea revealed that God's heart had not changed: "I will heal their backsliding, I will love them freely, for My anger has turned away from him. I will be like the dew to Israel; he shall grow like the lily, and lengthen his roots like Lebanon. His branches shall spread; his beauty shall be like an olive tree, and his fragrance like [the cedars of] Lebanon" (Hosea 14:4-6). Israel didn't deserve it, but God planned to love them anyway—that's how grace works.

Hosea, through his own personal pain, leveled a heavy message on Israel, but the result would be repentance, and so restoration. We don't know if Hosea's marriage worked out, but he faithfully delivered God's message, trusting that God can change the heart turned fully over to Him. "For the ways of the LORD are right; the righteous walk in them, but transgressors stumble in them" (v. 9). Think of Hosea not with a finger pointed at sinners, but like God, with open arms ready to restore relationships broken by sin.

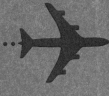

JOEL, AMOS, AND OBADIAH
FLIGHT PLAN

Facts

Joel

Author

Little is known of Joel the son of Pethuel other than what is described in his book (Joel 1:1), the second book of the Minor Prophets.

Date Written

The date of composition is unknown. Some scholars suggest that the wording, phrasing, and descriptions found in the book indicate it was written during the reign of Joash, king of Judah (825–796 BC).

Amos

Author

Amos, a herdsman from the village of Tekoa, near Bethlehem, wrote this book (Amos 1:1), the third of the Minor Prophets. Amos grew up in the southern kingdom of Judah, but was sent by God to prophesy to the northern kingdom of Israel.

Date Written

Amos ministered during the reigns of King Uzziah of Judah and King Jeroboam of Israel. He most likely wrote his book during this time, anywhere from 792 to 754 BC.

Obadiah

Author

Little is known about the author of the book of Obadiah (Obadiah 1), the fourth of the Minor Prophets, besides his name.

Date Written

That Obadiah prophesied against the Edomites provides the only clue to when his book was written. Edom fell to Babylon in 553 BC, so Obadiah most likely recorded his prophecy before that date—typically thought to be anywhere between 840–553 BC.

Landmarks

Joel

A popular notion in Joel's day was that the day of the Lord would actually serve to deliver and bless Israel and bring judgment on the surrounding nations. But Joel had a very different message. Along with the prophets Isaiah (see Isaiah 2:10-21), Jeremiah (see Jeremiah 4:5-9), Amos (see Amos 5:18-20), and Zephaniah (see Zephaniah 1:7-18), Joel declared that the day of the Lord would mean punishment for unfaithful Israel as well. A major theme of his book is that restoration and blessing can come only after a purging through judgment and subsequent repentance.

> **Restoration and blessing can come only after a purging through judgment and subsequent repentance.**

Amos

Amos didn't just record God's words against the Gentile nations surrounding Israel; he also delivered God's words of judgment against Israel itself, as the Lord gave him visions of how He would mete out His judgment on the people. However, this divine message ended with words of hope: a promise of restoration for the faithful remnant of God's people.

Obadiah

Obadiah's brief vision from the Lord was directed to Edom, also known as Esau (named after the brother of Jacob, son of Isaac). Obadiah warned against pride and retaliation against the Lord's chosen people, and also described how possessions and position will ultimately count for nothing on the day of the Lord.

Itinerary

Joel
- The Lord's Affliction (Joel 1:1–2:17)
- The Lord's Restoration (Joel 2:18–3:21)

Amos
- The Roaring of Judgment (Amos 1–2)
- The Reasons of Judgment (Amos 3–6)
- The Representations of Judgment (Amos 7–9)

Obadiah
- God's Pronouncement Against Israel's Rival (Obadiah 1-16)
- God's Promise of Israel's Revival (Obadiah 17-21)

Gospel

Joel

One of the most remarkable prophecies of Joel was the prediction and promise of the Holy Spirit in Joel 2:28-32, quoted by Peter on the day of Pentecost: "It shall come to pass in the last days, says God, that I will pour out My Spirit on all flesh" (Acts 2:17). God poured out His Holy Spirit on the early church in Jerusalem after Jesus's sacrificial death and resurrection, but the passage in Joel also predicts that a similar outpouring will come upon Israel in a greater capacity in the end times.

Furthermore, Joel's predictions of devastating judgment and the eventual day of the Lord line up with the description Jesus gave in Matthew 24:21: "Then there will be great tribulation, such as has not been since the beginning of the world until this time, no, nor ever shall be." As with most Old Testament prophecies, Joel's prophecy had a double fulfillment: The plague of locusts pointed to the approaching Assyrian invasion of Judah, but it also pointed to the ultimate day of the Lord in the end times.

Amos

Amos's name and mission—that of *burden-bearer*—foreshadowed Christ's mission and work on the cross. Amos carried the weight of a difficult message—a prophecy of judgment on Israel and her enemies—but that message ended with God's promise to rebuild David's dynasty and restore His people to the land He promised would be theirs (Amos 9:11-15). In a similar way, Jesus came to bear our burdens—the crushing weight of our sin—with the ultimate goal of restoring us to a right relationship with God and giving us the promised land of heaven as our inheritance.

Obadiah

We can see redemption's scarlet thread in Obadiah by jumping ahead to New Testament times and comparing two very different kings. Herod was an Idumean—one of a few remaining descendants of Edom. He nicknamed himself "the Great," but we know him primarily for killing babies in Bethlehem in a manic hunt for the Christ child. His successor, Herod Antipas, had John the Baptist executed for condemning Antipas's marriage to his former sister-in-law Herodias. He wasn't about to let the truth of God stand in the way of his own lust—much like the sinful Edomites of old. In short, the Herod family motto could be summed up as "What's in it for me?"

Antipas faced off against the other king—the King of the Jews, Jesus Christ—taking part in the trial before His crucifixion (Luke 23:7-12). But Jesus's motto was "What's in it for *you*?" His philosophy centered on doing what was necessary to get you right with God. The Herods planned only for themselves—typically Edomite in their pride and arrogance. But Jesus has a future and a hope planned for you. Even the extremely brief book of Obadiah, so focused on God's judgment of an unrepentant nation, points us to this glorious King (Obadiah 21).

History

Joel

Because we know nothing of Joel other than what is included in his book, it's hard to pin down his time frame. Many of the words and descriptions he used indicate he lived near Jerusalem and might even have been a priest. A generally accepted time frame for his ministry is 825–796 BC.

Amos

Amos prophesied during the reigns of Uzziah of Judah (792–740 BC) and Jeroboam II of Israel (792–753 BC). Amos was a contemporary of Hosea, Isaiah, and Micah, but came after Obadiah, Joel, and Jonah. At this time in its history,

Israel was rich and stable, yet the country was turning from God and treating its poor with injustice.

Obadiah

While we don't know the exact time period during which Obadiah wrote his book, we do know that the Jews and the Edomites had a long history of animosity. The Jews traced their lineage back to Jacob, while the Edomites traced their lineage to Jacob's estranged twin brother, Esau. Because God chose Jacob over Esau to carry on His promises, tension and mistrust festered between the two groups for centuries.

Travel Tips

Joel

The book of Joel highlights the certainty of God's judgment and the assurance of God's Spirit. As believers, we have the Holy Spirit living in us (John 16:13; 2 Corinthians 6:16; 2 Timothy 1:14). We must be beacons of light, love, and truth as we anticipate the day of the Lord.

- God's warnings are meant to draw us back to Him. Like a warning sticker on an appliance, the signs of the end times as foretold in the Bible serve as a wake-up call to be aware and attentive, setting your sights on God.

- Before the ultimate peace comes the ultimate war. Even though massive armies will gather against Israel in the end times, Jesus Christ will singlehandedly win that battle—and the entire war. Joel's call to arms reminds us to prepare for spiritual warfare, to be ready for persecution, and to stand for God in a world that is becoming increasingly hostile toward Him.

- God can restore sin-wasted and afflicted years in your life. God is in the business of restoration. No matter what stage of life you're in right now, it's not too late to seek Him with your whole heart. Don't settle for anything less than God Himself.

> God is in the business of restoration. No matter what stage of life you're in right now, it's not too late to seek Him.

Amos

The book of Amos carries a real punch—and sometimes that's just what we need. In the busyness of everyday life, it's easy to become complacent about spiritual matters. We are saved by God's grace alone, but He still expects us to grow in holiness and be about His business, living out a balance of His love and justice.

- To whom much is given, much shall be required (Luke 12:48). God held the Jews accountable for what He had given them—His Word, the prophets, an inheritance of land. In the same way, we as believers will be held accountable for what we do with what Jesus has given us (Matthew 25:14-30).

- In the Bible, a *woe* is really a *whoa*—a *slow down*! When you read the word *woe*—a cry of lamentation and warning—look at it as a command to slow down and ponder the warning that's coming. These things aren't fun to read or think about, but we ought to take every word of God to heart, trusting the Holy Spirit to speak to us through them and, in the case of Amos, lead us away from the thoughts and deeds that end in woe.

Obadiah

Obadiah's message reminds us that God will defeat His enemies and establish His kingdom. He is the mighty Savior, extending mercy and grace to His people, Israel, whom He delivered from Edom and will redeem in the last days.

- Pride leads to destruction (Proverbs 16:18). Edom's greatest sin was pride: The people thought their stronghold and reputation for wisdom would protect them as they fed their feud with Israel that stretched back all the way to Jacob and Esau. But God held Edom accountable—and will hold present nations and peoples accountable—for unrepentantly abusing and persecuting His people, whether that be Israel or the church.

- God protects His people because of who He is, not who we are. In Obadiah, we see God stand up for and protect His people even though they were sinners, idolaters, and adulterers. When you feel far from God, don't soak in the mire of your failure—take a step back toward Him. He will always be there. Our God is faithful to finish what He started in us (Philippians 1:6), and our salvation is perfectly secure in Him.

Our God is faithful to finish what He started in us.

In Flight

The Minor Prophets are similar to modern technology. It seems the smaller our personal gadgets get, the more powerful they are. God packs a punch with just a few words, so even though the books of Joel, Amos, and Obadiah aren't lengthy, they are powerful. From a topographical view, Joel spoke to the south—Judah and Jerusalem; Amos addressed the north—Israel and its capital, Bethel; and Obadiah went east and spoke to the nation of Edom. It's as if God was assigning them different points on a compass.

Joel: The Day of the Lord

Joel preached to Jerusalem and Judah in the ninth century BC, using an immediate occurrence to predict the ultimate circumstance. Keep that bifocal approach in mind as we fly over—God warning through a natural event of both a coming judgment and the final one. The natural event was a horde of locusts plaguing the region, but prophetically it represented the Assyrian conquest of Israel in 722 BC, as well as the day of the Lord, an end-times period of God's judgment of the whole world.

The Lord's Affliction (Joel 1:1–2:17)

Judah was under an assault of insects—a historical plague of locusts. Joel asked the people, "Has anything like this happened in your days, or even in the days of your fathers? Tell your children about it, let your children tell their children, and their children another generation" (Joel 1:2-3). This was a memorable bunch of bugs, a crop-consuming contagion for the ages.

Joel mentioned four types of locust—chewing, swarming, crawling, and consuming (v. 4). They could have been four different varieties, or four developmental stages of a single kind. But either way, they were everywhere and eating every green thing in sight. Locusts are common in that region, and sun-darkening swarms surfaced every once in a while to wreak havoc on crops. In his prophecy, Joel tied the immediate damage they were causing to a coming event that would be even worse—an invading nation that would make the ruin the locusts were causing look mild by comparison. "A nation has come up against My land, strong, and without number; his teeth are the teeth of a lion, and he has a fangs of a fierce lion. He has laid waste My vine, and ruined My fig tree; he has stripped it bare and thrown it away; its branches are made white" (vv. 6-7).

Beyond the plague of locusts was God's judgment of Israel—the future assault of Assyria—but Joel looked even farther ahead, to the ultimate Day of Judgment. "Alas for the day! For the day of the LORD is at hand; it shall come as destruction from the Almighty" (v. 15). This is the long view, a progression of judgment dwarfing the locust plague and the Assyrian invasion: "the day of the LORD."

Mentioned five times in Joel and more than two dozen throughout the Bible, the day of the Lord is not a twenty-four-hour day but a process by which God will intervene supernaturally in man's affairs through His judgment. It's different than "the day of Christ" mentioned by Paul in the New Testament; the day of Christ describes the time when Jesus returns, first to take His church with Him, and to return with His people to reign on earth for 1000 years. The first part, known as the rapture—an event Paul called "the blessed hope" (Titus 2:13)—will initiate the worldwide judgment called the tribulation. That's the day of the Lord, a seven-year period of devastating judgment on the world and all who have rejected Christ (Revelation 6–19). The day of the Lord will lead to the day of Christ, when Jesus returns to earth to defeat His enemies and establish His kingdom on earth.

As a foreshadowing of the great and terrible day of the Lord, a shattering judgment for Israel's sin would come: "Blow the trumpet in Zion, and sound an alarm in My holy mountain! Let all the inhabitants of the land tremble; for the day of the LORD is coming, for it is at hand: a day of darkness and gloominess, a day of clouds and thick darkness, like the morning clouds spread over the mountains" (Joel 2:1-2). These images of doom would herald the arrival of the nation God would use to humble and punish His wayward children—Assyria. "A people come, great and strong, the like of whom has never been; nor will there ever be any such after them, even for many successive generations" (v. 2).

Even with judgment approaching, Joel called the people to repent, both personally and nationally. God called each individual to look inwardly: "Turn to Me with all your heart, with fasting, with weeping, and with mourning. So rend your heart, and not your garments; return to the LORD your God, for He is gracious and merciful" (vv. 12-13). Then He called the nation to gather and seek Him: "Blow the trumpet in Zion, consecrate a fast, call a sacred assembly; gather people, sanctify the congregation" (vv. 15-16). Everyone, from children to priests, was to gather before God and ask for His mercy.

If they did, God would move to save them:

> Then the LORD will be zealous for His land, and pity His people. The LORD will answer and say to His people, "Behold, I will send you grain and new wine and oil, and you will be satisfied by them; I will no longer make you a reproach among the nations. But I will remove far from you the northern army, and will drive him away into a barren and desolate land, with his face toward the eastern sea and his back toward the western sea" (Joel 2:18-20).

There is a lot going on in those verses with both near and far views. Most *immediately*, it is believed that the locusts came from the north, decimating the vegetation as they moved south. *Intermediately*, in 722 BC, Assyria also came from the north, sweeping over the northern kingdom of Israel before God stopped them in Judah. *Ultimately*, the northern army could also be the very force prophesied in Ezekiel 38–39, Gog and Magog, long thought to be a coalition of Russia and its allies that will attack Israel during the last days.

Regarding the eastern and western seas—the Dead Sea and the Mediterranean, respectively—other prophecies point to an end-times coalition against Israel that will be decimated, their corpses piled up between Israel and the Mediterranean coast (Zechariah 14; Ezekiel 39). Though apparently Israel did not respond to Joel's call for repentance in time to prevent Assyria's attack, God would bring all His people back to the land after their captivity in Babylon—a promise kept that would point to Israel's ultimate restoration after the day of the Lord.

The Lord's Restoration (Joel 2:18–3:21)

After the day of the Lord will come the day of Christ, the kingdom age in which Jesus will rule from an earthly throne in Jerusalem for 1000 years. As devastating as God's judgment will be, His restoration of His people will be wonderful: "I will restore to you the years that the swarming locust has eaten" (Joel 2:25). No pain, no gain. Every hard thing that God did—and will do—to catch His people's attention and turn their hearts back to Him will be worth the pain.

The key to God's redemption of those lost years will be Him pouring out His Spirit in the end times:

> It shall come to pass afterward that I will pour out My Spirit on all flesh; your sons and your daughters shall prophesy, your old men shall dream dreams, your young men shall see visions. And also on My menservants and on My maidservants I will pour out My Spirit in those days. And I will show wonders in heavens and in the earth: blood and fire and pillars of smoke. The sun shall be turned into darkness, and the moon into blood, before the coming of the great and awesome day of the LORD (vv. 28-31).

In the midst of terrifying wonders and signs of God's judgment will come a tremendous blessing: the gift of His Holy Spirit. This will be the silver lining, the dawn that follows the deepest darkness.

The apostle Peter quoted this passage on the day of Pentecost, when the fledgling church received the Holy Spirit (Acts 2). Just as the locust plague and Assyrian invasion predicted the future judgment on the world, Joel's prediction of God pouring out His Spirit on the Jewish nation in Jerusalem pointed to the greater outpouring on Israel and the world in the last days. That outpouring began with the church age, as God began to give His Spirit to both Jews and Gentiles, based on each individual's faith in His Son Jesus Christ. Joel's prophecy won't be completely fulfilled until the end times, something he pointed to when he said, "It shall come to pass that whoever calls on the name of the LORD shall be saved. For in Mount Zion and in Jerusalem there shall be deliverance" (Joel 2:32).

Joel proclaimed God's challenge to the nations that will rise against Israel in the end times, telling them to prepare for war, sort of a reverse prophecy of Isaiah, when earth's armies will "beat their swords into plowshares" (Isaiah 2:4). Joel asserted, "Beat your plowshares into swords and your pruning hooks into spears" (Joel 3:10). This is the preamble to the Battle of Armageddon, the gathering in the "valley of decision" (v. 14) to face off against Israel and its God in one final fight. The momentous nature of the occasion will be reflected in nature itself, with sun, moon, and stars fading out. "The LORD also will roar from Zion, and utter His voice from Jerusalem; the heavens and earth will shake; but the LORD will be a shelter for His people, and the strength of the children of Israel" (v. 16). The day of the Lord will be a time of fearsome judgment for God's enemies, but a time of great mercy for His people as He ushers in the kingdom age.

Amos: The Denunciation of Nations
The Roaring of Judgment (Amos 1–2)

Amos wasn't a professional preacher or priest, but a southern rancher—a herdsman from a rural village in the south near Bethlehem whom God called to deliver a tough message to Israel's enemies. He was a contemporary of the prophet Hosea, and they both preached to the same group, the northern kingdom of Israel, at the same time in history. Their styles, however, were completely different. Whereas Hosea ministered from a broken heart, Amos was more up in people's faces with his message, a series of reprimands roaring God's judgment against nations that had stood against His people.

Amos didn't waste time getting down to business, letting several nations know they were due for a dose of God's wrath. "For three transgressions of Damascus, and for four, I will not turn away its punishment" (Amos 1:3). Each subsequent nation received the same opening idiom: "for three transgressions...and for four." The idea is that each of them had committed multiple infractions against God, and Amos was telling them that they had finally gone too far, placing the straw that broke the camel's back. If you've read through the Old Testament, particularly the prophets, these nations form a familiar list—Damascus, Gaza, Tyre, Edom, Ammon, and Moab—all of whom frequently opposed God's covenant people.

Amos detailed the various reasons why each nation was now subject to God's judgment, but the common theme was that each of them had, in some way, harmed Israel. Matthew 25 details an end-times judgment known as the sheep and goat judgment—a parsing out of people and nations based on how they treated Him, shown in the kindness and comfort they showed "the least of these My brethren" (Matthew 25:40). That judgment will deal primarily with the treatment of a special group of 144,000 messianic Jews set apart by God as His witnesses during the tribulation (Revelation 7), but the judgment Amos prophesied was a precursor of the same type of condemnation for Israel's enemies.

Picture this fiery country prophet, preaching up a storm, saying, "Moab is toast! And so is Ammon. Edom? Toast!" And his audience is nodding, saying, "Yeah—that's right! Edom and Ammon are toast!" Then he says, "Judah is toast!" And the crowd quiets down, thinking, *Well, we guess that's all right; we don't really like those guys down south.* But then he gets to Israel, his northern audience, and the crowd goes silent. "For three transgressions of Israel, and for four, I will not turn away its punishment" (Amos 2:6). The bull's-eye had been narrowed from its outer circle, Damascus, closing in ring by ring until Amos's message hit dead center: Israel.

Amos wasn't afraid to strike too close to home, and his was a message consistent with what other prophets had been saying: God was fed up with His people's willful disobedience and disrespect of His law and His worship, and He would use other nations to discipline them in an effort to get them to repent and return to Him. But those other nations wouldn't get away with taking credit for being instruments of Israel and Judah's punishment. God would not turn away from Judah's punishment "because they have despised the law of the LORD, and have not kept His commandments" (v. 4), and Israel would not escape judgment "because they sell the righteous for silver, and the poor for a pair of sandals" (v. 6).

God judged the other nations for sinning against God's general revelation—the natural order He set in motion, including their own consciences. For example, every civilization we have records from had some kind of law against murder. In a general sense, people understand that taking another human life is wrong. But the Jews had His special revelation, His Word and the prophets; they should have known better. They had a specific commandment prohibiting murder, as well as a whole set of laws against idolatry and fornication and injustice. Peter wrote, "The time has come for judgment to begin at the house of God; and if it begins with us first, what will be the end of those who do not obey the gospel of God?" (1 Peter 4:17). The time for those other nations was on the way; but first, God would deal with His people.

The Reasons of Judgment (Amos 3–6)

Having established that God's judgment was coming, Amos then preached five messages, prophetic sermons covering the reasons behind judgment in greater detail. The first three messages begin with the phrase "Hear this word," and the last two start by proclaiming "Woe to you." All five address Israel, God's chosen people, and because of their special relationship to God, it made their sin more painful and even less pardonable.

In fact, that's the first reason they were being judged—because of their privileged position. "Hear this word that the LORD has spoken against you, O children of Israel, against the whole family which I brought up from the land of Egypt, saying: 'You only have I known of all the families of the earth; therefore I will punish you for all your iniquities'" (Amos 3:1-2). God didn't liberate the Philistines from Egypt, or protect the Syrians for forty years in the wilderness. He chose the Israelites—the descendants of Abraham, Isaac, and Jacob—with whom He had made ironclad covenant promises.

And no doubt there were people in the crowd who heard Amos's words and raised questions. "How could a God of love judge us? We're the chosen people." But that's why God could judge them—because they were the chosen people. Punishment is commensurate with privilege. To whom much is given—oral and written revelation from God—much shall be required (Luke 12:48).

Furthermore, Israel was being judged because they had received prophetic revelation. When God did something, He told His people His plans through His prophets: "Surely the Lord GOD does nothing, unless He reveals His secret to His servants the prophets" (Amos 3:7). God told Noah He would flood the world, Abraham that He would destroy Sodom and Gomorrah, Joseph that He would send famine on Egypt, and Moses that He would send plagues on Egypt. Israel couldn't say they hadn't been warned that they had sinned and that it would lead to punishment.

As Amos rolled through these sermons, God's rationale was overwhelming. Israel had oppressed the weak and poor of its own community, covering it up with holier-than-thou worship, refusing to turn back to God when He sent various diseases, defeats, and droughts (Amos 4). He even broke out a lamentation—a funeral dirge, or maybe just a typical country song—a "worry, don't be happy" take on Israel's dark future: "Therefore I will send you into captivity beyond Damascus" (Amos 5:27). Assyria awaited.

And just in case anyone down in Judah heard his message and thought they were exempt, Amos pointed his finger down south: "Woe to you who are at ease in Zion [that is, Jerusalem] and trust in Mount Samaria, notable persons in the chief nation, to whom the house of Israel comes...Woe to you who put far off the day of doom, who cause the seat of violence to come near" (Amos 6:1, 3). "Woe" is an expression of grief, of lament over someone's death. Israel and Judah should have paused and taken it to heart, letting God's Spirit work, but there is little indication they did.

The Representations of Judgment (Amos 7–9)

As you might expect with a prophet, God gave Amos some pretty wild visions to explain both what He was doing and the reasons behind it. Chapter 7 features a three-part vision: a swarm of locusts representing the coming Assyrian invasion, a consuming fire likely foreshadowing a drought, and a plumb line (a tool used to make sure walls were level during construction) measuring Israel against the truth of God's word. Amos begged God to hold off on the first two, citing Israel's inability to withstand those natural disasters, and God amazingly agreed to relent for a time. But Amos didn't protest the plumb line; he knew God would hold His people accountable for the way they had failed to respond to His word and ways.

Amos also ran into some opposition—a priest named Amaziah who tattled on him to King Jeroboam, saying that Amos was threatening his life and reign (Amos 7:10-11). Amos told Amaziah, "Look, I herd cattle and prune trees for a living. I'm not here for me, but because God called me to prophesy—and He has a word for you: Your wife will have to take up prostitution, your children will die violently, your land will be sold off, and Israel will be taken captive." *You like apples, naysayer? How do you like these apples?*

Speaking of fruit, Amos's next vision involved a basket of ripe fruit (Amos 8). God said, "The end has come upon My people Israel; I will not pass by them anymore" (v. 2). The ripeness of the fruit indicated that Israel was ripe for harvest; their sin was ready to be plucked from the tree of their disobedience and disrespect for God. Sometimes a harvest is a time of evangelism—guiding souls ripe to receive Christ to salvation. But here, it's sickle time, a precursor of Jesus treading on the winepress of God's wrath (Revelation 19:15).

The final vision Amos received was that of a two-part trailer, or a preview of coming attractions: one featuring God's judgment, and the other a scene of future blessings. Both are terse and impactful, summarizing key scenes from Israel's punishment as a preview in Amos's mind of what God would do on a grand scale in the full-length motion picture. The first image is of the inescapability of God's judgment: "Though they dig into hell, from there My hand shall take them; though they climb up to heaven, from there I will bring them down" (Amos 9:2). He would sift Israel like grain, sorting out the sinners, and no one would escape. "'Behold, the eyes of the Lord God are on the sinful kingdom, and I will destroy it from the face of the earth; yet I will not utterly destroy the house of Jacob,' says the Lord" (v. 8).

After His wrath subsides, God will restore Israel:

> On that day I will raise up the tabernacle of David, which has fallen down, and repair its damages; I will raise up its ruins; and rebuild it as in the days of old…I will bring back the captives of My people Israel; they shall build the waste cities and inhabit them; they shall plant vineyards and drink wine from them; they shall also make gardens and eat fruit from them. I will plant them in their land, and no longer shall they be pulled up from the land I have given them (vv. 11, 14-15).

The restoration of Israel to statehood in 1948 is a fulfillment of the physical aspect of that, but the spiritual renewal is yet to come—an event reserved for the tribulation-era selection of the 144,000 Jews (Revelation 7).

Obadiah: The Doom of Edom
God's Pronouncement Against Israel's Rival (Obadiah 1-16)

Obadiah had one specific focus, like a quick punch to the gut: pronouncing God's judgment on the nation of Edom. Like a one-hit wonder, Obadiah came out of nowhere, hit hard and fast, and was gone. The most we can tell about him comes from the meaning of his name: "servant of the Lord." The bigger question for some might actually be "Who is Edom?"

Located east of the Dead Sea (and east of Israel), Edom was a nation descended from Esau, Jacob's twin brother and son of Isaac. They had one of the most famous sibling rivalries of all time, struggling in the womb and fighting outside of it, and the bad blood continued with their descendants. Esau was also known as Edom, which means "red," because of his hair and complexion. God renamed Jacob *Israel*, so throughout the Old Testament, we read about conflict between Edom and Israel.

The Edomites had a historically huge ego, much of it fueled by their impregnable capital city, Petra. If you've ever seen *Indiana Jones and the Last Crusade*, you'll recall the huge temple carved into sandstone cliffs, set back in the narrow crack of a deep canyon (called the *siq*)—that's Petra. You can visit its ruins today, but you'll have to go almost single file and probably turn sideways to get through a few of the passages in the cliffs. It's been said that at one time twelve men could guard the whole city because it was so hard to get to. The Edomites developed a big head about their natural defense system, and God told Obadiah to set them straight:

> "The pride of your heart has deceived you, you who dwell in the
> clefts of the rock, whose habitation is high; you who say in your
> heart, 'Who will bring me down to the ground?' Though you ascend
> as high as the eagle, and though you set your nest among the stars,
> from there I will bring you down," says the LORD (Obadiah 3-4).

Why was God upset with Edom? For this simple reason: they had tormented Israel, His chosen people. "For violence against your brother Jacob, shame shall cover you, and you shall be cut off forever" (v. 10). Did I mention that Petra is an archaeological site, a set of ruins? It has been for centuries. Edom was a prime example of Solomon's warning: "Pride goes before destruction, and a haughty spirit before a fall" (Proverbs 16:18).

Edom not only abandoned Israel in its hour of greatest need—standing aside as the Babylonian army breached Jerusalem's gates in 586 BC—but they enjoyed the show and followed the Babylonians through the walls, sacking and looting. Obadiah clarified their errors: "You should not have gazed on the day of your brother in the day of his captivity, nor should you have rejoiced over the children of Judah in the day of their destruction; nor should you have spoken proudly in the day of distress" (Obadiah 12). They even stood outside the burning city and slaughtered those who tried to escape (v. 14).

God's Promise of Israel's Revival (Obadiah 17–21)

God would administer a serious spanking for Edom's sin, but He also promised to restore Israel: "The house of Jacob shall be a fire...but the house of Esau shall be stubble...and no survivor shall remain" (v. 18). He even offered a glimpse of the kingdom age, when all of Israel's enemies would be destroyed and God's people would return to their homeland: "Then saviors shall come to Mount Zion to judge the mountains of Esau, and the kingdom shall be the LORD's" (v. 21). God's covenant with His people Israel is an everlasting one, and nothing can separate God's people from God's promises for His people (Jeremiah 31:35-37).

Nothing can separate God's people from God's promises for His people.

JONAH
FLIGHT PLAN

Facts

Author

The author of the book of Jonah is unknown, but it was probably either someone familiar with the history of Jonah or Jonah himself. The only Old Testament reference to Jonah, other than in this book, is found in 2 Kings 14:25, which mentions "Jonah the son of Amittai, the prophet who was from Gath Hepher," a small town near Nazareth. Jesus Himself referenced the events in the book of Jonah (Matthew 12:39-41), giving strong support to the historical validity of the story.

Date Written

The book of Jonah was written during the reign of Jeroboam II of Israel, sometime between 793 and 753 BC.

Landmarks

Our current flight carries us out over the deep blue sea of the book of Jonah. Jonah's story is a classic example of what God can do not only through the words of a prophet but also in the life of a prophet. God told Jonah to go and preach to Nineveh, but Jonah was disobedient and fled to Tarshish instead. In spite of his defiance, God redirected his path and brought him to repentance in a unique place: the stomach of a fish. In a complete 180-degree turn, Jonah went and preached to the people of Nineveh, who repented of their sins and glorified God.

Itinerary

- Running from God (Jonah 1)
- Running to God (Jonah 2)
- Running with God (Jonah 3)
- Run-in with God (Jonah 4)

Gospel

Jesus used Jonah's adventure in the belly of the fish as a sign of His own burial and resurrection: "For as Jonah was three days and three nights in the belly of the great fish, so will the Son of Man be three days and three nights in the heart of the earth" (Matthew 12:40). Jesus physically died and physically rose again; thus, to call the story of Jonah a myth would imply that Christ's death and resurrection was a myth too. Of course, some people would use that very reason to challenge the veracity of both stories. But within the context of the Bible, a literal interpretation best fits the story of Jonah, given the historical record of Jonah's existence provided by 2 Kings 14:25 and the ancient Jewish historian Josephus, and Jesus's view of the not-so-tall tale.

The book of Jonah also shows the great lengths to which God will go to reach the lost and offer them forgiveness. Despite Jonah's unwilling and reluctant heart, God still used him to get a message of mercy to an unrepentant people. Hundreds of years later, Jesus Christ would go to even greater lengths to offer salvation to the entire world.

History

Jonah lived during the rule of King Jeroboam II (793–753 BC). This was a time of wealth, territorial expansion, and peace for the northern kingdom of Israel. But the nation was rebelling against the Lord, treating its own people poorly and playing with the practices of foreign religions. Because of this, God allowed the Assyrians to conquer and take Israel captive in 722 BC. It was to these very same Assyrians—to their capital city of Nineveh—that God called Jonah to preach the repentance of sin.

Travel Tips

While the book of Jonah highlights God's incredible capacity to forgive, it should also cause us to stop and examine the condition of our hearts as we serve the Lord. Even our stubbornness can't thwart His plans to reach as many as possible with the good news of salvation. God's mercy and grace should astonish and soften even the hardest places of our hearts.

- God loves mercy. Consider any Ninevites that might be in your life—people you would prefer God "dealt with" in swift and forceful fashion. When you feel a Jonah-like level of grumpiness toward another person—even if it's justified—remember God's grace and forgiveness toward you when you were still a sinner (and even now as a forgiven sinner).

- There's nothing harder to escape than your own comfort zone. Jonah got upset when God withered the plant that had grown up and provided shelter for him. God used the opportunity to point out just how unjustified and ungodly Jonah's griping was—God had just shown mercy to an entire city of lost, sinful people, but Jonah cared more about his own comfort.

- Exposure to scriptural truth does not guarantee a godly life. Jonah shows us the picture of a man who did not allow Scripture to penetrate and change his heart. He lacked the personal grace to match his intellectual understanding of God's grace.

- God gives second chances (and second-second chances and third-second chances and so on). God chased Jonah down and gave him another chance to preach to the people of Nineveh (Jonah 3:1). We shouldn't take for granted that Christianity is the story of second chances. Everyone who comes to Christ must realize that they need a second chance and that God is ready and willing to grant it.

> **We shouldn't take for granted that Christianity is the story of second chances.**

In Flight

Running from God (Jonah 1)

Jonah is a minor prophet with a major message. As God's first foreign missionary, he started history's biggest revival on record—but he resisted almost every step of the way. In fact, why Jonah ran from God is far more important than the details of the fish story—what was going on inside this runaway prophet is more meaningful than what was going on inside the fish (it probably just had indigestion, whereas Jonah had a transformation).

The fish story in question deserves a little attention, however, mostly because a lot of people see it as impossible or a myth—a cautionary tale Jewish parents told their kids at bedtime to get them to do what they were told. While it certainly might work in that way, it's even more convincing to see it as it really is, a historical narrative. For one thing, the book reads like a historical account—a recounting of facts, not a symbolic allegory or retelling of a dream. For another, the meticulous Roman-Jewish historian Josephus wrote of Jonah's adventures as real events.[31]

And most convincing, Jesus Christ Himself viewed Jonah's time in the belly of the fish as real, drawing a direct comparison between Jonah's three days and nights and His own coming three days in the "belly" of death. Furthermore, Jesus referred to Jonah's resulting ministry in Nineveh as a factual event (Matthew 12:39-41). You cannot take Jesus Christ seriously unless you are willing to believe a book that He Himself took seriously. Bottom line: If Jesus said it really happened, that's good enough for me.

Jonah, like Jesus, was from Galilee, a little village called Gath-Hepher only about four miles from Jesus's boyhood home of Nazareth. His name means "dove," which is ironic considering his hawk-like personality. Jonah was anything but peaceful, gentle, or a symbol of cooperation and peace. Maybe that's a reason God chose him—to give another example in His running menagerie of servants voted Least Likely to Be Used by God.

God took this unpeaceful dove and sent him to preach repentance to Nineveh, the capital city of Assyria, a fearsome and dreaded empire that would eventually conquer the northern kingdom of Israel. God said, "Go...cry out against it" (Jonah 1:2), and you'd think Jonah would like to have had the job of denouncing his enemies. But instead, he went the opposite way, heading south to Joppa and catching a boat west toward Tarshish. Here's the thing: "Jonah arose to flee to Tarshish *from the presence of the* LORD" (v. 3, emphasis added). Clearly he didn't want anything to do with the frightening Assyrians, but he was actually fleeing from God, not them. You'd think a prophet would know better. *God will never find me on this boat!* Um, wrong.

God didn't accept Jonah's prophetic resignation. Surely Jonah knew how that had worked out for Moses—*Oh Lord, I can't speak well*—but that God told him what to say. Or Jeremiah, whose frustration with being persecuted led him to quit, only to find that he couldn't because God's word burned in his heart like a flame. God had to knock Saul of Tarsus off his high horse to get him to open his eyes (Acts 9:1-6). God is willing to do things the hard way if you're hardheaded, like Jonah was. "But the LORD sent out a great wind on the sea, and there was a mighty tempest on the sea, so that the ship was about to be broken up" (Jonah 1:4). A dramatic refusal to serve required dramatic means to get this prodigal prophet back on track.

Jonah wasn't dealing with a pair of important truths: One, there's no escaping God; and two, God loved him too much to let him get too far off track. Solomon once noted, "Harsh discipline is for him who forsakes the way" (Proverbs 15:10). If you won't listen to the still, small voice of God, you may want to buy storm insurance! In that respect, the sailors aboard Jonah's ship showed more sense than he did, praying to their gods and throwing cargo overboard to try to stay afloat. And while the pagans prayed, Jonah sawed logs.

Soon the sailors realized that this guy was at odds with his God, and thus the reason for the storm. They were correctly freaked out, caught between maritime laws of safe passage and fear of this thundering God chasing down His wayward prophet. What had just been an issue between Jonah and God now involved them. A disobedient child of God is a menace to everyone—spouses, children, co-workers, friends, and even strangers can be affected by your sin.

To Jonah's credit, he took the blame. When the sailors asked him what they were supposed to do with him, he told them, "Chuck me overboard, and the sea will calm down." God ended up being glorified not by His own prophet but because the sailors made offerings to Him so He wouldn't be mad they threw His prophet into the water: "Do not charge us with innocent blood; for You, O LORD, have done as it pleased You" (Jonah 1:14).

Jonah should have said, "Give me five minutes so I can repent and ask God to forgive me. Then everything will be fine." He admitted he knew God, admitted it was his fault they were in danger, but did nothing to make things right. Even when the sailors rebuked Jonah for his disobedience, he maintained it. Their hearts were softened by their circumstances and the consequences, but Jonah's was hardened. By God's grace, he only ended up in a fish's belly rather than Davy Jones's locker.

People have made several suggestions about what kind of creature this fish was. But it doesn't really matter whether it was a huge Great White, a whale shark, or a sperm whale—it could've been a giant minnow, if God wanted it to be. What matters most is that "the LORD had prepared a great fish to swallow Jonah" (v. 17). God had a job for Jonah to do, so He kept him from drowning, assigning a fish or whale of some sort to carry him without digesting him for three days—and, in the process, humbling His runaway prophet.

Running to God (Jonah 2)

Inside the belly of the whale, Jonah's heart was changing. He hadn't prayed when God called him to go to Nineveh, or when the storm came up, or when he got tossed overboard, or even when he got swallowed. But now, after three days and nights at the Whalegut Spa, "Jonah prayed to the LORD his God from the fish's belly" (Jonah 2:1). A man can only take so much, and that fish belly was like a full trash can in August in East Texas—smelly, hot, and humid.

What's impressive is the quality of Jonah's prayer, both the sincere desire to seek and honor God and the language, which drew on Jonah's clear knowledge of the Scriptures—phrases from Psalms, Lamentations, and Job. Instead of "O Lord, it stinketh!" we read, "I cried out to the LORD because of my affliction, and He answered me. Out of the belly of Sheol I cried, and You heard my voice" (v. 2). He admitted he had messed up, and was receiving his just desserts as a whale's appetizer.

Drawing on the sentiment of Psalm 120 and the style of Lamentations 3, Jonah called out: "For You cast me into the deep, into the heart of the seas, and the floods surrounded me; all Your billows and Your waves passed over me. Then I said, 'I have been cast out of Your sight; yet I will look again toward Your holy temple'" (vv. 3-4). There are nuances from no fewer than eleven different texts of Old Testament Scripture in Jonah's prayer. There was enough repentance to get God to make the fish vomit him up on the beach, but there's a warning here: Exposure to scriptural truth does not guarantee a godly life. If you know the words of the Bible but don't take them to heart, it's practical atheism. To run from God, then, is to end up whale vomit—digested in the belly of your own pride.

If you know the words of the Bible but don't take them to heart, it's practical atheism.

For Jonah, though, there was a takeaway: "Those who regard worthless idols forsake their own Mercy" (v. 8). Was Jonah carrying a little statue in his pocket, worshipping a false god? No, but if an idol is anything that replaces God as first in your life, Jonah had one: himself. He set his will and agenda above God's, claiming to know God but pushing away what God wanted him to do. An old Jewish proverb says, "There's no room for God in the one who's full of himself." Jonah was full of Jonah, but when the belly of the whale was emptied, so was Jonah's pride. "I will sacrifice to You with the voice of thanksgiving; I will pay what I have vowed. Salvation is of the LORD" (v. 10).

Running with God (Jonah 3)

The biggest miracle in the book isn't the giant fish but the giant revival—the biggest spiritual mass-conversion in recorded history. The Great Awakening in the mid-1700s and the Second Great Awakening in the first half of the nineteenth century saw millions come to a living faith in Christ—a large percentage of the population at the time.[32] A good night for the Billy Graham Evangelical Association is a conversion rate of five to ten percent of the crowd, which could be hundreds or even thousands of souls saved. But in Nineveh, the number was 100 percent. "The people of Nineveh believed God, proclaimed a fast, and put on sackcloth, from the greatest to the least of them" (Jonah 3:5).

God wanted Jonah to complete the task of evangelism to the Assyrians of Nineveh. At this point, after such a bad start, He could've said, "You've been sufficiently reminded who's in charge, but I'm going to give the job to someone more enthusiastic." Instead, God gently and graciously told Jonah, "Arise, go to Nineveh, that great city, and preach to it the message that I tell you" (v. 2). It's one thing to be forgiven by God, but quite another thing for God to say, "I'm going to give you a second chance." Yet so often, that's exactly what He does.

So Jonah went to Nineveh, "an exceedingly great city, a three-day journey in extent" (v. 3). C.F. Keil, the respected Old Testament archaeologist, described Nineveh as a complex of four walled cities clustered together around the Tigris River.[33] The outer walls were one hundred feet high[34] with a sixty-mile circumference, and had 1500 guard towers and fifteen gates, each named after one of the gods the Ninevites worshipped.[35] As Jonah walked through the city, the largest of its time, he gave a simple, direct message: "Yet forty days, and Nineveh shall be overthrown!" (v. 4).

We don't know if that was all of his message, but it's all that's quoted. The impact was huge. It's impossible to overstate this. No one argued with him or took a shot at him; he wasn't arrested or mocked. Instead, the people repented, mourned their sin, and fasted—all of them, "from the greatest to the least" (v. 5). There were 120,000 children in Nineveh—signified by the phrase "persons who cannot discern between their right hand and their left" (Jonah 4:11)—which meant a general population of around 600,000, and they all turned from evil to God, who "relented from the disaster that He had said He would bring upon them" (Jonah 3:10).

The odds against Jonah's success were high. From a historical point of view, it's easy to see why he tried to get as far as he could from Nineveh. The Assyrian kings were known for brutality toward their enemies. They took captives from conquered lands back to Nineveh, dragging them by pierced lips for hundreds of miles. They peeled the skin off others, and piled up enemy heads outside the city gates.[36] Success wouldn't have been possible without God—but with God, it was inevitable. Even the king responded—either Adad-narari III (811–783 BC) or Shalmaneser IV (783–773 BC),[37] the two Assyrian kings during Jonah's time—and "he arose from his throne and laid aside his robe, covered himself with sackcloth and sat in ashes" (v. 6).

If it all seems unlikely, it was. How rare is it for one man to walk into hostile territory, give a simple warning about coming judgment, and everyone just turns to God? And it was for real too. God saw the Ninevites' conversion as genuine, because He held back His judgment. While God alone can truly change hearts, He often uses personal or cultural biases to get people's attention. In the case of Nineveh, He may very well have used their own superstitions to convert them.

The Assyrians had assimilated the worship of a Philistine deity, Dagon, into their own religious practices. Dagon, powerful and mysterious, supposedly controlled the seas and was revered throughout the Assyrian empire. They had probably heard the story of how, when the ark of the Hebrew God had been captured and taken to Dagon's temple in Philistia, the statue of Dagon had fallen on its face before the ark (1 Samuel 5:2-4). Imagine, then, their reaction when a prophet belched from the belly of a great fish—and very possibly bleached white by the digestive juices in its stomach[38]—entered the city like a bad omen and preached repentance and the power of that very God. Perhaps this is what Jesus meant when He stated that "Jonah became a sign to the Ninevites" (Luke 11:30). Jonah didn't perform a sign; he *was* the sign! And now Jonah went from running from God to running with Him, and the result was a massive spiritual shift in the least likely city in the world.

Run-in with God (Jonah 4)

Imagine the entire population of New York City converting like that, or London or Las Vegas. Picture everyone in Dubai, Beijing, or Baghdad turning their hearts to Christ. Words like *amazing* or *astonishing* fall short in trying to describe the wonder of such a thought. But it's a great thought, isn't it? This is a scene worth rejoicing over and celebrating wholeheartedly. That's what happened in Nineveh, but the man God used to accomplish the revival didn't rejoice: "It displeased Jonah exceedingly, and he became angry" (Jonah 4:1).

Why? Because Jonah knew God would forgive the Assyrians. That's why he headed for Tarshish in the first place—"for I know that You are a gracious and merciful God, slow to anger and abundant in lovingkindness, One who relents from doing harm" (v. 2). We don't know any ancient Assyrians, so it's harder to understand why Jonah begrudged them the mercy they received. Put it in a different historical setting, though. Picture Jonah as a Jew from the orthodox part of New York in the 1930s, whom God sent to Berlin to preach repentance to the Nazis. Picture him as a twenty-first-century Jew being sent by God into Mosul to cry out against ISIS. From those perspectives, his anger is much easier to grasp. He wanted his enemies punished, not spared.

What a contrast between God's nature and Jonah's—God is merciful and slow to anger; Jonah is mafioso mean. He wanted God to give the Ninevites what they deserved—swift, final justice for their hatred of the Jews. Barring that, he would rather have died than see Assyrians saved. "Therefore now, O LORD, please take my life from me, for it's better for me to die than to live!" (v. 3).

God again showed special grace for his angry prophet, asking him, "Is it right for you to be angry?" (Jonah 4:4). He was asking, "Why aren't you excited about something I'm excited about? Why aren't you glad that I am merciful?" But Jonah didn't want a perspective check. He went outside the city limits, sat down, and sulked "till he might see what would become of the city" (v. 5). Jonah still thought God might let Nineveh have it, but instead, God gave Jonah a plant to shelter him from the sun. "So Jonah was very grateful for the plant" (v. 6)—the first time we see him express thanks for anything, by the way.

The next day, though, God killed the plant, sending a hot wind and letting the sun beat down on Jonah's head. Jonah quickly shifted back into wishing he was dead. God asked Jonah, "Is it right for you to be angry about the plant?" And Jonah said, "It is right for me to be angry, even to death!" (Jonah 4:9). Amazingly, once again, God did not respond to Jonah's anger with His own. Instead, He tried to guide him through the right way to think about the matter:

> You have had pity on the plant for which you have not labored, nor made it grow, which came up in a night and perished in a night. And should I not pity Nineveh, that great city, in which there are more than one hundred and twenty thousand persons who cannot discern between their right hand and their left—and much livestock? (vv. 10-11).

Jonah was more upset about a soulless plant than 600,000 souls who would all face eternity without God. He couldn't move out of his own comfort zone, his own ideas about right and wrong, and see that God truly doesn't want anyone to end up on eternity's scrap heap. Some people, however, just won't be counseled. They mistake their righteousness for God's, wrapping their limited understanding in a rag of holier-than-thou behavior, and not even God Himself can change their minds. God is going to do what He knows is best for the most people—for anyone who will receive His blessings on His terms.

God is going to do great things. Will you make yourself available to Him for His purposes?

We don't have a neat little bow wrapped around the end of Jonah's story; it ends with questions. The question God posed to Jonah might very well be asked of each of us: "Is it right for you to be angry?" What angers you? There are plenty of options to choose from. And it's really easy to stay distanced from the world's problems, preserving your sense of security or even self-righteousness. Will you stay in your comfort zone, cut off from God's heart and desire to use you in His work? Or will you take the opportunity to let His heart fill yours, and open your eyes to the needs of the lost all around you? You know the truth: God is going to do great things. Will you make yourself available to Him for His purposes?

MICAH, NAHUM, AND HABAKKUK
FLIGHT PLAN

Facts

Micah
Author

The author of the book of Micah was the prophet and poet Micah of Moresheth. Moresheth was a small village near Jerusalem in the southern kingdom of Judah. Little is known about Micah other than the meaning of his name—"Who is like the Lord?"—his hometown, and the fact that he prophesied during the reigns of three kings of Judah: Jotham, Ahaz, and Hezekiah.

Date Written

Micah wrote his poetic prophecies between 730 and 720 BC.

Nahum
Author

Nahum is identified as the author of the book that bears his name (Nahum 1:1). We don't know much about Nahum other than that he was an Elkoshite—a native of a city identified in historical records as Elkosh, or Alqush, on the eastern banks of the Tigris River near modern Mosul in Iraq. Some, however, believe it to be a small village in the region of Galilee.

Date Written

Because Nahum prophesied against the Assyrian Empire, the date of his book could be placed during the reigns of Manasseh (696–642 BC), Amon (642–640 BC), or Josiah (640–609 BC). During this period of Judah's history, the Assyrians had all but destroyed the culture and religious life of the Jews but hadn't yet fallen to Babylon.

Habakkuk

Author

Habakkuk the prophet wrote this short book (Habakkuk 1:1). Little else is known of him.

Date Written

A reference to the Chaldean (pre-Babylonian) Empire in Habakkuk 1:6 indicates that Habakkuk probably wrote this book after the decline of the Assyrian Empire and prior to Nebuchadnezzar II's raid on Jerusalem. This puts the book's composition sometime between 612 and 605 BC.

Landmarks

Micah, Nahum, and Habakkuk all represented God to the southern kingdom of Judah. Micah spoke to the common people of Judah, the farmers and villagers; Nahum addressed all the people, leaders as well as commoners; and Habakkuk wrote as the priest he was, having a dialogue with God. Micah's theme was "God is moving"—yes, His judgment was approaching, but afterward, the future would be glorious. Nahum's theme was "the Ninevites are going," a reassuring message in the midst of their trials that God would punish Judah's enemies. Habakkuk's dialogue warned that "the Babylonians are coming," a reminder to smug believers that God is active and aware of their arrogance and ready with an answer they won't like.

Itinerary

Micah

- The Exposé (Micah 1–3)
- The Expectation (Micah 4–5)
- The Exaltation (Micah 6–7)

Nahum

- Judgment Announced (Nahum 1)
- Judgment Executed (Nahum 2)
- Judgment Rationalized (Nahum 3)

Habakkuk

- The Burden (Habakkuk 1)
- The Watch (Habakkuk 2:1)
- The Vision (Habakkuk 2:2-20)
- The Prayer (Habakkuk 3)

Gospel

Micah

Micah delivered one of the most well-known messianic prophecies in redemptive history a full 700 years before the events of the Gospels took place, a prediction of the little town of Bethlehem becoming the birthplace of the Messiah (Micah 5:2).

Micah not only prophesied about Jesus's first coming; he also prophesied about His return. The deliverer born in Bethlehem would have the heart of a shepherd, nourishing His people (v. 4)—that's Jesus's first coming—and bringing peace to the earth (v. 5)—that's His second coming.

Jesus Himself said, "I am the good shepherd. The good shepherd gives His life for the sheep" (John 10:11). And He did just that on the cross, giving His life for us so that we might have peace with God and receive the forgiveness of our sins. In the prophetic words of Micah, He "cast all our sins into the depths of the sea" (Micah 7:19). Jesus laid down His life and rose again, and now we wait for Him to return and reign in everlasting peace.

Nahum

Nahum shows that God is both merciful in salvation and righteous in judgment. Although Nineveh's response to Jonah's warning had been immediate and widespread, it hadn't lasted. A people steeped in evil had been shown the light but had gone back to the darkness. God showed grace to Assyria in Jonah's day—a reflection of what Jesus did in His first coming. But Nahum showed what Christ will do when He returns. He made it clear that judgment comes for those who reject the Lord and continue to live an unrepentant lifestyle.

Many of us don't like to see God how Nahum described Him—as a jealous avenger (Nahum 1:2). Yet any view of God that doesn't take into account His justice and holiness is incomplete at best and erroneous at worst. If God doesn't judge sin, then He's not righteous. It's true that He is slow to anger and doesn't relish judgment, desiring everyone to come to repentance (2 Peter 3:9). But make no mistake about it—He will judge.

> ## Any view of God that doesn't take into account His justice and holiness is incomplete at best and erroneous at worst.

Even the cross of Christ is both merciful and just—because God allowed His Son to take the just punishment for our sin, He can extend mercy to those of us who believe. And during the harshest times of widespread judgment in the future tribulation period, He will continue to offer salvation to those who receive Jesus as Lord and Savior. For those who repent and turn to Him, He will be, in the words of Nahum, "a stronghold in the day of trouble" (Nahum 1:7).

Habakkuk

Habakkuk is one of the most important writings in all of Scripture—so much so that one of its verses is cited multiple times in the New Testament as a central tenet of the gospel. The great doctrinal books of Romans, Galatians, and Hebrews all refer to, mention, or build on the famous verse "the just shall live by his faith" (Habakkuk 2:4), using it to point to the all-important truth that Jesus justifies His people by their faith in the finished work He did on the cross.

History

Micah

Micah prophesied during the reigns of Jotham (750–732 BC), Ahaz (735–715 BC), and Hezekiah (715–686 BC). This era was one of Assyrian dominance: The Assyrians conquered Samaria, the capital city of Israel, and destroyed parts of the southern kingdom of Judah. Micah preached around the same time as Isaiah, Hosea, Jonah, and Amos.

Nahum

Nahum prophesied the fall of Nineveh, which occurred in 612 BC. If Nahum lived between 648 and 620 BC, as is commonly projected, then he saw the reigns of three different kings of Judah during his lifetime: Manasseh, Amon, and Josiah, as well as the final kings of Assyria: Ashurbanipal, Ashur-etil-ilani, and

Sin-shar-ishkun. Ashurbanipal in particular was known for his cruelty and evil works. During his reign, Nineveh was at its zenith of wealth and power. Nahum was most likely a contemporary of the prophets Zephaniah and Habakkuk, and possibly Jeremiah.

Habakkuk

Habakkuk lived during the reign of King Josiah (640–609 BC). Several significant cultural and religious events occurred around this time: Josiah's religious reforms (622 BC), the fall of Nineveh (612 BC), and Babylon's attack on Jerusalem (605 BC), among others. Josiah's religious reforms were largely unsuccessful; much of the nation continued in idolatry and corruption, the two major sins Habakkuk addressed in his book. Habakkuk prophesied at the same time as Nahum, Zephaniah, Jeremiah, Daniel, Ezekiel, and Obadiah.

Travel Tips

Micah

The book of Micah reveals that God wants you to "do justly, to love mercy, and to walk humbly with your God" (Micah 6:8). Sometimes believers are accused of "being so heavenly minded that they're no earthly good." Micah reminds us to put into practice what we know divinely to be true; otherwise, we can do no earthly good.

- God has an immediate and an ultimate plan for His people. It's easy to focus on the trials and tragedies of this life and lose sight of what's coming. Micah reminds us that God uses hardships to mature us and times of rejoicing to remind us of His goodness, whetting our appetites for Christ's triumphant return.

God uses hardships to mature us and times of rejoicing to remind us of His goodness.

- Corruption works outward from the core of a nation—or an individual. Selfishness, lust, greed, and laziness are default settings. When you read God's Word daily, pray constantly, attend church regularly, and live life with other believers, you fill yourself with the things of God so that in times of trail or temptation, the fruit of the Spirit pours out of your life.

- God has a big eraser; let Him use it. "You will cast all our sins into the depths of the sea" (Micah 7:19). Confess your every sin to the Lord—everything that weighs you down in running this race—and let Him refresh your soul.

Nahum

God's jealousy isn't like human jealousy. He wants our solitary devotion, and He deserves it. He wants all of you—no affairs with the world, with other people, with work, with entertainment, with politics, or with religion.

- Who can stand blameless before God? Only Jesus. He alone can plead our case before the Lord. When you accepted Jesus as your Savior, He replaced your self-righteousness (your "good deeds," which are like filthy rags to Him) with His righteousness, the only righteousness that can match your need for salvation and forgiveness, giving you access to God.

- If Christians won't proclaim God's goodness to the world, then who will? The clock is ticking during this age of grace, and now more than ever, you need to stand for God's truth, balance it with God's compassion, and trust that God will judge any wrongs done to you as He sees fit.

Habakkuk

Habakkuk reminds us to ask God the right questions. In times of trouble, it's so much easier to ask "*How* can I get out of this?" rather than "*What* can I get out of this?" Our tendency to avoid suffering at all costs can blind us to the all-important truth that our loving, sovereign Lord works all things—even the very worst of things—together for our good.

- Commit your problems to God. When life is beating you up and you don't understand what's happening or what to do, get in God's Word and remind yourself of what you know to be true—that God is good, righteous, full of grace, loving—and He wants the best for you.

- Train your heart to wait on the Lord. In times of trial, respond the same way as Habakkuk: "I will stand at my watch...I will look to see what he will say to me" (Habakkuk 2:1 NIV). Be vigilant in watching for God's hand in your circumstances. He will see you through the worst of times because He has already taken care of the most important thing: where you will spend eternity.

- God can handle your tough questions. Approach Him with honesty and faith, but not with the expectation that He owes you a response. Faith is not supposed to silence all your doubts so that you never struggle with them again; faith is meant to make you sure of God and confident of His care.

> God can handle your tough questions.
> Approach Him with honesty and faith.

In Flight

Micah: God Is Moving

The Exposé (Micah 1–3)

If you have ever wondered during a hardship, *Is this ever going to get any better?* or *Why is God allowing this?*, the book of Micah is for you. This prophet spoke of God's temporary plan but also His ultimate design for His people—a divided nation oppressed by both local leaders and foreign powers. "Hear, all you peoples! Listen, O earth, and all that is in it! Let the Lord God be a witness against you" (Micah 1:2). Micah spoke in courtroom language, as if a case was being tried before God, who was acting as the judge, key witness, and prosecutor.

Micah exposed the sins of Samaria and Jerusalem, the capitals of the northern kingdom of Israel and the southern kingdom of Judah. Their kings and leaders had influenced their people for the worse, guiding them in idolatry and injustice. Like worms hidden at the center of an apple, they had corrupted and polluted their communities. Rotten from the core, they were companions in oppression. They would become bedfellows in judgment.

The execution of their sentence was going to be terrifying: "Behold, the Lord is coming out of His place; He will come down and tread on the high places of the earth. The mountains will melt under Him, and the valleys will split like wax before the fire, like waters poured down a steep place" (vv. 3-4). Though this kind of geographical destruction won't actually happen until the end times, it's a powerful metaphor for the oppressive might Assyria—as a tool in God's hands—would bring against Israel and Judah, enhanced by the fact that it was their own fault.

Micah focused on revealing the abusive leadership of Israel and Judah's wealthy ruling class: "They covet fields and take them by violence, also houses, and seize them. So they oppress a man and his house, a man and his inheritance" (Micah 2:2). The kings of God's people were acting like thieves, ripping off the poor because they could, but God wasn't letting them get away with it.

God was also done with false prophets and the people's lack of discernment about their lies. "If a liar and deceiver comes and says, 'I will prophesy for you plenty of wine and beer,' that would be just the prophet for this people!" (v. 11 NIV). The people would rather listen to faulty pundits under the influence of alcohol than true prophets like Micah under the influence of the Holy Spirit. The only preaching they tolerated led them down the broad path of living only in the moment, a worldview of either *everything is good so let's party*, or *nothing is good so let's get wasted*.

The prophets cursed anyone who argued against them. Micah's word to them warned that God was going to cut them off: "Therefore you shall have night without vision, and you shall have darkness without divination; the sun will go down on the prophets, the day shall be dark for them...Indeed they shall all cover their lips; for there is no answer from God" (Micah 3:6-7). God was aware of the situation, and He would move to expose the wolves among His people, starting with the ones hanging out inside the sheepfold. Israel and Judah's judgment was on their heads: "Because of you Zion shall be plowed like a field, Jerusalem shall become a heap of ruins, and the mountain of the temple like the bare hills of the forest" (v. 12).

The Expectation (Micah 4–5)

After pronouncing doom on the cities of Samaria and Jerusalem and proclaiming the perils of ignoring God's call to live faithfully, Micah predicted the restoration of Israel. It was a twofold promise: the first fulfillment would come after their Babylonian exile, and the second will come in the end times—including the arrival of the Messiah, who will usher in a period of peace and security. Micah referred to the last time first: "It shall come to pass in the latter days that the mountains of the LORD's house [Mount Zion] shall be established on the top of the mountains, and shall be exalted above the hills; and peoples shall flow to it" (Micah 4:1). In saying this, Micah echoed the words of his contemporary, Isaiah (Isaiah 2:2-4).

God's future plan includes not only Jerusalem but a little town not far from the capital called Bethlehem. Micah predicted the Messiah's birthplace seven centuries before Jesus came: "But you, Bethlehem Ephrathah, though you are little among the thousands of Judah, yet out of you shall come forth to Me the One to be Ruler in Israel, whose goings forth are from of old, from everlasting" (Micah 5:2). The future deliverer of Israel, Jesus Christ, would be born in Bethlehem. God orchestrated a number of world events in order to make this happen. Caesar Augustus, for example, decided to hold a census of the Roman Empire at just the right time, forcing a carpenter in Nazareth named Joseph to pack up his pregnant bride Mary and return to his hometown of Bethlehem just in time for the birth.

Micah also spoke clearly about the expectations of Messiah's second coming. "He shall stand and feed His flock in the strength of the LORD, in the majesty of the name of the LORD His God; and they shall abide, for now He shall be great to the ends of the earth; and this One shall be peace" (vv. 4-5). Like Isaiah, Micah shifted from the near future to the distant future, speaking of Christ's millennial reign and then shifting to the rise of Assyria, who would be evil shepherds, in contrast with the Messiah (vv. 5-6). Jesus is the Good Shepherd, laying His life down for His flock, leaving them in the care of human leaders until He returns to lead them (John 10:14-16).

The Exaltation (Micah 6–7)

Micah ended his book with multiple predictions of redemption and restoration through the promised Messiah. This section is written in the form of a prayer and confession of sin from the people to God, exalting Him as their only hope. Once again, Micah played lawyer, with Israel and Judah being the defendants. Micah asked on God's behalf what He had done to them that they had behaved so badly. He recorded their response in the form of four questions, each one suggesting an outward mode of worship—and each one showing a hidden motive that proved how far their hearts were from God.

The people first asked, "With what shall I come before the LORD, and bow myself before the High God?" (Micah 6:6). To bow is to show humility, to recognize another's superiority, so they were asking God, "Do you want me to show intensity in my worship?" Humility is a good thing, but you can bow down and still be driven by pride. If you make an extreme gesture in a worship service, like bowing down, check your motivation. Because if the thought enters your mind that others will notice and think that you're humble, you're already off track.

Their follow-up question was about the quality of their offerings: "Shall I come before Him with burnt offerings, with calves a year old?" (v. 6). Leviticus 5 said to bring a spotless lamb on the Passover—a lamb of the highest quality. That is, we should worship God with our very best. Once again, though, the sounds of worship can be top-shelf—great musicians, first-rate production values—but if the hearts of the worshippers aren't drawn toward God and His excellence, the sounds are a clanging gong, annoying and empty.

If it's not about quality, they then asked, is quantity the right way to worship? "Will the Lord be pleased with thousands of rams, ten thousand rivers of oil?" (v. 7). The Bible tells us to pray constantly. The way to walking closely with God is to die to ourselves, but even that can done with the wrong attitude—hypocritical shows of spirituality made not to invoke God but to impress others.

> ## The way to walking closely with God is to die to ourselves.

The final question reached to a much deeper place in the heart: "Shall I give my firstborn for my transgression, the fruit of my body for the sin of my soul?" (v. 7). God forbade human sacrifice among His people (Deuteronomy 12:31), but it was a common practice carried out by the pagans in an attempt to appease their gods. Such a tremendous sacrifice was supposed to show total commitment, even to the point of cruelty and harshness.

But God didn't want any of those things because He knew the inherent flaws in the attitude behind them. Instead, He reminded the people what authentic worship looked like: "He has shown you, O man, what is good; and what does the Lord require of you but to do justly, to love mercy, and to walk humbly with your God?" (Micah 6:8). Those three elements sum up the law—loving God with all your heart, soul, and strength, and loving your neighbor as yourself—and they show that worship is more than thirty minutes of singing "church songs" each weekend.

Micah felt the hollowness of the false worship surrounding him: "Woe is me! For I am like those who gather summer fruits, like those who glean vintage grapes; there is no cluster to eat of the first-ripe fruit which my soul desires" (Micah 7:1). Everywhere he looked around him, his countrymen were driven by greed and hypocrisy, so he looked upward to God and offered a personal petition for mercy: "Shepherd Your people with Your staff, the flock of Your heritage, who dwell solitarily in a woodland, in the midst of Carmel; let them feed in Bashan and Gilead, as in the days of old" (v. 14).

God was the only hope His people had, if they would only recognize their need for Him. Micah's name means "Who is like God?," and Micah praised Him accordingly: "Who is a God like You, pardoning iniquity and passing over transgression of the remnant of His heritage? He does not retain His anger forever, because He delights in mercy. He will again have compassion on us, and will subdue our iniquities. You will cast all our sins into the depths of the sea" (vv. 18-19).

As Corrie ten Boom said, "When we confess our sins...God casts them into the deepest ocean, gone forever. And even though I cannot find a Scripture for it, I believed God then places a sign out there that says, No Fishing Allowed."[39] Micah recognized that God was moving, especially in the hardest times, working His will and ready to forgive any who turn from sin to Him. Though God's goodness is sometimes a severe mercy, He is faithful to restore and provide reason to rejoice again.

Nahum: The Ninevites Are Going
Judgment Announced (Nahum 1)

A century-and-a-half after Jonah preached repentance to the city of Nineveh came the prophecy he would have preferred to give: Nahum's message about the complete destruction of Nineveh. The Ninevites repented—all of them—after Jonah's warning, but a handful of generations later, they had gone back to their old ways, and were even worse than they had been before. This time, God sent a prophet in Nahum, who by his condemnation of God's enemy offered comfort to worried believers.

Nahum described his vision as the "burden against Nineveh" (Nahum 1:1). "Burden" can mean a prophetic utterance, but it can also mean a heavy load. In Nineveh's case, the people would bear the burden of God's wrath detailed in Nahum's message. Though Nahum would dump the bulk of the burden on Nineveh, he began by describing the God they had offended: "God is jealous...The LORD will take vengeance on His adversaries, and He reserves wrath for His enemies; the LORD is slow to anger and great in power, and will not at all acquit the wicked" (vv. 2-3). Picture a slow, 150-year-long boil coming to a steam, almost ready to be poured out.

Anyone who thinks God is passive, weak, or detached is greatly mistaken. Micah demonstrated that God is moving, even in ways and places where we can't detect Him, and He cares about us and our choices. Eight times in the Bible, He is called *jealous*. Don't think of sinful, human jealousy, but that God will tolerate no rivals. There are no other gods beside Him, and He wants all of your heart, and all of the reverence and awe that is due to Him. Fortunately for us, God is also slow to anger—"longsuffering toward us, not willing that any should perish but that all should come to repentance" (2 Peter 3:9).

> **God is moving, even in ways and places where we can't detect Him, and He cares about us and our choices.**

And, as Nahum noted, "The LORD is good, a stronghold in the day of trouble; and He knows those who trust in Him" (Nahum 1:7). That little note of consolation, like a sunbeam breaking through the gathering clouds, was meant to serve as comfort for the Jews who had been suffering under Assyria's cruel hand, but even more comforting was what came next: "With an overflowing flood He will make an utter end of its place"—that is, of Nineveh as a great city—"and darkness will pursue His enemies" (v. 8).

Judgment Executed (Nahum 2)

Nahum warned the mighty Ninevite army to brace itself for its impending doom—not that it would do any good. "The shields of [Nineveh's] mighty men are made red, the valiant men are in scarlet. The chariots come with flaming torches in the day of his preparation, and the spears are brandished" (Nahum 2:3). Their intimidating armor, weapons, and chariots—painted red to strike fear in their foes and hide their own wounds so that they appeared invincible[40]—would come to nothing against God: "'Behold, I am against you,' says the LORD of hosts, 'I will burn your chariots in smoke, and the sword shall devour your young lions; I will cut off your prey from the earth, and the voice of your messengers shall be heard no more'" (v. 13).

Nineveh's end would be total devastation, described the way their terrified victims must have felt through all of their conquests: "She is empty, desolate, and waste! The heart melts, and the knees shake; much pain is in every side, and all their faces are drained of color" (v. 10). Check out the words "empty," "desolate," and "waste" in Hebrew. They are, in order, *buqah*, *mebuqah*, and *balaq*. Nahum used them because they're onomatopoetic—that is, when said aloud, they sounded like breaking pottery—a powerful image of God shattering the mighty Assyrian Empire.

Judgment Rationalized (Nahum 3)

God had told Jonah to go preach against Nineveh, "for their wickedness has come up before Me" (Jonah 1:2). Nahum laid out some of the details of the city's evil behavior, justifying its divine judgment. "Woe to the bloody city! It is all full of lies and robbery. Its victim never departs. The noise of a whip and the noise of rattling wheels, of galloping horses, chattering chariots! Horsemen charge with bright sword and glittering spear. There is a multitude of slain, a great number of bodies, countless corpses—they stumble over the corpses" (Nahum 3:1-3).

Assyrian brutality was the terror of its time. Archaeological records of King Ashurbanipal's practices toward conquered enemies depict gruesome acts, skinning people and displaying their skin publicly, walling others up alive, and impaling men on poles in a precursor of crucifixion.[41] God was putting an end to all that, with Nahum crying "Woe!" to their bloody behavior.

Their walls would fall like ripe fruit shaken from trees, and there was nothing they could do about it. They had the opportunity to turn and follow God, but their habitual rejection of Him sealed their judgment. "Your injury has no healing, your wound is severe. All who hear news of you will clap their hands over you, for upon whom has not your wickedness passed continually?" (v. 19).

Habakkuk: The Babylonians Are Coming

The Burden (Habakkuk 1)

Habakkuk was a prophet puzzled by an issue we all face: How can a loving God who is supposed to be all-powerful allow evil to exist? The argument goes like this: If God exists, and evil exists, God is not who He says He is. If He is loving but unable to do anything about evil, then He is not all-powerful. If He is all-powerful but doesn't stop evil, then He is not all-loving. Theologians call the problem *theodicy*—how do we deal with evil in the world contrasted with the thought of a good and all-powerful God?

Related to that dilemma is the question of why bad things happen to good people (and why good things happen to bad people). Wouldn't life make more sense if only bad people got diseases and had accidents and were killed by other bad people? That way, if you were a good person, you could have some kind of guarantee that things would go well for you. It sounds fairer that way, at least to us humans.

Though Habakkuk was a prophet, presumably of solid enough character that God chose him to deliver a message, he shared those questions and doubts with us— and he shared them with God. His book is a conversation of sorts about God's judgment against Judah. "O Lord, how long shall I cry, and You will not hear? Even cry out to You, 'Violence!' and You will not save" (Habakkuk 1:2). He was bugged about his own country. He couldn't believe that, after all the ways Judah had turned against God, that God hadn't done anything about their behavior.

It was the time of national deterioration and degradation. Godly people were suffering, wicked people were prospering, and Habakkuk prayed and waited—a long time. "Why do You show me iniquity, and cause me to see trouble? For plundering and violence are before me; there is strife, and contention arises. Therefore the law is powerless, and justice never goes forth. For the wicked surround the righteous; therefore perverse judgment proceeds" (vv. 3-4).

But then God finally replied. "Look among the nations and watch—be utterly astounded! For I will work a work in your days which you would not believe, though it were told you" (v. 5). God was going to bring judgment in the form of Babylon—"the Chaldeans, a bitter and hasty nation" (v. 6). Swift and deadly, the Babylonian army would sweep across the region, dismantling the current powers, Egypt and Assyria, with alarming ease—and God was going to let them have their way with Judah.

This was not what Habakkuk expected or hoped to hear. Perhaps he had been hoping for revival—maybe something like God had done back in the days of King Josiah, the sixteen-year-old who had restored the temple, cleaned out idolatrous priests and practices, and kept the first Passover in generations (2 Kings 22–23). But the Babylonians? *Look, God, I know I said we're bad, but they're* really *bad!* "O LORD, You have appointed *them* for judgment; O Rock, You have marked *them* for correction" (Habakkuk 1:12, emphasis added). Habakkuk's prophetic vision turned out to be quite a burden.

The Watch (Habakkuk 2:1)

In the midst of Habakkuk's disappointment and confusion, he did the right thing: He decided to wait on God, to watch and see what the Lord would do. "I will stand my watch and set myself on the rampart, and watch to see what He will say to me, and what I will answer when I am corrected" (Habakkuk 2:1). Notice he assumed that he would be off target if he assumed to understand all that God was doing, thinking about what he would say when God corrected him. That's a good policy.

> ## When it comes to God, never give up what you do know for what you don't.

As Habakkuk waited, he reminded himself of what he knew to be true about God. "Are you not from everlasting, O LORD my God, my Holy One?...You are of purer eyes than to behold evil, and cannot look on wickedness" (Habakkuk 1:12-13). When it comes to God, never give up what you do know for what you don't. A crisis shakes us up, but God is not moved or changed. Reason can only take you so far, and then you have to trust that the things that confuse you are clear to Him, and that He will be true to Himself—holy and just in judgment but willing and able to restore anyone who confesses sin and returns to following Him.

The Vision (Habakkuk 2:2-20)

God's answer followed Habakkuk's patient faith. "The Lord answered me and said: 'Write the vision and make it plain on tablets, that he may run who reads it'" (Habakkuk 2:2). In other words, "Take notes—write legibly and large, because I want everyone to read this, young and old alike."

Even though Habakkuk had waited for God's reply, the Lord wanted His prophet to assure His people that, though Babylon would come and administer a divine spanking, God would punish them in due time. "Though it tarries, wait for it; because it will surely come, it will not tarry" (v. 3). God isn't limited to a human perspective on time; He exists outside of it, and sees all things as if they were happening right now. His sense of timing, then, is different than ours, and He requires His people to trust that whenever He acts, it's in His good and perfect time, taking every possible factor into account.

"For the vision is yet for an appointed time; but at the end it will speak, and it will not lie" (v. 3). God would deal with Babylon, but He was also telling Habakkuk to look beyond even that moment in the future, to a time when God will make everything right. "The earth will be filled with the knowledge of the glory of the Lord, as the waters cover the sea" (v. 14). This echoes a number of predictions woven throughout the Major and Minor Prophets—from Isaiah 6:3, 11:9, 40:5, and 52:10 to Jeremiah 31:34 and Zechariah 14:9—anticipating both the millennial kingdom of Christ and the establishment of the new heaven and earth, where the glory of God will provide all the light needed (Revelation 21:23-25).

In the meantime, though, as God's people wait for deliverance, they are to live with expectation: "The just shall live by his faith" (Habakkuk 2:4). This is a cornerstone verse in the Bible; Paul quoted it three times in the New Testament, and Martin Luther based the Reformation on its promise. God's people had failed in trying to achieve salvation by being good and obeying God's law; Habakkuk's prophecy here pointed to the new covenant God would make through Jesus Christ—a promise of salvation based not on human works but on faith in His work.

The Prayer (Habakkuk 3)

Habakkuk responded to the vision with a prayer, looking ahead to what God predicted. "O Lord, I have heard Your speech and was afraid; O Lord, revive

Your work in the midst of years! In the midst of the years make it known; in wrath remember mercy" (Habakkuk 3:2). He saw God's judgment, His use of Babylon to invade the land, ruin the crops, trample the vineyards, and steal the flocks. "When I heard, my body trembled; my lips quivered at the voice; rottenness entered my bones; and I trembled in myself, that I might rest in the day of trouble" (v. 16).

Though God would permit devastation, Habakkuk praised Him: "Yet I will rejoice in the LORD, I will joy in the God of my salvation" (v. 18). That's an incredible statement of trust. He wasn't celebrating the judgment, but that God would avenge His people on Babylon, and that He had good plans for His people beyond that. His prayer was that God would simply do as He had said He would—that even in the midst of suffering and destruction, God would be merciful to Judah.

When faced with an impending trial, Habakkuk asked the difficult question—what was God trying to show him through the hardship? He concluded that it was worth rejoicing because suffering in the hands of a loving God can be used for ultimate good. That's the message of the cross in a nutshell: The most vicious, horrible thing ever done in history happened to be the very best thing that could happen for the world because now our sins can be washed away and now we can be right with God because of that finished work on our behalf. It's the same message in both the Old and New Testaments: The just shall live by faith.

> The most vicious, horrible thing ever done in history happened to be the very best thing that could happen for the world.

ZEPHANIAH AND HAGGAI
FLIGHT PLAN

Zephaniah

Author

The author of the book of Zephaniah was the prophet Zephaniah, a prophet with a royal bloodline, the great-great grandson of King Hezekiah. Zephaniah 1:1 lists his father and other grandfathers: Cushi, Gedaliah, and Amariah. Zephaniah was probably born around 648 BC.

Date Written

Zephaniah was the last of the prophets to prophesy before the fall of the southern kingdom, Judah. He preached during the reign of King Josiah, so his book likely dates between 640 and 609 BC.

Haggai

Author

Haggai the prophet wrote the book that bears his name (Haggai 1:1). He was the first of the postexilic prophets, sent by God to the Jews who had returned from exile in Babylon to rebuild the temple in Jerusalem.

Date Written

Haggai's date of authorship is very specific: "In the second year of King Darius, in the sixth month, on the first day of the month" (Haggai 1:1). This means Haggai wrote his book between August and December of 520 BC.

Landmarks

Zephaniah

Zephaniah was a prince of the royal house of Judah and served as a prophet during the reign of King Josiah. His book addressed the social injustice and moral decay of Judah and her neighbors, pointing to and warning them of the coming day of the Lord and His wrath upon the nations, including Israel. He was a prophet of the eleventh hour, whose ministry led to reform and revival during his lifetime—but at the last possible moment before God's judgment of Judah.

Haggai

The tenth of the twelve Minor Prophets, the book of Haggai takes us on a brief journey of hard work and determination. God sent Haggai to preach to the restored community of Jews in Jerusalem after their return from exile in Babylon. Haggai encouraged his fellow Jews to finish rebuilding the temple, which had been destroyed by the Babylonians in 586 BC. His theme? *If you build it, He will come.* If God's people would put His glory and honor first by rebuilding His temple, He would come and meet them there and pour out His blessings. But first, God's people had to understand the reasons they were struggling to finish the temple.

Itinerary

Zephaniah

- Look Within (Zephaniah 1:1–2:3)
- Look Around (Zephaniah 2:4–3:8)
- Look Beyond (Zephaniah 3:9-20)

Haggai

- Israel's Struggle with Selfishness (Haggai 1)
- Israel's Struggle with Nostalgia (Haggai 2:1-9)
- Israel's Struggle with Unconfessed Sin (Haggai 2:10-19)
- Israel's Struggle with Unbelief (Haggai 2:20-23)

Gospel

Zephaniah

Zephaniah's prediction of the kingdom age points to Christ as the Lord within Israel (Zephaniah 3:5), the righteous Judge of all earth's nations (v. 8), and the reigning "King of Israel, the LORD" (v. 15). Zephaniah warned Judah that *a* day of the Lord, a more immediate and local series of judgments, was coming—first against the Jews for their idolatry, and then for the nations whom God would use to punish them. These judgments would serve as a type (a preview) of *the* ultimate day of the Lord, when God will judge the entire world in the end times. But mercy is as much a characteristic of God as justice is—displayed most obviously in the person of Jesus Christ—and we see this aspect of the Lord's character in the book of Zephaniah too.

At the end of time, when all God's enemies are defeated and Jesus is dwelling as king among Israel, Zephaniah's words will be completely fulfilled: "The LORD your God in your midst, the Mighty One, will save; He will rejoice over you with gladness, He will quiet you with His love, He will rejoice over you with singing" (v. 17). What a wonderful image of the crowning work of redemption! Revelation describes how even during the tribulation God will set aside and protect a group of 144,000 Jews who believe in Him, and Zephaniah framed the picture of Israel in the millennial kingdom after the day of the Lord. God's heart is to save as many people as will come to Him. He proved this by sending His own Son, Jesus Christ, to die for the sins of the world.

> **God's heart is to save as many people as will come to Him.**

Haggai

The scarlet thread of redemption appears in Haggai as the symbol of the signet ring—the royal mark of God's approval of Zerubbabel as the builder of the temple (Haggai 2:23). For God to "use" Zerubbabel like a signet ring signified two things: First, that God would be with Zerubbabel and give him the authority to rebuild the temple when Israel returned to Jerusalem from exile. Second, that Zerubbabel signified royalty and was precious in the Lord's sight. He was descended from the house of David and thus in the genealogy of Jesus Christ (Matthew 1:12-13; Luke 3:27). As a member of David's royal line, he represented the Messiah, who came through that line and eventually will establish His millennial kingdom on earth.

In other words, on both these counts, Zerubbabel had God's mark of approval—the stamp of His signet ring.

Hebrews 12:26-28 hearkens back to this passage and reveals God's plans for the end times. God will shake loose and get rid of anything that's based on the world and its ways so that all that's left is of His kingdom. Jesus taught His followers to pray, "Your kingdom come. Your will be done on earth as it is in heaven" (Matthew 6:10). Only those who are part of the new covenant of Christ, covered by His blood shed on the cross, will be part of that unshakeable kingdom.

History

Zephaniah

The book of Zephaniah dates to around 620 BC, during the second half of King Josiah's reign. Josiah's six-year reformation project was completed in 622 BC (2 Chronicles 34). Though this project was meant to bring about spiritual revival, many Jews remained stuck in their sinful ways, continuing the practices of idolatry and injustice in the land of Judah. This may be why Zephaniah specifically preached against Baal worship and idolatry. Zephaniah was a likely contemporary of several prophets: Nahum, Habakkuk, Daniel, Ezekiel, Obadiah, and Jeremiah. At the time of Zephaniah's writing, Nineveh had not yet been destroyed (its destruction, foretold in Zephaniah 2:13, and also predicted by Nahum, came in 612 BC).

Haggai

The Babylonian captivity of the Jews occurred between 605 and 536 BC. It began with Nebuchadnezzar invading Judah and ended with King Cyrus of Persia (the nation that conquered Babylon) signing a decree in 538 BC that allowed the Jews to return to Jerusalem. Cyrus's successor, Darius (522–486 BC), reissued the edict, causing the temple to be rebuilt within four years (Ezra 4–6). In 536 BC, Zerubbabel returned to Judah to begin the temple restoration, bringing with him about 50,000 Jews. After some opposition (Ezra 4–6), the temple was completed in March of 516 BC.

Travel Tips

Zephaniah

Zephaniah's message of God's tough love ended with rejoicing in God's future deliverance of His people and sovereign rule on earth. It's important to keep God's end game in mind as you face suffering and persecution in your daily life.

- Suffering tests your faith in God's sovereignty. When the winds of adversity blow against you—sometimes from all directions—don't believe the lie that God doesn't allow such adversity to happen to His kids. Instead, consider the truth that God not only allows bad things to happen, but sometimes causes them to happen because He wants to bring something good from it (Romans 8:28).

- Use Zephaniah's three exhortations to the people of Judah—look within, look around, and look beyond—to guide your thoughts and actions as you engage with your culture and anticipate the day of the Lord.

  - First, look within yourself. Are you worshipping God "in spirit and truth" (John 4:24)—with your whole heart? Are you renewing your mind and actively rejecting the lies of your culture by praying and reading the Bible regularly?

  - Second, look around. Zephaniah prophesied God's wrath on several nations for their poor treatment of His people. No matter what trials you face in this life, God will uphold you and avenge you if necessary. Don't worry about your enemies; instead, focus on living out a balance of love, grace, and truth that marks a true child of God.

  - Third, look beyond. Zephaniah rounded out his book by looking at the healing and restoration God's people will one day experience during Christ's 1000-year reign on earth. As believers, we have every reason to rejoice in the Lord, because the future He has laid out for us is glorious!

Haggai

Haggai reminded God's people not to neglect God's work—or God Himself. "Consider your ways!" was his cry throughout his book (Haggai 1:5, 7). Without God as your number one priority, life becomes a treadmill—a lot of hard work that doesn't get you anywhere. Remember: Seek His kingdom first, and everything else will fall into place (Matthew 6:33).

- Don't neglect your relationship with God. You can be the right person in the right place doing the right work and still forget to connect with Him. When life gets busy, the first thing we tend to do is skip church or tithing or devotionals, trying to live by our own power instead of God's. Be careful to spend time with God in prayer, in His Word, and in fellowship with other believers.

- Obedience to God leads to productivity for God. When Haggai rallied the people to start work on the temple again, they were, in a very real sense, working out their own salvation (Philippians 2:12). Working out your salvation doesn't mean working *for* salvation; rather, it means deciding to obey and serve God *because* you are saved and want to please Him.

- When God tells you to be strong, He will give you the strength you need to obey (Haggai 2:4). This is the message God brings His people every time He lays a difficult task before them: be strong. He will fill you with His Spirit and anoint you; His might in you will accomplish His work through you.

> When God tells you to be strong, He will give you the strength you need to obey.

In Flight

Zephaniah

Look Within (Zephaniah 1:1–2:3)

Zephaniah spoke of a God who, like a surgeon, wounded His people in order to heal them—a God who through judgment brings blessing. Sometimes, as with Israel and Judah, sin has settled so deeply into people's hearts—become so much a part of their everyday lives—that they will respond to God only through hardship. Zephaniah's ministry in King Josiah's day inspired the young monarch to begin spiritual reforms in Judah (2 Kings 23).

Even though Josiah was only sixteen, he read the law to the people, confirmed their covenant with God, cleansed the temple in Jerusalem of idols, and destroyed all the altars of Baal in Samaria and Judah. So even though sin had divided the kingdom and led to years of struggle, God was faithful through a prophet and a king to bring a time of blessing. That's the pattern Zephaniah focused on in his book.

First, though, he had to wake Judah up to the reality of their sin—the things they had done that would bring on God's judgment. "I will stretch out my hand against Judah, and against all the inhabitants of Jerusalem. I will cut off every trace of Baal from this place, the names of the idolatrous priests with the pagan priests—those who worship the host of heaven on the housetops"—that's astrology—"[and] those who worship and swear oaths by the LORD, but who also swear by Milcom"—an Ammonite deity also known as Molech (Zephaniah 1:4-5).

Basically, a lot of people were worshipping God—going to the temple, offering sacrifices to Yahweh—but they were also worshipping other gods from surrounding nations. That blending of worship is called *syncretism*—a buffet-style approach to religion. But you can't pick and choose without consequences—especially if you are trying to choose the one true God *and* something else. It just won't work. On a practical level, it is pure hypocrisy. You can't truly call yourself devoted to a God who said He would tolerate no other gods. On a personal level, whenever you try to have it your way and God's way, God's way always ends up second, and you become one of those "who have turned back from following the LORD, and have not sought the LORD, nor inquired of Him" (v. 6).

> On a personal level, whenever you try to have it your way and God's way, God's way always ends up second.

Practical unbelief infected all aspects of society. Zephaniah warned Jerusalem's merchants in the market district—the Fish Gate, Second Quarter, and Maktesh mentioned in Zephaniah 1:10-11—that "all those who handle money are cut off...their goods shall become booty, and their houses a desolation" (vv. 11, 13). In 586 BC, the Babylonian army would break through Jerusalem's walls at the Fish Gate, wiping out the Judean economy right off the bat.

Zephaniah then mentioned the coming of "the great day of the LORD" (v. 14)—a phrase used by many Old Testament prophets to describe a catastrophic time of God's judgment—through His direct intervention in human affairs. "That day is a day of wrath, a day of trouble and distress" (v. 15). Typically the term is used eschatologically—that is, speaking of the end times—but sometimes it is used in a local, more immediate way, which is what is happening here. Zephaniah predicted not *the* day of the Lord but *a* day of the Lord—a preview in the near future of what is to come in the end times.

With God prepared to wield Babylon like a whip against Judah, Zephaniah warned the people to look within themselves, to see their sin as a community, and repent of it:

> Gather yourselves together, yes, gather together, O undesirable nation, before the decree is issued, or the day passes like chaff, before the LORD's fierce anger comes upon you, before the day of the LORD's anger comes upon you! Seek the LORD, all you meek of the earth, who have upheld His justice. Seek righteousness, seek humility. It may be that you will be hidden in the day of the LORD's anger (Zephaniah 2:1-3).

Zephaniah's name means "the LORD will hide." And here he offered hope that, in the day of the Lord's anger, the people might be hidden from the worst of it. It is God's character to shelter His own from the full brunt of His wrath. That doesn't mean God's kids don't suffer, but the comparatively faint buffeting of trials that come from the world are very different than the full brunt of judgment that comes from the Lord. God preserved Noah's family, hidden in the ark, above the flood. And He preserved His people, hidden by lamb's blood on their doors, from the final plague on Egypt.

A pretribulation rapture, in which I believe, fits the same pattern, with God's people being removed from earth to spare them from the full impact of His wrath during the tribulation. As Paul said, "God did not appoint us to wrath, but to obtain salvation through our Lord Jesus Christ" (1 Thessalonians 5:9). But to obtain salvation, we must each look within, to see if we are in right standing with God. That was Zephaniah's charge to Judah.

Look Around (Zephaniah 2:4–3:8)

Zephaniah then told Judah to look around at all the different surrounding nations that God was also going to judge. The Lord allowed Babylon—and before them, Assyria—to be His chastening rod, to spank His wayward children. He used Nebuchadnezzar and Shalmaneser and other rulers to get His people to turn back to Him. But whereas the intent of these nations was to humiliate and obliterate Israel completely, God's desire was to restore them to a right relationship with Him. So He wasn't pleased with the arrogant, godless way that these nations messed with His people, and He was going to punish them for what they had done.

God addressed four representative nations, each from a different cardinal direction relative to Israel: the Philistines to the west, Moab and Ammon to the east, Assyria to the north, and Ethiopia to the south. "The LORD will be awesome to them"—and not the good kind of awesome, either—"for He will reduce to nothing all the gods of the earth" (Zephaniah 2:11). God told His people to look around, because even though He would use these nations to punish them, none of them would escape His ultimate judgment: "All the earth shall be devoured with the fire of My jealousy" (Zephaniah 3:8). Mess with God's people, and you mess with God.

Look Beyond (Zephaniah 3:9-20)

Afterward, God called His people to look beyond the judgment of Jerusalem and the other nations to the blessing to come. "Then I will restore to the peoples a pure language, that they all may call on the name of the LORD, to serve Him with one accord" (Zephaniah 3:9). The idea behind "pure language" isn't totally certain. It could be a cleansing of hearts for worship, a contrast between the idolatry that had been going on to the words from a heart committed to seeking God and, therefore, worthy to call on His name. Historically, it could mean that, when the Jews returned from exile speaking the language of Babylon, God intended to restore the use of Hebrew among His people.

Beyond that, though, it could also refer to the kingdom age, when Christ rules from Jerusalem after the tribulation—a time when a sincere worship of God will be possible and not just an ideal. During the kingdom age, purified hearts will utter pure worship. Whatever the case may be, it's certain that hearts will be turned to God. "The remnant of Israel shall do no unrighteousness and speak no lies, nor shall a deceitful tongue be found in their mouth; for they shall feed their flocks and lie down, and no one shall make them afraid" (v. 13).

And, as a more definite prediction of the glory of the end times, Jesus Christ will be in the midst of God's people: "The king of Israel, the LORD, is in your midst; you shall see disaster no more. In that day, it shall be said to Jerusalem, 'Do not fear; Zion, let not your hands be weak. The LORD your God in your midst, the Mighty One, will save; He will rejoice over you with gladness, He will quiet you with His love, He will rejoice over you with singing'" (vv. 15-17). Because God delights in His children, He made a way back to Him through Christ, and in the end, all His children will celebrate His presence among them.

Haggai

When you turn the page in your Bible from the end of Zephaniah to the beginning of Haggai, you make a historical leap in time from before the exile to the first postexile prophet. Haggai wrote a brief but powerful message to Israel's leaders. As you'll recall from our flights over the books of Ezra and Nehemiah, in 539 BC,

King Cyrus of Persia (who had conquered Babylon and inherited the exiled Jews) issued a decree sending back to Jerusalem as many Jews as wanted to go rebuild the temple and the walls.

Of the million-and-a-half or so Jews dispersed around the Persian Empire, only about 50,000 returned. They began with great enthusiasm, though, clearing out the debris from the ransacked temple courts. They built an altar and made animal sacrifices, and seemed to be off to a flying start. But after a few years, having laid the foundations for the new temple, they stopped building. They left God's work for their own interests and personal affairs, a turn made easier for them to justify by the persecution they faced from the locals.

Israel's Struggle with Selfishness (Haggai 1)

God was going to let His people drift only so far from His purposes, though. He sent four individuals to get everyone back on task: the governor, Zerubbabel, the high priest, Joshua, and two prophets, Haggai and Zechariah, all of whom inspired the people to honor God and resume the work. Haggai, for his part, laid out the reasons that the people of Israel had lost their enthusiasm.

The first reason Israel stopped building God's temple was that they became selfish. They put their own interests before the Lord's. Haggai told Zerubbabel and Joshua that God was aware of the situation: "This people says, 'The time has not come, the time that the LORD's house should be built'" (Haggai 1:2). Sixteen years had passed since they laid the foundation and quit the work, saying, "No, this isn't the time." Haggai asked them, "Is it time for you yourselves to dwell in your paneled houses, and this temple to lie in ruins?" (v. 4).

The people seemed to have forgotten that God had pledged that Judah would be in exile for seventy years, and that, after that time had gone by, against all odds, God would bring them back into the land of their ancestors, the land He had promised so long ago to Abraham, Isaac, and Jacob. That time had come, but they were saying, "No, I don't feel led to build God's house—maybe after I'm done building mine." And Haggai confronted them: "Consider your ways! You have sown much, and bring in little; you eat, but do not have enough; you drink, but you are not filled with drink; you clothe yourselves, but no one is warm" (vv. 5-6). In other words, when you invest in yourself and neglect to honor God, what you have is less satisfying and amounts to little compared to all the blessings He wants to give you. Selfishness kills satisfaction.

The phrase "consider your ways" appears four times in the book. It was Haggai's way of calling for self-evaluation, of challenging each individual to assess priorities and count the cost of their choices. They were taking a one-step-forward-two-steps-backward approach, pursuing their agenda as they neglected God's work. There was a simple solution: Be obedient. "'Go up to the mountains and bring wood and build the temple, that I may take pleasure in it and be glorified,' says the Lord" (v. 8). Whenever you obey God, He is glorified.

When you love God supremely, when you're willing to obey Him in every aspect of your life, you show people, even unbelievers, how great He is. You make Him famous—you glorify Him—because you're obeying His Word. God used Haggai's words to glorify Himself among His people, to stir up Zerubbabel and Joshua's spirits, and they got the people fired up and back on task (v. 14). Paul said, "Work out your own salvation with fear and trembling; for it is God who works in you both to will and to do for His good pleasure" (Philippians 2:12-13). You don't work *in order* for God to save you; you work for God *because* He saved you, and when you obey His call on your life, He gives you the energy and vision to succeed.

Israel's Struggle with Nostalgia (Haggai 2:1-9)

The second reason the Jews stopped building the temple involved their memories of the first temple. Financed by David and Solomon, the first temple reflected the wealth and glory of Israel's unified kingdom—the high point in their history. The second temple was a much humbler building, and the people became paralyzed by their own nostalgia. They were discouraged that the new building wasn't as grand as the old one.

Haggai passed on God's recognition of this, asking them, "Who is left among you who saw this temple in its former glory? And how do you see it now? In comparison with it, is this not in your eyes as nothing?" (Haggai 2:3). God had seen the response of a group of old-timers who had seen Solomon's temple and wept that the new one was like a cardboard box compared to the former structure (Ezra 3:12). The new generation had been stoked to see any temple to God built, but the nostalgia prevented many of the older generation from enjoying the accomplishment.

> **Walking forward while looking backward is a recipe for an unhappy life.**

Walking forward while looking backward is a recipe for an unhappy life. It's good to appreciate what God has done, but it's even more important to respect what God is doing now. In the case of the second temple and the rebuilding of Jerusalem, God was aware that there was a ways to go. But the important thing is that He promised to be with the people. He told Zerubbabel and Joshua, "Yet now be strong...and work; for I am with you" (Haggai 2:4).

Israel's Struggle with Unconfessed Sin (Haggai 2:10-19)

A few months later, another reason for stopping the work became clear: unconfessed sin. Haggai brought this factor to light by asking the priests a few questions about the law. First, he asked them, "If a sanctified object touches something unclean, would it make the corrupted item holy?" The answer, they said, was no—in fact, it would defile the holy object. He followed up by asking what would happen if an unclean object touched another unclean object. They answered correctly that it would be unclean still.

"Haggai answered and said, 'So is this people, and so is this nation before Me,' says the LORD, 'and so is every work of their hands; and what they offer there is unclean'" (Haggai 2:14). Impurity is more easily passed on than purity. If you're healthy and you touch your sick child, which is more likely: that your kid will get healthy, or that you will get sick? These people were going through the motions in their work on the temple and in the sacrifices they offered there, and God called them on it.

Doing God's work requires seeking God's heart.

Attitude goes a long way—for good or bad. Doing God's work requires seeking God's heart, and that means we have to watch out for sourness and complacency in our own hearts. Haggai called God's people to purify their hands and hearts before continuing the work God had given them to do.

Israel's Struggle with Unbelief (Haggai 2:20-23)

The final reason the Jews had stopped the work was simple unbelief. Haggai's final words addressed Zerubbabel personally, looking to encourage him. I can't help but think that, as Zerubbabel looked around, he was feeling discouraged. Israel had been crushed by a mighty empire, and another had risen to take its place. How would they ever stand against their imposing neighbors again? And the job itself was imposing—clearing the wreckage and rebuilding city walls and the temple.

He had only a few thousand people to do the work, and they had already lost their enthusiasm for doing it.

Haggai told Governor Zerubbabel to look toward the future—to what God was going to make out of this humble restart:

> "I will shake heaven and earth. I will overthrow the throne of kingdoms; I will destroy the strength of the Gentile kingdoms. I will overthrow the chariots and those who ride in them; the horses and their riders shall come down, every one by the sword of his brother. In that day," says the LORD of hosts, "I will take you, Zerubbabel My servant, the son of Shealtiel," says the LORD, "and will make you like a signet ring; for I have chosen you," says the LORD of hosts (Haggai 2:21-23).

Zerubbabel, in other words, would be the symbol of God's authority and approval—His signet ring. He was from David's line, and Jesus would be one of his descendants. These small beginnings, these first faithful steps, would lead to the greatness of the kingdom age, when Jesus will return to conquer His enemies and establish His reign on earth.

God promises blessing to those who commit to His work.

God promises blessing to those who commit to His work. "Is the seed still in the barn? As yet the vine, the fig tree, the pomegranate, and the olive tree have not yielded fruit. But from this day I will bless you" (v. 19). In the midst of life's busyness, never forget to embrace whatever it is that God has called you to do. As David put it, "Delight yourself also in the LORD, and He shall give you the desires of your heart" (Psalm 37:4). That doesn't mean God will give you whatever you want and then you'll be happy with Him. But if you enjoy Him, spend time in prayer and in His Word, serving His people, God will give you the desire for what He wants you to desire.

ZECHARIAH AND MALACHI
FLIGHT PLAN

Zechariah

Author

Zechariah, a priest, wrote the book of Zechariah. His father, Berekiah, and grandfather, Iddo, were priests. Zechariah was born in Babylon, but his father returned to Judah with his family in 536 BC, following the leadership of Zerubbabel (Nehemiah 12:4, 16).

Date Written

"In the eighth month of the second year of Darius, the word of the LORD came to Zechariah" (Zechariah 1:1). This dates to October through November of 520 BC.

Malachi

Author

Malachi is the author of this book (Malachi 1:1). The Bible is silent regarding his family and background. The name *Malachi* simply means "messenger"—perhaps a title, not necessarily a specific person. Whoever Malachi was, scholars generally believe he (along with Zechariah) was part of the Great Synagogue—a group of priests and leaders who collected and preserved the canon of revealed Scripture.

Date Written

Malachi prophesied during the time of Nehemiah. We know this because he mentioned that the temple in Jerusalem had been completed, that sacrifices were being made (Malachi 1:7-10; 3:1-8), and that a Persian governor was ruling the Jews. Malachi may have authored this book sometime between 433 and 430 BC.

Landmarks

Zechariah

The book of Zechariah offers an expansive prophetic view of the future. Along with the prophet Haggai, he was instrumental in inspiring his fellow Jews to rebuild the Lord's temple in Jerusalem (Ezra 6:14). The first eight chapters of Zechariah have to do with that work, and the remaining six chapters look to the future (some scholars believe these chapters were written thirty years later).

The book as a whole outlines God's program for His people during the "times of the Gentiles" (Luke 21:24), preparing them for their deliverance through the coming Messiah. Though Zechariah wrote about the temple construction that was happening in his day, his eyes were fixed on the future restoration of Jerusalem and the coming Messiah. His book is chock-full of prophecies about the Messiah, Jesus Christ, and he is the most-quoted minor prophet in the New Testament.

Malachi

Malachi is the thirty-ninth of the sixty-six books of the Bible, the last of the Minor Prophets, and the last book in the Old Testament in the Christian ordering of the books. The book of Nehemiah closes out the Old Testament historically, but Malachi closes it prophetically. He wrote about 100 years after the temple had been completed and the system of sacrifices had been reinstituted, and his book serves as the prelude to the 400 years of prophetic silence between the Old and New Testaments.

Malachi picked up where Ezra and Nehemiah left off, rebuking the priests for neglecting their duties to the Lord, being careless in their worship, and returning to former ungodly practices. The book ends by predicting the coming of the Lord and John the Baptist: "I send My messenger, and he will prepare the way before Me" (Malachi 3:1).

Itinerary

Zechariah

- The Immediate: Rebuilding the Temple (Zechariah 1–8)
  - Temple Visions (Zechariah 1–6)
  - Temple Requirements (Zechariah 7–8)
- The Ultimate: Retribution, Restoration, and Reign (Zechariah 9–14)

- Jesus's First Coming: Messiah Rejected (Zechariah 9–11)
- Jesus's Second Coming: Messiah Accepted (Zechariah 12–14)

Malachi

- The Assertion (Malachi 1:1-5)
- The Objection (Malachi 1:6–3:15)
- The Reaction (Malachi 3:16–4:6)

Gospel

Zechariah

No Minor Prophet book reveals more of the scarlet thread of redemption than Zechariah. Three of the eight rapid-fire visions the Lord gave the prophet pointed either to the first coming of the Messiah (who is called "the BRANCH" in Zechariah 3:8) or to Christ's end-times reign. In a cruel twist of fate, the very temple Zechariah inspired the people to build was the place where he was murdered, according to Christ (Matthew 23:35). Jesus referenced Zechariah's murder as He lamented the scribes and Pharisees' failure to recognize not only Him but also all the prophets God sent before Him: "See! Your house is left to you desolate; for I say to you, you shall see Me no more till you say, 'Blessed is He who comes in the name of the LORD!'" (Matthew 23:38-39).

With those words, Jesus referred to when He would ride into Jerusalem on the colt of a donkey, fulfilling Zechariah 9:9: "Behold, your King is coming to you; He is just and having salvation, lowly and riding on a donkey." Immediately following that prophecy is a description of Christ's second coming: "He shall speak peace to the nations; His dominion shall be 'from sea to sea, and from the River to the ends of the earth'" (v. 10). In the end, the Messiah will quell all militant, warlike action around the world and bring peace.

Now, Zechariah didn't know when either of these events would occur—that the Messiah riding into Jerusalem on a donkey would take place 500 years after his time, or that the Messiah's people would still be waiting for His second coming 2000 or so years after that. Both comings of Christ were prophetically foreshortened, being compressed into these two consecutive verses.

Malachi

Malachi's mysterious identity illustrates an important point: The messenger is not necessarily as important as the message. This is highlighted in Malachi's unique prophecy about a messenger who would clear the path for the coming Messiah: "Behold, I send My messenger, and he will prepare the way before Me. And the Lord, whom you seek, will suddenly come to His temple, even the Messenger of the covenant, in whom you delight" (Malachi 3:1).

Of course, we know now that John the Baptist was "My messenger," but imagine reading this 400 years before John arrived on the scene. All you would know was that someone named Malachi—a *messenger*—was predicting that someone God called "My messenger" would come and proclaim another Messenger—"the Messenger of the covenant"—and that Messenger would turn out to be the long-awaited Messiah. The lesser, unnamed messengers in this passage simply serve to point to the ultimate Messenger, Jesus Christ.

History

Zechariah

Zechariah ministered as a postexilic prophet, preaching after the Jews returned from exile in Babylon, beginning in 536 BC. After overcoming opposition (Ezra 4–6), the people completed the temple in March of 516 BC. Zechariah was a member of the Great Synagogue, a group of priests and leaders who collected and preserved the canon of revealed Scripture. He was a contemporary not only of Haggai the prophet but also of Zerubbabel the governor and Joshua the high priest.

Malachi

Malachi wrote his book at a time when the Jews had been free from Babylonian captivity for some time. Many of the problems Ezra and Nehemiah faced with the Jewish people were also problems Malachi tackled: marriage messes, tithing troubles, and social sins. Xerxes of Persia was the reigning king, but other than collecting taxes, he left the Jews to themselves. Malachi's heart cry was for the people to repent of their sins and return to true worship and faithfulness to God.

The book of Malachi was the last prophetic word before a period of 400 years of so-called silence from God, which was broken by the coming of the Messiah, Jesus Christ, and the writings of the New Testament. In biblical history, those 400 years of silence between the Old and New Testaments are known as the intertestamental period (ca. 400 BC to AD 25).

Travel Tips

Zechariah

Zechariah reminds us that rather than seeking certainty, God's people should seek God Himself. He is our certainty, our protection, and our provider. We can take comfort and have faith in the fact that He has everything under control.

- Faith cancels out fear. Henry Ward Beecher said, "Every tomorrow has two handles. We can take hold of it with the handle of anxiety or the handle of faith." The purpose of anxiety and discomfort is to draw you closer to God, and fear and faith are mutually exclusive. So grab hold of faith, and find out what God has in store for you.

- Let God rebuke Satan. As Zechariah recorded, "The Lord said to Satan, 'The Lord rebuke you, Satan!'" (3:2). God was the one who defeated Satan at the cross, and God is the one who gives us victory over him today. Instead of trying to talk to Satan, talk to God about him, and then let Jesus answer the door when the devil comes knocking (James 4:7).

- Don't despise "the day of small things" (Zechariah 4:10). Be faithful in the smallest details of life at home, at work, and with friends, family, and complete strangers. Even if God is the only one who notices your efforts, that's all that matters. He honors those who honor Him and are faithful in everyday matters.

Even if God is the only one who notices your efforts, that's all that matters.

Malachi

Malachi marks the end of our journey through the Old Testament, leaving us—even today—with a myriad of unfulfilled prophecies and promises. Of course, we don't have to wait 400 years to see God fulfill the promises having to do with the first coming of the Messiah—we can turn the page in our Bible and go right to the Gospel of Matthew. On the other hand, the church has been waiting 2000 years for Jesus to return a second time, take His church to be with Him, and establish His kingdom on earth. As we wait, we can glean some valuable lessons from Malachi about what God expects of us.

- God wants His people to tithe. The only time in Scripture God told His people to test Him was when it had to do with tithes and offerings: He challenged them to see whether He would bless them abundantly if they honored Him with their tithes (Malachi 3:10). Give because of all that He has given you—and give from a cheerful heart (2 Corinthians 9:7). You can't outgive God, but you can dishonor Him by not giving.

- God wants His people to act like His people. It's through His grace alone that you're saved, but once you are saved, you need to *respond* to His grace. What you do reflects on who you are—and *whose* you are. We're not called to be perfect but to grow in certain characteristics and in faithfulness to God. The Lord is looking for people who worship Him in spirit and truth (John 4:23).

God wants His people to act like His people.

- Leaders can't afford to become lazy. God used Malachi to call out the priests for shirking their duties (Malachi 2), growing comfortable and apathetic. When God puts you in a position of leadership, work hard to keep your eyes on Him in everything you do, leading those entrusted to you with all integrity and uprightness of character.

- God hates divorce (Malachi 2:16). He loves those who have been divorced, though, and He knows what it's like to be divorced (Jeremiah 3:8). Part of the reason the Bible says He hates it is because it's a sin and He knows the damage and hurt it causes. The good news is that divorce can be forgiven. But God keeps His commitments, and He expects us to do the same.

In Flight

Zechariah

The Immediate: Rebuilding the Temple (Zechariah 1–8)

Temple Visions (Zechariah 1–6)

Zechariah was born in Babylon and came to Jerusalem postexile—in contrast with Daniel, who was born in Jerusalem and taken to Babylon in the first wave of the exile. Zechariah was from a priestly family, and prophesied at the same time as Haggai. Where Haggai's book was short and sweet, making his point in straight-forward, even blunt fashion, Zechariah took fourteen chapters to unspool a series of visions—a mystical counterpart to Haggai's practical approach. And where Haggai was more in-your-face, Zechariah was beholding God's face. God used both of them to motivate the people to finish building the temple, the center of worship and community.

Zechariah's style is unusual, similar to the apostle John's as he recorded the apocalyptic visions of the book of Revelation. God gave Zechariah a rapid-fire series of eight visions about the rebuilding of the temple, and a pair of burdens, or oracles, regarding the millennial reign of the Messiah. It's that dual, near-and-far pair of lenses that many Old Testament prophets used, and Zechariah employed them to encourage his people, the fewer than 50,000 Jews who had returned from Babylon and were feeling insecure and insignificant as they took on the massive task of rebuilding Jerusalem's walls and temple.

The people looked around the rubble of the broken walls and the ruins of the temple and saw the legacy of their fathers' failure to follow God. Zechariah told them, "Do not be like your fathers" (Zechariah 1:4). They didn't have to follow that ear-plugging example, ignoring the prophets God sent to warn them to turn from their idolatry. God would hold them responsible for what they did, not what their fathers had done.

A few months later, God gave Zechariah a series of visions, eight in one night—a strange, symbolic journey covering the challenges facing Israel and God's strength and faithfulness to see them through it. From our 30,000-foot vantage point, we'll just hit the highlights:

Vision 1: An angelic horseman among the myrtle trees (Zechariah 1:8-17). The myrtle—better known as the laurel, a hardy evergreen, difficult to uproot, that grows low and strong—is an emblem of Israel. Like the myrtle, Israel would not be easily removed from their land, and God promised to meet them there: "I am returning to Jerusalem with mercy; My house shall be built in it" (v. 16).

Vision 2: Four horns and four craftsmen (Zechariah 1:18-19). Horns are symbolic of power and pride; these are the four world powers that dominated Israel (as in Daniel's vision, Babylon, Persia, Greece, and Rome). The craftsmen were the people and ways by which God would bring down each of those powers because of their mistreatment of Israel.

Vision 3: A man with a measuring line (Zechariah 2). This vision was symbolic of how God would build Jerusalem, "the apple of His eye" (v. 8), in the future. The city would spread well beyond its walls because of God's favor to it (v. 4). From about a dozen square acres in David's day to more than 45 square miles today, Jerusalem is still in that process of growth.

Vision 4: Joshua the high priest (Zechariah 3). Zechariah was Jerusalem's spiritual leader at the time, dressed in dirty rags and standing before the Angel of the Lord. Satan stood to his right, accusing him and the nation as a whole. But the Lord rebuked Satan (v. 2), cleaned up Joshua, and told Joshua he was a symbol of the Messiah to come—"My Servant the BRANCH" (v. 8), the offshoot of David's line.

Vision 5: A golden lampstand flanked by two olive trees (Zechariah 4). Perhaps the most famous of these visions, this menorah—a seven-branched candlestick—represented the lampstand in the temple that the priest had to fill with olive oil daily to keep it burning. What Zechariah saw was an automated menorah, continuously supplied with oil directly from the trees, which represented Zerubbabel and Joshua, the governor and high priest. Oil is a symbol of the Holy Spirit, and God wanted Zechariah to tell Zerubbabel that the temple would be built "not by might nor by power, but by My Spirit" (v. 6). What Israel couldn't do in their own strength, God would accomplish as a move of His Spirit.

Vision 6: A flying scroll (Zechariah 5:1-4). This billboard-sized scroll—fifteen by thirty feet, the exact measurement of the Holy Place in the temple—had writing on both sides, "the curse that goes out over the face of the whole earth" (v. 3). Specifically, thieves and perjurers would feel God's wrath as judgment for failing to keep God's standard as given in the Word of God.

Vision 7: A woman in a basket with a lead cover (Zechariah 5:5-11). The woman's name was "Wickedness" (v. 8), a symbol of sin, and she was carted off by two winged women (who represented the cleansing work of God's Spirit) to Shinar (that is, Babylon). The meaning was that Israel was to leave behind all that they had learned in Babylon, all of those wicked practices, some of which threatened to make a comeback in Jerusalem.

Vision 8: Four chariots (Zechariah 6). These are not the four horsemen of the apocalypse from Revelation 6, but God's angelic agents, surrounding and protecting Israel in all directions. God then told Zechariah to take up a collection from the exiles to build the temple; their investment was possible because God had secured their safety from the nations around them. "And this shall come to pass if you diligently obey the voice of the LORD your God" (v. 15).

Temple Requirements (Zechariah 7–8)

A few years later, Zechariah addressed a delegation that had come down from the northern part of Israel to meet with the temple priests in Jerusalem. They had been fasting and mourning once a year to mark Israel's exile and the fall of Jerusalem and the temple. They wanted to know if they should keep doing so, but God had a question for them: "During those seventy years, did you really fast for Me—for Me? When you eat and when you drink, do you not eat and drink for yourselves?" (Zechariah 7:5-6). It seemed that ungodly selfishness, not godly sorrow, caused their tears.

Part of the reason Israel had been sent into exile centered on this distinction: God doesn't want empty, religious observances; He wants people who live out the heart of the law—justice and mercy and compassion for each other. Instead of commemorating a disaster their sin had brought on them, how much better would it be to listen to and obey God's Word (vv. 7-12)? Maybe it wasn't the direct yes or no the delegation had been looking for, but God wanted to know if the people were willing to change. "I am zealous for Zion with great zeal...I will return to Zion, and dwell in the midst of Jerusalem" (Zechariah 8:2-3). He was committed to them; would they commit to Him?

The Ultimate: Retribution, Restoration, and Reign (Zechariah 9–14)

Jesus's First Coming: Messiah Rejected (Zechariah 9–11)

The last six chapters feature two oracles with a threefold focus: the Gentile nations, the Jewish nation, and the Messiah. The thread of the prophecies weaves in and out amongst them, beginning with a pledge by God to destroy some of Israel's enemies (Zechariah 9:1-8), which is followed by a prediction featuring both comings of the Messiah (vv. 9-10).

As we've seen before, the Old Testament prophets mostly received their visions in one big screenshot. The currently expanding gap between Jesus's first coming and His second wasn't apparent to them; they just called 'em like they saw 'em. Their perspective was a lot like flying over a mountain range: from a distance: the range looks postcard-flat, but as you go over, you see the peaks and valleys. For Zechariah, that included a prediction of Jesus's first coming—the King coming on a donkey's colt (Zechariah 9:9)—coupled with a prediction of His second—He'll stop a war against Israel and bring peace to the nations (v. 10; see also **Gospel** on page 376).

Zechariah then spoke of the blessings God had in store for a reunified Israel in the messianic kingdom, promises of rain and green fields but also of deliverance from bad leadership and the restoration of Israel's pride in belonging to God. "I will strengthen the house of Judah, and I will save the house of Joseph. I will bring them back, because I have mercy on them. They shall be as though I had not cast them aside; for I am the LORD their God, and I will hear them" (Zechariah 10:6).

A preview of the Messiah's rejection came next. In a move reminiscent of Ezekiel's dramatic enactments of prophecy, Zechariah took a pair of staffs and named them—"Beauty" and "Bonds" (Zechariah 11:7), also commonly translated as "Favor" and "Union." At key moments, he cut each of them in two, symbolizing first a breaking of God's covenant with His people, and second the bond between Judah and Israel. The people picked up on the symbolism of these gestures, but they also saw Zechariah take action; he drove out the false religious leaders (v. 8).

But even a true shepherd couldn't stand serving this flock—and they couldn't stand him either (v. 8). Zechariah told them they were on their own, and, as a symbolic gesture, told them to settle up with him for his service. They paid him thirty pieces of silver (v. 12), the exact wages Judas was later paid for betraying Jesus, the Great Shepherd. According to Exodus 21:32, thirty pieces of silver was the price for a slave that had been gored by an ox. That's how little the people thought of Zechariah—and how little Judas thought of Jesus.

God told Zechariah to throw the thirty pieces of silver "to the potter" (Zechariah 11:13)—basically, the poor box in the temple. Judas, of course, threw his blood money on the temple floor, and the Jewish leaders purchased a barren field with it, called *Akeldama*, or "field of blood." Judas later hanged himself there (Matthew 27:3-10). All of these things pointed to Jesus's first coming—His rejection by His people, compounded by betrayal and shame.

Jesus's Second Coming: Messiah Accepted (Zechariah 12–14)

Zechariah's second oracle brings Jesus's second coming into view. God promised that He would punish all the nations who had relished their roles as punishers of Judah and Israel. Though Assyria, Babylon, Persia, Greece, and Rome either had or would attack and subjugate the Jews, God described a future battle when all the earth's nations would rise against Israel—something we know as the Battle of Armageddon.

On that day, God will protect and avenge His people: "I will strike every horse with confusion, and its rider with madness; I will open My eyes on the house of Judah, and will strike every horse of the peoples with blindness...It shall be in that day that I will seek to destroy all the nations that come against Jerusalem" (Zechariah 12:4, 9).

When God defends His people, He will also pour out His Spirit on them (v. 10). At that point, they will have the eye-opening and heart-wrenching experience of recognizing Jesus as their Messiah—and that they failed to acknowledge Him the first time He came to them. "They will look on Me whom they pierced. Yes, they will mourn for Him as one mourns for his only son, and grieve for Him as one grieves for a firstborn" (v. 10).

Ancient Jews believed this prophecy referred to the suffering of the coming Messiah, In the original Hebrew text, there are two untranslated letters next to "Me"—*aleph* and *tav*. They are the first and last letters of the Hebrew alphabet, what the Greeks called *alpha* and *omega*, or in English, *the beginning* and *the end*. "They will look on Me, the Alpha and Omega, whom they pierced." It's a remarkable fingerprint of the Holy Spirit, an almost-hidden prediction of Jesus that matches one of His most powerful self-descriptions: "I am the Alpha and the Omega, the Beginning and the End...who is and who was and who is to come, the Almighty" (Revelation 1:8). God declared that they pierced "Me"—affirming the deity of Jesus Christ.

After the people of Israel grieve their ultimate failure, God will provide them with His ultimate restoration: "In that day a fountain shall be opened for the house of David and for the inhabitants of Jerusalem, for sin and for uncleanness" (Zechariah 13:1). This fountain was opened on the cross, but its flow of cleansing blood will only be widely accepted among God's people in the last days. It's one of those near-far moments in the prophecy.

The last chapter of Zechariah speaks of that final battle again, this time featuring the physical return of Christ. "In that day His feet will stand on the Mount of Olives, which faces Jerusalem on the east. And the Mount of Olives shall be split in two, from east to west, making a very large valley; half of the mountain shall move toward the north and half of it toward the south...Thus the LORD my God will come, and all the saints with You" (Zechariah 14:4-5).

After Jesus lifted off the Mount of Olives in front of His disciples (Acts 1:9), some angels came and asked them why they were staring at the empty sky with gaping mouths. "This same Jesus...will so come in like manner as you saw Him go into heaven" (v. 11). When Jesus returns with His church to defeat His enemies and claim the earth, His touch-down will have an appropriate impact, splitting the Mount of Olives in two.

Zechariah skipped the battle details, though, and went straight to the kingdom age: "In that day it shall be that living waters shall flow from Jerusalem, half of them toward the eastern sea and half of them toward the western sea"—the Dead Sea and the Mediterranean (Zechariah 14:8). Unlike the seasonal flow of water that dries up every summer in Israel, this one will be perennial—making the desert "blossom as the rose" (Isaiah 35:1). "It shall come to pass that everyone who is left of all the nations which come against Jerusalem shall go up from year to year to worship the King, the LORD of hosts, and to keep the Feast of Tabernacles" (Zechariah 14:16). Keeping the feasts of Passover, Pentecost, and Tabernacles will be a regular practice during the millennium (Ezekiel 44:24). Though Zechariah was murdered in the very temple he helped inspire the Jews to complete (Matthew 23:35), he pointed to God's ultimate plan to reconnect with His people—and all people—through Jesus Christ.

Malachi

The book of Malachi is an intensely personal conversation between two parties: God through His prophet—called Malachi, or *Messenger*—and the people of Israel. It breaks down into three parts: an assertion, followed by an objection, and then a reaction.

The Assertion (Malachi 1:1-5)

Maybe you've heard people reduce the Old Testament to "God is a God of vengeance" and the New Testament to "God is a God of love." Both are massive oversimplifications stemming from the unwillingness to dive in and actually read the book. The last book of the New Testament, Revelation, is all about God's wrath against evil and His just judgment against a calloused world. The last book of the Old Testament, Malachi, begins with this proclamation to Israel: "'I have loved you,' says the LORD" (Malachi 1:2). Just in case all the years of tough love didn't prove it, He just came out and said it—a direct assertion.

But Malachi didn't call this prophecy a "burden" for nothing. Right after God expressed His love for Israel, Israel responded: "Yet you say, 'In what way have You loved us?'" (Malachi 1:2). *You love us, God? How?* God answered them by giving a direct contrast: "Was not Esau Jacob's brother?...Yet Jacob I have loved; but Esau I have hated" (vv. 2-3). In other words, "I chose *you*. And you say, 'Prove it.'"

The root of all of Israel's problems lay in their failure to believe in the love of God. That's probably the root of all of our problems, going back to Eden. When Satan tricked Eve into doubting God's best intentions for her, planting a seed of doubt in her heart that grew into disobedience, it set a pattern for all of mankind.

We'd rather believe the devil when he leads us to believe God has neglected us than the pattern of love God has shown time and time again. But here, as the Old Testament wraps up, God makes it clear: He loves His people, whether they believe Him or not.

> **God makes it clear: He loves His people, whether they believe Him or not.**

The Objection (Malachi 1:6–3:15)

Once God made it clear that His care for Israel was not in question, He engaged in a sort of debate, presenting His complaints about Israel's behavior, stating their questions in response, and then answering them. Being omnipotent, He can do that kind of thing and be right on target.

Over the next few chapters, God complains to His people about them. In chapters 1, 2, and 3, He objected to their cheating, their apathy, their mixed marriages with worldly and ungodly people, their divorces, their theft, and their pride and arrogance. The back-and-forth nature of the dialogue suggests that loving Israel was often more heartbreaking than rewarding, more exasperating than enriching.

> God: "If I'm the Father, where's My respect? You priests don't respect My name."
>
> Priests: "How have we disrespected Your name?"
>
> God: "With your dirty, corrupt offerings."
>
> Priests: "What's corrupt about our offerings?"
>
> God: "You say My altar doesn't deserve your first and best. You offer blemished animals. Try giving lame gifts like that to your human leaders and see where it gets you. I'm not taking your bored, halfhearted offerings anymore."
>
> Priests: "Why not?"
>
> God: "I've seen how you cheat on your wives and divorce them. I see you shortchange your tithes and offerings. You wear Me out!"
>
> Priests: "How do we wear you out?"

What exasperating and irritating excuses! "You have wearied the LORD with your words; yet you say, 'In what way have we wearied Him?' In that you say, 'Everyone who does evil is good in the sight of the LORD, and He delights in them' or, 'Where is the God of justice?'" (Malachi 2:17). The people were exhausting God's patience with their religious show fueled by their lack of any real relationship with Him. They let temporary, earthly matters get in the way of looking at God as their protector and provider. The result was lukewarm religiosity.

"'Return to Me, and I will return to you,' says the LORD of hosts. 'But you said, "In what way shall we return?" Will a man rob God? Yet you have robbed Me! But you say, "In what way have we robbed You?" In tithes and offerings'" (Malachi 3:7-8). Here's what was happening: the people of Israel were holding back their tithes, saying "Things are tight this month," which forced the priests, who were sponsored by those tithes, to go out and work in the fields. God's ministry through the priests was being hindered because the people didn't trust that God would meet their needs. In that way, they robbed God, but they were actually robbing themselves because God responded to their faithlessness by shutting off the rain, which spoiled the crops.

God dared them to act boldly: "'Bring all the tithes into the storehouse, that there may be food in My house, and try Me now in this,' says the LORD of hosts, 'if I will not open for you the windows of heaven and pour out for you such a blessing that there will not be room enough to receive it'" (v. 10). While the general rule is not to put God to a foolish test, here He dares His people to believe in Him in a practical, bottom-line way. That was the best way to satisfy His objections: *Reverse your tightfistedness and watch My openhandedness!*

God was about to go to heavenly radio silence for four centuries, and, since then, only individuals have had that promise opened up to them over the years. But this Scripture anticipates a time when all the people of Israel will put their money where their mouths are and trust Him completely—a time that won't be fully realized until the kingdom age. But before the kingdom age, there had to be a King, and Malachi predicted His arrival.

The Reaction (Malachi 3:1–4:6)

Malachi, the messenger, foretold a messenger—John the Baptist—who would herald the greatest Messenger of all, Jesus Christ. "Behold, I send My messenger, and he will prepare the way before Me. And the LORD, whom you seek, will suddenly come to His temple, even the Messenger of the covenant, in whom you delight. Behold, He is coming" (Malachi 3:1). One messenger would point the way, and the other Messenger would be the Way.

The prediction that He would come to His temple means that there had to be a temple for Him to come to. Jesus came to the temple that Zerubbabel rebuilt and Herod the Great greatly expanded and supplemented with continuous construction—and which was razed by the Romans in AD 70. All of that fit Malachi's prediction. Furthermore, Malachi predicted a bridge between the Old and New Testaments. "Behold, I will send you Elijah the prophet before the coming of the great and dreadful day of the LORD. And he will turn the hearts of the fathers to the children, and the hearts of the children to their fathers, lest I come and strike the earth with a curse" (Malachi 4:5-6). Elijah the prophet had lived several centuries before this time, and it would be another four after Malachi before God spoke again, so what's the deal with saying He would send Elijah?

When Jesus referred to John the Baptist as "Elijah who is to come" (Matthew 11:14), He didn't mean that John was some reincarnation of Elijah, but that John was a prophet in the tradition and style of Elijah—a powerful, no-nonsense spiritual heir. As the angel told John's father Zacharias, before John was born, that John would "also go before Him [the Messiah] in the spirit and power of Elijah, 'to turn the hearts of the fathers to the children'" (Luke 1:17). The angel quoted Malachi 4:6 to verify this spiritual lineage. While talking with John and Peter on the Mount of Transfiguration (Matthew 17:10-13), Jesus confirmed that John was Elijah's spiritual successor, and that, in keeping with Malachi 4:5, the actual Elijah would return at some point in the future, likely as one of the two witnesses of Revelation 11.

Finally, notice that the final word of the Old Testament is "curse" (Malachi 4:6). Shortly after Genesis opens up, we find a garden in which the curse is introduced, and according to Malachi, the curse was still in operation. But the New Testament ends with a blessing, with John recording a future in which "there shall be no more curse" (Revelation 22:3). And the last line of Revelation says, "The grace of our Lord Jesus Christ be with you all. Amen" (v. 21). The difference between curse and grace is Jesus Christ. "For the law was given through Moses, but grace and truth came through Jesus Christ" (John 1:17).

The Old Testament closes unfulfilled—all sorts of predictions and prophecies waiting, pregnant with promise—but with a message of hope. God's reaction to His objection was to act according to His assertion: He loved His people and would deliver them, once and for all. The curse still lingered, but the cure was on the way.

The curse still lingered, but the cure was on the way.

NEW TESTAMENT

MATTHEW, MARK, AND LUKE
FLIGHT PLAN

Facts

Matthew

Author

Though the Gospel of Matthew does not name its author, church tradition asserts that Jesus's disciple Matthew, originally named Levi, wrote the account. Matthew was a tax collector who became a disciple of Jesus.

Date Written

The date Matthew was written is unknown. Most Bible scholars project it to be between AD 60 and 70, but it also may have been written as early as AD 38.

Mark

Author

The gospel of Mark does not name its author. However, church historians from as early as AD 130 have attributed its primary authorship to John Mark, the relative of Barnabas and traveling companion to the apostles Paul and Peter. Modern scholars have generally concluded that Mark received most of his information from Peter, and some consider Mark's Gospel to be Peter's account of his experiences with Jesus.[42]

Date Written

The date of authorship is unknown. It's possible that Mark was the earliest of the Gospels to be written, sometime between AD 60 and 68.

Luke

Author

Early church writers and scholars agree that the unnamed author of this Gospel was most likely Luke, the physician and traveling companion of Paul (Colossians 4:14; 2 Timothy 4:11; Philemon 24). Luke was a Gentile (non-Jewish) believer and was the only non-Jewish author of a New Testament book.

Date Written

Like Matthew and Mark, Luke was probably written between AD 60 and 70.

Landmarks

Matthew

The gospel of Matthew gives us our first look at the person who is at the center of not just the Bible but all of history: Jesus Christ. Matthew is the first book in the New Testament, the first of the four Gospels, and the first of the three Synoptic Gospels, which also include Mark and Luke.

Matthew presented Jesus Christ as the true Messiah and King of the Jews. He wrote in Aramaic, most likely for the benefit of the Jews scattered abroad who had no access to the apostles' teaching. His skill at record-keeping made him quite capable of presenting the facts of Jesus's life right alongside Old Testament references to Him. In particular, Matthew quoted a number of prophecies fulfilled by Jesus's first coming to convince Jews of Jesus's messiahship and authority.

Mark

The Gospel of Mark focuses on Christ as a servant (Mark 10:45). The two themes of this verse—service and sacrifice—are unpacked throughout the book. Mark is full of action, presenting Jesus as the faithful worker and servant of the Lord effectively going about and accomplishing His work.

Mark's purpose was simply to announce the words and works of Jesus Christ. At just sixteen chapters long, it is the briefest of all the Gospels, suiting the simple, straightforward approach favored by its intended audience, the Romans.

Luke

The Gospel of Luke is the most complete account of Jesus Christ's life, from His birth and ministry to His crucifixion and resurrection. Luke provided specific details about Christ's life on earth, adding to the reliability and trustworthiness of his historical account. As the third and longest of the Synoptic Gospels, Luke took a methodical and orderly approach to his account, focusing on Jesus's teachings about salvation and His fulfillment of Old Testament prophecies regarding the coming Messiah.

In particular, Luke emphasized Christ's humanity as God's Son—targeting his Greek-speaking, human-centric audience. The book also stresses Christ's kindness toward the weak, suffering, and outcast. Luke 2:11 announces Jesus as the "Savior, who is Christ the Lord." "Savior" identifies His mission; "Christ the Lord" identifies Him as the true Jewish Messiah. Luke 19:10 gives us his whole book in a nutshell: "The Son of Man has come to seek and to save that which was lost."

Itinerary

Because we are taking such a compressed look at these three Gospels, our **In Flight** text doesn't have room for a breakdown of each book. However, I want to give you an itinerary of important themes and sections in each book for your own information and study:

Matthew

- Preparation for the King (Matthew 1:1–4:11)
- Principles of the Kingdom (Matthew 4:12–13:52)
- Proofs of the Kingly Power (Matthew 13:53–18:35)
- Parables of Kingdom Life (Matthew 19–25)
- Passion and Power of the King (Matthew 26–28)

Mark

- The Servant's Identification (Mark 1:1-11)
- The Servant's Industry (Mark 1:12–8:26)
- The Servant's Incomparability (Mark 8:27–16:20)

Luke

- The Sending ("the Son of Man has come"): Jesus Introduced and Identified (Luke 1:1–4:13)
- The Seeking ("to seek"): Jesus Revealing and Restoring (Luke 4:14–21:38)

- The Saving ("to save that which was lost"): Jesus Sacrificed and Sovereign (Luke 22–24)

Gospel

Our word *gospel* comes from the Old English word *godspel*, which was translated from the Latin phrase *bona annuntiatio*, which itself was translated from the Greek word *euangelion*.[43] All of these words mean the same thing: "good news." It's important to realize that the four Gospels—the four proclamations of this good news—serve less as biographies and more as testimonials to the most astonishing historical event ever: God became flesh and walked among us in the person of the Messiah, Jesus Christ.

Think of the Gospels as a fourfold picture of Jesus Christ—a string quartet, if you will. Each book is a different instrument and has a slightly different sound, focusing on a different aspect of the person of Jesus, but together, all four play in beautiful harmony.

- The key word in Matthew's gospel is *fulfilled*; as Jesus fulfilled prophecy after prophecy about the Messiah, Matthew made note of it and quoted those Old Testament prophecies in his writing, looking to persuade his Jewish audience.

- Mark was written for a practical and on-point Gentile audience: the Romans. Mark portrayed Jesus as God's obedient servant, focusing on what He did. The key word in this gospel is *immediately*—a word that sets the book's intense pace and focus on activity and movement.

- As a physician, Luke was especially interested in portraying Jesus as fully God yet fully man. Jesus Himself used the key term *Son of Man* to emphasize this dual nature of humanity and exalted status. This title identifies Him with us, our struggles, and our weaknesses more closely than any other messianic title, also highlighting our great need for forgiveness.

Luke included a genealogy of Jesus in his book, although he took a left turn at King David and instead of tracing Jesus's lineage through Solomon (as Matthew did), he traced it through another one of David's sons, Nathan. Scholars believe he took this detour because he was tracing Mary's genealogy, while Matthew was following Joseph's genealogy.

What's the difference between the two? The line of Joseph established Jesus's legal right to rule as a son of David, and the line of Mary proved that He was also the physical, biological descendant of David. Taken together, the two genealogies establish an airtight case for Jesus as both the Son of David and the Son of Man— as the true Messiah and coming King.

History

When we open the book of Matthew, 400 years have passed since the last Old Testament book, Malachi, was written. The four centuries between Malachi and Matthew have been nicknamed the silent years—not because nothing was happening in the world, but because God didn't speak to His people during this time.

When we left Malachi, the Medo-Persian Empire ruled the world. When the book of Matthew opens, we quickly see a new leading power in Europe and the Middle East: Rome. In between the two, Greece under Alexander the Great had conquered Persia and most of the known world. One of the four dynasties that replaced him, the Seleucids, ruled the region surrounding Israel, called Judea. A group of priests led by the Maccabees resisted the Seleucid king Antiochus and won their independence, only to be reconquered a century later by Rome. The Jewish desire to see Rome overthrown simmered constantly throughout these years.

The Romans put a descendant of the Edomites on the throne of Judea, Herod the Great, who built up Zerubbabel's temple into a majestic complex, but also ordered the slaughter of innocent children as he hunted the foretold Messiah. His son, Herod Antipas, succeeded him in Jesus's day, reigning over the region of Galilee and Persia (4 BC–AD 39). Tiberius Caesar was the Roman emperor from AD 14–37, and Pontius Pilate was the Roman procurator of Judea from AD 26–36.

During this time, synagogues also popped up throughout Judea, holdovers from the exile in Babylon when gathering in groups to learn the law was the only way for Jews to practice their faith. The Scriptures the Jewish people studied during this time, known as the Septuagint, had been carefully translated into Greek by scholars in Alexandria, Egypt, in 285 BC, reflecting Alexander's influence on culture and religion throughout the Mediterranean. In fact, one of the dominant languages of the Roman Empire was Greek (though the Jewish people by and large spoke Aramaic).

Historically, the four centuries in between the Old and New Testaments were anything but silent, yet nonetheless they set the stage for God to break His silence by sending the Messiah.

Jesus showed us the Father's love as He gave us life and taught us how to live.

Travel Tips

The events of Jesus's life—which were just as historical as they were prophecy-fulfilling—shook the world. His teachings, His full immersion in the human experience, His deep interaction with people all gave mankind its first face-to-face look at God. Jesus showed us the Father's love as He gave us life and taught us how to live.

- The world's idea of what it means to be blessed—having health, wealth, and beauty—is the opposite of what Jesus taught in the Sermon on the Mount: Happiness comes from being poor in spirit, mournful, and meek (Matthew 5:2-12). It's a paradox, but it's also consistent with Scripture: God honors those who humble themselves.

- When you're living in the will of heaven, expect the wrath of hell. If you are being led by God's Spirit, you can count on the enemy attacking you. Just as Jesus's baptism was followed immediately by His temptation, you also can expect that the more business you do with God, the more interest you'll draw from the devil. Remember, though, the devil has already been defeated. God is the ultimate victorious one, and you belong to Him—not the devil.

When you're living in the will of heaven, expect the wrath of hell.

- Jesus is the Great Liberator. Matthew included the names of four women in his genealogy of Christ—something that just wasn't done at that time in Jewish history. Jesus recognized women, talked with them, healed them, and made them part of His plan to shake up the world. Feminists didn't liberate women; Jesus did.

- The Golden Rule (Matthew 7:12) is the summary statement of God's kingdom ethics—how we as His children are to treat others. It sets Christianity apart from all other belief systems. Instead of *not* doing what you *don't* want others to do to you, Jesus told us to *do* the right thing—to be loving, kind, and gracious.

- Disciples should always become apostles. *Disciple* means "learner," while *apostle* means "messenger." Once you've been equipped by the Lord, go out, serve Him, and share His good news.

- Worry is the result of reversing our priorities. So often we seek our own comfort first and expect the kingdom of God to fit in where it can. Even though Jesus made it clear we are a priority to God, we seldom make Him our priority. And when He's not our priority, that inevitably leads to us worrying about the very things Jesus told us not to worry about (Luke 12:22-34).

- Jesus wants you to develop a forgiving heart. He said that when you're praying, if you remember that you're holding something against someone, forgive that person in your heart (Mark 11:25). You don't need to tell him—just forgive him. We all need forgiveness. Don't withhold from others what God freely gave you.

In Flight

We're going to cover Matthew, Mark, and Luke all at once. Collectively known as the Synoptic Gospels because of their similarities in synopsis, or structure, they follow the same basic geographical outline: the early part is Jesus's Galilean ministry, the latter part is His Judean ministry, followed by His betrayal, crucifixion, and resurrection. John's Gospel, as we'll see in the next chapter, has a completely different structure.

I mentioned that the Gospels provide four different lenses through which to view Jesus Christ—like different instruments in a string quartet, playing in beautiful harmony. As a movie, the Holy Spirit directs the action from four separate camera angles. Each Gospel targets a different audience and reflects a different aspect of Jesus: for Matthew, He is the Lion of Judah—the promised Messiah; for Mark, He is God's Servant, dedicated to the mission of salvation; for Luke, He is the Godman, full of compassion, healing, and grace. Also, Matthew underscores what Jesus *said*, Mark emphasizes what Jesus *did*, Luke reveals what Jesus *felt*, and as we'll see next chapter, John showcases who Jesus *was*.

Matthew

Matthew wrote to the Jews about their Messiah, showing Jesus's connection to the lines of Abraham and David—that Jesus was the fulfillment of the promises God made to them, the historically anticipated Messiah. Matthew organized his material into five sections (see **Itinerary** on page 393).

Originally, Matthew was known as Levi, a recognition of his connection to that priestly tribe. Somewhere along the way, he became a tax collector, one of the most hated occupations in the land, working at a toll booth in Galilee. That's where Jesus found him and said, "Follow Me" (Matthew 9:9). Matthew instantly obeyed, stopped being a collaborator with the Romans, and became a follower of Christ. That he ended up writing the Gospel that addressed Jews most directly shows Christ's redemptive power: Matthew went from accomplice to apostle.

Matthew began with Jesus's genealogy—His earthly genesis: "The book of the genealogy of Jesus Christ, the Son of David, the Son of Abraham" (Matthew 1:1). He carefully established Christ's origins right away, because his focus was to portray Jesus as the King of the Jews, the fulfillment of Old Testament prophecy. Matthew understood that, if someone were to claim to be the Messiah, the first question a Jew would ask would be "What tribe are you from, and where were you born?" His audience knew that such a claim required scriptural verification—that person would have to fulfill certain predictions made about the Messiah over the centuries.

The genealogy Matthew presented established Jesus's credentials, including the timing: "All the generations from Abraham to David are fourteen generations, from David until the captivity in Babylon are fourteen generations, and from the captivity in Babylon until the Christ are fourteen generations" (v. 17). These three sections of fourteen generations emphasize something called *literary symmetry*. Matthew was bringing to the fore the three great epic periods in ancient Jewish history. The first was the patriarchy from Abraham to David, both of whom received messianic promises from God. The second great period was the monarchy, from Israel's greatest king, David, until the exile to Babylon. The third period, the captivity, followed the exile all the way up to the time of Jesus Christ. Matthew was grounding Christ's claim to be Messiah in Israel's history, a compelling argument for his audience.

As Matthew gave the account of the birth of Jesus Christ (vv. 18-25), he connected the events to prophecy. Following the angel's instructions to Joseph to name the baby Jesus, Matthew wrote, "So all this was done that it might be fulfilled which was spoken by the Lord through the prophet, saying: 'Behold, the virgin shall be with child, and bear a Son, and they shall call His name Immanuel,' which is translated, 'God with us'" (vv. 22-23, quoting Isaiah 7:14).

When Jesus came to be with us, He was known as Jesus, son of Joseph, of Nazareth. *Christ* is a title, not a surname. In Greek, it's *Christos*, the equivalent of the Hebrew *Mashiach*, or *Messiah*. And *Messiah* means "Anointed One," evoking a priest's inauguration, when olive oil was smeared or poured over the head of a new priest. That signified that God's Spirit was being poured out on him, making him suitable to minister.

For generations, Jews anticipated this special deliverer, the Anointed One of God, who would liberate God's people from oppression and set up His kingdom. In fact, a common Jewish prayer, uttered by the orthodox every morning, said, "I believe with a full heart in the coming of Messiah and even though He may tarry, I will wait for Him on any day that he may come."[44] Matthew was telling them, "This is the day—He has come."

Matthew emphasized what Jesus said to show the fulfillment of Jewish prophecy. He included three big discourses—sermons—to support his claim: the Sermon on the Mount (Matthew 5–7), the kingdom parables (Matthew 13)—seven parables unique to Matthew's Gospel—and the Olivet Discourse, given in its fullest recorded version (Matthew 24–25).

Mark

If you look at the number of chapters in Mark's Gospel (sixteen), it appears to be the shortest of the four, but if you were to take out Matthew's three major discourses, Mark would actually be longer. Mark was probably the first Gospel that was written. Tradition says that John Mark, the credited author, took dictation from the apostle Peter, so that Mark's gospel is actually Peter's account. The early church apologist Justin Martyr even referred to Mark as the "memoirs of Peter."[45]

Mark had his challenges along the way. Some scholars think he was the young man who fled naked from the Garden of Gethsemane when Jesus was arrested (Mark 14:51-52). Even though that poor guy isn't identified by name, it suggests a certain fearfulness—a tendency to crack under pressure. It might be one reason why John Mark became a bone of contention between the apostle Paul and his companion Barnabas. Mark, who was the nephew of Barnabas, had gone with them on their first missionary journey, but had chosen to leave them in the middle of the journey and go home (Acts 13:13).

When it came time a year later to head out again, Paul flatly refused to take Mark, feeling that he had deserted them the first time around. Paul and Barnabas ended up choosing other companions and going their separate ways (Acts 15:37-40). God's work was still accomplished on both missions, and we know that

Paul and Mark eventually reconciled at some point, because Paul later told Timothy, "Get Mark and bring him with you, for he is useful to me for ministry" (2 Timothy 4:11).

As far as the Gospel he either wrote or recorded, Mark wrote an action-packed account of Jesus as the Servant of God. Whereas Matthew and Luke give us photographic slides of the life of Jesus, Mark delivers a rapidly moving motion picture. The key verse tells us, "The Son of Man did not come to be served, but to serve, and to give His life a ransom for many" (Mark 10:45). Mark starts quickly too—no genealogy, just "the beginning of the gospel of Jesus Christ, the Son of God" (Mark 1:1). The next verse uses Scripture to introduce John the Baptist, and we're off and running. With a style like the rapid running of the early cinematic characters the Keystone Cops, Mark showed the determined mission of Christ through action-packed scenes.

Mark, in fact, is the only Gospel without some type of genealogy. Here's why: He was picturing Jesus as a servant. No one, especially in his Roman audience, cared about the pedigree of a slave. Since the emphasis is Christ as an obedient slave, a servant on the move, no genealogy was required. Mark contains less teaching and a whole lot more action than the other Gospels. You'll see conjunctions—connecting words like *and, now, then, immediately, straightaway*—giving the impression of Jesus going from one thing to the next, always focused on the mission. That is interesting in light of Mark's own difficulties in staying with a task; perhaps his approach reflects Peter's straightforward manner, but also his own hard-earned appreciation for perseverance in God's work.

Mark set his tone right away. In the first chapter alone, we read the word *and* eighty-five times, *now* and *then* seven times each, and *immediately* eight. I'll emphasize those words in a standard passage:

> It came to pass in those days that Jesus came from Nazareth of Galilee, *and* was baptized by John in the Jordan. *And immediately*, coming up from the water, He saw the heavens parting *and* the Spirit descending upon Him like a dove. *Then* a voice came from heaven, "You are My beloved Son, in whom I am well pleased." *Immediately* the Spirit drove Him into the wilderness. *And* He was there in the wilderness forty days, tempted by Satan, *and* was with the wild beasts; *and* the angels ministered to Him. *Now* after John was put in prison, Jesus came to Galilee, preaching the gospel of the kingdom of God, *and* saying, "The time is fulfilled, *and* the kingdom of God is at hand. Repent, *and* believe in the gospel" (Mark 1:9-15).

Mark didn't mess around. His view of Jesus was as a man of action and intention. In the very next sentence, Jesus had moved on to Galilee, where He called His first disciples, Simon and Andrew (vv. 16-18). Directly afterward, we see Jesus calling James and John, the sons of Zebedee, and off they went to Capernaum, "and immediately on the Sabbath He entered the synagogue and taught" (v. 21). Mark's approach continues throughout the book and gives the vivid impression of Jesus moving from task to task, God's obedient Servant.

It's no surprise, then, that Mark quickly arrived at the final week of Jesus's life on earth. What's interesting is that he spent just under half of his Gospel on it (Mark 10–16). During His final week on earth, Jesus was betrayed, arrested, tortured, crucified, and resurrected. That's quite a week! Its events are the collective focus of all the Gospels, the New Testament, and the Bible as a whole. In every book of the Bible you can find the scarlet thread of redemption—God's plan of salvation woven into the fabric of His interactions with mankind. One way or another, all of Scripture points to the cross, the ultimate sacrifice of God to redeem us from sin and death.

> **The cross was God's plan all along.**
> **All Old Testament history anticipates it,**
> **all New Testament history looks back to it.**

The Gospels focus more explicitly on this message than anywhere else in the Bible. Mark, with his fast pace and focus on Christ's servanthood, is a powerful demonstration. In all four Gospels, only four chapters are spent on Jesus's life before He began His public ministry. Eighty-five chapters deal with the last three-and-a-half years of His life, and twenty-nine of those are spent on the last week—thirteen on the day of His execution. The cross wasn't an accident or an afterthought, or God reacting to Jesus's suffering like it was unanticipated. Jesus is "the Lamb slain from the foundation of the world" (Revelation 13:8). The cross was God's plan all along. All Old Testament history anticipates it, all New Testament history looks back to it.

Mark moves quickly toward that crucial moment, following the same pattern as Matthew—Galilean ministry, Judean ministry, final week—but without the major discourses. Mark ends with Jesus's resurrection, His call to "go into all the world and preach the gospel to every creature" (Mark 16:15), and His ascension into heaven, where once His work was completed, He "sat down at the right hand of

God" (v. 19). The final six verses are Jesus's call to His followers to become servants as He was, to take up His mantle and share the good news of salvation everywhere.

Luke

The Gospel of Luke is the most complete narrative of the life of Jesus. It also follows the most natural reading sequence; you can go directly from the end of Malachi, which ends with the prediction of the Messiah's forerunner, and pick the story up with Luke's account of an angel addressing that forerunner's father, a priest named Zacharias (Luke 1:5-25). Speaking of the man the world would know as John the Baptist, the angel told Zacharias that his son would "also go before Him in the spirit and power of Elijah, 'to turn the hearts of the fathers to the children,' and the disobedient to the wisdom of the just, to make ready a people prepared for the Lord" (v. 17, quoting Malachi 4:5-6). We go right from the prediction to the fulfillment, which makes the 400-year silence seem a lot shorter to us than it did to the Jews who waited all that time.

Luke was a Gentile (non-Jewish) physician with a thorough, methodical approach to what he did. One of the results is the most comprehensive chronicle of Jesus's life, including twenty miracles, seven of which are found only in Luke's account. As a doctor, Luke wrote more about the healing ministry of Jesus than both Matthew and Mark combined. He also recorded twenty-three parables, eighteen of them unique to Luke—including such classics as the parable of the prodigal son and the parable of the good Samaritan. Luke noted some well-known songs of praise—from the virgin Mary's "Magnificat" (Luke 1:46-55) and the song of Elizabeth, the mother of John the Baptist (Luke 1:42-45), to the Christmas praises of the angels and shepherds (Luke 2:13-20) and the song of Simeon, who finally got to meet the Messiah he had awaited all his long life (Luke 2:25-32). Luke also documented one of my favorite stories, when Jesus walked incognito with two disciples along the road to Emmaus (Luke 24:13-32). Obviously all of these merit deeper, fuller consideration, but even from 30,000 feet, they stand out as landmarks.

Luke also demonstrates how God superintended the writing of the Bible. Luke opened by writing,

> Inasmuch as many have taken in hand to set in order a narrative of those things which have been fulfilled among us, just as those who from the beginning were eyewitnesses and ministers of the word delivered them to us, it seemed good to me also, having had perfect understanding of all things from the very first, to write to you an

orderly account, most excellent Theophilus, that you may know the certainty of those things in which you were instructed (Luke 1:1-4).

Thus begins an account in which the author, Luke, culled research from a variety of first-person sources, arranged it, and recorded it for posterity. It's an excellent example of human cooperation with divine inspiration—the model God used to write the entire Bible.

As Paul wrote to Timothy, "All Scripture is given by inspiration of God" (2 Timothy 3:16), where "inspiration of God" literally means "God-breathed." Here's what that does and doesn't mean: When we say the Bible was inspired by God, it wasn't dictation—God saying, "Here, Paul, write this down"—or concept inspiration— "I really feel like God wanted me to say this." Rather, as Peter put it, "Prophecy never came by the will of man, but holy men of God spoke as they were moved by the Holy Spirit" (2 Peter 1:21). "Moved" here is a nautical term, used by sailors to describe hoisting their sails and letting the wind determine their course. Basically the men who wrote Scripture hoisted their sails and God carried the vessel of their writing to the destinations He wanted it to reach. God is big enough to do that— to move men by His Spirit to write the words and nuances of meaning He wanted set down. Luke is a perfect illustration of that.

Most scholars believe Luke was originally from Troas, in Asia Minor (modern-day Turkey). Some hold that when Paul was in Troas and received a vision of a man from Macedonia saying, "Come over to Macedonia and help us" (Acts 16:9), the man was Luke. We don't know for sure, but that could have been how Luke came to join Paul's missionary team and gain firsthand access to the experiences he later recorded in the book of Acts. Luke was a doctor, probably owned by Theophilus (Luke 1:1). It sounds crazy, but, a few thousand years ago, doctors were often purchased as well-treated slaves. Wealthy aristocrats owned their personal physicians, which seems strange to us, because today it often seems the other way around. *Theophilus*, which means "friend of God," could be an actual name or a pseudonym made up to protect the man's identity.

Fittingly, there are many medical terms in Luke's Gospel. It's laden with them— right from the start. Luke opens by citing "Those who from the beginning were eyewitnesses and ministers of the word" (v. 2). "Eyewitnesses" comes from the Greek *autoptes*, which means "a detailed examination." We get the word *autopsy* from the root, and the idea is that Luke's sources observed and dissected the life of Jesus Christ. And the word "ministers" comes from a term used to describe medical interns. Right away, Luke established himself among those who were observers, researchers, and interns of the great Physician. They studied His life, analyzed it, synthesized different sources, and then Luke wrote his account.

It makes perfect sense, then, that Luke's emphasis is the humanity of Jesus Christ. He wrote for a Greek audience, playing off of the Greek ideal of the perfect man, an ideal going back to their golden age—a man perfectly trained, taught, and capable to rule with wisdom and balance. Luke took this idea to the ultimate level, introducing the Greeks not just to a good man but the God-man—fully God, fully human. And so he used the phrase "Son of Man" more often in this book than do the other Gospels. A key characteristic of this perfect Man is His real compassion, His genuine care for people, which Luke emphasized through his frequent accounts of miraculous healings.

Speaking of compassion, let's note something unusual about the ministry of John the Baptist. Elizabeth, his mother, had been barren, so the news of her pregnancy was cause for rejoicing in and of itself. The fact that the baby was also divinely ordained was also special, and the joy doubled when Elizabeth's young cousin Mary came to visit and share her own miraculous news. "It happened, when Elizabeth heard the greeting of Mary, that the babe leaped in her womb; and Elizabeth was filled with the Holy Spirit" (Luke 1:41).

Here's what I want you to notice: John the Baptist's ministry began when he was in utero—about nine inches long, maybe a pound and a half—and he jumped for joy in the presence of His Savior, a womb away but very much on the way. If there's ever a debate as to when life begins, this should end the debate for you as a Christian. This is a clear indication life begins at conception.

Like Matthew, Luke included a genealogy, but there are some differences. His is in reverse order of Matthew's. Matthew moved forward from Abraham to Joseph, while Luke moved backward from Jesus to Adam. Most scholars believe that Matthew contains Joseph's genealogy, while Luke shows Mary's. The names are pretty much the same until Luke gets to King David. Then he takes a right turn, tracing Jesus's line not through Solomon and the royal lineage, but through another son of David named Nathan. How could Jesus as the Messiah have two seemingly conflicting lines?

It seems like a dilemma, but here's the solution: In the Old Testament, multiple prophecies said the Messiah would come through the royal line of Judah and through the house of David. However, the kings of Judah acted in such blasphemous ways for so long that God got fed up with their degenerative behavior and placed a blood curse on King Jeconiah, who descended from David: "Write this man down as childless, a man who shall not prosper in his days; for none of his descendants shall prosper, sitting on the throne of David, and ruling anymore in Judah" (Jeremiah 22:30). Sure enough, none of Jeconiah's descendants sat on the throne of David. He was succeeded by his uncle, and then his line was cut off.

By Jesus's time, there hadn't been a Davidic dynasty for hundreds of years. So now we have a contradiction. God said the Messiah would come through David's line, but God had cursed that royal line. The problem is solved by the genealogies. Matthew recorded the line of Joseph, Jesus's legal father, which gave Jesus the dynastic rule because Joseph's genealogy goes back through the royal line to David. Luke established Jesus as the biological descendant of Mary, whose lineage can also be traced back through David. The two genealogies, then, cover all the bases. Joseph gave Jesus the legal right to rule, and Mary provided His biological claim to David's throne. God used the virgin birth to get around the curse on the kingly line so that Jesus has both the legal and physical rights as King and Messiah.

Luke follows the same synopsis as Matthew and Mark, covering Jesus's Galilean ministry (Luke 1–9), Judean ministry (Luke 10–19), and the final week and subsequent events (Luke 20–24). In these final chapters, Luke presented Jesus as Christ the King, the messianic man, feeling the grief of Israel's future. As Jesus drew near to Jerusalem before the final week of His earthly life,

> He saw the city and wept over it, saying, "If you had known, even you, especially in this your day, the things that make for your peace! But now they are hidden from your eyes. For the days will come upon you when your enemies will build an embankment around you, and surround you and close you in on every side, and level you, and your children within you, to the ground; and they will not leave in you one stone upon another, because you did not know the time of your visitation" (Luke 19:41-44).

Jesus was holding His people, the Jews, accountable to recognize a certain day—the day when God sent their Messiah to them, offering salvation. Daniel had predicted the very day when Jesus would be presented to Israel as the Messiah (Daniel 9:24-27). Luke showed its fulfillment here.

I'll close with the story of the one sermon of Christ's I wish was recorded along with what we have, a postresurrection appearance of Jesus that has caused me yearning since I first read it. It's a story of a couple of disciples walking from Jerusalem to the town of Emmaus about seven miles away. Jesus had recently been resurrected (Luke 24:12), and these two were discussing all that had happened the previous few days—Jesus's arrest, trial, and crucifixion. They were disappointed, disillusioned, and confused because they had left everything to follow Jesus. They believed—past tense—that Jesus was their deliverer. Now they thought, *He's dead. What now?*

As they were walking along, Jesus joined them on the road, but they didn't recognize Him. "And He said to them, 'What kind of conversation is this that you have with one another as you walk and are sad?'" (v. 17)—as if He didn't know. "Then the one whose name was Cleopas answered and said to Him, 'Are you the only stranger in Jerusalem, and have You not known the things which happened there in these days?' And He said to them, 'What things?'" (vv. 18-19). They go on and tell Him His own story, up to His resurrection, which they were finding hard to believe.

Jesus admonished them, going on to explain how everything that had happened to Him—remember, they still didn't know who He was—had been predicted centuries ago. "Beginning at Moses and all the Prophets, He expounded to them in all the Scriptures the things concerning Himself" (v. 27). Don't you wish you had that Bible study on record? Jesus went on a little further with them, even ate a meal in their company, and then, finally, revealed Himself: "Then their eyes were opened and they knew Him; and He vanished from their sight" (v. 31)—an impressive feature of His resurrected body. "And they said to one another, 'Did not our heart burn within us while He talked with us on the road, and while He opened the Scriptures to us?'" (v. 32). My heart burns with curiosity just thinking about what they must have heard!

We know all the scriptures predicting the Messiah and how Jesus fulfilled many of them when He was here and how He will fulfill the rest when He returns. But to hear Jesus Himself teach on that? What a gift to those followers. And that's what I want you to focus on as we come in for a landing: When Jesus showed up to these guys, He didn't do a miracle, but a Bible study. Sure, He did the cool vanishing act at the end, but He gave them a scriptural rundown of messianic prophecy. I'll bet He went back to Genesis, the first writings of Moses, covering Genesis 3 and the prediction of the seed of the woman bruising the head of the serpent.

No doubt Jesus spoke of Mount Moriah in Genesis 22, when Abraham offered his son to God on the same place where Jesus would be crucified. He probably took them to Exodus and the Passover, the smearing of the blood on the lintels and the doorpost, then to the tabernacle and its symbolic arrangement and sacrificial foreshadowing. He must have taken them back to the bronze serpent in the wilderness, lifted up by Moses to heal the people in their sin, just as the Son of Man would be lifted up. All those pivotal historical moments pointed to Him, and He pointed that out to them. "Behold, I have come—in the volume of the book it is written of Me—to do Your will, O God" (Hebrews 10:7).

Finally, in the burning of the two disciples' hearts as Jesus spoke to them, we see something beautiful. Jesus took something familiar, the Scripture they had grown up with, and applied it in a brand new way to their hearts. When Jesus Christ is revealed to you in His Word, it will set your heart on fire. I hear Christians all the time saying, "I want a new experience with Jesus." You don't need anything new. What you need is the familiar, newly applied to your current situation. God's Word is a living thing, able to cut through the complacency of familiarity if you'll let it.

> **When Jesus Christ is revealed to you in His Word, it will set your heart on fire.**

This is God's good news for you—that, through the blood and resurrected life of Jesus Christ, He has made a way to refresh your spirit and set your heart aflame. The patterns of the Synoptic Gospels show us again and again God's concern and compassion for all people—His desire to walk with us in all our walks of life, and how His Word, Old Testament and New, fuels and guides our steps.

JOHN
FLIGHT PLAN

Facts

Author

The author of the Gospel of John was an eyewitness to the events described in the book (John 21:24-25). Though the author did not name himself, ever since the time of the early church, it's been traditionally believed that it was John—the son of Zebedee, the brother of the apostle James, and the disciple whom Jesus loved (John 13:23). John was originally a fisherman from Galilee.

Date Written

Of the four Gospels, John's has the latest date of composition, written sometime between AD 80 and 90.

Landmarks

The Gospel of John is the most "spiritual" of all four Gospels. The book centers on the person and work of Jesus Christ; however, more than His *activity*, John is mostly concerned about Jesus's *identity*. His emphasis, even more than what Jesus did, is who Jesus is. The book's spiritual depth and focus on the incarnation of the God-man Jesus Christ sets it apart from the other Gospels.

While John doesn't follow the synoptic pattern of describing Jesus's ministry in Galilee and Judea, there is a strong final-week emphasis. One-third of the book deals with Jesus's last eight days, from Palm Sunday to Resurrection Sunday. And, of course, John is where we will find the most famous verse in the entire Bible, and the most often quoted, John 3:16: "God so loved the world that He gave His only begotten Son, that whoever believes in Him should not perish but have everlasting life."

John's overarching theme is found in the frequency of his most-used words: the name *Jesus* and the title *Christ* are found about 170 times, and the word *believe* appears about 100 times. John wanted us to believe that Jesus is the Christ, the Son of the living God (John 20:31). His Gospel is built around seven sweeping segments, all centered on the Son of God.

Itinerary

- The Incarnation of the Son of God (John 1:1-18)
- The Presentation of the Son of God (John 1:19–4:54)
- The Confrontation with the Son of God (John 5–12)
- The Instruction of the Son of God (John 13–16)
- The Intercession of the Son of God (John 17)
- The Execution of the Son of God (John 18–19)
- The Resurrection of the Son of God (John 20–21)

Gospel

Like each of the Synoptic Gospels, the book of John has its own focus, presenting Jesus as God. Together, all four form a fuller picture of Jesus Christ than any one of them could on their own. And when we look at all four Gospels this way, Old Testament history and symbolism come together to create a stunning portrait of Jesus as the pinnacle of redemptive history.

John is a studied portrait of the life of Jesus. Most of his material is unique among the Gospels, especially the seven statements Jesus made about Himself, using the phrase "I am" to identify Himself with God and as God. Unlike the other Gospel writers, John didn't include any parables, but he did record seven specific miracles that point to Jesus's divinity—five of which are found only in his account.

Another unique aspect of John's Gospel is his description of the preexistent Jesus. In relation to God, Jesus has always existed (John 1:1-2). John described Him as "the Word" by which God spoke the universe into being (John 1:3) and as the light that illuminates everyone's life, pointing them toward the truth and love of God (John 1:4). The idea of "the Word" was something that first-century Jews and Gentiles were familiar with. The Jewish scriptural commentaries called the Targum contained a reference to God as *Memra*, which means "the Word." This title referred to Jesus's act of speaking the world into being (Colossians 1:16).

The Greeks, on the other hand, looked at the organization and order of the universe—the predictable patterns of seasons and stars, day and night—and came up with a concept to account for it: *Logos*, or "the Word."[46] So when John opened his book by saying, "In the beginning was the Word, and the Word was with God, and the Word was God" (John 1:1), he knew his audience would grasp what exactly he was trying to say about Jesus Christ.

But for all the mystery and wonder present in his Gospel, John's focus was simple. Throughout his book, he used the title *Jesus Christ—Christ* meaning "the Anointed One" or "Messiah"—about 170 times, and the word *believe* about 100 times. His theme rings loud and clear, even to us today: Jesus is God, and here are all the reasons you should believe in Him.

History

John wrote his Gospel a few decades after the resurrection of Jesus, and after the dispersion of Jews and Christians under the persecution of Nero (AD 54–68) and the destruction of the Jewish Temple (AD 70). During the latter years of his life, John saw the Roman emperors Vespasian (AD 69–79), Titus (AD 79–81), and Domitian (AD 81–96) come to power. Some scholars speculate that John wrote during Domitian's reign. John may have lived in Ephesus when he wrote his Gospel and epistles, but he was exiled to the island of Patmos around AD 95, where he wrote the book of Revelation. John died around AD 98 and was the last of Jesus's original twelve disciples to die.

John didn't explicitly name himself in the Gospel that bears his name, only referring to himself as the disciple whom Jesus loved (John 13:23; 19:26; 21:7, 20). However, many early church fathers, including Irenaeus (a disciple one generation removed from John) attested that John wrote the book.[47]

Travel Tips

In his Gospel, John laid down his own eyewitness account of the truth to solidify the fact that Jesus was God. His rock-solid presentation didn't come a moment too soon, as the early church was already experiencing both physical and spiritual attacks for their faith in Jesus. The steadfast truth and belief John presented to his readers is critical for sustaining faith in every age.

- Jesus knows your heart. Many people believed in Jesus because of the signs and miracles He performed—not because they were desperate to be healed but because they wanted a show. Jesus is omniscient (all-knowing), so He knows if you're playing church or you're truly committed to Him.

- Jesus helped the helpless. The saying "God helps those who help themselves" is not biblical. Not only is it not in the Scriptures, but it also goes against the work we see Jesus do over and over again in His earthly ministry. He helped the helpless and the hopeless, not those who helped themselves. No matter how much of your own strength you have to fall back on, it will eventually fail you, whereas God never will.

- Jesus cleans the fish He catches. He loves you as you are, but He also loves you too much to leave you that way. Jesus washing the disciples' feet (John 13:1-20) paints a vivid picture of His ongoing work of sanctification in His people. He saved you—caught you and reeled you in—and He'll continue to work on making you more like Him, cleaning your feet, as it were, as you walk through a dirty world.

- Jesus valued prayer. Prayer is far too often the Christian's most underused resource. If Jesus, who was fully God and fully man, felt the need to pray no fewer than a recorded nineteen times in the Gospels, how much more do we need to pray, being fully human? We could all use more time on our knees.

> **Prayer is far too often the Christian's most under-used resource...We could all use more time on our knees.**

- Jesus forgives your worst mistakes. How many times have you, like Peter, denied Jesus? Even if you've never outright said, "I don't know Jesus," what have your actions indicated? Peter committed acts of self-confidence, disobedience, and self-absolution, indirectly denying Christ, until he got to a point where he denied Christ directly. But rather than shake your head at Peter, instead rejoice that Jesus restored him (John 21:15-19) and used him to accomplish great things. After all, Peter's pitfalls are the same ones many of us are prone to get caught in too.

In Flight

The Incarnation of the Son of God (John 1:1-18)

John was the most theological of all the Gospel writers. We see it in his prologue, what we might call the third genealogy of Christ. Matthew began his genealogy with Abraham because he was writing for the Jewish community. Luke ended his with Adam, the first man, because his focus was the Son of Man. But John, in establishing Jesus's identity as God, went all the way back to the beginning—before the beginning, actually, to the pre-incarnate state when Jesus was with the Father in eternity past.

"In the beginning was the Word, and the Word was with God, and the Word was God. He was in the beginning with God" (John 1:1-2). That sounds very similar to Genesis 1:1, complementing that beginning, where God created the heavens and the earth, with more specific information: Here, at the beginning of the world, was the Word. It's a strange, impersonal way to introduce such a significant Person—at least until we put it in its historical context (see **Gospel** on page 409).

The Word was a familiar term for first-century Jews and Greeks, and it helped John underscore his emphasis: Jesus Christ is Himself God. The language John used was unmistakable even to the enemies of Jesus, who said, "For a good work we do not stone You, but for blasphemy, and because You, being a Man, make Yourself God" (John 10:33). They didn't like it, but they understood what Jesus was saying about Himself.

Further establishing his claim, John made it clear that Jesus was both Creator and Incarnation. "All things were made through Him, and without Him nothing was made that was made" (John 1:3). And while Jesus is God, He was also fully a man: "The Word became flesh and dwelt among us" (v. 14). John's Gospel and three epistles (1 John, 2 John, and 3 John) are careful to establish this amazing truth. Part of the reason for this was because the truth was already under attack. When John wrote all his works, a prevailing false teaching was sweeping the early church, a teaching called Gnosticism.

The Gnostics claimed that Jesus Christ wasn't really human, existing in a fleshly body, and that He just appeared to be a man. John responded in no uncertain terms that the opposite is true: "Many deceivers have gone out into the world who do not confess Jesus Christ as coming in the flesh" (2 John 7). John kept both sides of his audience—believing and unbelieving—in mind as he wrote. "Who is a liar but he who denies that Jesus is the Christ? He is antichrist who denies the Father and the Son" (1 John 2:22). He established his credibility not by name but by virtue of his eyewitness experience, writing about that "which was from the beginning, which we have heard, which we have seen with our eyes, which we have looked upon, and our hands have handled, concerning the Word of life" (1 John 1:1).

The Presentation of the Son of God (John 1:19–4:54)

Once He began His ministry, Jesus made Himself known, presenting Himself to a number of people: to John the Baptist as the Lamb of God, calling the early disciples, at a wedding in Cana through a miracle, to Nicodemus in Jerusalem on the matter of spiritual rebirth, and to a Samaritan woman gathering water at a well.

John the Baptist's role as the forerunner of the Messiah had been foretold in the Old Testament. He was also Jesus's cousin. He knew Jesus, but when Jesus presented Himself to John for baptism at the Jordan River, John saw his cousin in a new light, as *the* Light (John 1:29). This revelation is in keeping with the apostle John's focus on Jesus's divinity throughout the book, including His omniscience.

Jesus knew everything, including what was in people's hearts. "When He was in Jerusalem at the Passover, during the feast, many believed in His name when they saw the signs which He did. But Jesus did not commit Himself to them, because He knew all men, and had no need that anyone should testify of man, for He knew what was in man" (John 2:23-25). John is building up to a contrast here based on Jesus's ability to discern between one group's "belief" based on Jesus's miracles, and the truth-seeking heart of the man Jesus would meet next, Nicodemus.

Nicodemus, an intelligent, scholarly man, misunderstood what Jesus was saying, but he asked Jesus to explain (John 3:1-2). He thought of Jesus as a teacher come from God, instead of Jesus as God come to teach, but here's what John was driving at: Jesus knew the difference between his heart and the intentions of the previous crowd, who just wanted a show, a miracle to tickle their fancies for the day.

Knowing Nicodemus's heart, Jesus cut right to the heart of the matter—how to get to heaven. "Most assuredly, I say to you, unless one is born again, he cannot see the kingdom of God" (v. 3). Unfortunately, the term "born again" has become a cliché, co-opted by the world and redefined as either an insult or to classify some evangelical subset of Christianity. But there's no such thing as a Christian who's not born again. That's what Jesus told Nicodemus. You have to be born again—literally, *born from above*—to get to heaven. And Christians are those who, given new life in Christ, go to heaven.

A little bit later in that same conversation, we come to the most often-quoted and well-known verse—what Martin Luther called "the heart of the Bible, the gospel in miniature" because it covers the whole scope of salvation. Here's a breakdown of John 3:16:

> The origin of salvation: "God"
>
> The motivation for salvation: "so loved"
>
> The object of salvation: "the world"
>
> The demonstration of salvation: "that He gave His only begotten Son"
>
> The requirement of salvation: "that whoever believes in Him"

The outcome of salvation: "should not perish but have everlasting life"

God is the origin of salvation. It's His plan—it has always been His plan—and ongoing desire for all people during this age of grace.

Nicodemus wasn't used to this concept. He thought that the way to get to heaven was by keeping rituals and ceremonies, going to the temple, offering sacrifices, and doing all the things he had been taught as a young Jewish man and now practiced as a priest and teacher. Jesus's requirement—belief in Him—must have sounded to Nicodemus the way it does to so many today—too easy, too simplistic to be true. If only more would take Jesus's follow-up assurance to heart: "God did not send His Son into the world to condemn the world, but that the world through Him might be saved" (John 3:17).

The Confrontation with the Son of God (John 5–12)

As Jesus made Himself known, a confrontation with the Jewish authorities was inevitable. Let's follow the course of events that built the tension between them that would end with Jesus's arrest, trial, and crucifixion:

John 5: Jesus healed a man on the Sabbath at the pool of Bethesda in Jerusalem, creating an uproar. Jesus didn't back down, responding, "My Father has been working until now, and I have been working" (John 5:17). The Jewish leaders didn't miss what He was saying—that He was equal with God, His Father—and they "sought all the more to kill Him" (v. 18).

John 7–10: Because of the Jewish leadership's desire to kill Him, Jesus avoided Judea, hanging around Galilee for a while before secretly going to Jerusalem for the feast. He taught boldly in the synagogue, criticizing the Jews for not recognizing Him as the Messiah (John 7:14-29). They tried and failed to arrest Him, and then when the crowds began to believe in Him, the Pharisees sent officers to confront Him (vv. 32-52).

John 8: The next morning, the Pharisees confronted Jesus at the temple with a woman caught in adultery, looking to trip Him up on the details of the law (John 8:6). Jesus stooped and wrote on the ground with His finger, then invited any of them who was without sin to throw the first stone at the woman (vv. 6-11). They dropped their rocks and left.

No one likes being busted, especially when you're the ones normally doing the busting, so the Pharisees tried to criticize Jesus for bearing witness to Himself (vv. 13-20), and later making a backhanded reference to what they considered

Jesus's illegitimate birth (v. 41). Jesus responding that they couldn't understand Him because they were children of their spiritual father, the devil (v. 44).

They accused Him of being demon-possessed and lying about His age when He claimed Abraham rejoiced in His coming (vv. 48-57). When He responded, "Before Abraham was, I AM" (v. 58), "they took up stones to throw at Him" (v. 59). Every confrontation with God's truth fueled their hatred.

John 9: After Jesus healed a man who had been blind from birth, another skirmish broke out, and Jesus told the Pharisees that one reason He had come was "that those who do not see may see, and that those who see may be made blind" (John 9:39). When they asked Him if He was saying they were spiritually blind, Jesus said, "If you were blind, you would have no sin; but now you say, 'We see.' Therefore your sin remains" (v. 41). *So, yeah, you're blind.*

John 10: Jesus, in identifying Himself as the Good Shepherd, essentially called Israel's religious leadership "hirelings" who flee their flock in the presence of a wolf (John 10:11-13). The Jews were conflicted among themselves, with some saying Jesus was demonic and insane and others claiming His words and works demonstrated the opposite (vv. 19-21). Finally, they asked Him directly, "If You are the Christ, tell us plainly" (v. 24).

Jesus's response illustrated the divide between them: "I told you, and you do not believe. The works that I do in My Father's name, they bear witness of Me. But you do not believe, because you are not of My sheep, as I said to you" (vv. 25-26). When He summed up by saying, "I and My Father are one" (v. 30), they "took up stones again to stone Him" (v. 31).

When Jesus asked them which of His good works they were planning to kill Him for, they said it wasn't for His works but because of His claim to be God (vv. 32-33). Jesus encouraged them to believe in His works as proof of His claims, but that only prompted them to try to arrest Him again (vv. 37-39).

John 11: Whatever battle lines had been drawn up to this point were blown out of the water when Jesus raised Lazarus from the dead (John 11:1-44). It was an unmistakable, undeniable sign that He was the Son of God. The Jewish leaders shifted from denial of His claims to plotting His murder (vv. 46-53)—"We've got to kill this guy fast before everybody starts believing in Him!"

John 12: Despite the desperate plan of the chief priests to wipe out the proof of Lazarus's resurrection by having Lazarus killed (John 12:10), Jesus embraced His destiny, ending His public ministry and heading for Jerusalem in what has been called the triumphal entry (vv. 12-16). As the people gathered and worshipped Jesus, the Pharisees lamented their own ineffectiveness, saying to each other, "You see that you are accomplishing nothing. Look, the world has gone after Him!" (v. 19). Some of the Pharisees even believed in Jesus, but they kept it to themselves because "they loved the praise of men more than the praise of God" (v. 43).

While on this path of conflict, Jesus made several important declarations about His identity—what we know as the seven "I am" statements of Christ:

- "I am the bread of life" (John 6:35)
- "I am the light of the world" (John 8:12; 9:5)
- "I am the door of the sheep" (John 10:7)
- "I am the good shepherd" (John 10:11)
- "I am the resurrection and the life" (John 11:25)
- "I am the way, the truth, and the life" (John 14:6)
- "I am the true vine...I am the vine" (John 15:1, 5)

The statements themselves are powerful—rich with the imagery of God's care and provision. What is even more remarkable, however, is that in the midst of Jesus's ongoing confrontations with the Jewish leaders, He never stopped speaking God's truth. The Pharisees and chief priests were powerful men, respected and feared for their authority, but Jesus didn't shy away once from their accusations or threats. Furthermore, He continued to teach, preach, and heal—the primary focal points of His public ministry.

When the Pharisees confronted Jesus, He stood toe to toe with them—but He did so on His terms and in His timing. When His own brothers wanted Him to go up to Jerusalem for the Feast of Tabernacles and do His works there, Jesus told them to go on ahead: "I am not yet going up to this feast, for My time has not yet fully come" (John 7:8). Jesus couldn't freely go out in public because He knew the Jews were after Him, looking to kill Him (v. 1).

A few chapters later, John recorded the end of Jesus's public ministry, its window of opportunity shattered by national unbelief (John 12:37-38). Many did not believe and, even among those who did, there was a greater fear of the Pharisees than of God—both of which were foretold. "Therefore they could not believe, because Isaiah said again, 'He has blinded their eyes and hardened their hearts, lest they should see with their eyes, lest they should understand with their hearts and turn, so that I should heal them'" (vv. 39-40). The ongoing confrontation between Jesus and the Jewish leaders had set the stage for the most important moment in history. Before Jesus would go to the cross, however, He still had words for His followers.

The Instruction of the Son of God (John 13–16)

Having withdrawn from public ministry, Jesus turned His focus specifically to His twelve closest followers. John recorded His private instructions in an intimate gathering at Passover—a feast charged with the fact that "Jesus knew that His hour had come that He should depart from this world to the Father, having loved His own who were in the world, He loved them to the end" (John 13:1). This is the scene we call the Last Supper.

Jesus broke bread and drank wine one last time with His friends, knowing two things: Judas would betray Him, but "the Father had given all things into His hands, and that He had come from God and was going to God" (v. 3). John portrayed Jesus as being absolutely in control: He knew who He was, knew where He came from, both pre-incarnate God and the Word made flesh. He knew God's plan for the cross, knew He was going to be glorified. John had noted Jesus's omniscience before in His public ministry; now, he touched on it again in this private moment, showing God's unchanging nature and the unstoppable nature of His promises.

What a special night. After Jesus wrapped a towel around His waist, "He poured water into a basin and began to wash the disciples' feet, and to wipe them with the towel with which He was girded" (v. 5). Beginning here and lasting all the way to the end of chapter 17, your red-letter Bible turns almost entirely crimson as Jesus shared His heart with His closest friends and followers. This was also a time of intense discipleship. While Jesus knew that He would be leaving them soon, they didn't. They could feel the weight of the moment, though, and were scared and shaken at this point, prompting Jesus to encourage them: "Let not your heart be troubled; you believe in God, believe also in Me" (John 14:1).

After breaking bread with His friends, Jesus washed their feet. This was more than Jesus being a good example, more than just a nice, intimate little meal punctuated by Jesus performing a kind service. Nor was He establishing a precedent, something He wanted them to practice every time they got together. That's not what this is about. Rather, Jesus was, in essence, acting out His entire ministry symbolically. Just as He rose from supper to wash their feet like a servant, He had risen to leave His throne in heaven and do the Father's bidding—serving mankind by washing their souls.

Jesus set the tone for all this at the Last Supper. He was, in part, preparing to return to glory. But He was also preparing His disciples for God's continuing plan for their lives, serving them, teaching them, encouraging them, and promising them the help of the Holy Spirit, who would pick up God's work in the hearts of all believers once Jesus had returned home to heaven. "These things I have spoken to you, that in Me you may have peace. In the world you will have tribulation; but be of good cheer, I have overcome the world" (John 16:33).

The Intercession of the Son of God (John 17)

John 17 is entirely devoted to Jesus's prayer to His Father on behalf of His disciples.[48] Jesus knew He had a limited amount of time left on earth, so He got His disciples together and passed on some very important principles and instructions. But then He went beyond instruction *to* them and made intercession *for* them. As He prayed for His followers, John wrote it down.

One of the remarkable things about this prayer is that it gives us the things that were on Jesus's heart as He faced His death. We can know His priorities as He looked toward—and beyond—the cross: first and foremost, the glory of God, but also the future of the disciples and the unity of the church, among other things. It's a long prayer, and it's truly the Lord's prayer. What we know as the Lord's Prayer in Matthew 6:9-13 is more accurately the disciples's prayer—how they should be praying and what they should be talking to God about. This is the Lord's own prayer to His Father, His heart for God as He faced the future.

"Jesus spoke these words, lifted up His eyes to heaven, and said, 'Father, the hour has come. Glorify your Son, that your Son also may glorify You'" (John 17:1). So begins Jesus's longest recorded prayer. Now, the Gospels show Jesus praying nineteen times. Among them, we see Him pulling a prayer all-nighter before choosing His disciples (Luke 6:12), getting up before dawn to pray the day in (Mark 1:35), withdrawing to pray by Himself (Luke 5:16), and laying hands on and praying for little children (Matthew 19:13-15).

Here's my point: Jesus was fully God and fully man, connected to the Father in a unique way every moment of His existence. If He still felt the necessity to depend on the Father in prayer for so much of His earthly life, how much more do we need to rely on God in prayer?

> If Jesus felt the necessity to depend on the Father in prayer...how much more do we need to rely on God in prayer?

The Execution of the Son of God (John 18–19)

Prepared by prayer, Jesus immediately stepped out to face the challenge before Him: His betrayal and arrest, examination before the authorities, torture, and execution. John mentioned that Jesus went out, crossing the Kidron Brook (John 18:1), and he did so for two reasons: First, because King David had passed over it when he left Jerusalem in mourning, driven out by Absalom's betrayal (2 Samuel 17:21-22). Jesus, like his ancestor, was also being betrayed.

Furthermore, John wanted to draw a parallel with the Passover: A stone conduit carried the blood of the sacrificed lambs—along with the water used to wash it away—out of the Temple Mount, where it emptied outside the city into the Kidron Brook. In Jesus's day, the brook was full and fast enough to warrant placing a bridge over it, so as Jesus, the Lamb of God, crossed that bridge, beneath Him flowed the blood of the Passover lambs. More than mere symbolism, this was the looming fulfillment of God's plan of redemption.

And Jesus knew it was His moment. He crossed the river, went into the Garden of Gethsemane, and went straight up to Judas, who was leading a detachment of soldiers, temple guards, and Jewish religious officials: "Jesus therefore, knowing all things that would come upon Him, went forward and said to them, 'Whom are you seeking?' They answered Him, 'Jesus of Nazareth.' Jesus said to them, 'I am *He*'" (John 18:4-5).

In the New King James, *He* is italicized, which means that word is not present in the original. In the original Greek text, it reads *ego eimi*, or simply "I am." It's the same phrase translated in the Septuagint (the Greek version of the Old Testament in wide circulation in those days) "I AM THAT I AM." In other words, Jesus identified Himself as God. "Now when He said to them, 'I am He,' they drew back and fell to the ground" (v. 6). This is the Word of God in action; the power in the mention of His name was enough to knock over a troop of soldiers. As Jesus would later make clear to Pontius Pilate, no one was going to do anything to Him that He didn't permit—including His arrest and execution.

And despite Peter playing whack-an-ear with the high priest's servant Malchus, the cross was something Jesus would have to face alone, something He alone could accomplish. Even so, it took a travesty of justice and a farce of a trial to bring Him to it. The soldiers tied up Jesus and took Him from the garden to Annas, the father-in-law of the high priest (vv. 12-13). Annas, unable to find any fault in Jesus, sent Him on to the high priest himself, Caiaphas. From there, Caiaphas, not wanting a murder to make him unclean on the eve of the Passover (v. 28), sent Jesus to the Praetorium, where He stood before the Roman governor of Judea, Pontius Pilate. After interviewing Jesus, Pilate had Him scourged, thinking this would satisfy the

Jews, because, as he told them afterward, "I am bringing Him out to you, that you may know I find no fault in Him" (John 19:4).

Pilate thought a severe beating would be enough to satisfy the Pharisees, but it wasn't. Puzzled by Jesus's unwillingness to speak in His own defense, Pilate told Him, "'Do You not know that I have power to crucify You, and power to release You?' Jesus answered, 'You could have no power at all against Me unless it had been given you from above'" (John 19:10-11). Pilate wanted to let Jesus go at that point, but the Jewish leaders threatened to let it be known that he would be no friend of Caesar's if he did so (v. 12). Pilate let his political ambitions and fears cloud his better judgment, but it all happened so that Jesus could fulfill His mission, securing our salvation through His unjust punishment and execution.

John caught up with Jesus again at Golgotha—what we call Calvary, the hill of crucifixion—where Jesus arranged for His friend to take care of His mother (John 19:26-27). Don't take that for granted. When a person is hurting or grieving that deeply, it is all-consuming. The loss, the presence of death, or the deep physical pain absorbs their attention. It is incredibly rare to even be able to think about anyone else. So for Jesus, in that kind of state, to be thinking about His mother's future was an act of great compassion. Furthermore, it was Jesus's last act: "After this, Jesus, knowing that all things were now accomplished, that the Scripture might be fulfilled, said, 'I thirst!'" (v. 28). He was given a sponge soaked in wine, and once He had "received the sour wine, He said, 'It is finished!' And bowing His head, He gave up His spirit" (v. 30).

The Resurrection of the Son of God (John 20–21)

It was hard for the disciples to grasp the immensity of Jesus's resurrection. When Mary Magdalene first reported that Jesus's tomb was empty, they ran to it and saw for themselves. John believed that He was risen, but neither he nor Peter could put it into perspective, because "as yet they did not know the Scripture, that He must rise again from the dead" (John 20:9). The newly resurrected Christ revealed Himself to Mary Magdalene first (vv. 15-18), and then appeared to His disciples twice, the second time convincing the previously absent Thomas that it was all for real (vv. 19-29). John told us that "truly Jesus did many other signs in the presence of His disciples, which are not written in this book; but these are written that you may believe that Jesus is the Christ, the Son of God, and that by believing you might have life in His name" (v. 31). Belief in Jesus's resurrection is the miracle that makes eternal life possible.

John wrapped up with a great chapter about the power of Jesus's resurrection to forgive, restore, and heal broken hearts and lives. Peter, rejoicing to see His Lord risen but shattered by his own weakness and betrayal and uncertain about what to do next, decided to go back to what he knew best—fishing. The other disciples followed suit, and they went out on a fruitless night of fishing in Galilee. The next morning, Jesus appeared, calling to them from the shore and asking about how their fishing had gone. They didn't recognize Him and told Him they hadn't caught anything, so He shouted to them to throw their nets on the other side of the boat.

The words must have struck a familiar chord to them, especially Peter, who perhaps thought of the time at Lake Gennesaret when Jesus had told him, "Launch out into the deep and let down your nets for a catch" (Luke 5:4). Peter had obeyed then, despite an equally fruitless night of fishing, and had been humbled by the net-breaking catch that followed. "Depart from me," he had told Jesus, "for I am a sinful man, O Lord!" (v. 8). Jesus had comforted him then, saying, "Do not be afraid. From now on you will catch men" (v. 10).

That had happened at the beginning of Jesus's ministry. Now, here at the Sea of Tiberias, after the resurrection of his Lord, Peter hauled in another unlikely catch. And the difference between fruitlessness and fruitfulness was the width of that boat. They were fishing on one side, torn by their anxiety over what to do next, and catching nothing. At Jesus's instruction and by His power, they threw their nets on the other side, and couldn't pull the nets back aboard because of the massive haul. John recognized Jesus first, and told Peter, who promptly dove into the sea and swam to shore (vv. 6-7).

The remainder of the chapter focuses on the reinstatement of Peter (vv. 15-23). Three times, Jesus said, "Peter, do you love Me?" Each time, Peter said, "Yes, Lord, I love You," and Jesus told him, "Feed My lambs." Jesus, denied by Peter three times, gave His beloved but impetuous son the opportunity three times to affirm his love for Him. Jesus didn't ask Peter, "Do you obey Me?" or "Do you believe in Me?" or "Do you believe this doctrine?" Jesus wanted to know the one thing that was more important than anything else: the status of Peter's relationship with Him. *Do you love Me?* Because if you love Jesus, then faith, belief, works, and everything else will follow.

If you love Jesus, then faith, belief, works, and everything else will follow.

John stamped his final statement by saying his testimony was true, and that "there are also many other things that Jesus did, which if they were written one by one, I suppose that even the world itself could not contain the books that would be written" (v. 25). John's words here could be a literary device or a statement of literal fact. It seems at first glance like exaggeration, but think of all the people who have been changed over the past 2000 years by their encounters with Christ. Their written testimonies alone would yield massive libraries!

There are millions of names written in the Lamb's Book of Life, each of them with a full story of individual experiences, interwoven with other individual experiences, all of them bound together by the scarlet thread of the redemption purchased by the blood of Jesus Christ. Their stories—my story and, I hope, your story too—are still being written, and, God willing, millions of other stories that have yet to be written will be.

ACTS
FLIGHT PLAN

Facts

Author

The book of Acts, also known as the Acts of the Apostles, is the sequel to the Gospel of Luke and the second book written by Luke. Luke was a physician, a traveling companion of the apostle Paul, and eyewitness to many of the events chronicled in Acts.

Date Written

Acts was written sometime after AD 60 and before AD 69. The book ends with Paul being imprisoned in Rome and doesn't provide any sort of conclusion to his trial (Acts 28). It also doesn't mention the fall of Jerusalem in AD 70. Because of this, we can assume Luke wrote Acts during the final events of Paul's life, before Paul was martyred for his faith.

Landmarks

The Acts of the Apostles details the post-Great Commission history of the early church: how it was founded and organized, and how it responded to the problems it faced. In his characteristically precise manner of writing, Luke told the story of how this rapidly growing community of believers received the power of the Holy Spirit—the promised Counselor and Guide—and were enabled to witness, to love, and to serve the Lord. This dynamic group of believers included folks from Jerusalem, Syria, Africa, Asia, and Europe.

The apostles were at the forefront of this group, witnessing to Jerusalem—and eventually the known world—about their faith in Christ through personal testimony, preaching, and defending the good news before the authorities. They shared the gospel with boldness and courage, even when faced with imprisonment, beatings, plots, and riots. In fact, the persecution they experienced was actually a catalyst for the spread of Christianity. Beginning in chapter 13, the book of Acts shifts focus almost exclusively to the missionary journeys of Paul, ending with his trip to Rome as a prisoner.

Using Acts 1:8—"You shall be witnesses to Me in Jerusalem, and in all Judea and Samaria, and to the end of the earth"—as a guide, we can divide the book of Acts into eight sections based on Jesus's call to be witnesses:

Itinerary

- The Gospel Witness to Jerusalem (Acts 1–7)
- The Gospel Witness to Judea and Samaria (Acts 8–9)
- The Gospel Witness to the End of the Earth (Acts 10–28)
  - A Witness of Faith in Christ Alone: Paul's First Mission (Acts 13:4–14:26)
  - A Witness in Open and Shut Doors: Paul's Second Mission (Acts 15:36–18:22)
  - A Witness in Conversions and Conflict: Paul's Third Mission (Acts 18:23–21:17)
  - A Witness in Chains: Paul's Arrest and Journey to Rome (Acts 21:18–28:31)

Gospel

Luke began the book of Acts by referring to the "former account [he] made"— the Gospel of Luke—about "all that Jesus began both to do and teach" (Acts 1:1). In our ongoing study of the scarlet thread of redemption, that word "began" is crucial. The Gospels recorded who Jesus was and what He did during His earthly ministry—but that was just the beginning of the story. Jesus didn't stop working when He ascended into heaven, but instead passed the baton to His apostles. And until He returns, He will continue the work He started, using men and women who are filled with the Holy Spirit and surrendered to His kingdom's cause.

Early on in church history, the book of Acts was given multiple names, including "The Gospel of the Holy Spirit" and "The Gospel of the Resurrection."[49] These titles serve as a reminder of whose story this is—God's. Redemption's scarlet thread wove itself throughout the history of the Old Testament—the fall in the Garden of Eden, the lives of the patriarchs, the kingdom of Israel, the prophets—and then burst into a bright splash of color in the New Testament, dominating the tapestry of the age of grace. The story of the early church shows us our ongoing role in the weaving of this tapestry: As God's agents, we are to spread the good news of Jesus

Christ. Everyone who puts their faith in Jesus becomes a joint heir with Him in His inheritance, but they also become His minister to a lost world, called to share His worship, His Word, and His ways.

Until Jesus returns, He will continue the work He started, using men and women who are filled with the Holy Spirit and surrendered to His kingdom's cause.

History

The book of Acts chronicles the period of time between Jesus's ascension and Paul's imprisonment in Rome in the mid-60s AD. This thirty-year period covers the founding of the Christian church and the earliest missions. The following chart shows some of the major developments in the church during this time and roughly when they occurred.

AD 30–35   Pentecost and the formation of the early church

AD 35–47   The church expanded into Judea and Samaria

ca. AD 44   James, the son of Zebedee and brother of John, was martyred

AD 47–48   Paul's first missionary trip

AD 49–52   Paul's second missionary trip

AD 52–57   Paul's third missionary trip

AD 60–62   Paul's first imprisonment in Rome

ca. AD 66–67   Paul's second imprisonment and martyrdom; Peter's martyrdom

The Roman emperors in power during this time were Caligula (AD 37–41), Claudius (AD 41–54), and Nero (AD 54–68).

Travel Tips

One of my favorite things about Acts is that it's an unfinished book. Jesus's work on this earth isn't done! That means Christians aren't just covered by Jesus's salvation, but also by His commission. Jesus is still working through His people, and you and I are part of what Peter, Paul, and the apostles began in Acts and many others have continued through the centuries.

- Persecution advances God's purposes. In typical paradoxical fashion, persecution doesn't hurt the church; it actually helps it grow. Jesus Himself said it's a fact of life for the Christian (Matthew 10:22). Instead of being surprised or hurt when the world persecutes us, we should prepare for it, keeping our focus on the Lord and the reward He promises to those who endure to the end—whatever that end may be.

> Instead of being surprised or hurt when the world persecutes us, we should prepare for it, keeping our focus on the Lord.

- Who is God to you? Saul's conversion to Christianity highlights two important questions every person must ask Jesus Christ at some point: "Who are You, Lord?" and "What do You want me to do?" (Acts 9:1-6). The Bible answers the first question, saying that Jesus is the Lord, the Son of God, and the Savior of the world. Once you accept that, you can go on to the second question, which can only be answered by surrendering your life to God. He will guide you and help you find your role in His greater plan.

- Legalism is dangerous. During the time of the early church, a group of people called the Judaizers taught that you had to keep the Law of Moses *and* give your life to Christ in order to be saved. Paul and Barnabas argued with them at length, because the Judaizers were trying to mix the law and grace (Acts 15). God's grace alone is what saves (Ephesians 2:8-9). We do good works in response to and as a result of being saved by God's grace, not the other way around.

- Who is the central character in the story of your life? The book of Acts ends abruptly, without even saying what happened to Paul. Why? Because Paul wasn't the central character of Acts—the Holy Spirit was, just as Jesus was the protagonist of the Gospels. The Spirit's work has continued long after the life of Paul, a work in which you, thousands of years later, play a part. The bigger story is God's. If you, like Paul, are content to play your part in His story—a story that encompasses all of history and every person in it—you will not find an easy, comfortable life but a satisfying and joyful one.

In Flight

The Gospel Witness to Jerusalem (Acts 1–7)

After reconnecting us with Jesus and His pre-ascension instructions to His followers (Acts 1:8), Luke showed us what was happening in Jerusalem. In a nutshell, the Holy Spirit came upon God's people (Acts 2:1-11). They began to preach boldly in the languages of everyone within hearing, which got them noticed by the people, which got them in trouble with the authorities, which got them arrested but did not stop them from continuing to preach the gospel.

After his humbling and restoration, Peter's boldness was now harnessed to the right message and the right attitude. When the apostles were mocked for speaking "the wonderful works of God" (Acts 2:11), he stepped up. "Peter, standing up with the eleven, raised his voice and said to them, 'Men of Judea and all who dwell in Jerusalem, let this be known to you, and heed my words'" (v. 14)—and then he preached the gospel, confidently, citing Old Testament prophecy about Jesus and tying it to recent events (vv. 22-36).

Unlike his previous bluster, Peter's words now carried the weight of fulfilled prophecy and the power of God's Spirit—both of which struck his audience: "Now when they heard this, they were cut to the heart, and said to Peter and the rest of the apostles, 'Men and brethren, what shall we do?' Then Peter said to them, 'Repent, and let every one of you be baptized in the name of Jesus Christ for the remission of sins; and you shall receive the gift of the Holy Spirit'" (Acts 2:37-38).

Boy, did Peter preach—and the message was all the more remarkable because it came from Peter! He was perhaps the most obvious example of the change in the apostles since we left them at the end of the Gospels. It wasn't but a month or two before that they had been huddled together in an upper room, scared to death. At the time, they could barely grasp the truth about Jesus, much less speak it. Now, they were bold. Earlier, Peter had stumbled when he spoke to the high priest's servant girl during Jesus's trial; now, he was articulate and well-spoken—in ways he as a fisherman had never been before.

What happened? How did these timid, obscure fishermen become poised, eloquent proclaimers of the gospel? Two reasons: a new presence and a new power. You'll see these themes running throughout the book. There was a new presence: The apostles had thought Jesus was dead, but seeing Him alive again, bodily risen from the dead, impacted them. They had despaired, but seeing Him alive in the glorified flesh gave them the greatest of hopes. They had written off their lives with Jesus as a fading dream, but now they experienced the power of everlasting life, of death being conquered. There was also a new power, the Holy Spirit. He had come upon and was filling this group of believers, something Jesus promised would happen. They hadn't waited in vain.

Now that the Holy Spirit had come upon them, they would become witnesses (Acts 1:8). More than fifty times in the book of Acts, the Holy Spirit is mentioned. In fact, this book could just as easily be called the Acts of the Holy Spirit. He regenerates people, baptizes people, commissions people for missionary service, and directs the affairs of the church—a constant, abiding guide and help to the church. This was what Jesus meant in the upper room when He said, "It is to your advantage that I go away" (John 16:7).

Jesus didn't wait long to explain Himself: "If I do not go away, the Helper [the Holy Spirit] will not come to you; but if I depart, I will send Him to you" (John 16:7). In other words, God's work would no longer be centered on wherever Jesus was at a particular moment. No longer limited by a human body, God's work would happen wherever believers would happen to be—all across the world—because the Holy Spirit would now be living in each of them, enabling this moment to become a worldwide movement, multiplying worldwide, from Jerusalem to Rome and beyond.

The Holy Spirit not only enabled the apostles to speak the good news with clarity and power, He helped them endure persecution. The rulers who had fought for Jesus's execution now turned their attention to these bold followers of the Man they thought they had successfully killed. Now these guys were out in public again, going on about this Jesus of theirs being risen and stirring the people up. Worse yet, they had healed someone—a man "lame from his mother's womb" (Acts 3:2).

That led to the arrest of Peter and John, which Peter, filled with the Holy Spirit, took as an opportunity to preach the gospel again (Acts 4:8-13). When the Jewish authorities forbade them to speak the name of Jesus, Peter replied, "Whether it is right in the sight of God to listen to you more than to God, you judge. For we cannot but speak the things which we have seen and heard" (vv. 19-20).

God's momentum carried through in Peter's leadership. He continued to do the kind of work that Jesus had done in His earthly ministry—preaching, teaching, and healing—which, like his Lord, also got Peter and the apostles arrested. An angel broke them out of jail and told them, "Go, stand in the temple and speak to the people all the words of this life" (Acts 5:20)—*Go tell 'em about Jesus!* And sure enough, the apostles were right back at it, which led to one Pharisee, Gamaliel, saying to his colleagues, "Keep away from these men and let them alone; for if this plan or this work is of men, it will come to nothing; but if it is of God, you cannot overthrow it" (vv. 38-39).

The apostles dealt with an in-house situation, a group of widows who felt neglected at the daily distribution of food. This led them to make a decision to appoint deacons—qualified, dedicated servants—who could take on that work while the apostles devoted their attention to the specific work God had called them to, the study and teaching of God's Word (Acts 6:1-6). One of those deacons, a young man named Stephen, "a man full of faith and the Holy Spirit" (v. 5), became the church's first martyr.

Stephen was a powerful witness to the gospel, doing "great wonders and signs among the people" (v. 8). This got him in hot water with a group called the Synagogue of the Freedmen, Jews from other parts of the region who tried but couldn't put up an effective argument against Stephen's preaching. Like the Jewish leaders had done with Jesus, they took the low road, stirring up others to accuse Stephen of blasphemy (vv. 9-15). Stephen's witness continued even when he spoke to the high priest—in fact, it got stronger.

Going back to Abraham and continuing the story of the Messiah's history through the patriarchs, Moses, Joshua, David, and Solomon, Stephen built a bulletproof case against the Jewish leaders (Acts 7:1-53). He called them to repent. "When they heard these things they were cut to the heart, and they gnashed at him with their teeth. But he, being full of the Holy Spirit, gazed into heaven and saw the glory of God, and Jesus standing at the right hand of God" (vv. 54-55). They picked up stones and killed him, taking off their outer garments and laying them "at the feet of a young man named Saul" (v. 58).

The Gospel Witness to Judea and Samaria (Acts 8–9)

Despite Stephen's death—or more likely, as we'll see, because of it—the gospel began to spread outside of Jerusalem, into Judea and Samaria. One of the deacons of the church of Jerusalem, Philip, decided to go up to Samaria and take a crack at sharing the gospel with Israel's old enemies. Not only did it work, it turned out to be a huge awakening—so many people responded so powerfully that the church in Jerusalem sent two heavy-duty bigwigs, John and Peter, up to Samaria to see what was happening (Acts 8:4-17). Philip's journey also included a trip to Gaza and an encounter with a high-ranking official under the queen of Ethiopia, a eunuch to whom Philip explained the book of Isaiah and its fulfillment in Jesus Christ, which resulted in the man's conversion (vv. 26-29). So the gospel was spreading through Jerusalem, Judea, and Samaria, just as Jesus had instructed (Acts 1:8).

The Gospel Witness to the End of the Earth (Acts 10–28)

God's choice of agent to spread the gospel to the "end of the earth" was as unlikely a candidate as could be imagined. Saul of Tarsus was a Pharisee, who—unlike many of his colleagues who didn't want anything to do with this new sect of Christ-followers—went after the early church full-on. This zealous radical gave Stephen's stoning an official thumbs-up, and then "made havoc of the church, entering every house, and dragging off men and women, committing them to prison. Therefore those who were scattered went everywhere preaching the word" (Acts 8:3-4). That's how Philip ended up going to Samaria and Gaza. Saul sought to eliminate the church; instead, he ignited its growth.

Saul considered himself a superior Jew and instrument of divine judgment against this cult of Christ-followers. Saul hated Christianity, to the point where it wasn't enough for him to chase down the Christians in Jerusalem and drag them to prison. He got permission to take his oppression bandwagon on the road to Damascus (Acts 9:1-2), little imagining that the One he persecuted would be waiting for him along the way.

Jesus got a hold of Saul, humbling him by leaving him no way to rely on his personal accomplishments, strengths, or ambitions to get out of the situation. As He told Saul, "It is hard for you to kick against the goads" (Acts 9:5). A goad was a sharp stick used to drive a stubborn animal onward; Jesus was talking about the conviction Saul was feeling at that moment. Saul surrendered and asked the Lord what He wanted him to do next; Jesus sent him into the city to wait.

Saul of Tarsus got saved. He was taken to Damascus, where he just hung out, blinded by his encounter with Christ and praying for a few days. Once his sight was restored, he started spreading the gospel message around the city (Acts 9:20), blowing people's minds not only with his message but his conversion. Bringing his zeal to bear for the glory of Christ, Saul quickly got on the nerves of the Jewish leaders in Damascus. To avoid being killed, he had to escape by being lowered in a basket down the city wall (vv. 23-25).

When Saul came to Jerusalem, he became quite a hot potato. The disciples, naturally, didn't trust him. They had a hard time believing that Saul of Tarsus, of all people, could be converted to the cause. A believer named Barnabas vouched for him, though, and they reluctantly let Saul into the fold (Acts 9:26-28). He got into it with the Hellenists—Greek Jews who had also opposed the church—and they tried to kill him. Finally, the church shipped him back to his hometown of Tarsus, where he stayed for many, many years in relative obscurity and isolation, until he went to Antioch. Once Saul got going, there was no stopping him, and the world would come to know him by his Latin name, Paul.

A Witness of Faith in Christ Alone: Paul's First Mission (Acts 13:4–14:26)

As the gospel begin to spread beyond Judea and Samaria, the bulk of Luke's account covered Paul's missionary journeys. Barnabas went to Tarsus to find Paul, while persecution increased in Jerusalem. King Herod beheaded James, John's brother, and arrested Peter, who was promptly broken out of prison by an angel (Acts 12:1-11). In the meantime, Paul and Barnabas headed to Antioch on their first missionary journey. Antioch was the third largest city in the Roman Empire at that time, an urbanized, multicultural, multiethnic hub of politics, travel, and trade. Paul joined the staff of the church at Antioch, and it became home base for their three journeys. After a while, the Holy Spirit sent them out to spread the good news (Acts 13:2-3).

Paul and Barnabas traveled from Antioch down to Seleucia (still in Syria), then sailed south to Salamis on the island of Cyprus and northeast to Galatia (modern-day Turkey). From there, they preached the gospel across the eastern part of Asia Minor, going to Lystra, Derbe, Iconium, Perga, and Attalia. Finally, they "sailed to Antioch, where they had been commended to the grace of God for the work which they had completed" (Acts 14:26).

The church gathered for a report on their travels, the first missionary conference (v. 27). It was a good report of God's work, even though Paul remained a real live wire. Everywhere he went, he got into trouble—and that was just Paul. He was a big mouth for Jesus. He didn't care what people thought of him, didn't care if he offended them in pointing out their theological errors; he wanted to get the message out, and he got it out.

Paul was unstoppable. After preaching the gospel in Lystra, they stoned him. They dragged him out of the city, thinking he was dead and planning to bury him. He wasn't, but where we would say "Get me out of here!" and head elsewhere, Paul stood up, brushed himself off, and went back into the city to preach again (vv. 19-20).

The defining moment at the Jerusalem conference was the insistence that salvation came through faith in Christ alone, apart from keeping the Law of Moses (Acts 15:1-29). The first battle of legalism versus grace was waged here, and the outcome affirmed the true nature of the gospel. After Paul gave his missionary report, Peter came to Paul's defense by showing that the Scriptures predicted salvation wasn't just for the Jews, but the whole world.

A Witness in Open and Shut Doors: Paul's Second Mission (Acts 15:36–18:22)

After working for the church in Antioch for a while, Paul and Barnabas decided to go back along their previous missionary route to check on all the churches where they had preached. This second journey started off on a fractious note, with Paul and Barnabas arguing over John Mark's inclusion in their group (Acts 15:37-38). Barnabas, Mark's uncle, wanted him to come with them, but Paul argued against it, saying. "This guy already ditched us once the first time around," which happened back on their first journey (Acts 13:13). They had a falling out over it, and Paul ended up taking Silas with him to Syria and Cilicia, while Barnabas took Mark and headed out for Cyprus (Acts 15:39-41).

What happened next was pivotal. Paul tried to head northeast into western Asia, but he and his team (which included a young man, Timothy, whose mother was a Jewish believer and whose father was Greek) "were forbidden by the Holy Spirit to preach the word in Asia" (Acts 16:6). They went westward instead, ending up in Troas, where Paul received a vision of a man telling him to come to Macedonia and help the believers there (vv. 9-10). God was clearly shutting certain paths to them but opening others. So Paul and company sailed west from Troas, across the Aegean Sea, coming to the "foremost city of that part of Macedonia" (v. 12), Philippi.

While in Philippi, Paul cast "a spirit of divination" out of a slave girl (vv. 16-18), which made her masters—who had been making a pretty penny off her "talents"—angry and got him and Silas arrested, beaten, and jailed. "But at midnight Paul and Silas were praying and singing hymns to God, and the prisoners were listening to them. Suddenly there was a great earthquake, so that the foundations of the prison were shaken" (vv. 25-26). Paul and Silas stayed put and ended up preaching to their warden, who converted to Christ, along with his whole family, and released them.

When the warden told them they were free to go, however, Paul said, "I don't think so." He identified himself and Silas as Roman citizens who had been unjustly beaten and jailed, and told their new brother that the magistrates could "come themselves and get us out" (v. 37). The magistrates freaked out because they had broken their own laws and ended up begging Paul and Silas to leave without making a stink, which they did. Paul couldn't have known it at the time, but it was the first small step on the journey that would eventually take him to Rome, where he would stand in chains for the gospel at the center of the known world.

There was a long road yet to travel, though. Paul and Silas went on to Thessalonica (Acts 17:1-9)—where they ran into conflict with the local Jews, who chased them off. The local church snuck them out of town and took them to Berea (Acts 17:10-14), where they ran into many fair-minded, Scripture-searching Jews but were chased off once again by the Thessalonian haters. Paul then sailed for Athens, leaving Silas and Timothy behind in Berea.

There, Paul sent for his colleagues, but while he waited he got into a debate with the Greek philosophers at the Areopagus (Acts 17:15-34). Paul left on his own terms and went to Corinth, where he took on work as a tentmaker and stayed for a year and a half. Over time, "many of the Corinthians, hearing, believed and were baptized" (Acts 18:8), but many of the local Jews took issue with Paul. Eventually he headed back to Antioch, where he took some time to regroup before heading out again.

A Witness in Conversions and Conflict: Paul's Third Mission (Acts 18:23–21:17)

It wasn't long before Paul hit the road again, going out to check in on many of the places he had previously visited. He went through Galatia, visiting the various churches there, and then headed south a bit, staying in the port city of Ephesus for about three years (Acts 19:1-20). It was the longest Paul stayed with any one church.

Of course, wherever Paul went, two things happened: conversions and conflict. It might have been easier if, in every city he came to, Paul had gone straight to the magistrate and introduced himself: "My name is Paul. I am an apostle of the Lord Jesus Christ—whom I will tell you about in a moment—and I am wondering if you could just tell me where the city jail is. I'd like to know where I'll be spending the night at some point while I'm here."

In Ephesus, a riot broke out after Paul's preaching resulted in people abandoning their idolatry, which led to fewer sales for a local silversmith named Demetrius, who riled up a mob to seize a pair of Paul's traveling companions (vv. 24-29). Paul wanted to go in and talk to the mob, but his friends held him back, realizing that his presence would be fuel for an already rapidly burning fire (Acts 19:30-31). A city clerk calmed everything down and dispersed the people, and Paul decided it was time to head over to Greece (Acts 20:1).

Paul traveled through Greece and Macedonia for three months, but wanted to get back to Jerusalem in time for the Feast of Pentecost. First, however, he wanted to check in with the church leaders from Ephesus, so he asked them to meet him in Miletus, where he had a solemn message to share. "Now I go bound in spirit to Jerusalem, not knowing the things that will happen to me there, except that the Holy Spirit testifies in every city, saying that chains and tribulation await me" (vv. 22-23).

Paul's faith resonates in his words, his sense of God's will, and his desire to do it. "But none of these things move me; nor do I count my life dear to myself, so that I may finish my race with joy, and the ministry which I received from the Lord Jesus, to testify to the gospel of the grace of God" (v. 24). He had a bigger vision of what God could accomplish through such difficult circumstances. He would argue that being chained to guards in Rome allowed him to lead some of them to

Christ, the first sparks of a revival that eventually swept Caesar's own household (Philippians 1:12-14).

A Witness in Chains: Paul's Arrest and Journey to Rome (Acts 21:18–28:31)

When Paul arrived in Jerusalem, he was indeed arrested. People recognized him in the temple and trumped up false charges against him, dragging him outside and beating him until Roman guards showed up (Acts 21:26-36). At the soldiers' barracks, Paul shared his testimony before the Roman guard and the Jewish high council, who were so infuriated with his seeming betrayal of Judaism that they wanted to kill him. He managed to stave off a worse beating than he took by claiming his rights as a citizen of Rome (Acts 22:22-30).

Paul's testimony before the Sanhedrin (the Jewish supreme court) landed him in the middle of a conflict between the two ruling parties, the Pharisees and Sadducees, that nearly got him torn apart (Acts 23:1-10). At what must have been a low moment for Paul, wondering if he would ever get to Rome, God Himself delivered encouragement: "Be of good cheer, Paul; for as you have testified for Me in Jerusalem, so you must also bear witness at Rome" (v. 11). Paul's path to Rome involved getting him safely out of Jerusalem first. A band of forty men planned to ambush him on the way to a council meeting and kill him, but Paul informed the Romans, who arranged for a huge military escort to take him to Caesarea and the governor of Judea, Felix (vv. 12-33).

Paul's case was tied up in court for two years while he stayed incarcerated at Caesarea in Herod's Praetorium before being sent to Rome (v. 35). While there, he went through three trials—court appearances before two governors (Antonius Felix and Porcius Festus) and one king (Herod Agrippa II). Members of the Jewish Sanhedrin in Jerusalem came to the first trial, wanting to protect their reputation against a former member becoming a follower of Jesus (Acts 24). Felix let Paul have visitors, and Paul even spoke with him and his wife about faith in Christ, but Felix held back on ruling on Paul's case and was succeeded after two years by Porcius Festus. He left his office with Paul still in chains.

Festus put Paul on trial again, but because he wanted to "do the Jews a favor, answered Paul and said, 'Are you willing to go up to Jerusalem and there be judged before me concerning these things?'" (Acts 25:9). Paul had already played this game before and was ready to cut to the chase, so he told Festus he hadn't wronged the Jews or anyone else, and appealed to Caesar (vv. 10-11). Paul knew he wasn't going to get any justice from the Jewish council in Jerusalem. So he decided to play his last card—his Roman citizenship—and appeal to a higher power, Caesar himself in this case. In a way, he made Festus's job easy for him, and off to Caesar he went.

Traveling in the prison section of a cargo ship carrying grain to Rome from Egypt, Paul got exactly what he wanted. He had written to the Romans years earlier, telling them, "Now no longer having a place in these parts, and having a great desire these many years to come to you, whenever I journey to Spain, I shall come to you" (Romans 15:23-24). He was getting something his heart had long desired—an opportunity to do God's will in the heart of the empire. He didn't care that he was going as a prisoner, and as a bonus, he would be traveling on Rome's dime. Rome, in fact, would end up unwittingly sponsoring all the evangelism Paul would do from jail, all the letters he would write to the churches.

When Paul finally arrived in Rome, he testified to the local Jews, some of whom believed after hearing what he had to say (Acts 28:17-29). He lived for two years under house arrest, chained to one guard after another. Or rather, they were chained to Paul—he had a captive audience coming in shifts, drawing the guards out of their own lives and sharing about Jesus. "Then Paul dwelt two whole years in his own rented house, and received all who came to him, preaching the kingdom of God and teaching the things which concern the Lord Jesus Christ with all confidence, no one forbidding him" (vv. 30-31).

And that's where the book of Acts ends. It seems abrupt, but then it's not the end of the story, is it? There is more to come. Luke didn't tell us what happened to the hero of the story, the main agent, because it's not Paul. The Holy Spirit is the main character, remember? He wasn't done working then, and He isn't yet. Luke told the story of Jesus in a Gospel and the story of the early church—primarily Peter and Paul—here in Acts, but the Holy Spirit has continued to do His work, down through the centuries, to you and me. We are part of the story, an ongoing account of God's desire to redeem as many as will believe in His Son, a work that will continue until Jesus returns for His church.

> We are part of the story, an ongoing account of God's desire to redeem as many as will believe in His Son, a work that will continue until Jesus returns for His church.

ROMANS
FLIGHT PLAN

Facts

Author

The author of the book of Romans was the apostle Paul (Romans 1:1). Also named Saul, Paul was a Roman citizen from the city of Tarsus (which is in present-day south-central Turkey). He was a tentmaker as well as a religious leader—a Pharisee, trained under the famous first-century rabbi Gamaliel. After persecuting the early church, Paul had an experience with the living Christ on the road to Damascus (Acts 9) and became one of the most influential early followers of Jesus, going on to write about half the books and one-quarter of the content of the New Testament.

Date Written

Paul wrote Romans around the year AD 57, possibly while in the city of Corinth on his third missionary journey.

Landmarks

Romans marks the beginning of the third major section of the New Testament. The *Gospel* section of the New Testament gives the fourfold testimony to Jesus Christ. The *historical* book of Acts shows the first thirty years of church history. And now the *epistles* present the correspondence of church leaders to Christians in different parts of the Roman Empire.

Paul wrote this powerful letter to the church at Rome to prepare the way for a visit he hoped to make there. He presented the basic ideas of salvation to a church that had not previously received the teaching of an apostle, and he also explained the relationship between Jew and Gentile in God's overall plan of redemption. Many Jewish Christians in Rome were being rejected by the more numerous Gentile Christians because these Jewish believers, though saved, still felt constrained to observe dietary laws and sacred days.

So Paul laid out for them the simple, basic gospel—God's plan of salvation, how both Jew and Gentile can be made right with God. This is the theme of

Romans, stated broadly as the "righteousness of God" (Romans 1:16-17; 3:21-22) and branching off into the ideas of justification by faith, sanctification, security, freedom from guilt, and submission to authority.

Romans is the most systematic of Paul's epistles. It reads more like an elaborate theological essay than a letter, emphasizing Christian doctrines concerning sin, death, salvation, grace, faith, righteousness, justification, sanctification, redemption, resurrection, and glorification, among others. Paul made widespread use of Old Testament quotations in the book, sometimes using them to carry his argument. He also expressed a deep concern for Israel and its present status, its relationship to the Gentiles, and its final salvation. Paul presented just about every major Christian doctrine in Romans, which I'll divide into four sections: God's wrath, grace, plan, and will.

Itinerary

- The Wrath of God (Romans 1:18–3:20)
- The Grace of God (Romans 3:21–8:39)
- The Plan of God (Romans 9–11)
- The Will of God (Romans 12–15)
- Paul's Greetings and Blessings (Romans 16)

Gospel

Romans is Paul's gospel manifesto and serves as a logical follow-up to the book of Acts, since Acts traced the movement of the gospel from Jerusalem to Rome, the capital city of the world's dominant empire at the time. Rome's power, influence, and infrastructure (Roman roads ran at least 50,000 miles all over Europe and Asia Minor, for example[50]) allowed the good news of Jesus to eventually reach "the uttermost part of the earth" (Acts 1:8 KJV).

During his third missionary journey, Paul stayed in Corinth for about a year and a half, and it was probably from this city that he wrote to the Roman believers. His message was simple, defining the very essence of Christianity: God's righteousness came through Jesus Christ. He declared that this *righteousness* (mentioned sixty-six times in the book) could not come by obeying the Law of Moses (the word *law* appears seventy-eight times) but only through faith in Christ (*faith* is mentioned sixty-two times). The patchwork of just these three repeated words helps us to see the essence of the message of the book of Romans: *Righteousness* doesn't come from our ongoing work to keep the *law* but rather by *faith* in the finished work of Jesus Christ.

Paul painted a stark picture of the human condition: we're all born under God's wrath, slaves to sin. While the world loves to celebrate mankind's so-called righteousness—our sincerity of belief and supposed basic goodness—Paul said that we are in fact "all under sin" (Romans 3:9). He quoted numerous Old Testament passages (Psalms 14:1-3; 53:1-3; Ecclesiastes 7:20) to underscore his point: that "there is none righteous, no, not one; there is none who understands; there is none who seeks after God" (Romans 3:10-11). And this is why the gospel is such good news: We can never be good enough or do enough good deeds to gain salvation, but because Jesus Christ came and died on the cross for our sins, we can be made right with God simply through our faith in Him.

> ### It's the wretched and poor in spirit...who place their faith and trust in Jesus and will be saved.

In Romans, Paul emphasized this essential aspect of the gospel over and over again: It's the wretched and poor in spirit—those who realize they are sinners—who place their faith and trust in Jesus and will be saved.

History

Paul wrote his letter to the Romans during the first years of Emperor Nero's reign (AD 54–68). Rome, a large and prestigious capital city, had a sizeable mixture of ethnicities, cultures, and religions, and the church there was almost certainly made up of both Jews and Gentiles. Acts 19:21 tells us of Paul's plans to visit the city.

Nero, the sixth Roman emperor, is famous for supposedly orchestrating the burning of Rome in AD 64 (rumors abounded that he threw his own private concert while the city was in flames) and then blaming the Christians for it.[51] In the months following this bizarre event, the Roman historian Tacitus reported some of the first officially sanctioned persecution of the early church.[52] According to *Foxe's Book of Martyrs*, Nero came up with all kinds of cruel punishments, including many

> that the most infernal imagination could design. In particular, he
> had some sewed up in the skins of wild beasts, and then worried
> by dogs till they expired; and others dressed in shirts made stiff

with wax, fixed to axletrees, and set on fire in his gardens, in order to illuminate them. This persecution was general throughout the whole Roman empire; but it rather increased than diminished the spirit of Christianity. In the course of it, St. Paul and St. Peter were martyred.[53]

Nero's persecution of Christians was only the beginning; the Roman Empire continued to oppress and kill Christians over the next two-and-a-half centuries. As the pattern goes, however, the church not only survived, but thrived during this time. The emperor Constantine eventually established tolerance for Christianity in the Edict of Milan in AD 313,[54] opening the door for it to become the official state religion decades later under Theodosis I.[55]

Travel Tips

The book of Romans challenges us with its in-depth exploration of doctrine, or teachings about what it means to be saved and follow Jesus. Doctrine should transform the way you think, act, and speak in the world and with other believers, ultimately making you more like Jesus.

- The dividing line between a saint and an ain't is salvation by grace. If you're not saved by faith in Christ alone, then you ain't a saint. Then you're still subject to God's wrath. Some think that if you're really good and a group of people looks back on your life and sees that you performed thirty miracles, you get canonized and they add a little halo to your church directory photo. That's not what *saint* means. If you are a believer in Christ right now while you're still here on earth, in God's eyes you are a saint—set apart for Him because of what He has done for you.

- Christians need to be real with one another. We often feel the need to put on a show in front of other people, especially believers, projecting an image of ourselves as having it all together—great job, great marriage, great faith. But every single person struggles with sin, doubt, fear, and worry to some degree (Romans 7:15-25). Fellowship is so important because you need that honesty, accountability, and encouragement that only other believers can provide.

- Let understanding and grace govern your conduct with other believers. In Romans, Paul described the difference between a strong Christian and a weak one. Physical strength isn't the issue; demonstrating grace and moral but non-legalistic reasoning is. Paul's instructions for weak and strong center on this idea: "Let each of us please his neighbor for his good, leading to edification" (Romans 15:2). Enjoy your liberty in Christ, but don't flaunt it.

> **Fellowship is so important because you need that honesty, accountability, and encouragement that only other believers can provide.**

In Flight

The Wrath of God (Romans 1:18–3:20)

Paul saw the world clearly and simply. There were only two groups of people in the whole human race—saints and ain'ts! The *saints* were believers and the *ain'ts* were unbelievers. He further divided the unsaved into three camps: pagans, moralists, and religionists. He wrote about them all: pagans—people who have no faith at all in God; moralists—people who rely on just doing nice, good things; and religionists—those who are strict adherents to their faith, usually Jewish people who trusted in their own self-righteous keeping of all the various commandments.

Paul made it clear that none of them were sitting pretty in God's eyes: "The wrath of God is revealed from heaven against all ungodliness and unrighteousness of men, who suppress the truth in unrighteousness, because what may be known of God is manifest in them, for God has shown it to them" (Romans 1:18-19). That phrase should chill the blood of any person who doesn't know God. God doesn't hide from people; rather, people ignore Him and His truth—with terrifying, everlasting consequences. Life, death, and eternity are not to be trifled with; accordingly, Paul pulled no punches.

It was, and remains, an unpopular message. Typically, if people acknowledge God's existence, they prefer to think of Him only as a God of love—which He is. As Paul would later write, "God demonstrates His own love toward us, in that *while we were still sinners*, Christ died for us" (Romans 5:8, emphasis added). However, until you do something with the love that He offers in Christ, His posture toward you is one of wrath. And don't fall for the line that God has operated under two different personas, one of judgment and wrath in the Old Testament and love and grace in the New. Not so. God is the same throughout the whole Bible, always perfectly loving and perfectly just, and His attitude toward sin has never changed: wrath, "revealed from heaven against all ungodliness and unrighteousness of men" (Romans 1:18).

> **God is the same throughout the whole Bible, always perfectly loving and perfectly just.**

Here is God's final verdict as He looks at humanity: guilty. The law of Moses made it impossible to have excuses for sin, "that every mouth may be stopped, and all the world may become guilty before God" (Romans 3:19). It's a pretty dismal picture Paul painted, and he makes it clear that keeping the law isn't enough—first, because it's just not possible, and second, because the purpose of the law was to reveal our sin problem. "Therefore by the deeds of the law no flesh will be justified in His sight, for by the law is the knowledge of sin" (v. 20).

Humanity has no hope to save itself, and we can't do anything about it. There's no ray of light, no silver lining, and no exceptions. You are guilty. I am guilty. The Pope is guilty, Billy Graham is guilty, Mother Teresa is guilty. Your grandparents are guilty. That brand new infant just born into your home is guilty. No one can stand on their own merits before God. His wrath is righteous and just.

The Grace of God (Romans 3:21–8:39)

The very next verse begins "But now" (Romans 3:21). Those two simple words show us a major shift in the book, from wrath to grace, transitioning between despair and hope, sin and salvation. And, oh, is it welcome! "But now the righteousness of God apart from the law is revealed, being witnessed by the Law and the Prophets" (v. 21). There's the phrase that turned over and over in Martin Luther's mind as he pondered salvation: "the righteousness of God." It's tied directly to the only way we can ever be in right standing with God: "Even the righteousness of God, through faith in Jesus Christ, to all and on all who believe. For there is no difference; for all have sinned and fall short of the glory of God, being justified freely by His grace through the redemption that is in Christ Jesus" (vv. 22-24).

Justified is an essential biblical term, legal in origin; it refers to *a verdict* that has been rendered. In ancient times, the accused would stand before a judge in a courtroom to hear whether the verdict was *guilty* or *not guilty*—condemnation or justification. So when Paul wrote the phrase "being justified freely by His grace," he was saying that God makes a legal declaration that you as a believer are righteous because of Christ's blood. *Justified* means that God treats me, a sinner, *just-as-if-I'd* never sinned. Thinking of being justified in this way (*just-if-I'd*) will help you remember its basic meaning.

> ## Justified means that God treats me, a sinner, *just-as-if-I'd* never sinned.

Paul had just made it clear that every one of us falls short of God's standards (Romans 3:23), so the idea that God declares someone righteous once he or she trusts in Christ, and then treats them as if they actually *are* righteous, is staggering. How is God doing that? "Through the redemption that is in Christ Jesus" (v. 24). Whereas *justification* is a legal term, *redemption* comes straight from the slavery block. To redeem someone referred specifically to a prisoner or slave being transferred to a new owner.

Jesus redeemed fallen mankind, enslaved to sin, because "God set [Him] forth as a propitiation by His blood, through faith, to demonstrate His righteousness" (Romans 3:25). *Propitiation* means "appeasement" or "satisfaction." What Jesus did on the cross appeased God's wrath, satisfied the requirements of lifeblood as the penalty for sin. It was something only Jesus, in His perfection, could do for us.

To summarize, then, you've fallen short of the glory of God—the mark of perfection. Everyone has. But because you trust in Christ, God legally declares you righteous; all the purity and righteousness of Christ is now credited to your account. Jesus redeemed you, buying you back from the slave market of sin by His blood, which satisfied the penalty of God's wrath.

As redeemed believers in Christ, with His life in us, we've also been set free from the consequences of sin and are free to really live. "For the wages of sin is death, but the gift of God is eternal life in Christ Jesus our Lord" (Romans 6:23). So what about the law? What is our relationship to the Law of Moses, the Ten Commandments, the regulations of the old covenant?

Paul explained that relationship as he talked about his own personal struggle. "We know that the law is spiritual, but I am carnal, sold under sin. For what I am doing, I do not understand. For what I will to do, that I do not practice; but what I hate, that I do" (Romans 7:14-15).

Follow Paul's thinking: Here's the common struggle for all redeemed people— we understand that there is a better way to live, to think and speak and act, but we don't always do what we know we should. Those of us who have been raised with a set of religious laws feel the guilt of breaking those commandments. We know that the high standard of what is right isn't always kept. We fall, we fail, we flail! It's an ongoing battle between the spirit and the flesh. Paul captured the struggle in classic fashion: "O wretched man that I am! Who will deliver me from this body of death? I thank God—through Jesus Christ our Lord!" (vv. 24-25). That's a statement of both despair and delight, of guilt and grace.

Paul unpacked the answer to his anguished question and showed the liberation that comes from the indwelling of the Holy Spirit. "There is therefore now no condemnation to those who are in Christ Jesus, who do not walk according to the flesh, but according to the Spirit" (Romans 8:1). He then used questions to make poignant statements, asking, "Who shall separate us from the love of Christ? Shall tribulation, or distress, or persecution, or famine, or nakedness, or peril, or sword?" (v. 35). In other words, no event, no catastrophe, no failure, no force, no person, no heartache—in short, no circumstance whatsoever—can ever stop God from loving you and fulfilling His salvation plan in you.

God's grace is truly amazing, and Paul summed up its magnificence: "I am persuaded that neither death nor life, nor angels nor principalities nor powers, nor things present nor things to come, nor height nor depth, nor any other created thing, shall be able to separate us from the love of God which is in Christ Jesus our Lord" (vv. 38-39).

Paul also presented a classic picture of God's sovereign care: "We know that all things work together for good to those who love God, to those who are the called according to His purpose" (v. 28). Such a soft pillow for weary hearts! This promise sets up His whole plan: "For whom He foreknew, He also predestined to be conformed to the image of His Son, that He [Jesus] might be the firstborn among many brethren. Moreover whom He predestined, these He also called; whom He called, these He also justified; and whom He justified, these He also glorified" (vv. 29-30).

The Plan of God (Romans 9–11)

Having established the breadth and depth of God's grace, Paul responded to some issues that had arisen among the Gentile believers concerning their Jewish neighbors. He addressed some key questions: Why did the Jews reject Jesus as their Messiah? And if God has a plan for them, how does their unbelief and rejection fit into that plan? These were questions that Paul had no doubt wrestled with himself, and his passionate heart for his people is interlaced throughout these statements. "Brethren, my heart's desire and prayer to God for Israel is that they may be saved" (Romans 10:1). The once zealously hardened rabbi who had gone to arrest messianic Jews in Damascus (Acts 9) now revealed his brokenhearted plea for Israel's salvation.

In confirming that Israel, God's elect, had rejected the gospel, Paul made it clear that God's word had not failed, nor had His promises. "But it is not that the word of God has taken no effect. For they are not all Israel who are of Israel" (Romans 9:6). Some Jews had, indeed, converted to the faith—just as Paul himself had—and that fact, coupled with God's promises for Israel in the future, were a great comfort to him. Even so, Paul used Old Testament Scriptures to underscore the point that the gospel message was for both Jews and Gentiles. Israel stumbled because the Jews didn't seek righteousness by faith but by works (vv. 30-33). They said they were right with God just because they worked hard to keep a set of rules. But that was never God's plan.

God's plan and promise are for *anyone* who would accept Jesus as Lord and Savior—Jew or non-Jew. "For there is no distinction between Jew and Greek, for the same Lord over all is rich to all who call upon Him. For 'whoever calls upon the name of the LORD shall be saved'" (Romans 10:12-13, quoting Joel 2:32). And even though Israel had now nationally rejected Jesus as their Messiah, that rejection didn't eliminate them from God's future blessings or from the promises He had already made to them. Though their failure to recognize their Messiah fell squarely on their own hardheartedness (vv. 19-21), their obstinacy wouldn't prevent God from carrying out His plan to include Israel in the future.

As a result, God temporarily set Israel aside, but this wasn't final; there will be a reinstatement. "God has not cast away His people whom He foreknew...At this present time there is a remnant according to the election of grace" (Romans 11:2, 5). In the meantime, however, Israel's rejection meant salvation for the whole world. Israel is the root of faith and salvation for the Gentiles, and any who are saved should remember that they are branches that God has graciously grafted onto the tree He first planted (vv. 15-22). Just as a felled tree still has some life in the root system, God's plan for the Jewish nation will one day bud, grow, and bear fruit again.

Israel, however, had a problem. Many of the Jewish people believed that they were the chosen of God, the elect, and that salvation was simply a matter of birthright. They thought being born a Jew was enough to receive God's kingdom. They didn't understand the distinction God had tried to make through so many prophets over so many years: He wants a contrite heart, not a conceited performance.

Paul sought to correct their misunderstanding. "For I bear them [Israel] witness that they have a zeal for God, but not according to knowledge" (Romans 10:2). He wanted Israel to be saved but made it clear that just because someone lived in Israel or was Jewish didn't mean he was saved. Each Jew needed the same Christ that every believer had received. "For they being ignorant of God's righteousness, and seeking to establish their own righteousness, have not submitted to the righteousness of God. For Christ is the end of the law for righteousness to everyone who believes" (vv. 3-4).

> ## God doesn't love you because of who you are but because of who He is.

Every time I go to Israel and see the Orthodox Jews fervently praying at the Western Wall, I think of those verses. Man is incurably addicted to working for his own salvation. For whatever reason, we struggle to say to God, "I am not good enough; I'm a failure, but I accept Your gift." We're like kids wanting to make their parents proud—*I am going to be good; I am going to earn their approval; I am going to pull up my bootstraps and make it happen*. That's a mark of responsibility with your human parents, but it just doesn't work that way with God. He doesn't love you because of who you are but because of who He is.

Often, though, our addiction to self-sufficiency and self-righteousness begins with ignorance. Like Paul said, we have zeal but not knowledge. We want to do what's right but we don't have a correct understanding of what God has said in His Word. The Jews didn't have a correct understanding of the Torah, of the revealed will of God in the Scriptures, and it caused them to reject Jesus as the Messiah.

Over and over again, Paul quoted the Old Testament to make his points, doing so more often in Romans than in all the rest of his letters. It was important for his audience to grasp the bigger picture—for the Jews to see how the Law and the Prophets pointed toward a Messiah for the entire world, and for the non-Jews to see that God's plan still included Israel nationally.

Paul acknowledged that it was a challenging message for both parties, but critical for both to understand and embrace. "I do not desire, brethren, that you should be ignorant of this mystery, lest you should be wise in your own opinion, that blindness in part has happened to Israel until the fullness of the Gentiles has come in" (Romans 11:25). In other words, some Jews will have hard hearts until all the Gentiles who will be coming to Christ over the centuries have done so—whatever that number may be. God alone knows it, but when mankind reaches that point, when that final Gentile individual converts, God will be done with the church age—the era of drawing the nations into the body of Christ through the work of the Holy Spirit, including the outreach of its members through missions and evangelism.

God's historical calendar will then turn from that dispensation—that manner of dealing with people—and turn back to the Jewish nation, restoring them during a period of time known as Daniel's seventieth week (Daniel 9). That's the tribulation period. Just before it begins, the church age will end with the removal of the church from the earth—known as the rapture (1 Thessalonians 4:16-17)—and the tribulation will begin, including a restoration process in which God will gather

144,000 Jews, 12,000 from each tribe, to be His witnesses on earth (see **Revelation: Parenthesis 1** on page 621). Until then, only God knows the number and time. The next person you see, or even you yourself, could be the last non-Jewish person saved.

At that point, and because God keeps all His promises, He will resume His program with the Jewish people. "For the gifts and the calling of God are irrevocable" (Romans 11:29). God won't ever take back His promise to bless Israel, along with the gifts of prophets, Scripture, promises, and the Messiah. His plan is the result of His will—to have His people, whether Jew or Gentile, live remarkable, redeemed lives.

The Will of God (Romans 12–15)

In the homestretch of Romans, Paul got down to the nitty gritty of living in light of all the truth he just spent eleven chapters establishing. That's why he began by saying, "I beseech you *therefore*..." (Romans 12:1, emphasis added). This is Paul's style. When you read his epistles, you'll notice that, whether the letter is long or short, he begins by laying a foundation, giving you concrete, doctrinal truth, and then shifting to the application of that truth—*therefore*, based on what you know, here's how you should live.

Paul begged his readers in Romans to, "by the mercies of God" (v. 1), apply to their lives all he had just covered: the knowledge that mankind is under God's wrath and judgment, that overflowing grace came to cancel out wrath, and that God has a plan for everyone—Jew or Gentile—based on faith in the grace that Jesus Christ purchased on the cross. In light of all that, Paul pleaded for people to combine doctrine and deeds, promises and practice: "Present your bodies a living sacrifice, holy, acceptable to God, which is your reasonable service. And do not be conformed to this world, but be *transformed* by the renewing of your mind, that you may prove what is that good and acceptable and perfect will of God" (vv. 1-2, emphasis added).

"Transformed" comes from the Greek word where we get *metamorphosis*, a process of physical change, like when a caterpillar transforms into a butterfly. It's a total change, wrought over time. Paul meant that your character changes from cherishing what the world values most to honoring what matters most to Jesus. As a Christian, you are following one of two value systems—the world's, or Christ's. The two are set against each other, but you are at all times being molded by one or the other. You are either valuing what the world values and adhering to its standards, its ways of thinking, or you are being sanctified, made more and more into the image of God in Christ. As British translator J.B. Phillips put Romans 12:2, "Don't let the world around you squeeze you into its own mould, but let God re-mould your minds from within."

You are either valuing what the world values... or you are being sanctified.

Paul's contention was that you become more like Jesus in two ways: generally and specifically. Generally, you present yourself to God: "Here I am, God; do whatever You want with me. I am Yours. You've got some great plans ahead for me and I don't want to miss any of them." Then, as you do that, He transforms your thinking from the world's perception to His wonderful perspective. Doing that will equip you to do two things: present yourself to the world as a representative of God and a witness to them, and present yourself to the body of Christ to serve the church.

Romans 13 covers the first part of presenting your renewed self to the world. Our relationship to society and the secular government is in view here, as we are called to submit to governing authorities and its laws. We do so because God has established them as rulers. In Romans 14 and 15, Paul dealt with the second part of presenting our renewed self to the church, the body of Christ. He identified two groups of Christians. One group he called "weak in the faith" (Romans 14:1), and the other, those "who are strong" (Romans 15:1). The weak ones are the legalists, who have strong moral convictions about the details of living out their faith—watch what you eat and what days you worship on—but an incomplete understanding of grace. Paul called these things "the scruples of the weak" (v. 1). Some folks in church are like this—it's all about the dos and don'ts, the rules and regulations.

Paul's exhortation to the strong was to bear with the weak, "and not to please ourselves. Let each of us please his neighbor for his good, leading to edification" (Romans 15:1-2). By strong, Paul meant those believers who have a broader understanding of Scripture and Christian liberty. Our liberty must never deliberately violate others' sensitivity. The convictions of the weak may be right or they may be wrong, but the stronger Christian shouldn't flaunt his or her understanding so that their weaker brother or sister suffers in walking with God. Sometimes the strong need to correct or admonish, but other times, they just need to love the weak. "Therefore let us not judge one another anymore, but rather resolve this, not to put a stumbling block or a cause to fall in our brother's way" (Romans 14:13).

Certain things are essential to the faith, but others are not. Paul understood the difference and encouraged stronger believers not to be judgmental about nonessential issues. If you agree with a brother or sister that Jesus is Lord, that He is the Son of God who came to die for our sins, rose from the dead, and will come again, it matters a lot less that they think all Christians should be vegetarians or worship on Saturdays or listen only to certain kinds of music.

Paul would say, "You know those things don't matter to Christ, but what does matter is that you don't scarf a cheeseburger in front of your vegetarian friend, or crank up the radio just to show your liberty." God's will is that we serve one another and build each other up: "Therefore receive one another, just as Christ also received us, to the glory of God" (Romans 15:7).

Paul's Greetings and Blessings (Romans 16)

Romans wraps up with an extensive list of names. At first glance, it might seem boring—maybe because your name isn't on the list. If it were, you'd be excited—*Hey, my name's in the Bible!* Paul included twenty-nine names in Romans 16, sending greetings and encouragement to people he hadn't met but knew about from others. Some were Jews, and others Gentiles; some were nobility, and others slaves. Paul greeted men and women unified by one thing: Jesus Christ. Because of Paul's ministry, prisoners were coming to Christ, and some of them were in Caesar's household. His attitude behind bars gave him an opening among the Romans. Paul was not just a soul-winner but a team-builder.

It's also noteworthy that nine of the names Paul listed belonged to women. He greeted them as sisters in Christ, co-laborers and fellow saints—all of which flies in the face of the bad rap Paul has gotten over the years, particularly from feminists, as a chauvinist. How many other ancient documents mention nine women by name and praise them for their hard work and importance to the ministry? None. There wasn't a sexist bone in Paul's body, simply because there is no room for it in the body of Christ.

Your name may not be written in one of Paul's letters, but I'll tell you where it is or can be written: the Lamb's Book of Life (Revelation 21:27). If you have received Jesus Christ as your Lord and Savior, as Sin-bearer and Substitute, your name is in His book as someone who belongs to Him, who has received His free gift of salvation and the eternal life that comes with it. And if your name isn't written in the Lamb's Book of Life, it can be.

> If you have received Jesus Christ as your Lord and Savior...your name is in His book as someone who belongs to Him.

1 CORINTHIANS
FLIGHT PLAN

Facts

Author

The apostle Paul authored the book of 1 Corinthians (1 Corinthians 1:1-2). Paul was a Jew from the esteemed tribe of Benjamin and a Pharisee who persecuted the early church before he converted to Christianity.

Date Written

Paul wrote 1 Corinthians from the city of Ephesus during his third missionary journey. He ministered in the city for more than two years (Acts 19) and most likely composed the letter around AD 55–56.

Landmarks

Much of what Paul covered in 1 Corinthians regarded Jesus's role as head of the church, the result of what Jesus did on the cross (Matthew 16:18-21). So much of what the Corinthian church was doing defied the headship of Christ, choosing worldly wisdom and ways over godly gratitude and grace. Where Jesus championed unity among His people, they broke off into factions, looking to lift themselves above other believers instead of following Jesus's example and lowering themselves to serve everyone. They were saved but selfish.

The results of operating in their own strength revealed themselves in sexual impurity and a lack of doctrinal clarity, particularly about Jesus's resurrection, which is what sets Christianity apart from other religions and Jesus apart from other religious leaders. Paul explored its importance in depth (1 Corinthians 15), and the kind of love it enables and promotes (1 Corinthians 13).

Jesus's resurrection is what sets Christianity apart from other religions.

On his second missionary journey, Paul came to Corinth—a city known for its depravity—and stayed for a year and a half, working as a tentmaker during the week and preaching in the temple on the Sabbath. While he was there, God told him, "Do not be afraid, but speak, and do not keep silent; for I am with you, and no one will attack you to hurt you; for I have many people in this city" (Acts 18:9-10). So Paul ministered boldly to a church torn by divisions, sexual immorality, divorce, and a host of doctrinal issues.

It's understandable that Paul was compelled to write so strongly to a church that had all but completely fallen into the dissolution its city encouraged. Through God's grace, Paul would later be able to rejoice over the church's repentance and acceptance of his God-given authority. First, though, he addressed in this letter a series of practical problems in the Corinthian church.

Itinerary

- Congregational Disunity (1 Corinthians 1)
- Spiritual Immaturity (1 Corinthians 2–4)
- Sexual Impurity (1 Corinthians 5–6)
- Marital Infidelity (1 Corinthians 7)
- Personal Liberty (1 Corinthians 8–10)
- Imbalanced Community (1 Corinthians 11–14)
- Doctrinal Perplexity (1 Corinthians 15–16)

Gospel

Most noteworthy in 1 Corinthians is the clear presentation of the gospel in its basic form in chapter 15. When reduced to its essence, the gospel is an event in history at a certain time, in a certain place, by a certain Person: "Christ died for our sins...He was buried...and...He rose again" (1 Corinthians 15:3-4). Some of these verses may've been used by ancient believers at the time of their baptism as a sort of confession of faith. In abbreviated form, Paul focused on the need for Christ's death, burial, and resurrection, giving us the very heart of the gospel itself.

The power of resurrected life in Christ fuels every objective we can have as believers, enabling us to love the way God loves us, with both righteousness and compassion for everyone we meet. Jesus died to make you right with God, and His resurrection makes it possible for you to love like God. Paul made it clear that such love must shine through in everything from marriage to taking communion to giving in support of God's work to loving your brothers and sisters in Christ.

The power of resurrected life in Christ fuels every objective we can have as believers.

History

The city of Corinth was a commercial crossroads for the Roman Empire. It became a melting pot of devotees to various pagan cults that was filled with a whole slew of nationalities and thousands of slaves. It was marked by a cultural and moral depravity neither surprising nor unusual in such a large seaport. Greek playwrights coined a phrase, *korinthiazesthai*, "to act like a Corinthian," which described a character who was either a drunk, a prostitute, a pimp, or some combo of the three.[56] Spread throughout the city, pagan temples encouraged widespread licentiousness. At one time, the temple of Aphrodite was reported to have 1000 temple prostitutes.[57] And those cultural corruptions seeped into the church at Corinth.

The name *Corinth* means "ornament,"[58] which was more an indication of its commercial value than its physical beauty. Corinth, located on the isthmus connecting the Peloponnesian peninsula to mainland Greece, was a natural center of trade and point of exposure to religions and ideas from around the world. A couple of centuries before Paul's time, in 146 BC, Corinth was destroyed by the Roman general Lucius Mummius.[59] In 44 BC, Julius Caesar rebuilt the city and quickly reestablished its importance as a trade center for the empire.[60] Paul helped establish the church of Corinth during his second missionary trip (Acts 15–18), sometime around AD 50.

Travel Tips

The church in Corinth had a whole score of problems Paul addressed at length in this letter. But we can take encouragement from this, knowing that the church today is not all that different from the New Testament church. It was filled with imperfect people—former sinners facing their own issues and challenges—all learning how to walk with Jesus day by day.

- Unity should be our goal as Christians. We might not agree on the nonessential issues of doctrine like what style of worship to use during services, but we should be like-minded when it comes to the core teachings of Scripture, especially regarding Jesus. God uses common men and women to spread an uncommon message: the good news of Jesus Christ. That end goal should never fail to bring us together.

- What's worse: doing wrong, or being wronged? When someone wrongs you, is your first impulse to forgive and let it go? Probably not—that's not natural. But as an act of your will and in compliance and obedience to Jesus (Matthew 5:39), it is supernaturally possible. Restoration of relationship should always be your goal, because it's God's goal.

- The church should not mirror the world. Paul reminded us that we're no longer to live in sin but instead live differently from the world around us (1 Corinthians 6:11). On one hand, we as the church need to take God's commands seriously, not allowing sin to flourish in our midst. On the other hand, we also need to embrace God's grace alongside His truth, love those who have fallen into sin, and do what we can to restore them to a right relationship with God and His church, being mindful that God loved us and bought us for Himself while we were still sinners (Romans 5:8).

- Navigate life's gray areas biblically. As Paul said, "All things are lawful for me, but not all things are helpful; all things are lawful for me, but not all things edify" (1 Corinthians 10:23). Consider two limitations: utility and charity. First, is what you're considering going to help you achieve your ultimate goal of representing Christ, becoming more like Him, sharing about Him? Second, if you do it, will others be hurt? Don't put your freedom ahead of someone else's walk.

Navigate life's gray areas biblically.

In Flight

Congregational Disunity (1 Corinthians 1)

After a year and a half in Corinth, Paul headed for Ephesus. From there, he wrote to the Corinthian church, and the first issue he addressed was disunity in their congregation. People were siding with different teachers that had come and gone from that assembly—he mentioned himself, Apollos, Cephas (Peter), and Jesus.

High on Jesus's list of priorities was praying for the unity of His future church (John 17:20-23). Because of that, Paul pleaded with the Corinthians "that there be no divisions among you, but that you be perfectly joined together in the same mind and in the same judgment" (1 Corinthians 1:10). One of the families had reported to him that these factions were causing division, threatening to break up a church that Corinth needed desperately. The problem wasn't with the leaders mentioned, but with the people who were choosing to rally behind a particular one, in effect creating an elite clique. It's human nature to try to make the group you're a part of the best, but that's not what Jesus or His church are about.

If it seems like your church isn't made up of the best and brightest—the most educated, financially successful, good-looking people—remember God's plan: "You see your calling, brethren, that not many wise according to the flesh, not many mighty, not many noble, are called. But God has chosen the foolish things of the world to put to shame the wise, and God has chosen the weak things of the world to put to shame the things which are mighty" (1 Corinthians 1:26-27).

I've long considered these to be my "life verses" because of God's great condescension to choose and use weak, insecure, and flawed people. God chooses to use those who are humbly committed to His glory. The world doesn't often think much of the people God chooses, which makes God's work all the more winsome and wonderful. This truth will also keep us from getting a big head, "that no flesh should glory in His presence" (v. 29). We are common people carrying an uncommon message.

We are common people carrying an uncommon message.

Look at the twelve apostles—in the world's eyes, they were just a gang of Galilean hicks—fishermen, a tax collector, a zealot, and other outcasts and nobodies. But Jesus loved them all, and He chose them even after a night of prayerful consideration seeking the Father's will. And that was Paul's point: The church is made up of simple vessels desiring to be used by God. His choice to use such weak, imperfect agents is a mystery, but the work of worshipping, equipping, and evangelizing gets done in such a way that only God gets the glory. If it's done any other way, it might look slicker or more efficient, but the work would be getting done in our strength and skill, and we would not learn to trust God as we should. The result would be empty, man-made, immature religion instead of God's amazing movement.

Spiritual Immaturity (1 Corinthians 2–4)

Paul then tackled the issue of stunted spiritual growth—both the cause and the effect of disunity. It's like this: When I was baby, my parents were stoked when I said my first words and took my first steps. But if I had still been stumbling around and saying, "Mama, Dada" at fifteen, it wouldn't have been so cute.

Paul, as a pastor, loved to see people respond to the gospel and come to Christ, but he wanted them to grow as believers, and when he didn't see that growth, it broke his heart. Many Corinthian believers failed to recognize the difference between God's inerrant wisdom and the world's passing and fickle understanding. Paul reminded them to listen to what their teachers had taught them: "We speak wisdom among those who are mature, yet not the wisdom of this age, nor of the rulers of this age, who are coming to nothing...These things we also speak, not in words which man's wisdom teaches but which the Holy Spirit teaches" (1 Corinthians 2:6, 13).

In order to mature, they had to focus on spiritual understanding, "the hidden wisdom which God ordained before the ages for our glory" (v. 7)—the knowledge of Jesus Christ, His atoning work on the cross, and the indwelling of the Holy Spirit in all who receive Christ. Paul framed the issue as three types of people: the *natural*, the *supernatural*, and the *unnatural*.

The *natural* man is simply a man as he is by nature—the unbeliever, for whom the things of God are "foolishness" (v. 14). He's governed by the appetites and fears of his fleshly nature, and because of that can't appreciate God any more than a blind man can a sunset. And even if he wanted to understand God, he couldn't, because the things of God "are spiritually discerned" (v. 14).

The *supernatural* man is "spiritual [and] judges all things, yet he himself is rightly judged by no one" (1 Corinthians 2:15). Because of the Holy Spirit in him as a believer in Christ, he inclines toward spiritual things: loving God and God's truth, cherishing what matters to God—loving others, Bible study, fellowship, sacrificial service, worship, and prayer. Once you shift from the natural to the supernatural, you lose your taste for natural things; their hold on you becomes habitual rather than essential. Because of your redeemed nature, God can help you break old habits and ways of thinking and behaving. You shift into that "Amazing Grace," blind-but-now-I-see mode of living, marked by grace and gratitude.

The *unnatural* man is caught in the middle, saved by God's grace but struggling with unsaved tendencies. The Corinthians were stuck in transition, going back and forth between the natural and supernatural, the carnal and the spiritual, and if that isn't addressed, the flesh will win out. They had enough of the Spirit to be saved but enough of the world to be miserable. If a wall divides the kingdoms of God and the world, a fence-sitter is in the worst possible position. Though they'll make it to heaven, they won't enjoy the abundant life that Jesus promised. Many Corinthian believers had become unnatural—neither fish nor fowl. Paul described them as "carnal" Christians (1 Corinthians 3:1), driven by the appetites of their flesh.

Paul addressed their stunted growth, saying, "I fed you with milk and not solid food; for until now you were not able to receive it, and even now you are still not able" (v. 2). He taught them simple, basic doctrines, but they couldn't stomach the greater, deeper, more tension-filled truths of God's Word. Being born again is just the start of the Christian life. The Corinthians weren't growing, and Paul saw the proof: "Where there are envy, strife, and divisions among you, are you not carnal and behaving like mere men?" (v. 3). Even worse, Paul noted, some of them had gotten "puffed up" (1 Corinthians 4:18), thinking they were able to have it both their way and God's way. That unnatural attitude carried over into their most important relationships and behaviors.

Sexual Impurity (1 Corinthians 5–6)

Corinth was the Las Vegas of the ancient world, a sexually permissive and debauched city, and some Christians there even thought that what happened in Corinth stayed in Corinth. Paul told them otherwise: "It is actually reported that there is sexual immorality among you, and such sexual immorality as is not even named among the Gentiles—that a man has his father's wife!" (1 Corinthians 5:1). Apparently there was a case of a certain kind of incest in the church, a man cohabiting with his stepmother, having a relationship with her.

Paul said even the Romans weren't doing that sort of thing—it was morally revolting to them.[61] But not only were the Corinthians aware of it, some were allowing it as a sign of their broad-mindedness. When tolerance becomes the highest value, even above truth, sin gets a strong foothold among God's people. "And you are puffed up," Paul said, "and have not rather mourned, that he who has done this deed might be taken away from among you" (v. 2). "Puffed up" describes a runaway ego, but it also suggests a metaphor Jesus used to describe sin's contaminating effect: leaven (Luke 12:1-3). Leaven is basically yeast; it causes bread dough to rise, and it only takes a little to affect an entire loaf.

The Corinthians were impressed with their own tolerance of their brother's sin. But Paul called them out: "Your glorying is not good. Do you not know that a little leaven leavens the whole lump?" (1 Corinthians 5:6). They weren't showing good judgment in their overly tolerant treatment of sin, which left them in a bad spot to be used by God in any capacity requiring discernment and judgment.[62] They were suing other believers in secular courts (1 Corinthians 6:1-2), but they should have been handling conflicts in a godly manner within the church.

That leaven—that lack of good judgment—had permeated their sexual conduct too. Paul instructed them to take a zero-tolerance policy: "Flee sexual immorality. Every sin that a man does is outside the body, but he who commits sexual immorality sins against his own body" (v. 18). "Sexual immorality" is one word in the Greek text: *porneia*. Not only is it the root word of *pornography*, it's a warning that any sexual conduct outside of God's stated biblical boundaries—sex outside of marriage, cohabitation, emotional and physical affairs, homosexuality—is outside of His will and subject to judgment. The world says, "That's so old-fashioned; relax," but Paul, in the face of sexual sin that might be shocking even by today's standards, said, "Run from it."

Sexual impurity involves the theft of a level of intimacy that's reserved by God for a committed marriage. Paul wanted these believers' lives to be fulfilling, and so he gave sound counsel—stay pure, fight for purity, and protect yourself, your relationships, and the church.

Marital Infidelity (1 Corinthians 7)

As part of his instructions about sexual impurity, Paul addressed both single and married believers in a long, complicated set of directives, set for the specific context they lived in. He was happy with his singleness because it freed him up to focus entirely on his ministry, and he offered his take on the matter: "I say to the unmarried and to the widows: It is good for them if they remain even as I am; but if they cannot exercise self-control, let them marry. For it is better to marry than to burn with passion" (1 Corinthians 7:7-8). In other words, it's better to get married than to let lust destroy your relationship with God, your witness, and your ministry.

Marriage is a commitment that curtails individual freedoms. To do it well requires levels of submission to God and each other that a single person doesn't have to consider. And in a time when the Roman government was killing Christians left and right, the idea of staying single had a unique appeal: If you had to run for your life or stand and be jailed or executed, it would be better not to have to worry about a spouse's welfare. So Paul said, "If you can stay single like me, great. But if not, better to get married than to let lust incinerate your walk."

Personal Liberty (1 Corinthians 8–10)

Personal liberty was Paul's next topic. Sometimes the solution to an issue is not plainly black or white. There are certain gray areas where we have to draw from black-and-white principles and bring them to bear in the fuzzy situation so we know what we're supposed to do. We have freedom in Christ and we live under His grace; our justification in Him means we're not under human laws or regulations in a bottom-line way anymore. The Old Testament paradigm had shifted, its morality fulfilled by a different motivation. Rather than strict obedience to the law, Christians are to consider God's heart to bless others.

When the pagan temples around Corinth were finished using the meat offered up for sacrificial offerings, they would sell it. Christians wondered: Should they buy this meat? Paul said, "An idol is nothing in the world" (1 Corinthians 8:4)—in other words, idols aren't real, so a mature Christian has freedom to eat the meat, knowing that there is no other God. Meat is just meat. But for some believers, the idea of eating that meat was offensive; for various reasons, in their minds, it remained a violation of God's Old Testament law and was to be avoided.

Paul's primary concern wasn't the meat, but the way some believers behaved. They were eating the meat in front of brothers and sisters who felt it was wrong, flaunting their liberty to the offense of other believers. "Beware," Paul said, "lest somehow this liberty of yours become a stumbling block to those who are weak" (v. 9). A greater law of love was at stake. Paul asked, "Because of your knowledge shall the weak brother perish, for whom Christ died?" (v. 11). Better to go vegetarian than eat meat that offends your Christian brother.

Our world and culture today are loaded with gray areas—things that the Bible doesn't address explicitly, or that grace has fulfilled with regard to the law's requirements so that we don't have to obey them anymore. But as you consider how you let that culture into your life—movies, books, music, websites, fashion, drinking, smoking, social media, and so on—first consider Christ's overarching commandment: to love God with all you are and to love your neighbor. Jesus told us to love each other in the church especially well because it creates a strong witness to the outside world (John 13:34-35). Biblical principles should provide the basis of your behavior, but in areas of nonessential doctrine, let love guide you through the gray areas. "Whatever you eat or drink, or whatever you do, do all to the glory of God" (1 Corinthians 10:31).

Biblical principles should provide the basis of your behavior, but in areas of nonessential doctrine, let love guide you through the gray areas.

Imbalanced Community (1 Corinthians 11–14)

When it came to appropriate worship, however, Paul didn't see gray areas in the Corinthians' shortcomings. They were misbehaving in preparation for taking communion, one of the two sacraments Jesus told the church to observe. The Corinthians would have a get-together they called a love feast before they shared the Lord's Supper—what we'd call a potluck. But they treated it like an opportunity to pig out and get drunk and carry those attitudes into sharing communion. The result was that some members didn't get the same portions and were "not feeling the love" because the food had run out.

Paul wasn't having it. "What! Do you not have houses to eat and drink in? Or do you despise the church of God and shame those who have nothing? What shall I say to you? Shall I praise you in this? I do not praise you" (1 Corinthians 11:22). He rebuked them, reminding them of what Jesus had meant when He broke the bread and drank the wine and warning them to take a good, hard look at themselves before partaking of those elements. "For he who eats and drinks in an unworthy manner, eats and drinks judgment to himself" (v. 29). Paul told them to eat their meals at home, and then come together focused on one another and Jesus.

The Corinthians also needed clarification about the proper use of spiritual gifts in the public assembly. Paul discussed the diversity of spiritual gifts and ministries in the body of Christ, explaining how they are governed by the Holy Spirit and meant to build up the body, not set individuals apart as special or talented. "The manifestation of the Spirit is given to each one for the profit of all" (1 Corinthians 12:7). Spiritual gifts are not supposed to be the focus of worship, nor are they to be ignored or abused. There is a wonderful range of gifts and an impressive variety of people to manifest them for God's glory and the church's benefit. Paul laid out the guidelines for gifts like prophecy, which is for believers, and speaking in tongues, which is for unbelievers and requires an interpreter (1 Corinthians 14:22-25). "Let all things," Paul said, "be done decently and in order" (v. 40). Spiritual gifts aren't to be treated as toys to play with, but rather as tools used to build.

Paul used the metaphor of the church as a body, with Christ as its head, to underscore this point. Just as a human body needs all its parts to function optimally, the church needs each member to play his or her part. God appoints people to play different roles—apostles, prophets, pastors, teachers, and so on—but never intended each person to be all of those things. And yet we should all be pulling for each other, not seeking the roles that we think are most important. "If one member suffers, all the members suffer with it; or if one member is honored, all the members rejoice with it" (1 Corinthians 12:26). Above all, the balance of roles and gifts was, and is, to be dictated by love—by what Paul called "a more excellent way" (v. 31).

First Corinthians 13 is well-known for Paul's inspiring and challenging exposition of Christian love. It's not the fleeting, inflammatory type of infatuation the world embraces but an expression of action, of the choice to seek someone else's best good. It's not self- but others-oriented, a reflection of God's love for us in Christ. Paul's point, in fact, is that anything you can do or accomplish is empty without love as a motivating force and ultimate objective. The striving to love like Jesus is what the church is all about, which is why Paul said, "Now abide faith, hope, love, these three; but the greatest of these is love" (1 Corinthians 13:13). Anything less amounts to nothing at all. What Jesus prayed for in John 17:26 is what Paul rallied for in this chapter—the authentic love that should be the hallmark of God's people.

Doctrinal Perplexity (1 Corinthians 15–16)

Paul wrapped up with an appeal for doctrinal clarity. There were some key gospel teachings that he knew the church at Corinth needed a firm grasp of in order to be able to follow his advice in the rest of the letter. First and foremost was Jesus's resurrection.

If I were to make a list of the ten greatest chapters in the Bible, 1 Corinthians 15 would have to be on it. It is the most extensive and comprehensive chapter on the bodily resurrection in all of the Bible. Paul laid out the importance of the resurrection and its implications for all believers. Jesus's bodily resurrection from the dead is one of the three big credentials that set Jesus apart from any other religious leader (the other two being His global impact on history and His fulfillment of prophecy). In this chapter, both Christ's own resurrection and ours are explained.

Some of the Corinthians, though, struggled to believe in resurrection. They of course believed that Jesus rose from the dead, or else they could not be Christians. Their struggle was with the resurrection of everyone else. As Paul asked, "How do some among you say that there is no resurrection of the dead? But if there is no resurrection of the dead, then Christ is not risen" (1 Corinthians 15:12-13). Think about what that would mean: If there is no such thing as resurrection from the dead, then Jesus is still dead. Christianity would be based on what some dead guy said 2000 years ago. And you couldn't trust anything that dead guy said, because He would by default be a liar, having told His disciples He was going to be killed in Jerusalem and raised to life again on the third day.

No resurrection means your faith is empty and your witness is false (1 Corinthians 15:14-15). Preaching the gospel would be ridiculous, because resurrection is at the heart of the good news. Worse, you'd still be stuck in your sin, and every believer who has passed into eternity believing such a lie would be gone forever

(vv. 17-18). If there is no resurrection, Christianity is a big joke, and Christians are laughingstocks worthy of pity.

But Christianity wouldn't have survived this long if it was just a hoax. If the Roman persecutions hadn't killed it off, any number of other conflicts and divisions over the centuries that followed surely would have. A long line of martyrs thought Christ was worth dying for. Why be killed for something you know isn't true?

Not only did Jesus rise from the dead, so will we. And both resurrections stand or fall together. Christ's precedes all others in importance, and all of ours require His. When Jesus rose from the grave He not only conquered death, He demonstrated that those who believe in Him will do the same (John 11:25-26).

Paul wrapped up these powerful insights about the resurrection with a thought that drove it home for the Corinthians. "Now Christ is risen from the dead, and has become the firstfruits of those who have fallen asleep" (1 Corinthians 15:20). "Firstfruits" were a high-quality sample of the harvest that the Jews offered to God each year. Jesus was just the firstfruits of the resurrected life available to all who believe in Him; in other words, *There's a whole crop of people out there waiting to be harvested, Corinthians, and you're part of it!* It's an amazing promise, just as real and true for us today as it was then.

The resurrection is the heart and pulse of the gospel message.

Without a doubt, the resurrection is the heart and pulse of the gospel message. It was the power that would enable the Corinthians to step up their game and follow Paul's instructions for their improvement—and that same power lives in us today, both to save us and help us grow in faith.

2 CORINTHIANS
FLIGHT PLAN

Facts

Author

The apostle Paul wrote the book of 2 Corinthians (2 Corinthians 1:1). Paul was around fifty years old and at the end of his third missionary journey when he penned this letter. Departing from Ephesus (where he had stayed for more than two years), he headed to Macedonia to pursue various ministry opportunities. It was in Macedonia that he wrote 2 Corinthians, hoping for a chance to make a personal visit to the Corinthian church.

Date Written

Paul wrote 2 Corinthians between AD 56 and 57.

Landmarks

Sometime after Paul wrote 1 Corinthians, false teachers infiltrated the church at Corinth, spreading opposition against Paul because they thought he was unqualified to be an apostle of Jesus Christ. Their misinformation began to erode the church's confidence in Paul, so he sent Titus as a representative to deal with the situation, and as a result, the majority of the church reconsidered their attitude and repented of their actions. Paul wrote 2 Corinthians to express his joy at their turnaround and to appeal to them to accept his authority.

Paul spoke more about himself in this letter than in any other. He explained his ministry in the first seven chapters, talked about the collection for the saints in chapters 8–9, and defended his apostleship in the last four chapters. Several times throughout the book—especially in his "fool's speech" (2 Corinthians 11:16-33)—he referred to the many hardships he had suffered for the gospel. Overall, though, as he explained his absence, enlisted their help, and established his own apostolic credentials, Paul's key word was *encouragement*. His affection for the Corinthian church, though stern in places, is clear throughout.

Itinerary

Gospel

God's plan to populate heaven with redeemed people centers on what may be called the Great Exchange: "He made Him who knew no sin to be sin for us, that we might become the righteousness of God in Him" (2 Corinthians 5:21). This verse is perhaps the clearest and most succinct declaration in the whole Bible of what theologians refer to as vicarious (or substitutionary) atonement—that God made Jesus a substitute for us, to pay for our sin.

As Isaiah wrote, "He was wounded for our transgressions, He was bruised for our iniquities; the chastisement for our peace was upon Him, and by His stripes we are healed" (Isaiah 53:5). The prophet was foreseeing this Great Exchange, God giving us His righteousness in exchange for our sin. To us it seems like God got a bad deal—all our failures, botches, shortcomings, abuses, infractions, and filthiness for all His righteousness, blamelessness, and perfection. But that was His plan all along: At the cross, God treated Jesus the way we deserve to be treated so that He could treat us the way Jesus deserves to be treated. This truth is the salient core of the gospel message.

If you take that to heart, all the hardship you go through in this life has a much greater purpose. That truth can help you see past the pain. "Our light affliction, which is but for a moment, is working for us a far more exceeding and eternal weight of glory" (2 Corinthians 4:17). Your suffering is not hopeless, but will be worth it in the end. Because Paul opened his heart to make these points, being straightforward and honest about his own personal hardships, they made a deeper impact on the Corinthians and still resonate with us today.

Your suffering is not hopeless, but will be worth it in the end.

History

Corinth was a prominent city in New Testament times, known particularly for its theatres, athletics, religions, and cultural life—and for the seedy side of each of those things as well. Being a seaport city it was ready-made for the sleazy-made-easy activities for which this traveler's town had become known. Paul visited the city multiple times to preach the gospel and encourage the Christians in the area. During his first visit to Corinth, sometime around AD 50, Paul stayed for eighteen months and helped plant the spiritual seeds that would germinate into the Corinthian church. During his second missionary visit (AD 49–52), he helped start the Corinthian church (probably in the year AD 52). It was during Paul's third missionary journey (AD 52–57) that he most likely wrote his letters to the Corinthians, addressing the issues found in each letter.

Travel Tips

Paul encouraged the Corinthians that suffering for the sake of the gospel has the greatest possible purpose: to glorify God by identifying with the suffering of His Son, Jesus Christ. Living the Christian life is not easy, but Jesus never promised it would be. The book of 2 Corinthians shows us that part of living that life is offering open hearts and hands to our fellow believers—not because it's easy, but because it's right.

- Don't waste your suffering. As an apostle, Paul experienced an abundance of persecution—and not just from the world, but from within the church as well. As hard as it may be, God has a purpose for whatever you're going through. Making the most of your suffering is a sign of true Christian maturity, which produces contentment and joy.

- Seek and promote forgiveness, especially in the church. Paul encouraged the church to restore an individual who had repented of an offense for which Paul had recommended forbidding his attendance in 1 Corinthians (2 Corinthians 2:7). Further, he told them to embrace the man again, "lest Satan should take advantage of us; for we are not ignorant of his devices" (v. 11). Allowing unforgiveness in the church would play right into the devil's hands, giving him a foothold from which to divide the congregation.

- Ministry is not an easy road. A lot of people think serving the Lord by working for a church must be great—you get to work with other believers for the glory of God, after all! While that's true, ministry is by no means easy. What Paul experienced—trials both in and outside the church, physical hardship, in-the-trenches spiritual warfare—isn't unusual; it's the norm.

- Cheerful giving is part of your faith. You can tell a lot about a person's spirituality (or lack thereof) from his attitude about money. Paul praised the Corinthians for willingly giving to his ministry (2 Corinthians 9:2). The spiritual benefits of giving follow the principle of sowing and reaping: give little, get little; give a lot, get a lot. "So let each one give as he purposes in his heart, not grudgingly or of necessity; for God loves a cheerful giver" (v. 7).

> **You can tell a lot about a person's spirituality (or lack thereof) from his attitude about money.**

In Flight

Paul's Corrections (2 Corinthians 1:1–2:13)

Paul opened his heart to the church he helped found at Corinth, extending God's grace and blessing His name—not because that was a spiritual-sounding thing to do, but because it was God's grace and blessing that had allowed him to survive a number of trials with a full heart, and he wanted those things to comfort the Corinthians too. "Blessed be the God and Father of our Lord Jesus Christ, the Father of mercies and God of all comfort, who comforts us in all our tribulation, that we may be able to comfort those who are in any trouble, with the comfort with which we ourselves are comforted by God" (2 Corinthians 1:3-4).

Part of Paul's purpose was to let the Corinthians know that he wasn't looming over their shoulders, looking to criticize and judge them. He was standing with them and pulling for them, and when he had in his previous letter sought to correct their behavior, it gave him no joy to use tough love. "For out of much affliction and anguish of heart I wrote to you, with many tears, not that you should be grieved, but that you might know the love which I have so abundantly for you" (2 Corinthians 2:4).

With that in mind, Paul encouraged the believers to consider forgiving and reinstating the man he had instructed them to correct previously—a man living an incestuous relationship with his stepmother (1 Corinthians 5:1-5). "This punishment which was inflicted by the majority is sufficient for such a man, so that, on the contrary, you ought rather to forgive and comfort him, lest perhaps such a one be swallowed up with too much sorrow. Therefore I urge you to reaffirm your love to him" (2 Corinthians 2:6-8). The man had repented, and Paul wanted them to practice the principle Jesus described: "If your brother sins against you, rebuke him; and if he repents, forgive him" (Luke 17:3). To leave a repentant brother unforgiven and unrestored would be to give Satan a chance to use his primary church-busting strategy: divide and conquer. After all, "we are not ignorant of [Satan's] devices" (2 Corinthians 2:11). Thus the letter's preliminary remarks were to give an encouraging course correction for this budding but hesitant congregation.

Paul's Explanation (2 Corinthians 2:14–6:10)

Paul wanted to explain and affirm his ministry in Corinth—the nature of, message, and motivation for what he had done and was doing. "Therefore, since we have this ministry, as we have received mercy, we do not lose heart" (2 Corinthians 4:1). He got personal, detailing his trials as an apostle. Paul's work had drawn attacks from inside the church as well as outside; he had been beaten and jailed for his ministry, but had kept going, drawn forward by his calling.

"We are hard-pressed on every side, yet not crushed; we are perplexed, but not in despair; persecuted, but not forsaken; struck down, but not destroyed—always carrying about in the body the dying of the Lord Jesus, that the life of Jesus also may be manifested in our body" (vv. 8-10). A lot of times, people don't know what goes into building a ministry. They see it at a certain point, after God has brought it to a certain level of prominence and development, but they don't know about the early days, when the pastor worked two jobs and every ministry was staffed by volunteers, when leased strip mall locations and offering collections in coffee cans were the norm.

But for Paul, all that was just part of the process. What motivated him was knowing he was in God's will on earth and that he would one day be with the Lord in heaven. "We know that if our earthly house, this tent [his body], is destroyed, we have a building from God, a house not made with hands, eternal in the heavens" (2 Corinthians 5:1). A glorified body, clothed in salvation, was the long-term payoff, and in the meantime, "the love of Christ compels us" (v. 14). The hardships were worth it because of the joy inherent in the message: "If One died for all, then all died; and He died for all, that those who live should no longer live for themselves, but for Him who died for them and rose again" (vv. 14-15). Paul embodied that message, living for Jesus and wanting to see those in Corinth receive it.

Paul's Exhortations (2 Corinthians 6:11–7:16)

Paul wanted the Corinthian church to embrace God's grace rather than diminish it by living small lives focused on worldly concerns and comforts. False leaders had infiltrated the church in Paul's absence and were turning its members against Paul by assaulting his character. In response to their agenda, Paul appealed to his track record with the Corinthians to listen to the godly truth he was sharing: "O Corinthians! We have spoken openly to you, our heart is wide open. You are not restricted by us, but you are restricted by your own affections. Now in return for the same (I speak as to children), you also be open" (2 Corinthians 6:11-13). Paul still had plenty of room in his heart for them, and he appealed to them in unguarded vulnerability.

Finding the balance between tenderheartedness and tough truth was essential. Paul hit on a principle that applied not only to the situation in Corinth but any of a number of potentially dangerous alliances for believers: "Do not be unequally yoked together with unbelievers. For what fellowship has righteousness with lawlessness? And what communion has light with darkness? And what accord has Christ with Belial [another term for Satan]? Or what part has a believer with an unbeliever?" (vv. 14-15).

The principle is sound, whether it's permitting a false teacher in church, dating or marrying a non-Christian, or forming a business partnership with someone who doesn't put Christ first. Paul wasn't saying we should end all associations with unbelievers. That would be self-defeating to the Christian agenda. He had written to the Corinthians before about this, warning them not to associate with sexually immoral people, but clarifying that he "certainly did not mean with the sexually immoral people of this world, or with the covetous, or extortioners, or idolaters, since then you would need to go out of the world" (1 Corinthians 5:10). Those are the very people God wants us to reach with the gospel. Rather, Paul was warning them to be careful around those who claimed to be believers but weren't living by God's Spirit or truth.

Paul went on to say, "Open your hearts to us. We have wronged no one, we have corrupted no one, we have cheated no one. I do not say this to condemn; for I have said before that you are in our hearts, to die together and to live together" (2 Corinthians 7:2-3). He had seen the good fruit of their previous repentance, brought about by his previous letter, and trusted that they would rise to the occasion again (vv. 8-12). The severity and tone of Paul's previous letter had produced its desired effect, and he now hoped that any rebellion the Corinthian church expressed against him would also cease.

Paul's Collection (2 Corinthians 8:1–9:15)

Paul shifted the emphasis to giving. He was taking up a collection for fellow believers in Jerusalem who were suffering through a financial crisis, perhaps due to persecution. Though Paul was addressing that local condition, this passage provides the most detailed model of Christian generosity and giving in the New Testament. He cited the example that the poorest churches in the region had given all that they could and doing so had given them great joy. He also noted how they managed it: "They first gave themselves to the Lord, and then to us by the will of God" (2 Corinthians 8:5). Their openness to receiving Jesus and then to taking in those who came in His name—who had lived out His love and truth among them—had inspired them to give out of what little they had. This was genuinely sacrificial giving.

The Macedonian churches had freely given "beyond their ability" (v. 3), demonstrating the biblical principle that it's okay to stretch your finances for God's work. While Paul spoke of giving proportionately to what they earned, he reminded the Corinthians that there would be an overall balance—that if they gave out of their abundance to supply what others lacked, at some point, others would do the same for them (vv. 12-15). He praised the Corinthian church for what they had done well and asked them to add this collection of funds to that list: "As you abound in everything—in faith, in speech, in knowledge, in all diligence, and in your love for us—see that you abound in this grace also" (v. 7).

Paul wasn't commanding them to give; he was asking them to test the sincerity of their faith. In doing so, he reminded them of the spiritual principle of reaping and sowing: "This I say: He who sows sparingly will also reap sparingly, and he who sows bountifully will also reap bountifully" (2 Corinthians 9:6). Jesus said something similar, encouraging believers in the hard aspects of following Him: "Give, and it will be given to you: good measure, pressed down, shaken together, and running over will be put into your bosom. For with the same measure that you use, it will be measured back to you" (Luke 6:38). You can never outgive God.

Knowing that God is faithful both when you have needs and to use you when others have needs, it only makes sense to give joyfully. That's why Paul said, "So let each one give as he purposes in his heart, not grudgingly nor of necessity; for God loves a cheerful [literally, *hilarious*] giver" (2 Corinthians 9:7). You can give out of sheer obedience, or you can enjoy doing it, knowing that you can't outgive God and that He loves it when you take pleasure in giving back to Him. You can be either a sad giver (doing it grudgingly), a mad giver (out of necessity), or a glad giver (cheerfully).

> You can be either a sad giver (doing it grudgingly), a mad giver (out of necessity), or a glad giver (cheerfully).

This reminds me of trips I've taken to Israel, during which we would make the journey from the Sea of Galilee to the Dead Sea. We would start at the Sea of Galilee, which is lush and green, children playing, trees, life in bloom everywhere. Go south a few hours, though, and you get to the Dead Sea, which is barren and dry, with nothing growing in or around it. The same source of water, the Jordan River, flows into both of them, so what's the difference? Why is one alive and the other dead? It's simple, really: The Sea of Galilee is alive because it has both an inlet and an outlet; it takes in water and it gives water out. The Dead Sea hoards everything; there's an inlet but no outlet other than evaporation. Because it never gives out, it has no flow; therefore, it's dead. That's a potent analogy for your life as a believer: You should be taking in God's blessing and giving it out. You'll bless yourself as well as others, and that was Paul's point.

Paul's Vindication (2 Corinthians 10:1–13:13)

In the final section of this letter, Paul sort of ruffled up his apostolic feathers and defended his own authority, credentials, and conduct. All sorts of charges had been leveled against him, mostly by the false teachers infiltrating the Corinthian church. But Paul humbly and firmly pleaded with the believers to hear him out:

> I, Paul, myself am pleading with you by the meekness and gentleness of Christ—who in presence am lowly among you, but being absent am bold toward you. But I beg you that when I am present I may not be bold with that confidence by which I intend to be bold against some, who think of us as if we walked according to the flesh (2 Corinthians 10:1-2).

It's hard to imagine that the great apostle Paul would have such ardent detractors, and it shows the kind of dynamic that can be present in *any* church.

Paul was aware of the accusations against him. "'For his letters,' they say, 'are weighty and powerful, but his bodily presence is weak, and his speech contemptible'" (v. 10). The posers spreading rumors in Corinth had apparently painted Paul as big and bad from a distance but a wimp up close.[63] Ironically, his enemies didn't hesitate to make fun of him from afar. It would be interesting to know how they fared up close. Empty trucks make the loudest noise!

For his part, Paul was prepared to defend his authority: "I consider that I am not at all inferior to the most eminent apostles. Even though I am untrained in speech, yet I am not in knowledge. But we have been thoroughly manifested among you in all things" (2 Corinthians 11:5-6). Paul wondered if his sin had been in preaching the gospel to them free of charge, implying that these new guys were taking advantage of his flock (vv. 7-10). These were the guys emulating not Christ but Satan, who "transforms himself into an angel of light...[and] his ministers also transform themselves into ministers of righteousness, whose end will be according to their works" (vv. 14-15). Paul was not pulling any punches here.

In order to defend himself, Paul admitted, "What I speak, I speak not according to the Lord, but as it were, foolishly, in this confidence of boasting" (v. 17). In other words, "I don't want to boast because it's not Christlike, but since you brought up my qualifications, let me clue you in a little." He could top anyone's claims. If they were Hebrews, he was a super-Hebrew—a Pharisee of high education and pedigree. If they called themselves ministers for Christ, he could outdo them "in labors more abundant, in stripes above measure, in prisons more frequently, in deaths often" (v. 23).

Paul had received visions of heaven and God so overwhelming and awe-inspiring that he wasn't allowed to repeat them (2 Corinthians 12:1-6). But the thing he appreciated most was that God kept him from getting a huge ego by giving him "a thorn in the flesh" (v. 7). This "thorn" was apparently some physical setback that humbled Paul and forced him to rely on God, who told him, "My grace is sufficient for you, for My strength is made perfect in weakness" (v. 9). That's what he wanted to brag about—that God kept him honest by balancing his blessings with permitted buffetings so that he would keep Christ first. The weaker the human instrument, the stronger the divine support required. Simply put, the weaker you feel, the harder you'll lean on Him.

The weaker the human instrument, the stronger the divine support required.

Though Paul hated self-commendation, he was forced into defending his apostolic authority.

> I have become a fool in boasting; you have compelled me. For I ought to have been commended by you; for in nothing was I behind the most eminent apostles, though I am nothing. Truly the signs of

an apostle were accomplished among you with all perseverance, in signs and wonders and mighty deeds...I will very gladly spend and be spent for your souls; though the more abundantly I love you, the less I am loved (2 Corinthians 12:11-12, 15).

Paul had some keen insight into how Jesus must have felt when His own people rejected Him and eventually crucified Him.

Being like Christ was more than enough for Paul, his weakness showing his Savior's strength. "I write these things being absent, lest being present I should use sharpness; according to the authority which the Lord has given me for edification and not for destruction. Finally, brethren, farewell. Be complete" (2 Corinthians 13:10-11). Like Jesus, Paul wasn't going to swing his authority around like a big stick, but he wasn't going to say nothing when God's work in Corinth was at stake. His final admonition to "become complete" was a single-sentence summary of the whole letter and an exhortation to live out what they had been taught was right in Christ—to "be of good comfort, be of one mind, live in peace; and the God of love and peace will be with you" (v. 11). As a spiritual parent, Paul wanted them to become mature in faith and in love.

Conviction should lead to commitment.

Conviction should lead to commitment. Paul demonstrated both—a quality that singled him out as a true apostle of Christ and that he helped foster in the Corinthians by urging them to give cheerfully to God's work. And in this final piece of advice to the Corinthians, he told them, "Grow up." They had learned what they needed to do to become mature Christians; it was up to them to own it and live it out.

GALATIANS
FLIGHT PLAN

⨍acts

Author

The apostle Paul wrote the book of Galatians (Galatians 1:1), addressing it to a group of church assemblies rather than to one. Paul was born in the city of Tarsus in the southern part of the region of Galatia (modern-day Turkey). After his conversion to Christ (around AD 34), Paul spent the remainder of his life ministering God's grace and preaching the gospel. He was executed for his faith around AD 67.

Date Written

While there are different theories regarding the date Galatians was written, they span the period from AD 47–55 (see **History** on page 472).

⌷andmarks

Paul's forceful little letter of Galatians addressed the Galatian church's legalism and the false gospel of works—more specifically, *Judaizing*, or requiring people to keep the Law of Moses. Galatians is a classic statement of the doctrine of justification by grace through faith alone, written to counter false teachers who were saying that a person must keep the Jewish law to be righteous before God. Much like Paul's epistle to the Romans, Galatians has played a strategic role in the history of the Christian church. The letter had a notable impact on the life of Protestant giant Martin Luther.[64]

In Galatians, Paul addressed problems raised by the oppressive theology of certain Jewish legalizers who had caused believers in Galatia to trade their freedom in Christ for bondage to the law. Paul also defended the gospel and his apostleship, described the differences between law and grace, and explained the practical application of these truths.

⌶tinerary

- The Personal (Galatians 1–2)

- The Doctrinal (Galatians 3–4)
- The Practical (Galatians 5–6)

Gospel

Galatians is the Magna Carta of the doctrine of Christian liberty. It declares total liberty in Christ from the religious laws of Moses, emphasizing that freedom from sin is accompanied by freedom from the law and doctrines of man. The law is a curse for us because we're not perfect and can never fulfill its demands. But because Jesus lived a perfect life and fulfilled its demands, He was able to take our place and take the punishment we deserved, becoming the curse for us, suffering its consequences, and defeating it once and for all by rising from the dead.

As Paul wrote in Galatians 3:13-14, "Christ has redeemed us from the curse of the law, having become a curse for us (for it is written, 'Cursed is everyone who hangs on a tree'), that the blessing of Abraham might come upon the Gentiles in Christ Jesus, that we might receive the promise of the Spirit through faith." Capital punishment by stoning was part of Jewish law, but crucifixion wasn't. Stoning was a holy remedy, but being nailed to a cross was considered to be defiling—an unclean death for an unholy people.

Paul's point was that Jesus died in a way that the Jews considered cursed. The weight of the true curse—our sins—was then placed on Him, and because of that, He was able to purchase for us freedom from sin and perfect liberty in Christ. He was the perfect substitute for us, the only One who could bear the weight of all our sin. Only Jesus could do it—and that's why salvation is a gift of God's grace and not something any human being could ever earn.

History

The history of the Galatia of Paul's day is shrouded in mystery. In the early part of the first century AD, the term *Galatia* had ethnic as well as political meaning. On the one hand, Galatians were ethnically Celtic people who had migrated from Europe. But politically speaking, *Galatia* could refer to several cities in the region (Antioch, Iconium, Lystra, Derbe, and Tarsus). The Roman emperor Augustus made the area a Roman province in 25 BC, meaning that Paul, who was born in southern Galatia, was also born a Roman citizen.[65]

There are two theories regarding the date Galatians was written. The north Galatian theory (also known as the geographical view) puts the date of authorship circa AD 55, when Paul was in Ephesus (sometime around or after Acts 19:1). The south

Galatian theory (or the political view) puts the date of authorship at AD 47–49, which meant Paul was in Antioch when he wrote the letter (sometime around Acts 15),[66] perhaps establishing the need for church-wide clarification on the doctrine of salvation by grace.

However, Paul's focus throughout the book is exposing the Judaizers' false teaching that salvation depended on keeping the Law of Moses, which was one of the major issues resolved by the first council of Jerusalem (described in Acts 15). Paul makes mention of his report to the council (Galatians 2:2), which suggests that he wrote the letter at the later date.

Travel Tips

Paul ended the letter of Galatians with some practical applications for those who embrace salvation by faith in Jesus Christ alone. True belief in Jesus will translate into a beautiful, holy, loving lifestyle—one that is markedly different from a lifestyle based on salvation by works.

- Hold to the true gospel of grace. The Galatians had turned to "a different gospel" (Galatians 1:6)—one based on works instead of grace. Paul said that if anyone preached a gospel other than the one he had preached, then "let him be accursed" (v. 8). No matter how sweet a preacher's words are—even if they come from an angel, as Paul said (v. 8)—if they don't match up with what the Bible says, they are false, and you are to reject them completely.

- Hold on to your liberty in Christ. Jesus set you free from the bondage of sin—from human nature and its shackles—so why would you chain yourself to those same things again (Galatians 3:1-3)? Jesus has set you free not only from sin, but also from manmade religious rules (John 8:36). You're free from any regulation anyone tries to add to the gospel, no matter how convincing it sounds or who is prescribing it.

> ### Jesus has set you free not only from sin, but also from manmade religious rules.

- To fully receive God's grace, you first must acknowledge your sin. No one can be good enough to earn their way to heaven. But unless you acknowledge you're a sinner, you'll never see your need for a Savior.

The law is a blessing only for the perfect; for the rest of us—and, yes, that's *all* of us—it's a curse from which only Christ can redeem us (Galatians 3:13). The law says, "Do this and live," whereas faith says, "Believe this and live."

- What does it mean to "walk in the Spirit" (Galatians 5:16)? The Holy Spirit lives in every single believer, energizing our new nature in Christ—our liberty and freedom from sin—while helping us resist the impulses of our flesh. Freedom in Christ is not about doing what you want, but doing what Christ wants: loving other people and having a servant's heart. That produces what Paul called the fruit of the Spirit: "love, joy, peace, longsuffering, kindness, goodness, faithfulness, gentleness, [and] self-control" (Galatians 5:22-23).

In Flight

Paul broke out the boxing gloves in his letter to the Galatians. He followed up his customary greeting of grace and peace by directly questioning the teachings of the false teachers who had infiltrated the church. He went on to deliver what we call a polemic—a strong written attack—against these false teachers, a group of first-century legalists called the Judaizers, who were perverting the gospel of Christ. Paul fiercely defended the doctrine of salvation through faith and God's grace—God's favor toward us that we don't deserve but that He offers freely.

The Personal (Galatians 1–2)

Paul opened with his standard blessing of grace and peace, but then got right down to business: "I marvel that you are turning away so soon from Him who called you in the grace of Christ, to a different gospel" (Galatians 1:6). It's astonishing, really; the Christians in Galatia heard the good news of Jesus Christ from the greatest teacher in all of church history, next to Jesus Himself. They sat under Paul's teaching, but when he moved on to the next stop on his missionary journey, they turned from his teaching toward people who badmouthed him and turned them from the truth. "There are some who trouble you and want to pervert the gospel of Christ" (v. 7) The Judaizers were reversing it, going backward to the fetters of the law instead of forward into the freedom of grace.

Paul and Barnabas had already fought against that teaching just after their first missionary journey, while they were living in Antioch (Acts 15). It was a critical battle: God sent Jesus to accomplish something no one else ever could have, and when

He did, something significant happened: The veil in the temple, which enclosed the Holy of Holies, tore from top to bottom (Matthew 27:51). This veil had symbolically separated the people from the presence of God, but its rending at Christ's death symbolized that anyone who received Him could now enter God's presence. Atonement's price had been paid, and the world changed forever.

History, however, tells us that the Jews quickly began to offer sacrifices again, indicating the veil had been either stitched up or replaced.[67] It was a typical human response. God removes a barrier; people put up another barrier as soon as possible, addicted to the self-sufficiency of their rituals and ceremonies. What God simplifies, we complicate. Paul wasn't having it. "But even if we, or an angel from heaven, preach any other gospel to you than what we have preached to you, let him be accursed" (Galatians 1:8). Like a doctor who knew he had to act quickly and decisively to save a patient, Paul moved to cut the cancer out.

What God simplifies, we complicate.

It wasn't that Paul didn't know what it was to be legalistic. He recounted his salvation, his "former conduct in Judaism" (v. 13), and how his advanced Judaism compelled him to persecute the church. Being Mr. Judaism meant he missed God's point—that only Christ's perfect sacrifice could save him—something that God spent a lot of time teaching Paul in isolation (vv. 15-19). Eventually the apostles in Jerusalem accepted him, and they all realized that God had given Paul a ministry to the Gentiles, just as He had given Peter a ministry to the Jews (Galatians 2:7). Above all, Paul made one thing clear—the driving thought behind his ministry: "I have been crucified with Christ; it is no longer I who live, but Christ lives in me" (v. 20). This deep, personal conviction was founded on the pure doctrine of the gospel—Paul's next topic.

The Doctrinal (Galatians 3–4)

Paul presented several arguments centered on justification by faith—the central teaching that a person is saved by believing in Jesus alone, not by doing good works to try and earn salvation. The Christians of Galatia had lost sight of this essential truth, and Paul's frustration was clear: "Oh foolish Galatians! Who has bewitched you that you should not obey the truth, before whose eyes Jesus Christ was clearly portrayed among you as crucified?" (Galatians 3:1). Why would anyone want to turn away from liberty in Christ and to bondage in anything—even the law? Why, when Christ set you free, would you say, "Now that I am free, I would like to be a slave of some other teaching"? Whoever these legalistic preachers were, they must have wowed the Galatians, awed them, persuaded them. Again, it's human nature to build up barriers, to try and give ourselves walls to scale and mountains to climb— even if the wall of sin revealed by the law makes Everest look like a speed bump.

It still happens. If you don't start first and always with God's Word, you're susceptible. People who aren't biblically astute may find a new book on the Christian bookshelf, read it, and feel as if they have gained new insight: "I never saw that before; I never knew that before; that has to be the truth"—not realizing that perhaps the reason they'd never seen it before is because it's just not in the Bible.

Paul wanted the Galatians to think through the matter, to look past their infatuation with religious liturgy and recall what he had taught them, the truth that had come from God Himself. "Did you receive the Spirit by the works of the law, or by the hearing of faith? Are you so foolish? Having begun in the Spirit, are you now being made perfect by the flesh?" (Galatians 3:2-3). If works couldn't save you in the first place, why would you return to them seeking spiritual maturity? It baffled Paul.

He reminded the Galatians of what Abraham, the father of the Jews himself, had done in response to God's Spirit: "Abraham 'believed God, and it was accounted to him for righteousness.' Therefore know that only those who are of faith are sons of Abraham" (Galatians 3:6-7). Back in Genesis 15, God had promised Abraham a nation's worth of descendants, and Abraham believed Him. It was a singular moment of simple faith in God and His promise. That genuine faith justified him in God's eyes—not his works and not the law, which wouldn't be given for another four-and-a-half centuries. That made Father Abraham, whom the Jews claimed as their source of righteous connection to God, a Gentile who receive God's justification through faith. God saved him because Abraham believed Him, and God credited it to his account. That's exactly how it works with Jesus.

Paul quoted the law to make his point. "For as many as are of the works of the law are under the curse; for it is written, 'Cursed is everyone who does not continue in all things which are written in the book of the law, to do them'" (Galatians 3:10, quoting Deuteronomy 27:26). No one could keep the law in its entirety, which meant that everyone was under its curse. "But that no one is justified by the law in the sight of God is evident, for 'the just shall live by faith'" (v. 11, quoting Habakkuk 2:4). The law is a blessing only if you keep every single bit of it, something that's simply not possible to do (as the system of sacrifices required by the same law demonstrates).

The law doesn't demand belief, only obedience. But Jesus said, "This is the work of God, that you believe in Him whom He sent" (John 6:29). He did what no one has ever done or could ever do. Jesus took the curse on Himself, redeeming anyone who believes in Him the way Abraham believed God, "that the blessing of Abraham might come upon the Gentiles in Christ Jesus, that we might receive the promise of the Spirit through faith" (Galatians 3:14). Anyone who receives Christ's sacrifice by faith has life, whereas the law can only bring death (**Gospel** on page 472).

Paul then acknowledged a reasonable question that would be asked in light of what he had just said. "What purpose then does the law serve?" (Galatians 3:19). Judaism was the only religion God ever gave to mankind and it served a distinct purpose: to reveal transgression. The law couldn't remove sin; it could only reveal sin—exposing its presence in human behavior. It was a placeholder from Moses to Jesus, keeping God's people in check until the Seed He promised Abraham had come. As Paul put it, "The law was our tutor to bring us to Christ, that we might be justified by faith" (v. 24). It instructed God's people on His righteousness, holiness, and mercy, making clear that there was no way any person, no matter how good or hardworking, could stand on their own merit before God. While new covenant grace makes us "come of age" as God's children, old covenant law keeps us stunted, stifled, and yearning for more.

The law revealed sin by pointing to the cross and the empty tomb.

The law revealed sin by pointing to the cross and the empty tomb. "When the fullness of the time had come, God sent forth His Son, born of a woman, born under the law, to redeem those who were under the law, that we might receive the adoption as sons. And because you are sons, God has sent forth His Spirit of His Son into your hearts, crying out, 'Abba, Father!'" (Galatians 4:4-6). After Adam and Eve fell, sin cursed mankind. The law revealed how pervasive and unavoidable its reach and grasp were, but God's plan was always to buy back His children from sin's chains and adopt them as His own children. The Son of God became a man to enable men (and women, of course) to become sons (and daughters) of God. That's what *Abba* means; it's the Aramaic term translated "Daddy," an indicator of the intimate relationship God wants to have with us. Only grace through faith makes that connection possible.

The Practical (Galatians 5–6)

Paul had described his personal relationship with the law and outlined proper doctrine on grace versus the law. He wanted to end by bringing all of that back to a practical level so that his readers wouldn't think the gospel of grace was going to lead to lewd, loose living free of accountability. Rather, it would promote holy living. "Stand fast therefore in the liberty by which Christ has made us free, and do not be entangled again with a yoke of bondage" (Galatians 5:1). Living by grace will promote true spirituality, not an unnecessary burden or a tangle of rules and regulations.

Those false teachers, the Judaizers, didn't like Paul's message because they thought preaching grace was in effect preaching lawlessness—that people would say, "Hey, cool, I'm under grace, so I can do whatever I want." They reasoned that the law was necessary to keep believers in line, but Paul's point was that God's grace will do in a person what the law never could. John Bunyan, the persecuted English author of *The Pilgrim's Progress*, beautifully summed up the difference in a poem:

> Run, John, run, the law commands,
> but gives us neither feet nor hands.
> Far better news the gospel brings:
> it bids us fly and gives us wings.

Paul's point was that the gospel of grace won't make you indulgent; it will make you like Jesus, a true servant to others. "You, brethren, have been called to liberty; only do not use liberty as an opportunity for the flesh, but through love serve one another" (Galatians 5:13). He repeated what Jesus had said—that the law could be summed up in two commandments: Love God first with all you are and have, and love other people the way you want to be loved (Galatians 5:14 and Matthew 22:37-40).

"I say then: Walk in the Spirit, and you will not fulfill the lust of flesh" (Galatians 5:16). The Holy Spirit living inside of you, a believer, energizes the new nature that has been put within you, helping you to live out your belief in Christ. When you were born physically, you possessed an old nature, driven by the impulses of the flesh, the instinct to sin. When you were born again spiritually, you received a new nature, God's Spirit within you. But "the flesh lusts against the Spirit, and the Spirit against the flesh" (v. 17). We are a kind of walking civil war then—our unredeemed humanness opposing our redeemed godliness, with our will in the middle.

Paul drew up two lists to contrast the works of the flesh and the works of the Spirit. Living according to your old nature, the flesh, produces all kinds of sin (Galatians 5:19-21), but living according to Christ produces the fruit of the Spirit: "love, joy, peace, longsuffering, kindness, goodness, faithfulness, gentleness, self-control" (vv. 22-23).

I'm sure you've never walked up to an apple on a tree and thought, *That tree is working really hard to make that apple. Look at that tree sweat.* That's the thing about fruit: to make an apple, the branch just has to hang in there. No stress. No strain. No strife. That's what Jesus said: "He who abides in Me, and I in him, bears much fruit; for without Me you can do nothing" (John 15:5). If you just hang in there, staying in fellowship with Jesus, reading the Bible, praying, having fellowship with other believers, you will produce fruit. You won't have to strive for it. Yes, you'll have to follow Him, showing your love through obedience, and that's not always easy, but your faithful discipleship makes you a rebel against the world's system of producing works in order to have value.

The law produces an outward *display* of spiritual-looking behavior, but it can be done without having any inward *desire* to please or serve God. That desire can only honestly come from giving all you are over to Christ's control. His Spirit in you will produce fruit. Paul talked about how this comes out in our treatment of people, especially those who are off-target in their walk. "Brethren, if a man is overtaken in any trespass, you who are spiritual restore such a one in a spirit of gentleness, considering yourself lest you also be tempted" (Galatians 6:1).

How different this was from the Judaizers, who pointed their fingers and said, "You have to keep the Law of Moses to be saved." The implication of wrongdoing for them was that the person who sinned wasn't truly saved. They had no sense of restoration and compassion; it was always condemnation. Rather than shooting its wounded, the church needs to follow God's lead and be in the business of restoration—the restoration of sinners to a right relationship with God, and of believers to a fruitful walk with Him.

When we do that, we will be able to bear "one another's burdens, and so fulfill the law of Christ. For if anyone thinks himself to be something, when he is nothing, he deceives himself. But let each one examine his own work" (Galatians 6:2-4). That's all about seeking the inward heart versus feeding the outward appearance. And Paul ended with a note of encouragement: "Let us not grow weary while doing good, for in due season we shall reap if we do not lose heart" (v. 9).

Paul had been through a lot to preach the gospel—beatings, scourging, and imprisonment—but his focus wasn't on what he had done: "God forbid that I should boast except in the cross of our Lord Jesus Christ, by whom the world has been crucified to me, and I to the world" (v. 14). He had walked in the grace of God, and exhorted the Galatians to follow his lead, resting in the finished work of Christ and the gifts of His Spirit. That grace can be hard to receive, but once you surrender to it, you'll see how your works pale in comparison to the fruitful, loving, life-producing, and life-affirming work of the Holy Spirit.

EPHESIANS
FLIGHT PLAN

Facts

Author

The apostle Paul wrote the book of Ephesians (Ephesians 1:1). Along with Philippians, Colossians, and Philemon, Ephesians is one of the four aptly named prison letters Paul wrote while imprisoned in Rome for preaching Christ (Acts 28).

Date Written

Paul was first imprisoned in Rome between AD 60 and 61. This particular letter was delivered to the Ephesian church by a man named Tychicus, a companion with Paul on his missionary journeys (Ephesians 6:21-22).

Landmarks

Second only to the book of Romans, Ephesians is perhaps the most thoughtfully written work of Christian theology in the New Testament. It addresses a group of believers who were ignorant of their wealth in Jesus Christ and were living as spiritually impoverished beggars. Paul wrote to motivate them to draw upon that wealth in their daily living, explaining their identity in Jesus Christ and the awe-inspiring gifts they had through Him. Paul also spoke of God's indestructible purposes, Jesus as the center of the universe and the focus of history, the living church, the new family of God, and Christian conduct.

One of the letter's major themes is how to build up the spiritual body of Christ. Paul spoke of the body as a bride (Ephesians 5:25-27), a temple (Ephesians 2:19-22), and a soldier (Ephesians 6:10-18). These images point to the importance of unity within the church and how the whole body must work together to achieve a common goal. Each member of the body must help, not hinder, God's work. From a practical standpoint, this means eliminating backbiting, gossip, unnecessarily negative criticism, envy, anger, and bitterness, as these things hurt the church.

Paul explained how God, through the church, is building up a family, a new society with new standards, values, and relationships. As members of that family, we must go beyond merely reading or hearing God's Word and put it into action.

Ephesians has been called both the crown jewel and the Grand Canyon of the New Testament for its depiction of the depth and breadth of God's rich plan of love, mercy, and salvation.

Itinerary

- The Believer's Wealth (Ephesians 1–3)
- The Believer's Walk (Ephesians 4:1–6:9)
- The Believer's Warfare (Ephesians 6:10-24)

Gospel

The book of Ephesians focuses on how God is building a spiritual family and a new society based on the truth of the gospel—and this society includes Jews as well as Gentiles (non-Jewish people). Paul summarized the basis for this new family early on in his letter: "Blessed be the God and Father of our Lord Jesus Christ, who has blessed us with every spiritual blessing in the heavenly places in Christ" (Ephesians 1:3). In that verse, we see the wealth of the inheritance in Jesus, in whom we have everything we'll ever need—because of the salvation Christ purchased for us on the cross and the wonder of what it means to be adopted by God.

Throughout the rest of his letter, Paul expounded on that theme, preaching what he called "the unsearchable riches of Christ" (Ephesians 3:8). Though these unsearchable riches are something you have to take on faith, Paul made it clear that people come into the family of God "according to the eternal purpose which He accomplished in Christ Jesus our Lord, in whom we have boldness and access with confidence through faith in Him" (Ephesians 3:11-12). The wonder and wealth of faith in Christ includes these simple but mind-blowing facts: God chose you, adopted you, and redeemed you. Because He picked you and then He placed you in His new community, you have eternal life to look forward to, as well as abundant spiritual life available to you right now.

History

The city of Ephesus was a great Roman commercial port along the coast of the Aegean Sea, located in what is now the country of Turkey. Ephesus boasted theaters, a library, a school of philosophy, and the Temple of Artemis (Diana), one of the seven wonders of the ancient world.[68] Paul visited Ephesus during his second missionary journey and stayed for almost three years (AD 50–53). The Ephesian church was founded toward the end of Paul's trip, near the beginning of his third missionary journey, and grew up under his teaching. Paul himself pastored the congregation for three years, and then his protégé Timothy stayed for another year and a half.

Jesus wrote a little postcard to the Ephesian church through the apostle John in Revelation 2:1-7, stating that though they had tested false apostles and persevered, they had "left [their] first love" (Revelation 2:4). By the time Christianity had become the region's dominant religion, Ephesus had lost most of its power and influence in the Roman Empire.[69]

Travel Tips

In typical fashion, Paul began the letter of Ephesians with doctrine (teaching) and ended it with application. Here we see the spiritual wealth God has for us, the way we should walk in that wealth, and the spiritual defenses God has provided to help us resist the devil and our own fleshly desires.

- Members of the body of Christ are wealthy for three main reasons: God's fatherhood, God's great forgiveness, and our new spiritual family—the believers with whom we share our lives. It can sometimes be challenging to work with other Christians, but what an amazing comfort and resource God has given us in each other! Through Christ, we are able to love, pray for, encourage, commiserate with, and hold each other accountable. Jesus is our foundation, strength, and unity (Ephesians 2:14-20).

- Walking with Christ means leaving your old life behind. More than just leave the old crowd you used to run with, you must start at the root of the problem and transform the way you think about the world in general. "For you were once darkness," Ephesians 5:8 says, "but now you are light in the Lord. Walk as children of light."

Submission is the oil that makes the
gears of relationships—especially family
relationships—run smoothly.

- Submission is the oil that makes the gears of relationships—especially family relationships—run smoothly. In Ephesians 5, Paul laid out the hierarchy of a godly marriage: a wife submits to her husband, and a husband sacrifices his life for his wife (vv. 22-33). The key to this marriage relationship, however, is found in both parties "submitting to one another in the fear of God" (v. 21). And that's the key to any Christian relationship: To love like Jesus, you need to voluntarily put other people first.

- Christianity is a battleground, not a playground. Regardless of your political or philosophical thoughts about war, you cannot be a spiritual pacifist or you will fall. You need to realize that when you became a believer, you defected from the kingdom of darkness and made the devil your enemy. The good news is that God Himself has provided you with spiritual weapons to use against that enemy (Ephesians 6:10-18).

In Flight

The Believer's Wealth (Ephesians 1–3)

Ephesus was considered the bank of Asia, the financial center of the Roman Empire, so it's fitting that Paul used financial language throughout the letter—*inheritance*, *fullness*, and *filled*, for example—to describe the spiritual wealth all believers have in Christ. He employed that phrase, "in Christ," more than two dozen times to underscore that relationship as an heir with Christ of God's spiritual riches. It's like a kid going into a bank and having access to his parents' funds because he's "in the family."

Paul wanted the believers in Ephesus to tap into their spiritual bank accounts. Too many were living like spiritual paupers instead of princes, failing to appropriate all that God had for them as His children. That God-given wealth includes "every spiritual blessing in the heavenly places in Christ" (Ephesians 1:3), including the blessings of being chosen by God to be holy and blameless in His eyes (v. 4). God "predestined us to adoption as sons by Jesus Christ to Himself, according to the good pleasure of His will" (v. 5). You might say that God sees you through rose-colored glasses, the blood-red lens of Christ's finished work on the cross.

> **God sees you through rose-colored glasses, the blood-red lens of Christ's finished work on the cross.**

The thought that God chose some people and not all people bothers some folks. There's little else more sacred to a human being than the right to choose, and yet some of us don't like to think that God also makes choices. And how do you even know God chose you? Well, I'll let you in on a little secret: If you receive Christ, then you will discover that He has. But what if you don't want to receive Christ? Then maybe God hasn't chosen you. "But that's not fair!" you might object. Then choose Christ. Only God has the destinies of all people sorted out, so why not trust Him with your life and accept His Son as your Lord and Savior? He promised that "all that the Father gives Me will come to Me, and the one who comes to Me I will by no means cast out" (John 6:37).

Besides, as Charles Spurgeon said, "I am sure He chose me before I was born, or else He never would have chosen me afterwards."[70] Once you accept that God predestined you for adoption as His child (Ephesians 1:5), you can enjoy your inheritance. In New Testament times, the process of Roman adoption gave the rights of inheritance to children of any age; in other words, you didn't have to wait to become an adult to become the heir of your father.[71] In the same way, if you have received Christ as Lord and Savior, you've been adopted by God and now share in His inheritance—an inheritance that you can enjoy from this day forward into eternity.

Furthermore, in Christ, "we have redemption through His blood, the forgiveness of sins, according to the riches of His grace" (Ephesians 1:7). When Paul penned Ephesians, the term *redemption* referred to the buying back of a slave with the intention of giving that slave his or her freedom. Up to one-third of some populations in the Roman Empire were made up of slaves,[72] so Paul's audience would have been familiar with the concept. And there are no second-class citizens among believers; all believers are rescued from the slave market of this world and all believers are rich in the spiritual assets given by God.

Paul wanted his audience to know just how dramatic this change was. Because of Jesus, we have gone not just from slavery to freedom, but also from spiritual poverty to spiritual wealth and, more profoundly, from death to life. "You He made alive, who were dead in trespasses and sins" (Ephesians 2:1). You were born into this world physically alive but spiritually dead, separated from God. You and I are sinners not just by choice but by nature. We are by choice "sons of disobedience...conduct[ing] ourselves in the lusts of our flesh" (v. 3), and we are also "by nature children of wrath" (v. 3).

Spiritually speaking, we as humans aren't just sick—we're dead (Romans 5:12-21). The theological term for our condition is *depravity*. This doesn't mean we're as bad as we can be; it means we're as bad *off* as we can be. And it explains why the human race hasn't been able to evolve out of our continuing cycle of warfare, crime, violence, and selfishness: we can't. No amount of education or wealth or self-improvement can rectify our fallen human condition, nor satisfy our souls' need for salvation. This is why, as Ephesians explains, "God, who is rich in mercy, because of His great love with which He loved us, even when we were dead in trespasses, made us alive together with Christ (by grace you have been saved)" (Ephesians 2:4-5).

God loved you before you ever felt you might need Him, when you were still caught up in your sins. And now that you've received His free gift of salvation through faith (Ephesians 2:8-9), you don't need to go through life worrying that God is holding things against you, living in fear of His wrath. He set you free, and you "are His workmanship, created in Christ Jesus for good works, which God prepared beforehand that we should walk in them" (v. 10); at the very least, breathe an ongoing sigh of relief and enjoy it!

God's wealth extends to your spiritual family, believers in your church, community, nation, and around the world. Paul expanded on how we fit together as a family, Jews and Gentiles together, all of us partakers of the same inheritance, the same grace, the same promise—all part of "the unsearchable riches of Christ" (Ephesians 3:8). Paul called it "the fellowship of the mystery" (v. 9), whereby God gives us each gifts, we share them with one another, and in sharing them, we build up the body of Christ. This mystery was kept secret in the Old Testament but revealed and unfolded in the New Testament.

The Believer's Walk (Ephesians 4:1–6:9)

We should live life in light of our wealth as sons and daughters of Christ and "walk worthy of the calling with which you were called" (Ephesians 4:1). Own your inheritance as a Christian—which, as you might expect, involves a paradox. To walk through life on that elevated level with Jesus, you have to walk before other Christians "with all lowliness and gentleness, with longsuffering, bearing with one another in love, endeavoring to keep the unity of the Spirit in the bond of peace" (vv. 2-3). To have a personal relationship with Jesus, then, isn't an isolating thing but an inclusive one, requiring you to live life with other believers.

While God gave each one of us grace and gifts, we are to use them to serve the church, "for the equipping of the saints for the work of ministry, for the edifying of the body of Christ, till we all come to the unity of faith and of the knowledge of the Son of God, to a perfect man, to the measure of the stature of the fullness of Christ" (vv. 12-13). There's really no place in God's plan for selfish living; He designed us for sacrificial serving. It's about the group, not the individual.

Paul also addressed walking before a world that rejects Him. "This I say, therefore, and testify in the Lord, that you should no longer walk as the rest of the Gentiles walk, in the futility of their mind, having their understanding darkened, being alienated from the life of God" (vv. 17-18). To truly follow Christ, Paul said, you have to "put off, concerning your former conduct, the old man"—the old you, that is—"which grows corrupt according to the deceitful lusts, and be renewed in the spirit of your mind, and that you put on the new man which was created according to God, in true righteousness and holiness" (vv. 22-24). Like ripping off old smelly rags and donning a new wardrobe, we are then to strut our new stuff on the "runway," surrounded by a worldly audience in hopes that our spiritual fashion would attract them to the Designer.

This is a simple but essential truth. More than leaving the crowd you once ran with, you leave the ways of the crowd, their values. "You were once darkness, but now you are light in the Lord. Walk as children of light" (Ephesians 5:8). That means no more of the old habits—lying, acting on anger, theft, leading others astray with your words and actions. Rather than being "partakers with them" in disobedience (v. 7), be "imitators of God as dear children" (v. 1). You're no longer part of the problem; you're part of the solution. Don't be afraid to be different than unbelievers are. Don't be afraid to stick out for the right reasons. "See then that you walk circumspectly, not as fools but as wise, redeeming the time, because the days are evil" (vv. 15-16). Step carefully, in other words; think about what you do and say as a follower of Christ. Live with precision.

If your Christianity doesn't work at home, it's not working at all.

The kind of walk that impacts the world starts at home. If your Christianity doesn't work at home, it's not working at all. That doesn't mean that people at home will always respond to your love and grace the way you want them to, but it does mean that those relationships are your first ministry and primary concern. Paul laid out the key to making family relationships work: submission.

Paul's instructions to husbands and wives are familiar to couples who have studied God's design for marriage, particularly where he talked about wives submitting to their husbands because the husband is the head of the wife (Ephesians 5:22-23). However, Paul's thought doesn't begin in verse 22. He started in the verse before, talking about how all believers should be "submitting to one another in the fear of God" (v. 21). It's not just an instruction for wives, but a principle for everyone in the family: Submit first to God.

After that, Paul described what submission should look like in family relationships: wives submit to husbands, husbands to God, children to parents, and so on. And for husbands, the command to love their wives like Christ loved the church (v. 25) involves a level of sacrificial love that can only be compared to Christ submitting Himself to the will of the Father when He went to the cross. That's how a husband submits to his wife, voluntarily putting his desires aside to love her in the most complete way possible. A husband has to be willing to die to all other rivals, including people, projects, and pastimes. He will then discover that his wife will most likely delight in submitting to his leadership.

We're to walk before believers, we're to walk before the world, and we are to walk at home by mutual submission. Whatever relationship you're working on, do it with "fear and trembling, in sincerity of heart, as to Christ; not with eyeservice, as men-pleasers, but as bondservants of Christ, doing the will of God from the heart" (Ephesians 6:5-7). What I have discovered is that, whether it's a husband and wife, children and parents, or employees and bosses, if each approaches the other with humility, willing to fulfill their God-given role in that relationship, then submission becomes the oil that lubricates the gears that make the relationship run smoothly. That's how you avoid the grind that life can become when relationships get messy; that's the pathway to joy.

The Believer's Warfare (Ephesians 6:10-24)

Finally, Paul wanted to prepare the Ephesians for where a walk with God would take them: the front lines of a conflict. Christianity is not a playground; it's a battleground. As a believer, you are in the fight. Paul said as much in his final words: "Finally, my brethren, be strong in the Lord and in the power of His might. Put on the whole armor of God, that you may be able to stand against the wiles of the devil" (Ephesians 6:10-11). Spiritual pacifism doesn't work, because whether you take Satan seriously or not, he is real. He hates you just because God loves you, and he is constantly at work to destroy what God loves. There's no fence-sitting for a Christian. Spiritually speaking, you have to fight, or you will be defeated; however, as Paul noted, you are not defenseless.

The first step is to know your enemy. In the Christian's case, he's been identified: the devil, and his minions. "We do not wrestle against flesh and blood, but against principalities, against powers, against the rulers of the darkness of this age, against spiritual hosts of wickedness in the heavenly places" (Ephesians 6:12). If you are accessing your wealth in Christ and walking with Him, you are a target—and that's good. It means that you have clearly identified yourself as God's child, and that all of God's resources are at your disposal. Before you worry too much that you're running around with a big bull's-eye on your back, you need to know what's in your weapons cache.

Those resources include spiritual weapons called "the whole armor of God" (Ephesians 6:13), which Paul advised you to put on every day, "that you may be able to stand against the wiles of the devil" (v. 11). Your arsenal is listed (vv. 14-18): the belt of truth to solidify your core, the breastplate of righteousness to guard your heart, the gospel of peace on your feet so you can walk like Christ, the shield of faith to protect you from enemy attacks, the helmet of salvation to cover your mind, and the sword of the Spirit—God's Word, taken to heart and employed in all situations. Last but not least you have prayer, which enables spiritual night-vision so you can be "watchful to this end with all perseverance and supplication for all the saints" (v. 18).

This is why you must never panic when engaged in spiritual warfare. You've got the leading edge. And you have lots of allies—God's own angels, the hosts (or armies) of heaven. "The LORD of Heaven's Armies is here among us" (Psalm 46:7 NLT). While a third of heaven's angels fell with Satan and are arrayed against you, two-thirds remain in God's service and are for you, employed to serve you (Hebrews 1:14). Don't get stuck on the demons, because they are outnumbered and outgunned—which they would be even if every angel ever created stood against Christ.

Remember your wealth in Christ—you are chosen, adopted, and redeemed—and that you are on the winning side. Spiritual warfare is real, and if you're not engaged, then you will be neutralized in your walk and in God's greater plans for you as His heir and ambassador. Fight the good fight with everything you can get your hands on and your heart around.

> **Remember your wealth in Christ—you are chosen, adopted, and redeemed—and that you are on the winning side.**

PHILIPPIANS
FLIGHT PLAN

Facts

Author

Paul is identified as the author of Philippians, along with his like-minded friend Timothy (Philippians 1:1). Paul wrote this letter while he was in prison awaiting the outcome of a trial, though it's not known exactly where he was imprisoned: Rome, Ephesus, Corinth, Caesarea, or elsewhere. The traditional view is that Paul wrote this while imprisoned in Rome, awaiting a final verdict regarding his case (Philippians 1:19-20), based on his reference to palace guards and those of Caesar's household (Philippians 1:13; 4:22). Timothy, a fellow Christian and constant companion of Paul's, tended to Paul during this time and probably delivered this letter to the Philippian church (Philippians 2:19).

Date Written

Depending on which prison Paul wrote from, several dates of composition are possible, ranging from AD 50 (if he was in Corinth) to AD 62 (if he was in Rome).

Landmarks

Nicknamed the Epistle of Joy, Philippians contains a message of longsuffering and joy in the face of persecution and hardship, written during one of Paul's stays in prison. Despite his trials, Paul rejoiced over the church in Philippi and encouraged them to live in unity and humility.

The church in Philippi might never have been founded and established if not for a vision that brought Paul to Macedonia (Acts 16:9-10). His extremely personal letter to the Philippians showcases his special affection for this caring and generous church. Paul expressed his love for the people there as well as his concern that they might drift away from all they had been taught. What's remarkable is Paul's personal expression of joy in spite of his imprisonment; the word *joy* appears five times in the book, and the word *rejoice*, eleven.

Paul's main concern was that the gospel was preached, no matter what happened to him. He showed an overwhelming devotion to Christ as he preached unity, humility, and dependency to the Philippian church, exhorting them to have joy in both their suffering and service to Christ. He also encouraged them to pursue for themselves the mind of Christ, the knowledge of Christ, and the peace of Christ. In closing, he reminded the Philippians that their true home was heaven.

Itinerary

- The Marvel of the Christian Life: Love (Philippians 1)
- The Model of the Christian Life: Christ (Philippians 2)
- The March of the Christian Life: Forward (Philippians 3)
- The Marks of the Christian Life: Peace and Joy (Philippians 4)

Gospel

Jesus Christ is, of course, the perfect model of the Christian life. In Philippians, Paul touched on one of the most remarkable aspects of Jesus's character: His humility and lowliness. No human being sets out to be humble and lowly. To most of us, that's equivalent to failing at life; we're constantly trying to make something of ourselves, climbing up higher on the ladder of life instead of stooping down lower. But that's a worldly way of living. Anyone can do that. Most everyone already does that. Jesus did the opposite. He was every bit as much God as the Father, but He gave it up to come to earth and serve mankind (Philippians 2:5-7).

Paul essentially gave us a backstage look at the incarnation and what Jesus went through in becoming a man. In Philippians 2:7, the Greek word that describes how He "made Himself of no reputation" is *kenoó*.[73] It means He emptied Himself when He became human, not of being God but of the prerogatives of God—i.e., the rights that are His because He is God.

You might say Jesus gave up His benefits as God: the glory He shared with the Father, angels praising Him at every moment, and the intimate company of the Father and the Spirit. Jesus also gave up His independent authority. While He was on earth, He submitted to the will of the Father: "I always do those things that please Him" (John 8:29). As Jesus prayed at Gethsemane, "Nevertheless not My will, but Yours, be done" (Luke 22:42).

When Jesus's job on earth was done, God restored Him to glory and gave Him "the name which is above every name" (Philippians 2:9), but He left quite an example for believers to follow. As His people, we are to humble ourselves like Jesus did, pouring ourselves out—casting aside what we think we deserve, want, or need—and being filled instead with the Spirit of God. In Philippians 2, Paul was basically saying, "When I tell you to be humble and love and serve one another, here's your model: Jesus Himself." You couldn't ask for a better one.

History

The city of Philippi in Macedonia was the gateway between Asia and Europe. Named after Philip II of Macedon (the father of Alexander the Great), the city was officially made a Roman colony in 42 BC after Marc Antony and Octavian defeated Julius Caesar's assassins, Brutus and Cassius, in a battle near the city.[74] Paul and his first two Philippian converts to Christianity, Lydia and the city jailer (Acts 16), founded the church there during Paul's second missionary journey (AD 50–53). It was the first Christian church established in Europe.

Travel Tips

Paul's chains and trials matured him in a way that a smooth-sailing, trouble-free life never could have. The result of him leaning hard on God and His grace brought balance to his point of view: "I know how to live on almost nothing or with everything. I have learned the secret of living in every situation, whether it is with a full stomach or empty, with plenty or little" (Philippians 4:12 NLT).

- Make plans but be ready for God to change them—and trust Him to know what's best for you when He does. Paul originally didn't plan to go to Philippi; he first traveled there because it was the only option the Holy Spirit gave him (through a vision in Acts 16:6-10). But Paul was grateful because God furthered the gospel through his trials and detours (Philippians 1:12).

- Enjoy being in the family business. Paul's joy and thankfulness were directly proportional to the growth of God's work. If you're a Christian, you're part of that family business, which means you should get involved in the global rescue operation God is overseeing. For reasons that we won't fully grasp this side of eternity, God has chosen to use people as agents to accomplish His work and His will, which is the salvation of all who are willing to come to Him through Jesus Christ.

Humility is the least natural and most important of all virtues.

- Humility is the least natural and most important of all virtues. Selfish ambition is at the heart of fallen humanity, as reflected in our values and culture. But Paul called all believers to be like Jesus, stooping lower and lower in humility rather than climbing higher and higher on the social ladder. You're never more like Satan than when you're selfish, and never more like Jesus than when you serve.

- When you're effective for Christ, Satan will target you. The Philippian church was being threatened with division because two women—possible founders of the church, but influential members of the fellowship nonetheless—had given Satan a foothold not just in their hearts but in the life of the church as a whole (Philippians 4:2-3). Paul knew that if they followed Christ's example of humility, they could resolve their issues and keep the church safe too.

- Your theology originates from one of two places: self-interest, or the interests of others. Think of these two approaches as two basins of water: The first is Pontius Pilate's basin; he washed his hands of the responsibility for Jesus's crucifixion in order to protect his own political agenda (Matthew 27:24). But Jesus filled a basin with water the night He was betrayed and lovingly stooped to wash the feet of His disciples—former fishermen, tax collectors, political zealots, and even a traitor (John 13:3-5)—modeling the others-oriented nature of His ministry. Which basin will you choose?

In Flight

The Marvel of the Christian Life: Love (Philippians 1)

Among Paul's opening words is a statement that, compared with his experience, doesn't make a lot of sense: "I thank my God upon every remembrance of you, always in every prayer of mine making request for you all with joy" (Philippians 1:3-4). His clear affection for the Philippians stood in contrast to a trio of contrary facts: he hadn't wanted to go to Macedonia in the first place, going only because God closed the door to his intended pathway to Asia and sent him a vision of a man telling him to come to Macedonia (Acts 16:9-10); further, he never found the guy in the vision, only a few women down by the riverside (Acts 16:13-15); and finally, he took a pretty serious beating and ended up in jail (not unusual for Paul, but still, not a reminder of good times).

You would think that looking back to his time in Philippi would make Paul sick to his stomach, remembering the frustration and pain he experienced in relation to his visit. But that wasn't the case. Instead, he was grateful "for [their] fellowship in the gospel from the first day until now" (Philippians 1:5). Paul didn't want to go to Philippi, but there he found confirmation that the gospel message produces a larger family—a group of fellow believers with whom to share life's ups and downs.

None of it was what Paul expected, from being taken in by Lydia, who received Christ after hearing Paul's words at the river, to Paul and Silas's jailer, whose whole family converted after Paul and Silas stuck around when an earthquake broke down the doors and loosed their chains (Acts 16:25-34). Whatever misgivings Paul had about Philippi dissolved in his gratitude for the work God had done through his presence there. As long as God's business was being done, Paul rejoiced and was thankful.

Even as he wrote the Philippians from another prison cell, Paul maintained a God-centered perspective. "I want you to know, brethren, that the things which have happened to me have actually turned out for the furtherance of the gospel, so that it has become evident to the whole palace guard, and to all the rest, that my chains are in Christ" (Philippians 1:12-13). Paul was in chains in Rome, but he also had a captive audience (literally—guards were chained to him in shifts throughout the day) for the gospel. God had used His secret agent, Paul, to gain entry into the emperor's own household, through Caesar's own Secret Service agents.

Can you imagine being chained to Paul the apostle? The impact that would make on your life? No wonder he was saying, "Hey! Don't feel sorry for me. Some of these guys are coming to Christ." And at the end of the letter, he greeted them from some of those saved in Caesar's household. There are no prison walls God can't penetrate, no chains He can't break, whether you're an inmate, an addict, or an unhappy housewife. Martin Luther translated the Bible into German while he was in prison. John Bunyan wrote *The Pilgrim's Progress* while incarcerated. Paul wrote four letters with his arms shackled in prison fetters. Some of your greatest work could take place now if you let God into that place of confinement and watch Him work.

> **Some of your greatest work could take place now if you let God into that place of confinement and watch Him work.**

That doesn't mean that jail life was a spa day, though. Even Paul grew weary of his chains, and he confessed as much. "For to me, to live is Christ, and to die is gain…I am hard-pressed between the two, having a desire to depart and be with Christ, which is far better. Nevertheless to remain in the flesh is more needful for you" (Philippians 1:21, 23-24). In a sense, he was between the Rock and a hard place—between the hope of heaven and the hope-sucking pain of a prison cell on earth. But the Rock, Jesus, helped him be useful in the hard place (1 Corinthians 10:4).

Paul always kept others in mind. It would have been a relief for him to end all the physical suffering he had endured as he spread the good news of Jesus, but he was willing to postpone heaven if God had further use for him, whether it was in ministering to prison guards or receiving visitors or writing letters to encourage the churches. Regardless of Paul's circumstances, his Christ-centered love for others made his life a marvel.

The Model of the Christian Life: Christ (Philippians 2)

Paul then unpacked the inspiration for his example: Jesus Christ. He wrote of the consolation he had because he belonged to Christ, the loving comfort and spiritual fellowship, the affection and mercy, which spreads from Jesus through the hearts and lives of His followers, and encouraged the Philippians to follow Christ's lead: "Fulfill my joy being like-minded, having the same love, being of one accord, and of one mind. Let nothing be done through selfish ambition or conceit, but in lowliness of mind let each esteem others better than himself" (Philippians 2:2-3). Humility is always a better path than superiority.

Paul was writing in the midst of a culture that hated humility, thought it weak, pathetic, subservient, and fruitless. But according to the very example of Jesus Christ, it's the supreme virtue. So Paul said, "Let each of you look out not only for his own interests, but also for the interest of others. Let this mind be in you which was also in Christ Jesus" (vv. 4-5). Selfish ambition is at the heart of fallen humanity; we all face it, all default to it in our original sinful nature. But to follow Christ is to take on His nature—humbly seeking to forgive, rescue, and restore.

Jesus Christ is our Savior, but He is also the model of the Christian life. So rather than thinking, *I've got to climb the ladder*, seeking to go higher and higher, Paul was saying, "Like Jesus, bend lower and lower—so low that you can see to serve people." That was Jesus's mindset, "who, being in the form of God, did not consider it robbery to be equal with God, but made Himself of no reputation" (vv. 6-7). This section of Scripture is really the theology behind the Christmas story—an infinite God condescending to become a human baby, born to a poor virgin girl and nestled in a feeding trough.

Being "in the form of God" (v. 6) means that, at all times, Jesus possessed the essential, unchangeable nature of God. In becoming human, "He humbled Himself"—not just by taking on a human body with all of its frailty, but by serving God by serving people—"and became obedient to the point of death, even the death of the cross" (v. 8). He humbled Himself by giving up His rights and benefits as God in heaven; He gave up His glory—angels praising Him every moment—and His intimate fellowship with the Father and the Holy Spirit. Jesus also gave up His independent authority; every moment He was here on earth, He submitted Himself to the will of the Father, to please Him and give us an example.

Jesus, in that sense, was the ultimate missionary. Think about it: Jesus must have experienced an intense case of culture shock in coming to earth! Just ask any missionary who enters a totally different society in a totally different country. At first it's exciting: you're making your mark in a foreign land for Jesus, giving everything for the gospel. After a few days, though, it can get old. No air conditioning, no hamburgers, no soft bed. You eventually get used to it, but the initial shock can be quite an experience. In a similar way, Jesus was the ultimate cross-cultural, cross-bearing missionary: He left heaven to come here, and He did it out of humility, for it was the Father's will that through Jesus's sacrifice on the cross we might be saved from sin (see **Gospel** on page 490).

The March of the Christian Life: Forward (Philippians 3)

A word of warning sneaks into the letter at this point as Paul's affection for the Philippians compelled him to give them a heads-up. "For me to write the same things to you is not tedious, but for you it is safe. Beware of dogs, beware of evil workers, beware of the mutilation [that is, circumcision]! For we are the circumcision, who worship God in the Spirit, and rejoice in Christ Jesus, and have no confidence in the flesh" (Philippians 3:1-3). What's all that about?

The problem was a group of spiritual scavengers who were devouring the gospel of grace and trying to drag Christians backward into the law instead of leading them forward into grace. Paul had often confronted these false teachers, called Judaizers, and he couldn't stand the thought of these "dogs" sinking their teeth into his beloved Philippians. He reminded them, "Look, I was a full-on Jew, born, raised, and trained, and I've left that behind." Following Christ was what mattered most to Paul, not bragging about being a super-religious Jew: "What things were gain to me, these I have counted loss for Christ" (v. 7).

Paul was marching forward for the sake of the gospel: "I press toward the goal for the prize of the upward call of God in Christ Jesus" (v. 14). He didn't claim to have it all figured out—to have arrived as the Christian version of the Pharisee he had once been: "Not that I have already attained, or am already perfected; but I press on that I may lay hold of that for which Christ Jesus has also laid hold of me" (v. 12). Paul wasn't perfect, but he was pressing onward.

It broke Paul's heart that some believers were being taken in by those "whose god is their belly, and whose glory is their shame—who set their mind on earthly things" (v. 19). He reminded the Philippians of the goal they were striving for: heaven. Your march forward will eventually take you into eternity: "Our citizenship is in heaven, from which we also eagerly wait for the Savior, the Lord Jesus Christ, who will transform our lowly body that it may be conformed to His glorious body" (Philippians 3:20-21). No matter how much work you put into your earthly body, it's still "lowly" compared to the glorified body awaiting you in heaven. The older you get, the more you notice (and admit) just how lowly your body is, and heaven starts looking better and better. It's worth pressing on for, through all the aches and pains of this life.

The Marks of the Christian Life: Peace and Joy (Philippians 4)

As Paul wrapped up, he touched on the key virtues that mark the Christian life: peace and joy. First, he encouraged peace with others—and he had a case study in mind. "Therefore, my beloved and longed-for brethren, my joy and crown, so stand fast in the Lord, beloved. I implore Euodia and I implore Syntyche to be of the same mind in the Lord" (Philippians 4:1-2). There seems to have been an argument between these two women; no details are given, just the request to be like-minded in the Lord. Paul knew, however, that any unresolved division in the church could give a Satan a foothold by which to destroy it, so he told them to sort it out. Peace within your church makes it a refuge from the clatter of this world.

Peace within yourself is mentioned next: "Be anxious for nothing, but in everything by prayer and supplication, with thanksgiving, let your requests be made known to God, and the peace of God, which surpasses all understanding, will guard your hearts and minds through Christ Jesus" (vv. 6-7). There's more to unpack here than our cruising altitude permits, but it's one of Scripture's great promises, directing the believer to take every concern to God in prayer, and leave it with Him, trusting He will do what is best. Replace worry with worship, panic with prayer, anxiety with adoration, and groaning with gratitude. If you treat this section like the command it's phrased as, you'll see how your obedience leads to peace.

Replace worry with worship, panic with prayer, anxiety with adoration, and groaning with gratitude.

Paul also emphasized rejoicing, expressing repeatedly his joy in the Christians at Philippi, but here he revealed how he had put it into practice himself: "I rejoiced in the Lord greatly that now at last your care for me has flourished again; though you surely did care, but you lacked opportunity. Not that I speak in regard to need, for I have learned in whatever state I am, to be content" (vv. 10-11).

He knew that the Philippians had always cared for him and supported his ministry (vv. 15-17), but while in jail in Rome, he had received another gift from them (v. 18). Paul's trust in God's sufficient grace meant that he didn't get anxious about financial support, and he rejoiced that the Philippians were in sync with God enough to continue to support his work in a difficult time. Contentment for the Christian begins with gratitude and is fueled by joy.

Paul also wanted his Philippian supporters to understand that they, as givers, would also be receivers of the ultimate blessing of contributing to God's work. He wasn't after their bucks but their benefit: "Not that I seek the gift, but I seek the fruit that abounds to your account" (Philippians 4:17). His comment is an inside glimpse into heavenly bookkeeping. Their support of his ministry meant that the souls saved as a result of Paul's missionary work would be credited to their side of God's account ledger—a reward in heaven for their participation in God's work. Besides, however else God would remunerate them, they would receive big hugs in heaven from people they'd never met, who would be there because they supported Paul and Silas financially.

As believers, then, we should be careful and prayerful about where we invest financially. Look to support ministries that are bearing fruit—bringing souls into the kingdom of heaven. That's the bottom line in God's books, as opposed to people begging for more resources, pleading and cajoling, saying they'll go under if you don't meet their financial need. God may use you to supply a need, but if the fruit's not there, your money and time shouldn't be either. I think Jesus was referring to this when He said, "I tell you, use worldly wealth to gain friends for yourselves, so that when it is gone, you will be welcomed into eternal dwellings" (Luke 16:9 NIV). Learn to look at the money you have as both a stewardship *from* God as well as an investment *for* God.

Supporting a guy like Paul is a sound investment. You know he won't let anything stop him from sharing the gospel, and the fruit of saved souls was evident everywhere he went. The Philippians saw even more proof as Paul signed off, saying, "All the saints greet you, but especially those who are of Caesar's household" (Philippians 4:22). Some of those soldiers Paul was chained to in Caesar's household were coming to Christ. As they served the king of Rome, Paul introduced them to the King of kings. When they switched shifts every six hours, they would want to know more about the letters Paul was writing, the truths he was discussing, the warnings he was giving. No doubt they brought their questions to him, and grew as a result.

Paul was always on the clock for Christ, a great example that any place you're at can become a fulcrum, a launching pad for you to share the gospel. No wonder he told us, "Rejoice in the Lord always. Again I will say, rejoice!" (Philippians 4:4).

COLOSSIANS
FLIGHT PLAN

Facts

Author

The apostle Paul is identified as the author of Colossians (Colossians 1:1). The word *apostle* means "to send." When Paul used the term *apostle* to refer to himself in Colossians 1:1, he was saying that he was sent as a messenger—in his case, on behalf of Jesus. What a wonderful thought, considering that Paul was once a persecutor of Christians before his Damascus road conversion around AD 34 (Acts 9).

Date Written

Colossians is one of Paul's four prison letters recorded in the Bible. He probably wrote several of these letters, specifically while imprisoned in Rome between AD 60 and 62.

Landmarks

The young church at Colossae had quickly become the target of heretical attacks. The so-called Colossian heresy included belief in ceremonialism, asceticism (severe self-discipline), angel worship, the depreciation of Christ (lessening or cheapening His identity as fully God and fully man), secret knowledge, and reliance on human wisdom and tradition. It's likely that the Colossian heresy was a mix of an extreme form of Jewish legalism and an early stage of Gnosticism. As an old saying puts it, "A lie can travel halfway around the world while truth is still putting on its shoes."

Paul's main purpose in this letter was to refute the Colossian heresy. To accomplish this goal, he exalted Christ as the very image of God, the Creator, the pre-existent Sustainer of all things, the head of the church, the first to be resurrected, the fullness of deity in bodily form, and the reconciler. Thus, he concluded, Christ in and of Himself is completely adequate, and we have been given the fullness of salvation through Him. The Colossian heresy, on the other hand, was altogether inadequate. As a mere human philosophy, it was empty, hollow, and deceptive, lacking the ability to empower the believer for new life in Christ.

> Christ in and of Himself is completely adequate, and we have been given the fullness of salvation through Him.

Itinerary

- Personal Issues: The Wisdom of Christ (Colossians 1:1-14)
- Doctrinal Information: The Preeminence of Christ (Colossians 1:15–2:23)
- Practical Instruction: The Application of Christ (Colossians 3:1–4:6)
- Relational Interaction: The Hidden Saints of Christ (Colossians 4:7-18)

Gospel

The book of Colossians contains the Bible's strongest written defense of Christ's preeminence—His position of unmatched superiority and His role as the most important person ever to exist. Both the Gnostics and Judaizers denied this aspect of who Jesus is, and the blend of both parties' philosophies in Colossae confused the church there.

Paul began his defense of Christ's preeminence by stating that Jesus "is the image of the invisible God" (Colossians 1:15). Paul understood that his audience was aware of two coexisting realities: the visible world that we live in and can detect with our five senses and the invisible world inhabited by unseen spiritual beings—i.e., God and His angels, and Satan and his fallen angels.

Where does Jesus fit in this hierarchy of things we can and can't see? Right at the top. He is "the firstborn over all creation. For by Him all things were created" (vv. 15-16)—in heaven and on earth, both the seen and unseen. As the *firstborn*—which is the Greek word *prototokos*, meaning first in importance or priority[75]—Jesus made everything that exists and holds it all together, sustaining the material universe in perfect balance.

What's the ultimate reason for all this? So "that in all things [Jesus] may have the preeminence" (v. 18). If Jesus is the preexisting one, the Creator and Sustainer of all that we can and cannot see, the incarnation and image of God Himself, and the founder of the church, it makes sense that He should occupy the preeminent, or most important, place in peoples' lives. God the Father assigned Him that preeminent position, and so should we. That's the full message of the gospel.

History

The ancient city of Colossae was located in modern-day Turkey along the Lycus River near the cities of Laodicea and Hierapolis. Laodicea (whose church Jesus called out for its lukewarm spirituality in Revelation 3) was the financial center of the area, while Hierapolis was known for its spas and supposedly healing waters.[76]

In Paul's time, Colossae had already fallen in prestige and prominence in the Roman Empire. Earlier in its history, especially around the fifth century BC, it had been a thriving city, known for its trade and clothing business.[77] The church at Colossae was founded during Paul's three-year stay in Ephesus during his third missionary journey (AD 52–57). Paul's friend Epaphras may have helped with getting the church started.

In the years after Christ's death and resurrection, a belief system that became known as Gnosticism began to take shape and work its way into religious circles, the church at Colossae not excluded. It was likely a blend of Gnosticism and Judaism that had taken root in the Colossian church. Simply put, the Gnostics believed that God is good, but everything in the material world is evil. Because of that, Jesus could not have had a physical body; He must have been what Gnostics called an emanation, or *aeon*—some part of God's essence that emanated out from Him. Because God is perfect, He would have nothing to do with an evil material creation, so from time past, they posited, various emanations simply came forth from Him and accomplished various deeds. One of these emanations created the world, for example, and another one came to earth as Jesus.[78] Gnostics also held that in order to become enlightened and saved, one must attain to a secret higher knowledge (*gnosis*) above that of Scripture. That's Gnosticism in a nutshell, and while it's certainly one weird nut, it had a lot of traction in Paul's day. It needed to be refuted.

Travel Tips

The church today desperately needs to take to heart the truths found in Colossians. Throughout the centuries, we as God's people have often gone off track, focusing on secondary concerns and losing sight of the only issues that matter. Paul's letter to the Colossians reminds us to keep Christ at the absolute center of everything because He is everything; nothing in this life matters as much as He does.

- Know who Jesus is. One of Satan's chief tactics is to hijack what God has done or said and twist it to his own advantage. In the mess of Gnosticism and Judaism that plagued Colossae, Satan's false teachers took sound biblical terms like *wisdom, knowledge,* and *spiritual understanding* and redefined them so that they pulled people away from what the Scriptures really taught. When you talk to nonbelievers, especially ones who claim to have a connection to Christianity, know how to define your terms. You'll find that the Jesus whom Paul described in Colossians, for example, is quite different than the Jesus of the Mormons or Jehovah's Witnesses. In your conversations with others, always start with a clear definition of who Jesus is and what He has done.

- Keep first things first. As believers, we all want to grow; we all want more than we've already experienced; we all want a deeper relationship with God. But growth in these areas does not come from any system that preaches that in order to be saved, you must have Jesus *plus something else*—Jesus plus baptism, Jesus plus social justice, Jesus plus marriage, Jesus plus the pro-life movement. You can't add to Christ. Who He is and what He did at the cross are complete. Putting those things—though they're valuable in and of themselves—at the same level of importance as Jesus makes you ineffective in your faith and unproductive as His agent in the world. Working for your own salvation is a sickness, and Jesus is the only one who can cure you of that seemingly inexhaustible addiction. You must trust that Christ alone is enough.

- Keep your eyes on Jesus every day. If He is first in importance in the universe, He must be first in your everyday life. If Jesus doesn't have first place in your marriage, your family, your work, your relationships, your hobbies, or your entertainment—both when everyone is looking and when no one is—can you truly say He is the Lord of your life? Think about it: When you hammer a nail, what do you look at? The nail—not the hammer or your thumb, because you hit what you're aiming for; you hit your target. In the same way, when you make Jesus your focus, you'll hit your target.

> If Jesus is first in importance in the universe,
> He must be first in your everyday life.

In Flight

Personal Issues: The Wisdom of Christ (Colossians 1:1-14)

Paul's mission and emphasis were always Jesus Christ, but here in Colossians, he focused on Jesus Himself in a specific and doctrinal way. He took the identity of Christ and made it a personal issue to them. He began by thanking God for the church at Colossae, and encouraging the people with his prayerful support: "We give thanks...because of the hope which is laid up for you in heaven, of which you heard before in the word of the truth of the gospel, which has come to you, as it has also in all the world, and is bringing forth fruit" (Colossians 1:3, 5). Whenever the true gospel message is preached there will inevitably be fruitful results; people will be affected by it.

There had been spiritual fruit in Colossae, but wherever there is fruit, there are fruit flies. The grace and love that flourished among them had attracted false teachers, so Paul had turned his prayers for the Colossians to their protection: "For this reason we also, since the day we heard it, do not cease to pray for you, and to ask that you might be filled with the knowledge of His will in all wisdom and spiritual understanding" (v. 9). Paul prayed for knowledge, wisdom, and spiritual understanding because these were the areas that were under attack from the Gnostics (see **History** and **Travel Tips** on page 501). He prayed that the Colossians would "walk worthy of the Lord, fully pleasing Him, being fruitful in every good work and increasing in the knowledge of God" (v. 10). Since spiritual growth cannot exist apart from spiritual knowledge, Paul wanted to see the fruit of a deeper love for God's Word.

> Spiritual growth cannot exist apart
> from spiritual knowledge.

The Colossians would need a clear, firm understanding of the truth to combat the subtle, attractive, and totally heretical teachings of the Gnostics. So Paul reminded them of what God had done for them: "He has delivered us from the power of darkness and conveyed us into the kingdom of the Son of His love, in whom we have redemption through His blood, the forgiveness of sins" (Colossians 1:14). The key to fighting this enemy would be turning their eyes toward Jesus and focusing on the truth about who He is and what He had done. It was a matter of the deepest significance, both for the church and each individual in it. Christ's sacrifice brought our status as children of God.

Doctrinal Information: The Preeminence of Christ (Colossians 1:15–2:23)

Paul then turned his attention to the most important issue at stake: the preeminence of Jesus Christ—the place of Christ in the world and in the church (see **Gospel** on page 500). Both the Jewish legalists and the Gnostics denied that Jesus Christ is the most important being in existence, so Paul emphasized that truth: "He [that is, Christ] is the image of the invisible God, the firstborn over all creation. For by Him all things were created that are in heaven and that are on earth, visible and invisible" (Colossians 1:15-16).

Sometimes I just want to land our plane and dig deeply into the rich soil of a verse or concept, and this is one of those moments. Even from 30,000 feet, however, we can observe some powerful truths. Notice, for example, that there is a visible creation and an invisible creation. Both are real; the latter is inhabited by spiritual beings like angels and fallen angels.

Now, when Paul described Jesus as God's *image* at the beginning of verse 15, he used the Greek word *eikón*, which means "likeness" or "portrait."[79] In other words, he was saying Jesus is the visible likeness of the invisible God. Think of it in terms of film photography: Before the days of digital imaging, you'd snap a picture, the shutter opened, light traveled through the lens and the shutter opening, and the silver halide crystals on the surface of the film captured what is called the *latent image* of a photograph.

If you looked at the film, you wouldn't be able to see anything, though the latent image is there. The light has altered the emulsion, though it is not visible yet. But when you apply certain chemicals called *developers* to the film, the reaction of those chemicals brings out the image, amplifying it—taking the invisible and making it visible. Up until Jesus came to earth, God was invisible. But in Jesus He developed a picture of Himself, capturing His character and nature in a way we could see and understand. The apostle John noted, "No one has ever seen God, but the one and only Son, who is himself God and is in closest relationship with the Father, has made him known" (John 1:18 NIV).

Furthermore, Jesus made it all: "All things were created through Him and for

Him. And He is before all things" (Colossians 1:16-17). Go back in time as far as you can—Jesus will walk out of eternity and meet you there. He is the only person who has ever existed before He was born, as John 1:1-3 makes clear: "In the beginning was the Word, and the Word was with God, and the Word was God. He was in the beginning with God. All things were made through Him, and without Him nothing was made that was made."

And not just that, but "in Him all things consist" (v. 17). "Consist" means "to cohere" or "to be held together tightly." Jesus is the superglue that holds the universe together. "And He is the head of the body, the church, who is the beginning, the firstborn from the dead" (Colossians 1:18). The church was Jesus's idea. He said He would build His church (Matthew 16:18), and He's been faithful to do that throughout history, calling men and women together to worship Him, learn about Him, and do His work. Paul wasn't overstating the importance of Jesus—that can't be done—just describing it.

That fact didn't (and hasn't) stopped various cults and false teachers from twisting key words like "firstborn" (v. 15). They'll say, "Jesus isn't God because He was born," or they conveniently take the phrase "firstborn from the dead" (v. 18) out of context, saying it means that Jesus was the first person raised from the dead. But that doesn't make sense, since Jesus raised people from the dead during His ministry and there were resurrections in the Old Testament. "Firstborn," then, can't mean first in chronological order; in fact, it means first in order of status or priority, and that's Jesus (see **Gospel** on page 500)—the most significant, important, and prominent of those who have been resurrected.

God made Jesus first and foremost so "that in all things He may have the preeminence. For it pleased the Father that in Him all the fullness should dwell, and by Him to reconcile all things to Himself, by Him, whether things on earth or things in heaven, having made peace through the blood of His cross" (Colossians 1:18-20). And that makes sense. If Jesus is the preexisting one, as Paul said, if He is the creator and the sustainer, the incarnate one who reveals the personality of God in human flesh, and if He is the originator of the church, He should occupy the most important place in our lives. If all of "the fullness" is in Him, then all you need is Him.

Paul was driving at this crucial truth: Jesus Christ was no second-rate Gnostic emanation, but the true and exact revelation of God the Father. As Jesus told Phillip, "He who has seen Me has seen the Father" (John 14:9). Paul wanted the Colossians to be sure they were focused on the real Christ,

> in whom are hidden all the treasures of wisdom and knowledge. Now this I say lest anyone should deceive you with persuasive words...Beware lest anyone cheat you through philosophy and

empty deceit, according to the tradition of men, according to the basic principles of the world, and not according to Christ (Colossians 2:3-4, 8).

The interesting thing about these false teachers is that they seemed to attach themselves to existing churches rather than going out and winning converts on their own. They wormed their way into congregations of young believers by teaching that Jesus by Himself wasn't enough. You needed Jesus plus the Jewish law, or plus this extrabiblical Gnostic revelation. And if those churches weren't rooted deeply in the truth, they were susceptible.

So Paul reminded the Colossians of some of those truths about Jesus: "In Him you were also circumcised with the circumcision made without hands, by putting off the body of the sins of the flesh, by the circumcision of Christ" (v. 11). Identifying with Christ through His crucifixion is the mark that sets Christians apart—not the physical circumcision of the Law of Moses.

Further, Paul said, they were "buried with Him in baptism, in which [they] also were raised with Him through faith in the working of God, who raised Him from the dead" (v. 12). That's what baptism symbolizes, not what baptism does. Baptism by itself does nothing; it only represents what Jesus did for you through His death and resurrection. Baptism can get you wet but it can't get you clean—where it really counts. Every sacrament is a symbol, not the substance. Every ceremony is completed in Christ (vv. 16-17); no ceremony can accomplish what Jesus did, so there is no way any of them can add to your salvation. Jesus "wiped out the handwriting of requirements that was against us, which was contrary to us. And He has taken it out of the way, having nailed it to the cross" (v. 14).

Everything else being taught by the heretics had "the appearance of wisdom in self-imposed religion, false humility, and neglect of the body, but are of no value against the indulgence of the flesh" (v. 23). If you never learn to rest in the grace God has given you in Christ, you'll never be satisfied, because religious rituals, rites, and ceremonies have no power to restrain your sinful impulse or bring you to God. Choosing holy-looking and holy-sounding things makes you feel good about yourself for a while, but they are poor substitutes for the substance of Jesus Himself.

Practical Instruction: The Application of Christ (Colossians 3:1–4:6)

Paul shifted from correction and doctrinal information to personal and practical application, the real-world working out of God's grace in the believer's life. He began with an *if-then* propositional formula: "If then you were raised with Christ,

[then] seek those things which are above, where Christ is, sitting at the right hand of God" (Colossians 3:1). When you seek heavenly things, values and virtues centered on Christ, you'll be able to "put to death your members which are on the earth: fornication, uncleanness, passion, evil desire, and covetousness, which is idolatry" (v. 5). Since the first part is true theologically and historically, the second part should also be true practically.

The battle of the flesh versus the Spirit, the old man against the new, was a familiar topic for Paul, and he tapped it again here: "But now you yourselves are to put off all these: anger, wrath, malice, blasphemy, filthy language out of your mouth. Do not lie to one another, since you have put off the old man with his deeds, and have put on the new man who is renewed in knowledge according to the image of Him who created him" (vv. 8-10). Break the habits that were part of your life before Jesus, and start doing what reflects your new life in Him: "tender mercies, kindness, humility, meekness, longsuffering; bearing with one another, and forgiving one another" (vv. 12-13).

You're not doing these things to earn salvation but rather to exhibit it. You are saved by grace and therefore have the power to show that grace by gracious behavior. "Above all these things put on love...[and] whatever you do in word or deed, do all in the name of the Lord Jesus, giving thanks to God the Father through Him" (vv. 14, 17). Paul got specific at that point, speaking of the way that love works in family relationships: "Wives, submit to your own husbands, as is fitting in the Lord. Husbands, love your wives and do not be bitter toward them. Children, obey your parents in all things, for this is well pleasing to the Lord. Fathers, do not provoke your children, lest they become discouraged" (vv. 18-21). God's power to change works! And it works first at home in the most primary of human relationships.

Notice how Paul thinks in this letter. He began by exalting Jesus Christ as the creator and the sustainer of everything. He then exalted Christ as the head of the church, and he observed that not only is He the head of creation and Lord of the church, but He needs to be the Lord of the kitchen, the living room, the bedroom, the weekend, and the boardroom. As the preeminent one, He ought to change your relationships, beginning at home, and then on out into the world. You don't add anything to Jesus; you bring Jesus into everything.

Not only is Jesus the head of creation and Lord of the church, but He needs to be the Lord of the kitchen, the living room, the bedroom, the weekend, and the boardroom.

Relational Interaction: The Hidden Saints of Christ (Colossians 4:7-18)

From time to time, Paul listed in his letters associates and coworkers who were important to him. Here he cataloged eleven people. It's tempting to skip over those names, but to Paul, these people were critical to his ministry and spirits. Anytime you see a successful endeavor, whether in ministry or otherwise, there are always unnamed people without whom it wouldn't have happened. Paul devoted the last chapter of this letter to them—the hidden saints. If you were to ask anyone in the first-century church, they would know who they were, perhaps because Paul wrote about them (Colossians 4:7-14). This follows Paul's policy to render honor to whom honor is due (Romans 13:7).

Someone once said that the greatest ability in the world is dependability. Whether you are depending on someone else or being depended on—and you'll play both roles before it's all said and done—ministry gets done only as a group effort. Because we're human, though, there are ups and downs along the way, relationships that need to be both nourished and restored. That's how God wants it, and it's what we see in other people Paul mentioned:

Tychicus, the "beloved brother, [and] faithful minister" (Colossians 4:7), mentioned five times in the New Testament as a partner with Paul on his third missionary journey. Perhaps he had traveled from Colossae to Ephesus to see that new preacher Paul everyone had been talking about, and he had been converted and committed himself to God's work. Paul trusted him to carry his letter to the Ephesian church (Ephesians 6:21).

Onesimus, another "faithful and beloved brother" (Colossians 4:9), had been a runaway slave—a criminal—who, as a fugitive, had run into Paul, been introduced to the gospel, and was restored to his master (the subject of the book of Philemon).

Barnabas's cousin *John Mark* (Colossians 4:10) had gotten homesick as he traveled with Paul and Barnabas on their first missionary journey, and abandoned them, which later caused a division between Paul and Barnabas (Acts 5:35-41). Here, it appears that everyone had been reconciled (also evident in 2 Timothy 4:11), always a good sign among believers.

Epaphras, one of the pastors at Colossae, also sent greetings. Paul mentioned that Epaphras was "always laboring fervently for you in prayers, that you may stand perfect and complete in all the will of God" (Colossians 4:12). Paul sent this letter back with his colaborer, a prayer warrior he clearly admired as much for his "knee-ology" as his theology. Later, Epaphras would be imprisoned with Paul (Philemon 23).

Luke the physician, Paul's traveling companion and the author of the Gospel of Luke and the book of Acts, was with Paul, as was the only person mentioned who provided not a good example but a cautionary tale: Demas (Colossians 4:14). Demas is mentioned three times in the New Testament. He was with Paul on his third trip, when Paul got arrested and beaten, but at some point, it all became too much for Demas, because the last we read of him is in Paul's final letter: "Demas has forsaken me, having loved this present world" (2 Timothy 4:10).

Demas was a guy who had the veneer of a dedicated Christian while all the while loving the things of this world—or at least, not being able to look past the persecution Jesus promised His followers in this life to the glory that awaited those who stayed the course. It's a sad testimony, but a reminder that persecution will separate the wheat from the chaff—the dedicated from the dabbler.

> ## Persecution will separate the wheat from the chaff—the dedicated from the dabbler.

Finally, Paul also wanted the Colossians to exchange letters with the church at Laodicea, which was only ten miles away (Colossians 4:16)—wouldn't it be wonderful to have that letter too!—a reminder that, in the early church, doctrine and correction were spread through such letters as the ones Paul wrote. They were taken as seriously as we take them today, revelations of God's Spirit moving among His people to educate, inform, and encourage them. Paul's epistle to the Colossians no doubt served to keep many on track as they focused on Jesus and refuted the lies of the heretics among them.

1 AND 2 THESSALONIANS
FLIGHT PLAN

Facts

Author

The first verse of each book identifies the apostle Paul as the author. Paul helped establish the church in Thessalonica on his second missionary journey (AD 49–52). He taught the church only for about a month, then was more or less forced by a group of unfriendly Jews to move on to Berea, Athens, and Corinth (Acts 17). After Paul was driven out, he wrote these two letters to address the issues the Thessalonian Christians faced.

Date Written

Paul wrote this first letter to the Thessalonians sometime during his second missionary journey, possibly from the city of Corinth, where Silas and Timothy had met up with him (Acts 18:1-5). First Thessalonians may be the oldest letter we have from Paul, dating from between AD 50 and 51. Second Thessalonians was written very shortly after 1 Thessalonians, possibly within a month, sometime in AD 51 or 52.

Landmarks

Written in the early days of the church, halfway through the first century, both 1 and 2 Thessalonians focus on things of the future. Because of that focus they are called eschatological epistles, or letters about the last days. First Thessalonians is about the Lord's return, and 2 Thessalonians is about the Lord's retribution.

First Thessalonians is about the day of Christ, another euphemism for His coming for the church—called the rapture of the church, our gathering together unto Him. Second Thessalonians is about the day of the Lord, an often-used phrase in Scripture referring to a period of judgment we call the tribulation. Paul wrote both letters to encourage the young believers in the hope of Christ's return and to educate them about the nature of the end times.

Itinerary

First Thessalonians
- Transmission of Faith (1 Thessalonians 1)
- Demonstration of Love (1 Thessalonians 2)
- Exhortation to Godliness (1 Thessalonians 3:1–4:12)
- Instruction for the End Times (1 Thessalonians 4:13–5:28)

Second Thessalonians
- Waiting for Christ's Return (2 Thessalonians 1)
- Warning about Christ's Rivals (2 Thessalonians 2)
- Working as Christ's Representatives (2 Thessalonians 3)

Gospel

Paul summarized the power of the gospel by describing the three tenses of the Christian life: past, present, and future.

> They themselves declare concerning us what manner of entry we had to you, and how *you turned to God from idols to serve the living and true God, and to wait for His Son from heaven*, whom He raised from the dead, even Jesus who delivers us from the wrath to come (1 Thessalonians 1:9-10, emphasis added).

"You turned to God from idols" (v. 9): This describes your past. At one time, you served the obsessions and distractions of this world—but then you turned and placed your faith and belief in God, trusting in Jesus's death and resurrection.

"To serve the living and true God" (v. 9): When you received Jesus as your Lord and Savior, you also decided to make God first in your life. In response to His love and salvation, you now love and serve Him through worship, obedience, and service.

"To wait for His Son from heaven" (v. 10): This describes our future expectation. Jesus will come back for us one day—first to take His church to be with Him, and then to establish His kingdom on earth.

These three tenses of the Christian life show up earlier in chapter 1, when Paul spoke of "remembering without ceasing [the Thessalonians'] work of faith [*the past*], labor of love [*the present*], and patience of hope in our Lord Jesus Christ [*the future*] in the sight of our God and Father" (v. 3). Notice the key words in that verse: faith, love, and hope. Faith looks back to a crucified Savior. Love looks up to a crowned Savior. And hope looks ahead to a coming Savior. It's a wonderful way to summarize the work of Jesus Christ and all that He has done, is doing, and will do for His church.

> Faith looks back to a crucified Savior.
> Love looks up to a crowned Savior.
> And hope looks ahead to a coming Savior.

History

Thessalonica was the capital of the Roman province of Macedonia. It was a seaport city, located on a major trade route to the East. Founded in 316 BC and named after Alexander the Great's sister Thessalonike of Macedon, it became the capital of the region in 148 BC. In the first century BC, it then became a free city—and a prosperous one at that.[80] Sometime after AD 50, Paul visited Thessalonica with Silas, Timothy, and Luke during his second missionary trip (Acts 17). The pair of letters he wrote to the Thessalonians shortly afterward are among the earliest of all New Testament writings, which also shows that the doctrine of Christ's return was paramount to the early church.

Travel Tips

First and Second Thessalonians secure our hope in Jesus's return for His church. In both letters, Paul made it clear we are to live in anticipation of the rapture and second coming of Christ, looking forward to the riches of heaven while living richly on earth and doing all we can to increase God's kingdom in the here and now.

- Keep your dependence on God fresh and authentic. In only three weeks, Paul unleashed the power of the gospel and trusted the Thessalonian believers to hold tightly to it. When problems and challenges arise, especially as you do God's work, they represent an opportunity to depend on Him and continue in your work the same way you began: on your knees in prayer, reading His Word, and trusting Him as you watch Him move.

> ## Keep your dependence on God fresh and authentic.

- Learn to live in anticipation of Jesus's return. Nobody knows how long it will be till He returns, but you can be sure that every single day draws it closer, and it *will* happen. Don't be led astray by those who claim that the doctrine of the rapture is false; know what the Word says, know your church history and your current times, and most importantly, know by the witness of the Holy Spirit within you that Jesus is coming soon.

- Everybody has faith in something. For the believer, growing in faith in God is crucial, and it takes two simple though sometimes difficult acts: immerse yourself in the Word of God, and exercise the faith God has given you. Paul praised the Thessalonians for their "patience and faith in all [their] persecutions and tribulations that [they endured]" (2 Thessalonians 1:4).

In Flight

1 Thessalonians
Transmission of Faith (1 Thessalonians 1)

Paul began this letter with words of gratitude, thanking God for the Christians in Thessalonica, remembering their "work of faith, labor of love, and patience of hope in our Lord Jesus Christ" (1 Thessalonians 1:3). He remarked on how the gospel had come to them, and how it was going out from them. He, Silas (called here Silvanus), and Timothy had taught them and set a godly example among them: "Our gospel did not come to you in word only, but also in power, and in the Holy Spirit and in much assurance, as you know what kind of men we were among you for your sake" (v. 5).

Even though Paul and his team had been in Thessalonica for only three short weeks—probably three weekends, as far as Paul teaching them was concerned—the Christians there had taken it to heart under difficult circumstances (the oppression that drove Paul out of town) and become a model church in the region. "From you the word of the Lord has sounded forth, not only in Macedonia and Achaia, but also in every place. Your faith toward God has gone out, so that we do not need to say anything" (v. 8). Take joy in seeing the work God accomplishes through you. The phrase "sounded forth" is the Greek word *exécheó*[81]—the root of our word *echo*.

The idea is that when we receive God's Word, it should resonate within us and then reverberate from us, bouncing off in waves through our lives and our witness to touch the lives of others.

The gospel came *to* them and now the gospel was coming *through* them. They had received the truth and then become transmitters of the truth. That's where the real joy of the Christian life is. It's not just that God has done a work for you and in you, but that God is doing a work through you to the world. What you hear with your ears and enjoy in your heart should then be heralded by your lips. The believers in Thessalonica were doing their part to transmit God's life-giving message.

The Thessalonians' lives reflected the work God had done in and among them, turning their hearts from idol worship to serving Him and eagerly awaiting the return of Jesus (see **Gospel** on page 511). Love, joy, and hope resulted from their faith, helping them face an uncertain present because they trusted in a certain future—a future about which Paul wanted to give them further encouragement and instruction.

Demonstration of Love (1 Thessalonians 2)

As I noted in **Facts** (on page 510), Paul had been driven out of Thessalonica after three weeks, traveling on to Berea and then Athens (Acts 17). The people who chased Paul away no doubt thought of this as a victory, not realizing that the Holy Spirit hadn't left with Paul, that the Spirit was living inside the converts and guiding them in the truths Paul had shared with them. Paul's enemies, however, were badmouthing him, calling him a charlatan, and Paul wanted to address that—to affirm his credentials and encourage the Thessalonians in case they were feeling uncertain about him.

"Even so we speak, not as pleasing men, but God who tests our hearts. For neither at any time did we use flattering words, as you know, nor a cloak for covetousness—God is witness. Nor did we seek glory from men, either from you or from others, when we might have made demands as apostles of Christ" (1 Thessalonians 2:4-6). Paul had the spiritual authority to command them, to impose his apostolic credentials, but he reminded the Thessalonians that he had, in fact, done just the opposite, being gentle and affectionate among them. "We were gentle among you, just as a nursing mother cherishes her own children" (v. 7). A nursing mother understands the critical nature of the dependence of her newborn, and doesn't make demands for her baby to stop crying for food or to recognize her authority and fall in line.

Paul and his companions got temporary jobs and worked for a living so they wouldn't be a burden on their fellow Christians, presenting a godly example not just when they were preaching on weekends but during the week as they labored to support themselves (v. 9). "You know how we exhorted, and comforted, and charged every one of you, as a father does his own children, that you would walk worthy of God who calls you into His own kingdom and glory" (vv. 11-12). Acting like both a mother and father, then, Paul rejoiced in his spiritual children's growth, and that they took to heart his demonstration of love. "For what is our hope, or joy, or crown of rejoicing? Is it not even you in the presence of our Lord Jesus Christ at His coming? For you are our glory and joy" (vv. 19-20).

Exhortation to Godliness (1 Thessalonians 3:1–4:12)

Paul looked forward to the day when he and his beloved Thessalonians would be reunited in glory forever. But he wanted to make sure they understood what it would take to make their time on earth count for Christ, anticipating Jesus's return as well as staying engaged in His work until then. "Now we live, if you stand fast in the Lord" (1 Thessalonians 3:8). The phrase "stand fast" describes a group of soldiers standing their post and holding their ground, following the orders of their commanding officer.

Above all, Paul encouraged them to love each other, just as he and his companions had loved them, "so that [God] may establish your hearts blameless in holiness before our God and Father at the coming of our Lord Jesus Christ with all His saints" (v. 13). In following the commandment Jesus gave that His followers should love one another so that the world would know they were His (John 13:34-35), the Thessalonian believers would shine God's light in a culture that had not only rejected God's messenger, Paul, but also the moral conduct he espoused. The love of a Christian allows the light of the gospel to penetrate.

The love of a Christian allows the light of the gospel to penetrate.

"Finally then, brethren, we urge and exhort in the Lord Jesus that you should abound more and more, just as you received from us how you ought to walk and to please God; for you know what commandments we gave you through the Lord Jesus. For this is the will of God, your sanctification: that you should abstain from sexual immorality" (1 Thessalonians 4:1-3). Both the Greek and Roman cultures held abstinence in disdain; sexual pleasure had long been part of the worship of Greek deities, and Romans took lovers wherever and whenever they pleased. Before the gospel took hold in that part of the world, promiscuity was the cultural norm.

Paul made it clear that God had better plans for His children, a higher level of moral purpose that included self-control, not self-centeredness: "God did not call us to uncleanness, but in holiness. Therefore he who rejects this does not reject man, but God" (vv. 7-8). It was not uncommon for believers to imitate the culture around them rather than imitating Jesus—or Paul himself, who invited them to heed his example on numerous occasions (in his appeal to his conduct in Thessalonica, as well as in 1 Corinthians 4:6 and 11:1). In that sense, not much has changed. Godly conduct in sexual matters—honoring your spouse and staying pure before marriage—doesn't mean that God is a prude, but that He has something far better for you than giving in to those impulses and desires. Our conduct toward each other and unbelievers regarding sex is just one of the ways we can "walk properly toward those who are outside" (v. 12).

I'm amazed at the depth of the topics Paul alluded to in this letter, given that he spent less than a month among the Thessalonians. Clearly, it wasn't just that they had heard the second greatest Bible teacher ever, after Jesus, but how they listened. As Jesus noted, "Take heed how you hear" (Luke 8:18). And you can hear God's Word in so many different ways in our culture today—radio, television, online, social media, books, and so on. Whereas the Thessalonians and other first-century churches hungered for a letter from Paul or Peter or John, we have to be careful not to let the volume of teaching available dampen our desire to know more of God as He reveals Himself in His Word.

Instruction for the End Times (1 Thessalonians 4:13–5:28)

In the last part of this first letter, Paul addressed one of the concerns that Timothy had reported after his visit to Thessalonica (1 Thessalonians 3:6). As a group of new believers, they had concerns. With all of their loved ones who had been dying under Rome's persecutions, perhaps they would miss the climactic event of Jesus's coming. And would their friends and relatives who had died miss out?

Paul clarified matters: "I do not want you to be ignorant, brethren, concerning those who have fallen asleep [that is, died], lest you sorrow as others who have no hope. For if we believe that Jesus died and rose again, even so God will bring with Him those who sleep in Jesus" (1 Thessalonians 4:13-14). What a great word of comfort—the sure hope that we will be reunited with other believers who have died before us! And here, Paul explained, is how that would happen:

> This we say to you by the word of the Lord, that we who are alive and remain until the coming of the Lord will by no means precede those who are asleep. For the Lord Himself will descend from heaven with

a shout, with the voice of an archangel, and with the trumpet of God. And the dead in Christ will rise first. Then we who are alive and remain shall be caught up together with them in the clouds to meet the Lord in the air. And thus we shall always be with the Lord. Therefore comfort one another with these words (vv. 15-18).

This is what we call the rapture of the church: At some unknown point, Jesus will come back for His church. The "dead in Christ"—those believers who have passed away—will experience their resurrection first, followed by those who are on earth, who will be instantly carried up into the clouds to meet the Lord.

When I bring this up, invariably someone will say the term *rapture* isn't in the Bible, and they're right; but the event we call the rapture is a biblical teaching. Jesus promised His followers that He would return for them (John 14:1-3), and Paul told the church in Corinth about it (1 Corinthians 15:51-52). Just because a word may not be in the Bible is not a valid argument that the concept is also absent. The word *Bible* isn't in the Bible, either, but it's the accepted term for the book containing God's Word. So the term *rapture* accurately describes what will happen when Jesus comes for His church. The phrase "caught up" in 1 Thessalonians 4:17 is the Greek term *harpazó*. Used fourteen times in the New Testament, *harpazó* can mean a number of similar things: to catch up or away, to take by force, to pluck, or to pull.[82] *Rapture* comes from the Latin Vulgate translation of 1 Thessalonians 4:17, which renders *harpazó* as *rapiemur*, related to the Latin *raptus*, which got turned into the English word *rapture*. Each of these words indicates we'll be going up and going up *fast*.

The rapture is a different event than the second coming. In the rapture, Jesus will literally lift His church to Himself somewhere in the atmosphere, and we'll be with Him from then on (v. 17). We don't know exactly when this will happen, but it will leave the earth without true Christians for a time. In contrast, the second coming will be a worldwide event seen by everyone. The Bible specifically tells us that Jesus will physically come all the way to earth 1260 days after a tribulation event called the abomination of desolation, which will occur in a rebuilt Jewish temple in Jerusalem (Revelation 11:2-3). But for unbelievers, God's final judgment will be harsh and unexpected—like "a thief in the night" (1 Thessalonians 5:2).

In the rapture, Jesus will come for believers. Like a groom coming to get his bride, Christ will come to take His bride, the church, to enjoy the "marriage supper of the Lamb" (Revelation 19:6-9). In the second coming, Christ will come with His people to the earth to execute vengeance on the Antichrist, judge the inhabitants of the earth, and set up His millennial kingdom (Revelation 19:11-21). The rapture is sudden, unpredictable; no one knows the day or the hour. The second coming, on the

other hand, is going to happen exactly 1260 days after the abomination of desolation. So three-and-a-half years after a distinguishable point in the tribulation period,
Jesus will come back to the earth to quell Armageddon and bring final judgment.

Paul called that final judgment "the day of the Lord" (1 Thessalonians 5:2), a
phrase mentioned twenty-three times in the Old and New Testaments. "The day
of the Lord" is not restricted to a twenty-four-hour period as much as it is a period
of time when God dramatically intervenes and changes the course of human affairs.
The day of the Lord describes the ongoing process of God's supernatural judgment—something that dates back to Old Testament predictions by Joel, Amos, Isaiah, and Daniel, among others. Here, in Paul's reference, the day of the Lord refers
to the last three-and-a-half years of the seven-year span of the tribulation, when
God's judgment will be poured out on the earth.

It will be the worst period of time in human history. For unbelievers, Jesus will
come in sudden judgment, with all the shock and disappointment of a burglary
(v. 3). In contrast, "you, brethren, are not in darkness, so that this Day should overtake you as a thief" (v. 4). As we look forward to Jesus's return, we should sound
forth to others the good news that through Christ, the day of the Lord can be a
time of rejoicing.

> As we look forward to Jesus's return, we should
> sound forth to others the good news that through
> Christ, the day of the Lord can be a time of rejoicing.

"But let us who are of the day"—that is, Christians saved from wrath and looking forward to Jesus's return—"be sober, putting on the breastplate of faith and love,
and as a helmet the hope of salvation. For God did not appoint us to wrath, but to
obtain salvation through our Lord Jesus Christ" (vv. 8-9). Even though God will
spare believers the wrath appointed for the rest of the world during the tribulation,
we are to be vigilant, wearing the armor of God Paul described in Ephesians 6:10-18
to protect us from the devil and his minions—the "principalities" and "powers" of
the "rulers of the darkness of this age, against spiritual hosts of wickedness in the
heavenly places" (Ephesians 6:12).

God wants His people to behave as though they are His and not fall into the
ways of the world—the system of influence ultimately under Satan's domain. Paul
drew the contrast out in his language. "You are all sons of light and sons of the day.
We are not of the night nor of darkness" (1 Thessalonians 5:5). And because we

are not "appointed to wrath," we can look forward with reassuring confidence to Jesus's return.

2 Thessalonians
Waiting for Christ's Return (2 Thessalonians 1)

A few months later, Paul wrote again to the Thessalonian church to clear up another matter that troubled them. And while typically the sequel of a movie or book lacks the punch of the original, it almost seems like Paul saved the best for last. If you have any appetite for end-times teaching, 2 Thessalonians is a treasure trove because it includes one of the main teachings in the entire Bible about an individual often referred to as the Antichrist. Though he isn't called the Antichrist in this letter, he is given three different names here: "the man of sin" and "the son of perdition" (2 Thessalonians 2:3), and "the lawless one" (vv. 8-9).

Before getting to him, though, Paul cleared up a misunderstanding in the Thessalonian church, "to give you who are troubled rest with us when the Lord Jesus is revealed from heaven with His mighty angels" (2 Thessalonians 1:7). Despite Paul's assurances in his first letter, the Thessalonian Christians were still concerned that the intense, ongoing persecution they were facing was part of the end times, as opposed to the kinds of trials that believers should expect to face simply because they belong to Christ.

Had they somehow missed Christ's return, and, if so, when would their persecutors be judged by God? Shouldn't they have been delivered from such harsh persecution by the Lord they had been waiting for to return? Paul expressed his admiration for them as they faced hardship, and encouraged them that it was a mark of their mature faith, the "manifest evidence of the righteous judgment of God, that you may be counted worthy of the kingdom of God, for which you also suffer" (v. 5).

Paul reassured them that although "it is a righteous thing with God to repay with tribulation those who trouble you" (v. 6), judgment on their enemies might have to wait until the end of the world—a certain event in a time yet to come, when Jesus would definitely make His return and judgment clear to the world "in flaming fire taking vengeance on those who do not know God, and on those who do not obey the gospel of our Lord Jesus Christ. These shall be punished with everlasting destruction from the presence of the Lord and from the glory of His power"—a powerful description of everlasting hell—"when He comes, in that Day, to be glorified in His saints and to be admired among all those who believe, because our testimony among you was believed" (vv. 8-10).

Warning about Christ's Rivals (2 Thessalonians 2)

Paul then clarified what events would happen in the end times, "concerning the coming of our Lord Jesus Christ and our gathering together to Him" (2 Thessalonians 2:1). Because of their faith in Christ, these believers were losing their jobs, being beaten, arrested, and killed—enough persecution to make them ask, "Did we miss the rapture?"

Paul encouraged them "not to be soon shaken in mind or troubled, either by spirit or by word or by letter, as if from us, as though the day of Christ had come" (v. 2). A certain series of events had to happen first, and certain characters had to come on the scene, before the end times would unfold.

> Let no one deceive you by any means; for that Day will not come unless the falling away comes first, and the man of sin is revealed, the son of perdition, who opposes and exalts himself above all that is called God or that is worshiped, so that he sits as God in the temple of God, showing himself that he is God. Do you not remember that when I was still with you I told you these things? (vv. 3-5).

In other words, Paul said, the end times couldn't happen until they had all been gathered together in the air with Jesus, kicking off the seven years of the Tribulation, and the man of sin—the Antichrist—had been revealed at the midpoint of the Tribulation, leading to three-and-a-half terrible years until Jesus returned to earth. In a sense, then, they could relax. They hadn't missed the rapture; it just hadn't happened yet. Furthermore, the time Daniel had prophesied (Daniel 9:27; 11; Matthew 24:15), when the Antichrist would set up an image of himself in the (rebuilt) temple in Jerusalem—the "abomination of desolation"—hadn't happened yet, either. [83] Even though "the mystery of lawlessness [was] already at work" (2 Thessalonians 2:6)— the spirit of the Antichrist in the world, looking to disrupt and destroy the church— the ultimate fulfillment of his appearance won't happen until the end times.

The Holy Spirit is the primary reason that the end times haven't happened yet. As Paul put it, "Only He who now restrains will do so until He is taken out of the way" (v. 7). The Holy Spirit keeps evil—the "mystery of lawlessness"—from completely overtaking the world. And when will He—the Holy Spirit—be taken out of the way to let evil fully run its course? Well, since the Spirit lives in believers and is the only power capable of restraining the evil of the Antichrist, He will leave when we will—at the rapture—setting the stage for the Antichrist's brief reign of terror.

When truth and grace are taken away from the earth, it's going to get ugly. This doesn't mean that the Holy Spirit will be gone altogether during the tribulation period. "Taken out of the way" doesn't mean being taken out of the world. He will still be working in hearts and drawing people to Christ during that dark period, giving them strength to face martyrdom for the sake of Jesus. But the Holy Spirit dwells in the church in a unique way, fulfilling the promise of Jesus to His disciples (John 14:16). When Christians are raptured, that powerful influence will be removed.

The salt and light we are to be in the world (Matthew 5:13-14) will be removed, leaving the world to fester like an infected sore in its immorality and godlessness. "And then the lawless one will be revealed, whom the Lord will consume with the breath of His mouth and destroy with the brightness of His coming" (2 Thessalonians 2:8). Satan's power will orchestrate the rise of the Antichrist, but Jesus's return will utterly demolish both of them. All the people who wish all the narrow-minded Christians would just disappear will one day get their wish. Until then, we must continue to be the salt that preserves goodness and the light that reveals the love of Jesus.

Working as Christ's Representatives (2 Thessalonians 3)

Paul's final words to the Thessalonians blended encouragement and exhortation. "Therefore, brethren, stand fast and hold the traditions which you were taught, whether by word or our epistle" (2 Thessalonians 2:15). Until Jesus returned, Paul was saying, stay true to what you've been taught about God and Christ, representing Him well in a world that can't comprehend Him without faith: "Finally, brethren, pray for us, that the word of the Lord may run swiftly and be glorified, just as it is with you, and that we may be delivered from unreasonable and wicked men; for not all have faith" (2 Thessalonians 3:1-2).

In 1 Thessalonians, Paul had addressed the type of people who had driven him out of the city, and who were misrepresenting him to the church there. Here, he added a postscript of sorts along the same lines: "We command you, brethren, in the name of our Lord Jesus Christ, that you withdraw from every brother who walks disorderly and not according to the tradition which he received from us" (v. 6). He reminded them of how he, Silas, and Timothy had conducted themselves while they were among them, in order to set an example.

"For we hear that there are some who walk among you in a disorderly manner, not working at all, but are busybodies" (v. 11). "Disorderly" indicates that some among them were out of line, not following Paul's example. And Paul told them to "work in quietness and eat their own bread" (v. 12). In other words, *mind your own business and don't be a mooch!* People like that, especially ones who call themselves believers, can wear you out. But Paul encouraged the true believers "not [to] grow weary in doing good" (v. 13).

That included treating in a Christlike way those who were out of order: "If anyone does not obey our word in this epistle, note that person and do not keep company with him, that he may be ashamed. Yet do not count him as an enemy, but admonish him as a brother" (vv. 14-15). Few things are more Christlike than holding an honest line against sin while still holding out the hope of reconciliation and restoration.

The church has been waiting for the return of Jesus Christ for 2000 years—or, as Paul said in another letter, "looking for the blessed hope and glorious appearing of our great God and Savior Jesus Christ" (Titus 2:13). Anyone who says that the rapture couldn't come at any moment doesn't know their church history very well. The earliest believers were eagerly awaiting Christ while living for Him in the meantime.

It's one thing to look at Paul's letters to the Thessalonians and see what he said about Christ's return. It's another to look forward to that event, whether you're napping in the grave or living your life above ground, anticipating that meeting with Him in the heavens. Take that hope into your heart, and then share it with others who have grown weary of the troubles of this world.

1 AND 2 TIMOTHY

FLIGHT PLAN

Facts

Author

The author of 1 and 2 Timothy is identified as the apostle Paul (see the first verse of each letter). Paul wrote three types of letters during his ministry: travel letters (which he wrote while on his missionary trips), prison letters (which he wrote while incarcerated), and pastoral letters (which he wrote to instruct specific individuals after he was released from prison). First Timothy is the first of his three pastoral letters (2 Timothy and Titus are the others).

Second Timothy doubles as a prison letter because Paul wrote it from a prison in Rome. In what was probably his last letter before his execution, Paul gave advice on church leadership and doctrinal concerns. It's also Paul's most personal letter, expressing his love and admiration for his friend Timothy.

Date Written

Paul most likely wrote 1 Timothy from Macedonia between AD 62 and 64, while he was on his third missionary trip. If 2 Timothy was indeed Paul's last epistle, it was probably written sometime in AD 66 or 67.

Landmarks

The book of 1 Timothy details the apostle Paul's advice and instructions to the young pastor Timothy, who was facing a heavy burden of responsibility in the church at Ephesus. The task before him was challenging: false doctrine had to be erased, public worship safeguarded, and mature leadership developed. In addition to addressing the conduct of the congregation, Paul talked pointedly about the proper conduct of a minister. Timothy needed to be on guard so that his youthfulness didn't become a liability rather than an asset to the gospel. Paul instructed him to carefully avoid false teachers and greedy motives and instead pursue righteousness, godliness, faith, love, perseverance, and gentleness as befitting a man of God.

Paul wrote a second epistle to his young protégé from a Roman dungeon. In it, he encouraged Timothy to stand strong for the faith, endure hardship, and preach the Word. The book was meant to serve as a set of final instructions on how to stand up for the faith.

Itinerary

First Timothy
- The Message of the Church (1 Timothy 1)
- The Members of the Church (1 Timothy 2)
- The Ministers of the Church (1 Timothy 3–4)
- The Ministry of the Church (1 Timothy 5–6)

Second Timothy
- The Present Calling: Stand Up for the Faith (2 Timothy 1)
- The Pastor's Character: Stand Up in Your Calling (2 Timothy 2)
- The Practical Concern: Stand Up as You Fight (2 Timothy 3)
- The Personal Charge: Stand Up till the End (2 Timothy 4)

Gospel

Paul summarized redemption's scarlet thread with elegance in a simple statement to Timothy: "[God] desires all men to be saved and to come to the knowledge of the truth. For there is one God and one Mediator between God and men, the Man Christ Jesus, who gave Himself a ransom for all" (1 Timothy 2:4-6). That's as succinct a statement of the gospel as you'll find in Scripture: it captures God's heart, plan, and provision for salvation. Those verses are tailor-made for sharing the message of God's good news—His promise of life in Jesus Christ.

Paul opened his final letter by identifying himself as "an apostle of Jesus Christ by the will of God, according to the promise of *life* which is in Christ Jesus" (2 Timothy 1:1, emphasis added). The heart of the gospel is God's promise of life—not the threat of damnation. Of course, the flip side of that promise is judgment and eternal punishment for those who reject it. Hell is real; Jesus spoke more about it than anyone else in the Bible, not as an allegory or figure of speech but as a real place. But the good news is found in God's promise of life—abundant life now and eternal life later. Paul's ministry wasn't about dangling people over the fires of hell but about explaining what God had done so that they could go to heaven. He won people by the warmth of God's love and by His promise of life.

Paul was a man of great character, and he never took any sort of credit for his salvation. He always threw the focus back on God's grace—how God mercifully chose us to be His own and chooses to use us in everyday life. What if God's love depended on our behavior? We might have a good day every so often—when we read our Bibles and pray and are "good." But other days, not so much. We could never be good or consistent enough to earn God's love, could we? But that's the point of grace: God loves you regardless of your level of goodness or holiness. When you understand grace the way the Bible teaches it, it frees you from man-made rules and regulations, as well as self-righteous protocols that often keep you from living out your salvation with any spiritual power and practical joy.

You can never earn your salvation, but you also can't understand salvation—or God's grace—without hearing or reading God's Word. Studying and applying the truths of the Bible doesn't save you, but it is essential to Christian living. That's why throughout 1 and 2 Timothy, Paul encouraged Timothy to hold fast to the Scriptures (especially 2 Timothy 3:14–4:5). The Lord has given us the Holy Spirit to help guide us into His truth (John 16:13), but we need to do our part by regularly seeking that truth where He has provided it for us—in the Bible.

> The Lord has given us the Holy Spirit to help guide us into His truth, but we need to do our part by seeking that truth where He has provided it for us—in the Bible.

History

The Ephesian church, where Timothy was a pastor, was the heart of Paul's ministry. Paul established the church in Ephesus, spending three years in that town. He then visited the church on his second and third missionary journeys and kept in close contact with the congregation throughout his life. Ephesus was located on the Aegean coast in what is modern-day Turkey. Athens gained control of the city in 454 BC, then lost it to Alexander the Great in 333 BC. In 133 BC, it was officially bequeathed to Rome.[84] Paul founded the church there in AD 53.

Timothy was from Lystra in the province of Galatia. His father was Greek, and his mother was Jewish (Acts 16:1-3). Timothy's mother and grandmother taught him the Old Testament Scriptures (2 Timothy 1:5), but he became a Christian under the ministry of Paul, possibly during the apostle's first missionary journey (AD 47–49). Paul then became Timothy's mentor and friend, and they traveled together during Paul's second and third missionary trips. Timothy was with Paul during Paul's imprisonment in Rome (AD 60), then became pastor of the church in Ephesus sometime afterward.

According to the early church historian Eusebius, Paul was executed under the reign of Emperor Nero sometime before AD 68.[85]

Travel Tips

Paul desired for Timothy to anchor himself and his congregation in God's Word—not so that they would be able to quote a set of rules and regulations, but so that they would grow in their knowledge of God and thus know how to care for and treat one another. Paul's words serve as a relevant reminder of both the joys and trials the Christian life can bring.

- Christians have dual citizenship. We are citizens of heaven as children of God (Philippians 3:20), but we are also called to be responsible citizens of earth. We are to pray not just for the leaders who agree with our political position or are sympathetic to our beliefs, but for all who are in authority (1 Timothy 2:1-2).

- The sole focus of our worship should be God. Paul recognized that dedicating even a short amount of time to focus on the Lord can sometimes be challenging, so he urged us to not only worship in church but also "pray everywhere, lifting up holy hands, without wrath and doubting" (1 Timothy 2:8). And during worship services, avoid doing anything that takes the focus off God and puts it on yourself.

- Money isn't the root of all evil—the *love* of money is (1 Timothy 6:9-10). Our culture's insistence that true satisfaction in life comes from the pursuit and accumulation of material things is a lie and a trap. Real prosperity is not found in things but in relationships—an intimate walk with the living God first and foremost, which brings true forgiveness of sin and relief from shame and guilt.

- Make your words count. Paul's last recorded words in the Bible are "The Lord Jesus Christ be with your spirit. Grace be with you. Amen" (2 Timothy 4:22). Every Christian should aim to finish their life as Paul did: with a strong emphasis on God's grace, power, and faithfulness. How can you make what you say and do count? By making *all* you say and do count.

> How can you make what you say and do count? By making *all* you say and do count.

In Flight

1 Timothy
The Message of the Church (1 Timothy 1)

As Paul addressed Timothy, "a true son in the faith" (1 Timothy 1:2), he got right down to business: "As I urged you when I was in Macedonia—remain in Ephesus that you may charge some that they teach no other doctrine" (v. 3). When it came to the faithful doctrine, or the revealed truth of God, Paul didn't want Timothy to put up with the runaway heresy of the Gnostics and other pseudo-Jewish mystics—the "fables and endless genealogies, which cause disputes rather than godly edification which is in faith" (v. 4).[86]

The Gnostic infection struck the church pretty early on, muddying the waters of scriptural clarity and confusing the new believers who didn't have regular access to an apostle and were often waiting on the latest letter from one to answer their questions. A serious battle for the faith was at hand, and Paul wanted Timothy to stand his ground and have no illusions about the work he was undertaking: "This charge I commit to you, son Timothy, according to the prophecies previously made concerning you, that by them, you may wage the good warfare" (v. 18).

Many Christians today do not know that they are in a war for the truth. Gnosticism may not be the threat today, but moral relativism, neo-atheism, spiritual liberalism, and various unbiblical approaches to Christianity are. We must still "contend earnestly for the faith" (Jude 3)—something we won't know how to do unless we familiarize ourselves daily with God's Word. That happens through individual study, but also through biblical teaching from the pulpit. You might think, *But I'm no Paul—how can I contend the way he did?*

Start by looking at Paul's self-description: By his own admission, he was "formerly a blasphemer, a persecutor, and an insolent man" (1 Timothy 1:13). But he recognized the key to his transformation and to being used by God: "The grace of our Lord was exceedingly abundant, with faith and love which are in Christ Jesus" (v. 14). God often uses the very people who are most aware of their inadequacies: Moses knew he couldn't speak well; Jeremiah recognized his youthful lack of experience; and Paul ranked himself as least among believers. These people are usually the easiest to work with, while the hardest to work with are those who think they have it all figured out. God often has to break down and humble those people and take them through a process of refinement till they come away saying, as Paul did in Romans, "O wretched man that I am! Who will deliver me from this body of death? I thank God—through Jesus Christ our Lord!" (Romans 7:24-25).

God loves to use flawed people to minister to other flawed people and glorify Himself.

Paul was the poster boy of unqualified people being used by the Lord. As he told Timothy in this letter, "For this reason I obtained mercy, that in me first Jesus Christ might show all longsuffering, as a pattern to those who are going to believe on Him for everlasting life" (1 Timothy 1:16). It's so easy to say that God's grace is amazing—you've probably sung the song dozens of times—but we often don't grasp the depth of that truth. God loves to take your inadequacy and turn it into potency! He'll take your weakness and eclipse it with His strength. He loves to use flawed people to minister to other flawed people and glorify Himself.

The Members of the Church (1 Timothy 2)

Paul then talked about the various groups of people who would be part of the church that Timothy would pastor, and he opened by calling them to the primary tool in any Christian's kit: prayer. "Therefore I exhort first of all that supplications [strong seeking], prayers [words addressed to God], intercessions [prayers on behalf of someone else] and giving of thanks be made for all men, for kings and all who are in authority, that we may lead a quiet and peaceable life in all godliness and reverence" (1 Timothy 2:1-2).

He didn't say to pray for people who agree with your political position, or for leaders who are sympathetic toward Christian principles: We are to pray for "all men" and "all who are in authority." As Christians, we have dual citizenship: the country we're citizens in, and heaven (Philippians 3:20-21). That fact should extend our perspective beyond any local factionalism or national ideology. If Paul could write that while Caesar Nero, the imperial madman and great persecutor of Christians, was in charge—and pray for him too—then you can summon the obedience to pray for your leaders today. You are to be a responsible citizen here on earth—something that will distinguish you and even give you opportunities to share the reason why.

"For this is good and acceptable in the sight of God our Savior, who desires all men to be saved and to come to the knowledge of the truth" (1 Timothy 2:4).

Paul also wanted Timothy to have sense of what to expect when the church gathered to worship and hear the Word. He began by continuing on the theme for prayer: "I desire therefore that the men pray everywhere, lifting up holy hands, without wrath and doubting" (v. 8). The idea here is that, as men lead in the public worship of the church, a common posture for prayer is to raise the hands.

Worship, however, isn't all about external posture, but rather, internal praise. It's not about how you look, but who you're looking to. Paul encouraged people to remember that church isn't meant to be a fashion show. He wanted "women [to] adorn themselves in modest apparel, with propriety and moderation, not with braided hair or gold or pearls or costly clothing, but, which is proper for women professing godliness, with good works" (vv. 9-10). So a woman should be known primarily for her godly behavior and attitude, not her style. And a "good work" along those lines would be to dress modestly so that the Christian men in attendance aren't distracted by her appearance. It's fine to dress nicely, to wear jewelry and makeup, but it's also important to respect that it's about making God the center of attention, not you.

The Ministers of the Church (1 Timothy 3–4)

Timothy also needed to know about the ministers of the church—those who would serve God and others in various capacities. The principal office in the early church was the position of bishop, which means "overseer" or "pastor." Paul listed the qualifications: "A bishop then must be blameless, the husband of one wife, temperate, sober-minded, of good behavior, hospitable, able to teach; not given to wine, not violent, not greedy for money, but gentle, not quarrelsome, not covetous; one who rules his own house well" (1 Timothy 3:2-4). The same general code of ethics applied to deacons as well (vv. 8-13), *deacon* being a term used both officially and unofficially to indicate both a specific office and a general term for anyone who serves in the local assembly of a church.

Paul warned Timothy about those who will fall away from the truth (1 Timothy 4:1-3) and the need to warn them and to teach the truth. "If you instruct the brethren in these things, you will be a good minister of Jesus Christ, nourished in the words of faith and of the good doctrine which you have carefully followed" (v. 6). Those who minister need to be spiritually fed themselves. People who constantly devote themselves to the spiritual needs of others can easily become more focused on their audience than on God. If you work in ministry, be intentional about digging into God's Word for yourself and discovering what God has to say to you personally. Public ministry should be the outflow of personal meditation.

Doctrine, by the way, is not a professional word, referring to something only theologians get excited about. Nor is it a cold, hard, outdated word. Some Christians treat doctrine like it's some dry and dusty old antique with no relevance for real people and real life. They'll even say, "I'm not into doctrine; I'm into Jesus." That may sound cool and super spiritual, but it's way off target biblically. Paul used the word *doctrine* twenty times throughout his writings; it simply means the good, solid teaching of biblical truth (1 Timothy 4:16). It's what the first Christians were primarily committed to (Acts 2:42). Without doctrine, we wouldn't have any knowledge of God, Jesus, or how to grow in our faith. It's how we get to know God for who He really is! For ministers to impart it to others, though, they must first be steeped in it themselves on a regular basis.

> **Without doctrine, we wouldn't have any knowledge of God, Jesus, or how to grow in our faith.**

The Ministry of the Church (1 Timothy 5–6)

Once the ministers are doing their job properly, God's ministry can flourish. Paul gave Timothy specific advice on how to treat all the different types of people who gather at church—men and women, young and old, rich and poor. As pastor, Timothy was to set the tone and hold the line, respecting older men and women as fathers and mothers and treating younger men and women as brothers and sisters (1 Timothy 5:1-2). The church was also to be a place of provision for those who had no other resources or income, like widows—but there was a level of discernment required: They were to honor widows who really were widows (v. 5). If a woman's husband died and she was one who sought the Lord and honored Him, and had no other means of support, by all means, the church was to support her. But if she was out every night living a wild party life, she was on her own.

Families were expected to take care of their own, and the church was supposed to support its leaders so they could focus on God's work: "Let the elders who rule well be counted worthy of double honor, especially those who labor in the word and doctrine" (v. 17). Paul also described a protocol for dealing with conflict involving an elder: "Do not receive an accusation against an elder except from two or three witnesses. Those who are sinning rebuke in the presence of all, that the rest may also fear" (vv. 19-20). You don't see a lot of open accusation in the church today because difficult issues can be circumvented by the accused just going to another church down the street. But back then, there was no other church—so believers had to protect their church from sin and sometimes that involved calling people out publicly so that the whole assembly would see the seriousness of the matter. Accountability helps develop purity.

Paul addressed the workings of another type of relationship common in his day but foreign to us today: that of the master and bondservant. By some estimates, anywhere from a third to a half of the Roman Empire was made up of either slaves or people in bonded servitude (that is, who worked for a master without having individual rights of citizenship).[87] But Jesus is the great equalizer, and it was common for both masters and servants to attend church—a relationship addressed half a dozen times in the New Testament. Paul said that servants were to honor their masters even though the distinction of their status didn't matter in Christ's new community: "Those who have believing masters, let them not despise them because they are brethren, but rather serve them because those who are benefited are believers and beloved" (1 Timothy 6:2).

Finally, Paul gave some plain old practical guidance, exhorting Timothy not to get caught up in either the "useless wranglings of men of corrupt minds and destitute of the truth" (v. 5) or the temptations of money, "for godliness with contentment is great gain" (v. 6). He told Timothy to obey his calling—upholding and teaching the Word of God: "O Timothy! Guard what was committed to your trust, avoiding the profane and idle babblings and contradictions of what is falsely called knowledge—by professing it some have strayed concerning the faith" (vv. 20-21). Like every minister, Timothy was to stand up for God's truth—he was to teach it, preach it, fight for it, warn of forsaking it, and exhort with it—guarding it as a sacred trust.

2 Timothy

The Present Calling: Stand Up for the Faith (2 Timothy 1)

Paul began his last letter, and his second to Timothy, by recalling Timothy's strong spiritual upbringing with his grandmother and mother—both believers who gave him a legacy of godliness. "I call to remembrance the genuine faith that is in you, which dwelt first in your grandmother Lois and your mother Eunice, and I am persuaded is in you also" (2 Timothy 1:5). Paul's next words make it seem as if Timothy needed encouragement—as if he got discouraged easily: "Therefore I remind you to stir up the gift of God which is in you through the laying on of my hands. For God has not given us a spirit of fear, but of power and of love and of a sound mind" (vv. 6-7). Perhaps young Timothy was a bit fearful or even reluctant to exercise his ministry with the kind of opposition that was present in Ephesus.

Times had gotten tough for Christians, primarily because of official Roman persecution, and Paul seemed to perceive that Timothy needed to buck up and stand firm in the face of the challenges of the day. "Do not be ashamed of the testimony of our Lord, nor of me His prisoner, but share with me in the sufferings for the gospel according to the power of God" (v. 8). As he so often did, Paul offered his own experience as an example, citing a few people who had turned away from him and one who had sought him out in prison (vv. 15-18). Despite the ups and downs, Paul remained steadfast in his faith and encouraged Timothy to do the same: "Hold fast the pattern of sound words which you have heard from me...That good thing which was committed to you, keep by the Holy Spirit who dwells in us" (vv. 13-14). Paul knew that little things can have a big impact, and that a small bit of encouragement could go a long way for Timothy's future service.

The Pastor's Character: Stand Up in Your Calling (2 Timothy 2)

Paul deployed a wide variety of metaphors as he called Timothy to stand as a pastor—a shepherd of the flock God had given him to steward. In just a few verses, we see that a godly leader is like a soldier, an athlete, a farmer, and a hired laborer:

Soldier: "You therefore must endure hardship as a good soldier of Jesus Christ. No one engaged in warfare entangles himself with the affairs of this life, that he may please him who enlisted him as a soldier" (2 Timothy 2:3-4).

Athlete: "If anyone competes in athletics, he is not crowned unless he competes according to the rules" (v. 5).

Farmer: "The hardworking farmer must be first to partake of the crops" (v. 6).

Laborer: "Be diligent to present yourself approved to God, a worker who does not need to be ashamed, rightly dividing the word of truth" (v. 15).

When Paul told Timothy to be "rightly dividing" the Scriptures, he drew on yet another metaphor—that of the tentmaker. Paul made tents by trade, and in those days, tentmakers worked not with fabric but animal skins, which required exactness in cutting and stretching in order to make the pieces fit. They had to cut straight lines, rightly dividing the material so that it would remain useful.

Each analogy has a common element: determination. Paul wanted Timothy to have no illusions about the fact that being a pastor required hard work and commitment. And this was a crucial juncture for Timothy. With the church under fire from the Roman government outside and wolves dressed as sheep on the inside, now was not the time for Timothy to throw in the towel. God's people deserve a pastor who spends time in God's Word—praying, studying, looking at the original language and history of the text, and determining its context and application. And God Himself deserves that effort.

The Practical Concern: Stand Up as You Fight (2 Timothy 3)

Paul wanted Timothy to know and teach the Scriptures because there were many teachers who were deviating from God's revealed truth and still calling themselves Christian leaders:

> Know this, that in the last days perilous times will come: For men will be lovers of themselves, lovers of money, boasters, proud, blasphemers, disobedient to parents, unthankful, unholy, unloving, unforgiving, slanderers, without self-control, brutal, despisers of good, traitors, headstrong, haughty, lovers of pleasure rather than lovers of God, having a form of godliness but denying its power. And from such people turn away! (2 Timothy 3:1-5).

Looking at that list, you'd think Paul was watching a modern-day news program and connected on social media. What's also alarming is that Paul compiled that list only thirty years after Christ's resurrection; a mere three decades and people were already falling away from the truth. Jesus once asked a haunting question: "When the Son of Man comes, will He really find faith on the earth?" (Luke 18:8). Paul told Timothy that "the church of the living God [is] the pillar and ground of the truth" (1 Timothy 3:15), so it makes sense that it would be the battleground for the issue of truth. Satan has always targeted God's truth, going back to Eden, and it is one of his key strategies to attack the church from outside with cults and moral relativism, and from within through division and strife. Pastors need to fight battles on their knees in prayer, and then on their feet in preaching.

As Paul also told Timothy, we need to turn away from those falsehoods if we are to stick to the truth. That starts always with the Bible: "All Scripture is given by inspiration of God, and is profitable for doctrine, for reproof, for correction, for instruction in righteousness, that the man of God may be complete, thoroughly equipped for every good work" (2 Timothy 3:16-17).

The Personal Charge: Stand Up Till the End (2 Timothy 4)

In light of the real threats and practical concerns the church faced, Paul drove his point home with a personal duty for Timothy:

Preach the word! Be ready in season and out of season. Convince, rebuke, exhort, with all longsuffering and teaching. For the time will come when they will not endure sound doctrine, but according to their own desires, because they have itching ears, they will heap up for themselves teachers; and they will turn their ears away from the truth, and be turned aside to fables (2 Timothy 4:2-4).

"Sound doctrine" literally means *hygienic* doctrine—clean, healthy teaching. One might wonder why anyone would ever turn away from good, solid, healthy Bible teaching. Here's why: It rebukes their ungodliness. The apostle John observed that, when Jesus, the Light of the world, came the first time, He was rejected by most because "men loved darkness rather than light, because their deeds were evil" (John 3:19). People may reject Jesus today by saying that He doesn't fit in with their belief system, or accept a watered-down version of Him that is unable to save anyone. But any rejection of Christ is an accommodation to their own behavior and preferences. This is why preaching is always part of the battle strategy—it assaults false teachings and ungodly "arguments and every high thing that exalts itself against the knowledge of God" (2 Corinthians 10:5).

In contrast, Paul told Timothy to "be watchful in all things, endure afflictions, do the work of an evangelist, fulfill your ministry" (2 Timothy 4:5). Paul sensed his time was short (v. 6), but he wanted his young protégé to imitate him in one more thing: fighting the good fight and finishing the race (v. 7). There are few things more disheartening than a well-run race that falls apart at the end, but few more praiseworthy than a hard race completed. In his final words, Paul reminded Timothy that the race was worth running: "I have kept the faith. Finally, there is laid up for me the crown of righteousness, which the Lord, the righteous Judge, will give to me on that Day, and not to me only but also to all who have loved His appearing" (vv. 7-8).

> There are few things more disheartening than a well-run race that falls apart at the end, but few more praiseworthy than a hard race completed.

Though the last several verses are a postscript describing the various trials and personal betrayals Paul was facing, it's fitting that he went out preaching, encouraging, and exhorting a young pastor to stay in the game and keep fighting for the gospel. And his very last words were ones of blessing: "The Lord Jesus Christ be with your spirit. Grace be with you. Amen" (2 Timothy 4:22).

Second Timothy is the last letter Paul wrote—his swan song. Even as he encouraged Timothy to be watchful and diligent, he anticipated the end of his earthly ministry: "I am already being poured out as a drink offering, and the time of my departure is at hand" (2 Timothy 4:6). Not long after Paul finished this letter, he met his earthly fate, executed on Caesar Nero's orders outside the Basilica Julia courthouse in Rome. Early church history records an undisputed tradition that he was beheaded.[88] And in that brutal moment, Paul the apostle went from the imperial city of Rome to the celestial city of heaven. May we all finish our races as well as he finished his.

TITUS AND PHILEMON
FLIGHT PLAN

Facts

Titus

Author

The author of the book of Titus is identified as "Paul, a bondservant of God" (Titus 1:1). The word "bondservant" refers to a slave, a person under the authority and ownership of a master. In other words, Paul was saying that he was under the authority of Jesus.

Date Written

The date of authorship is unknown. Titus may have been written between Paul's imprisonments in Rome (AD 62 and 65 and thus between Paul's two letters to Timothy.

Philemon

Author

"Paul, a prisoner of Christ Jesus" (Philemon 1) is identified as the author of the book of Philemon. This is the last of Paul's prison letters—those he wrote while incarcerated in Ephesus, Caesarea, and Rome. Sometimes called the Polite Epistle, Philemon is one of the few writings of the New Testament whose scriptural canonicity has not been challenged.

Date Written

Philemon was written at the same time as Paul's other prison letters, during his first imprisonment in Rome, between AD 60 and 62.

Landmarks

Titus

The book of Titus is basically a church operations manual designed to establish basic elements of church order and witness. In it, Paul emphasized the need for purity in leadership and soundness in doctrine. He probably wrote to Titus before traveling to Nicopolis (Titus 3:12), where he spent the last free winter of his life.

This brief letter focuses on Titus's role and responsibility in the organization and supervision of the Cretan churches. As was typical of his letters, Paul frequently stressed the importance of sound doctrine—the wholesome biblical teaching that he knew every church needed. The letter is structured around three different manifestations of God's grace, each one functioning as the basis for orderly instruction and behavior in the church.

Philemon

Philemon is a personal letter. It differs from all of Paul's epistles in that it is neither doctrinal nor intended for general church instruction. Paul focused on applying the principles of brotherly love and forgiveness to personal life. He wrote to Philemon, an active Christian in the church at Colossae and one of his converts, on behalf of Onesimus, Philemon's runaway slave who had come to Christ after fleeing to Rome and had been instructed by Paul during Paul's first Roman imprisonment.

This is the only private letter of Paul's that has been preserved, and the only letter of its type in the New Testament besides 3 John. In keeping with his ongoing emphasis that believers ought to be responsible citizens, Paul felt that Onesimus should return to his master in fulfillment of his Christian duty. We don't know how Onesimus had wronged Philemon—only that Paul urged Philemon to forgive and accept Onesimus as a new brother in Christ.

Itinerary

Titus

- Order in Leadership (Titus 1)
- Order in Discipleship (Titus 2)
- Order in Stewardship (Titus 3)

Philemon

- Ethics in Christ (Philemon 1-9)
- Equality in Christ (Philemon 10-13)
- Exoneration in Christ (Philemon 14-21)

Gospel

Titus

Paul's summary statement to Titus highlights two key elements of the gospel—its means and its mark. God's grace is the gospel's means, and it is marked by our hope in Jesus's return: "The grace of God that brings salvation has appeared to all men, teaching us that, denying ungodliness and worldly lusts, we should live soberly, righteously, and godly in the present age, looking for the blessed hope and glorious appearing of our great God and Savior Jesus Christ" (Titus 2:11-13).

Notice that we are looking for something called the "blessed hope." It is not called the irresponsible hope—as in, "I can check out of my civic responsibilities because I'm getting raptured out of here." It's also not called the escape-route hope: "I'll live how I want and then turn to Jesus at the last moment." It's called the *blessed hope* because believing that Jesus could come back at any time keeps you vigilant and on your toes, keeps you honest, and inspires you to live a pure lifestyle.

What we do while we're waiting for Jesus to come back should be driven and motivated by the grace with which He purchased us—though we shouldn't treat that grace like a get-out-of-jail-free card or a license to disengage from living a responsible life. Paul called our hope in Jesus's return *blessed* because it causes us to live a holy life that's pleasing to the Lord.

> **What we do while we're waiting for Jesus to come back should be driven and motivated by the grace with which He purchased us.**

Philemon

Paul's letter to Philemon shows the love and mercy of Jesus Christ in action. Paul expressed his love for Philemon and Onesimus—both owner and slave—but recognized that a bill still had to be paid on Onesimus's behalf (Philemon 18). His offer to pay the debts Onesimus owed is a beautiful picture of what Jesus has done for us. On the cross, Jesus took our debt on Himself and paid what we owed God—the cost of sin's wages, which is death. "He made Him who knew no sin to be sin for us, that we might become the righteousness of God in Him" (2 Corinthians 5:21). We were slaves of sin, and He paid to set us free.

History

Titus

The legacy of Paul's life is apparent: Through his various missionary journeys, he preached the gospel and touched the lives of many people throughout Asia Minor and Europe. It seems that Paul ministered on the island of Crete for a short time before leaving Titus there to continue the work (Titus 1:5), much like he had with Timothy at Ephesus (1 Timothy 1:3). Besides a short stop there on the way to Rome (Acts 27), no further ministry of Paul is mentioned. Originally colonized by the affluent Minoans in 3000 BC, during Paul's time, under Roman rule, Crete was largely a rural culture.[89] The church was probably started there sometime in the AD 50s.

Philemon

One of the biggest historical themes of Philemon is slavery. Slaves in the Roman Empire were typically treated as a commodity—that is, worth only what they could be sold for. In some places, up to one-third of the population was enslaved.[90] Slavery wasn't based on race; it included prisoners of war and foreigners, as well as those who owed debts they could not pay. Some families were forced to sell their children into slavery in order to survive.

But slaves could find freedom, and many did; sometimes owners would set a slave free, and other times a slave would formally purchase freedom through labor. A formally freed male slave could become a Roman citizen with full rights, so there was incentive to work hard and be obedient to one's master.[91]

While some Roman slaves performed menial tasks, many were well-educated in philosophy, science, and medicine. Slaves were used in most every aspect of life except public office.[92] When the gospel came to town and a church was born, slaves and owners mingled together in the new Christian community to worship and learn God's Word.

Travel Tips

Titus

The book of Titus reminds us that God is a God of order, not chaos. Jesus built and continues to build His church based on His historical act of grace at the cross; our response to His love and mercy is to obey Him and do what is good and right. That response begins with church leaders.

- Paul called for church leaders—elders, bishops, and pastors—to have integrity. *Integrity* implies *wholeness*, consistently giving Jesus control of every area of your life and "holding fast the faithful word as [you have] been taught" (Titus 1:9). Integrity doesn't mean perfection, but it does mean that false criticism won't stick because you live above reproach in all your ways.

- A church should be unified. Discipleship is all about learning and growing together as one body in Christ—"in all things showing your-self to be a pattern of good works...that [you] may adorn the doctrine of God our Savior in all things" (Titus 2:7, 10). What a wonderful thought! By your godly and inclusive behavior toward others in the body of Christ, you further beautify God's truth.

- Good doctrine produces both responsible citizenship and a protec-tive attitude toward God's church (Titus 3:8-9). Some people come to church not to worship or learn but out of their own ulterior motives and purposes. But a healthy body can purge its own illnesses. We have a responsibility to keep the body of Christ focused on God and to counter divisive attitudes in a gracious but firm way.

By your godly and inclusive behavior toward others in the body of Christ, you further beautify God's truth.

Philemon

Paul's letter to Philemon reveals his unfailing belief in God's sovereignty and grace: God allows certain things to happen and then weaves them together into the tapestry of His greater purpose. This letter gives us real insight into Paul's heart, consideration, and tact. He had no doctrinal ax to grind, no admonitions to make, no problems to address. He just wanted two people he cared about to come together in the peace and grace of Christ.

- Your ministry starts at home. When Paul referred to "the church in [Philemon's] house" (Philemon 2), he may have meant Philemon's ministry to those who lived in his home—that is, his family. The home is a place where husbands are to minister to their wives, husbands and wives to their children, and older siblings to younger siblings by setting a godly example and by cultivating, shepherding, and guiding one another closer to Jesus.
- Freedom in Christ surpasses earthly labels. Unless Jesus is your master, you are enslaved to something that will never fully satisfy and will certainly never give you the freedom to be who God intended you to be. But when you belong to Jesus, you become free—free to, like Paul the apostle, relate to any fellow Christian as your brother or sister, regardless of their status, wealth, gender, ethnicity, or anything else that formerly would have divided you from them.

God loves to restore broken people.

- God loves to restore broken people. Paul echoed this truth when he wrote to restore the relationship between Onesimus and Philemon (Philemon 15-16). Think of all the people and circumstances that led to your salvation—how God orchestrated so many details to bring you into a right relationship with Him. If He was in control of all that, you can trust that He'll also work everything in your life—the good, the bad, and the ugly—together for your good.

In Flight

Titus

Order in Leadership (Titus 1)

Paul's impact on the church in Crete is proof that, as long as God has someone who is willing to be used, He can make a lot out of very little. After only a brief visit to this island, and later in an unplanned stopover while he was a prisoner bound for Rome (Acts 27), Paul left his companion Titus to shore up the local church, which had probably originally been founded after the Day of Pentecost, when Cretans in Jerusalem heard the Spirit preach the gospel in their own tongue (Acts 2:11) and were converted. This letter represents Titus's marching orders to shore up the work God had begun there.

Titus, a convert of Paul's, had been with Paul at the Council of Jerusalem (Acts 15), a prime example of a Gentile convert to Christianity (Galatians 2:3). He had served the church in Corinth (2 Corinthians 8:6, 16-17), and also accompanied Paul on his third missionary journey. Titus had also organized a collection for poor saints in Jerusalem (vv. 10, 17, 24). Paul had trusted him to hand-deliver the epistle of 2 Corinthians, and now he was calling this trustworthy saint to straighten out the church in Crete. "For this reason I left you in Crete, that you should set in order the things that are lacking, and appoint elders in every city as I commanded you" (Titus 1:5). Titus was a solid Christian who got the job done.

The church in Crete needed strong leadership and solid, doctrinal teaching, and Paul was confident Titus would provide both. Titus was the kind of a guy who didn't just give messages but helped people forge their way through a time of crisis. Furthermore, Paul asked him to "set in order" what was needed. The phrase in Greek, *epidiorthoō*, has the root word *ortho*, which is where we get words like *orthopedist*. Paul was telling Titus, "You need to be like a spiritual orthopedist, aligning crooked lives with Scripture, straightening and setting the bones of their faith in a healthy way." A biblical splint is the best cure for a broken church.

Titus was to do so by appointing elders (Titus 1:5) who would help him confront false leaders (vv. 6-10) and teach sound doctrine (Titus 2:1). To make sure Titus knew what to look for in a leader, Paul listed the right characteristics for qualification: above reproach in behavior, a faithful husband, believing children, and not accused of "being wild and disobedient" (Titus 1:6 NIV). Similarly, a bishop—an overseer—was also to have excellent character: "blameless, as a steward of God, not self-willed, not quick-tempered, not given to wine, not violent, not greedy for money, but hospitable, a lover of what is good, sober-minded, just, holy, [and] self-controlled" (vv. 7-8). False teachers spread spiritual infection and require holy doctors to offset their contagion.

The terms "elder" (Greek, *presbyteros*) and "bishop" (*episkopos*) were used interchangeably in the New Testament, along with the term for "pastor" (*poimēnos*). This was indicative of how simple early church government was: leaders of godly character guided, instructed, and protected the church. *Integrity* was the key word—especially regarding God's Word: A leader was to "[hold] fast the faithful word as he has been taught, that he may be able, by sound doctrine, both to exhort and to convict those who contradict" (v. 9). The standard for shepherds was high because of their tremendous impact on the sheep.

Order in Discipleship (Titus 2)

The church in Crete needed to be discipled—taught by a strong believer like Titus what it meant to follow Christ. Even more importantly, they needed to learn together—as a true fellowship in the body of Christ. As he had in his letters to Timothy, Paul laid out the network of relationships in the church that needed to click—older men and women setting good examples for the younger men and women, respectively, and bondservants treating their masters with respect.

It's human nature to gravitate toward similar types of people when we get together, but the all-encompassing nature of Christ's sacrifice and the fact that earthly distinctions will be rendered useless in heaven means we have to push past our comfort zone and interact with all sorts of people in the church. Young people should learn from the experience and (one hopes) wisdom of older folks, and older people are often energized by the enthusiasm and spiritual zeal of young believers. Singles and married couples can give each other needed reality checks about each other's lives. Creative types need to mesh with protective ones, each realizing the value the other brings to God's family.

Titus was to lead the way. Paul told his friend, "Exhort the young men to be sober-minded, in all things showing yourself to be a pattern of good works; in doctrine showing integrity, reverence, incorruptibility, sound speech that cannot be condemned, that one who is an opponent may be ashamed, having nothing evil to say of you" (Titus 2:6-8). Paul reminded Titus that true discipleship wasn't about putting on a religious appearance but preparing for the endgame—living godly lives until the return of Jesus Christ. "For the grace of God that brings salvation has appeared to all men, teaching us that, denying ungodliness and worldly lusts, we should live soberly, righteously, and godly in the present age, looking for the blessed hope and the glorious appearing of our great God and Savior Jesus Christ" (vv. 11-13). Salvation produces transformation, which in turn leads to the anticipation of Christ's return.

Salvation produces transformation, which in turn leads to the anticipation of Christ's return.

Notice that Jesus's return is called the "blessed hope," not the reckless hope or the escape-route hope. Many outside the church (and some inside) accuse Christians of checking out of life or civic responsibility, as if the rapture provided the ultimate diplomatic immunity. In fact, that's the last thing the blessed hope is. Believing Jesus could return any minute teaches you to live in constant anticipation, living a pure lifestyle. As the apostle John wrote, "Everyone who has this hope in Him purifies himself, just as He is pure" (1 John 3:3).

Order in Stewardship (Titus 3)

Once the church in Crete had established solid leadership and the firm practice of discipleship, the next challenge—as it always is—would be the stewardship of representing Christ to the world. Paul advised Titus on how to coach people in the role of being stewards—caretakers—of God's greatest gift, the gospel. Their attitude outside of the four walls of the church building was essential to their success as citizens of both earth and heaven.

As a Christian, your home in heaven is guaranteed, but you still have to be responsible in this life. To that end, Paul told Titus, "Remind them to be subject to rulers and authorities, to obey, to be ready for every good work" (Titus 3:1). Though your ultimate ruler is a King greater than any earthly ruler ever could or will be, you still need "to speak evil of no one, to be peaceable, gentle, showing all humility to all men" (v. 2). Any unbeliever who crosses our path is an opportunity.

Paul's summary statement boils down to this: Solid doctrine will produce sensible duty, reflecting God as stewards in this world: "These things I want you to affirm constantly, that those who believe in God should be careful to maintain good works. These things are good and profitable to men" (v. 8). That role as God's ambassadors to the world requires representing God faithfully in the community—at work, while traveling, in everyday interactions with each person you encounter.

Part of that stewardship—that watchful care and vigilant protection—also means guarding the church itself. Paul knew that some came to church not to worship God in spirit and truth (John 4:23-24) but with ulterior motives. Not everyone who attends church is there to grow in their faith; some want to gather a following or use the church for their own purposes. Paul told Titus to identify them by their behavior and then deal with them decisively. Especially problematic were hovering legalistic religionists looking for an opportunity to assault grace-filled congregations. "Avoid foolish disputes, genealogies, contentions, and strivings about the law; for they are unprofitable and useless. Reject a divisive man after the first and second admonition, knowing that such a person is warped and sinning, being self-condemned" (Titus 3:9-11).

"Divisive man" is the Greek word *hairetikos*—as in *heretic*. So when someone chooses to divide the church with incorrect interpretations of Scripture or self-willed disobedience, "reject" him or her. This means that you reject their ideas, warning them that they are incorrect in a specific area and that their teaching or action is dividing the church. After a second warning, you are to reject them by cutting them off from the fellowship of the church. This follows the pattern given by Christ Himself (Matthew 18:15-17). Of course, at that point, you also need to seek counsel from the leadership of your church, but your goal is to protect the body of Christ, doing so with humility and compassion, but also with determination and commitment. That was the model of order Paul wanted Titus to establish in Crete, and it still holds today.

Philemon

Ethics in Christ (Philemon 1-9)

Paul's shortest letter in the New Testament is also his most personal, and it features a controversial subject: slavery. That's still a loaded word even in modern times, particularly in America, but Paul dealt with it in his day too. Specifically, the issue was one unique to the early church: How do you deal with someone in the church who is a runaway slave and his master happens to be the guy who hosts the church meetings in his house? The situation required an ethical response, and Paul provided one.

"Paul, a prisoner of Christ Jesus, and Timothy our brother, to Philemon, our beloved friend and fellow laborer, to the beloved Apphia, Archippus our fellow soldier, and to the church in your house" (Philemon 1-2). Paul was familiar with the church in Colossae, which had been founded by his friend Epaphras (Colossians 1:7; 4:12-13). He had written the people a letter and likely received regular reports on them from Epaphras and Tychicus (who had delivered his letter to them). And apparently he knew Philemon, and was probably responsible for his conversion (Philemon 19).

Philemon must have been a prominent church member at Colossae. He was wealthy enough to have a large house with several slaves, and perhaps even host the Colossian church in his home. It's also possible that when Paul referred to the church in Philemon's house he could have been talking about his ministry to his own family. Apphia and Archippus were likely Philemon's family, possibly a wife or daughter and a brother or son. Ministry starts at home, cultivating those relationships and showing the love and grace of Christ among those you know best. Either way, Philemon was living his faith out among the Colossians.

Paul praised Philemon for his reputation of "love and faith" (v. 5), and because "the hearts of the saints have been refreshed by you" (v. 7). Paul was setting the table for a request—something that was the right thing to do in Christ but would be difficult by the social and cultural standards of that day. He appealed to Philemon to warmly receive a runaway slave, Onesimus, whom Paul had converted to the faith while the slave was on the run.

Slavery worked a bit differently in the Roman Empire than it did in American history (see **History** on page 539), but slaves were still considered personal property. When a slave ran away, the full force of the law was against him or her, and there were even slave-catchers who hunted fugitive bondsmen, seeking to profit from the missteps of any runaway servant. Anyone harboring a runaway was breaking the law, and the authorities employed bounty hunters to recover them. A captured slave (in Latin, *fugitivus*) was branded on the forehead and often sentenced to hard labor or even death rather than returned to the owner.[93] The church, then, was a radical equalizer for slaves and masters under normal circumstances, but for a runaway, there was an added element of risk for both parties. In Christ, however, everyone involved could do the right thing.

Equality in Christ (Philemon 10-13)

Being a follower of Christ overrode all other labels, so when a church was established in a town, it often brought slaves and owners together as equals. As Paul had written, "There is neither Jew nor Greek, there is neither slave nor free, there is neither male nor female; for you are all one in Christ Jesus" (Galatians 3:28). That was the grounds on which he was appealing to Philemon to take Onesimus back. "I appeal to you for my son Onesimus, whom I have begotten while in my chains [that is, led to Christ while still in prison], who once was unprofitable to you, but now is profitable to you and to me" (Philemon 10-11).

Consider the deeper meaning of Paul's request. The name *Onesimus* means "useful" or "profitable," something Onesimus had not been before coming to Christ. Because Paul offered to pay any debt Onesimus owed (vv. 18-19), it's thought that Onesimus must have stolen money or property from Philemon before running away to Rome. He probably thought he could get lost in the busyness of the capital city, but Jesus found him and directed him to Paul. And because Onesimus now belonged to Christ, he had begun to live up to his name.

Paul, being Paul the great writer, enjoyed the play on words, but his point was rock solid. Philemon had an obligation to treat Onesimus differently now that they were fellow Christians. "I am sending him back. You therefore receive him, that is, my own heart, whom I wished to keep with me, that on your behalf he might minister to me in my chains for the gospel" (vv. 12-13). The bridge between uselessness and usefulness is the simple touch of God's grace.

> ## The bridge between uselessness and usefulness is the simple touch of God's grace.

Exoneration in Christ (Philemon 14-21)

Paul, being Paul the great apostle, could have demanded that Philemon comply with his request. Instead, he modeled the love and grace he wanted Philemon to show Onesimus: "Without your consent I wanted to do nothing, that your good deed might not be by compulsion, as it were, but voluntary. For perhaps he departed for a while for this purpose, that you might receive him forever" (vv. 14-15). In other words, this breach of temporal human law had come under God's providence so that it could lead to an eternal benefit for both men. If Philemon had read Paul's letter to the Romans, particularly Romans 8:28, he would have recognized Paul's point: God works all things together for good for those who love Him—*and, Philemon, if you believe that, here's an opportunity for you to put it into practice.*

"For perhaps he departed for a while for this purpose, that you might receive him forever, no longer as a slave but more than a slave—a beloved brother" (vv. 15-16). Paul wasn't requesting that Onesimus be freed from slavery but that Philemon forgive him and receive him as a brother. "If then you count me as a partner, receive him as you would me. But if he has wronged you or owes anything, put that on my account" (vv. 17-18). Paul was drawing out the example of Christ, who paid a debt on the cross that no one can afford—not even a wealthy person like Philemon.

While Paul figured that Philemon would respond favorably to his request, he still felt it necessary to remind Philemon of a powerful truth: He was indebted to Paul for his own salvation. "I, Paul, am writing with my own hand. I will repay—not to mention to you that you owe me even your own self besides" (v. 19). Onesimus owed Philemon a large material debt, but Philemon owed Paul an even greater spiritual debt—one that couldn't be repaid, only honored. Again, Paul was confident that Philemon would do the right thing, but he wanted to remind him of the bottom line. "Yes, brother, let me have joy from you in the Lord; refresh my heart in the Lord. Having confidence in your obedience, I write to you, knowing that you will do even more than I say" (vv. 20-21).

What Paul told Philemon to do with Onesimus is exactly what Jesus Christ has done with us. We were slaves of sin, but He has forgiven us. We have been set free, exonerated of the cost of our sin. Paul knew that his love for Onesimus wasn't enough to fix the problem. Love had to pay the bill. "God so loved the world" by itself isn't enough to do anything, but God giving His only begotten Son paid sin's bill—and that's everything.

Roman law demanded branding, punishment, and even death for a slave who ran away; God's holiness and righteousness demand that sin be punished as well. But the difference is that God created a way to pay that debt, giving all who receive the gift of salvation equal standing by the blood of Christ, and offering them eternal life through His resurrection. Along the way, He restores relationships and heals broken hearts.

HEBREWS
FLIGHT PLAN

Facts

Author

The author of the book of Hebrews is unknown. A number of people have been suggested, such as Paul, Luke, Clement, Barnabas, Apollos, and others, but it still remains a mystery. Whoever wrote Hebrews knew Greek, was steeped in the Old Testament Scriptures, had a well-organized mind capable of ordering numerous details to produce a well-reasoned argument, and was inspired by the Holy Spirit.

Date Written

The date of composition is uncertain. It's possible that Hebrews was written before AD 70 because it does not mention the destruction of the Jewish temple or refer to Christian persecution. In a document that is so heavily Jewish, this is remarkable.

Landmarks

The book of Hebrews takes us on a journey of mystery, wonder, revelation, and faith. Although we don't know who penned it, this well-written letter reveals an author who wanted Jewish believers to continue in the grace of Jesus Christ—and Jewish unbelievers to embrace it—rather than try to escape persecution by bowing to the rites and rituals of Judaism.

Hebrews is basically a sermon about Jesus. It begins by exalting Jesus's greatness, then goes on to explain what He did on our behalf as the ultimate High Priest, ending with a challenge to embrace His finished work on the cross. The overarching theme of Hebrews is, simply put, the superiority of Jesus Christ—a matter with both doctrinal and practical applications.

Itinerary

- The Doctrinal (Hebrews 1–10)
  - A Better Messenger (Hebrews 1–2)

- A Better Moderator (Hebrews 3:1–4:13)
- A Better Mediator (Hebrews 4:14–7:28)
- A Better Ministry (Hebrews 8)
- A Better Monument (Hebrews 9)
- A Better Method (Hebrews 10)
- The Practical (Hebrews 11–13)
  - A Better Manner (Hebrews 11:1–12:2)
  - A Better Mindset (Hebrews 12:3-29)
  - A Better Mercy (Hebrews 13)

Gospel

This book drips with the gospel on every page. One of the most prevalent images in the book of Hebrews is Jesus as the great High Priest who has ushered in the new covenant:

> Seeing then that we have a great High Priest who has passed through the heavens, Jesus the Son of God, let us hold fast our confession. For we do not have a High Priest who cannot sympathize with our weaknesses, but was in all points tempted as we are, yet without sin. Let us therefore come boldly to the throne of grace, that we may obtain mercy and find grace to help in time of need (Hebrews 4:14-16).

What a marvelous passage! We all need God's mercy and grace—and lots of it—and that's what the new covenant provides. Because of what Jesus did for us in giving Himself as our atoning sacrifice, we don't have to come before God with fear and trembling, shaking in our boots because of our sin. No, we can come boldly before His throne and ask for His help. As our High Priest, Jesus is the Mediator, the go-between between us and God. Through His death and resurrection, He built a bridge that spans the chasm between holy God and sinful man.

History

Because little is known about the author of Hebrews or the date it was written, the history surrounding it is fuzzy at best—though that hasn't stopped people from guessing who might have written it. Around AD 200, Tertullian held that Barnabas was the author. More than 1000 years later, Martin Luther posited that Apollos was the author. He reasoned that Apollos was a good speaker and knew his Old Testament Scriptures (Acts 18), which made him as good a candidate as any.[94] But probably the most prevailing opinion about the writer of Hebrews is that it was Paul.[95]

Let's look at Paul's candidacy for a moment. Because Paul wrote so much of the New Testament, we know his writings have certain hallmarks and characteristics. The thing is, Hebrews doesn't have these hallmarks. Paul typically opened with a greeting of grace and peace to whomever he was writing (as did Peter, James, and John), but this book doesn't have that greeting. Also missing is Paul's standard ending, where he signed with his own hand and made comments to specific people. Hebrews doesn't mention its author or audience; in fact, it's less of a letter and more of a formal sermon with carefully laid out themes.

Whenever Paul quoted Scripture in his letters, he quoted from the original Hebrew text, but the author of Hebrews used the Septuagint—the Greek translation of the Old Testament. Finally, the author of Hebrews put himself in the category of those who heard the gospel secondhand—the salvation "which at the first began to be spoken by the Lord, and was confirmed to us by those who heard Him" (Hebrews 2:3)—whereas Paul said he had received the gospel directly from Jesus Himself (Galatians 1:11-12).

So who wrote Hebrews? Whoever it was knew Timothy (Hebrews 13:23), so that helps narrow the list of possibilities: perhaps Barnabas, Silas, Luke, Philip, or Aquila and/or Priscilla. But if I were to venture a guess other than Paul, I would say Apollos. He was a Jewish Christian, so he had a deep understanding of Judaism, and the Bible indicates he was an educated and eloquent speaker who taught the Scriptures accurately. He also would likely have known Timothy. But ultimately, God superintended the writing of all the books in the Bible, so human authorship is a secondary concern at best.

Travel Tips

The central message of Hebrews is simple: Jesus Christ is superior. He is a better messenger than the angels, a better moderator than Moses, and a better mediator than a Jewish priest. In Him, we have a better covenant than that which was established in the Old Testament, a better method than ritual sacrifices, and a better monument than the tabernacle or temple. Because of Christ's superiority, the new covenant of Christianity is superior to all other religions and religious practices.

- Jesus is a better messenger than God's angels. The author of Hebrews knew that some Jews might equate Jesus with angels or even categorize

Him as inferior to them, so he made it clear that Jesus had "become so much better than the angels" (Hebrews 1:4), which means we don't need to pray to a guardian angel or, for that matter, any other envoy or go-between.

- Jesus is a better moderator than Moses. A great man of God, Moses stood in the gap between the Lord and His people, moderating the covenant He had made with them through the law. Yet Moses was just a member of the household of faith, whereas Jesus is its architect and builder (Hebrews 3:3).

- Jesus is a better mediator than any Jewish priest. Under the old covenant, a priest's job was to act as the mediator between man and God. Jesus, on the other hand, was—and is—the perfect Mediator between man and God. As a man, He identifies with our weaknesses and our need for forgiveness, and as the perfect, holy God, He was able to make the ultimate atoning sacrifice for our sins (Hebrews 4:14-16). Now He lives forever as the one true Mediator, interceding to the Lord on our behalf.

- Jesus has a better ministry than the law: the ministry of grace. When He established the new covenant, His sacrifice was once for all: "With His own blood He entered the Most Holy Place *once for all*, having obtained eternal redemption" (Hebrews 9:12, emphasis added). We now have freedom from sin and access to God, completely ours for the asking. Jesus's atonement could never be repeated—and never needs to be!

- Stay focused on following Jesus. Don't let anything keep you from running your race—attitudes, habits, relationships, anything that keeps you from "looking unto Jesus" (Hebrews 12:2), who is the goal and the prize all in one.

Because of Christ's superiority, the new covenant of Christianity is superior to all other religions and religious practices.

In Flight

The Doctrinal (Hebrews 1–10)

A Better Messenger (Hebrews 1–2)

Right away, we see the theme of Christ's superiority: Jesus is a better messenger than any God had previously sent—primarily angels and prophets. "God, who at various times and in various ways spoke in times past to the fathers by the prophets, has in these last days spoken to us by His Son, whom He has appointed heir of all things, through whom also He made the worlds" (Hebrews 1:1-2). Through the centuries, God had spoken in many different ways and at different times—directly to Adam and Eve in the garden, then by angels, then via Moses and the Levitical priests, and later by various prophets. But God's ultimate revelation was in and through Jesus Christ. Jesus Christ is God's last word on the subject of salvation!

All that God ever wanted to say was said in Christ, and anything we ever needed to know about God can be found in Christ. Jesus is God's perfect messenger, "having become so much better than the angels, as He has by inheritance obtained a more excellent name than they" (v. 4). Angels were prominent in Judaism, from the two cherubim guarding Eden's gates with flaming swords to the two placed atop the ark of the covenant to the seraphim crying out "Holy, holy, holy" in His presence (Isaiah 6:3).

> All that God ever wanted to say was said in Christ, and anything we ever needed to know about God can be found in Christ.

Angels helped to bring God's words and His law to men (Hebrews 2:2; Galatians 3:19)—but Jesus was a better messenger (something with which no angel would argue) because of His personal excellence as the Messiah and the importance of His message (Hebrews 2:1-3). Jesus willingly "made [Himself] a little lower than the angels"—human, in other words—"for the suffering of death crowned with glory and honor, that He, by the grace of God, might taste death for everyone" (v. 9). He made the angels, along with everything else, and they exist, like everything else, to glorify Him—a message carried through the gospel, that great news of God's love and His Son's supreme sacrifice.

A Better Moderator (Hebrews 3:1–4:13)

As important as angels were in Judaism, Moses was even more prominent. An amazing man chosen by God to help deliver His people, Moses was also the moderator of God's law. He was Israel's diplomat to God and God's ambassador to Israel. He was the great lawgiver. Even more, "the LORD spoke to Moses face to face, as a man speaks to his friend" (Exodus 33:11). As great as Moses was, Jesus did an even better job of carrying God's word to mankind.

"Consider the Apostle and High Priest of our confession, Christ Jesus, who was faithful to Him who appointed Him, as Moses also was faithful in all His house. For this One has been counted worthy of more glory than Moses, inasmuch as He who built the house has more honor than the house" (Hebrews 3:1-3). Moses was part of the household of faith, special and anointed, but still human, still flawed. Jesus designed and built that house, something we've seen over and over in the Gospel section of our FLIGHT Plans—the Old Testament pointed to Him, His first coming as Messiah and His second as King. Moses'ss greatest legacy was that he was a foreshadowing of Christ (Deuteronomy 18:15-19).

And whereas Moses was unable to enter the Promised Land because of his disobedience, and even under Joshua, Israel failed for an entire generation to inherit the land God promised—the land of God's rest and peace—Jesus fulfilled God's promise of rest. "He who has entered His rest has himself also ceased from his works as God did from His" (Hebrews 4:10). By God's grace, Jesus made it possible for anyone—Jewish or otherwise—to make peace with God. He moderated God's new plan of salvation for all mankind (a much better deal than the old one).

A Better Mediator (Hebrews 4:14–7:28)

God's plan of salvation required the perfect person to carry it out. The Law of Moses had instituted priests to serve as mediators between God and men, carrying the sacrifices and rituals necessary to pay sin's cost. However, the priests were human, subject to sin like everyone else, and they had to conduct cleansing rituals and sacrifices in order to approach God on behalf of the people. Jesus became a perfect Mediator, sinless and able to pay the ultimate price for sin on behalf of everyone who believes in Him.

Having such a priest makes all the difference. "Seeing then that we have a great High Priest who has passed through the heavens, Jesus the Son of God, let us hold fast our confession. For we do not have a High Priest who cannot sympathize with our weaknesses, but was in all points tempted as we are, yet without sin. Let us therefore come boldly to the throne of grace, that we may obtain mercy and find grace to help in time of need" (Hebrews 4:14-16). We all need God's mercy—and we need it often. There aren't enough doves and oxen and bags of grain to cover all the sacrifices we need to make over the course of a lifetime. But Jesus did it once and for all.

God assigned Jesus the honor of becoming our High Priest, following the tradition of God having called Aaron and the Levites to be priests under the law (Hebrews 5:4-5). Jesus was from a different tribe, however—Judah—and a different order of priests, "according to the order of Melchizedek" (v. 6). Melchizedek was the peculiar character in Genesis 14 to whom Abraham offered a tithe. He was a "priest of God Most High" (Genesis 14:18) and brought out bread and wine as he blessed Abraham.

Also, in one of David's messianic psalms, God promised that the Messiah would be "a priest forever according to order of Melchizedek" (Psalm 110:4)—quoted here in Hebrews 5:6—a prediction of Jesus as High Priest. Because Jesus was from the tribe of Judah, not Levi, and a priest in the same order as Melchizedek, who served God before the law, He alone qualifies in a priestly sense to operate outside the parameters of the established law. "If perfection were through the Levitical priesthood (for under it the people received the law), what further need was there that another priest should rise according to the order of Melchizedek, and not be called according to the order of Aaron?" (Hebrews 7:11).

Jesus was operating under a different plan, a different system—one set up by God before the foundation of the world (Hebrews 4:3). His superiority as Mediator between God and men established the new covenant under His priesthood, and He Himself is the Way between us and God.

A Better Ministry (Hebrews 8)

Because we have a better messenger than the angels, a better moderator than Moses, and a better mediator than Aaron and his boys, we have a better ministry, based not on the old covenant of law but the new one of grace. The author of Hebrews made it clear that this new covenant was in God's mind ages before the events of the Gospels. He quoted a well-known Old Testament passage to underscore this point: "Behold, the days are coming, says the LORD, when I will make a new covenant with the house of Israel and with the house of Judah...I will put My laws in their mind and write them on their hearts; and I will be their God, and they shall be My people" (Hebrews 8:8, 10; quoting Jeremiah 31:31, 33). Those days that had been predicted have now come.

Under the old covenant, the priest represented God to the people and the people to God. You couldn't just rush into the Holy of Holies in the temple your-self and approach the Lord whenever and however you wanted; sin blocked your access to Him. In order to atone for the nation's sins and to open up that access to God, the priest carried out rituals, ceremonies, sacrifices, and careful observances according to Old Testament law. Because the priest was himself a sinner, he had to offer a sacrifice for his own sins before he could offer one for the sins of the peo-ple. The entire setup was at best a temporary fix, a transitory and provisional solu-tion to the sin problem.

But then Jesus Christ came and that changed everything. Under the old cove-nant, all priests came from the tribe of Levi, beginning with Moses and his brother Aaron and continuing down that family line through the centuries. But Jesus came from the tribe of Judah, indicating that God was setting up a totally new covenant with a new priesthood. And that's exactly what Jesus did. He is a better mediator, a better High Priest, of a better covenant. Jesus "has obtained a more excellent min-istry, inasmuch as He is also Mediator of a better covenant, which was established on better promises" (Hebrews 8:6).

The problem with the old covenant lay in humanity's inability to keep it. "If that first covenant had been faultless," Hebrews 8:7 tells us, "then no place would have been sought for a second." Whereas the old covenant tried to control con-duct—*don't do that; do this instead*—the new covenant aims at changing charac-ter. Whereas the old covenant was more outward than inward, the new covenant is inward and then outward. When you come under the new covenant of Jesus Christ, you experience a heart change, a spiritual rebirth that enables you to do what you couldn't under the law. And Jesus is a superior High Priest because He was a supe-rior sacrifice. Sinless and perfect, He offered Himself on the cross so that we could have access to God—not just on a high holy day when a priest made a sacrifice, but every moment of every day.

> **Jesus is a superior High Priest because He was a superior sacrifice.**

A Better Monument (Hebrews 9)

We also have something a whole lot better than a temple in Jerusalem or a tab-ernacle in the wilderness. "Even the first covenant had ordinances of divine service and the earthly sanctuary. For a tabernacle was prepared: the first part, in which was the lampstand, the table, and the showbread, which is called the sanctuary; and behind the second veil, the part of the tabernacle which is called the Holiest of All" (Hebrews 9:1-3). The tabernacle was a mobile sanctuary and had to be moved wherever God moved. Even when the temple was built as a stationary structure, it didn't provide a lasting remedy because the sacrifices that took place there had to be made continually. The temple in Jerusalem was to the Jews a monument of God's covenant to them, yet sadly became nothing more than a mausoleum of broken laws and a dying religion.

Christ's sacrifice was permanent, providing a superior monument. "Christ came as High Priest of the good things to come, with the greater and more perfect tabernacle not made with hands, that is, not of this creation. Not with the blood of goats and calves, but with His own blood He entered the Most Holy Place once for all, having obtained eternal redemption" (Hebrews 9:11-12). The phrase "once for all" is critical. Christ's atonement was a completed single work, never to be repeated. His blood was sufficient to satisfy God's requirements, because "not even the first covenant was dedicated without blood" (v. 18), and "without shedding of blood there is no remission [of sin]" (v. 22).

Everything related to the Old Testament system of sacrifice, though, pointed to a reality in heaven: "It was necessary that the copies of the things in the heavens should be purified with these [that is, the tabernacle, the altar, and the vessels used in sacrifices], but the heavenly things themselves with better sacrifices than these. For Christ has not entered the holy places made with hands, which are copies of the true, but into heaven itself, now to appear in the presence of God for us" (Hebrews 9:23-24). In other words, Jesus never went into the Holy of Holies in the tabernacle or temple; He entered the holiness of God's actual presence in heaven after having offered Himself as a sacrifice for our sin. In doing so, He paid off our sin forever.

Now, the tabernacle—a scaled-down, comparatively low-budget model of heaven—takes up a lot of space in Scripture, fifty chapters compared with the two devoted to creation. And the one thing clear in all of the details about its construction, furnishings, and ministry is that it had one door. There was only one way to enter it; that is, there was only one way to approach God—from the east side, where the tribe of Judah encamped. You had to pass their banner, with its lion insignia, to enter the place of fellowship with God. Jesus said, "I am the door. If anyone enters by Me, he will be saved, and will go in and out and find pasture" (John 10:9)—not to mention John 14:6: "I am the way, the truth, and the life. No one comes to the Father except through Me."

If you were the high priest walking into the Holy of Holies in the tabernacle, you saw the menorah on the left, the only source of light. Jesus said, "I am the light of the world" (John 8:12). On the right side was the table with the showbread; Jesus said, "I am the bread of life" (John 6:48). Jesus's "I am" statements are represented throughout the tabernacle, but He embodied what they only symbolized.

That was also true of the tabernacle structure itself. The enormous fence that surrounded it was plain-looking white linen. Peering over the white cloth you could see the top of the Holy Place, which was covered with animal skins. Not attractive. But when you got inside, it was beautiful, made of costly materials, gold utensils and vessels, rich textiles ornately embroidered and dyed in expensive hues—especially the Holy of Holies, which was constructed of wood covered in gold. Interestingly, Jesus is depicted in a similar way. Isaiah had described the Messiah's physical appearance such that it brought to mind the tabernacle's outer fence: "He has no form or comeliness; and when we see Him, there is no beauty that we should desire Him" (Isaiah 53:2). His blood, however, is precious (1 Peter 1:19), His work as High Priest is incomparable (Hebrews 4:14-16), and He is the King of kings (Revelation 19:16).

The tabernacle and the temple were monuments testifying to heaven, their riches and splendor and their cleansing sacrifices just a shadow of Jesus's monumental accomplishment and what His sacrifice purchased for us. The access that was restricted in the old, symbolically shown in the temple, was removed, so that anyone who believes can come directly and boldly to God through Jesus Christ.

A Better Method (Hebrews 10)

Hand in hand with the better monument Jesus established is the improved method we have for entering into a right relationship with God. Aren't you glad you don't have to bring an animal sacrifice when you go to church? Can you imagine dropping your sheep off at the door on Sunday morning and then hanging around waiting for the priest to kill and bleed it, purifying your way into the sanctuary? That was basically what the priests used to do in the temple, and they were always busy.

At the time of the writing of Hebrews,[96] the daily sacrifices were still taking place. "Every priest stands ministering daily and offering repeatedly the same sacrifices, which can never take away sins" (Hebrews 10:11). The job was never done because sin was never completely atoned for—until Jesus. "But this Man, after He had offered one sacrifice for sins forever, sat down at the right hand of God" (v. 12). That's a remarkable statement. Priests were always on their feet because their job was never ended. But Jesus, as our High Priest, sat down. He sat down because the job was finished—just as He had said at the cross before He died (John 19:30). The old method of sacrifices would never again be required to pay sin's debt because His blood had paid it in full.

The Practical (Hebrews 11–13)

A Better Manner (Hebrews 11:1–12:2)

Having established the doctrinal foundation for Jesus's superiority, the writer of Hebrews shifted to the application of that truth. The life of faith is superior to life under the law because faith produces what the law could never produce—the behavior that God requires. The driving principle of faith has a long heritage, going way back before the law ever existed. So the author summoned what he would later call a "cloud of witnesses" to testify to the power of faith—examples of people who lived by faith by the principle of trusting God with their lives.

Hebrews 11 is known as the "Hall of Faith" because of the encouraging examples of faithful people we can look to for inspiration. It begins by defining its main term: "Now faith is the substance of things hoped for, the evidence of things not seen" (Hebrews 11:1). "Things not seen" includes the atomic, subatomic, and quantum particles that form creation: "By faith we understand that the worlds were framed by the word of God, so that the things which are seen were not made of things which are visible" (v. 2).

The names recorded here are all well-known, but it's the faith exhibited by these people that sets them apart—their unyielding belief that God was worthy of honor and obedience and trust:

> "By faith Abel offered to God a more excellent sacrifice than Cain" (v. 4).
>
> "By faith Enoch was taken away so that he did not see death" (v. 5).
>
> "By faith Noah, being divinely warned of things not yet seen, moved with godly fear, prepared an ark" (v. 7).
>
> "By faith Abraham obeyed when he was called to go out" (v. 8).
>
> "By faith Sarah herself also received strength to conceive" (v. 11).

The list goes on—Isaac, Jacob, Joseph, Moses, Rahab, David, and so on—and their testimonies are summed up at the end of the chapter: "All these, having obtained a good testimony through faith, did not receive the promise, God having provided something better for us, that they should not be made perfect [that is, completed in their faith] apart from us" (v. 39).

Faith trumps legalism and religion. Faith produces what mere rules and human morals never can: the holy behavior that God requires. Many people put their faith in science—in empirical data and what their senses can perceive. Oftentimes they criticize a life of faith, claiming that it's impractical—but everyone puts faith in something. And biblical faith is far more than positive confession or wishful thinking. It has "the *substance* of things hoped for, the *evidence* of things not seen" (Hebrews 11:1, emphasis added). Put another way, biblical faith is based on evidence and rooted firmly in the character of God.

> **Faith produces what mere rules and human morals never can: the holy behavior that God requires.**

Faith is practical. We have a whole group of people who have finished the race before us and are cheering us on, exhorting us to follow their example—everyone from Jesus to Moses to Paul to William Wilberforce to Martin Luther King to the believers you've known who have passed away. "Therefore we also, since we are surrounded by so great a cloud of witnesses, let us lay aside every weight, and the sin which so easily ensnares us, and let us run with endurance the race that is set before us" (Hebrews 12:1).

The use of the race metaphor suggests the practical nature of faith, modeled in Jesus Himself. We run our race, "looking unto Jesus, the author and finisher of our faith, who for the joy that was set before Him endured the cross, despising the shame, and has sat down at the right hand of the throne of God" (v. 2). Keep your eyes on Him as you go through the ups and downs of life, knowing that He will be your strength and inspiration in this race of life, and your reward and glory as you cross the finish line into the next.

A Better Mindset (Hebrews 12:3-29)

You can rest assured that you are putting your life in good hands because of the hope that only Jesus offers. He faced hardship, rejection, betrayal, violence, and shame because He felt you were worth it. "Consider Him who endured such hostility from sinners against Himself, lest you become weary and discouraged in your souls" (Hebrews 12:3). Jesus never offered a trouble-free life, only a redeemed one. Your great High Priest paid the price so that your trials and troubles can have significance.

The author of Hebrews knew that his audience was facing persecution for their faith in Christ and that they were tempted to go back to the relative safety of Jewish rituals and sacrifices. But because bad things happened to Jesus, they would also happen to His followers. They needed to be ready to endure persecution because there was hope in it. There was hope because it was temporary. As miserable as their suffering might be, it would have an end—and even if that end was in death, eternal glory in heaven awaited them.

Furthermore, suffering is purifying. You are God's child, and He will allow hardship into your life to help you learn and grow in your faith. "If you endure chastening, God deals with you as with sons" (Hebrews 12:7). Just as fire purifies precious metals, so trials purify faith. God won't take His eyes off you. That's a better hope than anything the law of Moses or any other religion can offer.

> ## Just as fire purifies precious metals, so trials purify faith.

A Better Mercy (Hebrews 13)

As the book concludes, the author offers an overarching instruction: "Let brotherly love continue" (Hebrews 13:1). The superior faith and hope enable us to love in a better way—by obeying God, seeking the best and highest good of our fellow believers, and "entertain[ing] strangers" (v. 2), showing hospitality and compassion to those whom God sets in our path.

Hebrews is summarized in one of the most beautiful benedictions in all of Scripture: "Now may the God of peace who brought up our Lord Jesus from the dead, that great Shepherd of the sheep, through the blood of the everlasting covenant, make you complete in every good work to do His will, working in you what is well pleasing in His sight, through Jesus Christ, to whom be glory forever and ever. Amen" (Hebrews 13:20-21).

Because of Jesus—our superior Savior and Good Shepherd—we have unrestricted access to the very throne of God. We can come boldly through prayer, in faith, knowing that our great High Priest is interceding for us always, and that He has adopted us as His brothers and sisters—coheirs with Him of the riches of God's grace, and able to do whatever works He has for us in this life.

A story is told of a group of soldiers in World War II who wanted to bury one of their buddies who had been killed. They took leave, found a nearby churchyard, and hoped to give him a decent burial. The only problem was that they were at a

Catholic cemetery and their friend was Protestant. They went to the priest, who shook his head with genuine regret and told them that their friend couldn't be buried in that graveyard unless he was Catholic. Seeing their despondency, he offered them a small plot just outside the fence, which technically wasn't part of the cemetery. Though they wanted to bury their friend among the honored dead, they took shovels in hand. Afterward, they mourned, telling stories about their friend before departing in sorrow.

They decided to get up the next morning and visit the grave one more time before going back to the battlefront. They came to the churchyard but couldn't find the grave of their friend. They looked all around the outside boundaries of the fence before going to the priest. "We've looked everywhere but can't find our friend," they said. "Can you help us?" The priest said, "After what happened yesterday, I couldn't sleep all night. So I got up, went out, and moved the fence. Your friend is now inside."

God has moved the fence. We were outside the fence, without access, but by the work of Jesus Christ, everyone has been offered entry. To receive Him by faith guarantees the way in. We're included because we are dealing with a system that is by far better because Jesus Christ is by far the best. He is the only Son from the Father, the only way to heaven, and the only hope for salvation—our perfect sacrifice, and the ultimate messenger, moderator, and mediator of the Father.

JAMES
FLIGHT PLAN

Facts

Author

The author of this book is identified as "James, a bondservant of God and of the Lord Jesus Christ" (James 1:1). The New Testament mentions several people named James, but the general consensus is that this work was written by James the half-brother of Jesus (Mark 6:2-3), who by Acts 15 was in charge of the church in Jerusalem.

Date Written

Because James did not mention the destruction of Jerusalem and used the Greek term that translates to *synagogue* instead of *church*, it's believed that the book of James is one of the earliest books in the New Testament, dated between AD 44 and 50—that is, within ten to fifteen years of Jesus's resurrection.

Landmarks

The book of James is distinct from most of the other New Testament epistles because of its unmistakably Jewish nature—addressed to the "twelve tribes" (James 1:1) and emphasizing faith in action. True Christianity is characterized by good deeds and a faith that works. Genuine faith, James argued, must and will be accompanied by a consistent lifestyle; it involves putting your faith where your hands and feet are. He used simple language and was obviously familiar with Jesus's Sermon on the Mount. His letter reads similar to Old Testament wisdom writings like the book of Proverbs.

Some people argue that there's a contradiction between James's emphasis on works (James 2:24) and Paul's emphasis on faith (Romans 3:28; Ephesians 2:8-9). But we must keep in mind that each author had a very different audience: James wrote to counter those who said that a Christian's conduct is irrelevant to salvation, and Paul was addressing legalists who said you needed works in order to be saved. James and Paul don't polarize; they harmonize. Throughout his letter,

James emphasized the importance of Christian maturity, describing the traits of the mature believer.

Itinerary

- Mature Christians Are Robust: Patient in Trials (James 1)
- Mature Christians Are Real: Practice the Truth (James 2)
- Mature Christians Are Restrained: Control the Tongue (James 3)
- Mature Christians Are Reserved: Poor in Spirit (James 4)
- Mature Christians Are Resigned: Persevere in Trials (James 5)

Gospel

Although Jesus is mentioned only a couple times in the book of James, He is at the center of everything James was driving toward. Because we have such a great salvation through Jesus, we have access to what we need to live out our faith: the wisdom of God. "If any of you lacks wisdom," James wrote, "let him ask of God, who gives to all liberally and without reproach, and it will be given to him" (James 1:5). We all need wisdom of some sort, don't we?

This is especially true when we're going through hardship—and the book of James certainly doesn't shy away from talking about that. In a trial, we tend to pray for deliverance rather than wisdom; that's simply part of our human nature. For the mature Christian, however, hardship ought to be embraced as an opportunity to learn, grow, and move forward in one's walk with God. It's by no means an easy process, but it's an important part of being sanctified—becoming more like Jesus. Instead of asking, "Lord, *how* can I get out of this?," develop an attitude that says, "Lord, *what* can I get out of this?"

> Instead of asking, "Lord, *how* can I get out of this?," develop an attitude that says, "Lord, *what* can I get out of this?"

When you're in a tough spot, ask the Lord for wisdom to deal with whatever circumstance you're facing—but make sure you do it with faith and assurance in your heart. James said that when you ask God for wisdom, you need to "ask in faith, with no doubting, for he who doubts is like a wave of the sea driven and tossed by the wind" (v. 6). Having faith doesn't mean you understand what God is doing or allowing in your life, but it does mean having confidence in His ability and then obeying whatever He tells you to do. Look at what Jesus did in His darkest hour in the Garden of Gethsemane: He first prayed for deliverance, then He prayed for God's will to be done no matter what. Then He went and did what was necessary (Matthew 26:36-46). He didn't waste a drop of His suffering. That ought to be our heart's cry in hardship: *Lord, let me not waste any of this!*

History

James had an unusual life. Growing up in the home of Joseph and Mary and living with his older half-brother Jesus must have been quite the experience! James had the rare opportunity to watch Jesus in all sorts of life situations, and in the end, he humbled himself and declared that he was Jesus's bondservant (James 1:1). Initially, Jesus's brothers—including James—didn't believe in Him (John 7:5). But after the resurrection, James's unbelief turned to unwavering belief (1 Corinthians 15:3-7). James became a leader in the early church (Acts 15) and headed up the Jerusalem council in AD 50. He was executed for his faith in AD 62.[97]

Travel Tips

James is chock-full of practical instruction on how to live out your faith and grow in your relationship with the Lord. "Draw near to God," James wrote, "and He will draw near to you" (James 4:8). The more like God we become, the nearer we are to Him, and vice versa. God is always present and always aware. But when we follow Him and obey His Word, our hearts are naturally drawn closer to His.

- Embrace trials. Two main factors drive Christian maturity: trials and temptations. We don't like either one, but we need both—the great paradox being that patience helps you endure trials but is also produced by trials. Growth as a believer cannot be achieved while being content to stay in safe waters. Where the water is smooth and undisturbed, the rocks beneath are sharp; where the water pounds the shore with waves, the rocks have been polished and smoothed into something beautiful.

> ## Growth as a believer cannot be achieved while being content to stay in safe waters.

- Be God's conduit of love and blessing. James reminded us to fulfill the "royal law" of Scripture: "You shall love your neighbor as yourself" (James 2:8). Because God has poured His love and His Spirit into our hearts through Jesus Christ (Romans 5:5), no one in our circle of influence should be starved for love, care, or consideration. Of course, not everyone in our lives is easy to love, but they don't have to be: God is the one who pours His love through us on other people.

- Loose lips sink ships. Gossip and careless speech can sink not just individual brothers and sisters, but entire churches. That's why James said mature Christians will control their tongue, and "the fruit of righteousness is sown in peace by those who make peace" (James 3:18).

- Growth hinges on practice. Being born again is just the beginning of your spiritual life. It has little to do with actual age, but is an ongoing process. Becoming mature in your faith requires patience, perseverance, and plenty of growing pains. James said that spiritual growth happens when you live what you believe, acting on the Word of God as you press on and keep walking in faith (James 1:22).

In Flight

Mature Christians Are Robust: Patient in Trials (James 1)

James is not a doctrinal book as much as it is a practical primer for seasoned believers. Everything he talked about hinges on two verses, both key components of Christian maturity: "Be doers of the word, and not hearers only, deceiving yourselves" (James 1:22), and "Faith without works is dead" (James 2:26). He wrote to Jewish believers—"the twelve tribes which are scattered abroad" (James 1:1)—scattered by the Roman government because of their faith in Jesus.

Facing persecution and harassment, these believers were going to have to mature in their faith in a hurry. James wanted to let them know that they were up to it—if they put their faith into practice. The first thing they had to do was embrace their suffering: "My brethren, count it all joy when you fall into various trials" (James 1:2). Trials are not an *if* but a *when*, yet even though we find no pleasure in them, there is purpose for them—"knowing that the testing of your faith produces patience. But let patience have its perfect work, that you may be perfect and complete, lacking nothing" (v. 3).

It's a classic paradox of the Christian faith that patience helps you endure trials but patience is also produced by those trials. One feeds the other. Stability doesn't come from a lack of hardship but of faith in the midst of it. And if you're not sure how to deal with the difficulty you're facing, you have the best possible resource: "If any of you lacks wisdom, let him ask of God, who gives to all liberally and without reproach, and it will be given to him" (James 1:5). When you are in a tough spot, going through a test or temptation, that's when you ask God for wisdom.

> ### Stability doesn't come from a lack of hardship but of faith in the midst of it.

Wisdom? Typically, in a trial, we ask not for wisdom but deliverance. But if trials produce patience and improve your faith, doesn't it make more sense to ask God what He wants you to do and learn? Rather than getting drunk or plotting revenge because you've lost your job, for example, instead, ask God what He wants you to get out of the situation. He will provide for you—but you can't afford to be wishy-washy about it. That's why James said, "Let him ask in faith, with no doubting, for he who doubts is like a wave of the sea driven and tossed by the wind" (James 1:6). Don't waste the experience you're going through by denying it, hiding from it, getting bitter or angry about it—and, in a lot of cases, wouldn't you rather learn the lesson only once? Being kept back in school because you flunked a test is a lot worse than suffering through studying for it the first time. It's the same in the school of faith.

James drew a distinction between being tested and being tempted. God allows testing and trials so that, with the proper attitude, you can grow in your faith. But temptation comes from the devil. "Blessed is the man who endures temptation; for when he has been approved, he will receive the crown of life which the Lord has promised to those who love Him" (v. 12). So, while you can ask God during a test, "What do You want me to learn from this?" you can't blame temptation on God. "Let no one say when he is tempted, 'I am tempted by God'; for God cannot be tempted by evil, nor does He Himself tempt anyone" (v. 13).

God permits testing and tailors it to our individual needs, which makes it a matter of step-by-step faith, trusting God all along the way. Temptation, however, follows a recognizable pattern: "Each one is tempted when he is drawn away by his own desires and enticed. Then, when desire has conceived, it gives birth to sin;

and sin, when it is full-grown, brings forth death" (vv. 14-15). James was dissecting temptation and showing us all of its stages, from desire to sinful action to harmful consequences. Testing comes from the outside; it's not your fault. But temptation comes from within, from your own desires—lust, greed, anger. God's purpose is to mature you and improve your life; Satan's is to neutralize you at a minimum and destroy your relationships, witness, and life if possible. A mature Christian is robust—sturdy, tough, able to learn and grow from hard times and to recognize temptation and seek God's wisdom in dealing with both.

Mature Christians Are Real: Practice the Truth (James 2)

James described authenticity as another mark of Christian maturity. A seasoned believer doesn't just talk about his faith, he lives it out in his everyday life. James gave an example from church life—two visitors attending a service. One is rich, one is poor, and the challenge is in how church members receive and respond to each. Will they show favoritism, imagining that the rich one can do something for them, or supposing that they can look good by being kind to the poor one?

God, of course, wants us to treat everyone with equal respect and love. "Mercy triumphs over judgment" (James 2:13). James said, "If you really fulfill the royal law according to the Scripture, 'You shall love your neighbor as yourself,' you do well; but if you show partiality, you commit sin, and are convicted by the law as transgressors" (vv. 8-9). It's a royal law because it came from our King—Jesus Himself, who summed up everything in the Old Testament in two commandments: loving God with all you are, and loving your neighbor as yourself (Matthew 22:37-40).

And the proof of that love, James said, is in putting your faith into practice. "What does it profit, my brethren, if someone says he has faith but does not have works? Can faith save him?" (James 2:14). This isn't a question of whether or not faith in Christ can save—it clearly can. What James asked was, "Can *that kind* of faith, disconnected from good works, help anyone, including the believer, to grow or advance God's kingdom?"

As he went along, James mentioned three types of faith: dead faith (vv. 14-17)—belief stuck in the mind but not evident from deeds; demonic faith (v. 19)—like the kind fallen angels have in response to what is true about God, doctrinally correct yet clearly cut off from righteous living; and dynamic faith (vv. 20-26)—belief put into behavior. "If a brother or sister is naked and destitute of daily food, and one of you says to them, 'Depart in peace, be warmed and filled,' but you do not give them the things which are needed for the body, what does it profit? Thus also faith by itself, if it does not have works, is dead" (vv. 15-17).

There's no contradiction between what James was saying here and the doctrine of salvation by faith (as Paul wrote about in Romans and Galatians, in particular). Earlier, James said of God that "of His own will He brought us forth by the word of truth, that we might be a kind of firstfruits of His creatures" (James 1:18)—that is, God gave us salvation as one of His "good and perfect gifts" (v. 17). Works, however, are the test of faith. You can tell the difference between dead faith, demonic faith, and dynamic faith by whether it actually impacts the person's behavior. It's a response to being saved, not a way to get saved.

Even so, James said, faith without works is dead. Actions demonstrate that the faith is real. Works show that faith works. Anyone can say they have faith, or say the right things to believe about God and Jesus, but real faith works—it becomes that person's practice in life, and God empowers the person to do the works He has set aside for them (Ephesians 2:10). According to Jesus, not everyone will pass that test, either: "Not everyone who says to Me, 'Lord, Lord,' shall enter the kingdom of heaven, but the one who does the will of My Father in heaven" (Matthew 7:21).

James anticipated how some might respond, saying, "You have faith, and I have works" (James 2:18). In other words, "You have your faith, and I'll have my works." But the two can't be separated. James said, "Show me your faith without your works, and I will show you my faith by my works" (v. 18). The former is dead, a matter of lip service, and the latter is proof of a vibrant, living faith.

Saying the right things won't cut it either. "You believe that there is one God. You do well. Even the demons believe—and tremble!" (v. 19). James was being ironic, of course. People claiming to be Christians are often capable of making accurate statements of belief. But think about it: Does Satan believe that there is one God? Yes; he used to work for Him. Does he believe that Jesus is the only way to heaven? He certainly does; that's why he momentarily thought he had won at the cross. Satan is as orthodox in his belief as anyone can be. He believes all the right things. However, what he does with that information is another matter altogether.

James's point was that talk is cheap. "But do you want to know, O foolish man, that faith without works is dead?" (v. 20). He cited Abraham as an example of faith working together with actions, saying, "By works faith was made perfect" (v. 22). Abraham's righteous deeds, including the belief that God accounted to him for righteousness (Genesis 15:6), completed his faith. His works justified him in the sense that they showed his faith was real, that he was bearing good fruit in his life as a son of a fruitful God. Obedience, then, proves relationship; it doesn't provide relationship, but it does verify the existence of true relationship.

Mature Christians Are Restrained: Control the Tongue (James 3)

In a key example of how to practice the truth, James observed that mature Christians have power over the tongue. Controlling our mouths is a struggle for all of us, but it's a necessary battle. Whether we speak a little or a lot, we need to make our words count. And for teachers, who are in a position to speak a lot more than the average person, there is a special level of accountability that comes with being known. "My brethren, let not many of you become teachers, knowing that we shall receive a stricter judgment" (James 3:1). You are always accountable to God for what you say, but especially as a Bible teacher, pastor, or group leader, because souls are at stake.

A pastor or Bible teacher is accountable to speak God's truth into people's lives, so it should be done with great preparation and prayer, and the challenge of harnessing the tongue to that purpose is even more daunting. "For we all stumble in many things. If anyone does not stumble in word, he is a perfect man, able also to bridle the whole body" (v. 2). The tongue, as the primary instrument of vocal communication, is incredibly powerful for such a small thing. But, as James noted, there are analogies: a tiny bit turns a huge horse, and a rudder directs a ship. "Even so the tongue is a little member and boasts great things. See how great a forest a little fire kindles!" (v. 5).

Words don't have to be true to have impact. Gossip has always been just as effective at causing damage as a match carelessly discarded in the woods. Just get enough people talking about something, even if it has only a little bit of truth, and you can destroy a whole reputation in no time flat. James took it even further than that, though: "The tongue is a fire, a world of iniquity. The tongue is so set among our members [that is, the parts of our physical body] that it defiles the whole body, and sets on fire the course of nature; and it is set on fire by hell" (v. 6). A reputation can go up in flames, and so can a person's whole character. More sins are committed with the tongue than any other single part of your body—gossip, lying, slander, insults, boasting, flattery, hypocrisy, and so on. The tongue can destroy.

And, James noted, it seems we can tame every kind of wild creature, but not our own tongues. "It is an unruly evil, full of deadly poison. With it we bless our God and Father, and with it we curse men, who have been made in the similitude [the likeness] of God. Out of the same mouth proceed blessing and cursing. My brethren, these things ought not to be so" (James 3:8-10).

There is a Greek myth about Proteus, who could change form whenever he wanted to, to whatever he wanted to be in that moment—a rock, a tree, a lion, a serpent. That shifting unpredictability is part of human nature. We can go from praising God to yelling at our kids in a hot minute. James asked, "Who is wise and understanding among you? Let him show by good conduct, that his works are done in the meekness of wisdom" (v. 13). Only by asking God for wisdom can we learn the restraint needed to tame our tongues.

Mature Christians Are Reserved: Poor in Spirit (James 4)

James further developed the concept of Christian restraint by encouraging his readers to show proper reserve and forbearance. We want to wait on God's leading, so that we don't act impulsively or rashly but with humility and consideration of others. That kind of spiritual maturity requires us to follow James's advice: "Let every man be swift to hear, slow to speak, slow to wrath" (James 1:19).

In order to behave that way, though, we need to acknowledge the root cause of conflict. James revealed it with a few questions. "Where do wars and fights come from among you? Do they not come from your desires for pleasure that war in your members?" (James 4:1). James used military language to describe a battle raging within each of us, and even in the church. "You lust and do not have. You murder and covet and cannot obtain. You fight and war. Yet you do not have because you do not ask" (v. 2). The dispersed group of Jewish believers James addressed were facing persecution from the world, but worse, they were taking altercations inside the church assembly and squabbling amongst themselves.

Further, they were asking the wrong question, wondering how to avoid outside persecution and how to get what they wanted. James challenged them to straighten out their priorities. "You ask and you do not receive, because you ask amiss, that you might spend it on your pleasures" (v. 3). In all of this, their own individual selfishness is the source of conflict: *you* lust, *you* murder, *you* covet, *you* fight—and "yet you do not have."

Conflict is a fact of life. No matter where you work, no matter where you go to church, no matter who you live next to, there will be disagreement and friction. So how do you deal with that? By being a mature Christian. You fight the temptation to push harder, argue more loudly, make your point more forcefully. You battle the desire to win—because what you consider a win is often a loss in God's book. You listen twice as much as you speak, and you bear in mind that "the wrath of man does not produce the righteousness of God" (James 1:20).

You show the reservation that Jesus demonstrated. There were no rocks in His hand when He turned away the crowd ready to stone the adulteress. He could have revealed all the sins that lurked in her accusers' hearts and prevented them from throwing stones, but He wanted their hearts to be convicted, so he just wrote on the ground. On the way to the cross, He could have called down a legion of angels to defend Himself or sent fire down from heaven as a message to Pilate and his henchmen, but self-defense was not His objective. Jesus showed us how to face the world without acting like the world. In fact, "friendship with the world is enmity with God" (James 4:4).

Jesus showed us how to face the world without acting like the world.

"Therefore He says: 'God resists the proud, but gives grace to the humble'" (James 4:6). That little word "resists" haunts me. It tells me that if I want to be at odds with God, the quickest way is to be proud. Whether I'm at home, at work, or out in the world, my pride will set God against me. Fortunately, "He gives more grace" (v. 6). God will always give you as much grace as you need to handle a conflict with humility, if that's your goal. Without humility—without that recognition that you can't stand before holy God, that you are desperate and needy before Him—you can't come to Christ. "Blessed are the poor in spirit, for theirs is the kingdom of heaven" (Matthew 5:3).

In and by His grace, though, you can root out the habit of conflict and turn from temptation. "Therefore submit to God. Resist the devil and he will flee from you" (James 4:7). Notice the order: Submit to God first, then resist the devil. Trust God to strengthen you as you actively turn away from doing things the devil's way. Don't bother talking to Satan. No need to verbally assault him, then drop the mike and walk away. Just walk away—turn from doing things his way. When temptation knocks, don't answer the door. Go find Jesus and ask if He wouldn't mind answering it. "Draw near to God and He will draw near to you" (v. 8).

In the Christian life, the way up is down. "Humble yourselves in the sight of the Lord, and He will lift you up" (James 4:10). If you make promoting God in your attitude and behavior your business, He will take care of yours. Pride divides whereas humility unites. That includes the way you speak of others and the way you do business; the former can have an eternal impact, and the latter may not go according to your plans. "You do not know what will happen tomorrow. For what is your life? It is even a vapor that appears for a little time and then vanishes away" (v. 14).

James wasn't saying it's bad to plan in advance. However, to plan your life apart from God, as if you can guarantee how it will go, is arrogant boasting. We are finite creatures of limited understanding. He has the big picture in mind in His infinite knowledge and uncontested sovereignty, so our humility is in recognizing that and trusting Him to do what is right, working all things together for good—especially when we don't understand why our plans have fallen apart. Maturity demands that you abandon the right to run your life, reserving it for God.

Mature Christians Are Resigned: Persevere in Trials (James 5)

Even as James called for these persecuted believers to trust God with their lives, he also took a shot at the wealthy (likely both those within and outside of the church) for their role in persecuting the poor. It was typical back then for the rich to oppress the poor because Roman law did little to prevent it, but James let his audience know that God was aware of what they were doing; they wouldn't get away with their abuses (James 5:1-6).

Then James turned his attention back to the persecuted, reminding them of the importance of perseverance. "Be patient, brethren, until the coming of the Lord. See how the farmer waits for the precious fruit of the earth, waiting patiently for it until it receives the early and latter rain" (James 5:7). Farmers have to wait on the weather; the one thing they can't control is the one thing that they need for their crops to grow. They are in it for the long haul, bearing the ups and downs with a larger picture in mind—a perfect analogy for the Christian life. Even a bumper crop, though, pales in comparison with what awaits faithful believers: "You also be patient. Establish your hearts, for the coming of the Lord is at hand" (v. 8).

Mature Christians persevere because they have hope. Hope lifts our eyes to a future justice. Jesus will return, set things to rights, and reward His faithful children. But until then, He strengthens those who are resigned to trust Him—not resigned in the sense that there is no other way to face hardship, but committed to the best, most hopeful way to face it. "Indeed we count them blessed who endure. You have heard of the perseverance of Job and seen the end intended by the Lord—that the Lord is very compassionate and merciful" (v. 11). What Job went through he didn't understand; instead, he persevered because of what he knew to be true about God, and he was able to praise God's name even in the face of tragedy and confusion.

Because of God's compassion and mercy, the mature believer's perseverance plays out in practical ways—praying for the suffering, forgiving sinners, singing cheerfully in the darkest times, confessing trespasses to and praying for other believers (vv. 13-16). In line with his earlier advice to ask God for wisdom, James reminded his audience that the "effective, fervent prayer of a righteous man avails much" (v. 16). Restoration is always a priority for God, so it should be for His people. "Brethren, if anyone among you wanders from the truth, and someone turns him back, let him know that he who turns a sinner from the error of his way will save a soul from death and cover a multitude of sins" (vv. 19-20).

> ## Restoration is always a priority for God, so it should be for His people.

James hoped that his audience would embrace that transforming truth: Mature Christians are shaped by trials and temptations into humble, hopeful believers who patiently persevere. Spiritual growth should happen as a result of a life connected to God, regardless of age and mindful of God's faithfulness throughout the process. God's resources are there for you—if you will only ask, and then act in faith on what you know. That's how you ensure that you'll grow up.

1 AND 2 PETER
FLIGHT PLAN

Author

The author of 1 and 2 Peter is identified as the apostle Peter in the first verses of each book. Peter was a disciple of Jesus, one of Jesus's closest friends, and "a witness of the sufferings of Christ" (1 Peter 5:1). He spent three years walking with Jesus, learning from Him and witnessing all that He did during His time on earth.

Date Written

First Peter was written sometime around AD 64, a time of declining condition for the church because of Roman persecution. Peter likely wrote 2 Peter shortly before he was martyred around AD 66, under the reign of Caesar Nero.

Landmarks

First Peter is essentially a handbook of conduct for Christ's ambassadors to a hostile world. Knowing that the persecution against believers would only continue, Peter carefully prescribed godly guidelines for believers to follow so they could bring honor to the One they represented. As they followed these guidelines and faced persecution head-on, the hope was that the true grace of Jesus Christ would become evident in and through them (1 Peter 5:12). In this letter, Peter also encouraged Christians to lift their eyes past the horizon of their present troubles and trials and look to their inheritance waiting in heaven, which can never perish, spoil, or fade. With that in mind, he laid out God's will and plan for believers.

In 2 Peter, the apostle gave the church both a stern warning and a soothing reminder. Seeing that false teachers were beginning to infiltrate Christian assemblies, and knowing that the church faced immediate danger, Peter wanted believers to grow in their faith so they could detect, combat, and withstand the spreading apostasy. To aid in this, he described the conduct of these false teachers in detail, including their ridicule of the Lord's second coming.

Peter also challenged believers to grow in specific godly virtues, becoming effective and productive in their knowledge of Jesus Christ. This knowledge is based on the authenticity and reliability of God's Word and is spurred on by believing in the sure return of the Lord Jesus Christ. The second coming of Christ, Peter explained, is the Christian's incentive for holy living in the present—the key to faithfully growing in the truth.

Itinerary

1 Peter

- God's Plan Includes Security (1 Peter 1:1-12)
- God's Plan Includes Surrender (1 Peter 1:13–2:10)
- God's Plan Includes Submission (1 Peter 2:11–3:7)
- God's Plan Includes Suffering (1 Peter 3:8–4:19)
- God's Plan Includes Service (1 Peter 5)

2 Peter

- Faithful Progress in the Truth (2 Peter 1)
- False Prophets Against the Truth (2 Peter 2)
- Future Predictions of the Truth (2 Peter 3)

Gospel

According to some proponents of the so-called health-and-wealth gospel, God will give you whatever you need to become physically healthy, financially wealthy, and always happy. While I certainly can't say what God will or will not do in your life, consider these facts: As a Christian, you follow the God whom the world despises. So while you are indeed God's child, and all of heaven's blessings and provision are at your disposal, and you will one day go to heaven, your life on this earth is a spiritual battle fought on a spiritual battlefield.

Like it or not, you've had an enormous spiritual bull's-eye on your back ever since you accepted Christ as your Savior. Even the Savior promised His disciples that they would have enemies simply because they were His friends (John 15:18-21)! Did you think Satan and all of hell would give you a standing ovation because you received Christ? By no means! You defected from the kingdom of darkness, and when you leave the enemy's camp, he will do all he can to wreck you.

But remember: God is sovereign and in control, and you are under His protection. You're in His family now, and there are so many wonderful benefits that come with that privilege. A rather unexpected blessing is that, when God allows you to suffer, He uses it for good. Just think of what He did through Jesus: He suffered and died an excruciating death on the cross, but this brought about the greatest good in all of history—salvation for the world.

Because you are God's, you will always be a target for those who set themselves against Him and His good plans. But as Peter said, "If anyone suffers as a Christian, let him not be ashamed, but let him glorify God in this matter" (1 Peter 4:16). Remember, you're on the side that wins in the end. God will be glorified in and through your persecution, and you'll get to spend eternity with Him, free from all suffering and sorrow. Part of the glorious gospel is the keeping power of God; the issue is, do you want to be kept?

> Remember, you're on the side that wins in the end.

History

Peter's original name was Simon, a common Jewish name, and his father was a Jew named John (Matthew 16:17). Peter grew up in the town of Bethsaida on the shores of the Sea of Galilee, then later moved to Capernaum. He first heard about Jesus from his brother, Andrew, around the year AD 27 (John 1:40-42). After that, he became one of Jesus's twelve core disciples. Jesus was the one who gave him the name Peter, which means "rock." Peter was privy to some of the most glorious moments of Jesus's life, such as when Jesus showed His divine nature at the transfiguration around AD 29 (Matthew 17:1-8).

During Jesus's trial, Peter, in his moment of weakness, denied Christ. But after the resurrection, Jesus restored Peter, paving the way for him to become a leader in the early church known for giving powerful sermons and doing mighty works (Acts 3–8). Around AD 40, Peter began his ministry among the Gentiles, and in AD 50, he was involved with the first church council at Jerusalem. He was executed under the reign of Emperor Nero around AD 66.[98]

Travel Tips

Peter has gotten a bad rap over the years. Nonbelievers know him best from the lame and erroneous jokes about heaven, where he stands at the gates with a clipboard, deciding who gets in and who doesn't. Believers, on the other hand, know him as the guy with foot-in-mouth disease, impulsive and strong-willed. But Peter was honest, loyal, passionate, and tenderhearted toward Jesus—probably the most human of the disciples and the one we can relate to the most (though we like to pretend we're smarter than him). Jesus took this rough-and-tumble fisherman, nicknamed him Rocky, and made him a fisher of men and a solid leader. We should be grateful for Peter's example and the Lord's awesome work in and through his life!

- Peter encouraged believers to grow by learning and ingesting God's Word: "Desire the pure milk of the word, that you may grow thereby" (1 Peter 2:2). Your spiritual growth is directly proportional to your spiritual hunger. If you are hungry for the Word, you will read it, dig into it, learn it, apply it, and grow. If it's an appetizer or occasional snack to you, your growth will be stunted. Your appetite grows depending on what and how often you feed it.

- Christianity works! If we follow Peter's advice to build on our knowledge of God and walk with Him, we'll see just how powerfully it does (2 Peter 1:5-8). Growing in the Lord isn't some magical process; it takes effort on our part to apply what God has given us for life and godliness, and it takes His power to sustain and enable us to do so.

- Defend against false teaching. Peter gave us three different ways to determine if someone is a false teacher: the test of character (2 Peter 2:10-14), the test of creed (vv. 17-18), and the test of converts (vv. 19-22). You can determine a person's legitimacy in the Lord by how he walks and by the fruit he produces; don't be fooled by outward appearances!

  - Character: Do you see the fruit of the Spirit in the person's character (Galatians 5:22-23)?

  - Creed: What do they say about Jesus—what's their creed? Is the gate they preach a narrow one, as Jesus said it must be (Matthew 7:13-14), or have they broadened it, departing from historic Christian truth?

  - Converts: Look at the people they influence. What do you see in terms of their holiness and joy? How's their prayer life? Have they become harsh and legalistic, loose and self-centered?

> Growing in the Lord isn't some magical process;
> it takes effort on our part to apply what
> God has given us for life and godliness.

In Flight

1 Peter

God's Plan Includes Security (1 Peter 1:1-12)

Peter wrote to a group of believers who had been scattered across Asia Minor by harassment, maltreatment, and persecution—"the pilgrims of the Dispersion" (1 Peter 1:1). He wanted to remind them that God was with them, especially in such dark times, that they were the "elect according to the foreknowledge of God the Father, in sanctification of the Spirit, for obedience and sprinkling of the blood of Jesus Christ" (v. 2). They were, as are all believers, called and chosen by God according to His plan that predates the foundations of the world (Ephesians 1:4).

Furthermore, Peter wrote, God has "begotten us again to a living hope through the resurrection of Jesus Christ from the dead" (1 Peter 1:3). His language brings to mind what Jesus told Nicodemus about the need to be "born again" to see God's kingdom (John 3:3). There is no more fitting description of what happens to a person at salvation than to call it a new birth. Peter picked up on that idea of rebirth to a new start—a "living hope"—as a child of God, given "an inheritance incorruptible and undefiled and that does not fade away, reserved in heaven for you, who are kept by the power of God through faith for salvation ready to be revealed in the last time" (1 Peter 1:4-5). "Let there be no mistake," Peter was saying. "God chose you, renewed you, and will keep you safe until His return. Your salvation is rock solid."

It's possible for people to be going to heaven but not enjoying the ride. When life gets bumpy or seems mundane, people sometimes question their destination and even their salvation. Peter reminded them that this was God's process, His plan, echoing John's words to the same effect: children of God "were born, not of blood, nor of the will of the flesh, nor of the will of man, but of God" (John 1:13). By virtue of your spiritual birth, you are also being spiritually kept.

So when you face persecution and the way is hard, God will still get you to heaven. "In this you greatly rejoice, though now for a little while, if *need* be, you have been grieved by various trials" (1 Peter 1:6, emphasis added). What "need" could trials possibly address? "That the genuineness of your faith, being much more precious than gold that perishes, though it is tested by fire, may be found to praise, honor, and glory at the revelation of Jesus Christ" (v. 7). Just as James discussed in his letter, mature Christians can rejoice in trials because God can make something good from them, burning away all the things that keep us from following Christ more completely. Trials have a way of clarifying what's essential and clearing away the superficial.

> ## Trials have a way of clarifying what's essential and clearing away the superficial.

At the time Peter wrote this letter, Christians were facing a new level of persecution brought on by the infamous great fire of Rome in AD 64. Up to that point, Christians had been unpopular, generally speaking, but still somewhat under the protection of being seen as a sect of Judaism, which was a government-permitted religion. After the fire, though, Caesar Nero diverted the blame for starting the blaze by pointing the finger at Christians—and persecution became policy.

It was relatively simple to fan the flames of hatred. Nero generated or exaggerated rumors about Christians, calling them cannibals because they "ate the flesh" and "drank the blood" of their Master (a twisted interpretation of the communion service). The equal status Christ gave men and women upset the balance in the Roman home, where wives were completely under their husbands' legal authority. The same happened with masters and slaves, the latter of whom formed about a third of Rome's population.

Christianity's damage to the status quo upset the equilibrium of the empire, and Rome fought back—imprisoning, torturing, and executing Christian men, women, and children as enemies of the state. Peter encouraged them to hold the line—saying that they were part of something that God had set in motion centuries ago, a grace revealed in part through prophets, a gospel so powerful and wonderful that even angels are awed by it (vv. 11-12). Prophets had predicted their salvation, and Christ had procured it.

God's Plan Includes Surrender (1 Peter 1:13–2:10)

Secure in their salvation, these believers could then fully surrender to God's will, trusting His plans and purposes. Peter offered a twofold method for surrender: reverence for God's will, followed by compliance to God's Word. "Therefore gird up the loins of your mind"—that is, be ready for action, be prepared in your thinking—"be sober, and rest your hope fully upon the grace that is to be brought to you at the revelation of Jesus Christ" (1 Peter 1:13).

Their hope—and ours—was that everything they could do to represent Christ well would be rewarded upon His return, but they had to follow Him "as obedient children, not conforming yourselves to the former lusts, as in your ignorance; but as He who called you is holy, you also be holy in all your conduct" (vv. 14-15). God will evaluate what His children do with the resources He provides, so "if you call on the Father, who without partiality judges according to each one's work, conduct yourselves throughout the time of your stay here in fear" (v. 17).

That fear, by the way, isn't terror or dread but a healthy respect for God. To fear God in this sense is to show reverence for Him—an awe of His love, grace, and power that produces humble submission to His will. From Peter's perspective, this is the best way to live life, focused on God and not on the things of this world. Both the riches and the troubles of this life burn up like dry grass, but these believers had "been born again, not of corruptible seed but incorruptible, through the word of God which lives and abides forever" (v. 23).

In light of God's gift, then, and in reverential awe of Him, we should commit to His Word and His ways. "Therefore, laying aside all malice, all deceit, hypocrisy, envy, and all evil speaking, as newborn babes, desire the pure milk of the word, that you may grow thereby" (1 Peter 2:1-3). Once you commit to following Jesus, your next desire should be to grow in that relationship. You do that by learning and applying His Word. The Bible should be precious to you because its promises apply to you. But if you don't apply Scripture, Peter said, you're being disobedient, and you will stumble (vv. 6-8). Part of your surrender to His control in your life is to accept that He wants you to anchor yourself in His Word.

> **The Bible should be precious to you because its promises apply to you.**

God's Plan Includes Submission (1 Peter 2:11–3:7)

With Christians in the crosshairs of a dangerous administration in Rome, Peter emphasized "having your conduct honorable among the Gentiles, that when they speak against you as evildoers, they may, by your good works which they observe, glorify God in the day of visitation" (1 Peter 2:12). Anytime someone gives you a hard time about being a Christian, it's difficult not to respond emotionally—to get angry and lash out, or to hit them over the head (figuratively speaking, of course) with Scripture.

To avoid those kinds of responses, you have to submit—to put God's will ahead of your own. Part of His will is that you "submit yourselves to every ordinance of man for the Lord's sake...For this is the will of God, that by doing good you may put to silence the ignorance of foolish men" (vv. 13, 15). We need to honor our dual citizenship—on earth and in heaven—by being responsible and humble citizens of each. Clearly if there's a conflict between obeying the government and obeying God, then we must obey God rather than men, as Peter himself said (Acts 5:29).

"This is commendable, if because of conscience toward God one endures grief, suffering wrongfully" (1 Peter 2:19). By submitting first and foremost to God, trusting that even your suffering can be used for good purposes in His hands, you are able to submit to earthly authorities—citizen to government (vv. 13-14), employee to boss (or servant to master, v. 18), wife to husband *and* husband to wife (1 Peter 3:1-7). "For to this you were called, because Christ also suffered for us, leaving us an example, that you should follow His steps" (1 Peter 2:21).

God's Plan Includes Suffering (1 Peter 3:8–4:19)

While it's not something that most Christians like to dwell on, part of God's plan includes the example of suffering that Jesus set. If Jesus Christ Himself was not exempt from suffering, then why do we think we ought to be? "For it is better, if it is the will of God, to suffer for doing good than for doing evil. For Christ also suffered once for sins, the just for the unjust, that He might bring us to God" (1 Peter 3:17-18). The salvation Jesus purchased for us came as a result of His suffering and carries with it the promise of heaven as well as the satisfaction in this life of doing God's will (1 Peter 4:1-2).

It shouldn't shock you, then, when you go through hard times. "Beloved, do not think it strange concerning the fiery trial which is to try you, as though some strange thing happened to you; but rejoice to the extent that you partake of Christ's sufferings, that when His glory is revealed, you may also be glad with exceeding joy" (vv. 12-13). This is what Paul called "the fellowship of His sufferings" (Philippians 3:10), knowing that when you are persecuted for following Christ, you are a partner in one of the deepest forms of fellowship anyone could ever have with Jesus (see **Gospel** on page 576).[99]

Peter said, "If you are reproached for the name of Christ, blessed are you, for the Spirit of glory and of God rests upon you. On their part He is blasphemed, but on your part He is glorified" (v. 14). Those who believe that suffering in this life can't be the will of God are missing the chance to know God better. All the blessings and necessities of heaven are at your disposal, but you are also living daily in a battle-ground. "Therefore," Peter said, "let those who suffer according to the will of God commit their souls to Him in doing good, as to a faithful Creator" (v. 19).

God's Plan Includes Service (1 Peter 5)

Peter wrapped up by turning his attention to the church, addressing leaders and youth specifically, and everyone else on a few general points. He wanted everyone in the body of Christ to grasp that God's plan for them included serving one another.

Speaking to his fellow elders, Peter encouraged them in their care for the church: "Shepherd the flock of God which is among you, serving as overseers, not by compulsion but willingly, not for dishonest gain but eagerly; nor as being lords over those entrusted to you, but being examples to the flock" (1 Peter 5:2-3). A position of leadership in the church isn't an opportunity to lift yourself up but to lift others up by word and deed.

Peter then spoke to the younger people, telling them, "Submit yourselves to your elders. Yes, all of you be submissive to one another, and be clothed with humility" (v. 5). Together, they would better be able to support each other, casting all their cares on God (v. 7), and resisting the devil, the roaring lion who constantly sought out the weak links in the flock for a way in (v. 8). Peter prayed God's blessings on all of them, that God, "after you have suffered awhile, perfect, establish, strengthen, and settle you" (v. 10). By loving and serving one another in the church, these persecuted believers would be able to withstand danger from the outside, and glorify God in their response to the world. The church can be a messy place sometimes because it's filled with imperfect believers and surrounded by indifferent unbelievers, but it's the best thing going (and it beats the alternatives).

2 Peter
Faithful Progress in the Truth (2 Peter 1)

If 1 Peter's theme is that Christians can expect danger from the outside, the theme of 2 Peter is that Christians can expect danger from the inside. This time, shortly before his death, Peter obeyed his call from Jesus to feed His sheep (John 21:15-18), warning them not of persecution but deception. False teachers were a constant danger in the early church; to recognize and root them out, believers would have to progress in their knowledge of and trust in God's truth.

Fortunately, God has provided all His children need, "as His divine power has given to us all things that pertain to life and godliness" (2 Peter 1:3). Once your salvation is secured, the rest of your walk with Christ, at least in this life, is a process of sanctification—being purified and made holy like Jesus. This process begins with us realizing that as Christians, we are "partakers of the divine nature" (v. 4).

Once we understand that, Peter said, we are then to make maximum effort to keep building on our faith, adding to our lives a progressive set of virtues. "For this very reason, giving all diligence, add to your faith virtue, to virtue knowledge, to knowledge self-control, to self-control perseverance, to perseverance godliness, to godliness brotherly kindness, and to brotherly kindness love" (vv. 5-7). This is the fruit of our salvation, not the root. These things don't save us; they are just our response to God's salvation—our cooperation with Him and His plans and purposes.

"He who lacks these [virtues]," Peter continued, "is shortsighted, even to blindness, and has forgotten that he was cleansed from his old sins" (v. 9). You need to remember where you've been and what you've been saved from so you can see where you're going and move forward. As you build on your faith and grow, becoming more and more sanctified, it will prepare you for the big move—the move to heaven.

If you're a believer in Christ, your ultimate destination is heaven; there's no question about that. But the manner in which you arrive is up to you. If you run your race well, investing all of yourself in what the Lord has called you to do, you can look forward to a victor's welcome. As Peter wrote, "Be even more diligent to make your call and election sure, for if you do these things you will never stumble; for so an entrance will be supplied to you abundantly into the everlasting kingdom of our Lord and Savior Jesus Christ" (vv. 10-11). Live in such a way now so that they'll roll out the red carpet for you later.

Live in such a way now so that they'll roll out the red carpet for you later.

Peter wanted to leave a written reminder of the things these believers already knew were needed to make progress in the truth. He reminded his readers that he was one of the few who actually walked with Jesus—thus, he was fit to tell them what he saw with his own eyes, to leave them a reminder based on an eyewitness account of Christ's life, death, and resurrection. Even more importantly, though, came the reminder to trust the objective truth of God's Word. "We have the prophetic word confirmed, which you do well to heed as a light that shines in a dark place...knowing this first, that no prophecy of Scripture is of any private interpretation, for prophecy never came by the will of man, but holy men of God spoke as they were moved by the Holy Spirit" (vv. 19-21). In other words, Peter said, "More reliable than what I saw and what I heard is the inherent unchanging objective truth of the Scriptures, the promises that have been made and were fulfilled in Jesus Christ."

False Prophets Against the Truth (2 Peter 2)

During the first few decades of church history, the big deception was legalism, promoted by the Judaizers. They taught that you had to keep the Law of Moses in order to be saved. They said Christ's sacrifice and grace weren't enough; you had to be circumcised and keep all the meticulous ceremonial laws. Peter wanted to make sure that the church knew about these false prophets and their battle against the truth. Having established the reliability of the prophetic scriptures about Jesus, he brought up an age-old enemy. "There were also false prophets among the people, even as there will be false teachers among you, who will secretly bring in destructive heresies, even denying the Lord who bought them, and bring on themselves swift destruction" (2 Peter 2:1).

In certain cases, tolerance is not a virtue, but truth always is—especially when it comes to directing people toward eternity. That's why Peter wanted us to be aware of the common characteristics of false prophets—so that we can recognize a cancer and cut it out of the body of Christ. Using our vocabulary but not our dictionary, false teachers distort truth and deny Christ, broadening the way to heaven and covering up their motives (see **Travel Tips** on page 577). Like their ultimate inspiration, the devil, they despise authority and want to set themselves up as the ones who decide what truth is.

But they have "forsaken the right way and gone astray" (2 Peter 2:15). The implication is that, at some point, they received the truth of Jesus Christ, but "after they escaped the pollutions of the world through the knowledge of the Lord and Savior Jesus Christ, they are again entangled in them and overcome" (v. 20). They've become the proverbial dogs returning to their vomit, and it would have been "better for them not to have known the way of righteousness, than having known it, to turn from the holy commandment delivered to them" (v. 21). All Christians have a responsibility to the truth—learning it, living it, and defending it.

To forsake that is to ensure God's judgment and wrath, because falsehood is never content to go it alone. Heretics want company. "Many will follow their destructive ways, because of whom the way of truth will be blasphemed. By covetousness they will exploit you with deceptive words; for a long time their judgment has not been idle, and their destruction does not slumber" (v. 3).

God will judge false teachers and prophets, because if He judged the angels who fell (v. 4), Peter said, then He certainly will judge people who fall into falsehood and teach false doctrine. They have been there in the past and will be there, threatening the church, until Jesus returns. The Bible says the church is "the pillar and ground of the truth" (1 Timothy 3:15), the guardian and bastion of truth in the world. So it makes sense that Satan has been attacking it from the beginning—just as he has attacked God's people and truth throughout time. We have to guard against that, holding the line for truth.

Future Predictions of the Truth (2 Peter 3)

After warning the church of the present threat in its midst, Peter turned to the future. Facing persecution, some believers were wondering when God was going to keep His promises of a better time to come. Peter named this as one of his main causes for writing a second letter:

> That you may be mindful of the words which were spoken before by the holy prophets, and of the commandment of us, the apostles of the Lord and Savior, knowing this first: that scoffers will come in the last days, walking according to their own lusts, and saying, "Where is the promise of His coming? For since the fathers fell asleep, all things continue as they were from the beginning of creation" (2 Peter 3:2-4).

That last sentence is a biblical definition of uniformitarianism—the erroneous philosophy that all things continue as they have been from the beginning of creation. "For this they willingly forget: that by the word of God the heavens were of old"—that is, they suddenly came into being by His word—"and the earth standing out of the water and in the water, by which the world that then existed perished, being flooded with water" (vv. 5-6). Basically, Peter said, "Remember the flood?" That catastrophe destroyed the world as it had once existed.

That huge change in the past was nothing compared to the change that will come in the end times—the fulfillment of those prophecies that pointed to God's final judgment. "The day of the Lord will come as a thief in the night, in which the heavens will pass away with a great noise, and the elements will melt with fervent heat; both the earth and the works that are in it will be burned up" (2 Peter 3:10). The real question, then, was not "When is God going to keep His promises?" but "Therefore, since all these things will be dissolved, what manner of persons ought you to be in holy conduct and godliness…?"(v. 11).

Safe to say, we're not supposed to be materialistic, right? If it's all going to burn, investing everything you have in this world doesn't make sense. We should be looking forward to the new, eternal heaven and earth that Jesus in His righteousness will rule, storing up treasure in heaven. It will be beyond belief—beyond our ability to conceive—and that future glory, a certain thing, should compel us to live our lives in a way that honors God. "Therefore, beloved, looking forward to these things, be diligent to be found by Him in peace, without spot and blameless; and consider that the longsuffering of our Lord is salvation" (vv. 14-15). Peter reminded us that a day is like a thousand years for God, and a thousand years is like a day. He has a different sense of time—and timing—than we have, but His is perfect.

So every day that passes in which people wonder where God is, or if He has forgotten His promise of judgment and justice, is another day in God's eyes that more people will come to salvation—and that should keep us patient. Because, when His judgment comes—and it will—each person's final decision will be locked in. There will be no turning back, no changing of minds—unbelievers bound for hell, apathetic believers squeaking in heaven's gates, and the just to their reward.

Peter signed off with a final warning—"Beware lest you also fall from your own steadfastness, being led away with the error of the wicked" (v. 17)—and a final encouragement—"Grow in the grace and knowledge of our Lord and Savior Jesus Christ" (v. 18).

Tradition says that when Peter was executed, he insisted on being crucified upside down because he insisted he wasn't worthy to die the same way Jesus had. Whether the account is true or not, the idea of a man who struggled to learn humility finally demonstrating it in such a profound moment is inspiring. What is clear from this letter, however, is that Peter obeyed his Master, feeding and loving His sheep until the day he joined Him in the perfect, incorruptible glory of heaven.

1 JOHN
FLIGHT PLAN

Facts

Author

Though 1 John doesn't name its author, it has long been thought that the apostle John wrote this letter. All five compositions attributed to John (his Gospel, three letters, and Revelation) have similar language, phrases, and themes. In fact, John has been nicknamed the Apostle of Love due to the frequent use of the word *love* in his works. John was the last of the twelve apostles to die, sometime between AD 98 and 100.

Date Written

John probably wrote this letter toward the end of his life after a long and fruitful ministry, possibly between AD 90 and 93.

Landmarks

The beloved apostle John wrote this letter to encourage believers to continue in their life of faith in Jesus Christ in accordance with the gospel they had been taught. First John 5:13 best sums up the letter's theme: "These things I have written to you who believe in the name of the Son of God, that you may know that you have eternal life, and that you may continue to believe in the name of the Son of God." John also warned his readers about false teachers and the ways of the world and proclaimed the preeminence of love—both God's love for us, and our dutiful response to love one another.

John wrote to define and defend the nature of Jesus Christ against heretical teachings that were creeping into the early church. Most notable among these teachings was Gnosticism. *Gnosticism* comes from the Greek word for knowledge, and it taught that anything physical or material is evil—that only the spiritual is good. This belief directly attacked the incarnation of Christ, because if matter is evil, then Jesus could not be a perfect physical man (see also **Colossians: History** on page 501). But John powerfully set forth Jesus Christ as the true Son of God—both undiminished deity and unprotected humanity—along with the revolutionary implications of that truth for our relationships with God and each other.

This letter is not organized in a typical manner, set out chapter by chapter in themes and sections. Rather, it reads more as a series of spirals—revolving topics or phrases that John introduced and then came back to repeatedly. These topics include comparisons (light versus darkness, truth versus lies, love versus hate, God's children versus the devil's children), discernment, happiness, holiness, and security. Each can be life-changing. There are a total of five spirals—revolutionary truths, if you will—viewed from different angles. These truths, when properly applied, will revolutionize your life with other people and with God.

Itinerary

- Revolution One: Friendliness
- Revolution Two: Holiness
- Revolution Three: Happiness
- Revolution Four: Perceptiveness
- Revolution Five: Security

Gospel

The gospel is good news! Sometimes we forget that simple but foundational truth. I think sometimes we *choose* to forget it as well—or at least live as if it doesn't matter. When we don't keep this at the forefront of our minds—the world-changing, astounding news that God is real, loves us, and sent His Son to die for our sins so we could have a right relationship with Him—we somehow figure we can just do what we want and let God's grace cover the rest.

On one hand, who could argue against or make small the immeasurable, unending wonder of God's grace—His unmerited favor shown to us on the cross? But on the other hand, we're not called to live however we want and just let grace do its thing (Romans 6:1). We have a responsibility to respond to grace by living according to God's revealed truth and walking in the light. There's no wiggle room there, according to John:

> This is the message which we have heard from Him and declare to you, that God is light and in Him is no darkness at all. If we say that

we have fellowship with Him, and walk in darkness, we lie and do not practice the truth. But if we walk in the light as He is in the light, we have fellowship with one another, and the blood of Jesus Christ His Son cleanses us from all sin.

If we say that we have no sin, we deceive ourselves, and the truth is not in us. If we confess our sins, He is faithful and just to forgive us our sins and to cleanse us from all unrighteousness. If we say that we have not sinned, we make Him a liar, and His word is not in us (1 John 1:5-10).

Christianity is the most countercultural philosophy in the world. Following Jesus is revolutionary because it means totally rejecting the world's way of thinking and living. Once you embrace the good news and receive the gift of grace and salvation in Christ, you then live it out in your thoughts, words, and deeds. This is part of stepping into the light of God's grace and walking in the gospel. It's like opening all the shades in a once-darkened room and letting the sunlight flood in. As you learn God's truth and put it into practice, you will be transformed; your life will become rooted in truth, joy, peace, and the assurance of heaven. Now that's good news!

Christianity is the most countercultural philosophy in the world.

History

After spending three years of his life with Jesus (AD 27–30), the apostle John became a leader in the early church (Acts 3–5). It's believed that after Paul and Peter's executions around AD 66–67, John pastored the church in Ephesus, located along the Ionian coast in present-day Turkey. After the Romans destroyed the Jewish temple in AD 70, John may have been the leading disciple who helped keep the Christian community together. He also probably began to write his Gospel account of Jesus around this time. In his later years, around AD 90, John wrote three letters (1, 2, and 3 John) to encourage Christians to keep the faith. He was exiled for this faith to Patmos, a rocky island about forty-five miles off the coast of modern-day Turkey, around AD 93. It was from Patmos that he wrote the book of Revelation.

Travel Tips

John followed Jesus for three years—he walked with Him from place to place, ate with Him, listened to Him teach, and watched Him as He interacted with people from all walks of life. John knew Jesus well. In 1 John, he expressed his great desire for his "little children" (1 John 2:1) to understand the revolutionary truth that Jesus is God; He will change your life when you follow Him with your whole heart.

- Following Jesus revolutionizes your relationships: "That which we have seen and heard we declare to you, that you also may have fellowship with us" (1 John 1:3). John shared the gospel so that others might join him in fellowship. *Fellowship* is so much more than hanging out over coffee and doughnuts. It is connecting with other Christians and going through life together, spurring one another on in spiritual growth.

- Following Jesus revolutionizes your holiness: "These things I write to you, so that you may not sin. And if anyone sins, we have an Advocate with the Father, Jesus Christ the righteous" (1 John 2:1). When we meditate on the truth and then act on it, sin's grip on us will diminish while holiness grows. And when we do mess up and stumble, we can fall back on the grace of our great Advocate before the Father—Jesus Christ.

> **When we meditate on the truth and then act on it, sin's grip on us will diminish while holiness grows.**

- Following Jesus revolutionizes your joy: "These things we write to you that your joy may be full" (1 John 1:4). Joy comes from receiving and embracing the message of the gospel—a sure sign that God's presence in your life is real. Knowing the authentic Jesus produces authentic fellowship with God and other believers, and that in turn produces joy.

- Following Jesus revolutionizes your discernment: "The anointing which you have received from Him abides in you, and...teaches you concerning all things, and is true, and is not a lie, and just as it has taught you, you will abide in Him" (1 John 2:27). Hone your ability to discern good from evil and truth from lies by reading and learning the Word. John called us to "test the spirits" (1 John 4:1)—in essence, to take something we've heard or been taught and check it against the truth of Scripture to make sure we're following that which is right and correct.

- Following Jesus revolutionizes your security: "These things I have written to you who believe in the name of the Son of God, that you may know that you have eternal life, and that you may continue to believe in the name of the Son of God" (1 John 5:13). Over and over again in this letter, John wrote about what we as believers *know*—not what we think or feel, but what we're sure of. Having faith in Jesus isn't based on wishful thinking or flimsy hopes but on the strong, confident assurance that through Him, we have eternal life.

In Flight

Revolution One: Friendliness

John had a knack for boiling down truth to its essence, explaining complex concepts in straightforward, practical language. He began by establishing his credentials as an eyewitness to the life and ministry of Jesus, and then explaining the purpose behind it all: fellowship with God. "That which we have seen and heard we declare to you, that you also may have fellowship with us; and truly our fellowship is with the Father and with His Son Jesus Christ" (1 John 1:3). John used the word *fellowship* a handful of times in this letter, and when you look at the context, it's clear that fellowship is more than sanctified hanging out. It's a partnership of believers based on the main thing we all have in common, Jesus Christ.

From John's perspective, true fellowship is a key measurement of the authenticity of our walk with Christ. "If we say that we have fellowship with Him, and walk in darkness, we lie and do not practice the truth" (v. 6). So much of what John said here is boiled down to the irreducible minimum—the most basic, foundational truth. It's alarmingly simple: If you claim to be a Christian but don't act like Jesus at all, you're lying. "But if we walk in the light as He is in the light, we have fellowship one with another, and the blood of Jesus Christ His Son cleanses us from all sin" (v. 7).

To be a Christian, then, is to live in community—not off on some farm somewhere, but in everyday life making our partnership with the body of Christ a significant part of our lives. One of the weakest links in the church today is fellowship, especially in the sense that we either resist or make it hard to let our guard down, to come as we are and be honest about our challenges.

We need to be genuine, seeking forgiveness for our mistakes and forgiving others when they're mistaken. "If we say that we have no sin, we deceive ourselves, and the truth is not in us. If we confess our sins, He is faithful and just to forgive us" (vv. 8-9). Any friendship hinges on the willingness to forgive another's imperfections; we support and challenge each other in order to promote unity and growth.

This is a world of big, impersonal institutions and a big, impersonal Internet, and the church can appear to be another big, impersonal institution. Many established churches, in particular, tend to concentrate on organization rather than the organism—the lives of the people that make it up. While discussing organizational structure and the accountability that comes with growth are both good and important, the most important aspect of any church is relationship, touching God's people through what God gives us—a chance to experience real community.

> ## A relationship with Jesus should revolutionize our friendships and fellowship.

Because it's much easier to go to church than to be the church, and always has been, John wrote to remind believers that we're all in this together with God. The fellowship he witnessed between Jesus and God the Father, between Jesus and His disciples, and among his fellow apostles transformed him. A relationship with Jesus should revolutionize our friendships and fellowship.

Revolution Two: Holiness

Part of the revolution that occurs when you choose to follow Jesus is that doing so separates you from the ways of the world. You're no longer obligated to follow the paths that emptied your life of meaning and purpose. The world overpromised and underdelivered constantly and your sinful indulgence in its ways left you more damaged. But your sins are forgiven, and feeling that weight lift off your shoulders is one of God's best blessings. That doesn't mean you're perfect (though you are going through a process of becoming more like Jesus—what we call sanctification); you're still going to make mistakes this side of heaven. But, John said, God still has you covered.

"My little children, these things I write to you, so that you may not sin. And if anyone sins, we have an Advocate with the Father, Jesus Christ the righteous"

(1 John 2:1). An advocate is a lawyer, so in Jesus, we have the best defense attorney in existence. "He Himself is the propitiation"—the payment or atonement—"for our sins, and not for ours only but also for the whole world. Now by this we know that we know Him, if we keep His commandments" (vv. 2-3).

Talk about a revolution. John said the truth should steer you away from sin, but it's a process that takes place step by step in the little decisions. If you can grasp the truths that John was sharing, if you let them seep into the soil of your heart, then you will see a diminishing of sin in your life. That's the process of becoming holy—becoming more and more like Jesus in how you think and talk and act.

Jesus freed you from the sin that is embedded in your very nature. He helped you change the way you look at sin—helped you recognize how pervasive and serious it is. John offered a reminder of sin's impact and of the greater impact of Christ. "Whoever commits sin also commits lawlessness, and sin is lawlessness. And you know that He was manifested to take away our sins, and in Him there is no sin. Whoever abides in Him does not sin. Whoever sins has neither seen Him nor known Him" (1 John 3:4-6).

Notice the difference between *sin*, singular, and *sins*, plural. The first is the root—the basic condition and nature of every person since the fall. Sins are the fruit of that twisted root—the acts we commit as a result of our essential brokenness. That's all part of our old nature. In Christ, though, we have a new nature. Even though the root remains in this life, we can go against our nature and prevent bearing the fruit of sin. And, as John wrote, that flows from the same principle: fellowship with God. Friendship *with* God leads to holiness *toward* God, which results in happiness *from* God. Your relationship with Him, and then with God's people, produces a holiness, which in turn produces happiness.

> Friendship *with* God leads to holiness *toward* God, which results in happiness *from* God.

Revolution Three: Happiness

John stated one of his main reasons for writing: joy. "These things we write to you that your joy may be full" (1 John 1:4). Joy isn't some manufactured emotion where we pretend to be happy in order to look like good Christians. It's not some fake pasted-on smile. Instead, it's a deep and profound experience that comes from acknowledging and living the truth. That begins with preaching the authentic message of the authentic Messiah. Responding to the gospel produces real fellowship with God and with each other that, in turn, produces joy. One follows the other; joy is the infallible sign of the presence of God and a partnership with God's people.

Some translations of 1 John 1:4 read "that *our* joy may be full," emphasizing that it's not about your personal happiness to the exclusion of everyone else around you, but it's a shared joy—one that is produced in concert with other believers. While as an individual you need a connection with God through Christ to be saved, you can't be disconnected from God's people and live a complete life. John wanted our joy to "be full"—to be an overflowing, abundant supply that comes in part from living life with our brothers and sisters in Christ. Christianity has often been viewed as someone giving in to God in a moment of weakness, with the result being a life without any more fun or enjoyment. While the first part is true—you can't really surrender to God until you recognize how desperate you are for His healing touch—the second part is way off target. Jesus liberates His followers from the pressure to conform to mankind's imperfect standards. Then, as we share this common experience with others who have also discovered it, our joy is amplified.

John wrote a lot in this book about sin—hardly a popular concept, then or now. No one likes to be told how messed up they are, so most avoid the topic, denying sin's existence or its effects. Sin is often seen as irrelevant and outdated, producing unnecessary guilt and shame from which mankind must free itself. You can trace the current manifestations of this to the philosophies of Darwin's evolutionary theory and B.F. Skinner's behavioral psychology, but it all goes back to humanity's basic tendency to resist God's higher ethics and standards. New philosophies are just old lies recycled and repackaged.

When you look at other religions or philosophies, they all try to come up with their own versions of why things are the way that they are. Whether it's Hinduism, Islam, Unitarianism, communism, or atheism, good and evil get redefined to fit an imperfect person's imperfect take on life. John said our peace and love come from God alone; He is our happiness. "By this we know love, because He laid down His life for us" (1 John 3:16). When you respond to what Jesus did for you by doing it for others—loving not "in word or in tongue, but in deed and in truth" (v. 18)—you can know that you belong to Him, and your sense of satisfaction will grow.

Revolution Four: Perceptiveness

After establishing the security and proof that believers have in following Jesus, John reminded his audience that they had a duty to defend what God had given them—to stand for His truth and guard His church. God has given us all the tools we need to tell good from evil, truth from lies.

> I have not written to you because you do not know the truth, but because you know it, and that no lie is of the truth. Who is a liar but he who denies that Jesus is the Christ? He is antichrist who denies the Father and the Son. Whoever denies the Son does not have the Father either; he who acknowledges the Son has the Father also (1 John 2:21-23).

Ours is the duty of discernment.

John used tough language in this context because Gnosticism was an ongoing threat, having infiltrated the Ephesian church in particular (1 Timothy 1:3-4). He warned believers that the fight was ongoing:

> These things I have written to you concerning those who try to deceive you. But the anointing which you have received from Him abides in you, and you do not need that anyone teach you; but as the same anointing teaches you concerning all things, and is true, and is not a lie, and just as it has taught you, you will abide in Him (1 John 2:26-27).

The threats were current and ongoing, and they will last until the end times. The Antichrist will someday come as the ultimate deceiver, but "even now many antichrists have come, by which we know that it is the last hour" (v. 18). Those lowercase *a* antichrists have taken many forms over the years, but all of them are deceivers, whether false prophets or teachers or those claiming to be Christ. Satan employs a twofold strategy: First, to keep all people in their lost and unsaved condition. Second, to target believers with ongoing deception in order to entice them back into ungodly living. All believers have tools of discernment, however, including our behavior. "Little children, let no one deceive you. He who practices righteousness is righteous, just as He is righteous. He who sins is of the devil, for the devil has sinned from the beginning" (1 John 3:7-8).

We also have the ultimate litmus test: what people say about Jesus Christ.

> Beloved, do not believe every spirit, but test the spirits, whether they are of God...By this you know the Spirit of God: Every spirit that confesses that Jesus Christ has come in the flesh is of God and every spirit that does not confess that Jesus Christ has come in the flesh is not of God (1 John 4:1-3).

If you live by the truth that Jesus was fully human and fully divine—live by it, not just say you believe it—then you can know you are His. Christianity is Christ! What a person believes about Jesus is all-important because He was the only one God uniquely sent into the world to save people (John 3:16). Anyone preaching and living something else has "the spirit of the Antichrist, which you have heard was coming, and is now already in the world. You are of God, little children, and have overcome them, because He who is in you is greater than he who is in the world" (vv. 3-4).

There's more to be being a Christian than showing up on Sunday and saying "God bless you," or thanking God after receiving an award or winning a game. Anyone can do that, and that's exactly the extent of what many do. Test the spirit, beginning with who they say Jesus Christ is. And then check their Scripture references—if they actually provide them—to see if they are on target doctrinally. And as you develop your discernment, remember to develop the parallel virtue of humility. To follow Christ is to be able to identify wolves in sheep's clothing, but it also means avoiding becoming an attack sheep yourself. "Be wise as serpents and harmless as doves" (Matthew 10:16). As John put it, "He who does not know love does not know God, for God is love" (1 John 4:8). That serves as a test for potential fakes and for us, to make sure we're staying true.

Revolution Five: Security

John's revolution continued with the various ways you can know you belong to Jesus. The word *know* appears more than thirty times in this letter; John wasn't saying, "I feel like Jesus was saying" or "Perhaps this is what Jesus meant"—over and over again. He wrote, "We know." John wanted us to feel secure and be assured.

It's pretty clear that, according to John, the Christian life is not built on empty wishes or flimsy hopes but a confident assurance that you *know* you are His, that you *know* you have eternal life with Him. And because it's John, he wanted you to know *how* you know. How do you know it's not a cultural conversion—where you show up at church and act Christian but never internalize the truth? How do you know it's not a ceremonial conversion—you went through baptism or confirmation or came up at an altar call but never did anything else? How can you be sure it wasn't just an emotional conversion, where you responded to pressure or reason instead of true conviction?

That uncertainty—that lukewarmness—is dangerous (Revelation 3:16), so here's how you can know that you're not just guessing what will happen when you die, or hoping that this whole Christian thing is real: *Are you living like it?*

Are you obeying God's Word? "Now by this we know that we know Him, if we keep His commandments" (1 John 2:3).

Are you believing His truth? "By this you know the Spirit of God: Every spirit that confesses that Jesus Christ has come in the flesh is of God" (1 John 4:2). "These things I have written to you who believe in the name of the Son of God, that you may know that you have eternal life, and that you may continue to believe in the name of the Son of God" (1 John 5:13).

Are you expecting Jesus's return? "Now we are children of God; and it has not yet been revealed what we shall be, but we know that when He is revealed, we shall be like Him" (1 John 3:2).

Are you conforming to His standards? "Now he who keeps His commandments abides in Him, and He in him. And by this we know that He abides in us, by the Spirit whom He has given us" (1 John 3:24).

Are you loving His children? "My little children, let us not love in word or in tongue, but in deed and in truth. And by this we know that we are of the truth, and shall assure our hearts before Him" (1 John 3:18-19).

Even from 30,000 feet, many of those statements jump out as bold assurances of faith. Seventeenth-century Puritan preacher Thomas Manton wrote, "None walk so evenly with God, as they who are assured of the love of God."[100] Each truth John laid out, based on the love and work of Christ, is potentially life-changing. His challenge to us today is to ask ourselves a question with total honesty: Do you want a revolution?

2 AND 3 JOHN AND JUDE
FLIGHT PLAN

Facts

2 and 3 John
Author

The author of 2 and 3 John is identified as "the Elder" (2 John 1; 3 John 1), indicating someone of mature age. Church history suggests that this was the apostle John. The style, word use, and themes found in 2 and 3 John are very similar to the other works John wrote.

Jude
Author

The author of Jude is identified as "Jude, a bondservant of Jesus Christ, and brother of James" (Jude 1). In the Gospels, a man named Jude is mentioned as a half-brother of Jesus (Matthew 13:54-55; Mark 6:2-3)—a son of Mary and Joseph who was born after Jesus. A man named Jude (or *Judas* in the original text, though not Judas Iscariot) is also mentioned as one of Jesus's twelve disciples (Luke 6:16). It's debated whether the author of this letter is the apostle, the brother of Jesus, or neither. The author did not identify himself as an apostle, but that could simply be a mark of humility. On the other hand, the author spoke about the apostles in the third person (Jude 17-18), so that seems to rule out the possibility that he was one of the Twelve.

2 and 3 John
Date Written

John probably wrote 2 and 3 John shortly after 1 John, sometime between AD 90 and 95. During this time, the apostle was finishing his work as a pastor in the city of Ephesus, unaware that his exile to the island of Patmos was right around the corner.

Jude

Date Written

It's unknown when Jude wrote this book. It's possible he wrote it before AD 70 because it doesn't mention the destruction of the Jewish temple, and it confronts certain recurrent false teachings that were prevalent in the early church (the theme of rejecting false doctrine is common to all the general epistles).

Landmarks

2 and 3 John

The books of 2 and 3 John, both written when the apostle whom Jesus loved was an old man, give us encouraging, personal snapshots of how a godly person handled difficulty.

Second John warns the church about the danger of the Gnostic teachers who denied the humanity of Jesus Christ in His incarnation. In it, the apostle John encouraged believers to continue walking in love but to also be discerning in their expression of love, cautioning them about receiving heretics into their homes and churches. In short, John's big theme in this little letter is being a lover of the truth.

In 3 John, the apostle praised the hospitality believers were showing to faithful, godly teachers. He desired these believers to have fellowship with their brothers and sisters in Christ, especially those who worked in full-time ministry. John used the examples of three different people in the early church to highlight three different ways to live—one bad and two good.

Jude

Jude wrote this letter as a sort of call to arms to the church to be constantly vigilant, standing strong in the faith and opposing heresy. Godless teachers were emboldening Christians to defect from the truth, saying that they could do as they pleased without fear of God's punishment, but Jude would have none of it. His letter was meant to motivate believers everywhere to take action by recognizing the dangers of false teaching, protecting themselves and other believers against that false teaching, and winning back those who had already been deceived.

Itinerary

2 and 3 John

- Balancing Truth and Love (2 John 1-3)

- Walking in Truth and Love (2 John 4-6)
- Standing for Truth and Love (2 John 7-13)
- Demonstrating Truth in Love (3 John)

Jude

- Contention for the Faith (Jude 1-19)
- Edification in the Faith (Jude 20-25)

Gospel

2 and 3 John

The gospel centers on an act of divine, transforming love: Jesus laid down His life that we might live. But that sacrifice was necessary because of one significant and sometimes hard-to-digest truth: We are dead in our sins by nature, and only God can save us. In other words, when it comes to the gospel, love and truth are inseparable. It's easy to look at the cross and acknowledge Jesus's love for us; it's another thing to know the truth of God's Word and live by it.

True believers cling to the Word of God and do what Jesus says. No extrabiblical stuff, no philosophy that says you need Jesus plus something else. As John wrote, "This is love, that we walk according to His commandments. This is the commandment, that as you have heard from the beginning, you should walk in it" (2 John 6). The gospel is precious enough to defend and those who herald it must equip listeners to do the same. Martin Luther wrote, "A preacher must be both soldier and shepherd. He must nourish, defend, and teach; he must have teeth in his mouth, and be able to bite and to fight."[101]

In the early church, false prophets came right to your door, but John instructed believers not to receive these prophets into their homes. Now, before you think, *Wow! That's harsh*, remember that churches in the early days met in homes, so John was really saying not to let false teachers into the *church*. Today, with wise preparation, we might have conversations with people who come to our doors teaching a different gospel. Even so, we need to protect the church—as well as our homes—from those who would lead us astray. The best way to do that is to walk in God's truth, growing in the knowledge of His Word.

Jude

Faith in Jesus Christ is a prize worth fighting for. It's not something we earn, but it is something we need to fiercely guard as the most important truth in the world: Jesus Christ, who was both fully God and fully man, died for the sins of the world so that we could be saved from death and hell when we believe in Him. Defending the gospel was the whole reason Jude wrote his letter in the first place, saying he "found it necessary to write to you exhorting you to contend earnestly for the faith which was once for all delivered to the saints" (Jude 3).

When Jude wrote about the faith that had been "once for all delivered to the saints" (v. 3), he was saying, in other words, that everything God wanted to say had been said and recorded by the New Testament authors by AD 100. All the other so-called revelations of God that have come after that time, including the Book of Mormon and the Qur'an, do not qualify as valid doctrine from God. Anyone who claims otherwise has to argue against or outright ignore Jude 3.

History

2 and 3 John

John wrote his biblical works after the dispersion of Jews and Christians under the persecution of Nero (reigned AD 54–68) and after the destruction of the Jewish temple in AD 70. The Roman emperors Vespasian (reigned AD 69–79), Titus (reigned AD 79–81), and Domitian (reigned AD 81–96) ruled during the latter years of John's life.

It was common for early Christians to meet privately in homes for worship and prayer (Romans 16:5; 1 Corinthians 16:19; Colossians 4:15; Philemon 2). Starting with the reign of Emperor Nero, Christians were systematically persecuted by the Roman government, so home churches provided safety and comfort. It was not until Constantine ratified the Edict of Milan in AD 313 that a tolerance for Christianity was enforced. [102]

Jude

Throughout his little letter, Jude referenced a number of events in the Old Testament to support his arguments. To the early church, the Old Testament was history, not some collection of made-up stories. Jesus Himself considered the Old Testament to be a source of authority (Matthew 4:4, 7, 10) and confirmed the stories of Jonah (Matthew 12:40), Noah (Matthew 24:37-39), and Adam and Eve (Matthew 19:4-6) as historical happenings.

Travel Tips

2 John, 3 John, and Jude

True love requires love for the truth. You can't throw out truth for love's sake. Even with the best of intentions, loving others without sharing the truth of the gospel with them is counterproductive and could even end up helping those who want to undermine the truth. In those cases, John's point seems to be, "It's not love if it's not based on God's truth," and Jude's point was that the truth was worth fighting for.

- Have the courage to address false teaching in the church. Oftentimes Christians don't want to deal with the fallout of drawing a line in the sand—even if it's over an essential theological issue—so we bend the truth and call it an act of love. But John said love and truth should never be separated (2 John 6-8). Jesus was God's love incarnate. His actions and words tell us that sometimes confrontation is demanded by a higher love—a love of God's truth.

- Love is rarely attacked, whereas truth almost always is. John wrote, "I have no greater joy than to hear that my children walk in truth" (3 John 4). Why didn't he say he rejoiced in his children walking in *love*? Because truth is the foundation of God's love, and it's the first Christian virtue the world attacks. The minute you say, "This is God's absolute truth for everyone," you'll be criticized. Love, on the other hand, is almost never condemned; the world simply lessens it by redefining it. But sincerity, good intentions, or love alone isn't what makes a Christian. Be gracious, but stick to the truth.

- One of the marks of a Christian leader is hospitality. Show faithful people the love of Christ by welcoming and hosting them in your home. Hospitality is also a way Christians can support other Christians who are doing God's work and need a place to stay, such as missionaries, traveling preachers, and musicians. John praised Gaius for displaying this kind of hospitality. What a blessing to give a fellow believer a welcoming environment as you break bread with them and provide a comfortable place to rest, sharing in the work of the Lord.

- Jude's tone and topics were serious, yet he still graciously opened his letter by saying, "Mercy, peace, and love be multiplied to you" (Jude 2). These three things are the very qualities we ought to display as believers who are contending for the faith.

- Balance truth with love when witnessing. While we want to contend earnestly for the faith, we don't want to do so contentiously (Jude 22-23). The nature of God's truth doesn't change no matter how you speak it, but nonetheless, speak it in love (Ephesians 4:15). The truth of the gospel, as powerful as it is, is so much less effective when spoken obnoxiously or with contempt. So, love people enough to tell them the plain truth, but tell that truth with respect and kindness.

True love requires love for the truth.

In Flight

2 John

Balancing Truth and Love (2 John 1-3)

John underscored a simple but important truth in this letter: True love requires love for truth. While Christians should be known for the way we love, we can't sacrifice truth on the altar of love. If your love has no parameters, then you are in danger of helping out those who are trying to undermine the truth. Just as he had in his first letter, John defined what love looks like in action; here, however, he did it on a more personal level.

Identifying himself as "the Elder" (2 John 1), John gently reminded his readers of his advanced age and continuing service to many regional churches. He addressed "the elect lady and her children, whom I love in truth, and not only I, but all those who have known the truth" (v. 1)—most simply and likely a mother he knew, perhaps one who hosted the local church in her home.

John mentioned her connection to him and other believers as a result of "the truth which abides in us and will be with us forever: Grace, mercy, and peace will be with you from God the Father and from the Lord Jesus Christ, the Son of the Father, in truth and love" (vv. 2-3). Notice in those first few verses the regular use of *love* and *truth*—two words at the heart of John's message in all his writings.

Christian love and truth, however, have a decidedly different meaning than their worldly counterparts. Unbelievers often misunderstand Christian love, interpreting it according to what the apostle Paul called a "darkened understanding" (Ephesians 4:18). They try to call Christians out, saying things like, "Aren't Christians supposed to be tolerant? How can you call yourself a Christian and speak out against that person or belief system?" They don't see love and confrontation as compatible. And in an age of rampant political correctness and moral relativism, we in the church often oblige them, not wanting to offend anyone.

Christian love is misunderstood not just by unbelievers but sometimes by believers as well. The world tends to believe that love means tolerating everyone and everything, never speaking out against people's choices or beliefs. Sadly enough, many Christians fall prey to this way of thinking. But just think of the many biblical examples that prove that love does not mean blind tolerance. Elijah, for example, stood against the prophets of Baal and the wicked King Ahab (1 Kings 18). Paul spoke against the legalism of the Judaizers on multiple occasions. And Jesus—love incarnate—criticized the hypocrisy of the Pharisees and Sadducees (Matthew 23:13-34), the wicked cunning of Herod Antipas (Luke 13:31-32), and the Nicolaitans' abuse of church power (Revelation 2:6). There's a balance. Sometimes confrontation is not only valid, it's demanded as a part of love (think of your parents while you were growing up).

Walking in Truth and Love (2 John 4-6)

Having a relationship with Jesus should affect every aspect of a believer's life. What we believe should always affect how we behave. That kind of integrity goes a long way. And so, John praised his reader, saying, "I rejoiced greatly that I have found some of your children walking in truth, as we received commandment from the Father" (2 John 4).

John exhorted the lady to remember that he was talking about a commandment Jesus Himself had given (back in John 13:34-35)—"that which we have had from the beginning: that we love one another" (2 John 5). John didn't mean that we love one another indiscriminately, without boundaries. He defined his terms: "This is love, that we walk according to His commandments. This is the commandment, that as you have heard from the beginning, you should walk in it" (v. 6). Truth and love are married in both doctrine and action—and as Jesus said about marriage between a man and woman, "let not man separate" it (Mark 10:9). Because, as John then warned, men were trying to do just that.

Standing for Truth and Love (2 John 7-13)

As we've seen over and over, false teachers were a threat from the earliest days of the church. "Many deceivers have gone out into the world who do not confess Jesus Christ as coming in the flesh. This is a deceiver and an antichrist" (2 John 7). They separated love from truth, making it a nice-sounding but ultimately empty idea—incapable of reflecting its greatest expression, the love of God in Jesus Christ.

One of the most loving things you can ever do is to tell someone the truth. What if doctors acted like all those misinformed preachers of tolerance? What if they looked at an X-ray, diagnosed a cancerous tumor, and then didn't tell you about it because they didn't want to hurt your feelings? What if they just figured it wasn't loving to give such bad news? You wouldn't thank them for holding back, would you? As hard as it would be to hear, you would want the truth. You would want to be told respectfully, gently if possible, but frankly, and with options for a course of treatment.

Similarly, and with far greater repercussions in eternity, witnessing is an act of love. John used the Greek word *agape* for this kind of love—an act of goodwill for someone's highest benefit, as God showed for us in Christ. Loving people enough to tell them the truth about heaven, hell, sin, salvation, and Jesus Christ is vital for their eternal spiritual health. It's absolutely essential that people hear that kind of life-changing truth—that God loved them enough to die for them. This love that John talked about walking in requires a proper outward expression.

Love doesn't mean you are tolerant, indulgent, lenient, or relaxed toward sin or doctrine. In fact, I'd call that *sloppy agape*. It's not true love. Not to tell people the gospel truth is a form of selfishness; you want to avoid a possible confrontation more than you want someone else to avoid hell. No one likes to be in someone else's crosshairs, but Jesus painted them on Himself because He loved you. Love and truth must never be separated. Paul wrote that love "does not rejoice in iniquity, but rejoices in the truth" (1 Corinthians 13:6). Love is not increased by decreasing the truth. In practice, whenever you compromise the truth, you actually destroy true love. True love requires loving truth.

> **Whenever you compromise the truth, you actually destroy true love. True love requires loving truth.**

John's primary concern here was that a lack of loving truth would open the door to false teachers. "Look to yourselves, that we do not lose these things we worked for, but that we may receive a full reward" (2 John 8). It was common in those days for traveling preachers to seek hospitality from the local church as they journeyed around the region. But not all of these travelers were deserving of hospitality:

> Whoever transgresses and does not abide in the doctrine of Christ does not have God. He who abides in the doctrine of Christ has both the Father and the Son. If anyone comes to you and does not

bring this doctrine, do not receive him into your house or greet him; for he who greets him shares in his evil deeds (2 John 9-11).

In other words, if we don't discriminate enough to keep false teachers from spreading their lies in our homes and churches, we will lose the reward that we would get for hospitality shown in the right way to the right people. To clarify, John wasn't saying you can't be courteous and pleasant to people who disagree with the Bible on minor matters, or those you're trying to evangelize. They may have misguided opinions about Jesus or questions that you can clarify and answer. But you do have to watch for those who have an agenda to undermine the basic truths of the gospel.

John signed off on this letter after writing only thirteen verses worth of material, saying, "Having many things to write to you, I did not wish to do so with paper and ink; but I hope to come to you and speak face to face, that our joy may be full" (v. 12). That verse echoes the hope that every believer has to look forward to: the glorious and joyous day when we will see God face to face and hear Him say, "Well done, good and faithful servant" (Matthew 25:23). On that day, John wrote, we will receive our "full reward" (2 John 8) if we continue walking in and standing for the truth.

3 John
Demonstrating Truth in Love

Third John is the shortest book in the Bible and the most personal of John's writings. First John seems to have been written to the general church population that John was overseeing in Asia Minor. Second John was written to the elect lady, whose name we don't know. But 3 John was written to Gaius, a specific individual. We don't know who Gaius was; that was a fairly common name. However, John used similarly phrasing in praising Gaius that he used with the elect lady and her children: "I have no greater joy than to hear that my children walk in truth" (3 John 4)—"children" in this case most likely meaning that Gaius was someone John brought to Christ himself.

John also continued his theme of truth, using the word six times in this letter, to go with the five times he mentioned it in 2 John. However, whereas 2 John says not to show hospitality to false teachers, 3 John flips the coin, with John encouraging hospitality to faithful teachers. So if the statement in 2 John is "True love requires love for truth," then 3 John tells us, "Love for truth requires true love demonstrated." If you love the truth, then, you're going to love those who stand for the truth, and you're going to show hospitality to those who bring it. Together, the letters provide a full-orbed picture of truth, love, and hospitality.

John was pleased to hear that Gaius was walking in the truth because that's not easy to do. Anytime you hold a line on what the truth is, you'll find out for yourself how difficult it is to find acceptance for biblical belief. When you think about God's character and nature, it makes sense that anything He would say would be true. Otherwise, He wouldn't be God. And when God says something is true, it will never be partly true or mostly true or true except in certain cases. It will be absolutely true and reliable because He is. But use the words *absolute* and *truth* together, and prepare for the sparks to fly.

Because of that, it's become popular in certain religious circles to make sincerity the highest standard—as in, "It doesn't matter what you believe, as long as you mean it." But all roads don't lead to God any more than they do to El Paso. If you took the wrong road, though you may be sincere, you'd still be lost. It's the same with getting to heaven. That's why it's praiseworthy to recognize those Christians who remained faithful to God's truth—and why John praised Gaius for living out his faith: "Beloved, you do faithfully whatever you do for the brethren and for strangers, who have borne witness of your love before the church" (3 John 5-6).

One particular area that John recognized was Gaius's hospitality to traveling preachers. "If you send them forward on their journey in a manner worthy of God, you will do well, because they went forth for His name's sake, taking nothing from the Gentiles. We therefore ought to receive such, that we may become fellow workers for the truth" (vv. 6-8). Gaius would share in whatever fruit came of these pastors' efforts in spreading the gospel just because he had been a good host to them.

Furthermore, Gaius's hospitality shows that he hadn't become cynical. He showed discernment in receiving teachers of the truth rather than just rejecting every teacher who came through town. Remember, John had written in 1 and 2 John that there were many false teachers. Unfortunately, not everyone in the church showed similar good judgment.

John commended Gaius, then contrasted him with someone in the church who was less savory: "I wrote to the church, but Diotrephes, who loves to have the preeminence among them, does not receive us" (3 John 9). Diotrephes wanted to be a big shot in the church, and his selfish behavior toward John, of all people, marked him for criticism, not praise. "Therefore, if I come, I will call to mind his deeds which he does, prating against us with malicious words. And not content with that, he himself does not receive the brethren, and forbids those who wish to, putting them out of the church" (v. 10).

Whoever Diotrephes was, he clearly didn't acknowledge John's authority as an apostle. He even went so far as to slander John rather than receive him. Desire for power and ego can drive anyone to such foolishness. Someone well said, "A man wrapped up in himself makes a very small package." Diotrephes was not showing his love for the truth, and John called him on it: "Beloved, do not imitate what is evil, but what is good. He who does good is of God, but he who does evil has not seen God" (v. 11). It's bad enough when nonbelievers provide bad role models—all the more when Christian leaders do. In fact, so-called Christian leaders who misrepresent the Lord and the gospel need to be exposed because of the damage they can do, both to themselves and others, on a level that can affect an individual's eternal standing with God.

In closing, John mentioned another believer who, like Gaius, was doing well: "Demetrius has a good testimony from all, and from the truth itself. And we also bear witness, and you know that our testimony is true" (v. 12). It's always good when you can wrap up on a positive note, and John did so here. There was more to say, but he wanted to save it for a face-to-face meeting with Gaius (vv. 13-14)—no doubt confident of getting the hospitality that a traveling minister of the true and living God could hope to receive from a truth-loving and truth-demonstrating believer.

Jude

Contention for the Faith (Jude 1-19)

Throughout the years, the book of Jude has been called the Acts of the Apostates, and rightly so. To believers today, Jude's warning against apostasy—the act of turning away from Christ—is more relevant than ever because we have been inundated with a whole slew of false teachings. As Christians, we must guard against teachings that distract us from the hard and steady truth written in God's Word. Vigilance is the best defense.

In calling the church to wage the right kind of war against apostasy, Jude's tone was scathing in its indictment. False teachers were committed to their cause, and the church needed to be committed to its cause—the gospel truth. He began his letter with one intention in mind, but switched to a spiritual call to arms. "Beloved, while I was very diligent to write to you concerning our common salvation, I found it necessary to write to you exhorting you to contend earnestly for the faith which was once for all delivered to the saints" (Jude 3).

By "the faith," Jude meant what is called "the apostles' doctrine" (Acts 2:42)—the body of Christian truth that the apostles promoted and taught about Jesus Christ—who He is, what He did the first time He came, and what He will do when He comes again. To "contend earnestly" means to put up a good fight, to speak and act on the truth with determination. "For certain men have crept in unnoticed, who long ago were marked out for this condemnation, ungodly men, who turn the grace of our God into lewdness and deny the only Lord God and our Lord Jesus Christ" (Jude 4).

Jude reached back to the Old Testament for three examples of those who turned from the truth: the delivered people of Israel who wandered in the wilderness, fallen angels, and Sodom and Gomorrah. In the first example, even though God had worked out an astonishing deliverance for His people and spoken to them through Moses, He "afterward destroyed those who did not believe" (Jude 5). God has also condemned those angels "who did not keep their proper domain" (v. 6), abandoning heaven to follow Satan and his rebellion. Finally, Jude cited Sodom, Gomorrah, and similar cities around them, who, "having given themselves over to sexual immorality and gone after strange flesh, are set forth as an example, suffering the vengeance of eternal fire" (v. 7).

The apostates in Jude's day—and those since then—were similar: "Likewise also these dreamers defile the flesh, reject authority, and speak evil of dignitaries" (v. 8). They even dared to speak things that angels—who are far more powerful and aware of the truth—wouldn't even say. Jude pointed to Michael the archangel, equal to Satan in power, who as he fought Satan rebuked him in the Lord's name, and didn't call out Lucifer on his own merits, avoiding taking undue authority for himself (v. 9). But *these* guys, said Jude, "speak evil of whatever they do not know; and whatever they know naturally, like brute beasts, in these things they corrupt themselves" (v. 10).

Standing for God's truth is a serious thing, and standing against it carries major repercussions: "Woe to them! For they have gone in the way of Cain, have run greedily in the error of Balaam for profit, and perished in the rebellion of Korah" (v. 11). Cain rebelled against God with his hard-hearted sacrifice, Balaam tried to speak for God but was motivated by money, and Korah's ego fueled a failed rebellion against Moses. Jude recalled a prophecy going back to Enoch, one of Adam's sons, foretelling judgment on all such people, for all their ungodly deeds and words against God (vv. 14-15). Jude's rebuke was strong, but his motives were pure.

Standing for God's truth is a serious thing, and standing against it carries major repercussions.

Jude reminded the believers reading his letter that Jesus's own apostles had warned them "that there would be mockers in the last time who would walk according to their own ungodly lusts" (v. 18). The fight was upon them, and continues today—the challenge from those who would change God's truth to fit their own agendas, and the challenge to those who stay true to stick to their beliefs and protect the church.

Edification in the Faith (Jude 20-25)

Jude then drew a direct contrast with the apostates: "But you, beloved, building yourselves up on your most holy faith..." (Jude 20). The Christian life can never be lived in neutral. You can't put your life on cruise control and just veg out in the spirit. It's not an option. You have to walk in the spirit and stay engaged. Otherwise, it's like trying to pedal a bicycle uphill in neutral—you'll only go backward.

Because the apostates are in the business of tearing down your faith, Jude would say, you'll be in the business of building it up. If you don't build, what exists will be torn down. How to build, then? For starters, begin by "praying in the Holy Spirit, keep yourselves in the love of God, looking for the mercy of our Lord Jesus Christ unto eternal life" (Jude 20-21). Pray first, anticipating attacks and asking the Holy Spirit to guide you into truth (John 16:13).

Then "keep yourselves in the love of God." Notice it's not "keep yourself in a place where God will love you." God's love in Christ is unmerited; once you're under Christ's blood, you're saved, but there's still the matter of obedience. Grace isn't a free pass on whatever you want to do. God's Word establishes boundaries; stay within them, where His love and blessing can reach you. God's love is like sunshine; it's always there, but we can block it by our behavior, losing the warmth and comfort of feeling His presence. Take Judas and John, for example. At the Last Supper, John drew closer to Jesus, even resting his head against Jesus's chest. Judas, however, was reviewing the details of his plot to betray his Lord. Jesus loved them both, but only John drew closer, keeping himself in Christ's love.

Similarly, Jude wanted these believers to draw close to God, even as they fought for His truth. "On some have compassion, making a distinction; but others save with fear, pulling them out of the fire, hating even the garment defiled by the flesh" (Jude 22-23). Jude called for the same discernment John wrote about—using Spirit-given judgment to encourage those who had doubts, to pursue those who were headed down the wrong path, loving sinners but not their sin.

In his closing benediction, Jude ended up at his original topic—the source of their common salvation. "Now to Him who is able to keep you from stumbling, and to present you faultless before the presence of His glory with exceeding joy, to God our Savior, who alone is wise, be glory and majesty, dominion and power, both now and forever. Amen" (vv. 24-25). All three books we've looked at tell us how to express our love in balance with truth. Whereas 2 John warned us to be careful about loving the wrong people and 3 John told us to be lavish with our love toward the right people, Jude admonished us to love all people enough to tell them the truth.

REVELATION
FLIGHT PLAN

Facts

Author

The author of Revelation identifies himself as John the apostle (Revelation 1:1, 4, 9). John wrote Revelation from the island of Patmos during the last years of his life (around AD 95–100). As punishment for his faith in Jesus Christ, John had been exiled to this rocky outpost in the Aegean Sea, home to a Roman penal colony.

Date Written

It's believed that John wrote Revelation between AD 95 and 96. Early church historians say he wrote the book at the end of Emperor Domitian's reign (AD 96).[103]

Landmarks

The book of Revelation, also known as the Apocalypse or the Revelation of Jesus Christ, is the most astonishing preview of the future ever recorded. Considered to be one of the most powerful books in Scripture, Revelation is a direct vision John had from God, who asked him to record it for future generations: "Write the things which you have seen, and the things which are, and the things which will take place after this" (Revelation 1:19). Written in symbolic language, this book employs many of the metaphors found in other parts of the Scriptures, which are key to understanding their meaning in Revelation. As a matter of fact, out of the 404 passages in this book, 360 quote or allude to the Old Testament.

Revelation was given to John to show the Lord's servants "things which must shortly take place" (Revelation 1:1)—in short, prophecies of things to come. "Shortly" means that, once they've begun, the events will happen quickly over a brief period of time. The book reaches back to the fall of Satan and forward to the doom in store for him and his angels, warning that the world's end and judgment are certain. But it also assures us of the glories of heaven for the faithful: After taking us through the events of the future great tribulation and the eternal fate of all unbelievers, Revelation offers a glimpse of heaven, the forever home awaiting God's people.

Itinerary

A simple outline for the book of Revelation is found in Revelation 1:19, where Jesus told John, "Write, therefore, what you have seen, what is now and what will take place later" (NIV):

- Part 1: The Vision—*What You Have Seen* (Revelation 1)
- Part 2: The Churches—*What Is Now* (Revelation 2–3)
- Part 3: The Future—*What Will Take Place Later* (Revelation 4–22)
  - Adoration: Jesus Glorified in Heaven (Revelation 4–5)
  - Tribulation: Judgment on Earth (Revelation 6–18)
    - *Judgment, Phase I—Seven Seals (Revelation 6)*
    - *Parenthesis 1: 144,000 Jews and Many Gentiles Saved (Revelation 7)*
    - *Judgment, Phase II—Seven Trumpets (Revelation 8–9)*
    - *Parenthesis 2: Two Witnesses, Cosmic War, the Antichrist and False Prophet, and Angelic Announcements (Revelation 10–15)*
    - *Judgment, Phase III—Seven Bowls (Revelation 16)*
    - *Parenthesis 3: The Fall of Babylon (Revelation 17–18)*
  - Second Coming: From Heaven to Earth (Revelation 19)
  - Millennium: Heaven on Earth (Revelation 20)
  - Eternal State: The New Heaven and Earth (Revelation 21–22)

Gospel

Jesus is the primary revelation of the book of Revelation. The Greek word for Revelation (*apokalupsis*) denotes an unveiling—think of a statue being unveiled in front of city hall. This book reveals Jesus Christ in His undiminished glory. He has always been God's Plan A, from before time began on this world. Because of that, He has been Satan's target since the fall (the devil's one major victory in the grand scheme of things). However, once God promised that Jesus would eventually defeat Satan (Genesis 3:15), Satan devoted himself to trying to cut off the line of the promised Messiah—something we see in the cosmic symbols of Revelation. "The dragon stood before the woman who was ready to give birth, to devour her Child as soon as it was born. She bore a male Child who was to rule all the nations with a rod of iron" (Revelation 12:4-5). Satan failed to stop Jesus's first coming and he won't prevent His return, either. The book of Revelation, then, gives us the full picture of Jesus—not only as Savior but as the coming Judge and King.

One day, Jesus will return and rule all the nations with a rod of iron, crushing Satan's head once for all, fulfilling the prophecy of Genesis 3:15. But before that time, Satan will make one final attempt to sabotage God's plan, unleashing his fury on mankind because he'll know his time is almost up (Revelation 12:12). During this time of tribulation, Israel will face persecution that will dwarf even the Holocaust. But Satan still won't win. The same Jesus who died on the cross as Savior will reign with His people as Sovereign.

When all is said and done, Jesus will come to judge the world and reign forevermore. This is the culmination of the gospel. "The kingdoms of this world have become the kingdoms of our Lord and of His Christ, and He shall reign forever and ever!" (Revelation 11:15). This is when the scarlet thread of redemption will be tied off, the tapestry completed.

History

Revelation was composed during Emperor Domitian's reign (AD 81–96), which saw widespread paganism and Christian persecution.[104] The total history covered in the book, on the other hand, spans from about AD 95 to an undisclosed time in the future—a time that only God knows (Matthew 24:36).

> **Reading Revelation is a blessing because in it we see a clearer picture of Jesus and are motivated to live our lives based on eternal values as we look to His second coming and eternal reign.**

Travel Tips

Revelation isn't some unknowable mystery of a book—it's really all about Jesus, the coming King and glorified Judge of all the earth. Reading Revelation is a blessing because in it we see a clearer picture of Jesus and are motivated to live our lives based on eternal values as we look to His second coming and eternal reign.

- Open your heart to Jesus. One of the enduring images of Revelation is that of Jesus knocking at a door, humbly requesting entry into the hearts of people with whom He wants to have fellowship (Revelation 3:20). Despite being rejected over and over again, Jesus still wants that intimate closeness with us.

- Why is Revelation so full of symbols? For one, symbolism can stand the test of time, transcending era, language, and culture. Symbols also arouse strong emotions in ways that straight facts can't. For example, talking about a world dictator is one thing; describing a beast rising out of the sea evokes the awe and terror he will one day provoke. Also, the symbols in Revelation have their roots in the Old Testament, which makes their interpretation more verifiable. The special blessing for those who take the time to study and believe this book (Revelation 1:3) begins with digging into its rich symbolism.

- There are four basic views of *eschatology*, or the study of the end times:

  - *Preterist:* This view holds that the book of Revelation was fulfilled by the time Jerusalem was destroyed in AD 70. One major event, however, doesn't fit in this view: Christ's physical reign on the earth—which, of course, has yet to happen.

  - *Historical:* This view claims that all of church history, from apostolic times to the present, is a panorama of the events of Revelation. To arrive at this specific view, however, one must stretch and bend a lot of history and prophetic interpretation.

  - *Allegorical:* In this view, Revelation isn't historical or literal but an allegory—a series of symbols that depict the ongoing battle between good and evil. To hold this view, you have to completely dismiss not only all the prophecies of Revelation but all the Old Testament prophecies about the end times.

  - *Futurist:* In keeping with the structure of the book, this view holds that part of Revelation has been fulfilled—i.e., the letters to the churches in chapters 1–3—while everything in chapters 6–22 has yet to be fulfilled. This view aligns best with Scriptures like Jesus's discourse on the end times in Matthew 24. It's also the only view that maintains a consistent line of interpretation based on the context, grammar, and history of the Bible as a whole.

In Flight

Part 1: The Vision—*What You Have Seen* (Revelation 1)

Exiled on the tiny, seventeen-square-mile island of Patmos, John received a vision of Jesus—but a Jesus he had only glimpsed before, during the transfiguration (Matthew 17:1-13). John had walked with Jesus, seen Him perform miracles and teach with passion. He had witnessed Him after His resurrection, nail holes in the hands and all. Here, in the Spirit, though, John saw the glorified Christ, the righteous Judge of all the earth—and what a sight He was!

With a voice somewhere between a heralding trumpet and a roaring waterfall, Jesus identified Himself as "the Alpha and Omega, the Beginning and the End...who is and who was and who is to come, the Almighty" (Revelation 1:8). John turned to face Him and saw "One like the Son of Man, clothed with a garment down to the feet and girded about the chest with a golden band. His head and hair were white like wool, as white as snow, and His eyes like a flame of fire; His feet were like fine brass, as if refined in a furnace" (vv. 13-15). Far from being *Gentle Jesus Meek and Mild,* this is Judge Jesus, mighty and riled, coming to execute judgment on the world, destroy evil, and set up His kingdom.

Standing in the midst of seven menorahs, Jesus held seven stars in one hand, a two-edged sword in His mouth, and looking at His face was like staring at the sun. John reacted in the only reasonable way: "I fell at His feet as dead. But He laid His right hand on me, saying to me, 'Do not be afraid'" (v. 17). Since the Lamb John had known was now the Lion, those words were welcome.

This, by the way, is the real power of Revelation: it gives a clearer, more complete picture of Jesus—both Savior and Judge, Lamb and Lion, Meek and Mighty. Jesus confirmed His identity—"I am He who lives, and was dead, and behold, I am alive forevermore. Amen. And I have the keys of Hades and of Death" (v. 18)—and told John to write down what He was about to show him.

Jesus revealed the meaning of the symbols: The seven stars in His right hand were "the angels of the seven churches" (Revelation 1:20), and the seven menorahs (called "lampstands") represented the seven churches for whom He wanted John to record letters. The penetrating light of Christ shows both His flawless discernment of His church and the impartial nature of His justice. A study of Old Testament symbols reveals that His flaming eyes and feet of brass are images of judgment. He began with the churches.

Part 2: The Churches—*What Is Now* (Revelation 2–3)

Jesus then dictated letters—postcards, really—to seven churches in the region, describing their spiritual state, "the things which are" (Revelation 1:19). There are three different ways we can apply the information given about these churches. First, they were actual churches. They existed in actual towns 2000 years ago in Asia Minor (modern-day Turkey). All are in ruins now, but in John's day, they were established local Christian congregations, and Jesus addressed them as such.

There is also a historical application. Each church may represent a different period of church history, from the apostolic church of the first century to the apostate church of the end times.

Finally, there is a timeless application for all churches in all eras. In every congregation, there are people who represent the seven conditions Jesus described so that effectively all seven conditions of these ancient churches can exist in any one congregation today.

For example, in any given service, there are likely some people who are like the church of Ephesus—busy, active, and discerning, but they've lost the spark of true, intense love and devotion for Jesus. Others are like the church at Smyrna, enduring great suffering for their faith in Jesus Christ—hassled, tormented, mocked for their Christian belief—yet still holding tightly to Him. Still others represent the church at Pergamos; they're compromised Christians who tolerate false teaching and doctrine.

Some Christians will be like their spiritual ancestors in Thyatira, a bit loose morally and spiritually, lacking discernment. Others will be like the church at Sardis, Christians in name but spiritually dead. Like those in the church of Philadelphia, others will be experiencing personal revival, keeping God's Word and honoring His name the best they can. Finally, more than a few will be like the church at Laodicea, lukewarm—neither hot nor cold but sort of complacent, apathetic, in danger of Christ's rejection.

As Jesus wrapped up His correspondence, He made a powerful statement to the church at Laodicea: "Behold, I stand at the door and knock. If anyone hears My voice and opens the door, I will come in to him and dine with him, and he with Me" (Revelation 3:20). How often that verse has been quoted as an appeal to unbelievers! *Look, Jesus is standing at the door of your heart right now, trying to get in, so don't leave Him out there in the cold; open up your heart to Him.* And while that is true in a general sense, it's not the context here. Jesus was trying to get into the *church*—among those believers who bore His name in Laodicea—and yet their hearts were lukewarm toward Him.

The preceding verse makes Jesus's intention clear: "As many as I love, I rebuke and chasten. Therefore be zealous and repent" (Revelation 3:19). He wasn't going to force His way into their hearts, but at the same time, if they rejected intimate fellowship with Him, they'd never get that fire back—that desire to know Him more and more and the corresponding power as a witness in the world.

Then, having revealed His heart for His church, Jesus turned John's attention to the pivotal events of the end times, taking His amazed disciple on a journey for the ages that revealed the end of the age.

Part 3: The Future—*What Will Take Place Later* (Revelation 4–22)

The church, the focus of the previous two chapters, won't come up again until the end of the book. It's virtually absent from here on out. The reason why is simple, but startling: Everything Jesus would show John from this point on would take place after the church age. After the rapture, the church will be removed from the earth, and the judgment of the tribulation will follow.

Adoration: Jesus Glorified in Heaven (Revelation 4–5)

After recording Jesus's letters to the churches, John received an invitation to heaven's throne room and the presence of God Himself. A trumpet-like voice told him, "Come up here, and I will show you things which must take place after this" (Revelation 4:1). He experienced in vision form what Paul described—a prophetic picture of what we call the rapture: "The Lord Himself will descend from heaven with a shout, with the voice of an archangel, and with the trumpet of God. And the dead in Christ will rise first. Then we who are alive and remain shall be caught up together with them in the clouds to meet the Lord in the air" (1 Thessalonians 4:16-17). I suggest that Jesus will shout the same words John heard: "Come up here!" From here on, John saw things above the fray of earthly tribulation—from a heavenly perspective.

What first caught John's eye in heaven wasn't Peter standing at heaven's gate, nor the fluttering of angel wings atop clouds as they played harps; nor did he immediately see the long-lost friends or relatives who had gone to heaven earlier. Instead, he was immediately drawn to God on His throne: "He who sat there was like a jasper and a sardius stone in appearance; and there was a rainbow around the throne" (Revelation 4:3). While it will be wonderful to reunite with beloved fellow believers—parents, relatives, friends, mentors—who have gone before you, the main attraction of heaven will be seeing God.

John arrived at a key moment in all of history: the redemption of creation. God held in His right hand a scroll closed with seven seals, and an angel called out,

"'Who is worthy to open the scroll and to loose its seals?' And no one in heaven or on the earth or under the earth was able to open the scroll, or to look at it. So I wept much" (Revelation 5:2-4). John felt the weight of the scroll's importance, the question at hand, and what was at stake.

"But one of the elders said to me, 'Do not weep. Behold, the Lion of the tribe of Judah, the Root of David, has prevailed to open the scroll and to loose its seven seals'" (Revelation 5:5). Scrolls were often used to record ancient real-estate transactions, and this one represents the biggest land deal of all. This scroll is the title deed to the earth. Though God created the earth and it belongs to Him (Psalm 24:1), Adam forfeited the responsibility of stewardship at the fall. The results for mankind and the planet itself were catastrophic. As Paul put it, "Through one man sin entered the world, and death through sin, and thus death spread to all men, because all sinned" (Romans 5:12).

But one Man, Jesus Christ, bought mankind back by His blood, and will redeem His creation. Here, John saw all of heaven acknowledging Christ's singular worth and unique authority and praising Him as He prepared to assert His ownership, cleansing the earth through judgment, purifying it as part of the process of its redemption—the tribulation.

Tribulation: Judgment on Earth (Revelation 6–18)

The bulk of the book covers what Jesus called the tribulation (Matthew 24:21), a seven-year period that includes various judgments: seven seals, seven trumpets, and seven bowls of wrath. Once these increasingly devastating judgments begin, they will happen quickly (Matthew 24:22), and then Jesus will return. In between chronicling these phases of judgment, John recorded parenthetical sidebars that give us further insight into specific tribulation events and people.

Judgment, Phase I—Seven Seals (Revelation 6)

The tribulation will be the most destructive, violent time in human history—worse than the Dark Ages, the Bolshevik Revolution, World Wars I and II, the Cultural Revolution, or the Holocaust. Referred to throughout Scripture as the "day of the LORD" (Isaiah 2:12; 13:6-9; Joel 1:15; 2:1-31; 1 Thessalonians 5:2) and also the "time of trouble" and "day of trouble" (Daniel 12:1; Zephaniah 1:15), and even, because of Israel's unique involvement, as "the time of Jacob's trouble" (Jeremiah 30:7). Written of more often than even the second coming of Christ, this unprecedented global outpouring of God's judgment will begin with the breaking of the first four of seven seals—the releasing of the four horsemen of the apocalypse:

The Antichrist (on a white horse): "He who sat on it had a bow; and a crown was given to him, and he went out conquering and to conquer" (Revelation 6:2).

War (on a red horse): "It was granted to the one who sat on it to take peace from the earth, and that people should kill one another; and there was given to him a great sword" (v. 4).

Famine (on a black horse): "He who sat on it had a pair of scales in his hand. And I heard a voice in the midst of the four living creatures say, 'A quart of wheat for a denarius [a day's wage], and three quarts of barley for a denarius; and do not harm the oil and the wine'" (vv. 5-6).

Death and Hell (on a pale horse): "The name of him who sat on it was Death, and Hades followed with him. And power was given to them over a fourth of the earth, to kill with sword, with hunger, with death, and by the beasts of the earth" (v. 8).

When Jesus opened the fifth seal, John saw all the martyrs who had ever died for Christ, crying out from under the altar of God, "How long, O Lord, holy and true, until You judge and avenge our blood?" (v. 10). They would have to wait a bit longer because their number would be increased during the tribulation.

The opening of the sixth seal unleashed a tremendous worldwide earthquake, accompanied by celestial signs: the blackening of the sun, the moon turning blood red, and stars falling from heaven like ripe fruit. People everywhere, from the mighty to the powerless, ran and hid, and everyone cried out, "The great day of His wrath has come, and who is able to stand?" (v. 17).

Parenthesis 1: 144,000 Jews and Many Gentiles Saved (Revelation 7)

Before the opening of the seventh seal, we have a break in the action, the first parenthesis. The answer to the question on everyone's lips is revealed, as we read of two groups who will be "able to stand." The first is a special group of 144,000 Jews, 12,000 from each of the twelve tribes of Israel (Revelation 7:4-8), and the second is an enormous group of Gentiles, "a great multitude which no one could number, of all nations, tribes, peoples, and tongues" (v. 9).

The first group, the messianic Jews, will come to saving faith in Christ through the testimony of the two witnesses, whom we'll see in Revelation 11. One hundred and forty-four thousand Jews will respond and be used by God to witness to people during the tribulation. Enabled by Spirit-empowered lives and words, they will conduct the greatest season of effective evangelism in history, and huge numbers of people will come to Christ. History's greatest revival is coming!

History's greatest revival is coming!

Judgment, Phase II—Seven Trumpets (Revelation 8–9)

John then saw Jesus open the seventh seal, followed by a half-hour's silence in heaven. The escalating tension was broken by the appearance of seven angels with trumpets, heralding the next phase of judgment. As each of the first four angels blew their trumpets, a natural disaster followed: burning hail torched a third of earth's trees and consumed all the grass (Revelation 8:7); a huge mountain-like object fell and turned a third of all the seas to blood, killing a third of the creatures in them (vv. 8-9); a giant star named Wormwood (a telling name, it turns out) fell and poisoned a third of the world's fresh water supply—rivers and springs (vv. 10-11); and the sun, moon, and stars were partially darkened, struck so that they produced a third less light than before (v. 12).

As awful as all that sounds, worse was still to come—three woes coming with the remaining trumpet blasts (Revelation 8:13). The fifth blast of the trumpet unleashed demonic scorpion-locusts from the abyss, creatures who tormented people for five months (Revelation 9:4-6). They didn't kill anyone—death took a merciless five-month break—they just stung and made people miserable.

The next woe—the sixth trumpet judgment—released angels of mass destruction upon the earth, four angels "prepared for the hour and day and month and year...to kill a third of mankind" (Revelation 9:15). These fallen angels, chained for millennia, led an army of 200 million horsemen on lion-headed horses that breathed fire, smoke, and brimstone, with stinging serpent-like tails; "and with them they do harm" (v. 19). The carnage John saw was mind-blowing.

Parenthesis 2: Two Witnesses, Cosmic War, the Antichrist and False Prophet, and Angels (Revelation 10–15)

Two Witnesses

The angel then informed John of God's plan to provide a unique pair of prophets in Jerusalem: "I will give power to my two witnesses, and they will prophesy one thousand two hundred and sixty days, clothed in sackcloth" (Revelation 11:3). Using the prophetic Old Testament calendar, 1260 days is three-and-a-half years—exactly half of the time allotted for the tribulation.

Although countless guesses have been tossed around as to who these witnesses will be, the one thing we know is that they will prophesy to Israel in the end times—and they won't be messing around: "If anyone wants to harm them, fire proceeds from their mouth and devours their enemies...These have power to shut heaven, so that no rain falls in the days of their prophecy; and they have power over waters to turn them to blood, and to strike the earth with all plagues" (Revelation 11:5-6).

To top it off, when they've finished their job, the Antichrist—"the beast that ascends out of the bottomless pit" (v. 7)—will attack and kill them. Then after three-and-a-half days God will raise them from the dead and call them home to heaven (vv. 8-12). People will be paying attention—especially the 144,000 Jews who will have converted to faith in Jesus as Messiah.

Cosmic War

The second parenthesis continues with a warning about the blowing of the seventh trumpet: "The second woe is past. Behold, the third woe is coming quickly. Then the seventh angel sounded" (Revelation 11:14-15), announcing the last set of judgments, which we'll see in Revelation 15. Before that, however, the vision shifts to a rare behind-the-scenes look at the age-old struggle between good and evil, light and darkness, the kingdom of Satan and the kingdom of God.

John saw symbols of the combatants in this cosmic war: a woman who would give birth to a Son (Revelation 12:1-2), and a fiery red dragon—none other than Satan himself (v. 9). This woman, clothed with the sun, moon, and stars, is decoded for us in Genesis as representing the nation of Israel (Genesis 37:9). The dragon's strength and authority are also symbolically shown: he has seven heads, which speaks of completeness—his massive intelligence. He has ten horns; a horn is always a biblical symbol of might. His crowns indicate his dominion over the world.

Since the Garden of Eden, Satan has done his best to wreck God's creation, destroy His people, and keep His Messiah from reversing the effects of sin. Joined by a rebellious third of the angels (symbolized in Revelation 12:4 as a third of the stars falling from heaven), Satan's original plan was to prevent the Messiah's coming (see **Gospel** on page 614). He failed there, and he will fail to destroy the world before Jesus returns to reclaim the earth and establish His reign.

That doesn't mean he won't keep trying. While God sheltered the woman (Israel) from the dragon for the second half of the tribulation (Revelation 12:6, 14-16), "war broke out in heaven" (v. 7). God didn't attack Satan *mano a mano* but sent Michael to defeat him, another indicator that Satan is no match for God. Satan and his minions will be dismissed from heaven once and for all (vv. 7-8), and he will turn his full attention to earth.

While rejoicing broke out in heaven for the victory of God's salvation, it will be "woe to the inhabitants of the earth and the sea" (Revelation 12:12). Satan will unleash his fury against the nation of Israel during the tribulation period. That will require the Israelis to flee and to hide, and the signal for them to run will be what Jesus called "the abomination of desolation" (Matthew 24:15), the midpoint of the tribulation, when the Antichrist sets himself up as God (2 Thessalonians 2:4).

The Antichrist and False Prophet

John's vision then turned to Satan's agent in this persecution. "I saw a beast rising up out of the sea, having seven heads and ten horns, and on his horns ten crowns, and on his heads a blasphemous name" (Revelation 13:1). This is the man whom Paul called "the man of sin" and "the son of perdition" (2 Thessalonians 2:3), whom John identified by his best-known name: the Antichrist (1 John 2:18; 4:3). All the heads and horns and crowns link him directly to the dragon, and Satan will "give him his power, his throne, and great authority" (Revelation 13:2).

The world is going to fall for him hook, line, and sinker. "They worshiped the dragon who gave authority to the beast; and they worshiped the beast, saying, 'Who is like the beast? Who is able to make war with him?'" (v. 4). Only believers, those who come to faith during the tribulation, will resist following him: "All who dwell on the earth will worship him, whose names have not been written in the Book of Life of the Lamb slain from the foundation of the world" (v. 8). Put in play after the breaking of the first seal of judgment (Revelation 6:2), the Antichrist will come as a peacemaker, winning the world over with eloquence and charisma—but God revealed his true nature: He is a beast.

To complete his unholy trinity, Satan will add to his Antichrist a False Prophet—"another beast coming up out of the earth" (Revelation 13:11). This evil sidekick will institute the Antichrist's worship, which will be tied closely to his economic plan—a malevolent and narcissistic uniting of a false church and an authoritarian state:

> He causes all, both small and great, rich and poor, free and slave, to receive a mark on their right hand or on their foreheads, and that no one may buy or sell except one who has the mark or the name of the beast, or the number of his name. Here is wisdom. Let him who has understanding calculate the number of the beast, for it is the number of a man: His number is 666 (vv. 16-18).

Angelic Announcements

The grand parenthesis continues with a parade of various announcements delivered by angels. Of particular interest is God's final worldwide offer of salvation, proclaimed in the heavens: "I saw another angel flying in the midst of heaven, having the everlasting gospel to preach to those who dwell on the earth—to every nation, tribe, tongue, and people" (Revelation 14:6). God will be putting His salvation on display at the most unexpected time. No matter where people live or what language they speak, they will hear and understand this last warning: "Fear God and give glory to Him, for the hour of His judgment has come; and worship Him who made heaven and earth, the sea and springs of water" (v. 7). No more excuses.

Judgment, Phase III—Seven Bowls (Revelation 16)

John then saw God's final judgment. Imagine all the times people have wondered when or if God would ever judge evil, from the Psalms to the martyrs under the altar in Revelation 6 and everyone in between who ever prayed, "How long, Lord?" Multiply that over millions of people over thousands of years; that's a lot of crying out for holy justice, isn't it? But all of that desire for reprisal and reparation will be nothing compared to the wrath our holy God has stored up for the wicked in the last days. "Then I heard a loud voice from the temple saying to the seven angels, 'Go and pour out the bowls of the wrath of God on the earth'" (Revelation 16:1). Here's a rundown:

The first bowl: "A foul and loathsome sore came upon the men who had the mark of the beast and those who worshiped his image" (Revelation 16:2). This one's pretty self-explanatory.

The second bowl: The sea "became blood as of a dead man; and every living creature in the sea died" (v. 3). This could be a mega-form of a red tide, when toxic red dinoflagellates discolor the ocean for miles, killing most fish in the affected area.

The third bowl: Rivers and springs "became blood" (v. 4). Whatever causes this will affect every living thing, but, as an angel said, particularly those who "have shed the blood of saints and prophets...You have given them blood to drink. For it is their just due" (v. 6)—ironic justice on top of killing thirst.

The fourth bowl: "The fourth angel poured out his bowl on the sun, and power was given to him to scorch men with fire. And men were scorched with great heat, and they blasphemed the name of God who has power over these plagues; and they did not repent and give Him glory" (vv. 8-9). This could be radiation burns resulting from the depleted ozone layer or solar flares—but the worst sunburn ever will only harden people's hearts at this point.

The fifth bowl: Wrath came down on "the throne of the beast, and his kingdom became full of darkness" (v. 10). Since the Antichrist's kingdom was already as spiritually dark as it gets, this must be tangible darkness—more than just the loss of light, a darkness that causes physical suffering, because the beast's subjects "gnawed their tongues because of the pain" (v. 10). Spooky, right?

The sixth bowl: The river Euphrates "was dried up, so that the way of the kings from the east might be prepared" (v. 12). This refers to the impending Battle of Armageddon (v. 16), with the dried riverbed creating a convenient path for an army of a couple hundred million who will march across toward Israel.

The seventh bowl: "The seventh angel poured out his bowl into the air, and a loud voice came out of the temple of heaven, from the throne, saying, 'It is done!'" (v. 17). In other words, God's judgment is over; the days have been cut short. "And there were noises and thunderings and lightnings; and there was a great earthquake, such a mighty and great earthquake as had not occurred since men were on the earth" (v. 18). That's quite a punctuation mark on earth's judgment, and then God will turn His attention to Satan's capital city, Babylon.

Parenthesis 3: The Fall of Babylon (Revelation 17–18)

The third pause in the action focuses on one aspect of the bowl judgments, the destruction of the Antichrist's ruling system, here called Babylon. Though Babylon was an actual city, the capital of one of the world's earliest empires, the Bible regularly uses the term to describe the world system—the spiritual kingdom and powers aligned against God. Revelation 17 details religious Babylon, using the image of a wicked, perverse woman "sitting on a scarlet beast which was full of names of blasphemy" (Revelation 17:3).

Revelation 18 covers commercial Babylon, the allure of luxury and riches that drew in earth's leaders, who "committed fornication with her" (v. 3)—that is, forsaking any integrity or principle to gain power and wealth. They led the Antichrist and False Prophet's charge against Christians, "and in her [Babylon] was found the blood of prophets and saints, and of all who were slain on the earth" (v. 24). And here, after the end of God's judgments, an angel announced her fate: "Babylon the great is fallen, is fallen, and has become a dwelling place of demons, a prison for every foul spirit, and a cage for every unclean and hated bird!" (v. 2). With Babylon's demise and the fall of the Antichrist, the stage will be set for the best part of the book, and the best part of the future—the glorious reappearing of Jesus Christ.

Second Coming: From Heaven to Earth (Revelation 19)

When you think of a battle, you think of a struggle—two sides losing casualties in a fierce contest of arms, skill, and strategy. That will not be the case in the greatest of all battles—the Battle of Armageddon. Jesus is going to mop the floor with His enemies: "The lawless one [the Antichrist] will be revealed, whom the Lord will consume with the breath of His mouth and destroy with the brightness of His coming" (2 Thessalonians 2:8). This is a total wipeout!

Think back to Psalm 2, where the world's rulers gather together against the Lord and His anointed, and God's response is to laugh: "The Lord shall hold them in derision. Then He shall speak to them in His wrath, and distress them in His deep displeasure: 'Yet I have set My King on My holy hill of Zion'" (Psalm 2:4-6). That will indeed be the case in the Battle of Armageddon—game over before it even begins. Jesus will take over the earth. There will be no vote, no counsels or committees to discuss a transition of power; He will take His rightful place as King, the culmination of all the hopes of His people throughout the ages.

John recorded the moment: "After these things [the tribulation] I heard a loud voice of a great multitude in heaven, saying, 'Alleluia! Salvation and glory and honor and power belong to the Lord our God!'" (Revelation 19:1). We will definitely be joining in that chorus of thanks and praise, all our sorrows, pain, and suffering over forever. And with the praises of His glory ringing out from heaven, Jesus will return:

> I saw heaven opened, and behold, a white horse. And He who sat on him was called Faithful and True, and in righteousness He judges and makes war. His eyes were like a flame of fire, and on His head were many crowns. He had a name written that no one knew except Himself. He was clothed with a rope dipped in blood, and His name is called The Word of God (vv. 11-13).

John described Jesus as treading the winepress of the "fierceness and wrath of Almighty God" (v. 15), absolutely crushing His enemies as if He were stomping on grapes in a vat. An angel called the birds to come to the field of Megiddo to feast on the flesh of God's enemies, and the Antichrist and False Prophet were captured and "cast alive into the lake of fire burning with brimstone" (v. 20), and "the rest were killed with the sword which proceeded from the mouth of Him who sat on the horse" (v. 21). Jesus spoke the world into existence (Colossians 1:16-17); here, His words completely demolish His foes.

The first time Jesus came, He was here for about three decades. This time, He will return for good, and His control will be permanent. The first time, He came as a helpless baby; this time, He will return as Warrior-King. Then, He was the Lamb; one day, He will return as the Lion. The world will be shocked as they look up and see, coming from the sky, a Person they will undeniably know to be Jesus Christ. And we will be coming with Him as part of the parade, with His angel armies, clothed in fine white linen and riding white horses (Revelation 19:14) to witness His victory and the establishment of His kingdom on earth, where He will reign for a thousand years.

Millennium: Heaven on Earth (Revelation 20)

Upon His return, one of Jesus's first official acts will be to imprison Satan. "Then I saw an angel coming down from heaven, having the key to the bottomless pit and a great chain in his hand. He laid hold of the dragon, that serpent of old, who is the Devil and Satan, and bound him for a thousand years" (Revelation 20:1-2). With Satan out of the way for ten centuries, the earth will get an extreme makeover.

Jesus will delegate authority to His saints, and the martyrs will finally get their reward, ruling with Christ during this period (Revelation 20:4-5). "Blessed and holy is he who has part in the first resurrection. Over such the second death has no power, but they shall be priests of God and of Christ, and shall reign with Him a thousand years" (v. 6). This thousand-year kingdom, this millennial reign, though the precise time is mentioned only here, has been predicted many times as a time of "regeneration" (Matthew 19:28) and "refreshing" (Acts 3:19). Other passages, such as Isaiah 35, describe this messianic age as a blossoming garden. We have trashed the earth, but the utter demolition of the tribulation will make that look like a soda can by the side of the freeway. Jesus will restore the world to Eden-like glory.

Despite Jesus ruling in person on earth, people will still have free will. Those born during the millennium will still be able to choose whether to give their hearts to Him or not. Enough will still choose not to do that, when God releases Satan from his prison at the end of the millennium, the devil will have an army to lead—called Gog and Magog (Revelation 20:7-8). This final rebellion will end decisively: "Fire came down from God out of heaven and devoured them" (v. 9). That's it. All the build-up, some of them no doubt planning their insurrection for decades, awaiting Satan's release, and *fwoosh!* It's over. One sentence, and all their scheming comes to nothing. But judgment still awaits.

While Christians will be held accountable for their actions and either given or declined rewards (2 Corinthians 5:10), forgiveness in Christ means their names have been recorded in His Book of Life (Revelation 17:8) and they are not in danger of hell. Our lives will be examined, but our salvation is secure. We will never be condemned for our sins. It will be a different story for anyone whose name is not recorded in that book.

Satan will be thrown into the lake of fire, joining the Antichrist and the False Prophet, and "they will be tormented day and night forever and ever" (Revelation 20:10). Final judgment will then come for all unbelievers, what we call the Great White Throne judgment. "I saw a great white throne and Him who sat on it, from whose face the earth and heaven fled away. And there was found no place for them" (v. 11). This is the most sobering moment in all of world history, past, present, and future.

John reported on the encompassing, eternal scope of this moment:

> I saw the dead, small and great, standing before God, and books were opened. And another book was opened, which is the Book of Life. And the dead were judged according to their works, by the things which were written in the books. The sea gave up the dead who were in it, and Death and Hades delivered up the dead who were in them. And they were judged, each one according to his works. Then Death and Hades were cast into the lake of fire (Revelation 20:12-14).

In this somber courtroom scene, there is no debate about guilt, only prosecution. There is no defense or jury, only the Judge. There is no appeal, only a sentence. No parole, only punishment. "This is the second death. And anyone not found written in the Book of Life was cast into the lake of fire" (Revelation 20:14-15).

Eternal State: The New Heaven and Earth (Revelation 21–22)

Finally, we reach the end of the end of days, stepping from time into timelessness. Jesus will terminate the old earth and create a new, eternal one. "Now I saw a new heaven and a new earth, for the first heaven and first earth had passed away" (Revelation 21:1). The new earth will have a new capital city: "I, John, saw the holy city, New Jerusalem, coming down out of heaven from God, prepared as a bride adorned for her husband" (v. 2). Human language falls flat here, wholly inadequate to describe our eternal home.

The Greek word John used for "new" indicates that it's a brand new, never-seen-before creation—not just a reboot or a resetting of time. An angel gave John a rundown of the New Jerusalem's dimensions—apparently it will be an enormous cube made of translucent gold and precious gems, extending nearly 1400 miles in each direction (vv. 16-21). And there will be no temple, "for the Lord God Almighty and the Lamb are its temple" (v. 22), and they will be its source of light too (v. 23).

> ## Human language...is wholly inadequate to describe our eternal home.

Best of all, we'll have the intimacy with God that He has always desired: "I heard a loud voice from heaven saying, 'Behold, the tabernacle of God is with men, and He will dwell with them, and they shall be His people. God Himself will be with them and be their God'" (v. 3). Because of that intimacy, "God will wipe away every tear from their eyes; there shall be no more death, nor sorrow, nor crying. There shall be no more pain, for the former things have passed away. And He who sat on the throne said, 'Behold, I make all things new'" (vv. 4-5). Heaven will not be what we expect, but beyond anything we could possibly hope for.

The Bible opened in the magnificent Garden of Eden, filled with God's good gifts and purposes, but then came the plot twist—sin and death entered the world, and paradise was lost. Yet God immediately promised a Deliverer, and continued promising that Deliverer throughout the millennia until Jesus Christ arrived. Jesus was born, grew up, lived, was killed, and then was resurrected, defeating sin and death. He ascended to heaven but promised He would return. And here we are today, hoping and waiting for Him to return and once and for all to defeat Satan, sin, and death and perfectly restore what's been lost.

The Bible's last sentence is the perfect counterpoint to its beginning: "The grace of our Lord Jesus Christ be with you all. Amen" (Revelation 22:21). We have come full circle. The fall brought a curse that permeated every part of creation. Now, at the end, we have grace. Sin brought a grimace to creation, but God poured in grace. Despite all the troubles in this world, all the broken hearts and suffering, a happy ending is possible for all of us if we will receive that grace. People of this world will often say, "Get real. This is it. This is the real world." I understand what they're trying to say, but there's more to it. This *is* the real world, but there is another world—a *really* real world. And that world is coming, the eternal reality God originally made you for, and Jesus is the door that will get you there. Despite all the diversity in the world, there are really only two kinds of people: saved and unsaved.

> ## Sin brought a grimace to creation, but God poured in grace. Despite all the troubles in this world, all the broken hearts and suffering, a happy ending is possible for all of us if we will receive that grace.

God loves all people and made the ultimate sacrifice so that everyone could be counted in the first category, but you have to choose Him. The book of Revelation reveals the future God wants to give you. If you've already received Jesus as your Lord and Savior, celebrate that future! But if you haven't yet received Him, will you do so right now? Jesus is waiting to embrace you as you are, forgive you of your sins, turn your life around, and take you on an adventure beyond your wildest dreams, with heaven as your destination. As we come in for a landing from our journey at 30,000 feet, all you have to do is say yes to Him, and your life can soar—forever!

BIBLIOGRAPHY:
WORKS REFERENCED

Alexander, David, and Alexander, Pat, *Eerdmans' Handbook to the Bible*, Grand Rapids, MI: William B. Eerdmans, 1973.

Baker, Warren, and Carpenter, Eugene, *The Complete Word Study Dictionary: Old Testament*, Chattanooga, TN: AMG Publishers, 2003.

Blomberg, Craig L., *From Pentecost to Patmos,* Nashville, TN: B&H Academic, 2006.

Bryant, T. Alton, *The New Compact Bible Dictionary,* Grand Rapids, MI: Zondervan, 1967.

Buttrick, George Arthur, *The Interpreter's Dictionary of the Bible, Volumes 1-4*, New York: Abingdon Press, 1962.

Comfort, Philip W., and Elwell, Walter A., *Tyndale Bible Dictionary,* Carol Stream, IL: Tyndale House, 2001.

De Silva, David A., *An Introduction to the New Testament*, Downers Grove, IL: InterVarsity, 2004.

Dever, Mark, *The Message of the New Testament,* Wheaton, IL: Crossway, 2005.

Easley, Kendell, *The Illustrated Guide to Biblical History*, Nashville, TN: Holman Reference, 2003.

Geisler, Norman, *A Popular Survey of the New Testament*, Grand Rapids, MI: Baker, 2007.

———, *A Popular Survey of the Old Testament*, Grand Rapids, MI: Baker, 1977.

George, Jim, *The Bare Bones Bible Handbook*, Eugene, OR: Harvest House, 2006.

Harris, Stephen L., *The New Testament*, Mountain View, CA: Mayfield Publishing, 1988.

Hoerth, Alfred, and McRay, John, *Bible Archaeology*, Grand Rapids, MI: Baker, 2005.

Holloman, Henry W., *Kregel Dictionary of the Bible and Theology,* Grand Rapids, MI: Kregel Academic, 2005.

632

Jensen, Irving L., *Jensen's Survey of the New Testament*, Chicago, IL: Moody, 1981.

———, *Jensen's Survey of the Old Testament*, Chicago, IL: Moody, 1978.

Johnston, Philip, *The IVP Introduction to the Bible*, Downers Grove, IL: IVP Academic, 2006.

Kaiser, Walter, ed., *Archaeological Study Bible*, Grand Rapids, MI: Zondervan, 2005.

Keener, Craig S., *The IVP Bible Background Commentary: New Testament*, Downers Grove, IL: InterVarsity, 1993.

Kitchen K.A., *On the Reliability of the Old Testament*, Grand Rapids, MI: William B. Eerdmans, 2003.

Knight, George W., and Edwards, James R., *Nelson's Student Bible Handbook*, Nashville, TN: Thomas Nelson, 2007.

Kurian, George Thomas, ed., *Nelson's New Christian Dictionary*, Nashville, TN: Thomas Nelson, 2001.

Lawrence, Paul, *The IVP Atlas of Bible History*, Downers Grove, IL: IVP Academic, 2006.

Lindsell, Harold, and Verbrugge, Verlyn, eds., *NRSV Harper Study Bible*, Grand Rapids, MI: Zondervan, 1991.

MacArthur, John, *The MacArthur Bible Handbook*, Nashville, TN: Thomas Nelson, 2003.

Marx, Christopher, *The Ultimate Timeline of World History*, Hauppauge, NY: Barron's Educational Series, October 2012.

Miller, Stephen M., *The Complete Guide to the Bible*, Uhrichsville, OH: Barbour, 2007.

Moule, C.F.D., *The Birth of the New Testament*, New York: Harper & Row, 1962.

Nixon, Brian, *The Master Teacher: Developing a Christ-based Philosophy of Education*, Costa Mesa, CA: Calvary Chapel Publishing, 2007, and *FAITH Bible Curriculum*, Trinity Southwest University and Veritas Evangelical Seminary, 2013–15.

O'Donnell, Kevin, *The Baker Pocket Guide to the Bible*, Grand Rapids, MI: Baker, 2004.

Richards, Lawrence O., *Illustrated Bible Handbook*, Nashville, TN: Thomas Nelson, 2003.

Robinson, Maurice, and House, Mark. *Analytical Lexicon of the New Testament Greek*, Peabody, MA: Hendrickson, 2012.

Sproul, R.C, ed., *New Geneva Study Bible,* Nashville, TN: Thomas Nelson, 1995.

Stearns, Peter N., gen. ed., *The Encyclopedia of World History,* 6th ed., New York: Houghton Mifflin, 2001.

Strong, James, *Strong's Exhaustive Concordance of the Bible,* Nashville, TN: Thomas Nelson, 1990.

Unger, Merrill F., *Unger's Bible Handbook,* Chicago, IL: Moody, 1967.

Willmington, Harold L., *Willmington's Bible Handbook,* Carol Stream, IL: Tyndale House, 1997.

Zodhiates, Spiros, *The Complete Word Study Dictionary: New Testament,* Chattanooga, TN: AMG Publishers, 1992.

————, *Key Word Study Bible,* Chattanooga, TN: AMG Publishers, 1991.

NOTES

1. Flavius Josephus, *Antiquities of the Jews*, 2.9.7, accessed May 12, 2016. According to tradition, Pharaoh's daughter told him, "I have brought up a child who is of a divine form, and of a generous mind...I thought proper to adopt him for my son and the heir of thy Kingdom." See http://penelope.uchicago.edu/josephus/ ant-2.html.

2. Douglas Main, "Israel Escapes Locust Plague—for Now," Live Science, March 6, 2013, http://www .livescience.com/27699-israel-escapes-locust-plague-for-now.html, accessed May 18, 2016.

3. Quoted in William Gallogly Moorhead, *Outline Studies in the Books of the Old Testament: Deuteronomy* (Grand Rapids: Fleming H. Revell Company, 1893), p. 6.

4. Flavius Josephus, *Antiquities of the Jews*, 5.1.29, http://penelope.uchicago.edu/josephus/ant-5.html, accessed May 25, 2016.

5. F.B. Meyer, *Christ in Isaiah*, CLC Publications, 1941, Kindle Edition (ch. 1).

6. BibleStudy.org, "What Happened to Goliath's Sword and Spear?", http://www.biblestudy.org/theplainer truth/what-happened-to-sword-and-spear-of-goliath.html, accessed July 20, 2016.

7. For example, Psalms 18, 34, 52, 54, 56, 57, 63, 124, 138, and 142.

8. Charles H. Spurgeon, "The Treasury of David: Psalm 59," The Spurgeon Archive, http://www.spurgeon.org/ treasury/ps059.php, accessed July 20, 2016.

9. Flavius Josephus, *Antiquities of the Jews*, 10.8.5, http://penelope.uchicago.edu/josephus/ant-10.html, accessed February 15, 2017.

10. Midrash *Tanhuma Qedoshim*, 10.

11. Rabbi Ken Spiro, "History Crash Course #43: The Jews of Babylon," Aish.com, http://www.aish.com/jl/h/ cc/48949881.html, accessed August 8, 2016.

12. Editors of *Encyclopaedia Britannica*, "Diaspora: Judaism," https://www.britannica.com/topic/Diaspora -Judaism, accessed August 8, 2016.

13. George A. Barton, "The Second Temple," Jewish Encyclopedia, http://www.jewishencyclopedia.com/ articles/14309-temple-the-second, accessed August 9, 2016.

14. J.N. Darby, *Synopsis of the Books of the Bible*, vol. 5 (London: Stow Mill Bible and Tract Depot, 1943), 374.

15. Herodotus, *The Histories*, translated by Aubrey de Sélincourt, revised by A.R. Burn (London: Penguin Classics, 1954, rev. 1972), pp. 429, 550.

16. Mark Cartwright, "Thermopylae," Ancient History Encyclopedia, April 16, 2013, http://www.ancient.eu/ thermopylae/, accessed August 12, 2016.

17. From Peter Kreeft's argument, quoted in Lee Strobel, *The Case for Faith: A Journalist Investigates the Toughest Objections to Christianity* (Grand Rapids, MI: Zondervan, 2001), p. 32.

18. P.T. Forsyth, *The Soul of Prayer*, Vancouver, BC: Regent College Publishing, 1916/2002, p. 47.

19. John Ortberg, *The Life You've Always Wanted: Spiritual Disciplines for Ordinary People* (Grand Rapids: Zondervan, 1997), 81.

20. Jerome K. Jerome, quoted at Brainy Quote, http://www.brainyquote.com/quotes/quotes/j/jeromekje137070 .html, accessed October 7, 2016.

21. Theodore Roosevelt, quoted at Goodreads, http://www.goodreads.com/quotes/62023-whenever-you-are- asked-if-you-can-do-a-job, accessed October 7, 2016.

22. Quoted by Dennis Rainey in *Staying Close: Stopping the Natural Drift Toward Isolation in Marriage* (Nashville: Thomas Nelson, Inc., 1989/2003), p. 1.

23. Flavius Josephus, *Antiquities of the Jews*, 11.1.3, http://penelope.uchicago.edu/josephus/ant-11.html, accessed October 17, 2016,

24. Harry A. Ironside, "Expository Notes on the Prophet Isaiah," 1952, https://www.studylight.org/commentaries/isn/isaiah-61.html, accessed October 18, 2016.

25. John F. Walvoord and Roy B. Zuck, *The Bible Knowledge Commentary: Old Testament* (Colorado Springs: David C. Cook, 1983), p. 1185.

26. Flavius Josephus, *Antiquities of the Jews*, 10.8.2. See http://penelope.uchicago.edu/josephus/ant-10.html.

27. Called Ithobaal III in Glenn E. Markoe, citing the works of Flavius Josephus in *Phoenicians* (Berkeley: University of California Press, 2000), p. 48.

28. Herodotus, quoted in John Thomas, *Anatolia; or, Russia Triumphant and Europe Chained* (London: Houlston and Stoneman, 1854), p. 66.

29. Flavius Josephus, *Antiquities of the Jews*, 1.6.1, http://sacred-texts.com/jud/josephus/ant-1.htm, accessed October 31, 2016.

30. Flavius Josephus, *The Wars of the Jews*, 1.1.2, http://www.sacred-texts.com/jud/josephus/war-1.htm, accessed November 3, 2016.

31. Flavius Josephus, *Antiquities of the Jews*, 9.10.1-2, http://penelope.uchicago.edu/josephus/ant-9.html, accessed November 11, 2016.

32. Patrick Morley, "A Brief History of Spiritual Revival and Awakening in America," June 30, 2015, http://patrickmorley.com/blog/2015/6/23/a-brief-history-of-spiritual-revival-and-awakening-in-america, accessed November 14, 2016.

33. Carl Friedrich Keil and Franz Delitzsch, citing Marcus von Niebuhr's *History of Assyria and Babylon Since Phul* (1857) in *Biblical Commentary on the Old Testament*, 1857–1878, www.biblehub.com/commentaries/kad/Jonah/4.htm, accessed November 14, 2016. C.F. Keil and F. Delitzsch, *Commentary on the Old Testament: Minor Prophets* (Grand Rapids: Eerdmans, 1946), pp. 379-417.

34. According to first-century BC Greek historian Diodorus Siculus, cited in Sir Austen Henry Layard, *Nineveh and Its Remains*, Vol. 2 (New York: George P. Putnam, 1849), p. 218.

35. New World Encyclopedia contributors, "Nineveh," *New World Encyclopedia*, http://www.newworldencyclopedia.org/p/index.php?title=Nineveh&oldid=986287, accessed November 14, 2016.

36. Daniel David Luckenbill, *Ancient Records of Assyria and Babylonia*, 2 vols (Chicago: University of Chicago Press, 1926–1927), sections 599, 800, and 810.

37. Enrico Ascalone, *Mesopotamia: Assyrians, Sumerians, Babylonians*, Berkeley: University of California Press, 2007, p. 1, cited in "Assyria," *The History Files*, http://www.historyfiles.co.uk/KingListsMiddEast/MesopotamiaAssyria.htm, accessed November 15, 2016.

38. Such a case was cited by A.J. Wilson, "The Sign of the Prophet Jonah and its Modern Confirmations," *The Princeton Theological Review*, 1927, p. 636. Wilson quoted from the account of a whaler, James Bartley, thrown overboard and swallowed by a sperm whale in 1891. The whale was later killed, and as it was being stripped for oil and fat, Bartley was discovered inside its stomach, unconscious. He recovered after a few weeks and resumed his duties, but his skin and hair were permanently bleached white by the whale's gastric juices.

39. Corrie ten Boom, *Tramp for the Lord* (New York: Jove Books, 1978), p. 53.

40. Robert Jamieson, A.R. Fausset, and David Brown, *A Commentary, Critical, Practical, and Explanatory on the Old and New Testaments*, 1882, http://www.sacred-texts.com/bib/cmt/jfb/nah002.htm, accessed November 18, 2016.

41. Simon Anglim, *Fighting Techniques of the Ancient World 3000 BCE–500 CE: Equipment, Combat Skills and Tactics* (London: Amber Books, 2013), pp. 185-186.

42. Peter Williams, "The Historical Reliability of Mark's Gospel," 2008, Theology Network, http://www.theologynetwork.org/biblical-studies/the-historical-reliability-of-marks-gospel.htm, accessed June 1, 2016.

43. Douglas Harper, "Gospel," Online Etymology Dictionary, 2016, http://www.etymonline.com/index.php?term=gospel, accessed June 1, 2016.

44. Jewish Virtual Library, "Jewish Concepts: The Messiah," http://www.jewishvirtuallibrary.org/jsource/Judaism/messiah.html, accessed June 24, 2016. (The prayer is a poetic version of the twelfth of Maimonides' 13 Principles of Judaism.)

45. Charles Evan Hill, *The Johannine Corpus in the Early Church* (Oxford: Oxford University Press, 2004), p. 338.

46. Kaufmann Kohler, "Memra," Jewish Encyclopedia, http://www.jewishencyclopedia.com/articles/10618-memra, accessed June 1, 2016.

47. Irenaeus, *Adversus Haereses*, 3.11.1 and 3.11.8, http://www.newadvent.org/fathers/0103301.htm, accessed December 12, 2016.

48. For a ground-level view of John 17, I wrote a whole book on this chapter, called *When God Prays*.

49. Mal Couch, *A Bible Handbook to the Acts of the Apostles* (Grand Rapids: Kregel Academic & Professional, 2004), p. 120.

50. *Encyclopaedia Britannica*, "Roman Road System," December 5, 2014, http://www.britannica.com/technology/Roman-road-system, accessed June 8, 2016.

51. *The Annals of Tacitus*, trans. Alfred John Church and William Jackson Brodribb (London: Macmillan and Company, 1876), pp. 301-302, 304.

52. Ibid, pp. 304-305.

53. *Foxe's Book of Martyrs*, eds. John Malham and T. Pratt (Philadelphia: J.J. Woodward, 1830), p. 410.

54. *Encyclopaedia Britannica*, "Edict of Milan," 2016, http://www.britannica.com/topic/Edict-of-Milan, accessed June 9, 2016,

55. National Geographic Society, "Rome Becomes Christian, Western Empire Ends," http://www.nationalgeographic.com/lostgospel/timeline_13.html, accessed June 9, 2016.

56. Jerome Murphy-O'Connor, *St. Paul's Corinth: Texts and Archaeology* (Collegeville: The Liturgical Press, 2002), pp. 56-57.

57. Strabo, *The Geography of Strabo*, ed. H.L. Jones (Cambridge: Harvard University Press, 1924), 8.6.20.

58. Roswell D. Hitchcock, "Entry for 'Corinth,'" *An Interpreting Dictionary of Scripture Proper Names* (New York: A.J. Johnson and Sons, 1869).

59. *Encyclopedia Britannica*, "Corinth," August 27, 2014, http://www.britannica.com/place/Corinth-Greece, accessed June 15, 2016.

60. Ibid.

61. M. Tullius Cicero, "For Aulus Cluentius," 14-16, from *The Orations of Marcus Tullius Cicero*, translated by C.D. Yonge (London: Henry G. Bohn), 1856.

62. While Paul's exact meaning isn't clear when he said, "Do you not know that the saints will judge the world?" (1 Corinthians 6:2), there are scriptural reasons to believe that believers will play some kind of role in executing God's judgment. The apostles will judge the tribes of Israel (Matthew 19:28), tribulation saints will reign with Christ during the millennium (Revelation 20:4), and it is possible that God will judge unbelievers based on the conduct of believers (Matthew 12:41).

63. One Apocryphal book, *The Acts of Paul and Thecla*, described Paul's physical stature as unimpressive, with a unibrow, thinning hair, bowlegged, and a large, crooked nose—but "he was full of grace, for sometimes he appeared as a man, sometimes he had the countenance of an angel." From *The Acts of Paul and Thecla*, trans. by Jeremiah Jones (1693–1724), http://www.pbs.org/wgbh/pages/frontline/shows/religion/maps/primary/thecla.htm, accessed December 12, 2016.

64. Greg Herrick, "The Epistle to the Galatians," Bible.org, May 20, 2004, https://bible.org/article/epistle-galatians, accessed June 23, 2016.

65. Tremper Longman III and David E. Garland, gen. eds., *The Expositor's Bible Commentary: Romans-Galatians* (Grand Rapids, MI: Zondervan, 2008), p. 550.

66. For a more in-depth look at these two theories, see Daniel B. Wallace, *New Testament: Introductions and Outlines*, "Galatians: Introduction, Argument, and Outline," February 2, 2009, https://bible.org/seriespage/9-galatians-introduction-argument-and-outline, accessed June 2, 2016,

67. Flavius Josephus, *The Wars of the Jews*, 5.5.4, http://penelope.uchicago.edu/josephus/war-5.html, accessed June 28, 2016. Writing in the first century, after Jesus's resurrection, Josephus described the veil in the temple in great detail, but did not indicate whether it had been repaired or replaced. Either way, because the Jews didn't see Jesus as the Messiah, they continued with their sacrifices until the Romans destroyed the temple in AD 70, as Jesus predicted (Luke 21:5-6).

68. Joshua J. Mark, "Ephesus," Ancient History Encyclopedia, September 2, 2009, http://www.ancient.eu/ephesos, accessed June 23, 2016.

69. Ibid.

70. Susannah Spurgeon and W.J. Harrald, *The Autobiography of C.H. Spurgeon, Vol. 1* (London: Passmore & Alabaster, 1897), p. 170.

71. David Neff, "Biblical Adoption Is Not What You Think It Is," *Christianity Today*, November 22, 2013, http://www.christianitytoday.com/ct/2013/december/heirs-biblicaliblical-take-on-adoption.html?start=1, accessed June 23, 2016.

72. Mark Cartwright, "Slavery in the Roman World," *Ancient History Encyclopedia*, November 1, 2013, http://www.ancient.eu/article/629, accessed June 22, 2016.

73. Bible Hub, "Kenoó," http://biblehub.com/greek/2758.htm, accessed June 27, 2016.

74. *Encyclopedia Britannica*, "Philippi: Greece," http://www.britannica.com/place/Philippi-Greece, accessed June 27, 2016.

75. Bible Hub, "Prototokos," http://biblehub.com/greek/4416.htm, accessed June 28, 2016.

76. David Padfield, "Colosse, Hierapolis and Laodicea," 2015, http://www.padfield.com/acrobat/history/laodicea.pdf, accessed June 29, 2016.

77. Ibid.

78. *Encyclopedia Britannica*, "Aeon: Gnosticism and Manichaeism," 2016, https://www.britannica.com/topic/aeon, accessed June 29, 2016. Got Questions Ministries, "What Is Christian Gnosticism?," http://www.gotquestions.org/Christian-gnosticism.html, accessed June 29, 2016.

79. Bible Hub, "Eikón," http://biblehub.com/greek/1504.htm, accessed June 28, 2016.

80. Mark Cartwright, "Thessalonica," *Ancient History Encyclopedia*, May 1, 2016, http://www.ancient.eu/Thessalonica, accessed June 29, 2016.

81. Bible Hub, "Exécheó," http://biblehub.com/greek/1837.htm, accessed June 29, 2016.

82. Bible Hub, "Harpazó," http://biblehub.com/greek/726.htm, accessed June 29, 2016.

83. Antiochus Epiphanes IV had desecrated the temple with an image of Zeus before Jesus came the first time, and had been defeated and the temple restored by the Maccabean Revolt in the second century BC. Antiochus came in the spirit of the Antichrist, but the ultimate fulfillment of the abomination will come when the actual Antichrist breaks a treaty he previously brokered with Israel and proclaims himself God in a future, rebuilt temple (Revelation 13:14-15). This lines up with Paul's words here in 2 Thessalonians 2:4.

84. Joshua J. Mark, "Ephesus," *Ancient History Encyclopedia*, September 2, 2009, http://www.ancient.eu/ephesos, accessed July 8, 2016. *Encyclopedia Britannica*, "Ephesus: Ancient City, Turkey," May 28, 2016, https://www.britannica.com/place/Ephesus, accessed July 8, 2016.

85. Philip Schaff, editor, *Nicene and Post-Nicene Fathers*, "Eusebius Pamphilus: Church History, Life of Constantine, Oration in Praise of Constantine" (Grand Rapids: William B. Eerdmans, 1956), chapter XXV, http://www.ccel.org/ccel/schaff/npnf201.iii.vii.xxvi.html, accessed July 8, 2016.

86. See **Colossians: History** (page 501) for more on the beliefs and threat of Gnosticism.

87. Walter Scheidel, "Human Mobility in Roman Italy, II: The Slave Population," *Journal of Roman Studies* 95, 2005, pp. 64-79.

Walter Scheidel, "Roman Population Size: The Logic of the Debate," Stanford University, 2007, p. 5, https://www.princeton.edu/~pswpc/pdfs/scheidel/070706.pdf, accessed January 10, 2017.

88. Eusebius, *Nicene and Post-Nicene Fathers*, Series II, Vol. 1, XXV.5, compiled by Phillip Schaff, https://www.ccel.org/ccel/schaff/npnf201.iii.vii.xxvi.html, accessed January 11, 2017.

89. John S. Bowman, "Crete: Island, Greece," *Encyclopedia Britannica*, September 24, 2015, https://www.britannica.com/place/Crete, accessed July 29, 2016.

90. Mark Cartwright, "Slavery in the Roman World," *Ancient History Encyclopedia*, November 1, 2013, http://www.ancient.eu/article/629, accessed July 29, 2016.

91. "The Roman Empire in the First Century: Slaves & Freemen," Devillier Donegan Enterprises, 2006, http://www.pbs.org/empires/romans/empire/slaves_freemen.html, accessed July 29, 2016.

92. Cartwright.

93. William Smith, "Servus," *A Dictionary of Greek and Roman Antiquities* (London: John Murray, 1875), pp. 1036-1042, http://penelope.uchicago.edu/Thayer/e/roman/texts/secondary/smigra*/servus.html, accessed January 12, 2017.

94. Zondervan NIV Study Bible, "Hebrews," *Biblica*, January 15, 2014, http://www.biblica.com/en-us/bible/online-bible/scholar-notes/niv-study-bible/intro-to-hebrews, accessed July 29, 2016.

95. Hampton Keathley IV, "The Argument of Hebrews," August 12, 2004, https://bible.org/article/argument-hebrews, accessed July 29, 2016.

96. That is, before AD 70, when Roman soldiers razed the temple in response to Jewish rebellion, fulfilling Jesus's prediction in Matthew 24:1-2, Mark 13:1-2, and Luke 21:5-6. The temple has not been rebuilt since, though end-times prophecy says it will be (Daniel 9:27; 2 Thessalonians 2:3-4; Revelation 11:1-2).

97. "Saint James: Apostle, the Lord's Brother," *Encyclopedia Britannica*, https://www.britannica.com/biography/Saint-James-the-Lords-brother, accessed July 29, 2016.

98. Norman L. Geisler, *A Popular Survey of the New Testament* (Grand Rapids: Baker, 2014), p. 262.

99. That doesn't include being weird or obnoxious, getting in people's face about God, and then when they reject you, saying you've been persecuted for Christ's sake. Jesus said, "Blessed are those who are persecuted for righteousness' sake" (Matthew 5:10), not "Blessed are those who are persecuted for antagonizing the unsaved."

100. Thomas Manton, *An Exposition with Notes upon the Epistle of James*, 1660, p. 57, http://www.ccel.org/ccel/manton/manton04.iv.html, accessed January 19, 2017.

101. Martin Luther, *The Table Talk or Familiar Discourse of Martin Luther*, trans. William Hazlitt (London: David Bogue, 1848), p. 183.

102. Dr. Sophie Lunn-Rockliffe, "Christianity and the Roman Empire," February 17, 2011, BBC, http://www.bbc.co.uk/history/ancient/romans/christianityromanempire_article_01.shtml, accessed August 15, 2016. *National Geographic*, "Roman Emperors Persecute Christians," 2016, http://www.nationalgeographic.com/lostgospel/timeline_09.html, accessed August 15, 2016.

103. Loren T. Stuckenbruck, "Revelation," *Eerdmans Commentary on the Bible*, eds. James D.G. Dunn and John W. Rogerson (Grand Rapids: William B. Eerdmans, 2003), p. 1535.

104. John Foxe, "The Second Persecution, Under Domitian, A.D. 81–96," *The New Foxe's Book of Martyrs*, rewritten and updated by Harold J. Chadwick (Alachua: Bridge-Logos, 2001), pp. 12-13.

BROADEN YOUR UNDERSTANDING OF EACH BOOK OF THE BIBLE

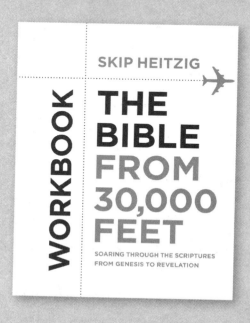

SKIP HEITZIG

WORKBOOK

THE BIBLE FROM 30,000 FEET

SOARING THROUGH THE SCRIPTURES
FROM GENESIS TO REVELATION

Get an unobstructed view of the heart of Scripture and study the Bible in a unique way with this companion workbook to *The Bible from 30,000 Feet* by Pastor Skip Heitzig.

Each chapter of this personal study offers an overview of one or more books of the Bible and provides stimulating questions to help you grasp the main message, understand the overall timeline of events, and then use that knowledge to stir your love and obedience to God.

You'll gain grander insights into God's ceaseless work and enjoy a clearer perspective on Bible history. Let your faith fly higher than ever before!

Great for both individual and group study.